KEN SCHULTZ'S

Fishing Encyclopedia

Worldwide Angling Guide

VOLUME 2

KEN SCHULTZ'S
Fishing Encyclopedia

Worldwide Angling Guide

Ken Schultz

IDG Books Worldwide, Inc.
An International Data Group Company
Foster City, CA • Chicago, IL • Indianapolis, IN • New York, NY • Southlake, TX

IDG Books Worldwide, Inc.
An International Data Group Company
919 E. Hillsdale Boulevard
Suite 400
Foster City, CA 94404

Copyright © 2000 by Ken Schultz

All rights reserved. No part of this book shall be reproduced, stored in a retrieval system, or transmitted by any means, electronic, mechanical, photocopying, recording, or otherwise, without written permission from the publisher. No patent liability is assumed with respect to the use of the information contained herein. Although every precaution has been taken in the preparation of this book, the publisher and author assume no responsibility for errors or omissions. Neither is any liability assumed for damages resulting from the use of the information contained herein.

Webster's New World is a registered trademark of Macmillan General Reference USA, Inc., a wholly owned subsidiary of IDG Books Worldwide, Inc.

The IDG Books Worldwide logo is a registered trademark under exclusive license to IDG Books Worldwide, Inc., from International Data Group, Inc.

For general information on books from IDG Books Worldwide's in the U.S., please call our Consumer Customer Service department at 800-762-2974. For reseller information, including discounts and premium sales, please call our Reseller Customer Service department at 800-434-3422.

For information on a multimedia version of this book, available from Tricom Intrtactive, Inc., please go to this Web site: intellipedia.com

To contact the author, please visit: www.kenshultz.com

Library of Congress Cataloging-in-Publication Data

This edition of *Ken Schultz's Fishing Encyclopedia*, which is published in 7 volumes, contains the entire contents of the work as previously published in a single volume: *Ken Schultz's Fishing Encyclopedia*, ISBN 9780028620572

This is Volume 2 of 7

Schultz, Ken, 1950–
Ken Shultz's fishing encyclopedia: worldwide angling guide/ Ken Schultz. — 1st ed.
p. cm.
ISBN 0-02-862057-7
Volume 2: ISBN 9781684427659 (hardcover) | ISBN 9781684427666 (paperback)

1. Fishing—Encyclopedias. 2. Fishes—Encyclopedias. I. Title.
SH411.S38 2000
799.1'03—dc21   99-033719
CIP

Manufactured in the United States of America

First Edition

Trademarks

All terms mentioned in this book that are known to be trademarks or service marks have been appropriately capitalized. IDG Books cannot attest to the accuracy of this information. Use of a term in this book should not be regarded as affecting the validity of any trademark or service mark.

Table of Contents

Introduction
vii

Acknowledgments
ix

Photo Credits
xix

Fishing Encyclopedia Entries

C
1

D
191

E
239

Appendix: Conversion Charts for Weights and Measures
269

Introduction

*"Ah, the gallant fisher's life! It is the best of any;
'Tis full of pleasure, void of strife, And 'tis beloved by many."*
—IZAAK WALTON

"All men are equal before fish."
—HERBERT HOOVER

W<small>HILE PRODUCING THIS FISHING ENCYCLOPEDIA I SPOKE TO MANY HUNDREDS OF</small> informed anglers. Nearly all of them thought the compilation of all things piscatorial was too overwhelming to contemplate because the angling universe is so enormous and diverse.

Certainly a modern fishing encyclopedia—if it truly provides a full field of knowledge—runs counter to the short and specialized tenets of today's journalism. Yet it is precisely because there is so much to the sport of fishing, plus an increasing profusion of specialized equipment and confusing terminology, that it was necessary to bring order and perspective to all of this in one definitive book.

Ken Schultz's Fishing Encyclopedia & Worldwide Angling Guide has been a long time in the making. I started thinking about it in 1991. Since work began in earnest in 1995, the project became even more expansive than expected, and indeed there were times when it was nearly overwhelming. As a result, the book (now a series of books) grew much bigger than originally planned, becoming 50 percent larger than any fishing encyclopedia that has heretofore been published.

As a result, however, this encyclopedia contains the equivalent of thirty standard-length books, meaning that there is ample space to devote to the species, equipment, techniques, locations, and ancillary matters that encompass the angling universe. Consider that nearly one-third of the encyclopedia series is comprised of the most comprehensive information on worldwide angling opportunities ever assembled. There is absolutely no place to find these details together; indeed, some elements of the *Worldwide Angling Guide* cannot be found anywhere else at all.

Likewise, the coverage of angling methods and equipment has never been addressed more comprehensively between the covers of any other book. In fact, *Ken Schultz's Fishing Encyclopedia* contains the most modern, illuminating, and extensive discourses on the basic elements of fishing tackle—baitcasting, big-game, conventional, flycasting, spinning, and spincasting—ever found in one place. Each of these entries undoubtedly contain more than all but the most scrupulous person will want to know.

Great lengths were also taken, however, to make sure that the less obvious subjects in the angling universe were included and reviewed in comprehensive fashion. For example, nowhere else is there a more extensive review of the principles, methods, and pros and cons of catch-and-release—perhaps the most important angling conservation development of the twentieth century.

Topics like fisheries management, angling-related travel, choosing guides and charter boats, and the care and preparation of fish for consumption, which are among many unglamorous subjects taken for granted elsewhere, receive complete explanation and review here. Likewise the otherwise oft-ignored subjects of ethics and etiquette—increasingly important issues as human pressures increase—are included.

Although there's an enormous amount of information in this series of books, every topic was approached with the intent to take nothing for granted and to present information in straightforward language. Angling is not like nuclear physics, and if it was half as complicated as some people try to make it, no one would enjoy it or have success. The extensive insertion of cross references is thus intended to direct you through a continuing stream of appropriate topics, so you can take any subject as far as you want to go. Some cross references appear within entry text next to topics that are more thoroughly reviewed elsewhere; many cross references appear at the end of entry text, either to direct you to the appropriate subject entry or to note related topics.

We've tried to make things easy to find and to place subjects where you're most likely to look for them, even if you're unsure of the proper terms or spelling. As an example, you'll find rainbow trout under the "T" entries (trout, rainbow) rather than under the "R" entries. Also, at the back of each book is a weights and measures conversion chart; this will be convenient for many readers since there's a liberal mix of metric and U.S. customary weights and measures throughout this book, just as there is at boat docks, fish camps, and tackle shops throughout the world.

Because the text is encyclopedic in format, however, it does not provide a full sense of the joy or spirit of sportfishing—the pleasure that makes it "beloved by many," as Izaak Walton said. Perhaps the accompanying photos help convey this. Photos and line art, incidentally, were planned and selected to reflect the broad, eclectic places and situations that so many anglers experience, as well as to reflect the great diversity of its participants. Angling is a very democratic recreation; as the quotation from President Hoover implies, the fish don't care who hooks them.

It is a special delight to publish this encyclopedia at the close of the twentieth century—a period with the most phenomenal sportfishing growth in the history of mankind—and at the advent of a new millennium. Knowing that the decades ahead will require proper stewardship of aquatic resources—something that anglers in particular have always demonstrated personal and financial support for—this text has been written and edited with sensitivity to conservation issues while also being realistic about the role that humans play as the highest predators and the diverse motivations they bring to angling.

In a sense, the sport of fishing is like a book with as many footnotes as main text. It is full of variables, especially individual skills, weather issues, peculiarities among species, habitat differences, and so forth. You may notice that the words "usually" and "generally" occur often in portions of the text. This isn't meant to be vague; it's because there are often no hard-and-fast rules in catching fish, no matter what you may have heard to the contrary. There are norms, but straying from norms is common for one reason or another, as any angler who has been humbled at a "hot" site at the "best" time of the season can attest.

While there is a wealth of reliable information here, a caveat is in order with regard to the contents of the *Worldwide Angling Guide*. Many of the countries profiled have not in the past provided, or do not currently provide, or may not in the future provide stable travel environments, especially to tourists of certain nationalities. Jungle fishing opportunities are especially among those that may present danger. Angola, Colombia, and Zambia come immediately to mind in this regard. Civil unrest can likewise make travel in certain places dangerous; recent troubles in Kenya, Indonesia, Russia, Uganda, and the Balkans serve as examples. The adventurous angler needs to use good judgment.

Things change the environmental order and aquatic resources, too. Yugoslavia hadn't been wrecked by bombs when that entry was written; Nicaragua and Honduras were leveled by Hurricane Georges right after those entries were written. Environmental changes sometimes radically alter the presence or availability of certain gamefish species, and in the more remote pockets of the world only native people and intrepid explorers are likely to know it.

On a final note, it is tempting to say, as marketers and publicists are wont to do, that this book contains everything an angler will ever need to know about fish and fishing. But new developments in fishing tackle will surely come along, changes in some habitats or in fish populations will alter the techniques and equipment used, and certainly natural changes will take place in some of the world's best angling spots. However, a lot of the fundamentals—the underlying principles of fish behavior, the function of basic equipment, and angling methodology—will be constant, making most of the information in this book relevant to the discerning angler even in years to come.

I expect to add to this body of knowledge in time, so if you think there's something that should have been included, if you have knowledge about fishing in a country that wasn't covered, or if you can suggest an improvement to any aspect of this book, please visit my website—www.kenschultz.com—and post a message about it.

Now, turn to any page and become absorbed.
—Ken Schultz

"If I fished only to capture fish, my fishing trips would have ended long ago."

—ZANE GREY

Acknowledgments

PRODUCING A BOOK OF THIS MAGNITUDE REQUIRED THE INVOLVEMENT OF A tremendous number of people and a great array of talents. This encyclopedia would not have gone beyond a mere suggestion, however, had it not been for the endorsement and encouragement of Natalie Chapman, a former publisher at Macmillan General Reference, now IDG Books Consumer Reference, whose confidence and vision made this book possible, and who gave me free rein to produce it as necessary. I'm also indebted to publisher Marie Butler-Knight, who took this project over in mid-stream, marshaled all the resources, and fervently shepherded the book to completion. Sincere appreciation is also extended to Renee Wilmeth and Kristi Hart, who directed the publisher's nitty-gritty editorial and production work with outstanding dedication and professionalism, plus a reassuring enthusiasm; to Pamela Benner, who paid excellent attention to details in the copyediting process and made good suggestions; and to many other directly involved personnel, particularly Beth Jordan, Faunette Johnston, and Jeanine Bucek.

This book could also not have been completed without the special assistance of my wife, Sandy, and my daughters, Alyson, Megan, and Kristen. They each helped in a variety of ways, especially by being patient. Sandy's assistance with a host of matters was very beneficial, and Kristen was particularly vital, pitching in for a second time during a desperate period with important research and writing assistance.

In order to make this encyclopedia truly comprehensive and of worldwide significance it was imperative to involve a host of contributors with expertise in technical fisheries matters, regional angling opportunities, and specialized sportfishing topics. I'm grateful for their participation and excellent contributions, the bulk of which made up the *Worldwide Angling Guide*. In particular, appreciation is extended to the incomparable Ed Migdalski, who provided technical scientific fisheries advice and vetted all of the fish art.

I'm also indebted to the late, and incomparable in his own right, A. J. McClane. His fishing encyclopedia of 1965 and 1974, though now outdated, was not only a phenomenal reference work, but a monumental achievement in an era before personal computers, electronic mail, fax machines, scanners, laser printers, and the various modern technology that made putting this book together far easier than it was in his time. Unlike me, he was unable to write and edit on a laptop computer in cars, planes, airports, hotel rooms, and other places, or receive electronically transmitted text. More significantly, McClane set a very high bar for what a real fishing encyclopedia ought to be, and provided a template for such a book for the twenty-first century. Without his accomplishment, it would have been much more difficult to plan and publish this book. (Aside to historians: four contributors to this project—Ed Migdalski, George Reiger, Jack Samson, and Bill Scifres—were also contributors to McClane's encyclopedia.)

Just as McClane, the contributors to this book, and the people at IDG Books Worldwide are the best in their fields, so is *Field & Stream* the largest and best fishing and hunting magazine in the world, and I've been privileged to be part of this publication continuously since 1973. I appreciate the confidence and opportunities provided me over that time by its editors. Those opportunities laid the groundwork for this encyclopedia. I'm especially grateful to Editor Slaton White and Managing Editor Mike Toth for allowing me leeway over the last several years that I've been working on this project.

Information, suggestions, encouragement, technical advice, reference paraphernalia, reviews and critiques, and assorted material assistance were received from so many individuals and organizations that some will likely be overlooked in these acknowledgments, for which I apologize.

I'm very grateful to the following individuals:

Blaine Anderson
John Anthon
Dick Ballard
Ron Ballanti
LaVerne Barnes
Cameron Baty
Susan Baumgartner
Gene Bay
Dick Bengraff
Virginia Benoit
Walt Boname
Toby Bradshaw
Eric Burnley

Cyril Calendini
Bill Chapman, Jr.
Jim Chapralis
Larry Columbo
David Cosby
Gary Dollahon
Lou Duarte
Todd DuPuis
Jack Erskine
Mike Fine
Paul Fuller
Riccardo Galigani
Ken Gangler

Acknowledgments

Guy Geffroy
Lois Gerber
Alessandro Giangio
Barry Gibson
Gary Giudice
Fred Golofaro
Jerry Gomber
George Gowen
Garry Gurke
Judy Hammond
Bill Hilts, Jr.
Bruce Holt
Dr. James Imai
Jimmy Kano
Nick Karas
Glenda Kelley
Gary King
Jason Klein
Bob Lang
Steen Larsen
Mike Leech
Bill Liston
Chun Liu
George Loechl
Paulo Loes
Frank Longino
Jim Matthews
John Mazurkewicz
Tom Melton
Paul Merzig
Ed Mesunas
Bill Miller
Gail Morchower
András Nagy
Andy Newman
Stuart Newman
Donald J. Orth
Tom Pagliaroli
Sheldon Pasternack
Dennis Phillips
Stanko Popovic
Norville Prosser
Jim Reist
Al Ristori
Milt Rosko
Gail Ross
Sharon Rushton
Pat Salimeno
Marty Salovin
Glenn Sapir
Christine Moore Serrao
Vin Sparano
Ron Speed, Sr.
Roy Stiner
Mick Thill
Roger Tucker
Jerry Valentine
Mike Walker
Ben Wechsler
Mark Weintz
Fenner Weller
Jim White
Anthony M. Williams
Dick Wood
Peter Yaskowski

I'm also grateful to the following companies and organizations (and specific people where noted in parenthesis):

American Sportfishing Association (Mike Hayden)
American Wire (Michael Shields)
Arkie Lures
The Atlantic Salmon Federation
Bay de Noc Lure Co.
Bead Tackle (Peter Renkert)
Bear Advertising (Dick Bear, Mark Malkin)
Big Jon (Jerry Livingstone)
Bullet Weights (Douglas Crumrine)
Bushnell Sports Optics (Barbara Mellman)
Cabela's Inc. (Tony Dolle)
Classic Fishing Products (Mike Richards)
C-Map USA (Pam Oldham)
Computrol, Inc.
Cossack Bait Products (Garry Shaw)
Cuba Specialty Mfg. Co. (Craig Osterhus, Dana Pickup)
Daiwa Corp.
Earie Dearie Lure Co. (Helen Galbincea)
EZE Lap Diamond (Donna Long)
Fin-Nor (Niels Stenhoj)
Flambeau Products Corp. (Jason Sauey)
Florida Keys and Key West Visitors Bureau
Flow-Rite of Tennessee (Don Zielinski)
Furuno
Future Fisherman Foundation
Garmin International (Steve Featherstone)
G. Loomis (Gary Loomis, Steve Rajeff)
Gudebrod
International Game Fish Association (Jim Brown)
Hudson River Foundation
Interphase Technologies
K-C Tackle (Raymond Packer)
L. L. Bean (Mary Rose MacKinnon)
L&S Bait Co. (Eric Bachnik)
Lowrance Electronics (Darrell Lowrance, Steve Schneider)
Luhr Jensen & Sons (Phil Jensen, Barry Ternahan)
Magellan Systems Corp. (Don Meyer)
Mann's Bait Co.
Marado Inc.
Old Town Canoe (Jim Kaiser)
O. Mustad & Sons USA (John DeVries)
National Freshwater Fishing Hall of Fame
Nomadic Expeditions (Denise Gogarty)
Normark Corp. (Ron Weber, Craig Weber)
The Orvis Company
Outdoor Technologies
Owner America Corp. (Kat Shitanishi)
Penn Fishing Tackle
Pradco (Joe Hughes, Bruce Stanton)
Scientific Anglers
Shakespeare Fishing Tackle (Mark Davis)
Sheldon's Inc.
Shimano American Corp.
Si-Tex Marine Electronics
Storm Lures (Sharon Andrews, John Storm)
Sufix USA, Inc.
Techsonics Industries
Len Thompson Lures (Richard Pallister)
Top Brass Tackle (Eric Cosby)
Tru-Turn Hooks (Wes Campbell)
Wisconsin Pharmacal
H. D. Wood Advertising
Worden's Lures
The Worth Co.
Wright & McGill Co. (George Large)
Yakima Bait Co. (Rob Phillips)
Zebco Corp. (Jenni Foster)

Gratitude is also due the following government agencies and government-funded programs (and the people noted in parenthesis), which provided research and reference materials, and, in some cases, other forms of assistance:

Alabama Cooperative Extension Service (Richard Wallace)
Alabama Department of Conservation and Natural Resources (Stan Cook)
Alabama Sea Grant Extension Program
Alaska Department of Fish and Game (Jon Lyman)
Alaska Sea Grant College Program (Kurt Byers)
Alberta Department of Environmental Protection

Acknowledgments

Arizona Game and Fish Department
Arkansas Cooperative Extension Program, Univ. of Arkansas (Nathan Stone)
Arkansas Game and Fish Commission (Keith Sutton)
Auburn University Marine Extension (Richard Wallace, William Hosking, Stephen Szedlmayer)
Brazil Embratur
British Columbia Ministry of Environment, Fisheries Branch
California Department of Fish and Game (A. Petrovich)
Canada Department of Fisheries and Oceans
Canadian Consul General
Cayman Islands Department of Tourism
Colorado Department of Natural Resources
Connecticut Department of Environmental Protection
Delaware Division of Fish and Wildlife
Florida Department of Environmental Protection, Marine Research Institute and Division of Marine Resources (Jim Lewis)
Florida Game and Freshwater Fish Commission, Division of Fisheries (Henry Cabbage)
Georgia Department of Natural Resources (Chris Martin)
Great Lakes Fishery Commission
Guam Department of Agriculture (Gerry Davis)
Hawaii Department of Land and Natural Resources, Division of Aquatic Resources
Idaho Department of Fish and Game (Jack Trueblood)
Illinois Department of Natural Resources
Indiana Department of Natural Resources (Jon Marshall)
International Center for Living Aquatic Resources Management/Food and Agriculture Organization of the United Nations
Iowa Department of Natural Resources (Steve Suman)
Kansas Department of Wildlife and Parks (Mike Miller)
Kentucky Department of Fish and Wildlife Resources (J. Beth Garland)
Louisiana Department of Wildlife and Fisheries
Louisiana Sea Grant College Program
Maine Department of Inland Fisheries and Wildlife (V. Paul Reynolds)
Manitoba Department of Natural Resources, Fisheries Branch (Carl Wall)
Maryland Department of Natural Resources (Eugene Deems, Jr.)
Maryland Sea Grant College Program (Jack Greer)
Massachusetts Division of Fisheries and Wildlife
Michigan Department of Natural Resources, Fisheries Division
Michigan Sea Grant College Program (Martha Walter)
Minnesota Department of Natural Resources (Tom Dickson)
Mississippi Department of Wildlife, Fisheries and Parks (Jim Walker)
Missouri Department of Conservation (John McPherson)
Montana Division of Fish, Wildlife, and Parks
Nevada Department of Conservation and Natural Resources
New Brunswick Department of Economic Development and Tourism
New Brunswick Department of Natural Resources, Fish and Wildlife Branch (Peter Cronin)
Newfoundland Department of Natural Resources
New Hampshire Fish and Game Department (Patricia Fleurie)
New Jersey Division of Fish, Game and Wildlife (Dave Chanda)
New Mexico Department of Game and Fish (Ruth Anderson)
New York Department of Environmental Conservation (Robert Brandt)
New York Sea Grant Program (David MacNeill, Mark Malchoff)
NOAA/Gray's Reef National Marine Sanctuary (Beth Kostka)
NOAA/National Marine Fisheries Service
NOAA/National Weather Service
North Carolina Division of Boating and Inland Fisheries (Fred Harris)
North Carolina Sea Grant
North Dakota Game and Fish Department (Terry Steinwand)
Nova Scotia Department of Fisheries (Murray Hill)
Nova Scotia Department of Lands and Forests (Barry Sabean)
Ohio Department of Natural Resources
Ohio Sea Grant College Program
Oklahoma Department of Wildlife Conservation (Nels Rodefeld)
Ontario Ministry of Economic Development, Trade & Tourism (Tom Boyd)
Ontario Ministry of Natural Resources
Oregon Department of Fish and Wildlife (Randy Henry)
Oregon Sea Grant (Pat Kight)
Parátur, State of Pará, Brazil
Pennsylvania Fish and Boat Commission
Portuguese National Tourist Office (Maria Joáo Ramires)
Prince Edward Island Department of Environmental Resources
Quebec Department of Recreation, Fish and Game
Rhode Island Division of Fish and Game
Rhode Island Sea Grant
Saskatchewan Department of Environment, Fish and Wildlife (Bruce Howard)

South Carolina Department of Natural Resources (Greg Lucas)
South Carolina Sea Grant Consortium (John Tibbetts)
South Dakota Department of Game, Fish and Parks
Spain Ministry of Commerce and Tourism
Tennessee Wildlife Resources Agency (Dave Woodward)
Texas Parks and Wildlife (Steve Lightfoot)
Tourism British Columbia
Tourism New Brunswick
Tourism Newfoundland and Labrador
Tourism Nova Scotia (Randy Brooks)
Tourism Prince Edward Island (Carol Horne)
Tourism Quebec (Siegfried Gagnon)
Tourism Saskatchewan (Gerard Makuch, Nadine Howard)
Travel Alberta (Peter Gregus)
Travel Manitoba (Dennis Maksymetz, Colette Fontaine, Gord Richardson)
University of Connecticut Sea Grant Marine Advisory Program (Nancy Balcom)
University of Delaware Sea Grant College Program
University of Florida Cooperative Extension Service
University of New Hampshire and University of Maine Sea Grant College Program
U.S. Fish and Wildlife Service
Utah Department of Natural Resources (Gerry Schlappe)
Vermont Department of Fish and Wildlife (John Hall)
Virginia Department of Game and Inland Fisheries (Mitchell Norman)
Washington Department of Fish and Wildlife (Nina Carter, James Chandler)
Washington Sea Grant Program (Kris Freeman)
West Virginia Division of Natural Resources (Hoy Murphy)
Wisconsin Department of Natural Resources (David Kunelius)
Woods Hole Oceanographic Institute (Tracey Crago)
Wyoming Game and Fish Department
Yukon Territory Department of Renewable Resources (Susan Thompson)

Finally, I'm also grateful to four student interns, whose early work compiling and organizing research materials was of much help—Kristen Schultz of Oberlin College, Alyson Schultz of Boston University, Mathew Kane of Hamilton College, and John Kuhner of Princeton University—and to Megan Schultz of Ithaca College, for website development and advice.

—Ken Schultz

About the Author, Artists, and Contributors

PRINCIPAL AUTHOR AND EDITOR

Ken Schultz has been a staff fishing writer and editor for *Field & Stream* since 1973. His feature articles and columns for that publication appear monthly, and he contributes to the magazine's nationally syndicated weekly radio show and to its website. Schultz is a frequent author of the outdoors column of the *New York Times*, and he previously was a syndicated newspaper columnist for Gannett. He has authored a dozen books on sportfishing and angling travel topics, has been a featured guest on CNBC, ESPN, and The Nashville Network, and appears regularly in assorted fishing segments for the Outdoor Life Network. A widely traveled angler, Schultz is a former holder of seven line-class world records and was inducted into the Fishing Hall of Fame in 1998. He lives in Forestburgh, New York.

THE ARTISTS

Steve T. Goione is a rising star in the world of fishing and boating art, working in mixed mediums to present his lifelong passion for angling in a dynamic and realistic style. Although he drew the distinctive pen-and-ink illustrations for this book as well as the cover, Goione is primarily a creator of fine art. From his studio in Toms River, New Jersey, he produces commissioned fishing scenes for private collections and limited-edition prints, and he has created original artwork for Sea World in Florida. Goione has also made a mark among boat builders and owners for commissioned renderings of big-game sportfishing craft, and he recently created original artwork for the latest products of Hatteras Yachts. A frequent guest artist on the big-game fishing tournament circuit, Goione appears at exclusive contests each year from Nantucket to Venezuela, and his work is regularly featured at fund-raising events for prominent conservation organizations.

David Kiphuth, whose renderings of fish appear in this book, has had a varied career in the field of art, having been a professional illustrator since 1969. His work has included portraiture, architectural renderings, maps, and book illustration. Kiphuth has created archaeological and scientific book and exhibit renderings for the Yale Peabody Museum, the Yale Department of Anthropology, and Yale University Press. He formerly maintained a studio and gallery in Branford, Connecticut, where he created and sold wildlife and nature art and animal portraits. Since 1989, he has been the staff illustrator for the *Gazette Newspapers* in Schenectady, New York. He lives in Saratoga Springs, New York.

THE CONTRIBUTORS

Brett Albanese of Virginia is a Ph.D candidate at the Department of Fisheries and Wildlife Sciences at Virginia Polytechnic Institute; he formerly worked at the Mississippi Museum of Natural Sciences.

Ken Allen of Maine is Associate Editor of *Maine Sportsman* and a prolific writer, photographer, newspaper columnist, book author, and guide.

Michael Babcock of Montana is Outdoors Editor of the *Great Falls Tribune*.

Ken Bailey of Alberta is Manager of Field Operations in central Alberta for Ducks Unlimited Canada; he is a prolific writer and President of the Outdoor Writers Association of Canada.

Dick Ballard of Missouri is President of Dick Ballard's Fishing Adventures and a foremost authority on Amazonian angling; he's sent anglers fishing around the world for 18 years, and established the first travel service for Bass Pro Shops.

Scott Bannerot of Pennsylvania and Florida has a Ph.D. in fisheries science and has worked in marine biological research and consulting; he is a photojournalist and a charter boat captain.

John A. Barnes of Bermuda is the Director of Agriculture and Fisheries for Bermuda; he authors a weekly fishing column in the Bermuda *Mid Ocean News*, and is an IGFA representative.

Rob Barraclough of Indonesia and England works in the oil industry and is a charter boat captain and freelance writer.

Carlos M. Barrantes of Costa Rica established the first two sportfishing camps in Costa Rica; he is an IGFA representative and was the first President of the Costa Rican Fishing Federation.

Cody Beers of Wyoming works for the Wyoming Game and Fish Department as Associate Editor of *Wyoming Wildlife* magazine and Editor of *Wyoming Wildlife News and Wild Times*; he is also a freelance writer and photographer.

Bob Berry of California is one of the world's top fish carvers and sculptors, and swept all divisions of the 1986 world championship of fish carving; he is a foremost competition judge, a former professional taxidermist, and author of the book *Fish Carving*.

About the Author, Artists, and Contributors

Mike Bleech of Pennsylvania is a writer and photographer whose work has appeared in most major U.S. fishing and hunting magazines.

Larry Blomquist of Louisiana is Publisher of *Breakthrough*, the world's largest taxidermy trade magazine, and one of the top competition judges in North America; he is a retired award-winning taxidermist, and former President of the National Taxidermists Association.

Fred Bonner of North Carolina is Editor of *Carolina Adventure* magazine; he is also a syndicated newspaper columnist, fisheries biologist, and an IGFA representative.

Judith Bowman of New York has been a foremost sporting books dealer for over twenty years; she produces two sporting book catalogs a year, with special emphasis on fishing.

John Brownlee of Florida is Senior Editor of *Salt Water Sportsman* and a former charter boat captain; he has served on the South Atlantic Fishery Management Council, is former Chairman of the Florida Conservation Association, and is an IGFA representative.

Eric B. Burnley of Virginia is the author of *Surf Fishing the Atlantic Coast* and a radio show host; he is a charter boat captain and Regional Editor of both *Salt Water Sportsman* and *The Fisherman* magazines.

Erwin Bursik of South Africa is Publisher of *Ski-Boat* and *Flyfishing* magazines of Durban, a member of the executive board of the South African Deep Sea Angling Association, and an IGFA representative.

Mac Campbell of Great Britain works for *Angling Plus*, a match fishing magazine, and has previously worked for *Sea Angler*, *Trout Fisherman*, and *Angling Times*.

Jim Casada of South Carolina is the author of many books, including *Modern Fly Fishing*; he is Senior Editor of *Sporting Classics* magazine, and outdoor columnist for the Rock Hill *Herald* and Greensboro *News and Record*.

Göran Cederberg of Sweden has been Editor of several international fact-packed large-format angling books, including *The Complete Book of Sportfishing*; he contributes regularly to north-European publications and has been chief editor of a Swedish sportfishing magazine.

Matthew D. Chan of Virginia is a Ph.D candidate at the Department of Fisheries and Wildlife Sciences at Virginia Polytechnic Institute; he formerly worked as a fisheries biologist for the U.S. Army Corps of Engineers.

Dawn Charging of North Dakota is Outdoors Director for the North Dakota State Tourism Department; she is also a writer and photographer whose family owns a successful fishing resort on Lake Sakakawea.

Homer Circle of Florida has been Angling Editor of *Sports Afield* magazine for 34 years; the dean of American outdoor writers, he is the recipient of numerous media and achievement awards, a former member of the Arkansas Game & Fish Commission, and a renowned television and video host.

Barry Ord Clarke of Norway is a professional photographer and writer and the author of several books on fly fishing and fly tying; he contributes regularly to most European fishing magazines, and is fishing consultant to Norway's largest private sporting estate.

Soc Clay of Kentucky is an accomplished and prolific fishing writer and photographer whose work has appeared in every major outdoor periodical in North America.

Angelo Cuanang of California is a Pacific Regional Editor for *Salt Water Sportsman* and a freelance writer and photographer.

Paula J. Del Giudice of Nevada is Outdoor Columnist for the *Las Vegas Sun*; a freelance writer, photographer, and book author; and former President of the Nevada Wildlife Federation.

Arthur De Mello of Uganda is a representative for the IGFA in Uganda.

Hansjörg Dietiker of Switzerland is Editor of the Swiss Anglers Magazine *Petri-Heil*, and an IGFA representative.

Philippe Dolivet of France is the Chief Editor of the French fly fishing magazine *Plaisirs de la Pêche* and a professional photographer; he is a fly fishing instructor and competitor, an ichthyologist, and an IGFA representative.

Gary Edwards of Wyoming is a longtime fishing guide and a television show host; he is the former Editor and Publisher of *Salmon Fever* magazine, and a former fly rod world record holder.

D'arcy Egan of Ohio has been a sportswriter for *The Cleveland Plain Dealer* for over 20 years; he authored the book, *Guide to Ohio Fishing*, and is host of the American Outdoorsman Radio Network.

Bill Ensor of New Brunswick works for the Fish & Wildlife Branch of the New Brunswick Department of Natural Resources; he was formerly marketing manager of fishing and hunting for the New Brunswick Department of Tourism, and is a longtime fishing guide.

Jack Erskine of Australia is a foremost big-game tackle designer and technical innovator who has helped design many of the modern rods, reels, and drag systems in use today.

Stan Fagerstrom of Oregon is one of the world's best known trick and accuracy casters, and has been featured at sport shows worldwide for half a century; he is also a book, magazine, and newspaper writer.

Jan Fogt of Florida is Editor of *The Bahamas Sportfishing Guide* and was the founding editor of *Bahamas Blue Water Magazine*; she is a contributing editor for *Sport Fishing* and *Marlin* magazines, and is also a book author.

Frank Fry of the Yukon Territory has worked with the Yukon Territory's Department of Natural Resources on various fishing projects.

Mike Garzillo of New Hampshire has been a newspaper columnist for 24 years; he is a regular contributor to various publications and a former regional editor for *Outdoor Life*.

Alessandro Giangio of Italy writes for Italy's premier fishing magazine, *Pesca in Mare*, and has been published worldwide; he has authored five books, is owner and master instructor of the Fishbuster Trolling School and Sportfishing Travel, and has a charter boat in Huatulco, Mexico.

Jerry Gibbs of Vermont is Fishing Editor of *Outdoor Life*, where his career as a staff writer has spanned three decades and made him one of North America's most respected angling authors; he has written several books and has been inducted into the Fishing Hall of Fame.

Barry Gibson of Massachusetts is Editor of *Salt Water Sportsman* and a longtime Maine charter boat captain; he is a former member of the New England Fishery Management Council, and former advisor to the International Commission for the Conservation of Atlantic Tunas.

Jerry Gomber of New Jersey has over twenty-five years of experience in design, development, and marketing of fishing rods and reels; during that period he has been responsible for several successful product innovations.

George Gruenefeld of Quebec and Saskatchewan is Editor of *Canadian Outdoor Publications*; he has written for many magazines in Canada and the U.S., is a book author, and was formerly Outdoors Editor for the *Montreal Gazette*.

Chris Hanks of the Northwest Territories is an anthropologist, freelance writer, and author of the book *Fly Fishing in the Northwest Territories*.

Steve Harper of Kansas is the Outdoors Editor of the *Wichita Eagle* and author of the book *Kansas Day Trips*; in 1995 he was named Conservation Communicator of the Year by the Kansas Wildlife Federation.

Dan Heiner of Alaska is an advertising agency executive and former editor and writer for *Alaska Outdoors* magazine; he is the author of four books on Alaska fishing, including *Fly Fishing Alaska's Wild Rivers*.

Bob Hodge of Tennessee is the Outdoors Editor of the *Knoxville News-Sentinel*; he was named the state's Best Outdoor Writer for 1996-97 by the Tennessee Sportswriters Association.

Grant Hopkins of Ontario is the outdoor columnist for the *Ottawa Citizen*, a frequent contributor to *Ontario Out of Doors*, and retired from the Royal Canadian Air Force.

John Husar of Illinois is the longtime outdoors columnist and general sportswriter of the *Chicago Tribune* and co-host of a Chicago radio show; he has worked for newspapers in Kansas, Texas, and New Mexico, and has covered the last nine Olympics.

Jim Imai of California has a Ph.D in physics and is Professor of Physics at California State University, Dominguez Hills; he is a Consulting Physicist for the Daiwa Corporation, and a leading authority on the design and performance of fishing reels and rods.

James Kano of Ontario is the Marketing Director of Japan Communications in Toronto and Outdoor Coordinator for the Press and Tourism division of the Ontario government; his articles have appeared online and in newspapers, guide books, and magazines.

Nick Karas of New York is the retired outdoor columnist for (New York) *Newsday* and a charter boat captain and ichthyologist; he has written for many national magazines and authored a dozen books, including *The Striped Bass* and *Brook Trout*.

Lee Kernen of Wisconsin is the retired Director of Fisheries for the State of Wisconsin; he is also a writer, fishing guide, and fisheries consultant.

Ronnie Kovach of California is a radio and television show host, educator, magazine writer, guide, and author of five books, including *Bass Fishing in California*, *Trout Fishing in California*, and *Saltwater Fishing in California*.

Steen Larsen of Denmark is one of Europe's leading sportfishing writers and photographers; he is a book author and lecturer, and contributes widely to many European angling publications.

Dick Lewers of Australia is Technical Editor of *Encyclopaedia of Australian Fishing*, author of seven books on angling, a former IGFA representative, 35-year columnist for *Modern Fishing Magazine*, and past President of the Australian National Sportfishing Association.

Bill Loftus of Idaho is the Outdoors Editor of the *Lewiston Morning Tribune* and the author of two guidebooks to Idaho.

Maurice Loustau-LaLanne of Seychelles is the Principal Secretary in the Ministry of Tourism and Transport for the Seychelles, and an IGFA representative.

Carl. F. Luckey of Alabama is a writer specializing in antiques and collectibles; he has authored ten books, including his best-selling, 618-page work, *Old Fishing Lures and Tackle*.

Joe Macaluso of Louisiana is an award-winning outdoors sportswriter/editor for the *Baton Rouge Advocate*; his weekly fishing reports have appeared in Louisiana newspapers since 1976.

Rosanne Macfarlane of Prince Edward Island recently received her Masters degree in Biology at

Acadia University; she works for the Department of Fisheries and Environment.

Dennis Maksymetz of Manitoba is Manager of Tourism Marketing for the Industry, Trade and Tourism division of the Manitoba government.

Don Mann of Florida is a longtime contributor to *Florida Sportsman*, a record-holding big-game angler, and book author; his articles and photographs have appeared in many publications.

Al Marlowe of Colorado has written numerous articles for outdoor magazines; he authored a trail guide for the Flat Tops Wilderness area and a fly fishing guide for the Colorado River.

Peter B. Mathiesen of Missouri is Executive Editor and Producer of the *Field & Stream Radio Hour*; he is also a magazine writer, photographer, and video and television show producer.

John McCoy of West Virginia is Outdoors Editor for the *Charleston Daily Mail*, Regional Editor for *Field & Stream*, and a frequent contributor to regional and national magazines.

Tom Meade of Rhode Island writes about the outdoors for the *Providence Journal-Bulletin*; he is the author of *Essential Fly Fishing*, and writes for various magazines.

Ed Migdalski of Connecticut is the retired Director of Yale University's Outdoor Education and Club Sports Programs, retired Ichthyologist for the Yale Peabody Museum, and holder of the current world record for the largest strictly freshwater fish (pirarucu) ever caught on rod and reel.

Kent Mitchell of Georgia has covered outdoor sports for the *Atlanta Journal-Constitution* for three decades; he has received the Communicator of the Year Award from the Georgia Wildlife Federation, and has authored three books on martial arts.

Bill Monroe of Oregon has covered the outdoors for his state's largest daily newspaper, *The Oregonian*, for 18 years.

Gary W. Moore of Vermont is a freelance writer and photographer; he is former Commissioner of the Vermont Fish and Wildlife Department and former Chairman of the Vermont Water Resources Board.

Sam Mossman of New Zealand is Special Projects Editor for *New Zealand Fishing News* magazine; he is the author of three books and hundreds of magazine articles, and has held five world and numerous New Zealand fishing records.

Perry Munro of Nova Scotia is a writer and artist who contributes to *The Atlantic Salmon Journal* and various other magazines; he is also an outfitter, master guide, operator of Maple Mountain Lodge, and a Director of Trout Unlimited Canada.

Iain Nicolson of Angola is an IGFA representative and has a Ph.D. in molecular genetics; he and his family pioneered fishing for blue marlin in Angola and collectively established six world fishing records.

Chris Niskanen of Minnesota is the Outdoors Editor of the *St. Paul Pioneer Press*.

Donald J. Orth of Virginia is a Professor of Fisheries Science in the Department of Fisheries & Wildlife Sciences at Virginia Polytechnic Institute.

Tom Pagliaroli of New Jersey is an advertising agency executive, freelance writer, and photographer whose work has appeared in various regional and national publications.

Ali Pasiner of Turkey is an attorney, the author of two fishing books, and a consultant to the Turkish version of the *Encyclopaedia Britannica*; he is also a writer, editor, and representative of the IGFA.

C. Boyd Pfeiffer of Maryland is a longtime journalist and photographer, a regular columnist for many angling magazines, and the author of numerous books on fishing topics, the latest of which is *Fly Fishing Salt Water Basics*.

Larry Porter of Nebraska has been on the sports staff of the *Omaha World-Herald* for over three decades and their outdoors writer since 1990; he has been named Nebraska Sportswriter of the Year three times, and is a former professional tournament angler.

Steve Price of Texas is a longtime Senior Writer for *Bassmaster* magazine and contributor to a wide variety of national sporting magazines; he is an accomplished photographer and author of several books.

Gareth Purnell of England is Editor of Britain's leading angling magazine, *Improve Your Coarse Fishing*, and former News Editor of *Angling Times*; he has fished annually in the World Freshwater Angling Championships since 1993.

George Reiger of Virginia is Conservation Editor of *Field & Stream* and *Salt Water Sportsman* magazines and the most widely respected conservation writer in North America; he has been a staff writer for *Field & Stream* since 1972, is the author of seven books on angling and marine ecology, and the recipient of numerous honors and awards.

Tim Renken of Missouri has been the outdoors writer for the *St. Louis Post-Dispatch* since 1963; he previously worked for the Nebraska Game Commission.

Len Rich of Newfoundland is the author of two books and many outdoor magazine articles; he operates Awesome Lake Lodge in Labrador, is a former Hunting and Fishing Development Officer for Newfoundland and Labrador, and is a past representative of the Atlantic Salmon Federation.

Tom Richardson of Massachusetts is Managing Editor of *Salt Water Sportsman* magazine, as well as a freelance writer and photographer.

Al Ristori of New Jersey is Saltwater Fishing Editor of the *Newark Star-Ledger*, Regional Editor of *Salt Water Sportsman*, Conservation Editor of *The Fisherman* magazine, and the author of several books;

he is also a charter boat captain and has served on the Mid-Atlantic Fishery Management Council.

Jim Rizzuto of Hawaii is Hawaii Editor for *Salt Water Sportsman* and *Western Outdoors*, a longtime columnist for *West Hawaii Today* and *Hawaii Fishing News*, and the author of the books *Modern Hawaiian Gamefishing* and *Fishing Hawaii Style*.

Nels Rodefeld of Oklahoma is an avid angler and hunter who frequently covers Oklahoma's hunting and fishing scene.

Milt Rosko of New Jersey is a writer for *Big Game Fishing Journal* and various other publications and a longtime authority on saltwater sportfishing; he is a photographer, book author, magazine feature writer, and lecturer.

Terry Rudnick of Washington has been writing articles on Northwest fishing subjects for more than 25 years; he is the author of the book *Washington Fishing, the Complete Guide*, and co-author of *How to Catch Trophy Halibut*.

Bob Sampson, Jr. of Connecticut is a writer, photographer, science teacher, and fisheries biologist; his work has appeared in numerous national and regional magazines.

Jack Samson of New Mexico is the retired Editor-in-Chief of *Field & Stream* and a former Associated Press columnist; he is Saltwater Editor of *Fly Rod & Reel* magazine, author of twenty books, and the first angler to catch both Atlantic and Pacific sailfish and all five species of marlin on a fly.

Ray Sasser of Texas is the Outdoor Editor of *The Dallas Morning News* and a freelance contributor to various magazines; he has been writing about outdoor sports for over 25 years.

Carl Werner Schmidt-Luchs of Germany is a contributor to *Blinker*, the largest angling magazine in Europe; he is a photographer, writer, and author of a dozen angling books.

Kristen Schultz of Massachusetts is a writer who recently graduated from Oberlin College; she works for an engineering consulting firm.

Bill Scifres of Indiana has been the Outdoor Editor of the *Indianapolis Star* since 1953; he is a book author, freelance writer, and photographer.

Eric Sharp of Michigan is Outdoor Editor of *The Detroit News*, and was formerly Outdoor Editor of *The Miami Herald*.

Luis Sier of Argentina is a newspaper columnist, a former magazine publisher, and an outfitter who operates several Argentinian fishing camps.

Jeff Simpson of South Dakota is an information officer for the State of South Dakota, a book author and freelance magazine writer, and former project developer for Cowles Creative Publishing.

DeWayne Smith of Arizona is an information officer for the Maricopa County Parks and Recreation Department; he covered the outdoors for over 30 years for *The Phoenix Gazette*.

Ryan Smith of Virginia is a research assistant with the Department of Fisheries and Wildlife Sciences at Virginia Polytechnic Institute.

Michael Snook of Saskatchewan is a freelance writer, conservationist, outdoor educator, and television producer.

Frank Sousa of Massachusetts is a writer for the *Springfield Sunday Republican* and the *Union News*, Editor/Publisher of *Northeast Woods and Waters*, and a freelance writer and photographer.

Vin T. Sparano of New Jersey is Senior Field Editor and retired Editor-in-Chief of *Outdoor Life*, for whom he worked for over three decades; he is a former syndicated columnist for *Gannett Newspapers*, and the author/editor of fourteen books, including *The Complete Outdoors Encyclopedia*.

Vladimir Stakic of Yugoslavia is Deputy Editor-in-Chief of the Yugoslavian angling magazines *Ribolovacka Revija* and *Ribolovacke Novine*, a freelance writer, and the author of three books of short stories.

Bob Stearns of Florida has been the staff boating/saltwater fishing writer of *Field & Stream* for 20 years and is the Electronics Editor of *Salt Water Sportsman*; the author of two books, he is a renowned fly fishing and light tackle expert, and has held two fly rod world records for sailfish.

Larry Stone of Iowa has been a writer and photographer for over three decades, and writes about the outdoors for the *Des Moines Register*.

Keith Sutton of Arkansas is Editor of *Arkansas Wildlife magazine*, a conservation publication of the Arkansas Game & Fish Commission, and a prolific freelance writer and photographer.

Ferenc Szalay of Hungary is Editor-in-Chief of *Magyar Horgász*, Hungary's premier fishing magazine; he is also President of the Hungarian National Committee for Match Fishing and Executive Board member of the Federation Internationale de la Pêche Sportive en Eau Douce.

Allan Tarvid of Texas is a contributing editor for *Sport Fishing* magazine and has authored hundreds of articles on electronics for sporting and commercial fishing and emergency service use; he has been a fishing guide and search and rescue diver.

Rikk Taylor of British Columbia is Editor and Publisher of *British Columbia Sport Fishing* magazine.

Mick Thill of Illinois and England is one of the world's top professional match fishing anglers and the first and only person to medal in the open water and ice fishing World Freshwater Fishing Championships; he is also a prominent float designer, and coach of the U. S. World Championship fishing teams.

Albert A. W. Threadingham of Fiji is an IGFA

representative for the Fiji Islands and Governor of the Hawaiian International Billfish Association and the Pacific Ocean Research Foundation; he is a former world-record fish holder.

Raj Tilak of Maryland and India is co-author of the book *Game Fishes of India and Angling,* and author of more than 200 research publications; he is experienced in fisheries and wildlife management, with extensive knowledge of gamefishes and their ecology in India.

Anssi Uitti of Finland works for the Finnish outdoor magazine *Metsästys ja Kalastus*, and his articles have appeared in *Urheilukalastus* (Sportfishing) and *Perhokalastus* (Flyfishing) magazines.

Luis Umpierre of Puerto Rico is a physician, Editor of *Notipesca* (Fishing News), President of the Puerto Rico Sportfishing Association, and advisory member of the Caribbean Fishery Management Council.

Rudy Van Duijnhoven of Holland is a freelance photographer and author; his work appears monthly in *BEET-Sportvissers* magazine, and he is European Correspondent for Fly Fishing in *Salt Waters* magazine.

Carlo Vernocchi of Italy and Zanzibar introduced modern big-game fishing to the Zanzibar archipelago of Tanzania in 1992; he is an IGFA representative and charter boat captain.

Victor Villavicencio of Manila is a representative for the IGFA in the Philippines.

Tsutomu Wakabayashi of Japan is the General Manager of the Japan Game Fish Association; he has written for several Japanese fishing magazines, and is an IGFA representative.

Steve Waters of Florida is the outdoors writer for the *Fort Lauderdale Sun-Sentinel* and occasionally writes for national magazines; he was formerly a newspaper writer and video executive in New York.

Tom Wharton of Utah has been Outdoor Editor of the *Salt Lake Tribune* since 1976; he has co-authored five books, and is past President of the Outdoor Writers Association of America.

Jesse E. Williams of New Mexico is the retired Chief of Public Affairs for the New Mexico Department of Game and Fish, and a former Colorado wildlife manager and environmental education supervisor.

Juergen Willms of the Yukon Territory has worked with the Yukon Territory's Department of Natural Resources on various fishing projects.

Jorge Xifra of Paraguay operates El Pescador, a sportfishing outfitting service; he is a writer, television show host, IGFA representative, and holder of four world fishing records.

Photo Credits

ALL PHOTOGRAPHS BY KEN SCHULTZ EXCEPT FOR THE FOLLOWING:

Ron Ballanti 2, 4, 16
Eric Burnley 236
C-Map 43
Garmin 45

Steve Goione 135
Nick Karas 253
Steen Larsen 104, 198
Penn Fishing Tackle 155, 158, 160, 163

Al Ristori 239
Mick Thill 125, 127, 256
Zebco 24

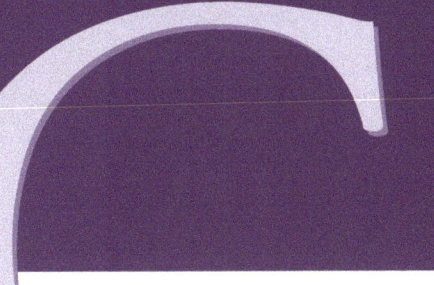

CADDISFLIES

Caddisflies belong to the scientific order Trichoptera, a term derived from *tricho,* meaning hair, and *ptera,* meaning wing, owing to the fact that hairs cover the wings. They are a large group of hardy organisms that have adapted to many types of aquatic environments. Their life cycle is different from that of mayflies *(see)* and stoneflies *(see)* since they have no nymph form; it consists of egg, larva, pupa, and adult stages, with most of the cycle being in the wormlike or grublike larva stage. Typically, caddisflies have one generation (hatch) per year, but many have several overlapping generations annually.

Many caddisfly larvae construct cases or houses out of a variety of different materials, including rocks, sand, gravel, twigs, leaves, or other debris, using a gluey substance secreted from their back end. The short, sticklike case is dragged along with the larva as it searches for food on the bottom of a stream or lake. Often, the methods and materials a caddisfly uses to construct its case can be helpful in identifying its taxonomic group. Certain caddisflies (family Hydropsychidae) are also known to spin webs for trapping food from flowing water. Fish eat the larva, case and all.

When it is time to mature, the caddisfly larva develops into its preadult stage, the pupa, in which the larva changes form inside the now-sealed cocoon-type case. The pupating period takes several weeks; then the pupa emerges, quickly migrates to the surface, and hatches into a winged adult. The appearance on the surface is brief, because most caddisflies appear suddenly, bounce a few times, and fly off, looking much like moths. The adults do not hold their wings upright at rest like mayflies, but fold them over their abdomen in tentlike fashion. The brief period of emerging pupa and winged adult provides quick foraging opportunities for fish.

Caddisfly

Larva

Adult

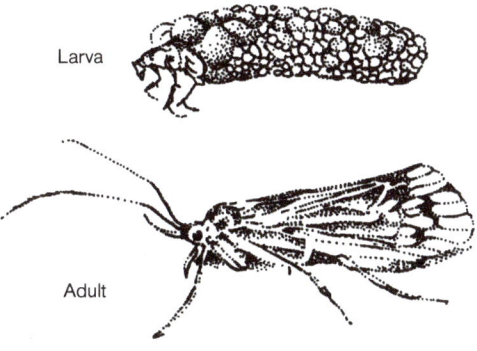

Caddisfly adults live from several days to several weeks depending on species. They mate in flight. Some females deposit their eggs on the water, alternately drifting and bouncing across the surface; yet other species land on the surface and swim to the bottom to deposit their eggs. Both behaviors provide significant feeding opportunity for fish, even more so than for other aquatic insects during the egg-laying period. The mating flights usually occur in the afternoon and evening, and may appear as a swarm. Hatches of caddisflies are drawn out well over the season.

Caddisfly larvae are up to $1^{1}/_{2}$ inches long and are mostly distinguished by these characteristics: three pairs of segmented and usually hooked legs on the upper middle section of the body; two small fleshy extensions at the end of the abdomen that may have a hairy or feathery appearance and end in a single hook; filamentous gills that may be present on the underside or end of the abdomen; and no antennae, or antennae that are very small and inconspicuous. They also have a characteristic motion, known as the caddisfly dance, of wiggling back and forth and then up and down in the water.

Caddisfly larvae may be confused with the larvae of dobsonflies, fishflies, alderflies, beetles, or aquatic caterpillars. Caddisfly larvae can be distinguished by the presence of single hooks on the end of each leg and at both tips of a slightly forked abdomen; dobsonfly and fishfly larvae have a forked tail with two distinct hooks on each fork, and similar beetle larvae have four hooks extending from a single point on the end of the abdomen. In addition, caddisfly larvae do not have long pointed tails (like alderfly) or caterpillar-like legs (like aquatic caterpillars or watersnipe fly larvae).

Like dobsonfly larvae, the caddisfly larvae may have fluffy gills on the underside (along the belly), but caddisflies do not have the fleshy or hairlike appendages protruding from the sides of the abdomen that are characteristic of dobsonfly, alderfly, fishfly, or certain beetle larvae.
See: **Aquatic Insects.**

CALIFORNIA

California is an angler's paradise. How could this not be the case in a state that covers nearly 159,000 square miles, has 2,674 square miles of inland water, and spans 3,400 miles of shoreline? California leads all of the states in numbers of

California

Yellowtail anglers enjoy a double hookup off Catalina Island.

licensed anglers, with more than 2 million, and it's small wonder. With thousands of lakes, and with people on the eastern boundary only 220 miles from the ocean, there is a plentiful and accessible array of fishing opportunities in the Golden State, almost all of them available year-round.

Near the Mexican border, anglers can experience sizzling saltwater action not only in the ocean, but also at an inland waterway, the Salton Sea. San Diego's city lake chain is home to world-class double-digit-size largemouth bass, and around the Los Angeles metropolitan area, Catalina Island and other offshore areas provide enviable opportunities for a variety of species, particularly yellowtail and huge white seabass. At nearby tiny Irvine Lake, trout anglers catch more trophy rainbows than anywhere else in the state.

Along the central coast, diversity in the salt extends from schools of albacore tuna to king and silver salmon, and in freshwater, from numerous bass lakes to trout streams. Farther inland, some of the finest mountain trout fishing in the country exists on both slopes of the majestic High Sierra.

Fishing is equally varied in Northern California. Large waterways like the Sacramento River Delta and San Francisco Bay yield striped bass, sharks, and sturgeon, while freshwater sites range from large Lakes Tahoe and Shasta to numerous small lakes and wild trout streams and rivers.

Getting a handle on the breadth of California's fisheries is a challenge, but separating the state angling opportunities into three broad segments—trout and salmon, warmwater/bass, and coastal and offshore fishing in saltwater—makes that challenge less daunting.

Trout and Salmon

Trout are the most popular gamefish species in both freshwater and saltwater in the Golden State, and California's wide range of trout waters is guaranteed to satisfy anglers, no matter how they fish or what means they use.

Numerous man-made impoundments in Southern California are within an hour's drive of many of the cities and towns between San Diego and Los Angeles. These lakes have unfairly received the reputation of being simply put-and-take reservoirs, but innovative stocking programs at many have resulted in annual catches of numerous trophy trout over 5 pounds.

Deeper Southern California lakes, including those in the San Diego reservoir system, sustain a trout population all year long. Many planted rainbows hold over through the winter and grow to healthy proportions. These trout lazily feed on abundant threadfin shad and are not restricted by short seasonal growth periods, as are trout in the colder and higher regions of the state.

In the northern part of Southern California, the complexion of the trout fishery changes somewhat. Trout in lakes such as Casitas share an important permanent niche in the lake ecology with warmwater species. These lakes have strong trout populations providing year-round sportfishing.

Trout are the primary sportfish in the midsection of California, through the Central Valley and into the High Sierra. Their dominance increases with elevation. Some High Sierra lakes, including Crowley, Bridgeport, and Twin, are renowned for their excellent trout fisheries. Many large rainbow and brown trout are consistently taken from these mountain lakes.

In Northern California, many small creeks, streams, and larger rivers sustain great trout fishing. Hotspots like the Owens, Truckee, and Walker Rivers have long been bonanzas for California fly anglers. This type of water is distinctly absent in the southern portion of the state.

Northern California possesses many semi-alpine lakes, such as Trinity and Shasta, that support warmwater species, including bass and trout. The Upper Sacramento River, Hat Creek, the McCloud River, and the Fall River are among the great trout waters, and thousands of pristine mountain lakes and streams are available throughout the region. Not to be overlooked are outstanding trout angling opportunities and extraordinary scenery in the far northeastern corner of the state.

Southern California. More trophy-size rainbows are taken from Orange County than from anywhere else in California. Irvine Lake, in particular, has an astonishing track record. Lake managers plant magnum-size hatchery-raised rainbows here. Although Riverside County has only a few trout lakes, they offer quality fishing. Lake Skinner is the top trout lake in this region, producing 1- to 2-pound fish nine months a year. San Diego County generates excellent winter and early spring fishing. Trophy-size trout are rare here, but the volume of fish at Poway, Jennings, and Cuyamaca is outstanding.

Lake Cuyamaca. Little-known Lake Cuyamaca is stocked with rainbows year-round, but the fishing is best in winter. Both bank and shore fishing are productive, especially along the log boom and the west shore. This is a scenic alpine fishery, where temperatures can drop to well below freezing during colder months.

Dixon Lake. Dixon is a small lake stocked with large quantities of pan-size rainbows from November through May. Trout in the 10-pound range add spice to the standard small plants.

Irvine Lake. A small reservoir in the foothills of Orange County, Irvine is a premier trophy trout fishery. Seasonal plants by the state are augmented with commercially raised rainbows that reach lunker size in a short time. Irvine has two trout seasons, one that starts in the fall and another that coincides with the High Sierra opener. It is estimated that more trophy-class fish over 5 pounds are caught at Irvine's spring opener than in all of the High Sierra lakes combined. Trout fishing is prime here from fall through late spring.

Lake Jennings. Covering only 85 acres, Lake Jennings has some of the best trout fishing in the region. It is regularly stocked from winter through early spring. Most trout are small, but a few 6- to 8-pounders are caught each year. Bank fishing is truly exceptional at Jennings. Boaters like to stillfish the deeper water near the dam.

Lake Miramar. Miramar excels in late winter and early spring, and produces quantities of trout following weekly plants. Trollers should try a flatline approach in the early part of the season. Bank fishing at Miramar can be highly productive, especially during midweek, when there's less pressure.

Lake Poway. A stellar trout lake lately, Poway is loaded with chunky rainbows, many caught from November through May. Most of the fish are under 2 pounds, but 5- and 6-pounders exist. Weed growth is heavy here, so it's necessary to keep your offering above the bottom.

Lake Skinner. Another notable trout impoundment, Lake Skinner doesn't have lunkers, but weekly plantings of 10- to 14-inch rainbows keep anglers busy. The prime spot is near the spillway, especially if the water is flowing over the dam, which churns up the bait and stimulates the bite. Sheltered coves in the east and south ends of the lake, and long rocky points, are also good trout-holding spots at Skinner.

Lake Wohlford. From January through the end of May this small Lake Wohlford steadily produces small rainbows. Shore anglers should try the boat docks as well as Oakdale and Willow Coves. Boaters like the buoy line by the dam and the cove across from the docks. Salmon eggs, marshmallows, and nightcrawlers are standard trout baits.

Los Angeles area. Trout fishing in the Los Angeles area can be challenging. The key to success is timing, with late winter through early spring best. Most trout here are planted pan-size rainbows; however, commercial stocking augments the state's program and provides larger specimens up to 10 pounds.

Two unexpected treats a short drive from the heart of Los Angeles are the West Fork of the San Gabriel River and the Upper Sespe Creek. These are bona fide wild trout rivers offering some of the most spectacular angling in the state.

Fly anglers should consider exploring the three major streams of the San Bernardino Mountains: the Santa Ana River, Bear Creek, and Deep Creek. Each has its own unique brand of fishing and all are excellent destinations for the angler seeking isolated waters in crowded Southern California.

Big Bear Lake. Big Bear is the largest lake in the San Bernardino Mountains and is considered the best of all Southern California trout lakes. This mountain reservoir has year-round angling, including ice fishing in the winter, with best results from late spring through fall.

Floating baits are particularly good here since they suspend above the weedy bottom. Shore casting is productive in the deep water at the west end of the lake. And trollers do well during the height of the season, with flatline and lead-core strategies excellent options.

Fly fishing can be spectacular at Big Bear during the summer. Both shore casting and fly trolling with traditional fly fishing gear work well. Bubble and fly rigs give bank anglers and waders an excellent opportunity to take quality 1- to 3-pound rainbows.

Lake Casitas. Casitas is one of the most popular recreational destinations in Southern California. In spite of the crowds, the lake produces some quality angling for rainbow trout, which are stocked from October through May. Trollers generally catch the larger fish.

Lake Piru. Piru provides considerable angling activity from December through March, when rainbows are planted. The trout fishing at Piru seems to be unaffected by changes in water levels, which can fluctuate seasonally. Shore anglers should focus on the west shore. Trollers have the greatest success in the summer.

San Gabriel River. The West Fork of the San Gabriel River, in spite of its proximity to downtown Los Angeles, has some of the finest wild trout waters in the West. Good options are the area past the Rincon Ranger Station, and the section below the second bridge where Bear Creek converges with the West Fork. Ultralight spinners and dry flies produce in this river. Spring and fall are best for fly fishing, although it may be necessary to scale down all the way to tiny size-26 dry flies for clear shallow areas.

Bay Area/Central Coast. The San Francisco Bay area has a wealth of sites that offer surprisingly good trout fishing. Some are small urban lakes, whereas others—such as San Pablo near Berkeley—approach 1,000 acres. San Pablo Lake experiences excellent fishing for trout in the 3- to 6-pound range.

At other bay-area lakes, such as Parkway or Del Valle, weekly trout plants during colder months produce outstanding shoreline action for stocked rainbow trout. Occasionally these metropolitan lakes are also stocked with huge 8- to 10-pounders—the fish of a lifetime for many people—just a few minutes from downtown San Francisco.

Southern Sierras. Trout fishing can range from terrific to tough in the waters of the Southern Sierras. Huntington Lake can be a standout in the early season. The Kern River also has remarkably good fishing for the stream angler.

Huntington Lake. Rainbows, browns, kokanee, and a few wayward brookies abound at Huntington Lake. There is some good boat and shore activity for 12- to 16-inch trout, as well as larger holdover fish. The angler on foot has some 14 miles of shoreline to explore. Early May can be an outstanding time to fish Huntington.

Kern River. The Kern is one of the most popular fishing holes in the state. Some of the best fishing is in the area above Lake Isabella, starting at Kernville. Early in the season, many small rainbow trout frequent these waters. Some anglers may encounter a lunker brown or jumbo rainbow using artificials. The higher up you travel, the better the chance of tying into a trophy specimen, especially on dry or wet flies.

Central Sierras. This area has sensational angling with minimal pressure. The lakes in the Carson Pass offer exciting trout fishing. Backpackers can select from scores of lakes in this region of the Sierras, and only a handful of hikers each season visits these remote alpine lakes, which are teeming with rainbows, browns, and brookies.

Emigrant Wilderness Area. There's a wealth of lakes in the 100,000 acres of pristine Emigrant Wilderness Area, which is located about 30 miles west of Sonora in the western Sierra Nevada. The forested terrain varies from rolling hills to ridges and granite domes. The best angling is at the lakes in the southwestern portion of this wilderness. Fly fishing is the best strategy, especially for native brown trout; natural baits are also a good choice. Hikers might consider packing-in a small inflatable boat.

Anglers venturing into this region to find some of these high-country lakes should carry a good topographic map and a compass, and perhaps a GPS unit. Many are not on marked trails, and some rock scrambling may be necessary. Be sure to file a trip itinerary with the local ranger's office and obtain required permits before heading into this remote wilderness.

Mokelumne and Merced Rivers. The Mokelumne and the Merced offer excellent fishing. The Merced River from below Crocker-Hoffman Dam to Merced Falls has a solid population of small rainbows. Both dry and wet flies produce on this river, especially for anglers willing to wade.

Numerous prime runs along the Mokelumne River are worth trying. This river is best fished by wading, or from a boat when the water is high. Dry-fly fishing can be outstanding from late spring to early summer. Although plenty of legal-size rainbows are planted along the Mokelumne each

A trout fishing scene in the western Sierras.

season, 16-inch-class fish can be found in the quiet, less-accessible deep pools.

Lake Tahoe. A magnificent crystalline body of water, Lake Tahoe is the jewel of the Central Sierras and home to gigantic mackinaw trout. Submersible research vessels have observed schools of these fish in the 40- to 50-pound range. Anglers trolling for mackinaws use a variety of methods; deep fishing with large jigs tipped with minnows can be successful at times.

There are also considerable numbers of rainbows, kokanee salmon, and even brown trout at Tahoe. Near-surface trolling, especially in the fall, is often successful. Locals prefer plugs that mimic rainbow trout or have dark finishes, and they tend to troll fast in this clear water, to give rainbows and browns less opportunity to study the lure.

Baitfishing is best from a boat at the mouth of Emerald Bay and at Logan Shoals. Fishing from shore is difficult but is most successful after a big wind, when the surface water is churned up with forage baits and other food.

Yosemite National Park. Trout fishing at Yosemite means getting out of the valley and up into the high country. The Tuolumne Meadows area off Highway 120 is easily fished. The Dana Fork area holds larger trout, as does the Lyell Fork area along John Muir Trail, south of the meadows. This beautiful trout stream meanders through the Upper Tuolumne Meadows and offers good brook trout fishing in the morning and evening. Plan on a four-hour hike.

Backpackers can choose Edith, Wilmer, or Tilden Lakes out of the Hetch Hetchy Dam area. These lakes hold both brookies and goldens. More than 300 significant lakes grace the Yosemite high country, but there is good fishing at only about one-third of them.

Eastern Sierras. The Eastern Sierras get more angling pressure than any other part of the Golden State. Two of California's most majestic rivers, the Walker and the Owens, tumble through this region and are known for trophy brown trout. In addition, both Bridgeport and Twin Lakes hold brown trout exceeding 30 pounds. Many lunker hunters spend long hours at these lakes in quest of the fish of a lifetime.

In the western U.S., there is perhaps no event that comes close to the excitement of the Lake Crowley Opener. This occasion signals the opening of the High Sierra season and is an essential part of the fishing year for hundreds of California anglers who visit the lake in quest of their first trout of the spring. The Eastern Sierras also hold dozens of other fine trout lakes and streams scattered throughout the magnificent wilderness lands of Inyo and Mono Counties.

Lone Pine, Independence, Big Pine area. The southernmost locales of the Eastern Sierras offer a series of fine mountain trout fisheries off access roads from U.S. Highway 395. There are creeks loaded with planted trout as well as trail heads into the wilderness areas. The high country provides good fishing opportunities at lakes ranging in size from 4 to 25 acres, at altitudes of 10,000 to 11,000 feet. Both rainbow and brook trout inhabit these lakes. The best months are June through September.

Bishop area. Bishop is one of the centers of Eastern Sierra fishing. The elevation of lakes in this area varies from 7,000 to 9,000 feet, although the higher-elevation lakes are accessible only in the warmer months. Bishop Creek, and the lake at its headwaters, are planted regularly and generate good angling. A few excellent trout lakes in this area are accessible by car. The headwaters of Bishop, Pine, and Rock Creeks are also good starting points for wilderness pack-in trout trips.

Lower Rock Creek, which runs from Tom's Place along Route 395 to Pleasant Valley Reservoir, is a very special trout stream. It holds both wild and planted fish, including large browns and rainbows. The upper reaches of this stream are accessible by a good trail and produce many wild brown trout. The last mile of Lower Rock Creek, before it empties into Pleasant Valley Reservoir, has an entirely different character. At the Los Angeles Department of Water and Power plant, Lower Rock Creek joins Pine Creek and the Owens River Aqueduct system to create a large river. Anglers catch many trophy browns and rainbows in this converging water. Pleasant Valley Reservoir is a highly underrated trophy trout fishery. There's a healthy population of medium-size rainbows in this impoundment, but the real treat is tackle-busting giant brown trout. There are a number of 20-pound-class fish here. Be prepared to do some serious rock hopping in order to get around the rugged shoreline. No boats are allowed, so all the hotspots must be approached along the bank. Early and late in the season are the best times, and it's good to use an outfit that permits long casting, as well as heavier line. Big spinners and spoons are a good choice, and magnum minnow plugs in rainbow trout finish are popular with lunker hunters.

Crowley Lake. As mentioned, there is probably no greater California fishing spectacle than the traditional opening-day extravaganza at Crowley, which is usually in mid-April and inaugurates trout season in the Sierras. Trout anglers from all over the West converge on this lake for the event. It is planted with hundreds of thousands of small rainbow trout each summer, and by the following season opener, these average almost a pound each. Trolling is the best method for catching larger rainbows and browns in the early season.

From August through October, a second (no bait) season goes into effect, as anglers gear up for trophy rainbows and browns. At this time of year, a legion of dedicated float tubers visit Crowley and work the weedbeds using flies that replicate small Sacramento perch, an important forage food for bigger trout.

The Owens River. The Owens produces many trophy-size trout. The two runs of the Upper Owens, from Benton Crossing and from Big Springs, are prime spots. The Owens Gorge below Lake Crowley also has a reputation for quality fish.

The Upper Owens River, which feeds Lake Crowley, is a meadow stream with open banks and excellent fly fishing water. Concentrate on the undercut banks in late evening. Good-size browns hold in these areas, and the section downstream out of Benton Crossing is especially good in the early spring for rainbows coming up from Lake Crowley to spawn. Excellent fly fishing here generates a lot of excitement.

Convict Lake. Located north on Route 395 a short distance above Crowley Lake, Convict Lake is one of the most beautiful spots in the Eastern Sierras, with rugged peaks surrounding clear, cold waters. Fishing for rainbows and lunker browns is generally best in late spring and early fall, but can also be good in summer months. It's possible to hike from Convict to about six small mountain lakes and numerous streams to find fishing and spectacular scenery.

Mammoth Lakes. Long recognized as a mecca for Southern California snow skiers, the Mammoth Lakes basin excels as a trout fishery in summer. This area is only a short distance off Route 395 above Crowley Lake. The town of Mammoth Lakes is a jumping-off point for a variety of good trout fishing experiences, including lake, stream, day-hike, and pack-in angling. There's a wide assortment of winding creeks and secluded mountain lakes in the immediate area.

One of the most popular local destinations is Twin Lakes, which offer good fishing for brookies, browns, and rainbow trout. Most are pan-size but can range up to 6 pounds. Lakes Mary, Mamie, Horseshoe, and George are accessible by car and provide good fishing using a variety of techniques.

The June Lake loop. Like Lake Crowley, the June Lakes area is a favored destination during the annual trout opener. June, Gull, Silver, and Grant Lakes offer sensational early-season limits and trophy trout. In general, bigger fish come from Gull and June. The best bank fishing is at Silver, and the largest volume of browns come out of Grant. Each has its own unique personality, but all offer great fishing as well as spectacular scenery.

Rush Creek. One of the most popular spots in the Sierras is Rush Creek in the June Lake Loop. The hottest stretch is just above Silver Lake. This creek is stocked weekly, so it usually has an ample supply of small rainbow trout. Rainbows and browns over 5 pounds are a realistic goal for the talented angler. The area between Silver and Grant Lakes is best for taking trophy fish.

Tioga Pass. The eastern gateway to Yosemite National Park, Tioga Pass is just north of the June Lake Loop. Ellery and Saddlebag Lakes along this road provide excellent fishing for the weekend angler. Ellery Lake holds quantities of rainbows, and almost all standard bait offerings produce. Saddlebag has rainbows, brookies, and some Kamloops; baitfishing or trolling are the best tactics here.

Twenty Lakes Basin offers excellent high-elevation fishing within a one-day hike from the Saddlebag area. Rainbows, brook trout, golden trout, and even cutthroats frequent Greenstone Lake. Shamrock, Odell, Lower Twin, and Potter are good for goldens. Leave prepared baits at home and try natural offerings.

Bridgeport Reservoir/Walker River. Bridgeport Reservoir is one of the most prolific waters for trophy brown trout in the state. Rainbows and browns from 1 to 4 pounds are common here; planted fish grow fast because of the abundance of food. Veterans start the season by trolling big trout-colored plugs for trophy browns; fan casting bigger spinners and spoons can also be productive. Early-season rainbows are caught by trolling; baitfishing is an excellent technique later in the summer.

The East Walker River flowing out of Bridgeport Reservoir is known for trophy brown trout; browns of 14 to 18 inches are common. Waders work the river in chest waders, using spinning or flycasting gear. Heavier tackle may be advisable, as it's possible to tie into a 20-pound brown.

Twin Lakes. The modest Twin Lakes are an excellent brown trout fishery, with specimens up to 25 pounds and tactics similar to those at Bridgeport. Bank fishing and trolling work particularly well. Most of the lunker trout landed at Twin Lakes are caught in windy, inclement weather or close to dusk, or both.

Northern Sierras. The Northern Sierras offer some of the most consistently good angling in California and experience limited angling pressure. For the person with time, these lakes provide an excellent alternative to the heavily pressured lakes elsewhere.

Lake Almanor. Trophy-size browns, rainbows, and king salmon (an experimental program that has been fairly successful) exist at Almanor, a lake with plenty of shoreline access as well as great fishing for boaters. Stillfishing with baits, and trolling—both around underwater springs—can result in a stellar catch. As water temperatures increase, trollers fish deep with flashing blades ahead of a nightcrawler.

Feather River. The North Fork of the Feather River flows along Route 70, between Lake Almanor and Lake Oroville, through the Feather River Canyon. Where accessible, the main river is good trout water. Perennial hotspots include the convergence of the North Fork with the East Branch of the North Fork, and the mouth of Yellow Creek, which are both just above the town of Belden. The Feather River has excellent fly fishing, and the North Fork supplies good baitfishing.

The Middle Fork of the Feather River is accessible along Routes 70 and 89 between Sloat and Portola. The annual stonefly and caddisfly hatch create good fly fishing opportunities. Tributaries out of Portola generate quality rainbows and browns early in the season.

Gold Lake Basin. Gold Lake is the most important trout fishery in this area. It is by far the largest lake and holds the biggest trout of all waters in this basin, including some mackinaws topping the 20-pound mark. Veteran anglers troll for these macs down to 100 feet during the summer months, and there are some bank fishing spots.

Truckee River. The Truckee River originates at Lake Tahoe and tumbles along Highway 89 toward the town of Truckee, then northeast along Interstate 80 to Nevada. The waters from Tahoe to Truckee possess pan-size rainbows and large native brown trout. Live baits account for some lunker browns here. Bigger browns and rainbows roam the 1-mile section below the Truckee lumber mill between Hirschdale and Floriston. The stretch of fast-flowing water that parallels Interstate 80 northeast of Truckee produces the best fly fishing action, and is one of California's finest fly fishing sites.

Yuba River region. Collins, Bullards Bar, and Englebright Lakes are located in the lower region of the Yuba drainage system, about 90 minutes northeast of Sacramento. These three reservoirs are fewer than 20 miles apart and provide fine trout fishing.

Collins is a 1,000-acre lake with an underrated trout fishery; it has ample populations of rainbows and browns supported by an expansive spring planting program. Bullards Bar is loaded with rainbows and kokanee salmon, mostly caught by trolling, with shallow action beginning in early February. Later in the season, kokanee range anywhere from 40 to 140 feet. Englebright Lake is another option for serious trollers; it has rainbows and browns, plus kokanee fishing that is frequently excellent.

North Coast. The North Coast is one of the most overlooked trout fishing areas in the Golden State. Trinity, Lewiston, and Whiskeytown Lakes are superb fisheries, and many different techniques work here. In the backcountry, Trinity Alps and the Trinity Divide are remote alpine lakes teeming with hungry trout. Even more remote is the Marble Mountain Wilderness, with scrappy brookies, rainbows, and browns. Trout fishing is restricted in this region to protect juvenile migratory fisheries.

The North Coast is home to most of the great steelhead and salmon streams in California. These include the Eel River, south of Eureka, and—farther north toward the Oregon border—the Mad, Redwood, Klamath, and Smith Rivers. These have legendary runs of steelhead and salmon, varying from late spring through early winter.

Lake Berryessa and Putah Creek. Lake Berryessa offers many opportunities for the angler, with rainbows that average 14 inches, trophy browns, and feisty Eagle Lake–strain rainbow trout. Trout season lasts from Memorial Day through mid-November. Baitfishing and flatline trolling are preferred methods at this lake.

The Trinity Alps Wilderness. More than 55 fishable lakes are located in these spectacular mountains northwest of Trinity Lake. Some are accessible by automobile; others require a multiday pack trip. Most are at elevations between 5,000 and 7,000 feet and hold brookies, rainbows, and browns. Live baits produce best in this area, with fly-and-bubble rigs a popular option.

Trinity Lake. A beautiful alpine lake, Trinity is on the southern edge of Trinity Alps, north of Redding. Trinity is heavily planted with 9- to 13-inch rainbows, and produces fish up to 20 inches that hold over each year. There is a smaller population of browns. Trolling generates good results at Trinity, especially in the dam area; stillfishing is productive in the west coves and the mouths of the feeder streams; and fly fishing is also an excellent option. Substantial numbers of kokanee salmon exist at Trinity; areas near the feeder streams are good later in the year for these fish.

Northeast Corner. *Pit River.* There's a natural fishery of 12- to 15-inch trout in the Pit River, with some up to 4 pounds. Fishing here requires caution while wading or shore fishing, because currents resulting from hydropower generation can be swift; watch for deep, hidden holes as well.

Lower Sacramento River. An excellent fishery for large native rainbows, the Lower Sacramento is often overlooked. Salmon can be caught from September through December, and fat rainbows are taken all year long. Anglers work The Lower Sacramento primarily in drift boats, from Redding to Red Bluff. Drift anglers who drag lures catch rainbows consistently. From late April through mid-September, the Lower Sacramento offers exciting fly fishing opportunities, especially for 10- to 22-inch rainbows.

Upper Sacramento River. One of California's premier trout waters, the Upper Sacramento has plenty of 10- to 14-inch fish, including wild rainbow and brown trout. There's the occasional brook trout here, among them trophy-size fish. The river's many deep pools are excellent for bait anglers, and the deeper pockets and tail-out areas provide good lure action; overall, however, these waters are known for outstanding fly fishing. Traditionally the best hatch has been from late July through early October.

Lake Shasta. Shasta's year-round fishery has one of the foremost trout populations in the state. Its 30,000 surface acres hold rainbow and brown trout, as well as Kamloops. Fishing is best in the early spring, when near-surface feeding peaks. Flatline trolling is particularly productive at this time. As water temperatures increase, the trout actively begin to pursue schools of threadfin shad; casters can score when they push the bait to the surface.

Warmwater/Bass

California is the most populous state in the nation and is also home to equally impressive numbers of bass, including northern- and Florida-strain largemouth bass, smallmouth bass, and some spotted bass. Since the 1970s, California has enjoyed a reputation for producing monster and near-world-record largemouth bass due to the cultivation and stocking of transplanted Florida-strain bass. Several 20-pound or better largemouths have made headlines, and anglers maintain an intense pursuit of both trophy and record-breaking fish in waters with big-bass potential. The Golden State's multitude of warmwater lakes and impoundments also feature outstanding angling for redear sunfish, bluegills, and black crappie. In addition, many reservoirs are home to popularly sought bullhead and channel catfish, as well as trophy blue catfish and striped bass.

Most California reservoirs are 1,000- to 3,000-acre impoundments, but some, like those on the Lower Colorado River and Lake Shasta, are expansive and complex fisheries. All receive a great deal of fishing attention, and the smaller ones, particularly near metropolitan areas, get very crowded. The following information is a brief summary of the top warmwater lakes.

San Diego Area. *El Capitan Reservoir.* El Capitan is one of the smallest big-bass fisheries in the state. At its maximum capacity, which is rarely reached due to seasonal water demands, the lake has only 1,100 surface acres and a bare 15 miles of shoreline. It is among the reservoirs in the famous

 Stories of sea monsters may have been based on surface sightings of the dorsal and caudal fins of two or more basking sharks—which grow to 50 feet—swimming one behind another as they often do.

San Diego City Lakes group managed especially as a trophy fish factory. March and April are the choice times to fish for bass, and the first few weeks after the lake opens can be sensational.

El Capitan has an excellent population of 2- to 3-pound black crappie, which are best fished in the early spring in shallow, brushy flats. The lake also features giant channel and blue catfish in the 15- to 30-pound range.

Lake Henshaw. At only 1,100 acres, Henshaw is another relatively small lake. Located in northern San Diego County, it is flat and has minimal visible shoreline; when looking across the lake, you might feel as though you were fishing on a flooded meadow. Anglers catch northern-strain largemouths here in modest numbers, and the lake receives little fishing pressure. The wind can howl across this unsheltered area and chill things down, even during the summer.

Henshaw is open and produces bass all year long. Spring is the best time, when the fish move shallow to the bank and are easiest to catch. The lake also has a solid population of pan-size black crappie, as well as bullhead and channel catfish.

Lake Hodges. Lake Hodges recurrently appears at the top of the list of best bass lakes in California. Many largemouths over 8 pounds are regularly caught from this 1,100-acre impoundment. Early in the season, the weekend crowds can be huge, with more than a thousand people sometimes waiting in line to get on the water.

Hodges is a premier flipping lake. In high-water years, miles and miles of tules line its shores. When the bass have moved up into the banks, tules almost anywhere on the lake hold some fish. Numerous coves and steep banks have excellent bass cover. Early spring, from March through May, is the best time to take a lunker-class fish. Fall action, using a variety of methods, can bring success.

Fishing for bluegills and crappie can be excellent at Hodges during the summer. In these warmer months, the lake produces limits of 3- to 5-pound channel catfish.

Lake Morena. Morena is a fine low-pressure alpine lake. It has been a true sleeper among Southern California bass fishing enthusiasts. Many Florida-strain largemouths between 7 to 10 pounds are caught here each year.

Winds can whip through this high-elevation lake, and it may get quite chilly. In good weather, however, the bass fishing is sometimes sensational, and just about every imaginable structure exists here. Morena turns on from late spring through summer. The water temperature—along with the bass bite—drops dramatically from late fall through winter.

Lower Otay Lake. Otay is one of the premier big-bass lakes in the world, and may be the best lake in the San Diego City system for early-season fishing. Otay annually yields a bumper crop of 8-pound-plus Florida-strain bass and is rivaled perhaps only by Lake Hodges for big fish. It's also legendary for immense catfish; both channel and blue catfish thrive here, and many double-digit specimens are landed from spring through fall.

Like most San Diego lakes, Otay is open only at certain times of the year. It is a tough lake in the hot summer months. For overall bass population, as well as trophy fish, the best time is in the spring and especially immediately after the lake opens in late January or early February.

Lake Sutherland. One of the smallest lakes in the San Diego chain, Sutherland has only 500 surface acres. This lake is also the most difficult to reach, stashed away in the hills outside the little hamlet of Ramona, about 45 miles northeast of San Diego. From late spring through summer, Sutherland is famous for its surface-busting Florida-strain largemouths, which can literally keep acres of water churned up for hours. The lake has an impressive population of these fish, and spring and summer are also good angling times.

Lake San Vincente. San Vincente is a famous impoundment in the San Diego City Lakes system. It has produced monster largemouths in the past, and there's an excellent possibility that a world-record bass swims in this lake. This canyon lake has only 1,000 surface acres and limited visible shoreline cover. Water clarity varies, ranging from very clear to stained. The fishing can be tough, however. Many anglers scale down to 6- or 8-pound-test line and learn to fish a variety of subtle baits. Mid-April through mid-May is the best period for sustained action. This is just before the spawn, when these Florida-strain fish move into shallower waters.

Los Angeles and Orange Counties. *Castaic Lake.* Castaic is one of the most popular fishing lakes in the state. Located 45 miles north of metropolitan Los Angeles, it hosts bass anglers from all over the West.

Castaic is comprised of two sections, the main lake and the after bay. The main lake covers about 2,500 acres, divided into two arms. Fishing is permitted in both arms, but water-skiing is allowed in only one arm—in the designated ski area. The after bay covers only 180 acres, with no powerboats allowed, but it has some of the best fishing at Castaic.

Weather permitting, this can be an outstanding bass lake, particularly for Florida bass, many of which are caught in double figures each year. Because the lake is heavily stocked with rainbow trout—a favorite big-bass delicacy—largemouths over 15 pounds are common.

Depending on fluctuations in water level, Castaic may have excellent shoreline brush or a lot of rocky banks. The bass hang around the steeper rocky walls, particularly those in the water-skiing area in the early morning and late afternoon. The longer rocky points and ledges in the fishing arm always seem to hold some bass, as does the buoy area at the far end of the ski arm. During the colder months, bass frequently move up from deep water during the day, particularly in the fishing-only arm. On this lake, the banks of coves traditionally are good during the spring spawn.

Lake Castaic also has a thriving striped bass fishery, and a number of fish from 15 to 20 pounds are registered each year.

Lake Irvine. Located almost in the center of suburban Orange County, Irvine has only 700 surface acres at peak water level. In the summer, it is heavily stocked with channel catfish and is open to night fishing. Many trophy blue catfish topping the 50-pound mark have been caught at Irvine. The lake has a solid population of black crappie as well as a small number of large white sturgeon. The bass fishing at Irvine can also be remarkably good. Many of the fish are 2- to 3-pounders.

Spring through fall is a good season for bass. Summer nights are also productive, especially during a full moon. Deep-water methods at this metropolitan lake can be effective too. Visit during midweek to avoid the heavy weekend pressure.

Pyramid Lake. A small impoundment north of Los Angeles, Pyramid has some of the best smallmouth fishing in Southern California, and modest populations of largemouth bass and striped bass. Although striper numbers aren't high, these fish can be good sized; 20- to 30-pounders are frequently caught. Spring and fall are the prime periods for bass; the stripers action runs throughout the year.

Riverside and San Bernardino Counties. *Big Bear Lake.* A longtime favorite of western anglers, Big Bear is 7^1/$_2$ miles long and more than a mile wide, with more than 22 miles of shoreline.

The bass fishery is primarily comprised of largemouths, but smallmouths are also present. The bass are commonly found along numerous weed lines scattered throughout the lake. Anglers can target bass near docks and boulders, as well as at the dam on the western end. Fishing excels from late spring through fall.

This mountain lake frequently freezes in midwinter. It can be windy and chilly even in midsummer. Big Bear also has a great black crappie population, which can produce terrific fishing from spring through fall.

Lake Elsinore. Elsinore is a relatively small body of water. It has had a diverse history, as the water levels vary greatly with local rainfall. The lake has considerable submerged structure, lots of shoreline brush, and groves of trees. The northern-strain bass are ample; catches include many 2- to 3-pound fish. Fishing is hampered by endless ski wakes and heavy pleasure-boat traffic from late May through September; however, the lake excels in November and December as well as in the early spring, when the water is cool and boaters are few.

Perris Lake. Perris was once home to world-record spotted bass, but this species is a rare catch now. Perris does have one of the most dynamic largemouth fisheries in the state, however, producing many bass over 10 pounds annually. There's also excellent panfishing here for redear sunfish, bluegills, and black crappie.

There are few prime fishing spots, so anglers must slow down and work with diligence and patience. The dam, submerged islands, and the brushy east shore are favored. Largemouths can be caught all year here, including midwinter. Spring is the best time for overall action.

Lake Silverwood. A small alpine lake of a little over 1,000 acres, Silverwood is a major recreational playground for weekenders throughout Southern California. Located in the mountains north of San Bernardino, Silverwood has year-round largemouth bass fishing, with lunkers topping 17 pounds.

The canyon lake can be miserably cold in this mountain setting, however, generating some rough wave action. An anchor might be necessary when the electric motor struggles; there are few places to take cover. Late spring is preferred for bass, as they spawn later here than at lower elevations. Striped bass numbers are not great, but 25- to 35-pound fish are always a possibility.

Lake Skinner. Skinner is one of California's truly underrated bass lakes. It covers only 1,200 acres when the water level is at its highest. It has somewhat unimpressive terrain—gentle sloping banks, a few rocky points, some mud flats—but a fair amount of tule growth when the lake is up. It is populated with pure-strain largemouths.

Skinner is an excellent summer lake. Many bass anglers prefer to fish it from June through September, when the fish are feeding actively on threadfin shad. The spring action is fair, but if the water level is up, look for some nice fish in the tules. Late fall and winter are also good for slower presentations and deep-water fishing.

Skinner also features a large population of small striped bass, but some fish over 30 pounds exist here. Most striper activity is in open water. The lake is open all year long and receives greatest angling pressure when rainbow trout plants start in late fall.

Ventura and Santa Barbara Counties. *Lake Cachuma.* For sheer scenic beauty, it's hard to beat the mountain setting of 7-mile-long Lake Cachuma. It has more than 3,200 surface acres, and most of the shoreline is accessible. Northern-strain largemouth bass and smallmouths are available here, although the former are most common. Largemouths over 10 pounds have occasionally been caught, usually on live crawdads. The coves at Cachuma always seem to hold some fish, and have good moss and aquatic plant growth during the summer and fall.

Cachuma can be productive year-round. Summer is toughest due to the heat and increased boat traffic. Spring is good, and there is usually a prolific bite in the fall. Bass are landed here in the dead of winter, particularly with deep-water tactics.

Lake Casitas. Scenic Lake Casitas may well be the most heavily used body of water in California,

Competitive casting began in the 1860s at the same time as organized baseball was starting; it preceded both professional basketball and football.

and draws bass anglers from all over the West. Just 78 miles from Los Angeles, it is the first choice for weekend anglers and campers. Casitas lures serious bass anglers in quest of a world-record largemouth. It has a thriving rainbow trout fishery that bulks up these Florida-strain bass in a matter of years. Numerous fish over 10 pounds are caught each spring.

It is a large lake by Southern California standards, with more than 30 miles of shoreline and nearly 3,000 acres of water at its highest level. With its gin-clear water, however, Casitas can be a very difficult lake to fish. The most successful bass anglers are proficient with light line and subtle baits and techniques. An excellent population of redear sunfish resides at this lake. Panfish anglers target redears all year, although early spring is best.

Casitas is an exceptionally good lake in late winter and early spring, especially from the first few weeks of February through the first week of April. It is particularly tough in the summer and then picks up again in late fall. Those seeking the bass of a lifetime should try to fish the lake when the first warm rains fall in the early spring. The rain stimulates feeding activity, and big female bass move up from deep water to feed on the shallower points and ledges.

Lake Piru. Piru is a 1,000-acre lake about 50 miles north of Los Angeles. The northern bass bite can be fantastic at times, and these fish are not as difficult to catch as largemouths in other waters. Many anglers rate it highly for deep-structure angling in the cold winter months. Piru's bass usually eat well from December through February. The more obvious choice is March through May, when the bass spawn and move up shallow. Piru is a tough summer lake.

Colorado River. *Lake Havasu.* Lake Havasu is an immense and varied waterway lying between California and Arizona on the Colorado River. It spans more than 45 miles, from Davis Dam to the north to Parker Dam to the south.

It was at Lake Havasu that striped bass were first introduced to the Colorado River in the 1960s, and stripers and largemouth bass have been the main attractions here, although the lake also has crappie, channel catfish, bluegills, and rainbow trout. Havasu covers 25,000 acres, making it smaller than the upstream reservoirs; however, 450 miles of shoreline provide countless nooks and crannies for angling exploration.

One of the largest freshwater fisheries enhancement programs in North America was instituted here in the early 1990s, resulting in nearly 900 acres of strategically placed artificial habitat around the lake.

Havasu's largemouth bass frequent the main body of the lake, which has a lot of structure, as well as in the main river arm. There are sheltered coves, steep canyon walls, broken rock, moss beds, reefs, rocky points, and some trees and deadfalls in the lake proper. Out in the main river heading north, there are many coves, endless tule banks, deadfalls, sandbars, and some steep walls. Sometimes, the "bite" can be good in the lake and off in the river and vice versa.

Havasu is literally a year-round fishery. Spring is always popular for more aggressively feeding fish. However, fall and winter are good in both the main lake and river. Summer can be a little tough, but if you can find sanctuary from heat, day cruisers, and skiers, the bass can be caught.

Lower Colorado River. The immense lower Colorado comprises one of the most unique bass fisheries in the Golden State. Situated along the California border at the southernmost portion of the state, the section of the Colorado River from Parker Dam to Mexico is especially fertile. The river snakes for endless miles, and the banks are sometimes lined with massive tule growth, at other times with thick brush and deadfalls. Occasionally there are steep canyon walls to cast to, along with hidden lakes or backwater pockets, plus numerous small coves off the main river channel.

The lower portion of the river has excellent all-around fishing during the fall and the early spring. Because the water doesn't get that cold this far south, look for good action as early as January or February, when the bass hold tight to the shallow cover. For consistently outstanding catches of northern bass, however, it is hard to beat this area in the fall.

Navigation can be dangerous along this stretch of the Colorado River, with the current and sandbars posing tricky boating. The Lower Colorado also has excellent channel catfish and monster flathead catfish, the latter sometimes weighing more than 30 pounds. Black crappie and bluegills are caught in the calmer backwaters.

Central California. *Lake Isabella.* Lake Isabella is the premier trophy bass lake of Central California. It has more than 11,000 surface acres, and people speculate that this might produce a world-record largemouth someday. The lake annually produces many Florida-strain largemouths over 10 pounds and has an excellent population of both northern- and Florida-strain bass. Isabella's winds are notorious, however, and can make fishing impossible; it is also a tough lake through much of the summer.

Lake Isabella is also one of the top black crappie fisheries in California. Anglers catch hordes of these panfish every year, fishing the shallow flats, particularly in the spring and summer.

Lopez Lake. Lopez has minimal angling pressure for largemouths or smallmouths. It covers only 950 acres but has more than 22 miles of shoreline. The banks of this canyon lake are steep, and most shorelines are rocky. There is little visual structure and few flats. Good dropoffs, many rocky points, and some good submerged structure do exist here. A thriving smallmouth fishery has blossomed, and more of this species is showing up in the catch.

Lopez is good in the spring and fall, but summer is tough.

Lake Nacimiento. Nacimiento has more than 5,000 surface acres and 165 miles of shoreline. Smallmouths outnumber largemouths by about three to one, which is understandable with the predominantly rocky shoreline. Bass are sometimes hard to come by, however, because the water level fluctuates dramatically. Just when the angler has the lake figured out, the water might be drawn down almost 100 feet. Nacimiento is an excellent winter bass lake from November through March. Anglers will find some decent activity in the spring, more so on largemouth than smallmouth bass.

Nacimiento has a prominent white bass fishery, too. These panfish generate terrific sport for hours at a time when they're chasing schools of bait. The summer months become especially tough between hot days and widespread water-skiing.

Lake San Antonio. San Antonio is a 16-mile-long, 5,500-acre lake on the edge of California's Central Valley. It boasts a thriving northern and smallmouth bass fishery. When the lake level is up, there is a wealth of shoreline and structure to fish, compatible with a wide range of approaches. The lake is divided into two distinct parts: The western arm has shallows and flats, with numerous coves and minor points. The eastern arm has deeper cover, steep rocky walls, and long, extended points. The bass are typically biting in either one half of the lake or the other, but usually not both. Spring and fall can be excellent periods to fish San Antonio for both smallmouth and largemouth bass, but summer suffers due to heavy boat traffic.

San Antonio also offers excellent striped bass fishing. Although the stripers are primarily small, anglers catch many of double-digit weight each year.

North-Central Lakes. *Lake Berryessa.* One of California's largest lakes, Lake Berryessa is more than 25 miles long, up to 3 miles wide, and drops to 275 feet. Spanning some 20,000 surface acres, Berryessa produces about an equal catch of northern-strain largemouths and smallmouth bass, with some of the former having been caught at 10 pounds. A few jumbo-size Florida bass thrive here, as well some spotted bass. Midspring and fall offer the best fishing; smallmouths move shallow in the early spring, sometimes feeding around the smallest streams that enter the lake. By late spring, these fish—along with the largemouths—move into the larger creek arms to spawn.

Clear Lake. Stretching out over 100 miles of shoreline, Clear Lake is the largest natural lake in California. Located about three hours north of San Francisco, it has one of California's finest bass fisheries. Anglers annually catch many largemouth bass between 5 and 7 pounds, and 10-pounders are common in spring and fall.

Clear Lake is not particularly deep, but it has rocky, brushy banks, extensive tule growth, and many grassy areas. Some anglers compare the terrain of Clear Lake to that of typical lakes in the southeastern United States.

Indian Valley Reservoir. A 4,000-acre lake that is somewhat off the beaten path, Indian Valley nevertheless has a good population of northern-strain largemouth bass. It is about 90 miles from Sacramento and a short distance from Clear Lake, and is loaded with structure. March and April are the best months overall, but the lake produces good catches from midsummer through late fall.

New Melones. A fairly large lake covering 12,000 acres and spanning up to 8 miles across, New Melones has a large contingent of northern-strain largemouths and has become a popular spot for avid Northern California bass anglers. Loaded with structure, it excels as a late-spring bass lake, yet fishing is consistently good from summer through early fall. Those who know the lake take a share of winter bass with deep-water techniques.

Pardee Lake. Pardee has a terrific population of both northern-strain largemouth and smallmouth bass. Largemouths over 10 pounds have been recorded, as well as smallmouths between 3 and 5 pounds. The lake covers more than 2,000 surface acres and has 43 miles of shoreline, with a lot of action taking place along rocky banks. The better areas for both species are the south arm of the lake, where the Narrows are formed, and the rocky points and coves where the river runs into the lake. The channel arm with the rocky shoreline around Shad Gulch and Cave Gulch can also be productive.

Pardee's bass fishing is remarkably good year-round, with May and June best. Angling pressure is very light. The bass bite can be outstanding during the first few weeks in February when the lake reopens.

Sacramento River Delta. A complex waterway, the Sacramento River Delta can be an outstanding bonanza at times. Both largemouth and striped bass frequent this river system. The key to fishing both is to monitor tidal flow and current. Its many smaller fingers, eddies, tules, sandbars, and backwaters make the delta an intriguing place to fish. This large river system also requires some knowledge of navigation, as ocean-class freighters and large big-wake-generating vessels share the water on a continuous basis.

Western Sierra Lakes. *Lake Camanche.* Resting in the heart of mother lode country, Camanche has over 7,600 acres and 60 miles of shoreline to fish. Largemouths and smallmouths lurk in its many grassy areas. It also has a small population of spotted bass, which often prefer slightly deeper water. April and May are excellent months, with summer tougher, and fall again productive.

Folsom Lake. Folsom is one of the largest reservoirs in Northern California. Covering nearly 12,000 acres, it offers a variety of opportunities for both northern largemouth and smallmouth bass, which are divided between the two major forks of the lake. Smallmouths primarily thrive in the north fork, and largemouths in the south fork. Two- to

 The cement that barnacles use to attach themselves to objects will not melt at temperatures above 6,000°F nor crack at −380°F.

4-pound largemouths are common; smallies run much less. Folsom is open all year but becomes a tough proposition in summer and winter. Anglers using deep-water tactics at the latter times. The best months are from April through June.

Lake Don Pedro. Don Pedro is one of Northern California's largest bodies of water, spanning nearly 13,000 surface acres at full capacity and offering in excess of 160 miles of shoreline. More than 26 miles long, this riverlike lake has numerous winding coves and creek inlets. It harbors an abundance of northern largemouths, with a few Florida-strain bass and a smattering of smallmouths mixed in. Most anglers pursue the fish from boats, and there is a wealth of good sites and cover. Although they make for tough fishing, March and April are the best bass months.

Lake Oroville. Lake Oroville lies behind one of the largest dams in the United States, and encompasses more than 15,000 acres in a deep canyon. The lake has primarily largemouths and smallmouths, but it holds a few spotted bass as well. Spring provides the best fishing at Oroville for northerns and bronzebacks, with summer tough, and fall good.

Northern Mountain Lakes. *Lake Almanor.* Lake Almanor offers fantastic smallmouth fishing. Like many California lakes, Almanor is a reservoir formed by a dam, in this case on the Feather River. A shallow lake, Almanor is about 13 miles long and up to 6 miles wide, and offers a magnificent view of nearby volcanic Mount Lassen from almost any place on the water. The smallmouth bass at Almanor are usually found in rocky areas or shallow flats, especially along the dam and the eastern shore. Smallmouth fishing is best from late spring through summer.

Lake Amador. Amador is a very small lake, with only 400 surface acres and a little more than 13 miles of shoreline, yet it is a genuine trophy bass fishery. Florida-strain largemouths were stocked initially at Amador in 1970, then again in 1973. From this initial plant, a quality hybrid population has emerged. Fish over 6 pounds are common, and a few top the 10-pound mark. The lake has a series of long, steep-sided arms and lots of underwater brushy structure. It is supplied only by runoff from surrounding creeks, so water temperatures vary widely with the seasons. The best fishing is during the spring spawn, when the water is clean.

Lake Shasta. With more than 30,000 surface acres and numerous coves, arms, and inlets, Shasta constitutes one of the largest and most varied inland waters in the West. The lake sports a year-round fishery and offers one of the state's finest smallmouth fishing opportunities. It also includes a thriving largemouth population; some of these bass have topped the scales at more than 10 pounds.

Spring is the best time overall to fish both bass species here. By April, the largemouths usually move to the backs of coves for the annual spawn. Smallmouths can also be caught in the middle of winter, which is a good time for a visit, especially with diminished crowds.

Trinity Lake. With more than 17,000 acres, 145 miles of shoreline, and some of the prettiest scenery in California, Trinity is one of the premier smallmouth fisheries in the state. It also has a thriving northern largemouth bass population that is sometimes overlooked with all the attention given to bronzebacks. April through mid-May is the best time for big bass of both species; action is also good from spring through October.

Saltwater Fishing

The Pacific coast of California has some of the finest saltwater angling in the world and is enjoyed year-round. Marine species range from marlin to salmon and from tuna to rockfish, and strategies to catch the various and diverse saltwater fish in Southern California are as unique as those used along the central and Northern California coasts.

Naturally, many marine gamefish are pelagic or migratory by nature, and follow currents. Migratory patterns greatly impact gamefishing opportunity along the coast from year to year. Whether large numbers of yellowtail, for example, are caught off San Diego depends largely on water temperature and coloration. When conditions are ideal, large quantities of bait species such as anchovies, smelt, sardines, and squid move offshore. If the water is too cold or too dirty, there is no bait and thus no yellowtail. Likewise, changing temperatures—as happens with the well-documented El Niño phenomenon—may spread the range of some species, or curtail it, in a given year. Similar ecological relationships govern the albacore tuna and salmon fisheries in the central and northern sectors. Not all saltwater fish are pelagic, however. The surf fishes, such as corbina and spotfin croaker, usually stay in the shallow-water zones all year along southern beaches.

Similarly, the many rockfish species popularly found around the Monterey Peninsula are permanent residents. Water temperature is the critical ingredient for activity. This is especially true near Point Conception above Santa Barbara and heading north. The coastline here is rugged and exposed to prevailing northwest winds, which tend to work with the current to bring up colder water from the depths. This action displaces the otherwise warmer surface layer. The process of wind and current "upwelling" typically occurs in the spring, so the inshore area remains cold year-round, in contrast to offshore waters that warm in summer along the southern coast. Thus the central and northern regions can sustain large populations of nonmigratory coldwater dwellers. The fishery in this part of California is stable; rockfish, lingcod, eels, and so forth are always available. On the other hand, Southern Californians are more dependent on optimal movements of warm, bait-laden currents

---

Fishing is mentioned often in The New Testament, albeit for food not sport; the fish that fed the biblical 5,000 is thought to have been tilapia.

for banner catches of such gamefish as bonito, barracuda, yellowtail, albacore, and bluefin tuna.

Surface-feeding pelagics such as tuna, yellowtail, and dorado have a tendency to aggressively strike fast-moving baits and lures. A combination of swimming metal jigs, spoons, and soft-plastic trolling lures produces consistently for these fish. In contrast, coldwater bottom dwellers like lingcod, salmon, grouper, and sheepshead are more inclined to strike slowly retrieved artificials, sometimes bounced off the bottom, or natural baits fished dead and deep.

When all of the variables—including water temperature, wind exposure, offshore topography, and proliferation of forage are considered—a very complex portrait of the California marine fishery emerges. The picture becomes even more intricate when lure selection and application are considered. As a result of all these elements, California offers one of the most dynamic and challenging saltwater fisheries in North America.

San Diego/Imperial County Area. Numerous sandy beaches that lie to the north and south of San Diego Harbor offer outstanding surf fishing. Torrey Pines, noted for its famous golf course, is also a good local barred perch spot. The Silver Strand, Ocean Beach, and Imperial Beach are similarly good perch and corbina stretches and experience minimal angling pressure.

The sportfishing catches of San Diego and Mission Bay often sample the offshore bite along these coastal waters. The Point Loma and La Jolla kelp beds are important fisheries for pelagic species.

In Ocean Beach, the short rocky spit near the pier can be a real hotspot. Few surf anglers try it, but the perch bite is phenomenal here at times.

The Point Loma kelp is a popular spot for the San Diego party boat fleet. Barracuda and bonito, as well as calico and sand bass, are found here, sometimes throughout the year. Yellowtail are another strong option in this kelp bed. Sheepshead, sculpin, shallow-water rockfish, and a few white sea-bass round out the catch.

Coronado Islands. The four rocky outcroppings of the Islas de los Coronados are technically in Mexican waters. They are about 7 miles off the Baja California coast and 10 to 12 miles south of San Diego Harbor. Sportfishing boats from all San Diego landings make runs to these islands, which are the yellowtail capital of the Southern California sportfishing fleet. Numerous other species abound off these desolate islands. South Island is the largest of the Coronados, and two smaller outcroppings to the north—Middle Ground and North Island—are also prime fishing targets.

San Diego Harbor and Mission Bay. Both San Diego Harbor and Mission Bay provide year-round angling opportunities. Anglers fish these bays either from shore or in small boats. Fish are abundant in the quiet waters. Species include halibut, bonito, barracuda, sharks, rays, mackerel, croaker, and perch, as well as sand and spotted bay bass. The deep edges of the main ship channel in San Diego Bay are excellent places to drift both lures and live baits. The areas near Harbor Island and Shelter Island Pier are noted hotspots. Fishing near the Coronado Bridge can be equally productive.

In Mission Bay the Ventura Bridge offers both bass and halibut action. Fish the pilings slightly north of this bridge. The seasonal weedbeds are prime territory for sandies and spotted bay bass. Fiesta Island is one of the premier spotfin croaker fisheries in the state when the run is on (usually a falling tide). The Quivara Basin has sporadic flurries of mackerel, bonito, and small barracuda. For bat rays, head to Mariners Point inside Mission Bay.

The Salton Sea. A unique inland sea, Salton lies in the middle of the Mojave Desert. It was formed when the Colorado River overflowed its banks at the beginning of the century. The Salton Sea has a higher salinity level than the Pacific Ocean, yet a number of saltwater species thrive here.

The prized gamefish is the orangemouth corvina, which can grow to more than 30 pounds. Both boat and shore anglers catch these fish all year long. Fishing can be best in midsummer using both lures and bait. The Salton Sea also has a modest population of sargo, small gulf croaker, and tilapia. Strong desert winds can kick up severe wave action, so boaters must be cautious.

Oceanside Area. Numerous interesting and varied opportunities exist around Oceanside. Landings inside Oceanside Harbor provide half-day and full-day excursions to the Barn Kelp and offshore islands for rockfish in the winter. A variety of pelagic species live here, including yellowtail, calico bass, sand bass, mackerel, white seabass, and halibut, as well as many bonito and barracuda.

Carlsbad Lagoon is an excellent source of spotfin croaker, big bat rays, halibut, and even a rare white seabass. Encino Lagoon and Oceanside Harbor are also worthwhile spots to try.

The Barn Kelp is one of the most prolific kelp beds for gamefish on a year-round basis. Farther north, the waters off the San Onofre nuclear power plant have been excellent sand bass territory when the spawning run is in full swing.

Orange County. *San Clemente Island.* San Clemente Island is an incredible bonanza for the saltwater angler willing to make the five-hour run from the Southern California mainland. Both party boats and private charters make full-day excursions to this isolated island.

Pyramid Head and China Point are favorite spots on the island's southeast end. The kelp beds are thick and provide sanctuary for big calicos. Bonito and barracuda also move along this kelp line. Yellowtail recurrently cruise the kelp, and it's a good place to catch live squid for bait in the winter. The White Rock sector on the middle of the eastern side of the island is another potential yellowtail stretch.

Opportunities for serious bass fishing exist at the isthmus on the far west side of Clemente. Bird Rock and Castle Rock on the outside are potential hotspots for calicos. The windward southwest side is an area to work for bluefin tuna. Shark hunters looking for blues, makos, and threshers can scout the channel between Clemente and Catalina Islands. Striped marlin are also a possibility.

Santa Catalina Island. Santa Catalina is the most popular of the offshore islands off the California coast. Located roughly 26 miles from the mainland, Catalina is 22 miles long and 7 miles wide. An abundance of saltwater gamefish can be caught around the island throughout the year.

Most private and party boat captains prefer to fish the leeward side of the island facing the mainland. The windward side can become rough from gale-force winds, with swells crashing into the rocky shoreline. The tip of the West End inside the floating kelp stringers is a favorite hotspot for big calico bass. Yellowtail, bluefin tuna, bonito, and barracuda breeze through this area.

Emerald and Cherry Coves, and the isthmus near the center of the island, are good areas for yellowtail. Halibut drifting occurs from Goat Harbor to the beaches north of Avalon. Bonito, barracuda, and some small shallow-water rockfish are also possibilities in this area. At the East End, near The Slide, yellowtail, bonito, and barracuda can be found cruising within a mile of the bank.

Rock-codding for deep-water species is best at both ends of Catalina. Striped marlin are possible in these areas. The West End and The Slide are also traditional hotspots for marlin.

Dana Point Harbor. Dana Point is one of the most diverse angling havens in Southern California. Gamefish—including halibut, sand bass, spotted bay bass, spotfin croaker, bonito, halibut, mackerel, and corbina—abound in the harbor basin. Along the outside rocks and jetties are sheepshead, opaleye, calicos, sculpin, sharks, and rays. To the north of the jetty, the rocks and kelp of South Laguna are prime calico bass haunts. In the offshore kelp, yellowtail, and a seasonal flurry of bonito and barracuda, can be found. Anglers working the sandy beach near South Laguna can also nail corbina, barred perch, croaker, and, occasionally, halibut.

Newport Harbor. One of the most interesting fishing sites in the region is Newport Harbor. This shallow bay sports a prominent population of spotted bay bass, sand bass, halibut, croaker, corbina, mackerel, bonito, barracuda, sand sharks, rays, and an occasional striped bass. Halibut can usually be found on the hard mud and sandy bottoms. Drift or troll the main channel for sandies and bay bass. The areas around the various boat docks and in front of the Balboa Pavilion are good spots for bass, perch, croaker, and the occasional halibut. Striped bass, in limited numbers, are landed in the Back Bay. Spotted bay bass are abundant in Newport Bay. Key-in on the dock pilings and under moored boats. Look for signs of eelgrass and places where currents converge. Spotted bay bass gravitate to this type of water. Corbina are frequently taken in the surf line or along Balboa Pier. Newport and Balboa Piers also have occasional runs of halibut and bonito.

Huntington Beach to Seal Beach. The Huntington Beach Pier is frequently invaded by schools of mackerel and small bonito. Most of the action here is on surfperch, a few halibut, tomcod, herring, and queenfish. At times there can be outstanding bonito action off this pier, as well as keeper-size halibut, yellowfin, croaker, and sargo. Seal Beach operates a sportfishing landing, and private craft can launch from Huntington Harbor. The beach below the bluffs to the north of Huntington Beach are good for barred perch. Windy Bolsa Chica State Beach between Huntington and Sunset Beaches is another barred perch stretch.

The beach around Surfside can produce a variety of fish ranging from sharks and halibut to corbina and yellowfin croaker. Small flounder, halibut, and turbot are taken in Huntington Harbor. For shallow-lagoon species, investigate the area around the Pacific Coast Highway bridge connecting Surfside and Seal Beach. The San Gabriel River Channel north of Seal Beach is another good spot for small bonito. The Huntington Flats and offshore oil platforms have been a favorite run for sportfishing and private boats. Halibut, bonito, and barracuda frequent the flats. The big news occurs when sand bass move in to spawn. The offshore oil rigs provide sanctuary for large yellowtail, as well as calico bass, bonito, and mackerel.

Los Angeles Area. *Long Beach Harbor and Palos Verdes area.* In the Long Beach harbor, fishing opportunities abound at jetties, piers, breakwaters, and even offshore oil islands. Anglers land bonito and mackerel off the Belmont Pier and outside the jetty and breakwaters. Spotted bay bass, sand bass, and calicos are popular species in the harbor. Halibut, croaker, perch, sharks, and rays are other possibilities. Spring is the best time for bass and halibut. However, the harbor can provide steady action throughout the year. The federal breakwater can be outstanding at night during the winter.

To the north, anglers can experience excellent surf casting for big calicos off the rocks on the Palos Verdes Peninsula. Sheepshead, surfperch, and opaleye are also available off these jagged bluffs.

King Harbor to Marina del Rey. King Harbor in Redondo Beach offers a variety of saltwater angling opportunities. Fish the breakwaters for bonito and mackerel as well as perch, opaleye, halibut, tomcod, smelt, and the occasional sand bass. The warm water inside the harbor yields bonito, barracuda, mackerel, and even yellowtail. Bonito fishing is outstanding from the pier. Outside the harbor, boaters can sample the pelagic gamefish that migrate into the area following schools of anchovies. To the north, Hermosa and Manhattan Beach Piers have excellent winter runs of barred surfperch. Good shallow-water surf fish can be found at 18th, 19th, and 26th Streets, especially for quality halibut.

Marina del Rey. There's good fishing inside Marina del Rey Harbor. Spotted bay bass, sand bass, and halibut are all possibilities. Other areas to work are the short breakwater and the long jetty. Big calicos and sand bass are good targets for night fishing; other species include tomcod, queenfish, small calicos bass, sand bass, halibut, bonito, and barracuda. Fish for bonito and barracuda on the ocean side of the jetty and toward the end. The sandy beach adjacent to the north of the jetty occasionally has some 1- to 3-pound corbina.

Santa Monica Bay to Malibu. This scenic stretch of coastline runs from the Santa Monica Pier to Bass Rock below Oxnard. The Santa Monica pier itself intermittently produces bonito, halibut, a stray calico or sand bass, mackerel, sharks, and rays. The Malibu Pier is on parity with Santa Monica for species variation and overall quality of fishing.

Beaches accessible from this point northward offer some other intriguing possibilities. Calico bass, halibut, cabezon, leopard sharks, barred perch, sargo perch, yellowfin croaker, and shallow-water rockfish are within a cast from the beach. Kelp beds and submerged reefs dot the public-access beaches from Malibu to Oxnard. Look for barred perch action at small rocky outcroppings. The larger rocks inside the bay near the Santa Monica Pier are outstanding for nighttime bass fishing. These rocks can be reached only by carefully maneuvering a small boat close to shore.

Private boats and sportfishers explore Santa Monica Bay for surface-feeding action. Skiff and party boat anglers sometimes get into hot bluefin tuna action in this bay. Here is also some of the best halibut fishing in the region, with anglers drifting over predominantly sandy bottoms. Coral Beach north of Malibu is an excellent spot for surf casting to offshore kelp beds. The surfer's reef to the right of the Malibu Pier is a legendary haunt for big calicos. Night fishing with heavy-duty tackle produces the best results. Other good fishing spots for barred perch, halibut, cabezon, sand bass, and calico bass are Latigo Canyon, Paradise Cove, and Leo Carrillo Beach.

Ventura and Santa Barbara Areas. *Ventura and Oxnard.* A wealth of kelp beds line this part of the coast. Ventura Harbor has good numbers of smelt, perch, and tomcod, as well as a few sand bass and halibut. Channel Islands Harbor has plenty of warmwater species, including sand bass, spotted bay bass, and a few calicos on the outside rock walls. Anglers pursue halibut extensively inside this harbor.

Halibut and barred perch are frequently caught along the windy beaches. Work below the naval base south of the pier. Offshore kelp beds are loaded with calicos, sand bass, barracuda, halibut, and even white seabass. Salmon activity also occurs in this area in late winter or early spring.

Channel Islands. The islands of the Santa Barbara Channel offer tremendous variety for anglers venturing out of Oxnard, Ventura, or Santa Barbara. Private and party boats fish Santa Cruz, San Miguel, Santa Rosa, or Anacapa Islands. Surface fishing in warmer months can be sensational here for calico bass, bonito, barracuda, yellowtail, white seabass, and sometimes migrating schools of albacore. These islands also offer excellent shallow-water lingcod and rockfish, and deep-water rock cod action. Winter and spring runs of both silver and king salmon also occur in the channel itself, as well as in the areas around San Miguel and Santa Rosa Islands.

Santa Barbara. This quiet seacoast city has a lot to offer the saltwater enthusiast. Private fishing boats and party boats ply the Channel Islands or One Mile and Naples Reefs to the north for some of the best shallow-water rockfishing on the coast. Surf casters can sample good perch and corbina action along the sandy stretches from Santa Barbara to Point Conception. Stearn's Wharf and the breakwater rocks are great spots for pier anglers and jetty jockeys.

The kelp south of Santa Barbara and Carpinteria is a hotbed for pelagic species. Bass, barracuda, white seabass, and assorted rockfish are local residents. Ledbetter Beach, Thousand Steps, Goleta, Shoreline Park, Refugio, El Capitan, and the Rincon Stretch are strong candidates for steady surf-casting action. Perch, halibut, corbina, sharks, bass, and cabezon can be caught from the beach. The harbor and breakwater are good places to look for perch, sand bass, and halibut. The water off Goleta Pier is a prime spot for both calicos and halibut on the drift.

Central California. *San Luis Obispo to San Simeon.* It is estimated that only about 10 percent of the beachfront area above Santa Barbara is ever fished, yet it can produce great fishing. Notable are rock cod and late-season albacore in the 30- to 50-pound range out of Avila Bay. Inside Morro Bay try for smelt, halibut, mackerel, or sand bass. Outside Morro Bay, rockfish are plentiful; these include blue, gopher, and copper rockfish, and also lingcod and cabezon. North of Morro Rock is a beach with excellent barred perch potential. Try the blowhole near Morro Rock for fork-tail and barred perch, as well as cabezon and starry flounder.

At Pismo Pier, fish for barracuda, halibut, corbina, and mackerel, plus barred, fork-tail, and walleye perch. Avila Pier and San Luis Pier are best for tomcod, shiner perch, and jack smelt. Offshore waters can sustain a good run of both king and silver salmon at times.

Cayucos, Moonstone, Sandstone, and San Simeon Beaches have great perch action. San Simeon Pier has barred, walleye, rubberlip, and piling perch, plus halibut and jack smelt. From Cayucos to Piedras Blancas, shallow-water rockfishing can be sensational for small-boat anglers.

The Nile perch of Africa is one of the largest gamefish in the world; its only North American relative is the wary, strong, and acrobatic snook.

Lingcod, cabezon, halibut, flounder, petrale sole, and even salmon can be caught off the nearshore reefs.

Monterey and Carmel Bays. Because of the broad variation in ocean conditions contained within this unique bay, Monterey-area fishing ranges from shallow-water rockfish to deep-water pelagics. The many piers, landings, beaches, rocks, and sloughs of the Monterey Bay area hold a variety of coldwater treasures, among them salmon, striped bass, perch, sanddabs, halibut, petrale sole, flounder, lingcod, cabezon, greenling, kelp and grass rockfish, sculpin, jack smelt, sablefish, and sharks. Party boaters, skiff anglers, surf casters, and rock hoppers alike can share in the bounty.

Rock anglers can also find abundant inshore rockfish. Greenling; olive, grass, and blue rockfish; cabezon; lingcod; and surfperch are all within casting range at 17-Mile Drive and Asilomar State Beach. Smelt, perch, and shallow-water rockfish are taken off the pier at the eastern end of Monterey Harbor. Occasional striped bass also show up here. Skiff operators can target rockfish, lingcod, and sanddabs inside both bays. In warm-water periods, bonito and barracuda can be an unexpected treat.

Salmon frequent the bay from early spring through fall. One good area is the mouth of the Salinas River. Albacore can occasionally be located in late summer as close as 10 miles offshore.

San Francisco Area. *Moss Landing to Santa Cruz.* Rockfish, perch, greenling, cabezon, lingcod, halibut, sanddabs, smelt, salmon, and striped bass are all landed in this area. The jetty and the beaches south of Moss Landing are excellent surfperch territory. Elkhorn Slough is famous for its shark and bat ray fishing, as well as sole and starry flounder.

The beaches north of Aptos range from sandy to rocky. Fish for cabezon, jack smelt, perch, and shallow rockfish from the shore and at Capitola Pier. Santa Cruz Pier also features lingcod, boccaccio, sculpin, sole, and starry flounder.

Numerous shallow reefs outside the Santa Cruz small-craft harbor sensational lingcod and rockfish populations. Other popular reefs lie off Soquel Point and Capitola.

Half Moon Bay. Pillar Point Harbor at Half Moon Bay is one of the most diverse fisheries in Northern California. Boats out of this harbor can fish the nearby reefs for copper, olive, yellowtail, black, canary, olive, and blue rockfish, as well as cabezon and lingcod. Salmon, striped bass, flounder, sanddabs, sculpin, perch, and jack smelt are sought too. Shore anglers can try their luck off the breakwater or pier for rockfish, perch, and sometimes salmon, lingcod, or striped bass. Poke-polers (anglers who use 12- to 16-foot telescoping rods to fish cut baits in rocky crevices) can work the adjacent rocky areas for rockfish, cabezon, and eels.

Fish the reefs outside the harbor for rockfish and lingcod. The stretch from Pillar Point to Moss Beach is a good area to prospect for bottom fish. Pier anglers can fish inside Pillar Point Harbor for perch, smelt, rockfish, sanddabs, and sculpin. Shore anglers can fish the jetties for surfperch, greenling, rockfish, cabezon, and lingcod, as well as flounder, sanddabs, and perch.

San Francisco Bay. Light-lining inside San Francisco Bay can be excellent for perch, smelt, flounder, shallow-water rockfish, and kingfish. The prized gamefish are striped bass, halibut, salmon, and sharks. Smelt and perch dominate catch totals at the Berkeley Pier. Jack smelt can be red-hot along the Burlingame shoreline. Wharves and piers on the San Francisco waterfront also yield starry flounder, smelt, and perch. An excellent perch bite often occurs on the stretch of shoreline from Coyote Point to San Francisco's airport. Other popular sites for perch include the Alameda Estuary and East Fort Baker under the Golden Gate Bridge on the Marin side.

The deeper channels around Marin—west of Angel Island, the Bay Bridge, and Hunter's Point—are longtime favorites for shark hunters. Anglers probe the waters off the greenhouse south of Sausalito, and the main channel between the Dumbarton and San Mateo Bridges in South San Francisco Bay. Leopard, soupfin, smoothhound, dogfish, and six- and seven-gill sharks can be taken almost anytime. Look for seven-gill sharks in spring and fall, and soupfin in spring and summer. Shark fishing is usually best at the top or bottom of a moving tide. The same holds true for halibut and sturgeon catches in this area.

Striped bass fishing is a seasonal event in San Francisco Bay. The best places to fish include Sausalito, Berkeley, Emeryville, Richmond, and the City of San Francisco. Stripers can be reached from shore as well as from boats. Fish Coyote, Oyster, and Hunter's Points, Candlestick Park, Mission Rock and Baker's Beaches, the Berkley flats, Alameda Rocks, the Raccoon Straits, Alcatraz, and Treasure and Angel Islands for major striped bass action.

San Francisco Bay produced this fine California halibut.

Farallon Islands. The Farallon Islands are 35 miles west of the Golden Gate and generate some of the finest bottom fishing in the West. Sportfishing and charter boats from Angler's Wharf, Berkeley, Sausalito, Pillar Point, and Emeryville fish these rocky outcroppings. King salmon and lingcod are additional quarries here. Be prepared for rough water and miserable weather at any time of the year.

Bottom fish taken from the islands include copper, blue, yellowtail, chili, golden eye, vermilion, and blue rockfish. Cowcod and lingcod round out the catch. Salmon are taken in the gulf between the islands and the mainland. Some of the largest lingcod caught in California are landed during the fall spawning period at these islands. Troll, drift, and mooch between Duxbury Reef and the Farallons in spring. Move from the San Francisco light buoy to Duxbury Reef in late summer through fall.

Northern California to the Oregon Border. Above San Francisco are numerous sandy beaches, docks, bays, piers, and rocky shorelines that host coldwater species. Tomales Bay, for example, is renowned for its shark population. Skiff anglers also enjoy some limited action on striped bass, salmon, perch, and starry flounder. Surfperch are the number one catch from the beach. Poke-polers target rockfish. Catch greenling, cabezon, and lingcod off the rocks and in outside waters all the way to the Oregon state line.

Bodega and Tomales Bays. Surf and jetty anglers as well as boaters can fish for schools of king salmon and quality rockfish north of San Francisco. Target the Cordell Banks for lingcod and rockfish. The Whistle Buoy off Bodega Bay is prime for chinook salmon. Fish the Bodega Bay wharf for smelt and perch. The rocks at Doran Park are excellent for shallow-water greenling, cabezon, and assorted rockfish. Carmel and Dillar Beaches are perfect for poke-polers. Wright's, Goat, Salmon Creek, and Portuguese Beaches are key places for smelt and surfperch. Lawson Landing at the mouth of Tomales Bay is the hotspot for striped bass, leopard sharks, and halibut. Hog Island is best for perch.

Fort Ross and Timber Cove areas. For excellent bottom fishing, try the reefs at Salt Point, Ocean Cove, Seal Rocks, Stillwater Cove, and Timber Cove. Look for big lingcod in the shallows in the winter. Target salmon from late April through the summer.

Crescent City. This quiet stretch of shoreline offers both salmon and bottom fishing. Rockfish specialists should try the St. George and South Reefs outside the harbor, and the 5-fathom curve from Three Sister Rocks to the harbor entrance for bottom fish. The catch includes black, blue, vermilion, China, and boccaccio rockfish. Pier anglers can catch flounder, perch, smelt, and greenling off Citizen's Dock. Lingcod, rockfish, and cabezon are year-round favorites in this cold water. Smaller silver salmon are caught in June, whereas August is best for king salmon. Poke-polers can fish the rocky outcroppings for rockfish, perch, and greenling. Surf casters can fish all year long here.

Eureka and Humboldt Bay. Four-mile-long Humboldt Bay has a solid population of walleye and redtail perch for surf anglers. Fish for shallow-water lingcod, black snapper, and greenling from the jetties. King salmon are also a possibility here, even from the rocky breakwaters.

Shelter Cove is a rockfish haven, especially for lingcod. The reefs off Ft. Bragg are excellent haunts for rockfish and salmon trolling. Prime targets include greenling, rockfish, cabezon, perch, and lingcod.

CALIFORNIA CURRENT

The California Current is an easterly offshoot of the North Pacific Current that flows southward and a bit eastward off southern Canada and the Pacific Coast of the United States to Baja California, Mexico, where it turns sharply westward into the North Equatorial Current. This is a flow of colder water, and it is slow and not as well defined as the Gulf Stream *(see)*, which is a warm northerly flowing current affecting the Atlantic Coast of North America.
See: Currents.

CANADA

Specific fisheries and angling opportunities in Canada are detailed elsewhere. Please refer to the individual province or territory listing. This entry provides an aggregate overview of sportfishing in Canada.

Like the United States, Canada has excellent sportfishing, but unlike any other country it has thousands of bodies of water that are far removed from population centers. With a larger landmass than the United States and less than one-tenth its population, most of which is concentrated in the southern portion of the country, Canada is a dream-come-true for anglers who want to fish in seclusion. Access to the most remote and roadless areas is not easy to afford or accomplish with limited time, however, and the open-water seasons are fairly short for most of the country.

Canada's abundant sportfishing opportunities range from the water-rich frozen tundra of the Arctic barrens to the wolf-inhabited boundary wilderness lakes on the U.S. border, from fiordlike Pacific coast bays with whales and salmon to tidal maritime island streams with sea-run brook trout, and from Great Lakes rich with trout and salmon to bush lakes rich with walleye and northern pike. Surrounded by three oceans, and covered with spruce forests, taiga, and tundra, Canada offers bass fishing in the shadows of metropolitan skylines, lake trout fishing in the company of caribou, salmon that are likely to be snatched by an eagle if left on a boat dock, and trophy walleye angling in central, drive-to rivers.

Pike, Lake Trout, and Walleye

By far the greatest overall angling effort in Canada is devoted to freshwater fishing, in part due to geography, as most provinces are located far from marine environments, and in part due to abundance, because there is more diversity inland. Lake trout, northern pike, and walleye are the top freshwater attractions. Certainly these fish are most widely distributed and available across the interior provinces and territories; pike and lake trout are favorites certainly of American visitors, who cannot do as well in their home states for these species as in Canada. Americans cannot find consistently fast pike action in most of the United States; and trophy pike are increasingly rare. In the U.S., a 15-pound pike or lake trout is a large specimen, but not one found regularly or with much certainty. Not so in Canada.

Except for the Maritime Provinces and British Columbia, all of Canada offers pike fishing. Pike are as plentiful in some waters as bluegills are in American lakes. In many of the former you can count on having lots of action, and in some of the more conservation-oriented waters you can catch and release your personal best.

The bigger pike generally come from the remote northern lakes in the heartland provinces of Manitoba, Saskatchewan, Ontario, and, to a lesser degree, northern Quebec, although some big pike are caught in the southerly reaches of the Northwest and Nunavut Territories, too. There's also good pike action in some of the bigger rivers and lakes within big-river systems, but the majority of the best fishing is in lakes, especially big lakes and places that aren't readily accessible from roads.

This is almost always a casting fishery rather than a trolling one. You seldom fish in big open-water areas, although you may have to cross large expanses of lake (which can sometimes be rough) to get from place to place. Pike fishing often takes you to some of the northern lakes' prettier locations: weedy back bays, meandering marshes, nooks and crannies. And there's a more visual element to the fishing. You see a lot of pike, whether they're cruising the shallows or chasing a lure. And, because the fish are fairly voracious, you sometimes get to see a cavernous mouth open and inhale your lure. It's an active game.

Anglers can have great action early in the season, especially for lots of fish. When northern lakes melt, the shallow bays and backwaters are the first to open and warm up, and pike cluster in these places, sometimes resting in water barely deep enough to cover their backs. You can do a lot of sight casting then. Weeds are sparse at best, and the water is ultraclear. You can also catch large fish, but because pike spawn in late winter or early spring, the early-season pike are not as hefty as they will be later, and the real monsters seem to be elusive.

On good pike lakes there is usually no bad time for pike. Later in the season, when the weeds are thick, most pike will be off the shoreline and in the weeds, and sight fishing opportunities are greatly reduced. Pike will have been feeding well and many will have better girth.

Lake trout are generally doing well in many parts of Canada, and with more emphasis on conservation of these old and slow-growing fish the future looks good. The better lake trout angling is usually in the upper half or upper third of the southern provinces, as well as throughout the Northwest and Nunavut Territories. Northern Manitoba and northern Saskatchewan provide some of the best opportunities for big fish, but the eastern and central tundra waters, as well as Victoria Island, are equally notable.

In the far north, rivers offer exciting lake trout fishing by casting, but seldom big fish; however, larger fish will prowl the turbulent inlet. In lakes, these trout are often structure oriented, and migrate to reefs, shoals, and islands to feed. They also cruise the shorelines. In lakes that warm up and create a thermocline, lakers will go to cool water below the thermocline in large open-water bowls. This is where their primary food, cisco and other lake trout, is found.

A lot of Canadian lake trout fishing is done in the upper 30 feet of water, and these fish are scrappy. The smaller ones, which sometimes thrash and roll wildly near the boat, can be a spunky nuisance. More than one angler, fishing in prime waters, has hooked and played a tenacious and drag-pulling laker for an hour or more.

In those far-north places where the water stays cold all season, you can catch lake trout in the upper strata all year long. In places that warm up in the summer and where the surface water reaches the 60s, the trout will positively go deep. It is late in the season that some of the heaviest fish are caught and the fewest anglers are out. Few far-north lodges stay open late in August or into September because of hostile weather and airplane delays. But those who do cater to knowledgeable, hearty anglers searching for trophy fish.

The busiest time for most lake trout lodges is the first few weeks of the season. Camps are usually full. Most bookings are made 8 to 12 months in advance, prior to knowing what the winter will serve up. A severe winter and/or a long, cold spring will delay ice out and possibly limit the places you can fish if you're scheduled at a lodge during the first or second week. But many anglers take that chance.

From big fish to lots of action, Canada's got whatever suits your walleye interests. Big and small lakes and big and small rivers, of which there are plenty in southern Canada, provide ample angling opportunity. Quebec, Ontario, Manitoba, and Saskatchewan lead the field, particularly the mid- to southern regions of those provinces.

You don't necessarily have to visit remote waters to find great walleye fishing. Although there's some fine walleye (called pickerel in many parts of Canada) angling in distant spots, seldom are the

To many people, angling in Canada is synonymous with remote wilderness, such as this scene at secluded Hunt Falls in northern Saskatchewan.

biggest fish found in those places. A 6-pounder, which is a good-size walleye, is relatively rare in most northern waters. The biggest fish may be closer to the border; such waters as Lake of the Woods, Rainy Lake, the Detroit River, Lake Erie, the St. Lawrence River, and the Bay of Quinte on northeastern Lake Ontario produce 8- to 10-pound or larger walleye and good overall numbers of fish.

For most of the season, from late spring through summer and into fall, walleye are located on rock reefs, sandbars, points, weed edges, and the like. In big lakes some walleye suspend in open water where there are schools of baitfish.

Lots of people fish walleye in near and far Canadian waters, from Labrador to Saskatchewan, and much of it is fish-on-your-own angling, either piloting a boat by yourself at a resort, or towing your own fish-catching machine to the designated site. The entire gamut of walleye tackle and techniques is employed, with fishing ranging from difficult to find in hard-fished waters to cast-after-cast easy in some remote fly-in lakes. The latter usually also offer good pike fishing, so there's good combination angling available.

There's a big rush in Canada when the spring walleye season opens, which varies by province and by district within provinces. Walleye have usually spawned by the time the opener occurs, but not necessarily. The angler rush subsides after the walleye disperse and migrate to summer grounds, becoming temporarily harder to locate.

Salmon, Charr, and Trout

To find Canada's other most heralded fish—salmon and charr—in their naturally occurring state, you have to migrate to all four extremities of the country. Salmon and charr are intensely popular in the coastal regions where they occur, but the anadromous coldwater species native to those areas are not available to the vast majority of Canadians without incurring substantial travel; this is even more so for charr than for salmon.

Atlantic salmon have been under tremendous pressures due to various factors, especially excessive commercial harvest in the North Atlantic. Naturally occurring Atlantic salmon are found in maritime Quebec, Newfoundland, New Brunswick, and Nova Scotia, all of which have well-known and storied rivers. Quebec's Gaspe Peninsula is easily accessed and has a significant amount of opportunity, but here and elsewhere the fish are subject to seasonal conditions and ocean events that cause fluctuations in the numbers and size of fish returning each year.

Angling for Canada's Atlantic salmon is almost entirely restricted to fly fishing, although land-locked populations exist (in Labrador and Quebec) and these can be pursued by various methods, including casting spoons with spinning tackle and trolling with various tackle types.

Overharvesting has had some impact on naturally occurring stocks of Pacific salmon (coho, chinook, sockeye, and chum salmon) off British

Columbia, but a greater impact has come from environmental changes, especially damming of rivers, and water-quality issues, some due to extensive logging. These fish, as well as sea-run rainbow trout (steelhead), however, are caught in rivers and coastal tidewaters, and the chinooks and cohos may range to large sizes, with the larger individuals usually caught in tidewater at the mouths of significant rivers.

Major runs occur at different times, and occasionally this can be adversely affected by commercial activities. British Columbia has 27,000 kilometers of coastline and more than 1,500 spawning rivers, so there's a lot of opportunity here, although the majority of resident and nonresident salmon anglers fish in the salt for the brightest, hardest-fighting, and best-tasting fish—so fresh they still carry sea lice. Anglers primarily mooch (a form of slow-trolling with cut-herring baits) or troll baits and lures with downriggers.

It is often forgotten that some of the most prolific salmon fishing in Canada occurs on its interior border with the U.S., in the Great Lakes, where Lakes Michigan, Erie, and Ontario in particular produce good numbers and sizes of chinook salmon, as well as cohos and steelhead. These fish have been introduced by Canadian and American wildlife agencies and are largely sustained through annual stocking, but provide ample opportunity throughout the year. Being close to major population concentrations (salmon and steelhead can be caught in view of Toronto skyscrapers) makes these fish accessible to a greater number of Canadians, even if they aren't native to that region.

Salmon, steelhead, and some trout are caught near shore in spring and late summer and in deeper offshore water later in midsummer, as well as in tributaries in late summer and early fall. Steelhead are caught through the winter in tributaries.

In northernmost Canada, fresh from the Arctic Ocean, naturally occurring sea-run arctic charr are perhaps the most exotic major Canadian sportfish, a species that relatively few anglers have caught, available for a limited midsummer period, and accessed almost entirely by fly-in air service.

Arctic charr inhabit many isolated interior lakes and most of the coastal rivers and streams that rise from lakes that can support spawning. The majority of charr are caught in rivers; however, the larger specimens are primarily caught in the lower stretches closer to the salt. Arctic charr rivers flow into the Arctic Ocean, Hudson Bay, and the Atlantic coastlines of Nunavut.

Charr do not run huge distances inland like Pacific salmon, and it is usually small specimens that are in the lakes. The charr that are caught early in the season are very bright fish, looking in coloration like a steelhead or fresh-run salmon, but they develop remarkable colors, and the later-season fish can possess beautiful shades of red and orange, plus spots. Nonspawning fish, especially the sea-run forms, tend to be silver.

The largest known arctic charr taken by anglers have come from the Tree River in the Nunavut Territory. The Tree River stock and related runs from the Coppermine and others rivers have consistently produced big fish. Chantrey Inlet in Nunavut also produces big charr, although it has a very small window of opportunity at ice out. More reliable are various rivers on Victoria Island, which have produced assorted line-class world records over the years. Although there are plenty of charr in the various rivers of Baffin Island, these waters have not been known for large specimens, and fish over 15 pounds have not been common there.

Various trout are available across Canada, from plentiful rainbows and cutthroats in British Columbia to brown trout in Alberta to brook trout in the eastern provinces. The best place in North America for large brookies is in Labrador; although some large fish occasionally come from northern Quebec waters. Brook trout, actually a charr and native to the continent, are favored by many eastern river and stream anglers, and sea-run brookies, or salters, are found in some of the maritime rivers.

Other Species

Other species with some following include bass, muskie, grayling, tuna, and halibut.

Both largemouth and smallmouth bass are found in Canada, with smallmouths more abundant and providing good fishing in southern Ontario, southern Quebec, New Brunswick, and Nova Scotia waters. One or both species are prominent in large and small inland lakes across this region, and smallmouths are prevalent in such large waters as Lake of the Woods, Georgian Bay, Lake Erie, eastern Lake Ontario, and the St. Lawrence River.

Muskies are likewise present in southern Ontario and Quebec, with especially large fish in Lake Huron/Georgian Bay and tributary waters, in the Ottawa River, and in the St. Lawrence River in both Ontario and Quebec.

Grayling are widely present in northern rivers and streams and are generally unavailable without making a fly-in trip. Few anglers make northern expeditions exclusively for these fish, which average $1^1/_2$ pounds, but they are popularly sought on light spinning and fly gear, as an adjunct to other fishing activities in the north. Halibut are just the opposite of grayling in almost every respect. They are caught off the northern British Columbia coast, primarily as a diversion to salmon, albeit in large sizes and with very stout tackle.

Bluefin tuna of enormous sizes are caught off Nova Scotia and Prince Edward Island. This fishery declined for a while but recovered in the late 1990s, with a federal quota placed on the total commercial and recreational catch. Although this species is generally in poor shape internationally, giant bluefins from 500 to 1,000 pounds are caught annually in the northwestern Atlantic under the quota system in late summer and early fall, and a portion of these

---

Cold-weather anglers can avoid life-threatening hypothermia by staying dry, eating high-energy snacks, covering extremities, and staying out of the wind.

are caught by anglers fishing out of charter boat from Nova Scotia or Prince Edward Island ports.

Related Topics
Visitors to Canada will find no lack of guides, charter boats, and services catering to anglers, especially in the well-known and well-publicized areas. Most lodges and camps have guides *(see)*, and charter boats *(see)* can be found in major inland waters and on the coasts. Lodges, camps, and other facilities dedicated to serving anglers are plentiful and are widely advertised in major outdoor publications in both Canada and the U.S. Outfitters exist who cater to canoe-camping and fishing trips, houseboat vacation and fishing trips, horse or foot pack trips, and so forth *(see: travel)*.

Canada is so large, and has such a plethora of angling opportunities, that it can be a bit bewildering for visitors from other countries who want to do some fishing. Prospective anglers therefore need to focus either on the region they plan to visit (perhaps on vacation) to discover the opportunities available and the common means of angling, or to focus on the species they wish to catch and then decide where to go to catch either many of that species or large specimens (at some places it is possible to do both).

Sportfishing in Canada is most popularly pursued from early spring through fall, but ice fishing has a large constituency, with perch, whitefish, and lake trout the major interests. Huge Lake Simcoe in Ontario bills itself as the "Ice Fishing Capitol of the World" and attracts up to 5,000 anglers per weekend in the height of the season.

There are regulations that restrict sportfishing by season, usually to protect spawning fish or fragile populations, and these are in place for most species of freshwater fish. For the most part, regulations regarding seasons, methods of fishing, catch limits, and licensing are determined by provincial and territorial governments. There is no national or federal sportfishing license in Canada, although each of the 14 provinces and territories requires a license issued by their government, which is valid only in waters within that jurisdiction, and in none is there a test or examination required to obtain a sportfishing license. Any person, whether resident or nonresident, can purchase a fishing license, although the nonresident fee is higher. Licenses can usually be purchased for varying time periods (a full year, a week, three days); they are most commonly acquired at stores selling fishing tackle, but are also obtained at some government offices, marinas, lodges, and camps.

Various provinces and territories are likely to have region-wide or water-specific regulations pertaining to the manner of fishing. Manitoba, for example, mandates the use of barbless hooks throughout provincial waters. These and other issues are addressed in a brochure or booklet provided when you purchase a fishing license.

Although some are not as productive as in the past, many of Canada's waters still provide good fishing. In some places, however, drive-in access has resulted in extraordinary fishing pressure. More logging roads have increased access to places few could previously reach in the summer, and these have gotten hammered.

Overfishing is one of the reasons why travelers who are able to fish without the convenience of having their own boat journey to fly-in locations, whether main lodge or outpost, to be assured of a high-quality Canadian experience. At such places there is a growing emphasis on catch-and-release (except small fish for lunch), including trophy specimens; using barbless or de-barbed hooks; using single-hook lures; and prohibiting fishing with bait to minimize injuring fish.

New owners, new customers, and a quality resource, have contributed to the acceptance and success of these policies. Younger and progressive owners have stepped in at many fly-in lodges across Canada. They have refurbished or built new deluxe or near-deluxe accommodations and made an enormous investment in the resource; most have exclusive outfitting rights. Aside from offering a good service, they must sink or swim with that resource. They, and most of their customers, recognize the resource is finite. People used to think there was no limit to the number and size of fish they could keep, even in lightly angled wilderness waters, and that there was no harm from fishing pressure. Now they know better.

Resource-protection changes have been well received by most conservation-oriented visitors. Considering the cost of such trips, no amount of killing fish, trophies or otherwise, would be of comparable worth, so quality of experience becomes the real issue. And the quality of experience is surely enhanced where there is enjoyable fishing opportunity.

CANARY ISLANDS
See: Spain.

CAN BUOY
A cylindrical buoy, usually green, used as an aid to navigation.
See: Buoys.

CANDIRU
The candiru is a small parasitic South American catfish.
See: Catfish.

CANDLEFISH
See: Eulachon.

CANE POLE
An inexpensive long pole, usually cut from a stalk of bamboo, unaccompanied by a fishing reel or rod

components, and used for making short-distance presentations, primarily of bait. Cane poles are usually from 10 to 15 feet in length; they are not cast, and have a fixed length of line attached to the tip. The line is no longer than the length of the pole, and the hooked bait, often with float or bobber, is usually lobbed or swung into the water.

Cane poles are used for stillfishing, primarily for panfish species, and hooked fish are retrieved by being jerked or lifted out of the water. Other materials may be used to make a "cane" pole, but the principal of operation remains the same.

CANINE TEETH

Pointed canine teeth are found in some carnivorous fish; they are usually larger than the surrounding teeth.
See: Anatomy.

CANNONBALL

See: Downrigger.

CANOE

Canoes are popular boats, widely used for fishing in flowing waters and in smaller lakes and ponds, and for accessing shallow backwaters and places where most other craft cannot be taken. Their popularity in part stems from the fact that they are relatively inexpensive compared to other fishing boats, eminently portable due to their light weight, easy to store and maintain, and durable. However, they are also more subject to capsizing because they're less stable than most other craft, although it is usually operator misuse or misjudgment, rather than the craft itself, that contributes to tipsiness or instability.

Canoes range widely in size, from mere one-person 10-footers to 24-foot models; the common lengths used by anglers are in the 15- to 17-foot range, although the longest canoes (which are heavy, broad-beamed, very stable, and commonly called "freighter" canoes) are used by anglers in some northern lakes, where they are also a primary means of transport for native people and wilderness residents.

Canoes are primarily open-interior craft with no closed storage compartments. The typical canoe tends to be narrower than other boats, and with limited leg room in the bow. The majority of canoes are double-ended, meaning that both the bow and stern are pointed; some models, however, have a square stern for the attachment of a small motor. Double-ended canoes are mainly paddled, but they can be poled or rowed with special attachments. They must be fitted with a near-stern cross-gunwale bracket to be used with a motor. Square-sterned canoes are propelled in the same manner.

Most canoes used with motors are operated with low-horsepower models, with the exception of freighter canoes. Electric motors are very useful on standard canoes, and can be attached to a square stern, a bracket, or in some cases to the gunwale. An electric motor moves a canoe along very nicely, and is a big aid for positioning while fishing, but it does nothing for portability. The heavy battery needed to power the electric motor negates portaging, and the same weight problem holds for gas motors.

Anglers have mixed feelings about canoes for pure fishing purposes. On the plus side, a lightweight canoe can be portaged over short, medium, and long distances to fish waters that other craft cannot reach. They are also easy to manipulate in shallow environments and in backwater spots that most other boats cannot access. If handled properly by paddlers, they are very quiet. They're also very good in shallow rivers and streams, and if you traverse whitewater.

On the minus side, canoes are highly susceptible to maneuvering problems, especially when paddling and when there's a wind. Many people who fish out of canoes spend more time paddling, positioning, maneuvering, and repositioning, than they do fishing, which means that they are not very effective anglers. This is especially so for anglers fishing alone, for those who do not care to anchor, or for those whose fishing is not helped by anchoring. Even when two paddlers fish out of a canoe, a little bit of wind or current means one angler must keep working the canoe while the other fishes. When anglers are guided from canoes, however, the guide does all of the critical maneuvering and position maintenance.

Another problem for many anglers is that it is unwise or at least risky to stand up in many canoes. Anglers see better, cast better, set the hook better, and play fish better when standing, but only the biggest, broadest, and most stable canoes permit this. The feeling of instability and of being pushed or pulled around by wind, current, or even the working of some lures, makes canoes a non-choice, or least-favored choice, for some anglers.

Canoes, especially smaller models and those propelled manually, are not good vessels on big waters,

Canoes are very popular for river fishing, although many places are best fished by getting out of the canoe and wading.

or in places where conditions can change suddenly into large waves and rough water. Although they can be paddled long distances, possible exposure to bad weather, heavy winds, and large waves restricts their useful practical range.

Materials and shapes. Canoes are made of aluminum, fiberglass, Kevlar, and various plastic composites. Aluminum has long been a favored material because it is light, durable, and maintenance free. But aluminum canoes tend to catch on rocks and are noisy and shiny, which can be detrimental to fishing in the very backwaters that a canoe is meant to access. Fiberglass canoes are less susceptible to being blown around because of greater weight and, in general, are less tipsy than aluminum. They are also durable and quiet, but their weight makes them tougher to portage long distances and harder for some people to lift, transport, or cartop by themselves. Kevlar canoes are expensive but lighter than fiberglass and also quiet, while plastic composites are moderately heavy but quiet and very durable. There are also wooden or wood/canvas canoes, which are expensive and require high maintenance, but are quiet, durable, and aesthetically appealing.

The length, width, and hull shape affect how a canoe paddles and maneuvers, and how much weight it can carry. Shorter canoes are generally lighter and more maneuverable. Longer canoes track better (stay in a straight line) and can hold more weight. Double-enders are easier to paddle than square-stern models.

Hull shapes are roughly analogous to the hulls on conventional boats *(see)*: flat, round, or some form of V, and with similar characteristics. Flat-bottoms are fairly stable, especially in flat water, but do not track very well unless they have a keel, which also aids turning; round hulls are unstable for the average user; V-shaped hulls (there are variations) are stable in rough water and track well. The keel line of the boat varies with the rocker, which is the degree to which the keel is straight or curved. A canoe without any rocker is considered to have a straight keel; it has more surface in the water and turns more slowly. A canoe with a lot of rocker turns quickly but is poor at tracking; it is more suitable to fast water than to flat water. Most canoes for fishing have a slight rocker, so they turn and track adequately.

For fishing and general outdoor use, a width or beam of between 32 and 39 inches is preferred; this is measured at the widest spot from the interior rather than at the gunwales because there are different designs to the sides of canoes. Sides that flare outward help keep water out but can be harder to reach over for paddling; sides that flare inward, called tumblehome, are easier to paddle but not as good at keeping water out. Straight sides are a blend of these and have less outward flare.

Canoe handling and loading basics. Canoes are paddled primarily with straight or bent-shaft paddles, the former preferred for general use because of versatility. A canoe usually turns away from the side the stern is paddled on, so direction is maintained by the stern paddler using a hook motion that twists the paddle through most of the stroke. It moves straight ahead when two paddlers keep their paddles vertical and pull straight back parallel to the keel line. To change direction, a paddler swings the paddle out in an arc; this is called a sweep, and the canoe will head in the opposite direction of the stroke. A solo paddler may find it best to sit in the bow seat facing aft, paddling stern-first as it were for better balance and control.

For some people, getting in and out of a canoe is often harder than controlling it. Canoes are meant to carry a load in the water, so they are weak and unstable when one end is on shore and the other unsupported. If you must get into a canoe that is partially on shore, keep your weight and center of gravity low, step in the center and keep hands along both gunwales; this can be aided by a companion who straddles the bow of the canoe and helps support it. Approach shore bow-first in still water and maintain stability for the bow occupant to get out, pull up the canoe slightly, and then straddle it for the rear paddler to exit. In flowing water, point the bow upstream when coming ashore to keep it from being swept into the current.

Canoes have a carrying capacity as do other boats, and this is identified on a capacity label in

Canoe Features

Keels
- Straight/no rocker
- Straight/slight rocker
- Curved/high rocker

Hulls
- Flat
- Round
- Modified-V
- Semi-V

Sides
- Flare
- Tumblehome
- Straight

the canoe. Remember that this weight includes paddlers. Be sure to situate the load so that there is a low center of gravity in the canoe, and evenly distribute the load for normal travel. When headed into a strong headwind, adjust weight to keep the bow down and stern high to achieve better directional tracking. You can move cargo forward or simply kneel in front of your seats to accomplish this.

Canoeists are well advised to wear properly fitting personal flotation devices *(see)*. Because canoes are more susceptible to capsizing than other craft, you have a greater chance of needing a PFD; water conditions, temperature, and other circumstances affect the situation, but be aware that a canoe can get away from paddlers pretty quickly in some situations, and a PFD that isn't on may not be accessible when needed. Be careful about making sudden moves in a canoe or shifting weight or cargo around. If you have to shift weight or change position, paddle to shore and make changes there. Be particularly careful where you are likely to encounter sudden waves from the wake of boats, and where there is current. In some situations it may be necessary to lash cargo to the canoe, and/or to use watertight bags for storing gear.

Anglers use canoes in both flowing and stillwaters and encounter different natural elements that can cause problems. In stillwater, waves, wind, and storms are likely to pose a threat, especially if you're laden down and traveling a far distance. Do not take unnecessary chances, and try to avoid problems (like heading for the lee shore when the wind starts to pick up, even if it means you have to paddle farther and it's less direct). In flowing water, you must know how to handle your canoe, and how to read a river for best navigation. An upstream **V**, for example, suggests rocks at the apex of the **V**; a downstream **V** suggests a gap between rocks. You may also need to scout ahead; where conditions are beyond your skill level (rapids, dams, fallen trees, whitewater) get to shore and portage or rope the canoe down. Remember that heavy rains or water releases can change a river's flow quickly. You should stay off water that is at or near flood stage.

One of the biggest problems with canoeing in rivers is that you are likely to encounter other anglers, including those who are wading or fishing from shore and have established their position. As an angler, you should be able to appreciate that the passage of a canoe over rising trout in a pool is going to put down those fish for quite a while, or that running right through the casting and fishing range of an angler is an uncaring if not hostile act. So make it a point to paddle behind an active angler, or to float by as far away as seems reasonable, or to ask if it's okay to move through the area the angler is fishing.

Canoes are perhaps the most frequently capsized craft, and for anglers, this not only poses obvious safety concerns, it can lead to the loss of a lot of gear. Anglers usually carry a fair amount of tackle, either in a box or satchel, and frequently leave it open. Be

Follow the depicted procedures to right a capsized canoe; helpers should apply their weight to the gunwale of the emptied canoe (bottom) to allow a capsizing victim to enter from the opposite side.

aware that if you capsize in this state, you can kiss just about all of your gear goodbye. It might be a good idea when fishing from a canoe to secure anything that you are not currently using. If all of your gear is in a closed tackle box, for example, you stand a better chance of getting the whole box (unless the water is really deep) and contents back, albeit soaked; if the box is open and you tip over, you'll lose a lot.

Regarding capsizing, if this happens in moving water, stay on the upstream side of the canoe to avoid being pinned against some obstacle. Hold onto the canoe unless you can increase your safety by letting go. When you reach a place where you can stand, bring the boat into the shallows to get the water out. In a lake or pond, a capsized canoe can be refloated by pulling it over the midsection of another, upright, canoe, but getting back into it without getting into the shallows is very difficult for many people.

If someone else is around, say in another canoe, they can help the capsizing victim refloat his canoe by pulling it, gunwales down, over the gunwales of their own canoe. The helpers can pull while the person in the water pushes. It may be necessary to rock or twist the capsized canoe to overcome suction. Once the bow and stern of the capsized canoe are out of the water, turn it over and ease it back into the water alongside the assisting canoe and preferably downwind. A light, athletic, and strong-armed person can get into the canoe by boosting in while the person(s) assisting lean on the opposite gunwale to help stabilize it.

See: Boat.

CANYON

A narrow, deep underwater valley with steep slopes, usually found far offshore in the ocean beyond the continental shelf. This underwater structure is often situated amidst powerful currents and attracts pelagic prey and predator fish, making it attractive to anglers who are able to reach such an area. In the northeastern United States, sportfishing the various Atlantic Ocean canyons is virtually an industry unto itself.
See: Offshore Fishing.

CAPE

The feathered skin of a chicken, from neck to the base of the back, which provides hackle for fly tiers.
See: Fly Tying.

CAPELIN *Mallotus villosus.*
Other names—Danish/Dutch/German/Norwegian: *lodde*; French: *capelin atlantique*; Japanese: *karafuto-shishamo*.

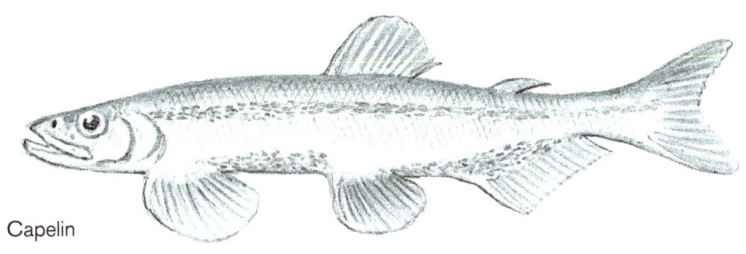
Capelin

A member of the smelt family, the capelin is an important food fish for cod, pollock, salmon, seabirds, and whales. It has commercial value; females are prized for their roe, and the meat is used as animal feed and fish meal. Like other smelts in flavor and texture, it is an excellent table fish, marketed canned and frozen and prepared by frying and dry salting.

Identification. The capelin has a large mouth with a lower jaw that extends below the eye. Males have larger and deeper bodies than females; also, the male has an anal fin with a strongly convex base, whereas the female has a straight anal fin base. Both sexes possess a single dorsal fin and extremely small scales. The body is mostly silver, and the upper back is a darker bluish green.

Size/Age. Capelin may reach a size of 9 inches, although they are usually less than 7 inches long.

Distribution. Capelin are found in the North Atlantic, especially in the Barents Sea up to Beard Island; in the White and Norwegian Seas; off the coast of Greenland; and from Hudson Bay to the Gulf of Maine. In the North Pacific, their range extends from Korea to the Strait of Juan de Fuca between Vancouver Island, Canada, and Washington, USA.

Habitat. Inhabiting saltwater, capelin are pelagic and live in the open seas.

Life History/behavior. Between March and October, capelin move inshore in large schools to spawn in shallow saltwater areas over fine gravel or on sand beaches; however, some may spawn at great depths. Spawning occurs more than once, and each female produces between 3,000 and 56,000 eggs; these are released at high tide and hatch in two to three weeks.

Food and feeding habits. Capelin feed primarily on planktonic crustaceans.

Angling. Capelin have no angling value, although they are used as food in some areas and are mostly caught in cast nets and dipnets.

CAPTAIN
See: Charter Boat Captain.

CARBON FIBER
A term for graphite.
See: Reel, Fishing; Rod, Fishing.

CAROLINA RIG
See: Soft Worm.

CARP

Although many freshwater anglers have a distinct affinity for certain species of fish, they often have a clear dislike or indifference for others, and in North America carp usually top the list of the latter. Carp, which are nonnative or so-called exotic species *(see)* in the United States, Mexico, and Canada, get little respect and have been the subject of intense, and unsuccessful, eradication measures. When considered in terms of weight (biomass), however, they are among the most abundant fish in North America, especially in the U.S.

Modern-day fisheries managers, whose predecessors were largely responsible for the ill-advised introduction of carp, mounted campaigns in the mid-1980s to encourage angling for these fish. Although a small carp following currently exists in North America, promotional efforts have produced little change in the appreciation of, or effort spent on, these fish. This trend continues despite the existence of large specimens in many bodies of water and despite the fact that when hooked, carp are among the strongest fish in freshwater.

Due to a small constituency, minor media attention, and plenty of other angling options, the methods of fishing for carp in North America lag behind those in Europe, where carp fishing is popular. Interest among North Americans may slowly increase, and methods become more focused, if populations of other important freshwater fisheries seriously decline. The abundant carp might then be more attractive. This is relatively unlikely, however, given the ingrained predispositions of anglers to certain styles of fishing. Meanwhile, because carp are abundant, relatively large on average, and overlooked by most anglers in the U.S. and Canada, these areas have relatively untapped potential for those who are interested in these species.

Carp

Scores of big carp mill near a marina at Lake Mead, Nevada

Species

Carp belong to the Cyprinidae family of freshwater fish, a large grouping of about 2,000 species that is abundantly represented in Europe, Asia, and North America but has no native species in Australia and South America. Cyprinids lack teeth in the mouth, although many have pharyngeal (throat) teeth for crushing hard foods and chewing plant material. Feeding habits vary; in many species, the mouth is somewhat protractile, or suckerlike, for feeding on the bottom, and many have sensory barbels on the chin or lips. Typically, the rays in the fins are soft, but in some (carp and goldfish) the first ray is spinelike. Most cyprinids are 6 inches or less in length, but they are highly important ecologically as food for larger fish; these include many species of minnows *(see)*, chub *(see)*, and others. Many of these smaller fish are used as bait. The few larger species provide sport for anglers or are harvested as food fish.

Types of Carp. The largest member of the minnow family, and a significant species to anglers, is *Cyprinus carpio*. Of the three varieties of *C. carpio*, foremost is the familiar and profusely scaled type that is primarily referred to as the common carp *(see: carp, common)*, which is also popularly referred to as the king carp or scaled carp. A second type is a scaleless version called the leather carp, sometimes referred to as the nude carp. The third type is one with a haphazard placement of a small number of oversize scales that is known as the mirror carp. The mirror and leather carp are actually domesticated, or cultivated, versions of the common carp as well as its predecessors. A related fish of increasing prominence is *Ctenopharyngodon idella*, the white amur, or grass carp *(see: carp, grass)*, an Asian species that is particularly adept at feeding on aquatic vegetation.

The above-mentioned fish are the ones people most commonly refer to when speaking of carp. Confusing terminology and identifications stew the pot somewhat, however, and fishing and scientific literature is full of references to fish that are, and are not, different from these. Mirror carp, for instance, generally have a smattering of scales, but may also appear with a full lateral representation of scales, or completely scaled, making these variants appear to be something other than mirror carp. The mirror carp with linear scales has two full rows of scales on each side, one running along the lateral line and the other below and alongside the dorsal fin. The fully scaled mirror carp is completely covered with scales of varying sizes and shapes, and is fairly rare. Mirror carp are scarce in North America, and it believed that no leather carp exist there; thus, common carp and grass carp are the major carp species on the continent.

The forerunners of the common carp in Britain are called wild carp, or wildies. This is not a separate species, as wild carp—like the common, leather, and mirror varieties—are designated *C. carpio*, but they are reportedly natural descendants of the original strains of common carp introduced to Britain. These slow-growing fish are smaller than common carp and possess a fully scaled body that seldom exceeds 10 pounds in weight. There is, however, a species called crucian carp (*Carassius carassius*) that is small, deep-bodied, and more closely related to the goldfish; it can reach a weight of $5^{1}/_{2}$ pounds and is of European and Asian distribution. Many carp are rather like goldfish; some of the carp cultivated in the Orient have gold-tinged scales, showing the close relationship of this species to the goldfish.

In addition to these fish, numerous other variations of common carp exist. They may be called European carp, German carp, Israeli carp, French carp, Italian carp, silver carp, snail carp, and bighead carp—all with some variation in color, body shape, or scale pattern.

Common carp average less than 5 pounds in weight through most of their range. A 10-pounder is ranked as a big fish in most places, but they can grow much larger. In North America, there are many carp in the 15- to 25-pound class; a relative lack of fishing pressure and low harvest suggest the possibility of many monster fish.

The all-tackle world record for common carp is a 75-pound, 11-ounce fish caught in France in 1987. How large these carp can grow is generally unknown; an $83^{1}/_{2}$-pounder was reported from South Africa earlier in the twentieth century. A 74-pound carp from Mississippi in 1963 is the largest reported North American state record, but it is unknown if this is the largest carp ever captured there. There are at least 14 state-record carp that weighed 50 pounds or better, and many states annually yield carp in the 25- to 40-pound range, and an occasional 50-pounder, some obtained through sportfishing and some through bowhunting or spearing. A few of these are grass carp and some are common carp. A 65-pound, 14-ounce grass carp taken in Arkansas in 1995 is the all-tackle world record for this species, and their ultimate size is unknown. Alabama and Arkansas have produced other 60-pound grass carp, and some states have produced 50-pounders.

The age that carp can attain is somewhat uncertain as well. An 1805 account of carp in a garden pond in Cambridge, England, mentioned a fish that had inhabited that pond for more than 70 years. A sixteenth-century Swiss naturalist cited a fish that was 150 years old. It is believed that the average longevity of carp in the wild is 15 years, and the life expectancy is much greater for those in cultivated ponds or aquariums. Large carp can clearly live 30 years, and perhaps as many as 50 years.

Carp are of primarily Asian origin and were widely transported and cultivated over centuries and broadly introduced in North America. In their native Asia, carp once graced the private fish ponds of emperors and were harvested only on festive occasions. Carp were among the first species of fish to be "farmed" as a means of controlling or increasing the population. European explorers transported carp to their continent, where these big minnows became choice fare on royal menus and were intensively raised in food ponds. In England, Izaak Walton, the ex officio patron saint of anglers and an oft-cited source by trout and fly fishing devotees, selected the carp as a favorite, calling it "the queen of rivers: a stately, good and very subtle fish" in his classic book *The Compleat Angler*.

Carp are sometimes reared in flooded paddies. In this way, protein and starch are produced simultaneously on the same acres, an important technique in overpopulated, protein-poor countries. Carp are often kept in special fattening pens before being sent to market; they can be shipped alive because they are hardy and will survive long periods out of water, as long as they are kept cool and moist.

Although their food value is underexploited and underappreciated in North America, carp are an important food fish elsewhere in the world. Its culinary popularity is due in small part to catches for personal consumption and in large part to commercial production and harvest. Carp are commonly used, for example, as an ingredient in gefilte fish, a favorite Jewish preparation, and they are valued in restaurants throughout Europe.

Many North Americans—anglers and non-anglers alike—turn their back on carp as a food fish, ostensibly because its flesh is tainted by the muddy or polluted waters in which it lives. In some situations, this may be true, but carp taken from many locations taste fine, whether consumed immediately or kept in cold, clean water for a while to eliminate muddiness (and firm up the flesh) prior to consumption. Carp can be prepared in a virtually unlimited number of ways, and in the U.S., where they are abundant, increased consumption would be appropriate not only for culinary reasons but also for environmental reasons, as they overpopulate many places.

North Americans' distaste for these fish stems in part from the carp's feeding habits and lifestyle. They subsist on tiny plants and animals, which they obtain by rooting along the lake or river bottom, often but not exclusively in mud. They draw-in the rich organic ooze with their suckerlike mouth and spit out or excrete bottom sediments. When spawning, they wallow in the mud and roil the water, sometimes causing stifling clouds of silt to settle over the nests and spawn of bass and other prized gamefish. Carp may also accidentally suck in the eggs or newly hatched young of these fish. The clouding of the water prohibits sunlight penetration, which in turn reduces plant and algae growth. This is not an attractive scenario, but then many people are fond of domestic pork even though the habits of pigs are not exactly regal. Moreover, catfish are prolific and omnivorous bottom feeders, known to eat dead fish even, yet they are appreciated by a large segment of the sportfishing public (although also unappreciated by some who are swayed by appearance and feeding behavior).

In addition to rooting around for food in turbid shallow environs, carp mate there and bring forth bumper crops of their own. A large female broadcasts her eggs over a wide area of shallows as she swims along, laying perhaps more than a million eggs in a season (a 20-pounder reportedly can produce 10 million eggs). The males fertilize the eggs by releasing clouds of milt in the areas where the eggs are laid. Neither the eggs nor the young get attention from the parents, but the carp population spirals upward because of the quantity of eggs and young produced. As a result, large populations of these fish exist in some waters, especially big lakes, reservoirs, and rivers.

The senses of carp are extremely well developed, more so than those of many other species. Their

Leather Carp

Mirror Carp

senses are in part responsible for their ability to adapt so well to so many environments, including areas that inhibit other species. Carp have a keen sense of smell, which explains why so many anglers offer them flavorful baits and lure them with advance chumming. Carp are reportedly capable of distinguishing one type of shellfish from another. They also have a highly developed sense of taste. Biologists report that carp have specialized taste buds in the skin of their snout, mouth, lips, and throat that are connected to the brain by nerves. Tests have shown that carp can differentiate between salty, bitter, and sweet substances, as well as between many extracts of fish skin and other fish tissues. They detect most of their food, especially in murky waters, by scent and then sample it with their barbels or lips. Sometimes curious, they will pick up a possible food item and taste it before ingesting it. They are also cautious and wary, however, and know when to avoid suspect items.

One seldom-addressed aspect of carps' acute senses is widely known by European anglers but is rarely detailed in the North American angling literature: carp (and some minnows) are supposedly capable of being alerted to danger through their sense of smell. Their skin possesses large cells that release sensory chemicals, called allomones, into the water when their skin is damaged by a predator. The scent of these allomones evokes a survival response in other similar fish, which scatter and possibly also seek cover. Does this imply that when a captured fish has been handled and then released, it alarms other fish? Some folks believe this is so, but there's no conclusive proof.

Goldfish. The goldfish *(Carassius auratus)* vies with carp in fame and for the length of time it has been associated with humans, although it has no significance in sportfishing and is primarily affiliated with aquarium collection. This cyprinid has been kept in ponds and aquariums in the Orient for many centuries.

Goldfish in the wild resemble carp in shape and sometimes in color, but they lack barbels under the chin. Those goldfish that escape captivity or that live in large outdoor ponds revert in only a few generations to their original natural greenish or black colors. They also grow to large size, weighing 2 pounds or more. For aquariums, they have been bred to produce a variety of shapes and colors, including rich black, red, yellow, and spotted, as well as the conventional gold. Some have bulging or telescopic eyes; others have tremendously enlarged fins. Goldfish are extremely hardy, which accounts for their ability to survive in small bowls and in poorly tended aquariums. When properly cared for in aquariums, they can live for more than 10 years.

Ecologists caution against the release of goldfish, intentionally or by accident. Although they will not breed in small aquariums, they will spawn and produce prodigious numbers in the wild. They can soon become so abundant that they crowd out native species. Because of this threat, in some areas there are laws prohibiting the sale of goldfish for bait (although carp minnows are used, deliberately or accidentally, for bait).

History, Attitudes, and Image

Carp present perhaps the greatest anomaly among freshwater species that exists in all of angling. When a species is abundant, hard-fighting, and respectable table fare, people will typically pursue it feverishly. Witness, for example, the historically recent introduction of Pacific salmon in the Great Lakes, which brought hordes of anglers out and spurred all manner of changes and evolution in equipment and fishing methods. But not so with carp in North America. Despite the abundance of carp and the large sizes attained—they reach heavier weights than most freshwater fish—they are largely ignored on this continent, to the bewilderment and envy of European devotees.

In the latest U.S. government surveys of angling participation, when respondents were asked what single type of fish they pursued most often, carp were not even represented among the 27 categories of response, which accounted for 98 percent of all replies. As mentioned earlier, in the U.S. the carp is generally more cussed than caught. By contrast, in Europe carp are less widely available yet far more highly valued. They are revered by many anglers and pursued with great devotion and fervor. And most of the carp caught are released. An evaluation of the history of carp and angling preferences may put attitudes and image into perspective.

Carp were native to Asia and known to both the ancient Greeks and Romans. They were apparently introduced to Great Britain in the mid-fifteenth century, although there are many different dates ascribed to this event. British writers have long attributed the spread of carp in England to their cultivation in monastery ponds, called stews or stewponds.

According to a report on exotic fish by the Sport Fishing Institute, carp "were apparently brought to the United States from Europe in 1831 and 1832 by a private citizen." The New York Department of Environmental Conservation reported that carp were first introduced into New York in 1831. The general introduction of carp in the U.S. occurred in May of 1877, when German fish culturist Rudolph Hessel arrived in New York with 227 leather and mirror carp, and 118 scaled carp for the U.S. Commission of Fish and Fisheries. These fish were first distributed by request to the constituents of congressmen in 1879, and by 1882 some carp had been distributed to every state and territory in the U.S. except Montana. A groundswell of complaints arose, and by 1896 federal carp stockings were discontinued. But the fish were then virtually everywhere, in many cases crowding out native species and spreading unhindered, with few enemies to keep them in control.

As the Sport Fishing Institute and many others have written, the introduction of the common carp to U.S. (and other North American) waters was a monumental mistake. Ironically, however, at the same time that carp were being distributed across the U.S., so were brown trout (also imported from Germany). And both American shad and striped bass were being moved from the East Coast, where they were indigenous, to the West Coast, where they were not indigenous. Today, the shad, striped bass, and brown trout exotic introductions are not looked upon with disfavor, at least by the general angling public.

Obviously there is some bias against the carp that cannot be ascribed to the mere fact that it is not indigenous to North America. This should evidently be attributed to the collective North American sense of what constitutes a sporting, or game, species. Although carp are not the sluggish fish that some people think, they are not an aggressive species in the same manner as many freshwater fish, and their diet is one that provides minor inspiration for people who like to cast lures or flies (that overwhelmingly imitate fish, aquatic insects, or terrestrials).

As Izaak Walton himself pointed out in *The Compleat Angler*, "if you fish for carp, you must put on a very large measure of patience." And in North America, unlike Europe, where there is an abundance of species of good size to pursue (several types of trout, salmon, and bass, plus pike, muskies, walleye, striped bass, catfish, and others), there has been little incentive to exhibit patience for a spooky, light-biting species that does not eat other fish, often scrounges for food, consumes vegetation, is considered by many an overgrown aquarium species, and primarily responds to odd bait preparations and oftentimes intensive chumming.

Europeans do a great deal of chumming (called feeding) for carp, and yet in North American freshwaters chumming is lightly, if at all, practiced for any species. It is illegal in some places, and at the very least it is viewed with disdain in others. Saltwater sportfishing enthusiasts in North America, on the contrary, rely heavily on some form of bait to catch fish, and chumming is the favored means of attracting many species of fish to a hooked bait. Granted, chumming in saltwater is largely done with ground, chunked, or whole fish, whereas chumming in freshwater (at least for carp) is accomplished with assorted prepared exotic, and some not so exotic (like corn), foods that are nevertheless not normally found in the water.

Naturally these attitudes, disparities, and contradictions provide a great deal of fodder for comparisons with fishing in Europe, where there are fewer prominent, large, and abundant freshwater species, and where angling traditions and attitudes differ. In England, not only are attitudes about carp and carp fishing more reverential, but there is great zeal about releasing the fish. Among the English, it is practically criminal to even think about keeping a carp because these fish are much less abundant. Carp farmers breed the fish for live sale to sporting syndicates; a 30-pounder might be worth more than $10,000. Yet in North America, carp anglers would not be questioned about keeping a carp (other than why they would want to eat it), and there is even a constituency for stalking and shooting carp with an arrow (legal in many places). This practice commonly occurs when the fish hold in the shallows and often when they spawn.

It is perhaps ironic that carp in Europe, especially in England, have been released so often that it is very difficult to recatch those fish, especially the old, large ones. They are either evidently crafty or become more so after being caught and released. One of the most intriguing footnotes with regard to carp surrounds the capture of the former British record, a fish of 44 pounds caught in 1952 and kept alive in the London Zoo Aquarium for 20 years after capture. The fish was visited and fed by Richard Walker, the angler who caught it. It would eat various baits, but never took the type of bait—reputedly a ball of bread paste—that Walker originally used to catch the fish. If this is indicative of the intelligence of these creatures, then it is no wonder that large specimens are very tough to catch on heavily fished European waters. Moreover, if carp in general are perceived to be hard to catch, requiring, as Walton said, a lot of patience, plus a lot of stillfishing, then it is little wonder that North Americans, having an abundance of more aggressive species with higher popularity quotients, do not warm to the different angling methods required to catch carp.

In North America, carp are not presently as difficult to catch as they are in Europe. Some anglers have terrific success in terms of numbers of fish, and many large ones are caught each year. So there is some question as to whether carp are as difficult to catch as many people believe, or whether they are just not well understood.

It will likely be a long time before carp are widely embraced by North American anglers, and before carp fishing is broadly recognized as an appealing sport. But for anglers with an open attitude, a follow-their-own-path mind-set, and an interest in pursuing a challenging and hard-fighting fish, the carp is a worthy quarry.

Angling for Carp

Whether you like their looks, food preferences, spawning habits, or other characteristics, carp are certainly a desirable fish to have on the end of a fishing line. They don't jump the way some popular gamefish do, but then the prized bonefish of saltwater also don't jump, opting instead to make blistering runs. Similarly, the hallmark of a fight with a carp is a streaking dogged run, the severity of which will depend on the size of the fish, the strength of your tackle, and perhaps whether the

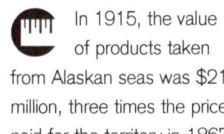

In 1915, the value of products taken from Alaskan seas was $21 million, three times the price paid for the territory in 1867.

environment is a river or lake. Big carp can take a lot of line off a reel in a hurry, and offer a lot of resistance throughout the fight, so there is little chance of horsing-in the large bruisers. And they fight until every last inch of line is retrieved. With a powerful sweep of its broad tail, this bronzed battler is off on a surging run that will test the finest tackle and overcome inferior equipment. Several determined runs and many minutes after being hooked, the fish may roll on its side to be led in. But that's not the end. Carp have a knack for rolling and flapping violently just as the net is swooping toward them, and many a good fish has escaped at this moment.

Hooking the fish, or, more appropriately, getting it to take your offering, is the biggest problem. Carp are not impulsive predators or ambush strikers. For the most part, they are not chasers or stalk-and-attack hunters. They are unlikely to strike a surface lure or diving plug, or, for that matter, most lures that are worked in a swimming manner and at a relatively fast (from their perspective) pace. When a lure is cast near them, they depart instantly. On occasion and where they are abundant, carp will strike a slow-moving jig, and either a weighted fly or a dry fly. Speed of movement is an issue but obviously not the major one. With all of the soft lures popular in North America, and especially with all the various types of soft worms and wormlike lures, one would expect plenty of accidental encounters with carp when using these items. In reality, however, there are darn few. So an angler who used plugs, spoons, spinners, surface lures, and most soft lures deliberately and exclusively for carp could cast or troll the paint off them, and then some, before realistically having a chance of catching carp in a natural environment. Nevertheless, carp are caught by anglers fishing for other species, mostly with some type of bait and looking for "whatever bites."

Deliberate fishing for carp requires a focused, not haphazard, approach, a good deal of patience, a knowledge of the habits of these fish, and slightly different equipment and tactics than are used for most popular freshwater species. As mentioned, many European anglers rank carp among the most difficult to catch of all freshwater fish. This is partly because carp are not exceptionally abundant, because there is intense pressure on them, and because of the natural cunning and wariness of the species. In the Old World, this sport is engaged in with a craftsman's care and with a degree of stalking and refined presentation that is uncommon among North American anglers. On the North American continent, with its bounty of big waters and variable species, anglers are not as refined in their approach or equipment, but they are moving in that direction.

Tackle. Tackle for carp varies. Ten-pound line is adequate strength, but if you want great sport and don't mind losing a fish or two, 4- to 6-pound line on an ultralight outfit will do nicely, especially if you're fishing unobstructed open water. Where carp in the 10- to 20-pound or better range might be encountered, it is important to have a quality line and a reel with a smooth-working drag. For big carp in waters with snags and a lot of thick grass or pad cover, it might be necessary to use heavier line, from 12 to 20 pounds in strength. Thin-diameter line is especially useful in carp fishing because it is less detectable yet has the strength of conventional-diameter line. A line with good abrasion resistance is also important.

Spinning, spincasting, and baitcasting tackle are all used to land carp, but spinning is probably the most functional method. The drag on many spincasting reels is often suspect, and if you hook a big fish, you must be able to apply pressure to it and count on a drag that is smooth and sturdy. Although most baitcasting reels are adequate in this respect, they are tough to use with light gear and might not be suitable for presenting the lightest terminal rigs and baits. Casting, as in cast-and-retrieve angling, is not a prominent aspect of carp fishing (except in some fly fishing and jig fishing situations), although casts are routinely made to put a bait into position; in many cases, this is more of a flip or toss than an actual cast. Where larger objects and weights are used, baitcasting reels will do the job, and they are certainly capable of handling the fight of a fish. Best to use a model with a flipping feature and, for large fish, one with a clicker.

Spinning gear, however, is a good choice for making all types of presentations, and midrange models with ample line capacity and a good drag are universally employed. Some anglers prefer spinning reels with a baitfishing or quick line-release feature.

Rod length is a matter of technique and preference. Lengthy rods with long handles are used by shore anglers, who prop these into rod holders while waiting for their bait to be picked up, and who need length when fishing close to shore for finicky fish. Using a long rod helps keep a close bait in

A float angler fishes for carp on a New York pond.

precise position and minimizes line interference—from the rod tip to float (see) or terminal rig. When targeting spots at a long distance, however, a long rod does not offer a significant holding advantage, although it does enhance distant bait placement and is more forgiving on light line strengths. Some anglers prefer them for controlling and playing a fish as well.

A long rod to most North Americans is 7 feet, but something in the 9- to 10-foot range might be more appropriate; 11- to 13-footers are common among European carp anglers. Many boat anglers can use their normal walleye and bass fishing gear, which includes rods that are in the 6- to $7^1/_2$-foot range and of light to medium action, but when specifically looking for big carp, it's necessary to gear up as one might for striped bass and to use a medium-heavy outfit.

Whatever length you settle on, look for a rod with a sensitive tip that will readily detect strikes, and a powerful butt for fighting the fish. A stiff rod might be useful for heavier fish, but casting soft baits with it will be more difficult, requiring more of a lob action than a cast; a softer rod with more flex will be easier on making bait presentations but also less punishing on a strong fish.

For those few who give fly fishing for carp a go, the primary needs are an 8- or 9-weight rod, a corresponding reel with ample backing capacity and an adjustable drag, and primarily a floating weight-forward line. A sink-tip line can be useful on occasion, but most fly anglers pursue visible, shallow fish, and a weighted fly will reach them without the benefit of a sink-tip fly line.

Bait. In North America, carp have been caught on an assortment of bait, primarily doughballs, corn, worms, processed baits, and commercially prepared baits, usually without chumming, although more anglers are using chum nowadays. They are also caught, although generally less often and more likely in Europe, on a variety of items that most anglers would find strange fishing items: cheese, beans, potato and carrot cubes, peanuts, rice, bread chunks, dog biscuits, cat food, and luncheon meat.

Doughballs are the most popular item used specifically for carp; these homemade concoctions are prepared from such ingredients as cornmeal, flour, syrup, anise oil, vanilla extract, among other offerings, and rolled into a ball. Much as been made by anglers about the various doughs and flavored concoctions that should be used for carp, and plenty has been said about favorite recipes for strange concoctions that are necessary to take carp (cornflakes mixed to a paste with strawberry soda is an overdone but popular example). Some sweet and flavorful product is almost always an ingredient. These concoctions are primarily items that produce a lot of scent and are meant to attract a wandering fish quickly. They are somewhat randomly effective but have taken a lot of carp, in part simply due to the abundance of unsophisticated fish. In Europe, such a bait is seldom used.

Many anglers who specifically target carp realize that the European style of attracting carp through elevated levels of chumming (which they call feeding or prebaiting) is much less of a hit-or-miss means of angling. In Europe, this chumming may be done for lengthy periods, perhaps several days, prior to actually fishing a location. In North America, few anglers do this. As previously noted, the legality of chumming in North America varies, not to mention that it is viewed with disdain by some anglers. Most of those who can legally chum do so while they are fishing, and a minority chum for a short period (perhaps a few hours or half a day) beforehand. A study of carp chumming by Nebraska fisheries personnel reportedly found that baiting drew carp within 6 hours and held them for about 24 hours. Of course, the effective time may depend on the type of water, where you place the chum, and the abundance of carp.

The chum used is often the same item that will be fished on a hook, although some chumming is done with groundbait. Groundbait is essentially made from crushed bread crumbs or stale bread, the latter being soaked, mixed into a paste, and stiffened with bran or cornmeal. These items are made into balls and tossed into the water, clouding and flavoring it. Other highly preferred chum, as well as hooked baits, are corn and boilies. "Boilie" is a British term for a small ball of processed bait made from assorted ingredients (milk and animal proteins, eggs, soy flour, wheat germ, coloring, and flavoring) that have been rolled together and boiled. They have a crusty shell that retards pecking by small fish. Corn is used straight from a can, but canned corn is usually soft, doesn't last, doesn't cast as well on a hook, and is taken by other non-target species. Carp prefer corn that has a bit more crunch to it. Anglers take hard-kernel field corn (maize), boil it long enough to soften it a bit (or let it sit in water for several days), and add sweetener. The result is a corn with more consistency than the canned version; it stays on a hook, is not attractive to other fish, and carp pick it up and try to crush it with their throat teeth.

When chumming, anglers distribute these baits over an area where carp are likely to move and feed, if necessary using a slingshot (catapult) or other throwing device to help reach the right locations. The hooked bait (called hookbait by the British) is fished among the chum. Corn, of course, is fished when corn has been used as chum, and bread or boilies are used with groundbaits. Anglers must strike a fine balance between overfeeding the fish, which could cause them to gorge and shut down; feeding too little, which can cause the fish to move on; and chumming just enough to attract them and trigger their interest. Overfeeding is not as much of a problem in North America, where there are more fish and more big waters, as it is in Europe. One of

the keys to the success of these items is that they do not attract, or are not consumed by, other species of fish, particularly pesky panfish and perch.

Hook size varies with the size of the bait. Many anglers use treble hooks for carp, especially with doughballs, but it's better to use single hooks. They're less likely to snag, are smaller and less obtrusive to finicky fish, and may make it harder to hook a fish, even though they seem to offer more points for hooking. A sharp and strong single hook, usually in size 6 or 8 but ranging from sizes 10 to 12, is the best bet.

Techniques. Many people believe that carp are strictly bottom feeders, but that is not the case. Although they primarily feed on the bottom, they also feed on or near the surface as well as at midlevels. Another popular misconception is that carp fishing is strictly a sit-and-wait affair. Although it is true that carp fishing is mostly a waiting game, anglers can opt to take a more aggressive approach and hunt for carp, stalk them, and cast to visible fish. Admittedly, these methods require care and stealth.

Because carp inhabit all types of environments, it is unnecessarily restrictive to expect predictable behavior or to limit one's pursuit to a single fishing method. In clear-water environs, for example, carp may depend very heavily on sight when feeding. In this case, they may be more susceptible to certain colors of baits, to striking jigs or flies that are cast ahead of them, and to using their vision in conjunction with smell or taste as a means of foraging. On the other hand, in muddy waters it is likely that they rely exclusively on smell or taste; vision then either plays an extremely limited role, or not at all.

Sight fishing for carp is not currently popular, because few anglers realize it is possible. Once it is recognized as a legitimate and potentially productive tactic, it might become more appealing. It is most likely to gain interest, possibly out of necessity, in waters that are experiencing a significant improvement in clarity, making sight fishing for carp routinely possible.

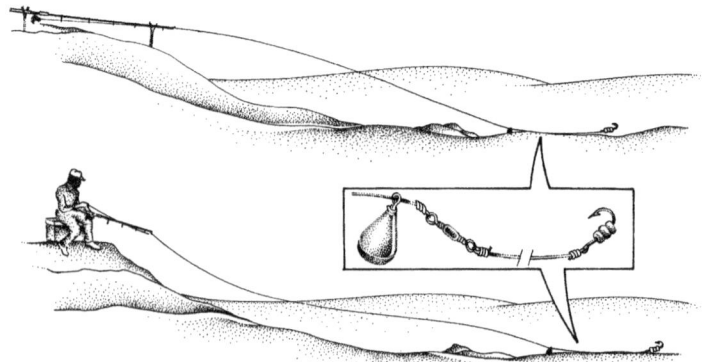

As described in the text, techniques for carp fishing from shore involve a tight-lined fixed bolt rig, depicted here in a rod holder (top), and ledgering, depicted here with a handheld rod (bottom). In both instances, the hook is baited with corn, and the area has likely been chummed.

The great majority of carp anglers, however, stillfish with baits, primarily from shore but also from boats. As previously noted, they employ an assortment of baits, and chum selected areas. Most shore anglers rest their fishing rod in a holder or otherwise prop it up (with the classic forked stick), and pay close attention to the rod tip, the line, a float if in use, and to any strike-indicating device.

Given the carp's proclivity for warmth, backwaters, slow current, and a tendency to root food out of the mud or rocks and suck it up, finding carp and learning where to concentrate one's efforts is not particularly difficult. Carp primarily inhabit shallow water in lakes and reservoirs, knowing that they can find baits better on a sand or gravel flat than in thick weeds. In backwaters, anglers work narrow, open areas between deep-water locales; carp funnel through these while feeding. They like weedbeds, if not for the plants then for the snails and other food items found under or within them. And they like shady spots, such as those found under overhanging trees and bushes. Well-aerated water and a choppy surface during windy weather are said to encourage feeding.

The favorite hangouts in rivers are at the head of pools, in eddies and slow-moving slicks, beneath undercut banks, and near banks beneath snags. They also hold along bottom structures where there is some relief from the current. In big rivers, they gather en masse below dam structures where eddying currents rotate against lock-and-dam walls or gate ends.

Carp usually scour the bottom when feeding, sometimes uprooting aquatic plants in the process. They consume much vegetation, as well as insect larvae, crustaceans, and small mollusks. They tend to hold in shallow areas, clustering in groups of fish that are akin to small schools. In ponds, lakes, and reservoirs, they seldom stay in one spot, preferring to roam in search of food. This tendency explains the popularity of chumming, as it helps attract and concentrate fish that would otherwise be on the move.

Many times these fish can be observed or intercepted in clear or murky shallow water near banks, as this is where much of their favorite food happens to be. In some places, such as municipal and community ponds where people feed ducks along the shoreline, carp hang out right under this frequent food supply.

In some nearshore muddy waters, carp create streaks of mud as they root along the bottom when feeding. They may also release trapped gas from the bottom. This appears on the surface as bubbles, perhaps in a trail, and is another giveaway that carp are present. Carp have a tendency to lie on the surface, seeming to bask in the sun, even in the middle of the day.

Fishing the edges of ponds and lakes, called margin fishing by European anglers, is a primary method of landing carp. Always fishing from the shore (they do not employ boats to the extent that North Americans do) with long rods, European anglers pursue the fish quite close to the shoreline. In sight fishing, this technique may entail dappling the surface with a bait to attract cruising or basking fish. For example, they may dapple a soaked piece of bread to a fish that is consuming small morsels of bait on or close to the surface. This is a game in which the bait is out of the water more than it is in it, and the angler watches intently for opportune moments to lightly deposit the bait on the surface, unencumbered by a weight or by line drag. Margin fishing sometimes encompasses bottom fishing.

Carp spawn in shallow bays, stream tributaries, or flooded fields and marshes from mid- to late spring or early summer. They are quite noticeable then as they thrash about and disturb the water. Often their backs are exposed, providing an obvious target for spear anglers or bowhunters. At other times of the year they frequently leap out of the water or roll or fin in shallow water or near the surface. Despite their sometimes obvious appearance in the water and their clearly raucous behavior when spawning in the shallows, carp are one of the most cautious of fish, and their wariness should not be underestimated.

When the water is clear, it is impossible to get close to carp without spooking them; casting overhand or waving a rod, or plopping a bait or float on the water close to a fish, is likely to immediately alarm it and send it scurrying. When the water is murky, anglers can maneuver closer, but they must still make a delicate presentation.

Bait presentations are usually made at varying distances from the angler, but seldom in water that is more than 10 feet deep, and often in depths of 3 to 6 feet. Once the bait is in the water, the angler places the rod in a rod rest, positioning the rod so that is pointed in the direction of the bait, preferably parallel to the water, and also pointed at the fish. Many people who watch the line or the tip indicator for a strike, angle the tip of the rod upward to observe the strike more easily. Europeans refer to these bait presentation styles as legering (called ledgering among North Americans).

A variety of bait rigs are used in this technique. For untutored carp in waters where they are abundant, some split shot placed a short distance from the bait might be sufficient. This rig is fished on the bottom, and the hook is set as soon as a pickup occurs. But most carp are more cautious than many unsuspecting anglers realize, and it is generally best to use a method that encourages the fish to pick up the bait but not sense the presence of bait or line. Bottom or near-bottom rigs intended for wary carp, therefore, are best embellished with a sliding sinker. This setup enables the fish to pick up the bait and perhaps move with it—a situation that is ideal in theory but not always possible in practice.

A common way to do this is with a bell or dipsey sinker that slides on the main line and is stopped by a barrel swivel. A leader is attached to the barrel swivel and a hook to the leader. An angler can hold the rod while keeping the reel in the freespool position (with the bail open) and guiding the line between thumb and forefinger, feeling for a strike on the taut line; or, the rod can be left in a holder. The bait is allowed to lie on the bottom or to float just a few inches above the bottom; a small piece of foam (or other commercially available item) is ideal for flotation. Theoretically, a carp venturing into a chummed area will see the higher bait first and take it before rooting on the bottom. Anglers who can legally fish two rods sometimes employ one of each setup.

Another favorite rig of carp anglers is a tight-line setup with a heavy sinker, known in Europe as a fixed bolt rig. This is similar to the rig described above in that a sliding sinker and bottom or raised bait are used, but the sliding weight is heavy, usually 2 or 3 ounces, and the main fishing line is kept tight to the reel, without slack. Here, the carp is expected to pick up the bait, instantly feel the tension of the weight, and bolt, thereby hooking itself.

Although hooks can be imbedded in bait, they can also be fished free of but close to the bait. The way to do this is with a so-called hair rig.

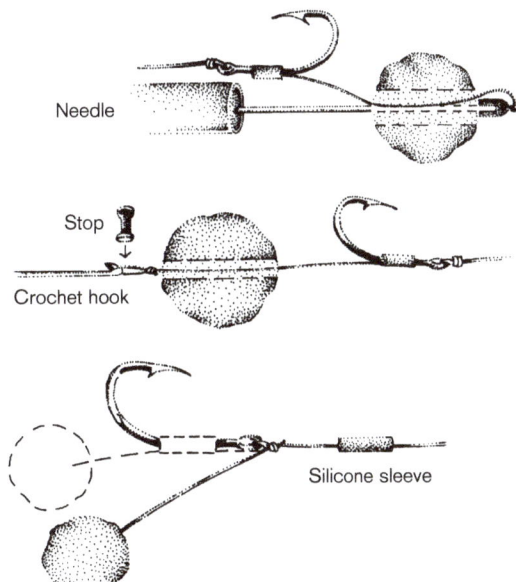

There are several ways to form a hair rig. The bait can be attached by tying line to it with a bait needle (top); by tying line to it via a crochet hook and a jamming stop (middle); or by pinning it with a silicone sleeve moved over the shank of the hook (bottom).

This sophisticated setup, originally tied with hair but nowadays constructed with fine monofilament or microfilament line, is also a self-hooking method of rigging. The fine line is tied to the eye of a hook and slid to the midpoint of the shank via a rubber stopper; threaded to the fine line is a boilie or corn kernels. A bait needle is necessary to thread the bait onto the fine line. The accompanying illustration shows this setup, but it's important to understand that the fine line should emanate from the shank of the hook for the best results. This placement allows the hook portion to enter the carp's mouth first but also ensures that if the rig is ejected by the fish, the hook will exit the mouth eye-first, greatly increasing the chance of a hookup.

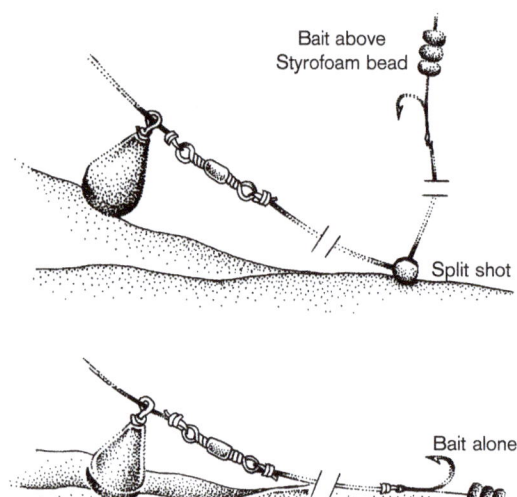

The bait on a bottom hair rig for carp can be raised slightly off the bottom (top) or lie directly on it, as circumstances warrant (bottom).

In current, or when the fish are not holding on the bottom, it may be necessary to use a float and also split shot that will force the bait downward yet be light enough to keep it drifting naturally.

With all of this emphasis on bait rigs and bait fishing, it seems odd to segue to fly fishing. Certainly not a mainstream tactic, fly fishing can nevertheless be productive for carp. The purists among trout and salmon fly anglers may balk at the thought, but sometimes flies make a lot of sense for carp; pursuing carp on fly tackle may be comparable to fishing for bonefish with flies (except the carp are bigger on average). Wherever carp are abundant, they often cruise along shorelines, singly or in small groups; if they happen to be slurping insects on the surface, a dry fly may catch them. Otherwise, a weighted fly (tied with the hooks riding up to avoid hangups) is the ticket.

Stalking and spotting, followed by careful casts, are the secrets to fly fishing for carp, a method that is sometimes extremely rewarding and sometimes not. If you think about it, a fly cast far enough ahead of the fish and resembling an insect or small crustacean has the potential to be a better lure than any other artificial and even most bait. As mentioned, however, these creatures spook easily, not unlike some more hotly pursued species. The challenges of presenting a fly without slapping the line on the water, or retrieving the line too fast and thus pulling the fly away from the quarry, can make fly fishing for carp as interesting as highly touted fishing methods aimed at species less widely available than carp (like bonefish).

CARP, COMMON *Cyprinus carpio*.
Other names—European carp, French carp, Italian carp, German carp, Israeli carp, leather carp, mirror carp, king carp, koi, sewer bass, buglemouth; French: *carpe, carpe commune*; German: *karpfen*; Japanese: *koi*; Spanish: *carpa*.

One of the largest members of the minnow family and a close relative of the goldfish, the common carp was also one of the first fish whose populations were regulated to increase production. Propagated for centuries and distributed widely, common carp are both beloved and despised. In North America, they are abundant but among the least-favored targets of freshwater anglers.

Three varieties of common carp exist, including the scaleless leather carp, the partially scaled mirror carp, and the fully scaled common carp, which is the most abundant of the three. In Europe and

Common Carp

Carp, Common

A common carp from Lake Oahe, South Dakota.

Asia, these carp have always been thought of as premier sport and food fish. In North America, however, the introduced common carp has wreaked economic and biological havoc. It was proclaimed a miracle fish for its economic benefits when it was first introduced across the continent in the 1870s, but then it began to crowd out native fish by reproducing too rapidly, damaging entire habitats, and exhibiting destructive feeding habits. It was soon regarded as a first-class pest and a hazard to natural ecosystems.

This view generally persists today, even though carp have not overcome most populations of other, more highly regarded, species. As a result, carp are harvested in huge quantities for commercial reasons, especially to curb their infestation of gamefish waters. In fact, many methods have been used and efforts made to rid American waters of common carp, including poisoning. Despite the favorable European outlook on carp, the effects this fish on waters in the New World is destined to remain a classic example of the problems that can result from introducing exotic species into new habitat.

Nevertheless, with eradication in North America virtually impossible, common carp exist in good supply and in relatively large sizes (compared to most other species), and provide an underutilized resource for anglers, not to mention an ample source of protein. In some circles carp are highly regarded as a food fish and can be prepared in many ways. The roe of the female has some food value and is often canned.

Identification. The common carp has a deep body form and a heavy appearance. Distinctive features include a short head, rounded snout, single long dorsal fin, forked tail, and relatively large scales. The mouth is toothless and suckerlike, adapted to bottom feeding, and the upper jaw projects slightly past the lower one. As in the goldfish, to which it is related, the common carp has a single serrated spine at the front of the dorsal and anal fins. Unlike the goldfish, however, the common carp has two pairs of fleshy barbels on either side of its mouth.

The pigmentation of the common carp ranges from gold to olive to brown with a yellowish coloring on the lower sides and belly and a reddish tint to the lower fins. Each scale on the upper sides of the fish has a concentrated dark spot at its base and a conspicuous dark rim. Juveniles and breeding males are usually a darker green or gray with a dark belly instead of a yellowish one, and females are lighter. Males develop tiny tubercles (temporary epidermal projections that help the male remain in contact with the female during spawning), which are found in a random pattern on the head and the pectoral fins. The common carp superficially resembles the bigmouth buffalo (*see: buffalo, bigmouth*).

Size/Age. Growing quickly and to moderately large sizes, the common carp is said to reach weights in the 80-pound range, although the average fish is considerably smaller. The all-tackle rod-and-reel record is 75 pounds, 11 ounces. The maximum life span is disputed but may be a half century; the average carp seldom exceeds 15 years of age.

Distribution. The common carp was one of the first species to be introduced into other countries. Its native range was restricted to temperate Asia and the rivers of the Black Sea and Aegean basins in Europe, specifically the Danube. At some point, the carp found its way to England, and in the nineteenth century it was brought from Germany to the United States. Today it is also found in South Africa, Australia, and New Zealand.

Habitat. Common carp are incredibly hardy and flexible in their preferences for living conditions. Primarily bottom-dwelling fish, carp like quiet, shallow waters with a soft bottom and dense aquatic vegetation. Although they favor large turbid waters, they also thrive in small rivers and lakes. They can live in low-oxygen environments and can tolerate temperature fluctuations and extremes, with the ability to survive in 96°F water for 24-hours. They tend to monopolize some of the bodies of water they inhabit.

Most of the time carp prefer to hold in quiet, shallow places with a muddy or sandy bottom, which they browse over. In some northern waters where the fish are abundant and such terrain is lacking or offers no food, carp will cruise over shallow, rocky flats and shoals, browsing along the rubble bottom. They are often observed during

the day in protected areas, sometimes adjacent to deep water, although they are seldom caught in deep water.

Life history/Behavior. By their second year, males are able to reproduce, whereas females are able to do so once they are three years old. Carp spawn in spring and summer, depending on latitude, becoming active once temperatures rise to the 60°F range. During the day or night, several males will accompany one or two females to shallow, vegetated waters and splash and thrash as the eggs are released and fertilized. A large female can carry millions of adhesive eggs, but the average amount is 100,000 eggs per pound of body weight.

The eggs go unattended, hatching in 3 to 10 days. The fry are born with an adhesive organ that they immediately use to adhere to bottom vegetation; after the first day, they must go to the surface and gulp air to survive. Common carp fry carry a large yolk sac, which they initially absorb for sustenance, later graduating to algae and plankton. They are quick to grow and may reach about 9 inches in length during the first year of their lives, if they escape the hungry jaws of their primary predators, which include northern pike, muskellunge, and largemouth bass. Juvenile carp make good baitfish, but their use is forbidden in some areas where trout are the main species.

Food and feeding habits. Omnivorous feeders, carp favor predominantly vegetarian diets but will feed on aquatic insects, snails, crustaceans, annelids, and mollusks. Aquatic plants and filamentous algae are the most popular food groups of the common carp. Their feeding habits are noteworthy, because they grub sediments from the bottom with their suckerlike mouths, uprooting and destroying vegetation and muddying the water. They have done severe damage to habitats by causing the loss of large quantities of plant life. This has proved detrimental to native fish populations and other animals.

Carp primarily spend their lives in small groups and are inclined to roam for food. They can gain several pounds a year in rich fertile environments but may remain smaller in those that are less fertile and where there is overcrowding.

Angling. The sporting value of carp is an issue that has been, and will continue to be, subject to much disagreement among the majority of anglers on both sides of the Atlantic, with most in the West devaluing it and most in the East, especially in Europe, extolling it. In the Old World, the carp has long been within ecological balance, seldom displacing the native fauna, so it has achieved a desirable status there. Because carp primarily eat aquatic plants, and not other fish, they are less receptive than many other species to the most commonly practiced methods of fishing in North America. Nevertheless, they are strong fish and hearty battlers, capable of stretching a fishing line and testing the skills of most anglers.

For more information and a detailed review of angling for carp, *see: Carp.*

CARP, GRASS *Ctenopharyngodon idella.*
Other names—white amur, amur, carp; French: *carpe amour, carpe herbivore, amour blanc;* German: *graskarpfen;* Japanese: *sogyo.*

A large member of the minnow family and an aquaculture species of worldwide importance, the grass carp is used for weed control because of its aggressive and herbivorous feeding habits. In the United States, where it was introduced in the early 1960s, it has become an extremely controversial species because of the biological damage it inflicts in the process of eliminating vegetation. In fact, there is growing concern that the introduction of the grass carp into nonnative waters will be as disastrous as was the introduction of its close relative, the prolific and destructive common carp. This species is called the grass carp by critics, whereas supporters often refer to it as the white amur to avoid the negative connotations associated in North America with the name "carp." It is commercially caught by seines in large quantities and prepared in a host of ways.

Identification. The grass carp has an elongate and fairly compressed body, a wide and blunt head, a very short snout without the barbels found on common carp, a short dorsal fin, and a moderately forked tail. The terminal and nonprotractile mouth has thin lips and sharp pharyngeal (throat) teeth especially suited to its feeding habits. The grass carp is covered with large scales; the ones on the upper sides of the body have a dark border and a black

Grass Carp

spot at the base, and give the fish a cross-hatched appearance. It is colored gray or green on the back, shading to white or yellow on the belly, and has clear to dark fins.

Size/Age. The grass carp grows quickly and to large sizes, some have been reported at 100 pounds in native waters. It can add 3 to 5 pounds a year to its weight under favorable conditions. The largest fish taken by rod and reel was a 65-pound, 14-ounce Arkansas specimen.

Distribution. Found originally in China and eastern Siberia, specifically in the Amur River basin from which it gets its name, the grass carp has been widely introduced to more than 20 countries. Only those in certain areas have been able or allowed to reproduce naturally; these places include the Danube River in central Europe, the Mississippi River in North America, and Russia and southern Africa. In the U.S., it was first stocked in Arkansas waters in 1963 and intentionally released in 35 states, although it has subsequently spread to other bodies of water where it was unwanted. In fact, many states have made it illegal to stock grass carp within their borders, unless a permit issued by the appropriate fisheries management agency has been obtained.

Habitat. Occurring in freshwater, grass carp inhabit lakes, ponds, pools, and backwaters of large rivers, with a preference for slow-flowing or standing bodies of water with vegetation. They are able to withstand temperature variation, extreme salinity, and low oxygen concentrations.

Life history/Behavior. Spawning takes place once a year over gravel bottoms in rivers, between April and September according to temperature; adults will migrate upstream to find acceptable spawning sites. The round eggs of the grass carp are semibuoyant and amber colored, hatching in 24 to 30 hours without the protection of the parents. After they absorb the nutrients in their yolk sacks in the first two to four days of their lives, the larvae feed on microplankton in quiet waters. The young hide in deep holes in riverbeds during the winter.

Food and feeding habits. Primarily vegetarians, grass carp have earned their name by eating aquatic plants and submerged grasses, adding the occasional insect or invertebrate. With the help of teeth on the pharynx, they tear off vegetation with jerking motions. Unlike common carp *(see: carp, common)*, grass carp do not muddy the water with their browsing, but their aggressive feeding habits cause other problems. Grass carp tend to break off the upper portions of grasses, leaving the roots to grow, so they are not as useful in eradicating vegetation as they are supposed to be. Also, grass carp cannot digest all the plant matter they take in, so instead of eliminating a vegetation problem, they make it worse by excreting plant material and distributing it to new areas. In addition, they contribute to increased water turbidity and to eutrophication. Finally, heavy browsing may stimulate faster than normal growth in certain kinds of plants.

Triploid grass carp. A technique that consists of exposing fertilized eggs to heat shock was invented by researchers in 1981 to produce sterile grass carp. This method creates nonreproducing fish of both genders. They are called triploid grass carp because they have three sets of chromosomes instead of the usual two sets (those fish are called diploid). They are as hardy as the ordinary variety of grass carp, but they have the benefit of not being able to overpopulate their habitats. They look like large creek chub, flourish in warm water, and may reach weights of 25 pounds or more. Triploid grass carp are useful in controlling unwanted aquatic plants, but the water clarity may deterioratedue to the substantial passing of plant material as fecal matter.

Angling. Grass carp are not a highly regarded species by a majority of North American anglers, for largely the same reasons as the common carp. However, they are strong fish that put up a tenacious fight, and they are known to jump. Where they are pursued by anglers, techniques are analogous to those for common carp, although these fish are known to feed on or near the surface, especially in locations where they have pared down the vegetation.

For more information on angling for carp, *see: Carp.*

CARP, LEATHER
The leather carp is a scaleless variety of the common carp *(see: carp, common)*.

CARP, MIRROR
The mirror carp is a partially scaled variety of the common carp *(see: carp, common)*.

CARRYOVER FISH
Stocked fish, usually trout, that survive at least one winter in the wild; also known as holdover fish.

CARVING
See: Fish Carving.

CAST
To throw an object that is connected to a rod via fishing line; also, the distant placement of an object via line and rod in the water, as in, "make a cast toward those lily pads."
See: Casting.

CASTER
A person who casts.
See: Casting.

CASTING

A fundamental element of many types of angling, casting is the act of throwing an object that is connected to a fishing rod via line. It is critical to some types of fishing but marginal or nonessential to others, and it may be enjoyed as a game or contest unto itself. The object cast is usually a lure or bait with hook(s), but it may be a hookless weighted object used for practice casts.

From an angling standpoint, the objective of casting is to present a lure or bait at some distance away from the caster's position, and to place it where it will be attractive to the species sought. In many instances, anglers cast to specific habitats, or targets, where fish may be present, or to roaming fish that must be intercepted; in such cases, accuracy—and possibly distance—are vitally important. Often, however, anglers cast blindly, seeking fish whose presence or precise location is unverifiable; in such cases, accuracy may have little or no significance, and distance may or may not be a factor.

Casting is done at close range in some situations, and at great distances in others. Some forms of angling require repeated, or continuous, casting throughout the day, whereas others require occasional or moderate amounts of casting. The weight of the objects cast varies with the species sought, the tackle, and the circumstances; thus, anglers must be adaptable and possess tackle suited to the conditions.

With few exceptions, casting is not difficult, and in some cases it can be an art form. Although a basic component of angling, it is one that many anglers do not master fully. Yet mastery is virtually guaranteed to contribute to success, if not greater enjoyment of sportfishing. In fact, many anglers prefer types of fishing that involve casting, especially those that require skillful casting (that is, accurate placement), because it is a measure of overall proficiency and an enjoyable activity in itself.

Two diametrically opposed principles govern casting. One requires the use of a weighted line to cast a nearly weightless object. This is the principle involved in fly fishing; a fly line carries a fly or fly-like object that is virtually weightless although not necessarily small or wind-resistant. This is a specifically focused activity that is detailed in the entry on flycasting tackle (see).

Arguably 90 percent of all sportfishing activity does not involve fly fishing; instead, a light or virtually weightless line is used to cast a weighted object. The weight of the object cast varies, but it is the terminal weight that carries the line forward or backward. This form of casting will be discussed in detail here—including the use of spincasting, spinning, and baitcasting tackle—although specialized forms of casting such as flipping (see) and pitching (see) are reviewed elsewhere.

Becoming Proficient

The majority of casters use spinning tackle (see) and spincasting tackle (see), and a significant number use baitcasting tackle (see). A few use conventional tackle (see). For the most part, casting requires placing a lure or bait at a moderate distance, generally from 30 to 60 feet in freshwater. It does require some competency to cast unerringly, particularly when circumstances are problematic—for example, when the wind is blowing, the boat is turning, or the current is changing your position. Often, and especially when lures are used, proficiency is necessary because the first cast made to a targeted location is most critical to success.

Many people do not take the time to fully master their equipment. As a result, they are able to cast well enough to get a lure or bait into the water, but not well enough to put it where they want it whenever necessary. This is never more obvious than when two people are together in a situation that demands the ability to put a lure in a specific spot. The one who can catches the fish; the one who cannot lags far behind. In some angling situations, this means not just being able to get your lures close to where you want them to go; it means pinpoint placement. Often, species of fish that live or forage in heavy cover—largemouth bass, peacock bass, and snook are examples—will not chase a lure that doesn't land in its dining area. Placing a lure or bait at the dining room door is often not close enough. Therefore, obtaining accuracy is a main element of casting proficiency.

Practice. Accurate casting is a function of experience. For most anglers, especially those who are new to fishing or to using a particular type of tackle, achieving proficiency, and especially accuracy, is derived from practice. Ironically, although casting is obviously important to many types of fishing, few anglers practice.

People accept practice as a part of almost every kind of participatory recreation, but few seem to relate the concept of practice to casting, with the exception of fly anglers. Yet, improving casting accuracy with spinning, spincasting, and baitcasting tackle through practice is essential to increasing success. Nothing can be done about many things that influence angling success, especially such variables as air temperature, wind direction, wind velocity, and water temperature, yet you can control your ability to put a lure on target by using quality, balanced equipment and by practicing. Beginners especially should not wait until they go fishing to learn to cast but should practice before they get near the water. Casting at targets in your yard or in a neighborhood park is good for everyone.

Targets. The best targets to start with are brightly colored plastic hoops or children's wading pools. They stand out well on yard grass and are about the right size. When you're learning to cast, you should set a pair of these out at 25 and 30 feet. Don't try to throw a foot farther until you can hit these targets consistently. You'll hit them often enough not to be totally frustrated, and you'll also be surprised how often you miss. Forget about distance and concentrate on accuracy. Resist the trap that most casting beginners fall into: putting a choke hold on their rod and winding up as if they were in the Olympic hammer-throwing competition. The objective is not to see how far you can cast.

Concentrating on accuracy is extremely important in the learning process. Physical strength has little to do with good casting. What does count is developing timing and coordination through practice. If you concentrate on accuracy until you're hitting those targets 8 times out of 10, then greater distance will come as a fringe benefit. If you do it the other way, by putting the emphasis on distance, you'll be in trouble from the beginning.

Casting weights. Practicing in the yard must be done with hookless objects known as casting weights or casting plugs. These are available in several sizes and in round or flat-sided versions, although they're not always easy to come by. Manufacturers should include them with their merchandise to foster practice, but none do. Some tackle shops don't carry them, although they might be able to order them. You may have to order them from a catalog merchant, and you may not have a choice of versions. It may be difficult to find the heavier weights (like the $^5/_8$-ounce size, which are better for baitcasting).

If you have a choice, flat versions are preferable to round for yard casting. On a hard surface the flat-sided weight is retrieved without much line twist. That's not true of the round type, which roll and spin and can cause twisted line. You don't need that, especially when learning.

If you practice much, the line tie at the end of your casting weight will eventually wear out and break. To repair this, get a small screw eye, like those used for hook hangers on lures, and screw it into the head of the plastic casting weight. If you're not successful in finding flat-sided $^5/_8$-ounce casting weights (or others for that matter), you can make them yourself by hollowing out the base of a $^3/_8$-ounce casting weight, adding sufficient lead shot, and covering the hole with epoxy.

Weight size varies with the tackle used. Once you've gotten some confidence by practicing at the learning distances, try using more targets and setting them at varied ranges. In actual fishing, you will be making one cast to an object that is 20 feet away, then to one that is 50 feet away, and then to another that is 35 feet away, perhaps from the same shore or boat position, with each cast separated by only a few seconds. You must be accurate at all distances at any given time, so position the targets at varied ranges. You might make a game of it, awarding yourself points for successful casts and setting some point goals, or you might cast with a companion in a friendly competition. Also try to make the targets more challenging as well. They might be plates, cups, tires, and the like. Finally, by changing the weight of the practice plugs, you can make the activity completely different. Not every lure cast will be the same weight nor, for that matter, as aerodynamic as a practice plug.

Spincasting

The spincasting reel is enormously popular because of its ease of use. No better reel exists for the child or adult who wants to enjoy fishing without working too hard at learning how to cast. Although it is fairly easy to cast a country mile with a spincasting reel, it is unfortunately the most difficult reel with which to learn accuracy unless you know the right technique. The problem centers around the pushbutton line-release device.

To operate a spincasting reel, you must depress the pushbutton and hold it in until you're ready for the casting plug to fly out. Many people unfortunately think they must press that button in again to stop the plug; even some manufacturer's manuals recommend this practice. As you'll discover the first time you try it, if you depress the pushbutton while the casting plug is airborne, the plug stops with a jerk and lurches back several feet. But if you don't stop the plug somehow, it flies too far and winds up in the brush or nearest tree, and if you've put much power into the cast while fishing, when you clamp down on the pushbutton again, the lure (and hooks) may come hurtling back at you. That could hurt.

To avoid this and thereby cast accurately, use the forefinger on your noncasting hand (the left forefinger for most people) to control the line.

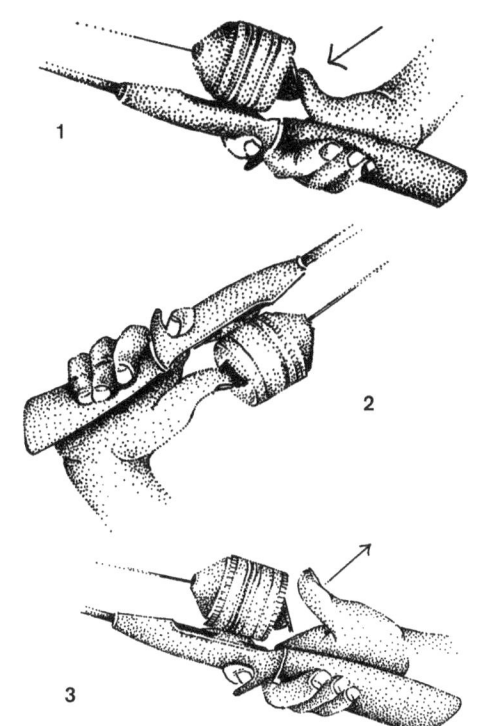

Casting with a spincasting reel begins by pressing the pushbutton with your thumb (1) and holding it throughout the backcast (2); release the pushbutton at the optimum point of rod flex in the forward motion of the cast (3).

Casting with a spincasting reel is essentially accomplished by pressing the pushbutton with your thumb (or the trigger with your forefinger) and holding it throughout the backcast, then releasing it at the optimum point of rod flex during the forward motion of the cast. When the button is released, line flows off the spool, through the opening in the reel cover, and out through the guides, carried by the weight of the object at the terminal end of the line.

Before making a cast, you should set the drag to the proper amount of tension (this is most critical) and adjust the position of the plug at the rod tip. The plug (or lure or bait, when fishing rather than practicing) should hang a few inches below the rod tip. You can get it to this position by reeling in the line until the lure is a few inches from the tip guide; if the reel is right at the tip, then pull a few inches of line off the reel drag, which will cause the lure to hang a few inches below the tip.

If you're right-handed, place the rod and reel in the palm of your left hand so that the handle of the reel is up and facing you. Extend the left forefinger to trap the line against the opening of the spool. Depress the pushbutton with your right thumb and point the rod tip at your intended target. Lift the rod back toward you swiftly, using your wrist and forearm (not the whole arm), and allowing the weight of the plug to flex the rod. In a continuous and unhesitating motion, and still using the wrist and forearm, bring the rod forward in an accelerated motion. Release the line and the pushbutton at the same instant during the forward stroke to cast the plug toward the target. While the casting plug is in the air, the line should flow across the tip of your left forefinger. To put the plug right where you want it, increase upward pressure with the left forefinger. With a bit of practice you will learn at what exact point in the forward stroke to release the line and the pushbutton, which is a major element in attaining the proper trajectory for accurate placement. Casting is the same for left-handed anglers, although hand positions are reversed.

Although these instructions belabor the act of casting, it is really a simple technique that almost anybody can master quickly. You'll quickly learn to feather the line with your left forefinger so that the plug drops right where you want it. Although spincasting does involve the use of both hands, your right hand still executes the casting stroke. The only function of the left hand is to get your left forefinger out where it needs to be to control the line. (Again, this text assumes a right-handed angler.)

When you are learning, and whenever striving for accuracy, get the rod and reel out in front of your body with both hands and make the rod follow an imaginary line from your nose to the target. Remember that the most important single phase of the spincasting technique is to have the line flowing over your forefinger while the plug is in the air. Once you get the feel for the control you have over the lure by simply lifting the forefinger slightly up against the line, you're on the way to accurate casting.

Proper casting, of course, is made easier with equipment of good quality. Some spincasting reels are junk. No one, especially a young beginner, can learn good casting with worthless equipment. Excellent spincasting reels are available in different sizes, and they come prespooled with line of appropriate strength. For beginners, a smaller size filled with 8- or 10-pound line is fine for starters. A smaller reel is easier for youngsters as well as for adults with small hands, to use in two-handed casting. It will be much easier to grip, and it lets them get their left forefinger out where it needs to be to achieve casting accuracy.

As for casting weight, use $^3/_8$ ounce. You can also use a $^1/_4$-ounce version, but a $^3/_8$-ounce weight is easier to work with, especially in the beginning. A 6-foot light or medium-light action rod is a good choice for use with spincasting reels, but it may be too large for youngsters. Choose a shorter one accordingly. Spincasting rods with an offset handle used to be common but aren't now, so you'll probably have to use a straight-handled rod. The reel sits up higher on such a rod and is not as easy to grip as it is on a rod with an offset handle, which places the reel lower in the seat. This is especially true with a larger reel. An offset handle is helpful when you use the two-handed technique, but you can manage otherwise.

Spinning

Spinning tackle started out as equipment for casting lightweight objects and for light angling applications. Today its foremost use is still in this area, although spinning gear that spans nearly all angling applications is available. Nevertheless, most casting with this equipment involves tackle on the lighter end of the spectrum, and tossing objects that weigh less than a half ounce (and in many freshwater applications at least half of that). Proper casting with spinning gear, especially when accuracy is required, involves more than just heaving. Although spinning tackle is easy to use, many people exhibit poor form when casting, especially inexperienced anglers. It is common to see many casters hold a spinning rod behind them and then throw their lure or bait forward, as if they were tossing a javelin or operating a catapult. It's not pretty, it's not effective for distance or accuracy, it may be dangerous to yourself or companions, and it can be a detriment to angling success. Effective casting starts with learning the basics properly.

One of the criticisms of spinning tackle, especially from freshwater bass anglers, is a lack of accuracy when fishing in tight quarters or when pinpoint accuracy in heavy cover is essential. If you have ever seen master casters exhibit their abilities at sport shows, you know that it's possible to be as accurate with spinning gear as with any other tackle; accuracy may not be as easy, but it is possible. As with all casting equipment, accuracy with spinning tackle requires that you stay in touch with your line while the practice weight is in the air. Spinning reel users usually do this by dropping the right forefinger to feather the line as it comes off the spool, which is moderately, but not superbly, effective, even in the hands of experts. There are other techniques you can utilize, and they will be described shortly.

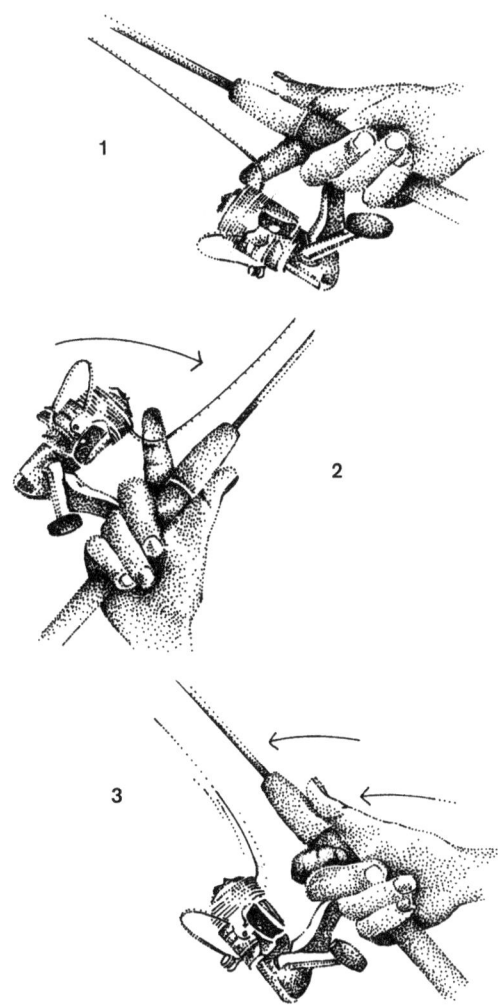

To cast most spinning reels, open the bail and use the tip of the forefinger to grip the line (1); then bring the rod back (2). As the rod comes forward, release the line (3) when the rod tip is pointing above the target.

Another criticism of spinning tackle is its tendency to produce twisted line or loose coils or loops on the spool. These will certainly adversely affect casting distance and accuracy. Line twist and how to avoid it are discussed in detail elsewhere *(see: line; spinning tackle)*. Recommendations for eliminating spool loops are given there.

Be attentive to the level of line on your spinning reel spool, especially when filling it up. Overfilling is a common mistake, and it contributes to loops and errant coils that lead to tangles and that hinder casting. Having too little line is better than too much when you are spinning, although you reach a point where too little line can impede achieving distance.

As with other kinds of equipment, every minute you spend practicing pays dividends when the time to fish actually comes. Practicing absolutely leads to increased fishing success. When practicing with spinning tackle, use $1/4$-ounce casting weights to start, and rods loaded with 6- or 8-pound-test line. You can change tackle components as your skills sharpen.

Basic casting technique. The basic method of casting with spinning equipment involves the following steps: Begin with the reel under the handle and facing away from you. Adjust the drag to the proper tension level. Hang the casting weight (or lure or bait when fishing) from 3 to 6 inches below the tip of the rod, and turn the handle to bring the bail roller close to the reel stem. If the weight is not in this position, reel it up to the tip and strip line off the reel by pulling on the line above the reel. Pull just enough line off the spool that the weight is the right distance below the rod tip, while at the same time bringing the bail roller close to the reel stem and extended index finger. The bail roller must be properly positioned to allow the finger to easily grab the line and to touch the lip of the spool.

To open the bail manually, grab the line at the roller with the tip of your forefinger and flip up the bail with your other hand. To open the bail automatically, depending on the reel, either extend your forefinger over the roller and grab both the line and the trigger, or simply grab the trigger.

Keep tension on the line with your finger; the tension will be released at the optimum point of rod flex in the forward motion of the cast. When this tension is released, line flows off the spool and out through the guides, carried by the weight of the object at the terminal end of the line.

To execute the cast, the reel should face away from you and you should be looking at the back of your hand. Point the rod tip at and slightly above your intended target. When you are learning, and whenever you're striving for accuracy, get the rod and reel out in front of your body and make the rod follow an imaginary line from your nose to the target. Bring the rod back sharply, using your wrist and forearm (not the whole arm) and allowing the weight of the lure to flex the rod. In a continuous and unhesitating motion, and still using the wrist and forearm, bring the rod forward in an accelerated motion, releasing the line with your forefinger during the forward stroke when the rod tip is pointing above the target.

The degree of flex in the rod will depend on the rod design and material; pure graphite rods require only a short hammering type of stroke, whereas more-parabolic composite or fiberglass rods require a back-and-forth motion. With a bit of practice, you'll learn what adjustment to make for the rod action as well as for different lure weights, and you'll learn at exactly what point in the forward stroke to release the line, which is a major element in attaining the proper trajectory for accurate placement. If the lure goes too high in the air, the line was released prematurely; if the lure lands a short distance in front of you, the line was released too late. It shouldn't take long to get the hang of it, which is one of the benefits of using this type of tackle.

The released line can be moderately controlled during a cast by allowing it to brush against an extended index finger from the rod-holding hand; the finger should be held near the spool lip. This is called feathering and is the most common method of controlling line that is cast from a spinning reel, although it is only moderately effective at achieving accuracy.

Better accuracy can be obtained by allowing the outgoing line to brush against the forefinger of the noncasting hand, although the open bail wire may make this difficult. To do this, the front of the reel has to be in the palm of the other (usually left) hand; extend the left forefinger out and press it against the lip of the reel's spool, keeping it there during the casting motions. When the cast is made and the weight released, keep the left hand in place and control the line by applying slight pressure on it with the left forefinger. This method puts your left forefinger on top of your line as it peels off the spool during the cast.

On some reels, the location of the open bail arm makes this two-handed method of line control a little difficult, but it can nevertheless be done. An improvement is removing the bail arm, as described later.

In lieu of feathering the line in either of these manners, many spinning reel users simply stop the cast altogether either by pressing the extended index finger against the spool, by closing the bail, or waiting for the end of forward momentum when the lure or weight reaches its target. Abruptly pressing a finger against the spool and closing the bail may cause the plug to stop abruptly and even lurch back toward you; allowing the lure to stop when it loses its own momentum is suitable only for open-water situations and cannot be used when obstructions are present or when pinpoint accuracy is necessary. These acts are not conducive to pinpoint casting, although they may be acceptable in situations where exact placement of a lure or bait isn't required.

Several options to the basic casting motion need to be pointed out. Although casting is often accomplished with one hand holding the rod and making the backward and forward motions, many people find it more comfortable and more secure to use two hands on the rod; they are able to attain greater distance and/or straight-line casts by using two hands. Two-handed casts are made by placing the secondary hand on the lower part of the rod handle and using both forearms and wrists to execute the proper motions; the secondary hand can be released from the rod while the casting weight is airborne, and moved up to the reel if desired. Many anglers use two hands for nearly all casting with spinning rods; when using large tackle and heavy lures, it is virtually mandatory.

Lowering your casting weight, lure, or bait a short distance below the rod tip is a necessary component of casting, but exactly how far is variable. You can put it too far or not far enough. This depends to some extent on the rod you're using as well as the weight of the object being cast. When using spinning gear, leave a longer drop from rod tip to practice plug than you would with a baitcasting outfit; timing on the cast seems to work out better if you do. Usually, the lighter the object you're casting, the longer drop you'll want between it and the rod tip. Practice will determine what works best for you. Try letting out different amounts of line between your rod tip and the plug. When you find out what you like best, stick with it.

An alternative to releasing the line with your forefinger after you've opened the bail is simply to drop the forefinger straight down to trap the line against the side of the reel's spool. When you cast, release finger pressure; then use the same forefinger to feather the line while the plug is in the air.

Line loops that form on reel spools often occur because of slack line that is momentarily present after a cast. To minimize slack line, don't crank the handle right away after a cast. Instead, reach out and manually close the bail arm with your left hand; then grab the line ahead of the bail roller with your left hand and pull off a few inches. Raise your rod tip at the same time. If you discipline yourself to do this after each cast, you'll eliminate a lot of problems; however, this technique obviously is not applicable in situations where you must begin retrieving the instant that your lure hits the water.

No-bail casting. To stay in touch with your line and improve accuracy while casting lightweight lures, consider removing the bail wire and learning

Spinning tackle is relatively easy to cast; with it you can cast light lures a significant distance.

to control the line with the forefinger of your non-casting hand, which then has unobstructed access to the reel and line.

The bail arm on a spinning reel is not an absolute necessity; in fact, early models did not have them, and many surf casters remove the bail arms on their reels to avoid malfunctions. The bail arm does nothing that your fingers can't do as well or better if you invest some time in training them.

Removing the bail arm gives you better control of your line by making it easier for your noncasting hand to access and feather the line for accuracy. Removal also eliminates many of the difficulties associated with spinning tackle, the most significant of which is the loop of line that forms occasionally on the spinning reel spool when you're using a bail. When you have a loop on the spool but don't realize it's there, the next cast will often result in a gob of line jamming up between the reel and the first guide of the rod. You'll lose time and patience untangling it, and you may have to cut the line. Since the bail contributes to the formation of that loop, you nearly eliminate that problem with a bail-free spinning reel.

When you take off the bail arm, leave the line roller in place, because the line roller is necessary for winding line on the spool. On some reels, the line roller and bail arm are integral and cannot be separated, in which case you cannot detach the bail arm without also removing the line roller.

To cast with a bail-less spinning reel, and assuming that you are right-handed, begin by holding the rod and reel with your right hand and palming the reel in your left hand. Extend your left forefinger and press it against the lip of the reel's spool. Flip the line off the line roller with your right forefinger; then trap the line against the front of the reel spool with your left forefinger.

Keep pressure on the spool while both of your hands raise the rod and flex it into motion. On the forward stroke, release the line with your left forefinger, keeping the left hand in place so that the forefinger can control the outflowing line as necessary.

Every second that the practice weight is in the air—and this is the real key to accuracy with a spinning reel—you must control the weight by applying slight pressure on the line with that left forefinger. This method puts your left forefinger on top of the line as it peels off the spool during the cast. The line is under your forefinger just as the line is under your thumb when using a baitcasting reel. If you practice this enough, you'll find that you can achieve a degree of accuracy with a spinning reel that comes close to the hallmark accuracy of baitcasting equipment.

Since the reel no longer has a bail that automatically picks up the line and directs it to the line roller, you must use your finger to put the line on the line roller. Once the cast is complete, simply reach down with your right forefinger and catch the line that is above the reel. Pull it up against the base of your rod and slightly back toward your body, then cradle it in the line roller as it comes around when you turn the reel's handle.

As you can see, in this procedure your fingers have simply replaced the bail. If you train them properly, they will work as well or better than the bail arm. Once you get the hang of this procedure, you won't even have to glance down to do it. It becomes almost automatic, and is accomplished in half a heartbeat. Always remember to pull up the line against the base of the rod with your right forefinger and slightly back toward your body before you crank.

It helps when using this method to raise your rod tip and put tension on the line as you get the line back on the spool. That little bit of tension helps prevent a spool loop from forming.

Baitcasting

Baitcasting tackle has a Jekyll and Hyde reputation. On one hand, it shines at providing accuracy, particularly where anglers need pinpoint lure placement; on the other hand, it gets rapped for being difficult to learn, being prone to spool overruns that produce horrible line snarls known as backlashes, and not being useful for casting lightweight objects. Some anglers still have a love-it or hate-it attitude toward baitcasting (also commonly referred to as levelwind tackle), despite the fact that the modern equipment has vastly improved.

Like all forms of tackle, baitcasting gear is a tool, and one that has an important place in angling. It is true that a person who has never used a baitcasting reel cannot pick one up and become an accurate or effective caster in a few minutes. However, if the rod and reel are of good quality and set up properly, and if a new user follows proper instructions and is willing to practice, he or she will soon be reasonably accomplished. Furthermore, that angler will be on the path to great proficiency as well as successful fishing with a form of tackle that is often preferable to spinning or spincasting.

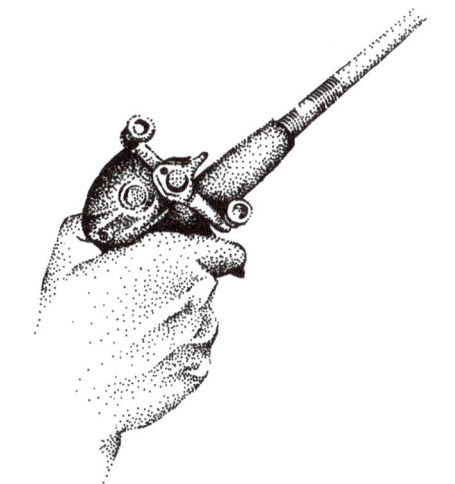

This is the common way to hold baitcasting tackle; turn your wrist so that reel handles face upward when casting.

Although baitcasting tackle is available for a range of fishing applications, its foremost use is in casting objects that weigh upward of $3/8$ ounce. Largemouth bass anglers, for whom baitcasting tackle is the preferred equipment choice, routinely cast lures weighing from $3/8$ to $5/8$ ounce, and some anglers use baitcasting gear for tossing lures and bait that weigh up to 2 ounces. Obviously, different models of rods and reels accommodate different applications, but effective casting, whether for distance or accuracy, always involves proper technique.

Baitcasting reels are noted for accuracy because they feature revolving spools that can be controlled constantly by the user's thumb. They are considered problematic because learning to apply appropriate thumb pressure to the spool in order to control it takes practice, and failure to control the spool produces an annoying overrun. To simplify casting, reel manufacturers have developed braking devices that apply tension to spools to prevent, or at least minimize, overruns, although not all reels have them and not everyone is benefited by them. Users must learn to cast without the aid of these devices so that they will be able to use any type of baitcasting reel under any circumstance.

Practicing with baitcasting tackle is as important, or more so, than with other gear, and practice does lead to increased fishing success. When practicing with baitcasting equipment in a yard or park, use a heavier weight than you would with other gear; a $5/8$-ounce weight is best for new users and helps achieve a feel for the game. You can practice with lighter weights after you've achieved a comfortable level of proficiency. Eventually you should practice with different casting weights because you'll be using a range of lure weights on the water, often switching between them.

No matter what you cast, you need good-quality equipment capable of doing the job. For beginners, a $5 1/2$- to 6-foot graphite rod of medium-light or light action is a good choice, accompanied by a reel spooled with 12-pound line. For a starting setup, avoid an overly large or heavy reel as well as a stiffer rod. This setup should provide a semblance of the balance needed when beginning to practice. Later you'll want different equipment for various fishing applications, but for learning, this is the best type of outfit.

The easiest line to cast with a baitcasting reel is the braided variety, because it is supple and lays nicely on the reel spool. But, if you aren't going to use braided line for your actual fishing—and the majority of people do not—then you might as well learn with the lines you'll actually be fishing with on the water. Many of the top-quality nylon monofilament lines available today have excellent casting qualities. Avoid bargain basement line, and seek a product that is reasonably limp and not overly elastic (see: line). When you put line on the spool, don't overfill it; overfilling can cause loose wraps that might catch each other. Don't underfill it either, because underfilling can adversely affect distance. If the ends of the spool have markers showing the maximum line capacity, put on enough line to stay even or slightly below them. Don't reel on so much that you cover up the markers.

Basic casting technique. Assuming that you are right-handed, the basic cast starts with holding the outfit in your right hand with your thumb on the spool. The drag should be adjusted for angling conditions, and the casting weight should be adjusted to the proper position at the rod tip. The weight (or lure or bait when fishing) should hang a few inches below the rod tip. You can get it to this position by reeling in the line until the lure is a few inches from the tip guide; if the reel is right at the tip, then pull a few inches of line off the reel drag, which will cause the lure to hang a few inches below the tip. With the weight in position, depress the freespool button or bar with your thumb and then rest it on the spool to secure the line.

To cast, take a relaxed stance with your rod and reel out in front of your body. Rotate your wrist to the left so your knuckles and the reel handle are up. This unlocks the wrist joint. The wrist does almost all of the work in a well-executed cast. When the wrist is turned so that the knuckles face up, the joint has greater flexibility and can work the rod so that the tip comes up far enough to provide the necessary casting power. Wrist action along with a slight upward movement of the right forearm is all the effort needed to cast properly.

To make the casting weight go where you want, draw an imaginary line from your nose to the target. Make your rod move back and forth along this line as you cast. The entire casting stroke should be executed out in front of your body; do not let the rod tip come back over your shoulder. If you keep your rod and reel out in front of your body as you cast, and your rod moves back and forth along this imaginary line, there's no way you can be off to the right or left of your target. You'll be off in depth in the beginning, but not to the left or right, and depth perception will improve with practice.

Casting in this manner keeps you from making the mistake of letting the rod tip come way back over the right shoulder. If you do that, your arm will be doing the work of the rod, and you won't be able to make the rod travel along that imaginary nose-to-target line that is helpful for achieving accuracy. Keeping the rod in front of your body forces it to work for you. There is tremendous strength in the modern baitcasting rod, but you have to load it up and put a bend in it so it will fire the casting weight where it needs to go. If you bring your rod back over your shoulder, you might as well have a broomstick in your hand.

With practice you'll develop and hone timing and coordination, which are the keys to casting success. Don't expect to knock the center out of your targets in the beginning. A good casting stroke is like flipping an apple off the end of a stick, or like hitting a nail right in front of your nose with a hammer. You release thumb pressure on the reel's spool at the same exact instant that you would smack the nail. Then you must be sure that your thumb stops the rotating spool as the practice plug lands.

Don't expect everything to come together for you within the first 10 minutes of practice. That's unlikely. As your skill develops, you'll find that you never completely remove your thumb from the reel except at the instant you let the practice weight fly out. You lift the thumb so that the spool can start, but you maintain contact to keep the line flowing smoothly and to slow the spool and drop the lure neatly into the target. This constant contact with the line as it pays out is what enables the expert caster to obtain pinpoint accuracy and, in some situations, a soft landing.

Although casting with baitcasting tackle is usually accomplished with only one hand holding the rod and making the backward and forward motions, many people find it more comfortable and more secure to use two hands on the rod, and are able to attain greater distance and/or straight-line casts by using two hands. Two-handed casts are made by placing the secondary hand on the lower part of the rod handle and using both forearms and wrists to execute the proper motions. This is easiest to accomplish on rods with a long, straight handle. Short pistol-grip handles are harder to use with two hands because of their short length and the bulb at the base; but if you take a knife and whittle down the bulb, then run sandpaper over it, you can make it two-hand friendly. Some anglers use two hands for almost all their baitcasting; when you're using big outfits and heavy lures, two hands are virtually mandatory.

Tension controls. Preventing an overrun by screwing down every tension control device on your baitcasting reel is indeed possible, but it is not a good idea, even for beginners. The key to becoming proficient and really accurate with baitcasting reels is to practice. Timing, coordination, and a trained thumb are developed through practice. Don't depend on mechanical features to eliminate your backlashes.

The best exhibition casters, who are able to unerringly put a casting weight into a cup at 40 feet by using a baitcasting outfit, find it unnecessary to use the magnetic antibacklash device or spool tension adjustment. They set the magnetic tension at or near zero and the spool tension so loose they can feel the slightest side-to-side movement in the spool if they use their thumb to push it back and forth. This kind of free-wheeling allows a baitcasting reel to perform at its best and enables accuracy with minimum effort—provided you practice.

This doesn't mean that you shouldn't use these controls at all as you learn. Read what the manufacturer has to say about tension controls in the manual supplied with the reel. But no matter what the best of these reels promises, realize that you will lose casting efficiency when you rely entirely on those controls.

A baitcasting tackle user shows good form by keeping his rod directly in front of him to help direct and follow a lure toward its target.

Most reel manufacturers suggest setting your controls so that a casting weight drops slowly when you take your thumb off the spool, and the spool stops turning as soon as the casting weight hits the ground. This technique is all right for starters, but strive to train your thumb so you can depend on it to control the spool.

First spooling. The following advice about putting on line arose from difficulties that were posed by baitcasting reels with V-shaped and semi-V-shaped spools. However, this advice has proven useful with all baitcasting reels and is an aid to effective casting, especially for people who are new to this equipment. Instead of putting new line on the reel by using the levelwind mechanism to guide the line back and forth, bypass the levelwind, tie the line onto the spool, and then carefully guide it onto the spool with your fingers as you reel. After you've filled the reel, run the terminal end of the line back out through the levelwind guide. You still use the levelwind guide when casting and retrieving; you just don't use it when you first fill the spool with line.

By doing this, you avoid a buildup of line along the sides, or edges, of the spool. Such a buildup leads to loops of loose line at the end of a cast, no matter how careful you are in thumbing the spool. Those loops will cut down on your efficiency and may cause a snarl or backlash. If you put on the line in a way that avoids edge buildup, you can minimize the likelihood of this happening.

Types of Casts

The basic casting information provided here for spincasting, spinning, and baitcasting tackle applies to all types of casts. The example used is the most common and straightforward situation, known as the overhead cast or the straight-ahead cast because the rod tip is raised vertically and the line is projected directly in front of the caster, whose eyes pick up the flight of the line and the cast object immediately. There are many situations, however, when it is not possible, or beneficial, to cast in this manner, either because of the nature of the cover in which some species are found or because of the necessity for accurate lure placement. Such situations give rise to a side cast, underhand cast, lob cast, and flip cast, which will be discussed shortly, and to such specialized procedures as flipping *(see)*, pitching *(see)*, and making bounce casts *(see)*, which are detailed separately because they are more involved.

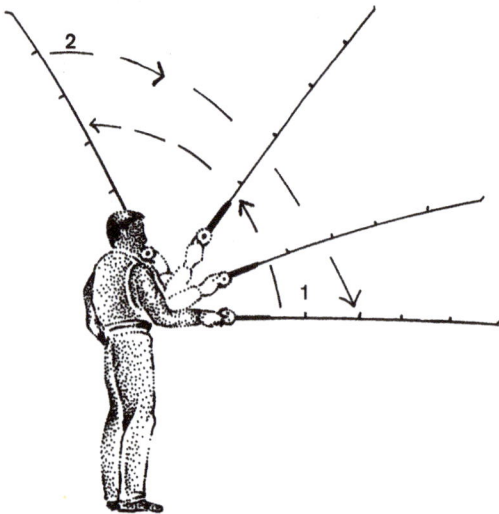

Shown is the basic overhead casting motion for spincasting, spinning, and baitcasting tackle. Note that the process starts with the rod aimed at the target and that the back cast (1) extends no further back than an imaginary 11 o'clock position before the forward cast (2) begins.

To recap the overhead cast, the wrist and forearm do all the work, using the top section of the rod for thrust. The cast begins with the rod low and pointed at the target. The rod is brought up crisply to a point slightly beyond vertical position, where flex in the rod tip will carry it back; then, without hesitation, the forward motion is started sharply, the lure being released halfway between the rod's vertical and horizontal positions. The entire casting action is a smooth, flowing motion; you are doing more than just hauling back and heaving.

The side cast, or sidearm cast, uses essentially the same motion as the overhead cast, except that it features horizontal movement. It begins with the rod low and pointed slightly outward. The wrist and forearm are used to flex the top section of the rod back and then forward, releasing the line just before the rod tip is pointed at its target, and following through with the forward motion after line release in order to bring the rod in front of you.

Getting the timing down, especially the proper moment to release the line, is a little more difficult and requires some practice, as does achieving accuracy, and accuracy is affected by the fact that the line, lure, and rod are not immediately aligned with the caster's eye and the lure is not as quickly picked up as it heads toward its target, although it does have a much lower trajectory than the overhead cast.

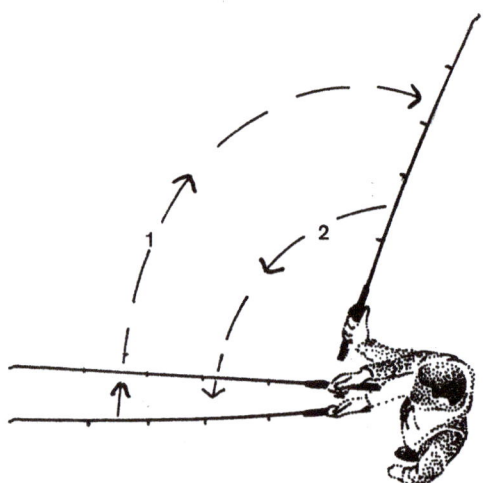

The dynamics of the sidearm cast for spincasting, spinning, and baitcasting tackle are the same as those for the overhead cast. The process starts with the rod aimed at the target, and the back cast (1) extends slightly past a perpendicular position before the forward cast (2) begins.

You can modify the conventional side cast into a side lob cast by starting with the rod tip pointed low toward the water and raising up the tip on the forward motion; this action raises the trajectory but produces a soft landing, which is good for shallow water. The same thing can be achieved by reaching across your body and sending the lure out with a backhand motion.

The conventional side cast is advantageous when overhead cover (like an overhanging tree limb) has to be avoided, or when there is a lot of wind; keeping the line and lure low to the water minimizes drifting off course and is a good way to deal with a blow. This cast is not very effective when distance has to be achieved, and it can be dangerous if performed next to another angler in a small boat, so you must be mindful of the position of your companions at all times.

To make an underhand cast, hold the rod waist-high, angled halfway between vertical and horizontal positions and pointed at the target. The rod must be flexed up, then down, then up again to gain momentum for the lure through the flex of the rod; on the second upward flex, the line is released.

This cast has very little arm movement but plenty of wrist action and can be useful when other casting motions are severely restricted. Many rods, however, are too stiff to permit this kind of casting.

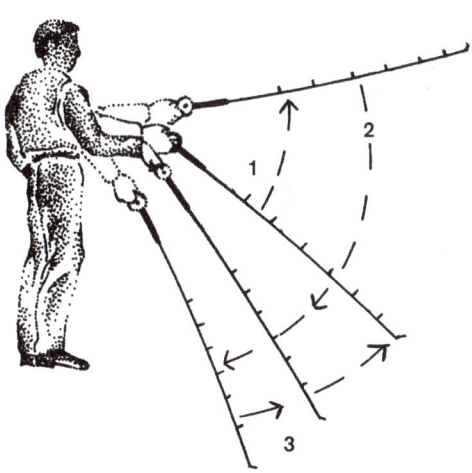

The underhand cast starts with the rod held waist-high, angled halfway between vertical and horizontal positions. From this attitude the rod must be flexed up (1), then down (2), then up (3) again to gain momentum for the lure through the flex of the rod; on the second upward flex, the line is released.

The flip cast is another cast used in special situations. Employed in tight quarters or for short ranges, the flip cast is a cross between the sidearm and underhand casts (different from flipping). It starts with the rod horizontal to your side, but you bring it backward only a short distance and then make a loop with the tip so that the tip springs around in a 270-degree arc and flips the lure straight out and low. This cast is used for short-distance (under 20 feet) work in areas where you can't bring your rod up or back for a conventional cast. It is a very efficient and very accurate cast when mastered but is almost impossible to accomplish while sitting down in a boat.

Another cast is the bow-and-arrow cast, which is a short-distance cast used with a limber rod in tight quarters. In this cast, you hold a lure by its rear hook in one hand and simultaneously release the hook and line from a freespooled reel. This cast is rarely used in actual angling situations, since many rods, especially graphite baitcasters, are not limber enough for it, and a flip cast will do just as well. Obviously you have to be careful about holding the hooks if you try this cast.

Casting Distance Issues

What angler, seeing a fish rise or break water just out of normal casting range, hasn't reached back and heaved a lure that extra distance to get the offering closer to the quarry? What person hasn't tossed a lure farther than normal to avoid spooking wary fish? What angler, caught up in the flow of casting and intrigued with testing his or her skills, hasn't "let one fly," especially downwind?

In football, a quarterback is said to "air it out" when he makes an extremely long pass. A long pass usually doesn't occur play after play in a game. However, a lot of anglers do "air out" their casts routinely. Unlike the quarterback, whose job is over when the ball leaves his fingertips, the angler has much to do until the lure or bait being cast returns to the tip of the rod. The distance of the cast has a substantial impact on fishing efforts.

Although surf anglers and people fishing in special situations, like casting to schooling (see) fish, have always had to make long casts, in recent decades the emphasis on achieving distance in casting, especially with the use of spinning, spincasting, and baitcasting tackle, has increased.

One reason is that most tackle manufacturers tout products whose chief virtue is achievement of distance. This claim is especially prevalent in spinning reels where spool design, line-wrapping systems, and spool rim materials have been modified to make it easier for line to flow off the spool. Rods, too, have had more attention with respect to enhancing distance, particularly guides and products that are part of a matched system. Baitcasting rod manufacturers started producing longer models for ordinary fishing years ago, mostly at the prompting of bass anglers, partially because longer rods help anglers cast greater distances.

The burgeoning of thin-diameter/conventional-strength lines as well as high-tech microfilaments (see: line) has intertwined with the distance-casting game. Better-quality lines have proven to be slick, limp, and eminently castable, and they improve ability to achieve distance.

Another, but lesser, factor, was an emergence of truly deep-diving plugs for freshwater fishing. To take advantage of the diving capabilities of these plugs, anglers must make long casts so that the lures run at the desired depths for the greatest amount of time possible in a cast-and-retrieve circumstance (this dovetails with longer rods). Thin-diameter lines allow lures to dive even deeper; combined with long rods and improvements in reels, they help the caster toss a lure almost as far as a quarterback can throw a football. And that's a long way.

So, casting a great distance with all forms of casting tackle except fly gear is now easier to accomplish than ever. But is it necessary? There is no correct answer; fishing success is influenced by too many different variables and situations/waters/lures/etc. Many anglers tend to think only in terms of the main advantages to casting greater distances: getting lures to fish they wouldn't have reached otherwise and covering more ground than otherwise possible to attract more fish.

Long casts are of course achievable, though perhaps not necessary. With some species of freshwater fish, and in some types of water, seldom do anglers need to cast great distances. Most walleye, largemouth bass, pike, and panfish anglers, for example, do not need to routinely make long casts because of the nature of the fish, the cover they inhabit, and the fishing techniques used.

The clarity of the water is one criterion for distance. Generally, fish in clear water are spookier than those in turbid water. The more difficult it is to see the lure as you drop it in the water, the murkier the water is; this is an indication that you can probably get fairly close to your quarry.

A prime benefit of getting close is simply the ease with which you can achieve accuracy. This is especially true when fishing in heavy cover, such as timber, or in places where casting is difficult, such as a small brushy creek. The effect of wind is also minimized at shorter distances; when using baitcasting gear, a shorter distance means that the chance of a backlash is lessened.

Backlashes occur in baitcasting reels when the spool turns faster than the line departs the spool; even highly experienced casters get backlashes when they give extra punch to their forward casting stroke in order to get a lure farther out. The best magnetic spool braking reels often cannot prevent such misfortune, although they are suppose to.

With practice and with continued long-distance casting in actual fishing conditions, you can lessen the chance of backlash and also increase accuracy. If you start long-distance casting efforts by not shooting for the moon at the start, but by building up to greater distances gradually (which is hard to do when a fish breaks water just a bit beyond your normal range), then you will overcome this problem.

One of the drawbacks to long-distance casting with any type of tackle is the loss of fish; at long distances, more fish that strike lures and get hooked are lost before being landed than fish that strike lures and are hooked at shorter ranges. How many more are lost cannot be known, but it is likely quite a bit. There is a good reason for this occurrence, though, and it is one that many anglers don't realize but can do something about.

The key here is hooksetting *(see)*. Anglers are more effective at setting the hook at short and midrange distances than they are at long distances. Most people simply do not set the hook well when a fish takes their lure a long distance away.

Sometimes the reason is that they don't detect strikes as well, and this may be a function of their attentiveness or their savvy, or more likely the tackle they are using. Not all rods are the same, for example, and it is possible to receive a strike but not feel it because the rod is soft and the fish nip the lure rather than slam it. With more appropriate tackle, such a thing won't happen. Nonetheless, certain types of lures are still hard to fish when cast long distances. Lures that you work by feel, which are generally made of soft material, and where you have to know what the lure is doing as you fish it, may not be struck the same way as other lures, so you have to be fully tuned into a long-distance strike when using these types of lures.

A noted fishing film once showed a largemouth bass swimming up behind a quickly moving diving plug, engulfing it, and then expelling it, all the while the lure kept swimming forward. The angler working that lure, which had two sets of treble hooks, reported that he never felt the strike. How could that be possible? As already mentioned, the reason could be that the rod wasn't sensitive enough, but it could also be that his line was too elastic. Elasticity, or stretch, in fishing line is an element that works against anglers where long-distance strike detection and hooksetting are concerned. In this particular instance, the fisherman used a nylon monofilament line that had 25 to 30 percent stretch, and the stretch had to be a factor in not detecting the filmed strike.

The stretch feature of line has been reviewed in detail elsewhere *(see: line)*, but it should be remembered that some lines stretch more than others; the greater the stretch, the more problem with lures (or hooks) that are a long distance away. The simple act of retrieving a hard-pulling plug can stretch some lines a little. Setting a hook and playing a fish, especially a large or strong fish, stretches some lines much more. It is harder to counter the effect of stretch when setting the hook if you have a long length of line. At short distances, you can generate more force and be more efficient at setting the hook.

You don't have to be an engineer to appreciate this fact. Take the hooks off a plug sometime, and with the help of a friend try a simple test. Soak the fishing line so that it absorbs water and you have simulated its condition when being fished. Have your buddy hold the rod as if retrieving a lure. Take a practice casting plug or hookless lure 40, 80, and 120 feet away, grasp it firmly in your hand at waist level, and tug on it to have your friend set the hook at each distance. Can you feel a difference in the force your friend applies? The force is more obvious if you use a scale or force gauge, because you're likely to measure a high percentage of loss from the shortest distance to the longest.

To counter the effect of line stretch, an obvious solution is to use a line with little or no stretch, provided that it offers the other characteristics that you need. Using such a line may remove or reduce

This angler gains casting leverage by using his left hand on the butt of the rod to propel a large lure a long way from the beach.

one of the problems associated with long-distance casts and long-distance fishing.

However, you also need to pay greater attention to the fine points. A super-sharp hook can make all the difference in landing or losing a fish that strikes a long distance away. Most long-distance fish are lost because the hook slipped out or was thrown when the fish jumped. A super-sharp hook penetrates easier and increases your chance of landing a fish. Sharpening your hook *(see: hook sharpening)* is a fundamental, but mostly overlooked, fishing technique.

Sharp hooks, of course, won't eliminate line stretch, but combined with a lower stretch line, they can make a big difference. You should also pay close attention to what you're doing. Be alert. Anticipate strikes at all times so you can react properly and swiftly. If you are casting surface lures, for example, make sure that slack is always out of your line.

The position of your rod, and your body, is important as well. The rod should be held at a low level; when setting the hook, you should be reeling and striking all in one motion, keeping the pressure on constantly and not yielding unless the fish is strong enough to pull line off the drag. Good hooksetting technique is never more important than when long distances are involved, and the same is true for fish-playing tactics *(see: playing fish)*. Fish that are a long distance off are harder to control than those up close. It is more difficult to keep a strong fish away from an obstruction when it is 125 feet from you than when it is 40. When fishing from a boat, you may have to maneuver the boat in order to change the angle of pull on a large fish and steer it away from obstructions. You have to anticipate and react quickly, however, to do this.

Rather than casting long distances as a matter of habit, you might try making a stealthier approach to fish. Wading river anglers know that it is possible to get fairly close to rising trout or to salmon in their lie by going slowly and as unobtrusively as possible, by not making excessive above-water motions, by keeping movement to the barest minimum in the fish's direct viewing window, and by being patient and not casting until achieving the most advantageous position for making the best possible presentation.

Pond and lake anglers, whether boaters or bank casters, should do likewise. Most lake and pond anglers are impatient; they want to cover lots of water, and in doing so they often don't make the best possible presentation. Certainly this statement isn't applicable where schooling fish are chased, but it is in most other circumstances.

Achieving distance isn't always necessary or advantageous, but when it is, there is more to being effective than just being able to air out a cast. You have to bring many elements together. However, when you do, you are usually on top of your game, and that means more success and enjoyment.

See: Baitcasting Tackle; Spinning Tackle; Spincasting Tackle; Surf Fishing.

CASTING BUBBLE

A small plastic float *(see)*, often transparent, used as an aid to casting and fishing with lightweight objects (like flies, tiny jigs, or unweighted natural bait) with spinning or spincasting tackle.

CASTING REEL

A term for baitcasting reel.
See: Baitcasting Tackle.

CAST NET

A circular net with fringe weights that is thrown for collecting baitfish. Cast nets come in various sizes and are used by anglers for collecting live bait. Shad, herring, and mullet are among the most common cast netting targets, and they are usually netted in shallow waters, although some netting takes place in the ocean in deep water, where large schools of baitfish are attracted to the surface with chum and then netted. In use, when a cast net is thrown, the full net opens as it hits the surface of the water, the weights carry it down quickly, the bottom of the net closes around fish, and the net is retrieved via a long connecting polypropylene line.

Using a cast net is the quickest way to catch a supply of bait in a short period of time, assuming that bait is plentiful and that you know where to find it. In some situations where live bait is necessary, anglers may spend a considerable amount of time trying to collect bait, even with a cast net, but the cast net is still most effective.

It takes practice to learn to throw a cast net properly, as it is usually necessary to cast the net to a specific place and to have it open fully to capture the greatest number of fish. You should practice throwing a net on a windless day and in shallow water. Face 90 degrees from where you want the net to land, place your weight on your back foot, and keep the net close to the water when throwing it. It takes a good back motion as well as a forward one to throw a cast net properly. Many cast nets come with 25-foot-long handline, but a 50-foot handline is better for deep-water use, current, and the inevitable problem situations. Don't wrap the handline around your wrist, and do not cast it over a rocky bottom, which invites hangup.

Cast nets come in different mesh sizes, different diameters, different weights, and with different strengths of mesh. They are commercially made and custom made, the latter preferred by people who gather bait professionally and by guides or charter boat captains who routinely use a cast net. Heavier weights and larger diameters are needed for deeper water use. The smallest cast nets have a 6-foot diameter and $1/2$-inch mesh, and weigh 10 pounds. They should be stored in a tall bucket when not in use, preferably one with large holes to allow drying and prevent rotting, and kept out of

With a portion of the net clenched in his teeth and the retrieval line wrapped around his right wrist, a guide uses a cast net to capture mullet. Getting the net to open fully is essential (3).

the sun; rinse the net in freshwater after use, and when it hasn't been used for awhile, soften it in warm water with fabric softener.

Using a cast net in freshwater and in some coastal or tidal waters may be illegal, or may require a permit. The overall diameter of the net may be restricted as well, and in some places there are regulations as to the number of nets that can be carried aboard a boat.

CATADROMOUS

Fish that migrate from freshwater to saltwater in order to spawn. Fish that do the opposite are called anadromous, and are more numerous. Freshwater eels are typical of catadromous fish; they are born at sea, migrate upstream to live and grow to adulthood, and then return to the sea to migrate to their spawning grounds.
See: Anadromous.

CATCH

(1) To capture a fish (usually by legal and sporting means in the recreational sense). A fish has been caught once it has been brought close enough to the angler to be secured and is restrained for unhooking, whereupon it may be kept or released.
See: Catch-and-Release; Landing Fish.

(2) The total number or poundage of fish captured from an area over some defined period of time. This includes fish that are caught but released or discarded, as well as those that are kept. With respect to saltwater fisheries, catch differs from "landings," a term referring to the number or poundage of fish unloaded at a dock by commercial fishermen or brought to shore by recreational anglers.
See: Fisheries Management.

CATCH-AND-RELEASE

"Catch-and-release" is a term that refers to the practice of catching gamefish by sporting methods and with sporting equipment and then releasing them alive. It is a concept rooted in angling ethics and tradition, and an action that has long been voluntary on the part of the angler—who chooses to release a fish that could be captured and retained for consumption. In the voluntary sense, catch-and-release is a personal, if not moral or ethical, judgment, and some practitioners believe that the spirit of catch-and-release has special meaning only when it is done voluntarily, especially with respect to fish that are notable for their size or scarcity. However, what was once primarily a voluntary action has increasingly become a legally mandated action for certain sizes, numbers, and species of fish. Thus, catch-and-release has become both personal philosophy and governmental policy.

Nevertheless, whether personal belief or management tool, catch-and-release has taken a long time for large numbers of people to embrace. It is widely debated by anglers and fisheries managers, and it is still evolving as more is learned about the factors affecting the survival of sport-caught fish that have been released, and as anglers learn and practice the proper methods of landing, handling, and releasing their catches.

Evolution of Laws

The notion of releasing fish that are not needed for consumption and that legally can be kept developed as a result of the actions of several groups of anglers: experienced anglers who had kept enough fish of a certain size or species that they didn't need to keep more, anglers who wished to extend their angling enjoyment by not keeping a legal limit and thus being able to continue fishing, and enlightened anglers who, perhaps most importantly, recognized that the removal of more fish of a certain size or species would be detrimental to a given water and fish population and might adversely impact future angling.

The modern-day genesis of catch-and-release angling advanced from a matter of individual conscience and choice into a movement as the result of a boon in angling participation in the latter half of the twentieth century, particularly through the 1960s and 1970s; other factors were the development of sophisticated sportfishing equipment, improved knowledge about fish, and the resulting increased pressure on fisheries populations. Many popular fisheries resources in North America were diminished or depleted in the decades following World War II. Although numerous factors contributed to this, and in varying degrees, the primary ones were water and air pollution, habitat destruction or alteration, commercial fishing, and sportfishing.

Sportfishing efforts in both freshwater and saltwater have long been targeted at selective species that have favorably appealed to the angling psyche. Bass, trout, salmon, crappie, and walleye, for example, have been leading freshwater favorites; striped bass, redfish, tarpon, tuna, and billfish are among the more popular saltwater species. Before pressure on these and other popular gamefish intensified, and before there was a more widespread collective modern-day sense of the need for conservation, anglers usually kept nearly all the fish that they caught in accordance with what were then very liberal limitations. Eventually, regulations regarding seasons, bag or creel limits, length limits, and methods of fishing were either enacted or made more encompassing and more restrictive.

At one time, anglers, as well as the general public, believed that recreational angling did not harm populations of fish, especially in freshwater where commercial fishing was generally less of a factor than it was in saltwater. Today it is recognized that this is not so; indeed, enough skillful anglers can decimate nearly any fish population over time if unchecked, with or without the contribution of other factors (pollution, commercial fishing, etc.). In some situations, skillful anglers can do this in a fairly short period of time, even while behaving according to legal limitations. Even if they do not decimate the entire population, they are still capable of changing population dynamics by selectively fishing for and keeping certain species or certain sizes (usually the biggest) of gamefish. An intense effort at catching, and then subsequently keeping, huge lake trout in northern Canada, for example, destroyed or gravely depleted many populations of slow-growing trophy fish from the late 1950s into the 1970s.

In response to changing situations, and in many cases at the request of various anglers' organizations,

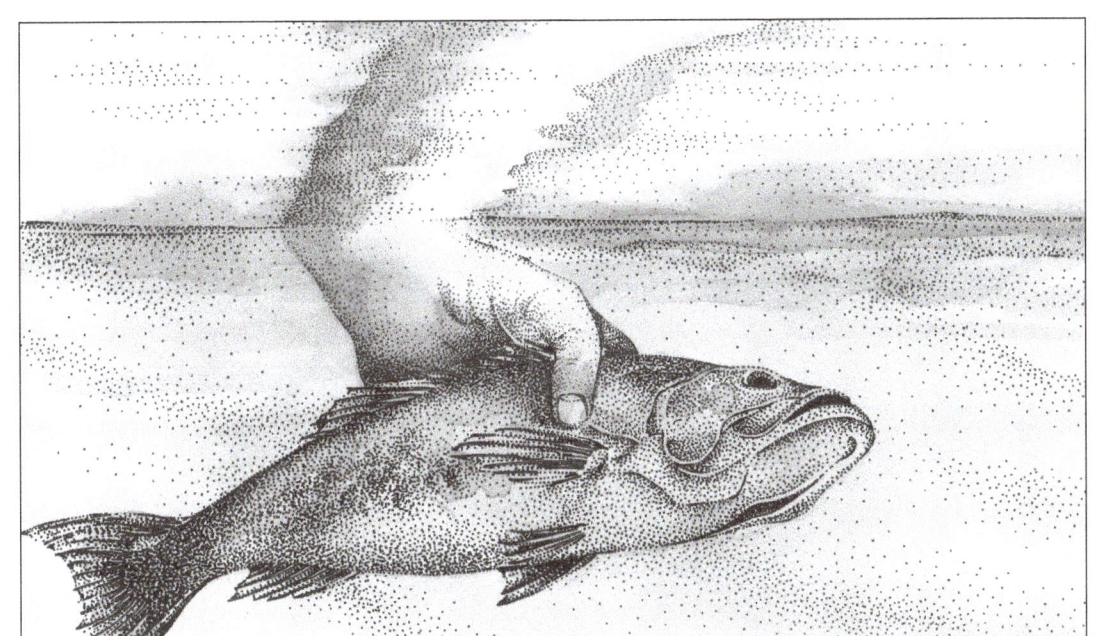

fisheries managers took action by implementing size or bag limits where there had previously been none, creating seasons, decreasing existing size or bag limits, specifying the terminal tackle that could be used, and taking other measures, such as creating slot limits, to maintain or improve specific resources.

Many fisheries management regulations pertaining to size, numbers, and seasons were established to allow young fish the opportunity to mature and to spawn. This is especially true in freshwater, and to a lesser extent in saltwater. Some regulations were established to achieve a specific objective, such as making available more trophy specimens of a certain species in a certain lake; releasing the larger members of a fish population is viewed as a way to foster the propagation and availability of larger specimens. Other regulations were established for what may seem an opposite reason: to address an imbalanced population of fish. In an unexploited, balanced population of fish, there should be many size groups (also called age classes), with fish in the medium ranges making up the bulk of the population, and with a good number of both small and large specimens. But where a fish population is exposed to angling, the usual result is that fish of all sizes are caught but the larger specimens are intentionally and disproportionately removed, which in time will significantly alter the structure of the population. It may lead to unbalancing it, with fewer size groups and fewer adult fish to reproduce.

Thus, by law, recreational anglers must release fish that they inadvertently catch out of prescribed seasons, or that do not meet size criteria, or that exceed the total number of fish allowable for a particular species. There are other reasons that fish must legally be released as well. For example, in certain places some species may not be kept if they are foul-hooked. This is a regulation based on sporting ethic rather than on biological management principle.

Indeed, some of the regulations concerning size and bag limits have more to do with social concerns—managing people—than with fisheries resources; although catch-and-release as a general principle has become more accepted, the extent to which it is accepted remains a dividing line between some groups of anglers. In fact, length-limit laws have actually had the unintentional effect of making larger fish more subject to exploitation. If anglers have to release all fish under a certain size, say bass under 15 inches, for example, some of them are much more likely to not release a legal fish after catching many "shorts."

Issues

To the nonangler, releasing a fish seems like a dubious decision—considering the expense that might be involved, the general uncertainty of achieving success, and the rejection of a fresh source of healthy food—unless it must be done to satisfy legal mandates. In terms of consumption, releasing fish that have been captured, regardless of the "sporting" means, runs contrary to mankind's long harvest tradition. Indeed, in most cultures of the world today, fish that are caught by rod and reel are almost always kept for consumption.

If you have been to some of those places, especially in freshwater, you might sarcastically say that this is why their fishing is not particularly recommendable, certainly not in comparison with the extent of the resources that exist in North America. Perhaps they needed to practice some measure of catch-and-release a long time ago.

Anglers who voluntarily release fish that they might otherwise keep do so for a variety of reasons. Some actually don't like to eat fish and don't even think about keeping them. Some like to eat fish but release them because of health advisories about consumption. Most, however, voluntarily release fish as a matter of conscience and because they are interested in seeing the fish they've just caught, and the population that it came from, continue to prosper.

Individual anglers, and some organizations representing anglers, advocate catch-and-release as a means of improving or maintaining the density of fish in a certain body of water, or the composition of the population, whether or not there are regulations in effect for this purpose. Although a high density, or number, of fish is not a guarantee of fishing success, it often translates into better fishing, especially for skillful anglers; greater numbers of fish are widely perceived as providing more opportunity for success and are therefore conducive to a good experience. Many anglers feel that voluntarily releasing all or most of the fish they catch in a given place helps ensure more fish for future fishing. Studies do back up this fact, although it may not be universally true. In some freshwater lakes and rivers, fish populations are sustained largely or entirely through stocking efforts. The fish that are voluntarily released in such places may not contribute to expanding the future population in those water bodies, although they may have the opportunity to grow into a much larger specimen that someone will have the pleasure of catching in the future. Nevertheless, anglers consciously choose to release their catches to foster the objective of ensuring more fish for future fishing, hoping that if enough other anglers do likewise, they will have a positive impact.

Most anglers who have fished for a long time and caught many fish of a particular species simply feel it is unnecessary to keep more of them, or more than what the anglers currently need to eat. In the early evolution of catch-and-release, this thinking became the basis for the motto: Limit your kill; don't kill your limit. Keeping only what they need, rather than taking the limit that the law allows, is probably the primary motivation today among knowledgeable and well-rounded anglers who voluntarily practice catch-and-release. When this motivation is combined with the rationale of choosing fish to keep based upon their condition, their size in relation to the fish population, or their species, an angler may be making the most intelligent decision. In other words, when an angler chooses to keep a fish, the angler can fine-tune the choices, perhaps choosing to keep a fish that has been wounded and has less chance of survival, instead of one that is in better shape, or perhaps keeping a fish that is smaller rather than bigger, when there are plenty of small fish available but few big ones. Perhaps the angler will choose to release a healthy spawning female fish so that its genes remain in the population pool or perhaps will choose to keep a specimen from an abundant species, rather than one from a species that is either less abundant or less intensively pursued.

Unfortunately, catch-and-release fishing has been touted by some as a panacea for improving fishing. This is simply not true for all species and in all situations. Moreover, some have preached this concept so aggressively that one could get the impression that keeping any fish is wrong, even if the law allows otherwise. Some newcomers to angling, particularly fly fishing, have embraced total catch-and-release out of a sense of being politically correct; this thinking puts them at odds with the many anglers for whom having a meal of freshly caught fish is appropriate not only for nutritional reasons, but also for the satisfying conclusion to an angling experience that it represents.

Some anglers deem it morally reprehensible to keep a particularly large fish. Others who rarely keep fish would however keep a particularly large

Most fish can be released quickly after capture, but it's always best to do so gently; this angler is releasing a bonefish.

one to send to a taxidermist. The former group needs to recognize that keeping or releasing a fish should remain a matter of choice and that, in some circumstances, it is not only acceptable but the right thing to do (when the fish is injured, for example; more on this issue later in the entry). The latter group needs to know that replica taxidermists *(see: taxidermy)* can produce fish mounts from fiberglass molds that are as good as skin mounts—and longer lasting; thus, in the case of trophy fish, it is possible to have the unique pleasure of releasing one of the rare members of a fish population and still have a representation to hang over the fireplace.

Compounding the acceptance of catch-and-release is the fact that regulations vary widely, and what is acceptable on one body of water is not on another. In certain situations, biologists have the challenging chore of convincing anglers to release small fish of a certain species at one lake, and then keep them at another. In some situations, regulations are applied unilaterally to many bodies of water, even when local conditions warrant having regulations uniquely tailored to fit the specific place or fish population.

Besides the sometimes confusing application of regulations, other factors enter into the issue of catch-and-release. For example, some species of fish, especially in saltwater, are available only seasonally because of migratory patterns. An angler who fishes for two days during that seasonally abundant period and keeps a legal limit of fish—say five fish—is not a game hog, yet someone who does this every day for 10 straight days is surely a game hog. However, if the latter angler kept just one fish a day for 10 days, the angler would have the same seasonal take as the angler who fished for only two days. On the other hand, an angler could fish for 10 days and not catch an average of a legal fish per day, but a more skillful angler could conceivably catch (and keep or release) a legal limit every day.

As the preceding examples have shown, the amount of fishing done by individual recreational anglers varies widely, and the skill level and success among anglers varies from novices to professionals. Thus, the amount of fishing that an angler does, and the amount of success that the angler experiences, has to be part of the equation in developing a personal catch-and-release ethic.

Anglers who fish often and with a high degree of accomplishment are the most likely to have an entrenched interest in catch-and-release, if they accept the fact that populations of fish can be harmed by excessive harvest. Yet many anglers who fish often take a holier-than-though approach to their sport, especially if they release all or most of their catch. A person who fishes 50 days a year, who enjoys good success, and who releases 95 percent of the catch, does not have a higher moral standing than the person who fishes only 5 days a year, who has relatively modest success, and who keeps most of the legal catch to eat. Furthermore, as will be illustrated in the following section, there is undoubtedly some mortality among the fish that are released by all anglers; even anglers who live-release every fish that they catch cannot claim to have no effect on the resource.

Of course, much of the effect that anglers have is very tightly focused. Many of the gamefish sought by anglers are among the top predators in their environment, yet they are also a small segment of the total food pyramid. There are approximately 22,000 species of fish in the world, but only a couple hundred are the quarries of anglers, and only a few dozen each in freshwater and saltwater are aggressively and intensively pursued by anglers. No wonder that things can get out of whack. However, this situation is all the more reason to take steps to ensure that those targeted species remain a renewable resource for the sake of biodiversity, recreation, and food.

Although anglers can have a serious impact on fisheries populations, and in some cases the most serious impact, they are just one of many influences. In the natural world, even in a perfectly balanced population not exposed to angling, a given number of gamefish, including specimens of catchable size, will die from natural causes every year. They are caught by predators (including each other), and they die of old age and disease. The percentage that is lost to natural causes varies in each situation, but they are annually replaced by new fish. When angling is introduced, some fish will be lost to angling-related mortality, and some, although fewer than previously, will be lost to natural causes. If the number lost to angling is in balance with the number lost to natural causes, so that the same percentage of overall mortality is achieved, the population will maintain itself, all other influences being equal. If angling-related mortality is negligible, there will be no net loss. But if angling-related mortality is equal to or greater than the natural mortality that would have occurred without angling, then the population will decline. Thus, it is desirable to keep angling-related mortality to acceptable levels. Fortunately, fish can be recycled, and they are a natural resource that can be enjoyed without being destroyed.

The rub is that simply releasing a fish that is breathing is not an assurance that the fish will survive. So to effectively practice catch-and-release, whether by choice or by mandate, anglers must know how to properly release fish, and they must understand what factors contribute to unintended angling-related mortality.

Survival Generalities

The most logical question to ask about releasing fish is whether they will survive after being hooked, played, landed, handled, unhooked, and returned to the water. The answer is that many, but certainly not all, will survive, and that survival depends on many factors.

Some fish, like this large Saskatchewan pike, need to be held stable in the water for a while until they can swim off on their own.

Many anglers have personally caught or seen fish caught that were undeniably previously landed and released by other anglers. Whether the fish had identifiable markings, cut-off hooks, or tags, it obviously survived previous capture. A small minority of anglers have had an opportunity to personally tag and release fish, and they or others have recaptured some of the tagged fish, a few of them many times. One angler reported in a letter to a popular periodical that a tagged bass in his pond had been recaptured over 20 times, and at least once it had been caught twice on the same day.

More significantly, numerous studies have been conducted by professional fisheries researchers on the survival of fish that are caught and released by anglers. Researchers have been evaluating this issue since the 1930s, long before catch-and-release became popular. Such studies have been done in controlled situations and with respect to most, if not all, of the most favored species of fish, particularly in freshwater. Trout and bass, being the most popular and prominent sportfish, have been especially well studied, and continue to be.

Although scientifically valid studies have proven conclusively that fish released by anglers can survive, the studies have not produced identical results or percentages of survival. In some cases, the methodologies were criticized—especially when released fish were confined to holding areas—and few attempts have estimated the survival of fish that are repeatedly caught and released (which may happen more often than is realized, and which is known to happen in "no-kill" sections of trout rivers). Moreover, many studies have specifically focused on hooking mortality to determine the effects of terminal gear. The effects of other factors, especially playing and handling the fish, are more difficult to assess; the general issue of stress has been less extensively studied, although the effects of stress on fish are fairly well established. The results of myriad scientific studies have been reported in many technical and popular publications. One of the most frequently quoted results is from a study of the heavily fished Buffalo Ford section of the Yellowstone River (devoted to only barbless flies and lures), where research indicates that cutthroat trout survived 9 to 10 catch-and-release occurrences per season.

Nevertheless, some general conclusions stand out in the collective body of scientific studies, chief among them that using bait is more detrimental to fish than using lures or flies, that barbless hooks cause slightly lower mortality than barbed hooks, that bleeding fish are unlikely to survive, and that deeply hooked fish are at much greater risk than fish caught around the edges of the mouth.

Injury and Stress

Fish primarily die before and after being released because of injury and stress. Some weakened or struggling fish may also die as a result of predation by other fish, birds, and some reptiles and mammals; this seldom accounts for a high mortality, although injury or stress may be an indirect factor. Death that occurs after release, usually out of sight of the angler and without the angler's knowledge, is called delayed mortality. Many fish that die from injury or stress do so within 24 hours after being released, the vast majority within 48 hours. Anglers can eliminate or reduce fish injury and stress, but to do so they should understand the physiological factors at work.

A general understanding of the biology of fish is contained in the anatomy *(see)* entry. Following is a synopsis of the key parts of the anatomy that play an important role in injury and stress.

Mucus. This is the protective coating of a fish that is a barrier to the entry of parasites, fungi, and disease organisms; it also seals in the fish's body fluids so that they are not diluted by the watery surroundings.

Air bladder. Located between the stomach and backbone, the air bladder performs several functions. Some species of fish use the air bladder as a compartment in which to store air for breathing; the fish falls back on this reserve when its usual supply of oxygen is shut off. The air bladder plays a part in aiding the equilibrium of density between the fish and the water.

Digestive system. The tongue, located just inside the mouth, is flat, rigid, and cartilaginous, and moves only when the base below it moves; the esophagus, or gullet (between the throat and stomach), is highly distensible and usually can accept any type or size of food that the fish can fit into its mouth; the stomach varies in shape and in most gamefish is elongated but may be saclike; and the intestines are generally shortened.

Gills. Fish breathe through their mouths and receive oxygen through the gills, which are much-divided thin-walled filaments where capillaries lie close to the surface. As the fish opens its mouth, a stream of water is drawn in and the gill cover is held tight, thereby closing the gill opening. Then the fish closes its mouth and drives the water over the gills and out the external openings. As water passes over the gills, oxygen is taken in through the walls of the fine blood vessels in the gill filaments and carbon dioxide is given off. The blood, well oxygenated, then travels through the fish's body. Gill rakers, located along the anterior margin of the gill arch, project over the throat opening and strain water that is passed over the gills; they also prevent solid particles from passing over and injuring the gill filaments.

Circulatory system. Fish blood passes from the heart to the gills for purification and then travels directly to all other parts of the body. The heart, blood, and blood vessels carry oxygen and nourishment to every living cell in the body and carry away carbon dioxide and other excretory products. The fish's heart is located close behind the fish's mouth. Blood vessels are largest close to the heart and become progressively smaller, terminating in a network of extremely fine capillaries that meander through the body tissues.

Pain. Since fish have a nervous system and sense organs, it would appear that they could feel pain; however, a fish's brain is not highly developed. There is no cerebral cortex (the part of the brain that stores impressions in higher animals), so the fish has little or no memory. Fish are essentially

The least harmful hooking areas are the jaw, snout, corners of the mouth, maxillary, and cheek. The most harmful hooking areas are the eye, tongue, isthmus, and gills.

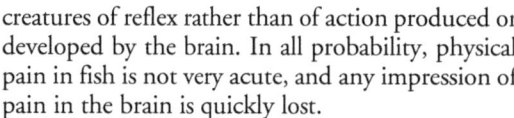

Transplanting fish was a common practice through the nineteenth century; as early as 1810, northern pike were transplanted to Maine and New Hampshire.

creatures of reflex rather than of action produced or developed by the brain. In all probability, physical pain in fish is not very acute, and any impression of pain in the brain is quickly lost.

Responses to capture. When a fish is hooked, it resists the capturing efforts of the angler. This struggling can cause stress. Where the fish is hooked and how it is landed, handled, and unhooked can cause injury, which may compound stress. How the fish is played by the angler, the length of time involved, how the fish is revived, and how it is released may cause injury and further stress.

The response of fish to these injury and stress factors varies widely between different species, and even between fish of the same species. In a general sense, some species are more resistant to rough-handling stresses than others, and such variables as water temperature, season (spawning), and even size of the fish make a difference in how fish react to the process of being caught and released. Thus, although one particular action may be identified as being harmful to a fish, or as causing stress, or as causing mortality, a number of actions may be collectively responsible.

However, much of the stress-related problems center around the gills, the respiratory system, and the circulatory system.

Gills. The gills are an especially sensitive area of a fish. Bleeding can come from even a slight nick, and bleeding in itself is a high-stress factor. A fish cannot breathe out of water; it gets oxygen from the water that is passed over the gills. Keeping a fish out of the water, whether to unhook it, photograph it, or weigh it, increases the stress load. When oxygen is low, fish breathe faster, trying to pass more water over the gills. If held out of the water for too long, a fish can suffocate. How long is too long? There is no stopwatch answer for this. The size and species of the fish, the temperature, and even humidity all play a role. However, lifting any fish by its gill flap, as many anglers do, is definitely harmful; it exposes the gill tissues to air and can result in tearing of the filaments. Touching and grabbing the gills can be very harmful. To reduce stress, anglers should minimize exposure of the gills to air, avoid touching them, and avoid grabbing a fish by the gills or lifting it by the gill cover.

Lactic acid buildup. As with most animals, vigorous physical exertion causes lactic acid to accumulate in the fish's muscles. This buildup occurs when the muscles are deprived of oxygen and the body incompletely metabolizes glucose. The same thing occurs in humans after strenuous exertion, and it produces the "oxygen debt" that long-distance runners and other athletes experience. When the exertion is over, if all other systems are functioning properly, the body metabolizes the lactic acid and restores the oxygen to appropriate levels. But this may not happen immediately; the more severe the lactic acid buildup, the longer it takes to return to normal.

Ordinarily, the metabolic process operates at a continuous balanced level, but there are natural times when lactic acid builds up in a fish. Chasing or escaping from predators, for example, is likely to temporarily build up lactic acid. The rigors of migration can produce moments of buildup; a fish that migrates up a river, like salmon or shad, may experience lactic acid buildup after it endures the hardships of running through a particularly difficult section of water, perhaps a falls that the fish must hurdle. After passing that difficult section, the fish will usually rest in a pool above that spot and recoup its energy, moving on when it has regained strength and when other factors tell it to do so.

As noted, the accumulation of lactic acid in a fish's muscles can lead to blood acidification and temporary disruption of many metabolic processes. If a captured fish is able to restore its blood acid (pH) level to normal or pre-stress levels, normal physiological processes return and the fish may survive after being released. If the blood chemistry balance is not restored, the fish will probably die. The volume of lactic acid generated is directly proportional to the duration of muscular activity.

In freshwater, most species of fish are landed fairly quickly, even on light tackle, by the average angler. There are some exceptions, such as salmon and big trout. In saltwater, more species attain large size and have a lot of strength, so there are more fish able to extend the battle with an angler. No matter what the environment, extended battles promote lactic acid buildup. The issue of playing fish so as to minimize lactic acid buildup is dealt with in more detail later in this section, but in general it is advantageous to land a fish quickly if you intend to release it, unless it has been hooked in very deep water. Playing the fish until it is exhausted, or "belly up," may lead to lactic acid poisoning and death. This eventuality may be prevented not only by playing a fish quickly, but also by unhooking it carefully and releasing it as quickly as possible.

Experienced anglers know that lactic acid buildup and the resulting stress work differently in fish. A rainbow trout, for example, will put up more struggle than a bullhead catfish. The coolwater trout is more likely to build up lactic acid than the warmwater bullhead; and the trout will not last long if kept out of the water, whereas the hardier bullhead may last a surprisingly long time. Anglers become acquainted with the fighting characteristics of the different species and should be able to recognize when certain fish need to be landed quickly and given more attention in the revival and release process. Some fish are so stressed after being landed (as well as handled for release), and their lactic acid level so high, that they have a greatly increased need for oxygen. This condition makes them harder to revive, and they may need more time to recover before they regain equilibrium and can swim off on their own.

Stress is the factor that initiates lactic acid buildup and this is compounded by injury, either because of where the fish is hooked or how it is handled later on. Bringing a fish to boat quickly, for example, while generally recommended, can have a drawback if the fish is so frisky that the angler, in efforts to unhook and release it, causes internal or external injury. Putting a stressed fish into a livewell may not be helpful either, if the well doesn't have sufficient aeration. In that case, the fish will struggle to get the oxygen it needs, thereby creating more stress rather than less. If the livewell is uncrowded, is properly aerated, and/or the water has been treated with conditioning agents, then stress can be reduced.

Thus, in the various stages of contact with a sport-caught fish, anglers may compound or mitigate stress, and it is important to have an understanding of the impact of all actions.

How a Fish Is Hooked

The catch-and-release experience starts with the angler becoming connected to a fish via rod, reel, line, and, of course, hook. A determining factor in the survival of a fish after release is where it is hooked. Where it is hooked is often a function of the angling technique, the terminal tackle employed, and the skills of the angler.

Many studies have proven that fish caught with bait suffer a much higher rate of mortality than fish caught with lures or flies. The studies differ in the percent of mortality of bait-hooked fish, but they agree that the use of bait generally results in deeply hooked fish and a significantly higher mortality. An analysis of the findings of studies conducted on lake- and stream-dwelling trout and salmon species showed an average mortality rate of 31 percent for bait-hooked fish, 4.9 percent for lure-hooked fish, and 3.8 percent for fly-caught fish.

While this is an alarming difference, it should be pointed out that the manner of fishing also effects deep hooking. Trolling with a lure or fly, for example, is unlikely to cause a deep-hooked fish. If an angler lets a fish run with either live or dead bait, and waits to set the hook, the likelihood is great that the fish will swallow the bait, and swallowing the bait will probably result in the fish being hooked deeply, especially in the esophagus or stomach. Removing a hook from these areas is usually difficult; it often cannot be done without taking the fish out of the water and hook removal in this instance may cause internal damage. If the hook is swallowed so deeply that it punctures the heart, which is just behind the mouth, or the liver or kidney, the fish is going to die.

Although such deep hooking is often a result of fishing with bait, it can also happen with lures Some lures, like plastic worms, for example, may be swallowed by fish if they are allowed to run with them, and deep swallowing of the lure can cause the same degree (if not more) of hooking mortality as bait swallowing. Indeed, some studies have shown

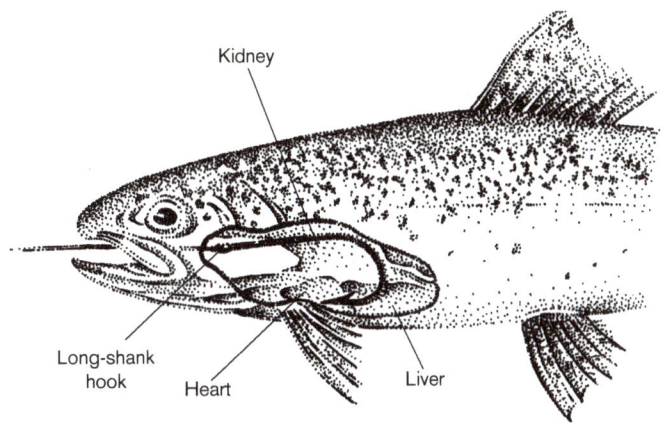

The kidney, heart, and liver are all vulnerable when a fishhook is lodged within the throat of a fish.

that live bait has caused no significant difference in mortality over certain types of lures that were likely to be taken deep. A study of live bait use compared with the use of Carolina-rigged plastic worms on largemouth bass, for example, showed a slightly higher mortality for the worms. This type of rig often is taken deeply, and anglers usually wait to set the hook *(see: hooksetting)*.

Obviously, one way that anglers using bait can reduce harm to fish is to set the hook quickly after a pickup or strike, rather than waiting for the fish to inhale it and then set the hook. This action is helpful, since most fish can inhale a bait item in an instant; however, it does not work for all species, and its success may depend on the type of bait used or species sought—pike and muskie, for example, will often hold a bait before consuming it rather than simply inhale it. Not all fish crush a bait and then turn it around to inhale; for those species, deep hooking can be avoided by being alert to a take and quickly reacting properly. Incidentally, some baitfishing with treble hooks is actually better than baitfishing with single hooks, since the trebles are harder to swallow (although the bait may act less naturally with the treble and the fish may detect a treble hook sooner than a single one). In some saltwater fishing, the use of circle hooks *(see: hook)* has gained popularity for baitfishing (especially for tuna) because these hooks usually catch in the corner of the mouth, causing less injury to a fish that will be released.

Most lures or flies are far less likely to be taken deep than bait hooks, in part because they are usually moving and anglers naturally react fairly quickly to a strike. As a result, most fish caught on lures or flies are hooked in body locations where the hook does not severely damage the fish. The lowest mortality of fish occurs when they are hooked in the jaw, the snout, the corners of the mouth, the maxillary, and the cheek. Hooking in the eye, the tongue, and the isthmus are a little more serious.

Being hooked in or near the gills is bad news because the hook may damage the gill filaments, either as a result of being hooked or as a result of hook removal. This type of injury causes bleeding and decreases the fish's chance of survival. Occasionally a single hook, whether used with bait or on lures or flies, will get into the gill area, but it is more common when a multihooked lure is used.

Studies have shown that fish caught on flies have a slightly lower mortality rate than those caught on lures, but the difference is so small that it has virtually no impact on the overall mortality picture. This negligible impact is the reason why special-use regulations established by fisheries managers generally prohibit the use of bait but permit the use of lures and flies, or specify single-hook lures and flies. Nevertheless, a belief persists among some anglers, primarily fly anglers, that people using lures, or hardware as it may derisively be called, cause more harm to the resource. Assuming that proper care is taken to unhook and release a fish, this is not so.

The use of treble hooks versus single hooks is another issue hotly debated. Here, too, some advocates of catch-and-release maintain that more harm is caused by trebles than singles. This is a split issue. Studies comparing the two have varying results. However, an evaluation of all studies on this issue concluded that there was no significant relationship between mortality and the number of hook points. This conclusion stands to reason in view of the slight difference in mortality between the use of lures and the use of flies (since nearly all flies have just a single hook). However, treble hooks on average are more difficult to remove from fish, which means that removing a treble hook usually takes longer than removing a single hook. A lure with multiple treble hooks, such as many plugs, may have two or three sets of treble hooks. Fish are often impaled by two or three hook points on multiple-treble-hooked lures; unhooking them may take longer, or one hook may cause no damage (in the corner of the mouth, for example) but another may damage a vulnerable area (such as the eye or the gill). Therefore, a reasonable conclusion is that the probability of injury to a fish is greater when a lure with multiple treble hooks is used.

In certain places, especially remote waters of northern Canada, the use of single hooks is either mandated by law or required as lodge or outfitter policy; and in some cases, those hooks must be barbless as well (barbed hooks have been banned throughout Manitoba since 1990). If an angler has a banned treble hook rather than the approved single hook, the guide will actually cut two of the points off the treble hook and pinch the barbs down on the hook before allowing fishing to start. These policies are in effect in waters where few fish—usually just one per person per day for shore lunch—are kept. The purpose of such policies is to minimize injury and permit quick release; these actions in turn help to maintain a large population of fish, all of which are slow-growing, and to increase the likelihood of big fish getting bigger. More comments on treble hooks versus single hooks follow later in this section.

As for barbless hook-related mortality, some older studies report no significant difference in mortality of fish caught on barbed versus barbless hooks; whereas some more recent ones show that fish caught on barbless hooks suffer lower hooking mortality than those caught on barbed hooks. Concerns that barbless hooks may cause deeper hook penetration, and thus facilitate injury, have proven groundless, and anglers who frequently, or exclusively, use barbless hooks do not report any findings that support these concerns. In fact, barbless hooks have the benefit of being easier and quicker to remove from fish, and this fact may contribute to a quicker release of the fish and less time spent out of the water.

With regard to some of these issues, it is reasonable to ask if mountains are being made out of molehills. For example, what is the difference if a barbless hook is removed in 18 seconds versus a barbed hook removed in 23 seconds, assuming that neither removal causes an injury? Or, is a 1 percent difference in fish mortality for barbless flies over barbed flies really important? Does it matter if fish-hooking mortality with a treble-hooked lure is 5 percent versus 4 percent for a single-hook lure? Maybe the differences are negligible if the fish is striped bass, the legal limit is one fish, and millions are around. But, maybe the differences are significant if the fish is a cutthroat trout in a special-regulation section of river that gets pounded by thousands of anglers.

A key issue in all these situations is the percentage of fish mortality. Studies of trout show mortalities of less than 5 percent for fish caught on lures and flies, and the percentages decrease from there with single and barbless hooks. But all of this has to be kept in perspective, because a fish that is caught on a barbless hook may still be mortally wounded if the angler rips out the hook, squeezes the fish hard while holding it for release, drops the fish on the ground or boat floor, and so forth. The hooks used and the location of hooking are just part of the picture. How the angler plays, lands, handles, and releases fish is also very important.

Playing Fish

The technical aspects of how to play a fish are discussed in detail in another entry *(see: playing fish)*. The intent here is to spotlight the effects of playing techniques upon fish that are to be released.

It was once axiomatic that the safest way to catch a fish was to play it until it was exhausted and then land it. That was in the days when many, if not most, fish that were caught were kept. It is true that an exhausted fish is less likely to thrash about and is easier to land and handle, and thus safer to the angler. But it is also true that an exhausted fish is more likely to be severely stressed.

As fishing tackle improved over the past half-century, the sport of fishing took on newer

---

Although there is only 1 family of catfish that lives in the freshwaters of North America, worldwide there are 30 families of catfish and more than 2,000 species.

dimensions with an increasing interest by anglers in catching large fish by using light tackle. Devotees, in fact, advocated light tackle in part to "give the fish a chance." The challenge of using light gear and employing above-ordinary angling skills created an interest in light-tackle usage that still runs strong today (see: light-tackle fishing). However, as more was learned about the physiological factors that affect hooked fish, the clearer it became that there is a correlation between stress in fish and the length of time that they're played, and that light-tackle use may cause some fish to be played for such a length of time that it affects their ability to survive when released. Ironically, although the use of light tackle may give the fish a better chance to avoid capture, it may give the fish less of a chance to survive the catch-and-release experience.

But the issue is not quite this clear-cut, and the solution to this dilemma is not necessarily to disavow the use of light tackle. Indeed, capable anglers can catch some fish quicker on light tackle than other anglers can catch them using heavier equipment. In fact, while it is hard to dispute the effects of lactic acid buildup over an extended playing time, what constitutes a long time and how much of a factor it is in causing mortality of fish varies widely among species and is complicated by the location of the hook in the fish, the temperature of the water, the size of the fish, environmental factors (like current), and other influences.

In general terms, large fish tend to have more difficulty with lactic acid buildup, and in some studies they have experienced a higher mortality rate than smaller fish. This fact, too, is ironic, because the larger fish are often the ones that many catch-and-release practitioners desire to see survive. In freshwater, most of the fish that are caught by anglers are landed in a relatively short period of time, either because of the skill of the angler or the type of equipment employed, or because most freshwater fish are small ($1/2$ pound to 2 pounds) and able to recover from lactic acid stress fairly quickly if they are not otherwise injured or mistreated. The scenario is a bit different in saltwater, where the average size is larger and where many sport-caught fish reach greater sizes than their freshwater brethren. Many species of saltwater fish are simply tougher than freshwater fish; and even on an equivalent-size basis, and assuming the use of identical equipment, they will be harder to subdue, which means landing them will take longer.

So how long is too long for large or strong fish? There is no guaranteed timetable, and no good way to measure the time. Where species in freshwater or saltwater are concerned, how you play a large or strong fish may be the most important factor of all. This is probably more important than whether you use a barbed or barbless hook or whether you use a lure instead of a fly. In some cases it may also be more important than whether you caught the fish on bait or not.

This issue of how you play the fish is central to what constitutes an exhausted fish, and it is admittedly a gray area. On the one hand, fish played to complete exhaustion may not survive. The key words are may not. If complete exhaustion meant certain death for a fish, then it would mean death for every animal that exercises itself to exhaustion, including long-distance runners and racehorses. Obviously, exhaustion cannot equate entirely with death. Some large and strong fish that are played to exhaustion can be revived and set free. Some cannot.

Indeed, the way that a fish is played may be the critical element. Playing a fish aggressively is more likely to result in breaking its spirit and saving its life. A tug-of-war can last longer and result in a "stubborn" fish that will not give up and cannot be resuscitated after capture. Fish of identical sizes can be played to identical times with different outcomes; one may be played aggressively by an experienced angler using light tackle and be successfully released, and the other fish may be played by an inexperienced angler using heavier tackle and be incapable of revival.

If you take the fight to the fish, no matter what the tackle, you often can convince the fish to give up. Anglers who fish for such powerful bruisers as tuna and billfish experience this frequently. If you are in a river playing a large fish, the battle might be prolonged if you move or lunge after the fish; whereas, by remaining motionless, you could actually fool it and make it feel less threatened, despite being on the end of your line (remember that you know what this means, but the fish doesn't), and you may land it quicker than you would have otherwise.

This gray area is evidently a psychological one. It is definitely an aspect of playing large and tough fish that many anglers give no thought to.

Landing and Handling Fish
The technical aspects of how to land a fish are discussed in detail in another entry (see: landing fish). The intent here is to spotlight the effects of landing and handling upon fish that are to be released.

One of the critical areas affecting the well-being of fish to be released is how they are treated once they are caught. Mishandling results in injury and stress, and is an aspect of catch-and-release that every angler can do something about.

Whether or not a fish is tired, its chance of survival is best if it never leaves the water, a feat that few anglers practice often enough. In some instances, frisky and obviously unharmed fish can be shaken off at boatside by leaving some slack in the line and jiggling the rod tip. This is especially true if single-hooked and barbless lures are used. An angler who is having great success and catching many fish while using multihooked lures should consider using lures with a single hook or pinching the barbs, rather than continuing to catch fish on the original lures, especially if the fish are repeatedly small and frisky.

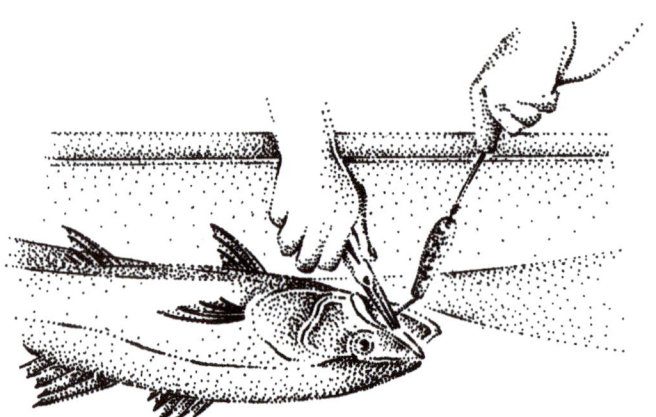

When fishing from a boat, you can easily release some fish without handling them by keeping the fish in the water at boatside and using pliers to free the hook.

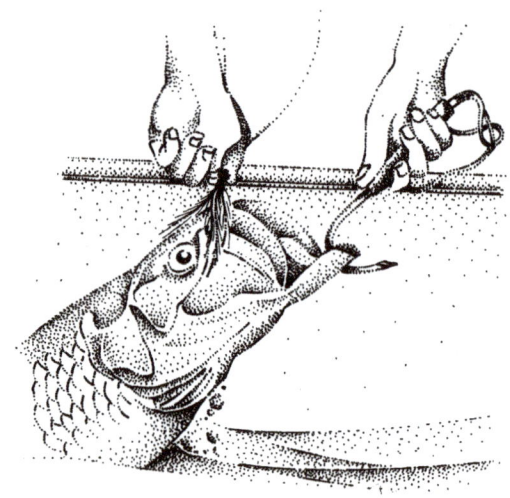

Lip-gaffing is one way to unhook a large fish without harming it. This may be a two-person operation, as depicted here, where one person lip-gaffs the fish and the other frees the hook.

Wading anglers can accomplish the task of keeping a fish in the water easier than boat or bank anglers can; some fish, like steelhead, can be grabbed by the tail and held with one hand and unhooked with the other hand, all while staying in the water. Or, the fish can be pinned against the angler's wet, wader-covered legs with one hand while the hook is removed.

Some fish can be unhooked in the water without handling. To do this, grasp the hook with needle- or long-nosed pliers and, without touching the fish (which may cause it to thrash about), quickly pull back and up on the point (in the opposite direction from which it is embedded) to free it. Once you have hold of the hook with the pliers, unhook the fish instantly in a quick wrist-twisting motion. This is usually, but not always, a two-person operation; one angler is holding the rod while the other reaches over (possibly holding the line lightly to steer the fish to an advantageous position) and, while the fish rests at the surface, uses pliers to quickly grab and free the hook. This is about as simple and as good a no-touch release as you can get. Unfortunately, this release method isn't always possible because of the size or behavior of the fish, the number of hooks or how the fish is hooked, the distance from water to gunwale of the boat, or other factors.

When you can't release the fish in the water, you have to land it by grabbing the fish by hand, netting it, cradling it, or gaffing it.

Gaffing. Gaffing *(see)* is usually a method for landing a fish that you intend to keep, because the gaff point snares the fish through its flesh. A fish landed this way is almost certainly a goner, so you can't gaff a fish that will be released. You can, however, safely gaff some species through the lower jaw with a short-handled lip gaff; these species are usually fairly large fish that are difficult to subdue for unhooking.

Tarpon, red drum, and striped bass are commonly landed in the lower jaw with a hand gaff and then freed by slipping the gaff hook point back out. These fish have fairly large mouths, and it is not difficult to bring the gaff down through the skin behind the lower jaw. There are no organs to damage here, so gaffing will not be fatal to the fish if it is done carefully, and this method is preferable to bringing the fish into the boat or trying to hold onto it.

Netting. Netting *(see)* can be harmful to fish and is a practice that probably should be reserved for fish that will be kept, but as with so many other aspects of catch-and-release fishing, this dictum is not absolute. A stream trout, for example, caught on a fly, can be landed and briefly held in a net without harm. A large salmon, caught on a multi-hooked plug, may pose a problem the instant that the hooks snare the side of the net as it is being raised around the fish. It's a situational thing.

Conventional round- or oval-shaped nets with deep mesh bags can damage the eyes and the jaws of fish and, possibly, the mucous coating. Cotton mesh nets are softer and don't seem to hurt the fish as much, but hooks are harder to get out of cotton mesh nets, and the nets are not as widely available today as nylon or rubber nets. One of the biggest problems in using a round or oval net is not actually the net itself, but the damage done to fish that are netted when a multihooked lure is used to catch the fish. The hooks inevitably grab the webbing of the net, and the fish thrashes and rips itself while pulling violently against the embedded hooks. If the fish rolls in the net with treble hooks, as pike and lake trout frequently do, then untangling becomes a real problem, and a good deal of time is lost before the fish can be unhooked. The situation is bad all around; some species may go into the net in good shape but come out with ripped skin, jaws, or eyes and be much worse off.

Cradling. Perhaps the best method of netting a fish that will be released, and one that deserves more attention, is to use a type of net called a cradle, or release cradle. This is not a net in the traditional handle-and-dipping sense, but it has similarities

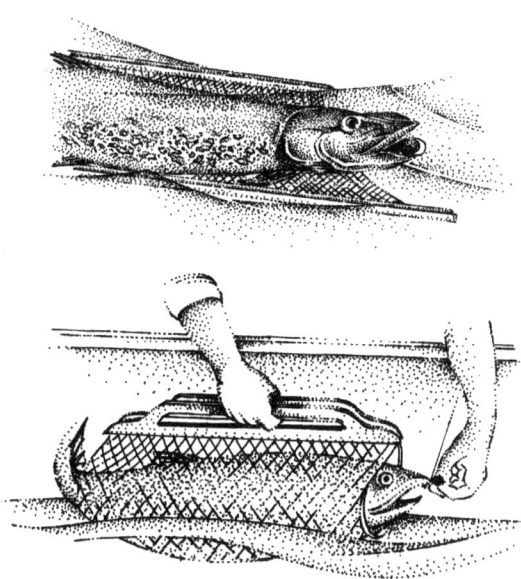

Cradles are an excellent way to handle some species of fish; a release cradle (top) provides optimal support for a long fish.

and is a benign way of landing and subduing a large or long fish so that it can be unhooked and released.

The most popular release cradles have two long narrow wood boards that are connected by $1/4$-inch soft-mesh knotless netting that is closed at the ends and that droops into the water to envelop a fish. The cradle is laid alongside a boat, and the netting droops into a trough below. The angler leads a captured fish alongside the boat and over the netting, and the net is folded up like a purse to enclose the fish, which remains full-length and in the water. Perhaps most importantly the cradle supports the full body of the fish in a horizontal position. Another version, usually homemade and intended for shorter fish, is smaller, with open ends and open-grip handle. In both cases, the fish stays relaxed in the net while the hook is removed, and the fish can be released without having to be handled. Moreover, you can rig the cradle up so that it's possible to weigh the fish and cradle while providing excellent horizontal support for the fish. It is very difficult to use a cradle when fishing by yourself, however; in that case, avoid a cradle or net altogether if possible and try to unhook the fish while it is in the water.

Release cradles, especially the larger ones, are more common among pike and muskie anglers, and are mostly a Midwest item, but the idea has broad application for landing freshwater fish and has some application in saltwater (although it is almost unknown there, perhaps because many saltwater boats have a high freeboard). If you can find a source for strong fine-mesh netting in 4- to 5-foot lengths, you can make your own cradle in both long and short lengths.

Hand-landing. When you land a fish without a net or gaff, you have to hold it somehow. Big fish are difficult to hold, and when brought into a boat, they are liable to be dropped or to squirm out of your hands and fall. Some fish, like a sailfish or big tarpon, might have to be held by two people in order to be properly subdued, supported, and unhooked. Nevertheless, large and small fish are often brought into boats to be released, and therefore are handled. In fact, in some cases, there is no other choice. In a big-water boat, for example, the freeboard makes it difficult, and unsafe under some conditions, for someone to lean over and attempt to hold and/or unhook a fish, especially if the boat is rolling with waves. In a low-freeboard craft, like a flats boat, bass boat, or jonboat, it is much easier and safer to get to a fish that is in the water.

Yet, even in these low boats, anglers regularly bring fish aboard for unhooking and release. Bass anglers, for example, often bring a fish into the boat, many by swinging it in because the fish is small and the line and tackle heavy enough to permit this. If they grab the fish by the lower jaw without letting it hit the floor or objects, then there's no problem. But if they swing it in and plop it on the floor, then pounce on it to unhook it, there is a problem.

The problem with physically handling a fish, as well as with letting a fish flop on the deck or floor of a boat or on the shore, is that the protective mucous coating may be removed, and the possibility increases of an infection that eventually may become grotesque and life-threatening. In addition, if the fish flops about while still hooked to a lure, the hooks on the lure may catch on some object (it might even be someone's leg or arm, which can be extremely serious) and cause further injury to the fish, which may also lead to infection. Such injury or exposure is likely more serious for freshwater fish than for those in marine environments because of the composition of saltwater; nonetheless, minimizing injury and exposure is always advisable whether the fish is in freshwater or saltwater.

Don't let a fish flop onshore or in a boat if you intend to release it. Wetting your hands before you hold a fish may help prevent removal of that protective mucus; however, many anglers maintain that wet hands make it harder to hold the fish, meaning that they have to grip it tighter. Using a sure-grip cotton glove that has been wetted is a good idea, and more anglers are using one to

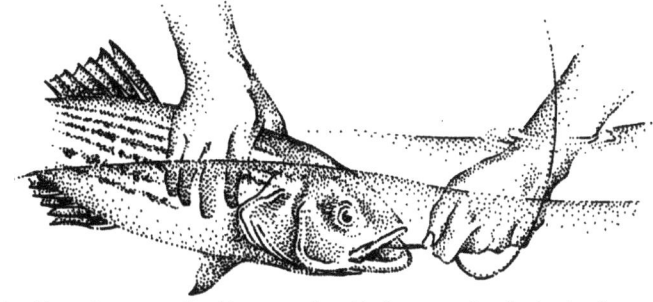

Lacking pliers, you should wet one hand before grasping the body of a small fish; keep the fish in the water while you free the hook with your other hand.

get a firm grasp on a fish and to minimize harm. However, don't grasp a small fish tightly around the middle of the body during unhooking, because you may cause internal damage. Admittedly, it's a fine line between holding a fish tightly enough to keep it from squirming free, but not so tightly that the internal organs are compressed. These organs are concentrated behind the mouth and the head, exactly beneath the "neck" or nape where many fish are likely to be held. Obviously, the smaller fish, with less meat at the nape, are more easily hurt by holding tightly there. Big freshwater fish, and many saltwater fish, can be held in that location without harm; for many, it is the best place to do so.

When holding and subduing larger fish, try placing a wet cloth or towel over the fish, at least over the head. This action usually has a calming effect and is especially useful for fish that may be held for a longer period, such as the extra few moments needed when tagging a fish or when unhooking a particularly hard-to-unhook fish.

Some fish have a handle that you can grab to facilitate holding, especially in the water. In a very few species that handle is the bill; mostly it is the tail. The tails of some fish are rigid enough to permit grabbing by placing your hand over the caudal peduncle just ahead of the tail fin. You can grab a jack or a tuna that way, and you can grab large salmon and pike by the tail. Smaller fish usually can't be grabbed that way, and the tails of many fish are not rigid enough to permit this. You can't grab a big largemouth bass securely enough by the tail, nor can you grab most trout (except really large ones) this way. You can hold bass by the mouth, however, and there are a few species whose mouths, lack of teeth on the jaws, or size may permit this. Bass are held by inserting the thumb inside the lower jaw and pinching the jaw against the bent forefinger, which is outside and pressing against the lower jaw. Some anglers wear a leather thumb guard for this, especially if they will be handling a lot of fish. However, larger and stronger fish that can be held by the jaw (anglers often call this the lip) are best secured by keeping the thumb outside and below the jaw, and putting the other four fingers inside the jaw, preferably (although not often) with a wet glove on.

Most fish cannot be hand-held by the mouth, usually because of teeth. One way to hand-land and hand-hold species by the mouth is with one of various jaw-gripping tools. These tools clamp over the lower jaw to secure the fish without requiring that the fish be touched by hand, and do no harm to the fish, although many models work best on smaller fish. For some species, a small lip gaff can be used to hold the fish for unhooking, although it should not be employed to lift the fish out of the water in such a manner that all the weight is placed on the jaw.

Many fish cannot, or should not, be supported by the lower jaw whether you are holding the jaw by hand or with a gripping device, but they can be gripped there while they are still in the water or while the rest of the body is being supported. Lifting fish up may or may not be a problem. The longer and heavier the fish, the more inappropriate lifting seems; yet lifting and briefly carrying fish, either headfirst or tailfirst, has been unharmful to many fish. Atlantic salmon have been tail-lifted, unharmed, by experienced anglers, although it's not something that ought to be done for very long.

In water, a fish maintains its equilibrium and balance, and body parts don't move around, but out of water, especially when held vertically, more pressure is brought to bear on internal organs and connective tissues. This is not necessarily harmful, although it can be, especially to larger fish (such as billfish) and/or fish that have already been severely stressed (don't forget that while you're lifting the fish vertically the fish is in need of oxygen). Therefore, keeping fish in a horizontal position, in or out of the water, is more in their best interests than lifting them vertically.

Smaller fish are less likely to be harmed when held vertically. Largemouth bass, which have been much studied, are commonly held vertically by anglers for unhooking and do not suffer from this position. However, most largemouth bass are small, and holding a 2-pound largemouth this way is not comparable to holding a 40-pound striper this way.

Holding fish under the gills, as previously discussed, is not appropriate, nor is putting your fingers in their eye sockets. It was once fairly common to grab some species by the cavity of their eye

A good gripping tool such as this helps keep hands away from fish and hooks, and facilitates unhooking for release.

sockets, but this sorry practice has become almost universally abandoned unless a fish is going to be kept. This practice causes obvious injury to the fish, and it may lead to infections.

One technique that anglers find helpful is turning a fish over and holding it upside down (out of the water with small fish and in the water with larger ones). This technique doesn't appear to cause problems for the fish and seems to tranquilize it. Some small fish, largemouth bass included, can be gently lifted with a hand placed under the belly.

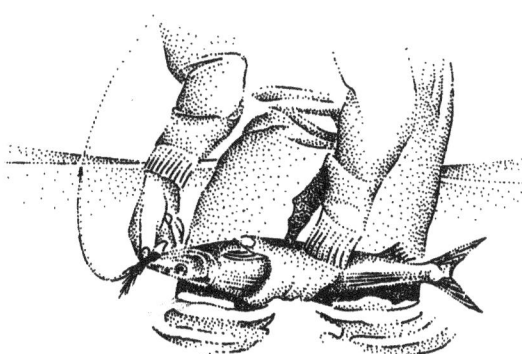

Before you unhook a small, frisky fish, try turning it upside down to tranquilize it.

This may be a good alternative for the angler when a fish has been caught on a lure with multiple hooks; however, it is really a technique for small fish, because proper balance cannot be supplied to larger fish this way, and a lot of pressure would be brought to bear on the internal organs.

When you do have to touch and hold fish, keep in mind that a minimum amount of handling is desirable in all cases, particularly in warm water. If fish must be taken out of the water, as previously explained, be conscious of their inability to breathe and of the length of time that they are forced to forego oxygen while being unhooked. Many of the fish that are held by anglers in the photographs in this book were released, even though they were held briefly out of water to take the photograph. When photographing fish, be prepared to take the photo quickly by having your camera available and ready to shoot (in other words, don't hold the fish out of water while you find your camera and load film into it). Of course, it helps if the fish are caught quickly and the water is cool.

The length of time that you hold a fish out of water—for unhooking, admiring, photographing, weighing, etc.—is one that has no set limit. For some exhausted fish, every second counts. For some hardy fish, a couple of minutes is no problem. If the fish has been landed pretty quickly, you should be able to tell its condition and whether there is a sense of urgency to the handling. Taking photos of a fish can put a fish in danger that is otherwise in fair to good condition. Not only is the fish held out of the water longer, but it is subjected to extra handling, sometimes by a couple of people, and this is often when fish get dropped or damaged. Photographing the fish without harming the fish is possible, although it is easier for people who have more experience in handling fish. In all cases, have unhooking tools, loaded camera, and other supplies at the ready. Dousing the fish with water is also a good idea; some saltwater anglers in large boats use a washdown hose to keep running water on a fish that is being unhooked and prepared for photographing prior to release.

As for weighing, lifting up a fish to weigh it is certainly not beneficial to the fish, and it prolongs the time spent out of water. Weighing occasionally leads to injury when a fish gets dropped, or when its gills are damaged from being touched or from the way the fish is hoisted for weighing. There are methods of estimating the weight of a fish *(see: measuring fish)*, and some grippers and nets have built-in scales so that the fish does not need further handling. If you absolutely have to weigh a fish, do it quickly, preferably with the assistance of someone else, and place the hook of the scale through the membrane behind the lower jaw, not under the gills or gill cover. Remember to be careful for your own sake as well as that of the fish, since some fish are especially difficult to handle, like a thrashing dolphin, and some are simply dangerous, like a bluefish, northern pike, or shark.

Unhooking Fish

A hook should be removed carefully, not in a jerking or ripping manner that might cause injury. Tugging at a hook could rip the flesh inside the mouth or on the cheek or other location, which could prompt bleeding or lead to infection. Ripping out a hook could also tear the jaw or the maxillary. So the best action is to try to remove the hook without damaging the fish. Removal is usually easier with barbless hooks than with barbed ones, and in both cases it means backing the hook point out rather than just grabbing and pulling, which is sometimes difficult. Of course, hook removal should be done quickly for the sake of the fish but also carefully to avoid hooking yourself.

If you are removing the point of a hook from a fish by using your fingers, be very careful; should the fish move or slip from your grasp, the potential

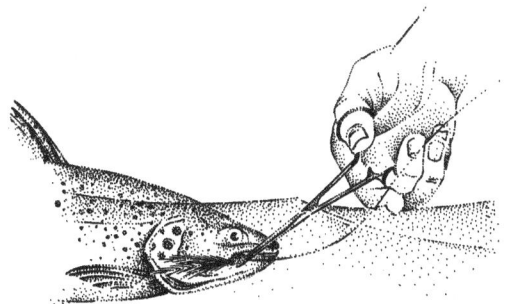

For small fish caught with a fly hook, use a hemostat to free the hook; the fish can remain in the water and often doesn't need to be handled.

for hooking yourself is great. People have been hooked in this manner, and one of the worst scenarios that you can imagine is getting a finger stuck on a hook that is still connected to the fish; this is definitely a possibility when a multihooked lure or a treble hook is used. Whenever you're unhooking a fish or otherwise handling it, whether with your fingers or with some tool, be careful not to hurt yourself, since the gill covers, fin spines, and teeth are some of the body parts that can cause a nasty cut, which may become infected.

For grabbing and freeing many hooks, the most popular tool is a long-nosed, or needle-nosed, plier. It is especially useful for midsized hooks and treble hooks on lures, which make up the bulk of hooks used by anglers. With a tapered head, it fits well into a fish's mouth, or fairly deep into the mouth. For strictly small hooks and for flies that anglers would prefer not to crush (or to tear the dressing) during removal, a standard or angled-head hemostat works fairly well.

These tools may not be adequate for fish with big mouths and large or sharp teeth, but other unhooking devices, usually with long arms and a trigger to secure the grip on a hook, are available. Jaw spreaders, which keep the mouth of toothy fish open for unhooking work, help a lone angler unhook fish, but you have to use the proper size for the circumstances and be careful not to rip the fish with the ends.

Still another tool is one that is used in saltwater by anglers fishing with fairly heavy line or leader, and is simply called a hook puller by many.

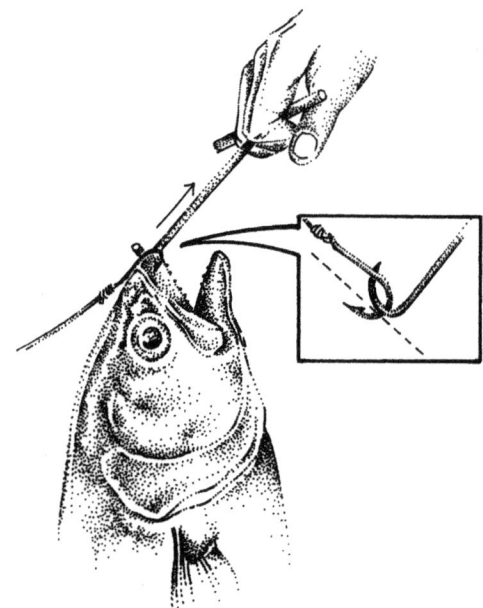

Small and intermediate size fish, especially in saltwater, are often unhooked with a hook puller, a tool with a crooked end. When a fish is lifted up with heavy line or leader, the hook puller is looped over the bend of the fishhook (inset), the fish is quickly raised up, and the fishhook point is pulled in the opposite direction, allowing the fish to fall back into the water.

It looks a lot like an old hauling tool for ice blocks, except the business end is hooked and is used to grab around the bend of a hook when a fish is lifted up with a heavy line or leader. With one hand on the line close to the hook and with the hook puller looped over the bend of the hook, the angler quickly raises up the fish and pulls the hook point in the opposite direction. This works best when the hook is embedded within a few inches of the jaws, and when the fish is not so large that it can't be lifted by the line or leader.

Perhaps the most contentious aspect of catch-and-release is whether to remove the hook from a fish that has been deeply impaled. This has primarily been a baitfishing issue, and for a long time the standard advice was to cut the line or leader off and leave the hook in the fish rather than to try to remove it and risk causing internal injury and bleeding. Many studies have found greatly increased rates of survival—sometimes two and three times better—if the hook is left in. However, hooks do corrode (depending on the type of hook, and they corrode faster in saltwater), and sometimes the hooks are passed through the anal vent. Although leaving in a hook may indeed be preferable to pulling it out, nevertheless a deeply swallowed hook that is well into the stomach may puncture vital organs; even if the fish is released, the damage is done. A hook left in the throat above the gills or the esophagus is not as serious.

Some recent studies contradict the cut-the-line advice, thus casting a cloud over the entire subject. They find that the survival of deeply hooked fish is good, or better, when the hooks have been removed. Whether or not to cut the line is usually a decision that anglers make based on circumstances at the exact moment and also based on such factors as the condition of the fish, the length of the fight, and the tools available for unhooking.

Sometimes the difficulty of unhooking a deeply caught fish is increased because of the size of the fish's mouth, the strength of the fish, the presence of teeth, and other factors. If two anglers work on a fish, one holding and controlling the fish and/or keeping its mouth open and the other working to free the hook, the unhooking time can be shortened and the need for resuscitation lessened. So, where a difficult situation exists, an angler should try to involve an extra pair of hands.

Where a difficult fish is concerned—a dangerous, toothy, or extremely active specimen—it may be helpful to place a wet rag or a wet cloth over the head of the fish to cover its eyes, and/or also to rest the fish on a soft surface (like an old and clean foam cushion). Saltwater anglers are more likely to do this, particularly with bluefish and small tuna, and it often has a calming effect.

The Release

With the hook out, it's time for the final act. In many cases, especially with small fish and with fish that have been landed quickly, simply putting them back in the water and letting go is all that has to be done; the fish is lively, makes a thrust with its tail, and disappears. Many anglers release fish rather cavalierly. They may be standing in a boat and, after unhooking the fish, just toss it back in the water. For the most part, this does not seem to hurt a fish, but it can't be good for them. Some people who have witnessed bass anglers on television do this repeatedly (as well as showing the fish off in a manner that some complain must be hurting its jaw) have written to major magazines complaining about this action, and it does seem to demonstrate indifference or to send a conflicting message, especially when anglers talk about what a great deed they are doing by releasing the fish. So it does not seem to be asking too much for anglers to bend over and release fish into the water more gently.

If a fish has been kept out of water for a while, if it has struggled mightily, and if it is stressed, then just returning the fish to the water may not be enough, no matter how gently it is done. A stressed released fish often turns over on its side or back, being too weak to maintain its equilibrium.

If you release a fish that seems to be okay but then turns over, retrieve it quickly, if possible, and hold it in an upright position in the water. Some released fish drift off and then turn over out of the angler's reach, or turn over when too deep to be retrieved. Therefore, you shouldn't let a fish go until it is clearly able to swim off under its own power. The fact that a fish is breathing doesn't mean it can do that. In fact, as noted previously, a stressed fish will breath more frequently in an effort to force oxygen over its gills because it is deprived of oxygen. Breathing just means that the fish isn't dead. You have to be patient.

To revive a fish, you need to keep it upright in the water. If you are in a river or a place with current, the fish should be headed into the current, not facing away from the current. You should not let a stressed

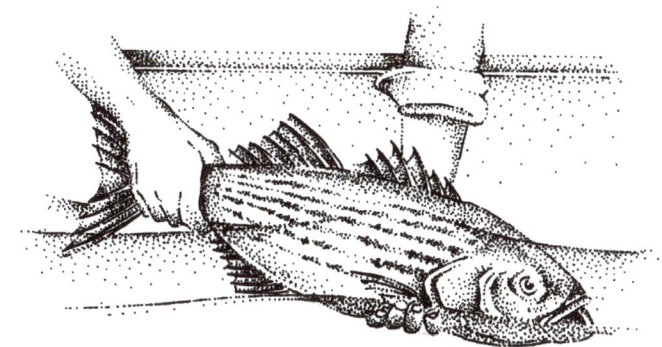

Before some fish can be released, you may need to revive them; this requires careful handling and moving the fish forward to pass oxygenated water over their gills.

fish free in a swift current, even after it has been revived, because it may not have the strength to resist the current, which could carry it away and bounce it on the bottom or against objects. In a river, a stressed fish should be taken out of strong current and released where the current is less. Sometimes, a fish released in the shallow backwaters of a river will rest there for a short while before moving, and it should not be rushed out before it is ready.

When you are reviving a fish, you can get oxygen to it by moving it forward to force water into its mouth and over the gills. Most instructions on this subject, including that provided by many fisheries agencies, advise moving the fish back and forth in the water to accomplish this. There is a minority viewpoint that advises against moving the fish backward, which makes more sense, but which may be subject to debate. The fact is, however, that a fish takes water into its mouth and forces it over the gills and out the external opening to take oxygen into the blood. The fish does not do this by swimming backward or by facing downstream. If you hold a fish facing downstream long enough in a strong current, it will die. That seems to indicate that moving water backward over a fish may not be helpful.

Moving a fish back and forth, to increase its oxygen intake, evidently does no good half of the time—when the fish is moving backward. Could a wading angler stir up sediment and induce suffocation from backward movement? Maybe. Could a person move the fish backward so quickly and abruptly as to do harm? Maybe.

Moving a fish forward only is admittedly harder to do for fish that cannot be held by the mouth by hand; however, with the right gripping tool, it may be possible. Mouth-gripped fish can be led forward in a circular or figure-eight pattern, especially if they are not big, but other fish, and large individuals, are harder to lead like this. Boat anglers can aid some fish by moving the boat slowly forward under outboard or electric motor power, but such fish have to be held by the head, or supported by the head and forward part of the body. You can seldom hold a fish by the tail alone and move the boat forward, because the fish gets turned sideways or backward.

In a river, be sure to face a fish upstream so that water flows into its mouth forcing oxygen over its gills; a chinook salmon is being released here.

If you hold a fish by the tail, you can usually move it forward and backward—an action that is easier to do and is at least somewhat helpful to the fish. Most of the time, such as when you're in clear open water, moving a fish backward and forward does not appear to be harmful, especially if you do not move it backward with the same vigor that you might move it forward. Even just moving it side to side may be helpful.

Cradling the fish with both hands is an alternative if you cannot move the fish forward. One hand holds the caudal peduncle, and the other supports the belly close to the pectoral fins. Hold the fish upright and keep it steady, perhaps moving it sideways if possible, until the fish recovers and can swim off on its own.

No matter what you do, the key is keeping the fish upright and supporting it, and giving it time. Devote whatever time is necessary to reviving a fish and getting it to the point where it can swim off on its own. It is not uncommon to devote 20 minutes to reviving a large fish, and some people have devoted an hour to a successful effort.

A fish is usually ready to go off on its own when it uses its tail muscles to try to swim. If it does this forcefully enough, you may let go of the tail immediately and the fish will dart off or swim slowly but assuredly away. It sometimes helps to poke the fish in the tail; this action provokes the fish into a short flight away and forces a burst of water and oxygen into its system, perhaps also giving it a boost in its recovery. If the fish swims off well on its own, this isn't necessary, but if it sits in one place and looks like it could be vulnerable to a predator's attack, then a slight poke with a rod tip, boathook, net handle, oar, or paddle might be worthwhile. Keep an eye on the fish as it swims off until you can no longer see it.

Finally, think about why the fish had to be revived in the first place. If you had played it better, could the fish have recovered quicker? What could you have done to decrease the stress before the fish was landed? Perhaps the fish needed revival because you held it out of the water too long for photos. Or perhaps it needed revival because you did not play it well enough. Ideally, you should be able to play a fish, no matter what the gear used, so that it is capable of swimming off immediately after you land and unhook it. Perhaps you need to improve your fish-fighting techniques to minimize the need for reviving fish.

Special Circumstances

Certain aspects of releasing fish and of catch-and-release in general deserve special consideration and more detailed evaluation.

Releasing deep-water fish. A general rule when releasing some fish and keeping others is to keep the ones that are caught in deep water rather than those caught in shallow water. Fish caught in deep water are usually harder to revive than those caught in shallow water, so being thoughtfully selective makes sense. However, if you do have to release deep-water fish, they should be appropriately cared for, since the deep water may cause a problem that is not experienced when shallower fish are released.

When some species of freshwater and saltwater fish are brought up from very deep water, they suffer a condition that is equivalent to what people know as "the bends," because pressure increases about 15 pounds every 33 feet in the water. This pressure has to be relieved; if it is not, the air bladder expands within the abdominal cavity, and the expansion may cause the stomach to protrude from the mouth. A fish in this condition, which is compounded by a sometimes drastic change in water temperature, will turn belly up if released and cannot recover until it has been "degassed."

Some species are able to belch the pressure away during retrieval, but in others it builds. Those in which it does not build have a pneumatic duct connected to the air bladder, allowing these fish to expel air and make more extensive vertical movements. Such fish include the various trout and salmon species, as well as carp and catfish. Those in which pressure builds are without this duct and cannot expel air; adjustment to pressure is slow, meaning that these fish cannot make rapid vertical movements. These species include largemouth and smallmouth bass, spotted bass, walleye, yellow perch, panfish species, striped bass, snapper, grouper, cod, hake, and black sea bass. Other fish, including lake trout and salmon, that have been brought up too quickly for their bodies to naturally adjust to the pressure changes, may still experience a problem, even though they have the natural means to overcome it.

How deep is deep enough to cause this depressurization? This is hard to say, but over 40 feet is generally thought to be deep enough to cause it in snapper and grouper, over 30 feet for walleyes, and over 60 feet for lake trout.

To relieve this pressure in trout and salmon, especially in lake trout, the fish can be "burped." Salmonids have an opening between the air bladder and esophagus that allows them to expel the air that bloats the air bladder. Burping is accomplished by holding the fish on its side or back and massaging or kneading the belly from the anal vent toward the head. This is sometimes difficult and may require a more active effort, actually squeezing the fish. A sound is made when the air is expelled. When the fish is ready to be released, hold it in the water at the surface with the head in the water, moving it forward or from side to side until it is fully recovered. To release it, there are two options. For fish that are large and too heavy to hold well, give the tail a quick squeeze to stimulate a vigorous dive. For fish that aren't so large and hard to hold, give the fish a vigorous shove or push headfirst and straight toward the bottom for a solid head start back down to the pressures and temperature from which it was taken. This thrusting tactic may also be helpful with other fish.

A large electric ray may have as many as a million generating units in its two special electric organs and can give an initial shock of more than 200 volts.

Burping is not suitable for other species because the air pressure cannot be naturally vented. It can still be expelled, however, using a technique that is called puncturing or venting by fisheries professionals and "fizzing" by some laypeople. Puncturing entails the insertion of a sharp object, usually a long needle, through the body wall of the fish to let the pent-up air escape through the puncture hole. The proper type of needle is a 16- to 20-gauge hypodermic needle obtained from medical or veterinary supply stores; a larger needle may be needed for very big fish. Where the needle is inserted into the fish may vary with the species. For walleye, the location is on either side of the fish approximately 1 inch above the anal vent; for snapper and grouper, it is just behind and above the base of the pectoral fin. The needle is inserted on a 45-degree angle under, not through, the scales, preferably when the fish is in a livewell. Hold the fish with its head slightly down and stroke the abdominal area to force air out. A sharpened pump needle also works, perhaps better because the air is quickly released through the hollow tube. If done correctly, the fish will be able to right itself in the livewell, and it then can be returned to the water.

A more detailed explanation of how to do this, and an illustration of location and technique, have not been provided here because this is a controversial topic still subject to testing and evaluation, although the California Dept. of Fish and Game, Ohio Dept. of Natural Resources, Florida Sea Grant, and the Southeast Office of the National Marine Fisheries Service have information on this subject available to the public. In general, puncturing is not recommended by most fisheries professionals because of concerns about inexpert handling by untrained anglers. The extra length of time that a fish would be held out of the water (where a livewell is not used) and the possibility of improper technique and perhaps further internal damage to the fish are other reasons why fisheries managers discourage the general public from this practice.

There is no direct evidence that puncturing or burping is effective against delayed mortality, and some research has indicated that untreated fish left on the surface of the water do recover on their own and return to deep water—unless they are discovered by sea gulls. Those who would attempt puncturing should probably practice first on deep-caught fish that would be kept for eating anyway. The difficulties inherent in releasing fish caught from deep water lend some credence to the belief that catch-and-release is primarily a shallow-water proposition, although the definition of deep and shallow is open to vastly different interpretations.

Anglers can take two other courses of action to help a deep-dwelling fish survive. The first is to play a deeply caught fish on a moderate and steady retrieve, rather than trying to bring it in as quickly as possible. A fast retrieve, which is the usual recommendation in most situations, does not give the fish time to adjust to changes in pressure naturally. Avoiding a fast retrieve may make the fish more suitable for release without degassing efforts. On the other hand, following this advice increases your chances of losing a fish because of the extra playing time, and there is no clear guide regarding how long a fish needs to adjust internal pressure. Moreover, in saltwater, bottom-dwelling fish, once they are initially hooked, often have to be played aggressively to keep them from diving into cover and cutting the line, and this aggressive fight carries through into the rest of the playing action.

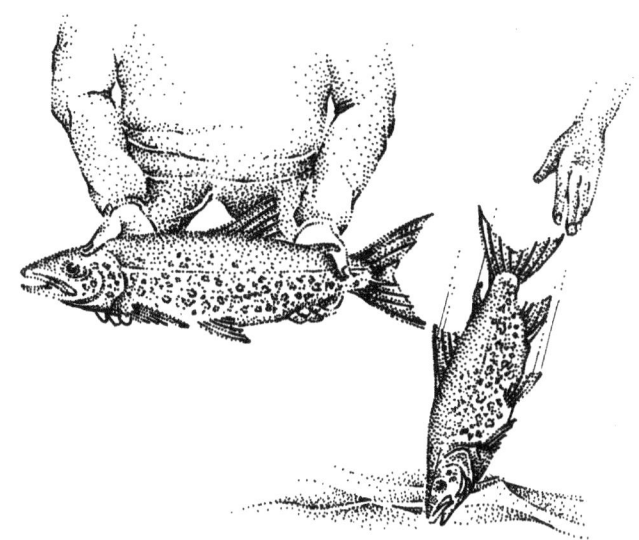

A fish caught in deep water may benefit from a deep-thrust head-first release action; support the fish horizontally until unhooked, and then quickly turn it head-first and plunge it into the water.

The second course open to anglers is to give the fish a good head start by thrusting it headfirst into the water when they release it. This is especially useful with lake trout or salmon, and is also useful for releasing tuna and amberjack that are small enough to be hand-lifted. To propel the fish forward, lift it by the tail and then thrust it headfirst into the water and as far as you can reach, as if you were stabbing a spear deep into the water. This quickly propels it downward.

Bleeding fish. Another general rule when releasing some fish and keeping others is to keep a fish that is bleeding rather than one that is not; bleeders, particularly those hooked in the gills, are less likely to survive than unharmed fish. This is not an absolute, however. In professional studies, and in the results of tag-and-release efforts of anglers, some fish that were bleeding when released have survived and been well enough to live for a long time and be caught again. Cuts or tears in flesh that cause a minor amount of bleeding may not be fatal; many anglers have caught fish that had been recently attacked by other predators, enough to create an open wound with some signs of bleeding, and the fish survived.

Fish that are bleeding from the gills, however, receive an extra dose of stress, and this is most likely to be critical. If there is a lot of bleeding, regardless of the cause, the appropriate action is to keep the fish if you can legally do so, rather than to cause it to become a mortality statistic that doesn't serve a meal purpose (although it may be food for other aquatic creatures).

However, the biggest dilemma is what to do when you land a fish that is bleeding but cannot legally be kept. Some anglers feel that keeping such a fish is an ethically appropriate act, but good intentions are hard to prove when confronted by law enforcement officials. If you don't release a fish that is bleeding, it will surely die, but if you have to release one that is bleeding, it might just recover.

Replacing treble hooks with singles. Suppose that you catch a large energetic fish on a plug. The fish is impaled by a barbed treble hook in the mouth. It flops over and over, hooking itself near the gills with another treble. When headed into the net, the fish rolls; the hooks catch in the net webbing. The net becomes a tangled mess, and some of the hook points are twisted out of shape; the flesh of the fish is ripped. You want to release it, but because the fish has been gashed and has been out of the water for so long during unhooking, it may succumb shortly to exhaustion or later to infection, or be easy prey.

Now imagine that you've cast a surface plug to heavy or close-to-shore cover. You lower the rod tip, take up slack line, and a fish strikes. You react reflexively and try to drive the hook into the fish, but it misses the lure. In a heartbeat, the tight-lined plug springs from the water toward you. Some people react fast enough to turn from this multihooked missile, but many take it in the arm, the chest, the hat, or even the face.

Similar things may happen when fish jump and throw lures, or when fish are close to the surface near the boat and the hook pulls out under extreme pressure. An accident may happen when you're trying to release a fish and it buries a hook into you.

You can't completely avoid these difficulties, but you can minimize the chance of them happening, especially when using plugs, almost all of which are supplied by manufacturers with multiple sets of treble hooks. To ensure individual safety and the well-being of fish that are released, use plugs with single, rather than treble, hooks. A detailed review of how to accomplish this is contained elsewhere *(see: plugs)*.

Single-hook use is required in only a few places in North America, so using a single hook is mostly a personal choice. By choice some anglers don't use live bait. Some won't troll. Some won't angle for various species during the spawning period. The issue of single hooks over treble hooks is also an individual choice, one that is based on your attitude. You don't have to take the treble hooks off all your lures, but there are times when a single hook is more appropriate than a treble for safety, fishing effectiveness, and the benefit of the resource.

Confining fish. Fish that are to be released should not be kept on a stringer or cooped up in a warm, poorly oxygenated container or well; you're reducing their survival chances significantly by doing this. In a well or container, cool water and abundant oxygen are vital. Don't cull unless you are keeping an injured fish and releasing a healthy one. Culling is replacing a fish on a stringer or in a well with another. In some places, once you have taken possession of a fish by confining it, culling by returning that fish to the water is illegal.

Generally a fish that has been confined is not as suitable for release as one that has been freshly caught. Livewells are very popular in freshwater and are especially geared for confining bass and walleye, although they are sometimes used to retain other fish. Although it is seldom beneficial to keep fish in these so-called livewells for later release (as opposed to instant, on-the-spot release), many people do this in freshwater. Most bass and walleye tournaments are based on the weight of fish caught, which are supposed to be kept in properly functioning livewells. That is the primary reason why livewells have proliferated in freshwater fishing boats. If you have to keep fish in a livewell, pay special attention to the water temperature and to the fish's need for frequent and ample aeration. In closed systems, the use of a stabilizing chemical, which decreases the fish's need for oxygen consumption and fights fungus infection and mucus loss, is beneficial. Using ice, noniodized salt, and some drugs (available from aquarium supply stores) are other measures that can be taken to aid fish that are detained for a long period prior to release, though this is something that relatively few anglers other than tournament anglers need to be concerned with.

General Guidelines for Releasing Fish
Plan in advance if you're going to keep or release a fish. This not only makes a difference in how you land the fish, but also helps you decide which fish you might keep that day and which ones you might release. For example, if you've made a decision to keep one or two fish, and you catch one early in the outing that is deeply hooked and/or bleeding, you might immediately decide to keep it since it is one that could have trouble surviving. If you haven't decided about keeping or releasing a fish until one is on the line, don't bring the fish into the boat and then decide, unless the fish has to be measured to see if it meets specific length requirements. The best course of action is to make the decision when the fish is in the water so that you can take proper steps from the start.

The major aspects of releasing fish have been detailed and explained throughout this section. In summary, to release a fish in good shape:

- Do not freespool a fish that has struck live bait.
- Set the hook quickly to keep bait or lures from being taken deep.

Like this walleye, many fish can be grasped behind the gills without injury, provided they aren't squeezed tightly.

- Play and land the fish quickly, unless it is taken from very deep water.
- Do not confine fish that will be released.
- Avoid netting; keep the fish in water whenever possible.
- Hold the fish firmly but gently; a wet hand, glove, or towel might help.
- Do not let the fish flop around.
- Keep fingers and objects out of the gills and eyes.
- Use a long-nose pliers or other tool for extracting hooks.
- If a fish is hooked in the esophagus or stomach, cut the line.
- Revive a tired fish by holding it upright and moving it forward or from side to side.
- Return the fish to the water gently and headfirst.

When you do keep a fish, be discriminating. The decision can be based on the condition of a fish or its size in relation to the fish population. You can choose to keep a species that is plentiful rather than one that is scarce. You can choose a nonspawner, a bleeder, or a small fish rather than one of the prime specimens.

Lastly, remember that even if you return all the fish you catch to the water, you're still having an impact. If the average delayed mortality rate for fish that are released after being caught is only 5 percent, and if you catch and release 60 fish in a few days or a week, chances are good that at least 3 of those fish will die. If the average delayed mortality is 10 percent, then 6 of those fish will die. And if you keep some of your catch, then the total impact you have is the number that you kept, plus a percent of those that died after release.

Considerations for Releasing Bass

Because largemouth and smallmouth bass are the most popular of all gamefish species, fishing pressure for them in many places is very intense, and there is a great deal of interest in, and adherence to, catch-and-release. Fortunately, largemouth and smallmouth bass, as well as their family cousins, are fairly hardy fish. Except under unusual circumstances, bass do not put up an extremely long fight, and they are fairly easy to land. They are not too disturbed by moderately respectful handling. They can be grasped without harm to fish or angler—in fact, you have a greater likelihood of injury than the fish because of the sharp points of multihooked lures. But bass are not immune to problems, and it is wise to avoid excessive or rough handling and excessive time held out of water. Try to minimize injury from multiple hooks, and avoid or minimize netting. Take special care of bass that are confined in livewells. Probably no fish are subjected to livewell containment more than largemouth bass, particularly by competitive anglers who retain the fish until weigh-in and then release them. Good handling, adequate water temperature, and ample oxygen are keys to their survival in livewells.

Bass are often hooked lightly and it is sometimes possible to free them from the hooks simply by letting them idle near the surface, lowering the rod tip, and putting slack in the line. You might try jiggling the rod tip. If this doesn't free the fish, then try freeing it while in the water using long-nosed pliers. If bass are not released in the water, it's best to grab them by the lower jaw. This hold provides the least possible physical contact and does the least damage. Few other species of fish can be grasped so handily. This landing technique requires caution, however, since a bass is usually hooked in a corner of the mouth, and the hooks are often exposed. If the lure has many hooks, the bass should be well subdued before a lip-landing attempt is made; an alternative in this situation might be to land the fish under the belly.

Soft plastic lures, especially worms, salamander and crayfish imitations, and grubs—many of them scented in part to encourage bass to hold onto them longer—are a prominent part of the bass angler's arsenal. However, some of these products or methods of using them could result in deephooking. The same is true, of course, for live bait. The manner in which bait or soft plastic lure users set the hook in a bass is a factor in the fish's survival later on. Waiting to set the hook should be avoided where possible.

Considerations for Releasing Trout

If proper care is taken of trout that will be released, the survival rate is very high; many studies have put it in the 95 to 97 percent range for stream trout when caught on lures and flies. The survival rate of trout that are released after being caught on live bait is about three times better if the hook is left in than if it is extracted. Thus, anglers should snip the line and not try to extract a small hook. If bait is used, a larger hook is less likely to get caught in the stomach than a small one. Most lure- and fly-caught trout are hooked in the jaws and the edges of the mouth, a few on the tongue, so it is relatively easy to get the hook out. On those occasions when a lure or fly hook is swallowed or manages to lodge in the gills, don't even bother with a token attempt unless the job looks easy; snip the line or tippet as close to the lure or fly as possible.

The less you handle trout, the better, but that is not always possible. Small stream trout squirm like eels, and often the hook cannot be removed without grasping the fish to keep it still. Here you can keep the fish in the surface water, but grab it around the body by gripping it behind the head and between the dorsal fin, trying to keep finger pressure off the soft belly and avoid squeezing it. Small fish can be completely encircled with a wet hand. Turning the fish upside down seems to have a tranquilizing effect. Only larger stream trout should be netted, usually when wading in deep rivers or fishing from a floating boat; if a net is used, keep it in the water with the fish and work the hook out while the fish is in the net and not struggling.

Make sure that you are not releasing the fish in swift current. Moving to the edge of the current is a good idea for releasing a large and tired fish, but take care not to stir up the shallows so much that it adds to the fish's breathing hardship.

Bigger trout, like lakers, are easy fish to injure in the landing and handling stages at all sizes. The big ones are fragile, and the small and medium-size ones have a notorious habit of wiggling and spinning. If they are captured in a net and the net lifted out of the water, the fish may continue to spin and cause itself problems because of the net and the lure. Large trout may be brought alongside a boat and held upright in the water for hook removal. They should not be brought into the boat if you are going to release them, although the cold water that lakers inhabit does help in preventing the onset of infection from the unintentional loss of their protective coating during handling. Methods of dealing with the release of lakers taken from deep water were previously described.

Considerations for Releasing Atlantic Salmon
Many of the advisements previously issued also apply to Atlantic salmon, but a few things are slightly different. Most Atlantic salmon fishing is with flies, by law or by custom/preference, so there isn't much at issue regarding deeply hooked fish. Salmon are fairly easily released if they haven't been played too long, so anglers should be able to achieve a high degree of survival for released fish.

Atlantic salmon are taken in rivers, virtually all by wading anglers who should move to a quiet location if possible to play and land the fish. By using a tippet of medium to heavy strength, an angler should be able to land a fish fairly quickly. The Atlantic Salmon Federation recommends breaking the leader on a fish that is not landed in 15 to 20 minutes, and not using a tailer to land a fish that will be released. When being released, the salmon should be kept in the water, held gently in a supported horizontal and upright position, and revived gently facing upstream. Give the fish plenty of time to recover.

Considerations for Releasing Marine Offshore Species
The National Marine Fisheries Service Game Fish Tagging Program advises anglers to simply tow such species as sharks and tuna slowly headfirst alongside the boat for tagging and before release. The forced flow of water over the gills will help revive the fish. The leader should be cut with cutting pliers as close to the hook as possible, allowing the revived fish to swim off. These fish can also be released by using a gaff as a dehooking tool. The technique requires the use of a V-notched stick or other device to depress the leader. The gaff hook is slipped over the hook, and simultaneously the leader is pressed down while the fish hook is popped back and out.

The same can be accomplished for billfish, although these species can be grabbed by the bill by one person while being tagged and unhooked by another. Holding the bill allows you to control the fish, which is very important. If you can reach far enough overboard (difficult if not impossible on many large sportfishing boats), hold the head of the billfish under the water, which in itself has a calming effect. When you grab the bill, place your hands so that the thumbs face each other; this position makes it easier to push the fish away if the fish thrashes. There are tools to slip over the bill for facilitating handling and hook removal.

CATFISH
Catfish comprise a large group of predominately freshwater fish that are distributed around the world. Some accounts peg the total number of catfish species worldwide at more than 2,200. South America is especially rich in quantity and species of catfish, and has some of the largest freshwater specimens. Many of the world's significant river systems are home to at least one species of catfish, and in most cases these fish rank among the largest fish of the river system. The same applies to large lakes, especially in reservoirs that are impoundments of large rivers. Many catfish are important for commercial and recreational purposes.

Angling for catfish is one of the most popular freshwater fishing activities, second only to bass fishing in some surveys, especially in the midsection of the United States. Despite high levels of participation, fishing for catfish is somewhat maligned, largely by omission, in most of the major outdoor media. Catfish, like some other species, are viewed with condescension in deference to other species with (subjectively) higher pedigrees and greater sporting virtues. In some U.S. locations, catfish are designated as gamefish by state fisheries agencies. They may be lumped in the negative-sounding category of "rough fish" (see) and treated to only incidental management. Catfish are the subject of (sometimes intense) commercial pursuit, and most of them are certainly short on color and beauty.

It is true that catfish lack some of the sporting attributes appreciated in other species. They almost never jump out of the water when hooked. Their fight is more bulldogging and bottom digging than sudden streaking; when hooked, a 20-pound river catfish does not fire 100 yards downriver the way a 20-pound salmon or steelhead would (although a 60- to 100-pounder might). They live in deep holes, often in turbid water, and their feeding habits are less than regal. Most people tend to fish for them in a laid-back, forked-stick, bait-on-bottom, wait-till-something happens manner. When you put all this together, it adds up to a fish that is relatively abundant but without a great deal of glamour and sex appeal.

Some of the perceived deficiencies of catfish might also be applied, incidentally, to other popular freshwater fish, especially panfish and walleye. Critics point out that stream trout and largemouth bass, most of which are rather small on average, are overhyped as gamefish and that the catfish deserves greater appreciation and better press than it gets. Indeed, looking at the abilities and habits of catfish, one finds an impressive fish that has adapted especially well to its niche in the environment, and one that is probably worthy of greater public attention. It is unlikely to get more respect, however, until it starts rising to the surface to take dry flies and/or aggressively attacks spinnerbaits and then cartwheels out of the water. Don't hold your breath. But don't ignore these fish simply because they lack the characteristics of other species.

Indeed, more Americans angle for catfish than they do for trout. There is arguably more national effort expended on catfish in a single week than in an entire year of Atlantic salmon fishing or bonefishing. This is partly because catfish are so abundant; the vast majority of anglers have access to some species of catfish. This attention is partly due to their importance as a food source; most species of catfish rank very highly as table fare, and people who catch catfish overwhelmingly tend to keep them, a practice that within reason is not harmful to most populations of catfish and is encouraged by fisheries managers. Another important reason for their popularity is that they are a fairly willing fish that is generally not too difficult to catch in smaller sizes; they don't require much sophistication in technique, tackle, or presentation methods. Like other species, most of the catfish caught are on the smaller side, certainly under 2 pounds, but on the right tackle they have spunk, and the bigger specimens can be a challenge to land, even if they don't provide the drama of some other species. Although their fighting virtues are short on style, the larger specimens are long on strength and rod-bending drama, not unlike many of the bottom-dwelling bruisers of saltwater.

As with other types of fishing, you can make angling for catfish as intricate as you like. But anyone can enjoy this activity, without special casting skills or highly sophisticated methods, and generally from almost any type of craft as well as from shore, so they clearly deserve a high popularity quotient.

Species

The majority of catfish are scaleless, but some are armored with heavy scales. They vary in size from tiny versions that are popular for aquarium use, the smallest of which grow no larger than $1/2$ inch, to huge specimens, the largest of which has been recorded at more than 600 pounds. Most catfish prefer the sluggish localities of lakes and rivers; some do best in fairly swift waters. Tenacious fish, they can stay alive out of water for a considerable time, especially if kept moist. They are characterized by having a single dorsal fin and an adipose fin; strong, sharply pointed spines in dorsal and pectoral fins; and whiskerlike sensory barbels on the upper and lower jaws. The head and mouth are generally broad, and the eyes small.

North American freshwater catfish. Members of the family Ictaluridae, North American freshwater catfish are distributed from Canada to Guatemala and contain about 50 species. These bottom-loving fish are important commercially; and many millions are harvested annually, some from natural environments and some from aquaculture or fish-farming operations.

Thousands of anglers pursue these fish, employing a wide variety of methods to catch them. All species obtained from fairly clear waters are delicious on the table. Many fish farms specialize in raising and marketing catfish. All members of this group have scaleless skins and a stiff, sharp spine at the leading edge of the dorsal fin and pectoral fins. Just in front of the tail, on the dorsal surface, is a fleshy adipose fin. Their eight barbels are sensory structures that help them to locate food.

Nearly all North American catfish live in sluggish streams or in the quiet waters of lakes and ponds. They are bottom feeders, taking both live and dead foods. They are typically active at night—although some are more active during the day than others—and on dark, overcast days or in roiled, murky water. Catfish spawn in spring and early summer, fanning a nest area in the sand or mud. One or both parents stand guard until the eggs hatch and then shepherd the young until they are large enough to fend for themselves.

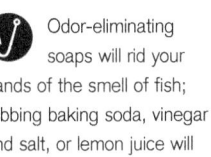 Odor-eliminating soaps will rid your hands of the smell of fish; rubbing baking soda, vinegar and salt, or lemon juice will also do the trick.

Perhaps the most abundant and best-known members of the clan of about a dozen species of the genus *Ictalurus* are the three principal species of bullhead: brown bullhead *(I. nebulosus; see: bullhead, brown)*, black bullhead *(I. melas; see: bullhead, black)*, and yellow bullhead *(I. natalis; see: bullhead, yellow)*.

Bullhead abound in freshwater from coast to coast in North America. In some regions they have been introduced by humans, either accidentally when a bait bucket containing a few baby bullhead was emptied, or intentionally when an angler stocked bullhead in his private pond. Settlers from the East carried bullhead over the Rockies to stock the waters with their familiar favorite. Until then, bullhead were not found west of the Rockies. Nature's way of moving bullhead into new habitats is more unique. The bullhead travel on the feet of wading birds that unknowingly carry the adhesive eggs with them from place to place. The eggs wash off as the birds wade, and in this way a new population of bullhead becomes established.

These catfish can survive in water that is so low in oxygen that the bullhead must come to the surface from time to time to gulp air. In these emergency conditions, the air bladder acts as an auxiliary lung. In the confinement of a pond in which conditions are initially favorable, bullhead may soon multiply beyond the food capacity. The result is an overpopulation of stunted, freakish fish—weird-looking creatures with oversize heads and shrunken bodies. Some years ago, biologists in Wisconsin poisoned a 9-acre pond that seemed crowded with bullhead. It contained nearly 250,000. The pond was supporting about 1,500 pounds of fish per acre, but not one bullhead was big enough to grace a skillet.

East of the Rockies, all three species are in abundance. Most common—and the species that has been introduced most widely—is the brown bullhead. In their original distribution, the black bullhead was the most widely distributed. In habits and flavor, the three species are scarcely distinguishable.

Also of commercial and recreational importance in some areas are the channel catfish *(I. punctatus; see catfish, channel)*, blue catfish *(I. furcatus; see: catfish, blue)*, white catfish *(Ameiurus catus; see catfish, white)*, and flathead catfish *(Pylodictus olivaris; see catfish, flathead)*. The largest is the blue catfish, which may tip the scales at more than 150 pounds. The record caught on rod and reel weighed 109 pounds. A 25-pound catch is considered large, however. Slate blue above and white below, this big catfish ranges throughout the large streams of the Mississippi River system but is most abundant by far in the deep, warm waters of the South. Small blue catfish are most easily confused with channel catfish. Both have forked tails, but the latter is more likely to have dark spots; they can be positively distinguished by anal fin ray count.

The channel catfish's maximum weight is uncertain, although a 58-pounder has been recorded; the average is less than 5 pounds. A young channel catfish has black spots over its bluish body, and its fins are also margined with black. The black becomes subdued or is absent in older fish. Of all the catfish, the channel cat shows the greatest preference for clear, flowing waters, but it does equally well in lakes and ponds. Because of its strong fight at the end of a rod and line, it rates favorably with anglers. It is stocked regularly in farm ponds to provide fishing fun as well as food and is a principal fish stocked in pay-as-you-fish ponds (white catfish are also popular here). The channel catfish is also the species most commonly used in catfish farming enterprises.

The white catfish lives primarily in streams feeding into the Atlantic, ranging southward from New England to Florida. Until the introduction of the channel catfish, it was the largest catfish inhabiting these waters. It reaches a known maximum size of about 22 pounds, but the average is less than 3 pounds. Growing much larger than the white catfish, the flathead catfish has a broad, flat head, and the lower jaw projects beyond the upper. It is known to reach weights exceeding 100 pounds; the average size caught by anglers weighs less than 5 pounds, although 20-pounders are not especially rare.

The foregoing North American catfish are not finicky about what they eat. They will accept almost anything offered for bait, although some are more finicky than others, and this is not to imply that they will strike anything at any time, only that they have eclectic tastes. Biologists have found strange collections of debris in the stomachs of catfish. But avid catfish anglers are especially likely to use a foul-smelling concoction called a stinkbait *(see)* for luring catfish. Most catfish, in fact, have taste glands located over much of their body, although these glands are concentrated in their long, sensory whiskers. Among the favorite stinkbaits are soured clams, ripened chicken entrails, coagulated blood, and a variety of cheese and doughball mixtures—all allowed to cure until they acquire a potent odor. A good catfish bait will attract some species from a long distance.

Finally, the North American freshwater catfish family includes the various madtoms *(see)*, about two dozen of which are in the genus *Noturus*. All are small, most of them less than 5 inches long. Madtoms are recognized by their unique adipose fin. Non-madtom catfish have a fleshy fin protruding from their back just ahead of the caudal fin. The adipose fin of a madtom is continuous with their caudal fin. Madtoms possess stinging venom in their dorsal and pectoral spines. The venom originates from cells of the skin sheath over the pectoral fin. The toxicity of the venom varies but approximates that of a bee sting, causing stab wounds to swell and become extremely painful. Some madtoms inhabit the fast waters of streams, living in the rapids or riffles; others prefer slow-moving streams or the stillwaters of ponds and lakes, much like other members of the catfish family.

The stonecat *(N. flavus; see: stonecat)*, is one of the largest of the madtoms, sometimes attaining a length of 12 inches, although it is usually less than half this size. It is found in the rubble and boulder riffles and runs of creeks and small to large rivers over most of the U.S. and southern Canada, from the St. Lawrence River system southward to Florida, westward to Oklahoma and across the northern tier of states to Wyoming, and north to Manitoba. It is occasionally caught by anglers and is of some importance as forage for game species. The tadpole madtom *(N. gyrinus),* seldom more than 3 inches long, occurs in much the same range but prefers sluggish waters. The freckled madtom *(N. noctumus)* is also small and has numerous black specks over its body. It is sometimes found in swift waters but may as frequently inhabit weedy, quiet waters. Some madtoms are fairly common, but most are rarely seen by anglers. A number of madtom species are on lists of protected fish.

South American freshwater catfish. There is enormous diversity of catfish throughout South America, especially in the Amazon and Orinoco basins, and they are members of several different families.

The names of these fish are sometimes confused among different languages, including native Indian, Portuguese, and Spanish, as well as English. The following general information concerns a few of the more notable catfish of South America. Most catfish there, especially the larger-growing specimens, are heavily valued for commercial distribution. Recreational fishing for most South American catfish is of some value for food but is a small part of the overall harvest. Until the late 1980s, many of the larger-growing species were substantial in size, but relentless commercial pressures have steadily lowered the average size of these fish, and the upper-end specimens are either nonexistent or far fewer in number.

The largest family of freshwater catfish in South America is Pimelodidae, which range from Mexico southward through South America except for the cold southern regions. These fish are reportedly the most abundant predators of other fish in the river channels and undertake upstream migrations to capitalize on prey that becomes concentrated during spawning runs or low-water periods. When these fish spawn, their young offspring drift or swim downstream to their nursery estuary. They are distinguished from other catfish mainly by their very large adipose fins. All have scaleless skins. The caudal fin is forked, and the medium-size, spined dorsal fin is high and located far forward on the body. The pectoral fins are also spineless. Typically, there are three pairs of long barbels that stretch back halfway or more along the body. Some of the numerous species in the more than 20 genera in the family are favorites with fish hobbyists.

Among the South American catfish encountered by anglers are various shovelnose catfish of the *Pseudoplatystoma* genus, which are called sorubim or (incorrectly) surubim by anglos or by an assortment of other names.

The tiger sorubim (listed as *Pseudoplatystoma tigrinum* and *Sorubim tigrinum*) and the barred sorubim *(Pseudoplatystoma fasciatum)* are among the species, but there is confusion between them. The shovelnose catfish is so named because its flat head is projected into a ducklike snout. The mouth projects down under the snout, conveniently located for picking up food rooted from the bottom.

The tiger sorubim of Brazil is known as *cachara* and *caparari* in that country and in Spanish as *tigre zúngaro*. The barred sorubim is listed as *doncella* and *rayao* in Spanish, and may also be called the tiger shovelnose catfish. The differences between these species are uncertain, although they have a zebralike pattern of vertical stripes, with dark spots on the back, flanks, and fins. They inhabit lagoons, narrow channels, and flooded forests and are more likely to strike lures than other Amazonian catfish. The *cachara* of Brazil is said to reach weights exceeding 20 kilograms and a length of more than 1 meter.

An apparently related fish, with spots but no stripes, is a shovelnose catfish known as *pintado* in Brazil *(Pseudoplatystoma coruscan).*

This fish, which may also be called the spotted sorubim or polka dot catfish, is a strong and tasty fish that is said to reach 80 kilograms in weight and nearly 2 meters in length. It sports a bluish gray color and black spots. It is found in river outlets, lagoon mouths, and channels, under floating plants, and along riverbanks, and is primarily caught at night.

A sorubim from the Trombetas River, Brazil.

74 Catfish

Blue Catfish

Barred Sorubim

Channel Catfish

Pintado

Flathead Catfish

Jurupoca

White Catfish

Dourada

Pirarara

Gafftopsail Catfish

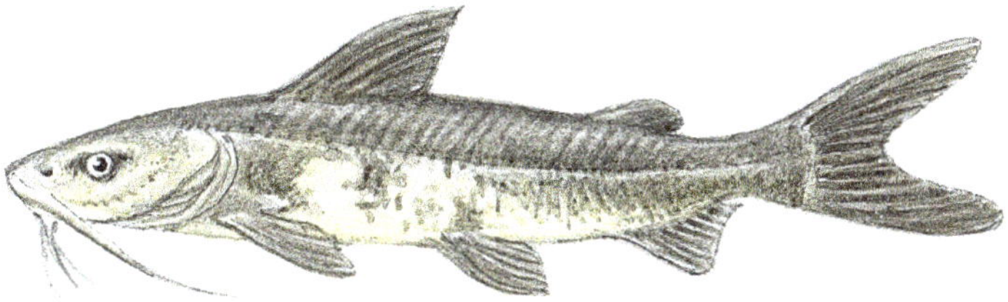

Hardhead Catfish

Wels

Walking Catfish

Jaú

Piraíba

A slightly different fish, reaching just 10 kilograms, is the *jurupoca (Hemisorubim platyrhyncos)*; it has a different mouth shape, with a lower jaw that extends past the upper and turns up.

Two prominent and large catfish are members of the *Brachyplatystoma* genus. The smaller of these, growing to 40 kilograms and nearly 5 feet in length, is known as *dourada* in Portuguese *(Brachyplatystoma flavicans)* and has been an especially important commercial species—one that has been heavily pressured.

Exhibiting a dirty gold color, it is easily distinguished and is also known as the golden catfish, although this terminology, as well as its Portuguese name, has caused it to be confused with the highly popular and sporty dorado *(Salminus maxillosus)*, which is also golden.

A larger cousin, *Brachyplatystoma filamentosum*, is called *piraíba*, a Tupi-Guarani Indian word that means "mother of all fish." Appropriately, the *piraíba*, which attains a reported weight of up to 300 kilograms (660 pounds), is the largest of South American catfish and one of the largest freshwater fish in the world.

This grayish catfish lacks the color of the *dourada* and is reputedly not valued for food in large sizes owing to hosting parasites. In pursuing this fish, some native Brazilians bait a small fish with a hook and tie that to a rope attached to the bow of their canoe. When a large *piraíba* is hooked, it may drag the canoe for several kilometers. Today a large specimen is one weighing more than 200 pounds.

Another member of this genus, incidentally, is the commercially valuable *piramutaba (Brachyplatystoma vaillantii)*. This light gray species, which reportedly grows only to 20 pounds but is especially valued for its flesh, has been heavily exported from Brazil.

Two other significant South American catfish are the *pirarara (Phractocephalus hemeliopterus)*, a colorful and hard-fighting species, and the deep pool-dwelling *jaú (Paulicea lutkeni)*.

The *jaú* grows to 100 kilograms and 1.5 meters, and ranges from a soiled yellow to solid black in color. It is a strong species that prefers rocky bottoms and quiet water below falls and rapids. The *pirarara's* colors blend yellow, brown, and deep red, and it is noted for producing a startling snort when it is taken out of the water. This fish has a short, stout body and a broad head with a thick bony plate. The broadtailed *pirarara* is a strong fighter that has been reported to 125 pounds and is desirable table fare.

These catfish are primarily predatory carnivores; when deliberately pursued by anglers, they are caught on whole or cut fish for bait. Some other South American catfish, presumably those seldom encountered by anglers, are herbivores. The armored catfish of the Amazon, for example, eat fleshy fruits, leaves, and mollusks, especially when the forests are flooded.

Sea catfish. Although the vast majority of catfish inhabit freshwater, some live in the ocean. Sea catfish of the family Ariidae are best known for the remarkable way they incubate their eggs. The male picks up the eggs as the female lays them and holds them in his mouth until they hatch. With 50 or more pea-size eggs, this can be a mouthful. More astonishing, when the eggs hatch, the male continues to serve the needs of his progeny by permitting them to use his mouth as a place of refuge. Up to a month may pass before the swarming mass of black baby catfish set off on their own. By this time, six or eight weeks have passed since the male has had a meal. Once his appetite is triggered, he does not hesitate to gobble up even his own offspring if they foolishly swim too close.

Sea catfish are found in tropical and subtropical seas throughout the world, sometimes straying into temperate waters that are warmed in summer. The sea catfish common in the Gulf of Mexico and along the southern Atlantic coast of the U.S. is *Arius felis*. Known as a hardhead catfish or hardhead sea catfish (*bagre gato* in Spanish), it reportedly ranges as far north as Massachusetts.

About 12 inches long and rarely weighing as much as 2 pounds, this greenish sea catfish has two barbels on its upper jaw and four on the lower. The tail is deeply forked. It is generally abundant, traveling in schools of a hundred or more. It frequents estuaries, and in some areas it enters freshwater. It is most often caught from bridges and piers in passages and inland waterways. Although edible, it is not generally consumed.

The gafftopsail catfish *(Bagre marinus)* occurs in much the same range as the sea catfish but is more abundant southward through the Caribbean and off northern South America, evidently extending as far as Brazil.

This species, also known as the gafftopsail sea catfish (*bagre cacumo* in Spanish and *bagre-fita* in Portuguese) grows larger than the hardhead catfish, usually twice the size. The gafftopsail has only two barbels on the lower jaw, is bluish above and silvery white below. The gafftopsail's most distinguishing feature is its high dorsal fin, the first ray drawn into a long, slim filament. The pectoral fins also end in long filaments. As does the sea catfish, the male carries the eggs, which may be as much as an inch in diameter, in his mouth until they hatch.

Other members of the sea catfish family, consisting of roughly 40 species in all, occur in warm seas throughout the world, but the family is notably absent from European waters. Sea catfish in Brazil, generally called *bagre*, are reported to attain a maximum size of 15 kilograms.

Other catfish of note. Among the numerous catfish, there are many odd species, including some that are armored, some that are parasitic, some that are dangerous, and so forth. This section briefly reviews a few species that have some angling significance, and a few that have no angling significance but are notable for their unusual characteristics.

One of the largest of all freshwater fish, which belongs to the Siluridae family of Eurasian catfish,

---

According to a U.S. Fish and Wildlife Service survey, 35.2 million people fished in 1996; they spent $37.7 billion on trips and equipment.

is the wels *(Silurus glanis).* The wels is said to exceed 12 feet in length and weigh up to 700 pounds, although the largest reported specimen was 3 meters long and weighed 200 kilograms.

Known also as the Danube catfish, it is found in eastern Europe and northern Asia, primarily in large lakes and rivers, although it has been known to enter brackish water in the Baltic and Black Seas. It inhabits deep-water environs but is reported to feed at night on ducks, voles, crayfish, and smaller fish. Typical of the family, its body is scaleless, the anal fin is long, and there are only two pairs of barbels, one on the upper jaw and one on the lower.

Fish hobbyists know the Siluridae family best for the glass catfish *(Kryptopterus bicirrhus),* a 4-inch species native to southeastern Asia. The body is so "glassy" that it reflects light in glittering rainbow hues and is transparent enough so that, particularly in young fish, the internal organs are visible. The dorsal fin consists of a single small ray, but the exceptionally long anal fin may contain as many as 60 rays. Unlike many catfish, this species thrives on the companionship of others of its kind. In nature, it lives in small schools.

Another large catfish is *Pangasius gigas* of the Pangasiidae family. Known as the giant catfish, this species is native to Indochina and the Mekong River basin, but is now listed as rare due to overexploitation. The giant catfish is said to weigh more than 250 pounds and exceed 7 feet in length. It has a deeply forked tail, a small adipose fin, a very long anal fin, a short but high dorsal fin, and a bristling of barbels (two or three pairs) around its mouth.

Catfish of the Clariidae family are unique in possessing an expanded, lunglike cavity in front of the gills and extending along each side of the spine as a much-branched or labyrinthic structure that is well supplied with blood vessels. As a result, these catfish can breathe air, enabling them to remain out of water for long periods if their bodies stay moist. They typically inhabit fouled or stagnant water that no other fish can tolerate. This auxiliary breathing apparatus makes the front of the body thick; the tail portion is thin, flat, and, in some species, almost ribbonlike. Both the dorsal and anal fins are long and spineless, and most species do not have an adipose fin. The body is scaleless, but the skin is thick and covered with mucus, an additional feature that makes possible its long exposure to the air.

The famed walking catfish *(Clarias batrachus)* is a member of this family. A native of southeastern Asia, it was imported to the U.S. as an oddity for fish hobbyists.

Some were either set free or escaped captivity in southern Florida. With snakelike movements and by using their pectoral fins as "legs," these catfish literally walk on land. When attempts were made to poison bodies of water to kill them, the walking catfish simply moved out of the undesirable water and traveled overland to a new home, leaving the native species to die.

Similarly, when ponds dry up during the dry season or in periods of drought, walking catfish keep moving to find pools with water. As a last resort, they bury themselves in the mud at the bottom of a pool of water where, like lungfish, they manage to survive until rains come again. Aggressive, reaching a length of about 8 inches, they do not hesitate to attack fish larger than themselves. There are about a half-dozen other species of walking catfish, some from Africa and some from Asia.

Among the smallest of all catfish, the few members comprising the parasitic Trichomycteridae family have a fearsome reputation. The species most responsible for this is the candiru *(Vandellia cirrhosa).* Only about 2 inches long, this little South American catfish enters the gill cavity of larger fish to suck blood. It has been known to enter the urethra of waders or bathers urinating under water; presumably it mistakes the urea for water exhausted from gills. Once inside, it erects its spines and lodges itself. The pain is agonizing, and the fish can be removed only by surgery. The candiru burrows in sandy bottoms and when disturbed from its natural hiding place, seeks any orifice or protective situation. It is native to the Orinoco and Amazon River basins in northern South America.

Another unusual and harmful tropical species is the electric catfish *(Malapterurus electricus),* an aggressive fish of the Malapteruridae family, sometimes exceeding 3 feet in length and weighing as much as 50 pounds. It is fearless, attacking and feeding on other fish. A large electric catfish can reportedly deliver a shocking 300 to 400 volts to kill small fish or stun large ones. The initial jolt is generally followed by a series of smaller ones. In addition to serving as a weapon of defense or as a means of overcoming prey, the electrical impulses may act as a sonar of sorts for navigation in the murky tropical waters where the electric catfish lives. The electric organs are located just under the skin along the full length of the body and tail. They are derived from glandular cells in the epidermis rather than from muscle tissue as in other fish capable of generating electricity. In polarity, the electric catfish is negative toward the head and positive toward the tail; this pattern is reversed in the electric eel.

The electric catfish holds among roots and rocks in sluggish or standing water in tropical Africa along the Nile (except Lake Victoria and the rivers of East Africa north of the Zambezi River), in Lake Tanganyika, in the lower Zambezi, Pungwe, and Lower Save Rivers, and throughout the Zaire system.

Catfish senses. It is no coincidence that catfish can thrive in diverse habitats and in waters that get extremely warm and stagnant, or that they are attracted to some vile-smelling concoctions offered as angling baits. Catfish are opportunistic feeders, similar to largemouth bass, and they are especially adaptable due to exceptional sensory abilities.

Catfish are believed to primarily rely on smell, taste, and hearing to feed, but this is only partly true. Some species and populations live in clear-water environments and are capable of being effective sight feeders. If you have observed catfish in an aquarium, you have probably noticed how their eyes move and follow things that get their attention. Some species, including channel catfish, may be susceptible to lures where the water permits reasonable visibility. Generally, catfish can see fairly well, but in many of their environments, especially large rivers and reservoirs, turbid water is common if not continuous and their vision is extremely limited. In these waters, hearing, taste, and smell play more important roles than vision in locating food, and these faculties may even be aided by taste and touch.

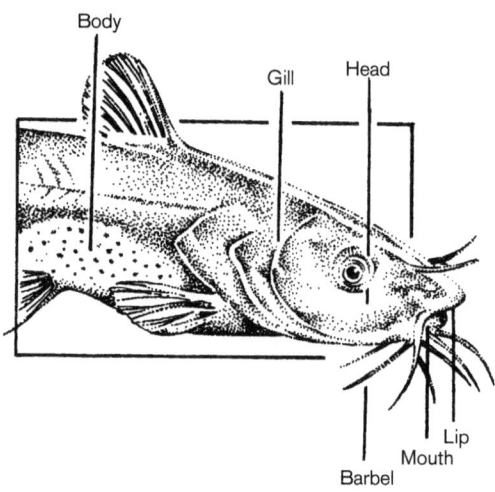

The catfish's exceptional external sensory faculties exist in each of the areas depicted above. The greatest sensitivity is in the barbels and lips.

Channel cats, blues, whites, and flatheads all have a finely developed sense of smell; bullhead have a less developed sense of smell than these species, but it is nevertheless better than that of most other fish. And like other fish, catfish smell as water enters their nares (nostril-like openings on the snout) and contacts an olfactory sac with many folds (catfish have more folds than do most other species). Catfish are first attracted by food odor; smaller fish will often feed, and taste the food, with their chin barbels before taking it. These whiskerlike appendages contain taste buds. Some catfish have taste buds all over their bodies—certain kinds can actually taste with their tails. The external taste buds greatly outnumber the internal ones, although the highest concentration of taste buds exists in the gills, barbels, and mouth. The combination of these intense senses allows catfish to be very aware of objects that produce odor, particularly prey fish, other predators, and other catfish. The distance at which they can detect odors is debatable, but some veteran catfish anglers believe that some catfish have the ability to follow a scent trail from up to 200 feet away. This may be more likely where there is current than in stillwaters.

Catfish also have excellent hearing ability. The otoliths in the inner ears are found in the bones of the skull, and these "ear bones" are connected to the air bladder. Vibrations are transmitted to the ear from the air bladder, which acts as a sounding board, allowing catfish to have greater detection of high-frequency sounds than that of many other species, including trout and bass. Low-frequency sounds are detected through the lateral-line system, a series of sensory cells running the length of both sides of the fish's body. The fish utilizes its lateral line to determine the direction of currents of water and the presence of nearby objects, as well as to sense vibrations both near and afar.

The highly developed senses of catfish work in combination to make these fish extremely adaptable and very capable of foraging effectively in places and conditions that inhibit other fish.

Angling for Catfish

As the profiles of the various bullhead and catfish indicate, these species inhabit a wide range of waters and locations. Channel catfish probably receive the greatest attention of the North American species, with proportionately less attention given to bullhead and blue catfish, followed by flathead and white catfish. Some aspects of angling for these species are uniform to all of them and some are different. One common but misunderstood element is that not all catfish are caught only on rotten baits. And not all catfish anglers smell bad, wear dirty overalls, and chew snuff. Today, catfish anglers might well fish from sleek and well-appointed boats instead of bare and battered jonboats powered by small old outboards, or they might spend considerable time wading and probing small rivers instead of lounging on the bank.

The diversity among catfish extends from species to their environment. Large catfish are generally the product of big waters, and the gargantuan specimens tend to be in the biggest river systems and in big lakes and reservoirs, especially those with abundant forage fish and in warm locales. Nevertheless, much catfishing occurs in smaller waters, particularly ponds, especially for bullhead and stocked white and channel catfish.

On the whole, anglers spend as many hours working these species after dark as they do during daylight hours. In the south, night fishing is a common practice; in the north, more anglers work this fish during daylight. But don't overlook fishing at night, as well as at dawn and dusk, when these fish are likely to be active.

Unlike most other freshwater species, catfish are the target of three distinctly different means of recreational fishing. These are noodling, setline fishing, and angling with rod and reel.

Noodling (see) involves taking fish directly by hand, which is an interesting and unique activity but not an element of sportfishing in the true sense. In setline (see) fishing, people use a line that

Anglers use a cane pole and a fly rod for small catfish on a Georgia pond.

is anchored at one point but is not connected to a hand-operated mechanical reel; it might be a trotline (see) or a simpler line attached to a limb, log, or jug, often not under the direct view and control of the person placing the line and not an instrument of sportfishing.

Fishing with rod and reel can run a gamut from cane poles for small specimens to heavy-duty levelwind reels and stout saltwater boat rods for big bruisers. For the majority of catfishing activities, anglers overmatch their tackle to the standard size of fish expected. Sometimes this is because a lot of catfishing requires bait-on-the-bottom presentations, using a heavy enough weight to keep the offering in place, and sometimes it is because of the possibility of hooking big and strong catfish in snag-laden habitat.

Catfish do not lend themselves to traditional trolling as a routine means of fishing, and very few catfish are caught in this manner. Their general bottom-hugging nature, the types of cover they are often associated with, and their general lack of midwater roaming and aggressive pursuit of forage are all unconducive to this method. In this respect, they are somewhat similar to largemouth bass. This is not to say that catfish cannot be aggressive; it is simply that trolling does not lend itself to most catfish environments. Stillfishing and drift fishing, how-ever, are the general methods of catfishing in all of their habitats, whereas casting is generally ineffective. On occasion, and in places where some species, especially channel cats, are abundant, some cast-and-retrieve fishing, especially using diving plugs or jigs tipped with baits, has merit. The tactile nature of catfish, and their general behavior, however, lends itself primarily to more passive presentation methods.

Tackle. Although in some circumstances and locations catfish are caught on flies, flycasting gear is rarely used for deliberate catfishing. Small fish in well-stocked ponds are an exception. Light spinning and spincasting tackle is particularly appropriate for the majority of catfish, especially bullhead and white catfish. For fish up to a couple of pounds, light-action outfits, short rods, and 2- to 8-pound lines are more than adequate. For variety, and in anticipation of midsize and some larger fish, light- and medium-action spinning or baitcasting gear, with 8- to 14-pound line and rods of $5^1/_2$ to 7 feet, is suitable.

The possibility of encountering large catfish (more than 15 pounds) in waters beset with thick cover, snags, and objects that a powerful fish can swim under or through and that enable it to break off, require heavier-duty tackle. For big cats, a sturdy light-duty conventional reel or medium- to heavy-duty baitcasting reel, spooled with a minimum of 17-pound line, is necessary. This should be coupled with a medium- to heavy-action rod; a shorter rod, in the 6- to 7-foot range, will suffice if there is little need for casting and you're using heavy line, but for regular casting and for cushioning light line, try a 7- to 9-footer. Line strengths used by big-cat anglers are often between 25 and 40 pounds, and some spool this onto heavy-duty levelwind reels with ample capacity.

Although this may seem like overkill, one does have to take into consideration the environment. A reservoir loaded with stumps and deadfalls and timber is a poor place to out-muscle a large catfish with light gear. And the biggest of catfish are individuals that can steam off with all of the line on a reel. Similarly, when fishing from shore in the wide environs of a tailrace, it may be necessary to use a surf casting outfit to propel a heavy weight out the necessary distance while having the line capacity to deal with the demands of proper presentation and playing fish.

Bait. If a researcher investigated all the articles ever written about the stuff that is used to catch catfish, they would probably include most of the items commonly found in a grocery store. No doubt everything from sardines to soap to pizza dough would have a recommendation and, indeed, catfish have eclectic taste. Anglers disagree greatly on which bait best attracts various species of catfish. On each sector of major waterways, there is someone who makes a home-brewed concoction that native catfish anglers swear by. Generally these contain cheese, anise oil, sour mash, ground corn, crushed shad, and sometimes a bit of rotten chicken liver. Most homemade bait works, but

According to Chinese legend, in the third century Tao Tzu Ming was fishing on a lake when a dragon surfaced from the water and carried him away to a sacred mountain.

fresh bait is usually are more productive. Items used to attract and catch the various catfish fall into these general categories: cut bait, which are pieces of dead fish; live baits; prepared bait, which includes dips, pastes, and various concoctions labeled stinkbaits; and miscellaneous bait, which include animal meat, cheese, blood, and sundry offerings.

Cut bait can include parts of various species of fish, often but not exclusively those that are present and abundant normally in the catfish's environment. Sometimes a whole dead fish is used for bait, especially in locations where there may be periodic die-offs of some species (like shad, which often happens in cold weather). Usually chunks and pieces of dead bait are used, and fished until they lose their freshness; fastidious catfish chasers with access to a lot of bait may re-arm with a new cut bait every time they reel in to check it. Fish used for cut bait include (but are not limited to) herring, gizzard shad, threadfin shad, mullet, suckers, chub, carp, shiners, smelt, and panfish, although in some locations it may not be legal to use certain of these species (particularly panfish). Dead shrimp and clams are also used for bait.

Cut bait is seldom used for bullhead, although small chunks might be tried where there are large individuals. Fresh cut bait is generally preferred, and a serious day of fishing for bigger catfish requires an ample supply of fresh cut baits (preferably just killed and not water-logged-soft and mushy).

Live bait runs a wide gamut of offerings but primarily includes fish and worms. Nightcrawlers, or even little wigglers or angle worms, are the main live bait for small catfish, especially bullhead. Most of the same fish used for cut baits are also live-bait candidates, where legal, especially herring, gizzard shad, shiners, mullet, suckers, and panfish, as well as goldfish. These bigger offerings are menu items for flatheads, blues, and channel cats. Other live bait that are used for catfish includes catalpa worms, leeches, crayfish, shrimp, hellgrammites, grasshoppers, crickets, and even frogs (a channel cat delicacy at times). Although many catfish anglers use treble hooks for live-bait fishing, a single hook (sized according to bait and fish, but running from 1/0 up to 6/0) does a good job. Preferences vary from a straight eye to an upturned eye and from a straight to an offset barb. Both the upturned eye and the offset barb help when the hook is set by presenting the hook's point at an offset angle in the fish's mouth. Although generally foreign to catfish angling, tuna circle hooks that have become popular for many saltwater bait applications may have merit.

"Prepared bait" is a pleasant and general term for a diverse bunch of doughs, pastes, dips, and general goop, some of it manufactured and sold commercially and much of it devised in repulsive home-kitchen experiments. Generally these odoriferous preparations are called stinkbait. Some are simply chunks of fish that have been marinated in some type of liquid long enough to turn them unbearably rancid; these are the crudest of preparations.

Most stinkbait is dip or moist preparations the consistency of paste or dough and can be molded and formed into shape on a hook. Dips may be between sour cream and cream cheese in consistency and include all types of smelly foods (cheese, ground chicken liver, ground oily fish, and the like) mixed with various liquids and fillers (like meal). A hooked sponge is thoroughly immersed in the dip, or a short soft-plastic ringed worm can be used as a dip holder. Paste-style stinkbait is like a dip that has been mixed with more filler and bonding agents so they can be formed into balls; pastes are fished with single or treble hooks buried in them. Stinkbait that is too loose to hold by themselves on a hook, but too firm to be a dip, can be fished in a net sack similar to the egg or spawn sacks used by river steelhead and salmon anglers, although it may be necessary to contain the bait in a small piece of plastic kitchen wrap, then poke holes in the wrap after the hook and net are secured.

All of these produce an odor that offends human beings, with pastes usually being less odiferous and rancid fish chunks being most offensive. These are especially effective on smaller catfish and are better for channel cats than blues or flatheads.

Miscellaneous bait is a catchall categorization for any of the catfish concoctions that people use that don't fit the prior molds. Perhaps the foremost of these is chicken liver, which has long been a popular offering. Frozen, rather than unfrozen or rotten, chicken liver is a popular bait for channel catfish, partly for its effectiveness and partly for its availability and general ease of use, as it lacks much preparation. Frozen liver holds well to a single hook, much longer than unfrozen new or aged liver; as it thaws, it exudes much more scent, making it more attractive. Use one section of liver (not both parts) and thrust a single hook in and out one time while the liver is still frozen.

Natural bait, whether cut or live, usually seems to be the best offering because it is what is normally found in the catfish's environment. Stinkbait, chicken liver, and assorted nonnatural items are not resident food, although it is possible in heavily fished locations that catfish can be conditioned to such foreign items if enough people use them. For larger fish (and obviously "large" varies with the locality and species), natural bait is generally a better item, although many catfish aficionados have distinct preferences for one of these categories over the others. It is disputed whether the more aromatic offerings are best in current or stillwater; in the latter environment, chumming is another scenario entirely. Dead bait is usually fished without a float, whereas live bait is fished either way. In big reservoirs, fishing a lively bait deep with a slip float is recommended. Natural bait should be changed often to be most effective, and live bait should indeed be lively.

Bullhead and small catfish tend to mouth and nibble bait, whereas larger fish may take it more readily. Blue and flathead catfish take bait more forcefully than do channel and white catfish, sometimes really nailing it.

Techniques. For the most part, fishing on or close to the bottom with some form of bait is the most reliable way to hook catfish. They will take artificials, but not nearly as well as some anglers might like, and lures are much less effective than baits. Flatheads are fairly susceptible to lures, and crankbaits are most productive. Channel cats are often caught by anglers who have tipped a jig with a minnow or a lively piece of nightcrawler. Some largemouth bass anglers, fishing with a jig-and-pork combo, have latched onto catfish. In big impoundments, anglers will catch some catfish while trolling plugs or while using jigging spoons or bucktail jigs, usually when seeking striped bass. Cats have even been known to run down schools of shad or river shiners just like walleye. Anglers are often surprised to land a channel catfish on a minnow-style plug while angling for bass or walleye. These are generally incidental catches; success seldom comes from deliberately casting lures for catfish. Stillfishing and drifting with some form of bait is the way to go.

As for bottom fishing, catfish will suspend, as mentioned earlier, and are more likely to roam at night to actively feed. This activity can take them away from the bottom. Catfish have been known to chase schools of bait (blues do this occasionally), but for the most part they are a less aggressive and more deliberate bottom or near-bottom feeder. To have continual success with these fish, they must be sought near or on the bottom of rivers and lakes.

A great deal of catfishing occurs in rivers, the natural habitat of most catfish species. Other popular locations include reservoirs, ponds, small lakes, and the backwaters connected to rivers, so strategies vary according to habitat. Bullhead fishing, for example, which focuses on small waters and stillfishing with worms, is a fairly straightforward bait-and-wait affair, but angling for channel cats is different. There are overlapping tactics and strategies, however.

In rivers, look to current cuts, stream mouths, gravel and rock bottoms, deep-cut riverbanks, shallow riffle areas with a hard bottom, river channels, and pools below riffles.

Deep holes or pools present good river catfishing opportunities. Channel cats work up into shallow water to feed, and move back into deeper water. Although some channel catfish are caught during daylight hours directly from within a hole itself, they are best caught as they move into the shallower areas upstream from the hole. This movement, throughout most of the season, occurs just prior to sundown and lasts for an hour or so after dark.

Flatheads, on the other hand, may refrain from feeding throughout the day and then begin foraging at dark. Unlike channel cats, flatheads venture only partway out of the deep hole to feed. If hole depth is 20 feet and the upstream area is 12 feet, a flathead may work only into 16 feet of water to feed, whereas a channel cat will work into the shallowest upstream point.

Obviously, holes and pools differ from place to place. Some are much longer than others, some deeper, some have more cover. Catfish are generally not found in the runs below a pool, and some pools taper so gradually into a run that it is hard to tell where the run actually starts. Cover, especially boulders near the head of the pool, is a likely place for catfish. Cover includes logs and fallen or sunken trees, which are likely places to get snagged but which frequently harbor catfish. If these and other objects slow fast current and provide a comfortable holding spot for catfish, they will probably serve as feeding stations, especially in deeper water. When fishing holes or pools, start at the end of a riffle and the top end of the pool; be careful to fish the head of the pool first, especially if there's cover. Then move down through the pool to the tail end, fishing any cover or snags as you get to them.

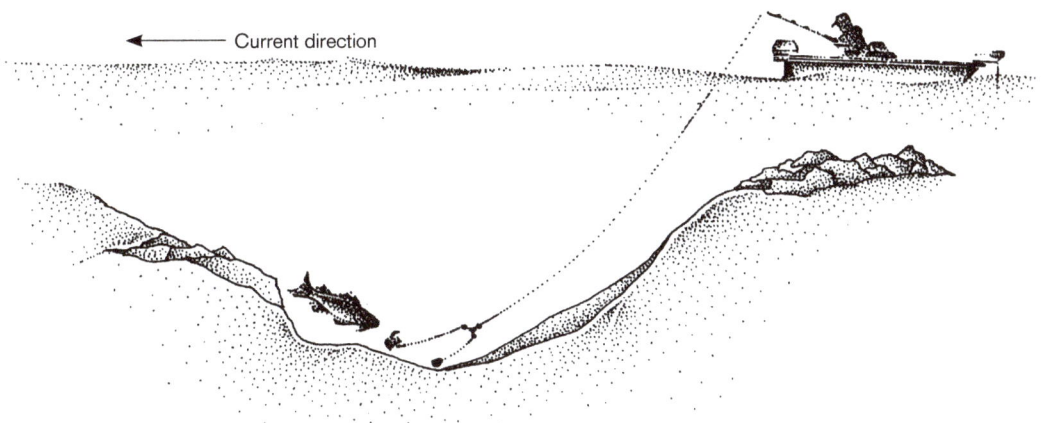

Catfish in rivers typically linger in deep holes and are best approached from upcurrent. A three-way bait rig is a good choice for this situation.

Sluggish rivers provide a multitude of wing dams and navigational structures, and catfish—especially flatheads—prefer to hold below these areas. Wing dams, in particular, are a favorite place for young individuals. Older, larger fish are more apt hold below a dam, lingering below open, churning gate waters, where dead, stunned, and mutilated fish are easily snatched up by the waiting fish.

In rivers with wing dams, anglers can harvest many channel and flathead catfish around riprap near these structures. In spring, they are found directly below the structure and close to it. Later, in warm weather, catfish will move up and around the wing dam and position themselves upstream from it.

Wing dams are man-made structures placed in large river systems to divert current flow toward the center channel. They consist of broken rock and are formed like a solid rock dock bed. In most cases, water runs over wing dams all the time, being deeper in the spring. On all wing dams, one end is anchored to the shoreline. Channel cats and large flatheads feed at these wing dams immediately after sundown. The sides of these hard structures are literally alive with crayfish and baitfish at sunset and during the first hour thereafter.

Catfish hold downstream from hydro dams where there is a dugout area followed by a hump. Constructed of hard material forced downstream with the current, the hump provides an ideal staging area for gamefish. The hump may come within 6 to 10 feet of the surface before falling off into the depths downstream; there the water may be 45 to 65 feet deep. Most of the channel catfish will be found in this area, as will trophy blue and flathead catfish. The hump will vary in form, but most are oval or egg-shaped. Look for channel cats to hold along the upstream sides. Flatheads and blue cats hold downstream from the hump.

Below many hydro dams, there is also an area of shoreline riprap that attracts catfish, which spawn here in small pockets and swirling eddies. Here, in early summer, along the outer edges in 5 to 8 feet of water, catfish feed on crayfish when they shed their shells.

Along this riprap you can catch catfish by walking from shore along the riprap structure downstream while your float and baits drift with the current. Use a slip float to keep the bait 3 to 4 feet deep; for bait try a black leech (spawning catfish love leeches) on a No. 8 hook, with BB-size split shot 6 inches above the hook. The leech hangs 3 to 4 feet below the bobber while drifting just off bottom. In some areas, where riprap literally runs for miles, an angler will walk his bobber three to four blocks before returning to his starting place to repeat the procedure. Later in the season, catfish move deeper off the riprap. Eventually they hold at a point where rock riprap and soft river bottom meet. Here they are best caught using standard fixed-place methods of bottom fishing.

When fishing areas other than the tailrace section of rivers, it's the mobile catfish angler who has the best chance of producing. Sitting on a hole and waiting for catfish to come and take a bait may deliver some success, and is a common means of catfishing, but there's no reason why catfish anglers shouldn't take a page out of the bass, stream trout, and walleye angler's book of methods by fishing likely places more intensively and aggressively, then moving on to look for more likely places. This enables an angler to cover a lot of ground and to look for fish rather than sitting and waiting for the quarry to get active or to come calling.

Keep in mind that river and stream catfish always feed into the current, and take advantage of their keen sense of smell, approaching them from above. Detecting a strike is a key to success, especially with smaller fish and with the particularly adept bait-nibbling channel cat. It's best to position yourself directly upstream of the area to be fished and to cast your offering directly downstream to the target. Once the rig rests on bottom in proper position, reel in slack line. This affords direct contact between sinker, trailing bait, and rod tip. Current-flow shifts will lessen and increase pressure on the rod tip at times. Keep constant pressure evenly distributed between the rod tip and bait by lifting and lowering the rod tip as pressure decreases and increases. When a catfish picks up the bait and moves slightly forward with it, a small vacuum around the bait is created in its mouth. The rod tip will slack off dramatically as the catfish crushes down. At this moment, drop the rod tip, reel hard, and set the hook.

Naturally, when some fish, including bigger ones, take the bait forcefully and move off, you should just point the rod at the fish, engage the gears, reel quickly, and set the hook. But, many times you need to detect that almost imperceptible pickup that creates slack line. Many people don't notice the slight slack in the line when the fish has food in a closed mouth and is confirming taste, and miss their opportunity because the fish then moves, detects something (the point of the hook or line tension), and then opens its mouth while the angler is just then setting the hook. In effect, the angler feels the "strike" when the fish is just letting go of the bait, and sets the hook when its mouth has opened.

If you simply cannot get the hang of strike detection (which many people cannot, because a common complaint in catfishing is missing strikes), and you've been hiding your hook inside bait, then fish with the hook more exposed. Catfish aren't dainty or ultrasensitive feeders and may not discern the hardness of a small light object like a hook (although the hook point is a different story). So try fishing your bait with the hook exposed; run it once through a cut bait, for example, rather than burying it inside, and make sure the point is exposed when any bait is impaled. This may induce more snags and lost terminal gear, but it also could produce many more landed fish, especially if you focus on setting the hook soon after getting a pickup.

Many anglers use egg sinkers on their bait rig, which allow catfish to run with the offering. There is some merit to this, as slow-water cats will pick up a bait and move sideways with it, mouth it a number of times before swallowing, and stay there. This presents good conditions for using an egg sinker. But where there is any significant current flow, and when fish are especially finicky, a bell sinker on a slip rig or three-way rig, or a bottom-walking sinker, may work better. Sinker weight will vary, depending on water conditions, from $5/8$ ounce to 2 ounces. Some conditions may require still heavier weight. The deeper and faster the flow of water, the heavier the sinker needed.

You may need to experiment with the length of leader from weight to bait, as well as with the distance fished behind the boat. Many people fish fairly close to the boat because of the general turbidity of water, but a longer length of line (120 to 150 feet) presents a different angle of line-to-bottom bait, and may be more effective at drawing pickups.

In lakes, reservoirs, and ponds, tactics vary a bit. Naturally, in big impoundments there is likely to be good catfishing in the tailrace water below the dam, and in the river (or rivers) that feed the reservoir. Current flow may vary with seasons and with demand for water, and levels and flow can change as water is stored or released, so these factors have an impact on fishing, although methods are generally similar to those already noted.

In big impoundments, places to focus your efforts are varied, but old riverbeds and channels are especially important. In these places, concentrate on the curves, bends, and deepest holes, and especially where two channels come together. Ledges, or any place where the lake bottom drops off to deep water out in the main lake, also produce catfish, as do humps that drop fairly abruptly to deep water. Flats may have catfish earlier in the season when the water is warming, and points are also worth trying but are often sporadic producers. The area near the dam, especially the face of it (if fishing there is permissible—many are cordoned off), and the riprap and boulders along the face can concentrate fish, including spawners.

Catfish are regularly caught at the mouths of tributaries, including small feeder creeks, and at the mouths of coves, backwater ponds, sloughs, and other areas that provide a funneling point for travel. Some anglers blanket the mouths of such areas with multiple baits to ensure getting the attention of cruising fish. Steep rocky timbered banks, especially in coves, and the back of coves, sloughs, and backwater ponds where there are stumps and timber along a sharply sloped bank, merit fishing effort.

Bullhead and small catfish favor soft-bottom backwaters and ponds with ample submerged vegetation. In ponds or small lakes where there is a weedline, bullhead are likely to be found along the deeper edge of the weeds, but in many places there

Big catfish are often found on the bottom of turbulent water below dam tailraces, such as this one on the Red River in Manitoba.

is no such delineation, and most weeds are thick and submerged in varying depths of water. In this case, look for them in the deeper portions, fishing your bait right above thick bottom-hugging weeds or on the bottom amidst sparser weeds. An inlet is a good place to concentrate efforts, as is the deep water near a dam if there is one, and also any areas that might funnel fish.

Fishing in ponds for catfish is often a sit-and-wait situation; in nonstocked ponds it usually takes time for cats to get to your bait. When fishing from shore, the question is whether to use a float with a bottom rig. Where there are bottom weeds, you'll probably need to use a fixed- or slip-float rig. When fishing from a boat, there is the added question of whether to drift or anchor. In stillwater, especially big impoundments, drift fishing is attractive to fish that are active and aggressive, and tends to produce more smaller fish; anchoring does not allow an angler to cover a lot of water, but it may help produce a bigger fish. In ponds, live baits (like nightcrawlers for small fish) are the main offering for bullhead; cut baits and stinkbaits are popular for catfish and blues. In impoundments, however, live or cut baits (shad or herring mostly), fished off the bottom, are the main tickets, and these can be fished on various rigs.

Of the various rigs used to pursue catfish in both rivers and lakes, certainly the most common ones are the slip rig and the three-way rig. The latter features a three-way swivel with a 5- to 8-inch drop line tied to a bell sinker, and a bait line of varying length tied to a hook. A slip rig usually employs a barrel or egg sinker (sometimes a sliding bell sinker), which slides on the fishing line above a swivel, and a variable-length leader attached to the lower end of the swivel. The slip rig gives the fish some slack line so it doesn't detect trouble when it picks up the bait. These rigs differ in one important way: The slip rig lets a fish run with a bait, whereas the three-way does not.

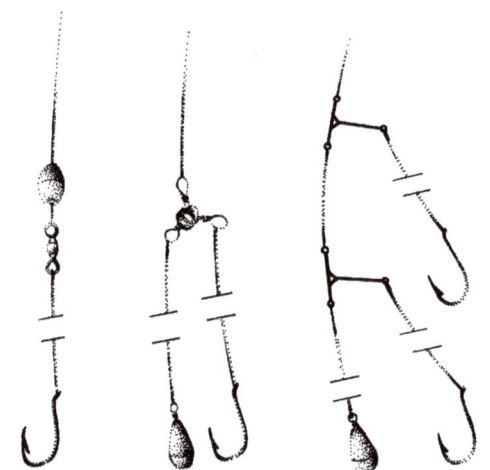

Shown from left to right are three common baitfishing arrangements used for catfish: the slip rig, the three-way rig, and the double-bait (or high-low) rig.

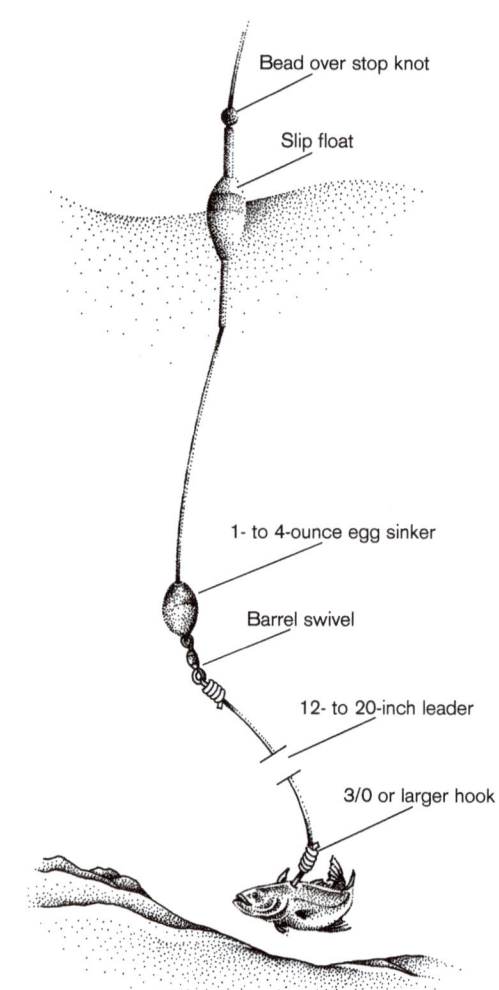

A live-bait float rig for large catfish.

If you're paying attention, there's no need to let a catfish run with the bait, nor is it necessary to delay setting the hook. In fact, by waiting you are likely to hook the fish too deep, which makes hook removal more difficult (and may make rerigging necessary); in most cases, a deeply hooked fish won't survive (which is fine if you intend to keep it but not if you don't or can't). For this reason, a three-way rig seems better; it seems even more useful when you consider that it doesn't snag in current as frequently as a slip rig.

A commonly employed third rig is a simple baited hook with a split shot placed roughly 8 to 15 inches above the hook on the fishing line. Fished like this, it's a snag getter in current, but when fished under a float—in both rivers and lakes—it has merit for drifting. You can also double-up on bait with a two-bait rig; in this setup, a bell sinker is used, and the baits are separated—one on the bottom and the other above the bottom—to avoid tangling.

The length of leader used in these rigs, or the length from shot or weight to hook, is subject to conditions, current, flow, and the angler's preference. Often the choice is a matter of habit. Many anglers stick with a midrange length of 10 to 15 inches, whereas some use leaders up to 3 feet long. Others prefer a leader that is just a few inches long. In heavy current, the greater the distance from weight to hook, the more the bait is likely to move, so this arrangement could produce more hangups than it would in lighter current. When a live baitfish is positioned on or close to the bottom, the bait's movement is enhanced and proper depth is achieved with a moderate length of 10 to 18 inches between the weight and the hook.

Although extensive information about handling and landing fish *(see)* is contained elsewhere, it is worth mentioning here that an angler must be careful when handling catfish, especially small ones that wriggle continuously. Catfish have sharp pectoral and dorsal spines that can inflict pain and cause wounds that can easily become infected. To avoid any chance of sticking yourself, approach small fish from their underside, placing your thumb against the back side of one pectoral fin and your index or middle finger against the back side of the other pectoral fin. Grasp the fish firmly with your palm across its stomach. The fish will be securely held and can be safely unhooked.

CATFISH, BLUE *Ictalurus furcatus.*
Other names—catfish, chucklehead cat, white catfish, forktail cat, Mississippi cat, Fulton cat, blue Fulton cat, great blue cat, silver cat, blue channel cat, highfin blue cat.

This is a popular species within its range and valued for its flesh as well as sporting value. The blue catfish is a strong, stubborn fighter. It can grow quite large, which enhances its appeal. It is considered good table fare and is widely pursued by commercial fishermen for the market. Its flesh is white, delicate, and tender, especially in smaller specimens.

Identification. Blue catfish are generally blue gray or slate blue and possess no spots or other markings, although they may be almost pale blue or silvery; their flanks taper in color to the belly, which is light gray or white. They have a deeply forked tail, and the anal fin has a straight margin. They resemble channel catfish *(see: catfish, channel)* and when small are most easily confused with that relative. Larger blue cats have a distinct humped-back appearance, with the hump occurring at and in front of the dorsal fin; their head is generally larger than that of a channel cat, and their body is less sleek. They can be distinguished from channel cats by their longer and straight-edged anal fin, which has 30 to 35 rays. In smaller specimens, a distinguishing characteristic is their lack of black body spots. Internally, the blue catfish has three chambers in the swim bladder, whereas the channel cat has two.

Like the channel catfish and the little-known yaqui catfish of Mexico, the blue cat has a deeply forked tail, a characteristic that distinguishes these three from the flathead catfish and bullhead, and to some degree also from the white catfish *(see: catfish, white)*, which has a moderately forked tail. As with other catfish, channel cats have heavy, sharp pectoral and dorsal spines, as well as long mouth barbels.

Size/Age. Blue cats are capable of growing to gargantuan sizes but are rarely found at the upper limits of their capabilities. Most anglers catch blues in the 5- to 20-pound range. Fish in the 20- to 50-pound class are not uncommon in waters with a good population of fish, but blue catfish in that range are infrequently caught and specimens exceeding that size are rare. The all-tackle world record for the species is a 109-pound, 4-ounce fish caught at Santee Cooper in South Carolina in 1991. A 116-pounder caught on a trotline was reportedly taken at Lake Texoma, Texas, in 1985, and in 1879 a 150-pounder from the Mississippi River near St. Louis was found at a local market and shipped to the U.S. National Museum. Historical accounts describe 100-pounders at the turn of the twentieth century, and individuals between 200 and 400 pounds have been reported but undocumented, perhaps being more lore than likelihood.

There is similar haziness concerning the blue cat's growth and longevity. Several scientific reports indicate that these fish grow up to 14 years of age, and they have been reported to live to 21 years, but greater longevity for the biggest specimens is evidently possible.

Distribution. Blue cats are native to the Mississippi, Missouri, and Ohio River basins in the central and eastern United States, extending north into South Dakota and south into Mexico and northern Guatemala. Dams and commercial harvest are among the factors that have affected their population and perhaps their size in some parts of their native range. They have been introduced with good success into some large river systems outside of that range, most notably in the Santee Cooper waters of South Carolina. They are now most abundant in the deep, warm waters of the South.

Habitat. Blue catfish inhabit rivers, streams, lakes, reservoirs, and ponds but are primarily a fish of big rivers and big lakes/reservoirs. They have been introduced into smaller lakes and ponds but seldom attain large sizes in such places. This species prefers the deep areas of large rivers, swift chutes, and pools with swift currents. Like the channel catfish, they prefer locations with good current over bottoms of rock, gravel, or sand.

Spawning behavior. Blue catfish spawn in the spring or early summer when the water temperature is between 70° and 75°F. Nests are constructed by one or both parents, usually among crevices and holes under logs and trees and in undercut banks. Secluded and dark places are often preferred.

Food and feeding habits. Blue catfish evidently eat most anything they can catch; their diet includes assorted fish, crayfish, aquatic insects, and clams. Herring and gizzard shad are part of their diet, especially when the catfish are larger and in places where these are abundant. Blue cats primarily feed on or near the bottom, and they are principally nocturnal foragers.

Angling. Blue cats are primarily caught by anglers bottom fishing with live or dead baits and with assorted stinkbaits. They are a strong fish that digs in; in larger sizes they are seldom immediately subdued. For in-depth angling details, *see Catfish.*

Blue Catfish

Channel Catfish

CATFISH, CHANNEL *Ictalurus punctatus.*
Other names—catfish, river catfish, fiddler, blue channel catfish, Great Lakes catfish, willow catfish, spotted catfish, forked-tail catfish, lady catfish.

The most widely distributed of all freshwater catfish, the channel cat is a significant component of recreational angling efforts as well as a mainstay of commercial fishing; its tender, white, and nutritious flesh is highly valued as table fare. It has been stocked widely in lakes and ponds, and provides the backbone of catfish farming activities. In some states, the sporty channel cat is ranked at or near the top among all species in angling popularity. Channel catfish have the potential to attain large sizes, although less gargantuan than other species, but their general willingness to strike baits, their wide distribution, and their high food esteem primarily account for their popularity.

Identification. Channel catfish are often recognized at a glance, owing to their deeply forked tails and small irregular spots on the sides. The spots may not be present in all specimens but generally are obvious in smaller individuals. These pigmented spots are most noticeable on younger fish, and obscure on older ones. Blue catfish *(see: catfish, blue)* also have a forked tail, but no spots, and the same is true for the yaqui catfish (*Ictalurus pricei;* a species in the Yaqui River drainage of Mexico). Channel cats are more slender than other catfish, perhaps owing to their native riverine existence, and they have a relatively small head. They are distinguished from white and blue catfish by their 24 to 29 anal fin rays.

The body of a channel catfish is pale blue to pale olive with a bit of silvery tint, but the color variation is subject to location and water conditions. Male channel cats during the spawning season may be entirely black dorsally, and other channel cats may be dark blue with little or no spotting, or uniformly light blue or silvery like the blue catfish *(see: catfish, blue)* or white catfish *(see: catfish, white).* Another feature distinguishing them from a blue catfish is the anal fin; this is shorter and more rounded on a channel catfish than on a blue catfish.

Like other catfish, channel cats have heavy, sharp pectoral and dorsal spines, as well as long mouth barbels.

Size/Age. The maximum age for these fish varies by latitude; some fisheries sources report a maximum longevity of 15 to 20 years, although it is believed it can exceed 20 years. Those commonly caught weigh from 1 to 7 pounds; fish exceeding 15 pounds are infrequent, and a 20-pounder would be considered extremely large. The all-tackle world-record specimen, a fish caught in 1964, weighed 58 pounds.

Distribution. Channel cats exist in freshwater throughout most of the United States and parts of southern Canada and northeastern Mexico. In the U.S., they are most abundant in the central region east to the Appalachian Mountains, and sparser on

A channel catfish from the Assiniboine River, Manitoba.

the West and East Coasts, where they are present mostly through introduction.

Habitat. The channel catfish inhabits rivers, streams, lakes, reservoirs, and ponds. Of all the catfish, the channel cat shows the greatest preference for clear, flowing waters, although it does equally well in lakes and ponds. It prefers clean bottoms of sand, rubble, or gravel in large lakes and rivers. Although it tolerates some amount of current, it is more likely to inhabit warm, quiet, slow-moving areas.

Spawning behavior. Channel catfish spawn in the spring or early summer when the water temperature is between 70° and 85°F. Nests are constructed by one or both parents, sometimes over open bottom but more likely among crevices and holes under logs and trees and in undercut banks. Secluded and dark places are often preferred. The male guards the eggs and aerates them, and has been reported to eat some of the eggs during incubation, although it guards the young until they disperse. Ten-inch females may lay only 2,000 eggs, whereas fish over 30 inches long may lay 20,000 eggs.

Food and feeding habits. Channel catfish are primarily but not exclusively bottom feeders. They are omnivorous and consume insects, crayfish, clams, snails, crabs, fish eggs, and assorted small fish, including sunfish, darters, shiners, and gizzard shad, plus a variety of plants.

Angling. The vast majority of channel catfish are caught by bottom anglers, but these fish sometimes linger on or near the surface, as well as at mid-depths. They are strong and provide a good fight on light tackle, although the smaller specimens are often overwhelmed by heavy-tackle users. Most anglers use some form of bait, and many find that channel cats prefer live baits over dead baits. For in-depth angling details, *see Catfish.*

CATFISH, FLATHEAD *Pylodictus olivaris.*

Other names—mud cat, muddy, shovelhead, shovelnose, yellow cat, appaloosa, goujon, johnnie cat, pied cat, Morgan cat.

A common and large-growing species, the flathead is one of the ugliest members of the freshwater catfish clan. Nevertheless, large specimens are commonly caught, and the fish provides a good struggle on hook and line. It is important both for commercial and recreational use, and produces good table fare when taken from clean environments.

Identification. The flathead catfish is distinctive in appearance and not easily confused with any other species. It has a squared, rather than forked, tail, with a long body and large flattened head. Medium to large specimens are rather pot-bellied and have wide heads and beady eyes. With their distinctly flat-looking oval shape, the eyes accentuate the flatness of the head, and the lower jaw further accentuates this trait by protruding beyond the upper jaw. Compared to that of other catfish species, the anal fin of the flathead is short along its base, possessing 14 to 17 fin rays.

Flathead color varies greatly with environment, and sometimes within the same environment, but is generally mottled with varying shades of brown and yellow on the sides, tapering to a lighter or whitish mottling on the belly. As with other catfish, flatheads have heavy, sharp pectoral and dorsal spines, as well as long mouth barbels.

Size/Age. Flathead catfish are a large and fairly quick-growing species, especially in the southern and warmer parts of their range. Most anglers encounter flatheads weighing from several pounds to 10 or 15 pounds; fish up to 20 pounds not uncommon, and fish to 50 pounds are a possibility in better waters. Many of the state records for flathead are in the 60- to 80-pound range, and the all-tackle world record, established in Kansas in 1998, is a 121-pounder. Flatheads do grow larger, however; Texas produced a 122-pounder caught on a trotline, and Arkansas has reported flatheads up to 139 pounds. The upper limits are generally unknown, although this species reportedly does not reach the maximum size of the blue catfish *(see: catfish, blue).* The chances of catching a really big flathead are better than those of catching a blue catfish, as the former species has a wider range and because more large flatheads seem to be available.

Flatheads have been reported to attain 30 pounds at less than 10 years of age, and presumably the largest specimens are 20 to perhaps 30 years old, although there is scant information on

Flathead Catfish

A flathead catfish from Lake Marion, South Carolina.

Food and feeding habits. Like its brethren, the flathead is omnivorous and opportunistic, and consumes diverse and available foods. Flathead catfish are primarily but not exclusively bottom feeders and consume insects, crayfish, clams, and assorted small fish, including sunfish, shiners, and shad. Adults consume larger prey, including bullhead, gizzard shad, and carp, and reportedly some terrestrial animals that have the misfortune of finding themselves in the water. Live fish are popular baits for flatheads, more so than other catfish species, as these fish are more reluctant to consume old and smelly bait. Although not exclusively nocturnal, flatheads are more active at night and may spend the day inactive in deep water or under cover. At night they may move shallower and feed at different levels.

Angling. Flatheads are popular with catfish anglers in large lakes and rivers and provide a strong and stubborn deep-digging fight. It takes time to subdue larger individuals, which are pursued with heavy tackle, especially because they exist in snag-filled environs. Bottom fishing with some form of natural or prepared baits is widely practiced, although live baits are very popular, especially for larger specimens. For in-depth angling details, see *Catfish*.

their absolute longevity. A Texas flathead that was tagged at 1.76 pounds was recaptured many years later when it weighed 31 pounds; analysis showed it to be 12 years old.

Distribution. Flatheads are native to the lower Great Lakes and the Mississippi, Missouri, and Ohio River basins from southern North Dakota to western Pennsylvania and south to northern Mexico, reaching as far east as the western tip of the Florida Panhandle. They are widely dispersed within that range and have been transplanted successfully well beyond this.

Habitat. This species is primarily found in large bodies of water, especially reservoirs and their tributaries, and big rivers and their tributaries. In rivers, they prefer deep pools where the water is slow, and depressions or holes, such as those that exist in eddies and adjacent to bridge pilings. They are also commonly found in tailraces below dams. Their chosen habitat often has a hard bottom, sometimes mixed with driftwood or timber. In large reservoirs, they are usually found deep, often in old river beds, at the junction of submerged channels, and near the headwater tributary.

Spawning behavior. Flathead catfish spawn in the spring or early summer when the water temperature is between 70° and 80°F. Nests are constructed by one or both parents, usually among crevices and holes under logs and trees and in undercut banks. As with other catfish, secluded and dark places are often preferred, and there is often a log or tree or other object at the nest site. The male guards the eggs and aerates them, and then guards the young until they disperse.

CATFISH, GAFFTOPSAIL *Bagre marinus.*

Other names—bandera, sailboat cat, gafftopsail sea catfish, gafftop cat, tourist trout; Portuguese: *bagre-fita;* Spanish: *bagre cacumo.*

This sea catfish is a common catch by both commercial fishermen and recreational anglers in the Gulf Coast, especially between April and August. Its dark, tender, lean meat is popular as table fare and has a moderate flavor.

Identification. The gafftopsail catfish has a steel-blue dorsal fin, silvery ventral fins, and a robust body with a depressed broad head featuring a few flattened barbels. The dorsal and pectoral fins have greatly elongated spines.

Size/Age. Mature gafftopsails grow to 36 inches and 10 pounds. Average small fish weigh less than a pound to $1\frac{1}{2}$ pounds and are 17 inches long. The maximum age is unknown.

Distribution. These fish range along the western Atlantic coast from Cape Cod to Panama and throughout the Gulf of Mexico, being abundant along Louisiana and Texas. They are absent from most of the West Indies and Caribbean Islands

Gafftopsail Catfish

but are present in western Cuba, and extend to Venezuela and possibly as far south as Brazil.

Habitat. Gafftopsails prefer deeper channels, particularly brackish water in bays and estuaries with sandy bottoms of high organic content. They prefer water temperatures between 68° to 95°F.

Life history/Behavior. Gafftopsail catfish move in large schools and migrate from bays and estuaries to shallow open waters of the Gulf of Mexico in winter. This movement and migration in gulf coastal and estuarine waters is related to spawning activity and environmental conditions. Spawning takes place in the waters of inshore mud flats between April and July, and has some unusual characteristics.

Gafftopsails reach sexual maturity at the age of two and are between 10 and 11 inches in length at the time. They have low fecundity, producing just 20 to 64 eggs per female; their eggs are believed to be the largest of all eggs produced by bony fish. Males carry the eggs and young in their mouths for 11 to 13 weeks until they are about 3 inches long; as many as 55 young have been reportedly carried in this manner at a time.

Food and feeding habits. Crabs, shrimp, and various small fish make up their diet, but like all catfish, gafftopsails have broad dietary interests.

Angling. Gafftopsail catfish are caught by some for their food value and by others as cut baits for angling for other species. They are primarily caught on live and cut baits, and occasionally on lures, including jigs and plugs.

For more angling information, *see Catfish*.

CATFISH, GOLDEN
The golden catfish is a South American catfish, also known as *dourada*.
See: Catfish.

CATFISH, HARDHEAD
The hardhead catfish is a sea catfish.
See: Catfish.

CATFISH, SEA
See: Catfish.

CATFISH, TIGER
The tiger catfish is a shovelnose catfish of South America, also known as sorubim.
See: Catfish.

CATFISH, WALKING
A walking catfish that uses its pectoral fins as "legs," which enables it to walk on land.
See: Catfish.

CATFISH, WHITE *Ameiurus catus*.
Other names—catfish.

White catfish are a common and popular fish with more limited range than other catfish species, and with commercial as well as recreational value. They have been successfully stocked in pay-to-fish ponds and are also cultivated for commercial bulk harvest. Their flesh is white and fine, and they make excellent eating, especially when caught from clean environments.

Identification. The white catfish looks somewhat like a cross between a channel cat *(see: catfish, channel)* and a bullhead *(see)*, owing to its slightly forked tail, broad head, and squat body. Midsize specimens are often thought to be huge bullhead. The white catfish has a moderately forked tail, which distinguishes it from flathead catfish *(see: catfish, flathead)* and bullhead, whose tails are not forked. Its anal fin is rounded along the edge and has 19 to 23 fin rays, fewer than in either the blue catfish *(see: catfish, blue)* or channel cat. Without close inspection, it could be confused with other catfish, although it doesn't possess the spots seen on young channel catfish. This fish is olive gray or slate gray on the head, and bluish gray or slate gray on its backs and sides, tapering to a white belly. As with other catfish, the white cat has heavy, sharp pectoral and dorsal spines, as well as long mouth barbels; its chin barbels are white.

White Catfish

Size/Age. White catfish are smaller than their blue, channel, and flathead brethren, but may grow larger than bullhead. The all-tackle world record for this species is a Florida fish that weighed 18 pounds, 4 ounces, but a 22-pounder has been reported from California. These are the known upper limits for this species, but it may grow larger. Most white catfish are small, averaging 10 to 14 inches, and are often confused with bullhead. They are a relatively slow-growing fish, reaching sexual maturity at three to four years. They have been reported to live 14 years but may get older.

Distribution. The native range of white catfish is freshwater and slightly brackish water of rivers along the Atlantic coast from southern New York to Florida. It exists along the Gulf Coast from Florida to Texas, and has been introduced to some inland waters in the eastern and western parts of the United States, including several New England states, plus Oregon and Nevada; it is well established in California.

Habitat. White catfish inhabit the silty bottom areas of slow-moving streams and rivers, as well as ponds, lakes, and the low-salinity portions of tidal estuaries. They generally avoid the swift water of large rivers and do not thrive in weedy or muddy shallow ponds.

Spawning behavior. This species spawns in spring and early summer depending on latitude, and its spawning behavior is generally similar to that of the bullhead. The parents build a nest on sand or gravel substrate, usually near shore and often in places associated with some form of sheltering cover; spawning occurs when the water reaches approximately 70°F, and the parents both guard the eggs and young.

Food and feeding habits. White catfish have a broad appetite and consume aquatic insects, crayfish, clams, snails, mussels, fish eggs, assorted small fish, and some aquatic plants. Adults primarily feed on fish and are active at night, although they are less nocturnal than other catfish.

Angling. Where they exist, white catfish are fairly abundant and aggressive, making them good targets for anglers, particularly bottom fishing enthusiasts. These fish produce a good fight on light tackle, although the smaller specimens are often overwhelmed by heavy-tackle users. Most people fish with some form of weighted bait. For in-depth angling details, *see Catfish.*

CATHODE-RAY RECORDER
A sonar device using a cathode-ray tube.
See: Sonar.

CAUDAL FIN
The tail fin, or the fin at the rear of the fish. The fleshy section connecting the caudal fin to the end of the body is called the caudal peduncle *(see).*
See: Fish.

CAUDAL PEDUNCLE
The fleshy tail end of the body of a fish between the anal and caudal fins. On some fish the caudal peduncle is rigid and provides a convenient "handle" of sorts for holding fish.
See: Caudal Fin; Fish.

CAYMAN ISLANDS
Just a one-hour flight from Miami, Florida, and well out in the western Caribbean, the three-island Caymans nevertheless remain relatively obscure to most big-game and inshore anglers. Yet the Caymans offer excellent light-tackle big-game fishing, plenty of flats with bonefish and tarpon, and reef fishing for numerous species, all on a year-round basis.

Perhaps the general lack of sportfishing attention given to the Caymans—which consist of Grand Cayman Island and the much smaller Little Cayman and Cayman Brac Islands—is due to their proximity to Cuba; Cayman Brac is less than 100 miles from Cuba's south shore islands, and Grand Cayman is about 200 miles away. Private boaters from the United States don't just run here for short periods, as they do out in the Bahamas.

The Caymans are not without visitors, however. With at least one beach classified among the best in the Caribbean, they attract many sunbathers and water-sports enthusiasts. And with outstanding reefs and tropical waters, the Caymans are explored underwater by thousands of divers each year.

The divers know well what some big-game anglers have learned by watching their sonar equipment: The bottom of the ocean drops off a long, long way just outside these islands. In fact, the word *dropoff* doesn't begin to explain what happens here, because these islands are mountains rising from the sea, part of the Cayman Ridge and a range of submarine mountains that extend all the way to the Misteriosa Bank.

Described as a "layer cake of life zones," the trenchlike dropoff outside Grand Cayman Island is known as The Wall. Here, the inshore reef plummets to 800 feet a few hundred yards from the island, and slopes to 3,000 feet within 3 miles. Beyond that it drops below 20,000 feet into the Cayman Trench, which is the deepest hole in the Caribbean.

If this sounds like the makings of big-game country, especially blue marlin and tuna, it is. With the blue water of the Windward Passage enveloping these islands en route to becoming the Yucatan Current, and year-long tropical water conditions, the stage is set for blue marlin. These fish are available here year-round and peak in abundance from May through July.

These aren't big blues; the island record to date is a 584-pounder, which is nothing to sneeze at but it is far short of the possibilities elsewhere in the Caribbean, especially out in the Indies. Blues here

---

Carp were brought to America from Europe; in 1831 carp stocked in a pond in Newburgh, New York, escaped and became established in the Hudson River.

are said to average 150 pounds, which makes this grounds for males (the smaller fish) and juveniles and for light-tackle efforts, including fly tackle. White marlin and sailfish are occasional catches during the year as well.

Yellowfin, blackfin, and skipjack tuna are also on the Caymans' offshore scorecard, as are dolphin and wahoo. Yellowfins are the most prominent tuna, average 30 to 40 pounds (the local record is 189 pounds), and are caught year-round. They are most abundant from April through August. Blackfins are more spotty, but opportunities to land them increase in July and August. Skipjacks are prominent from October through January and average 12 pounds.

Dolphin average 10 pounds here but run much larger in the period of peak abundance, from April through September. The wahoo fishing has been excellent in the past; these are very plentiful but lightly pursued, especially from December through March, sometimes very close to shore at Grand Cayman. These species are all caught close to Grand Cayman, of course, as well as at the Cayman Banks, which is a large shoal area about 10 miles west of Grand Cayman. Deep peaks and valleys here affect the currents, and both attract and hold baitfish schools.

Inshore, there is fishing for bonefish, tarpon, permit, pompano, and barracuda, although, again, for relatively small fish. Loads of baby tarpon exist in the mangroves and inland brackish waters of Grand Cayman and also at Little Cayman. Five- to 15-pound fish provide phenomenal action to light-tackle casters in shallow waters along the coasts and throughout the year; the fishing occurs along the mangrove shores, in the ditches on Grand Cayman, and in a popular brackish lake at Little Cayman. Larger fish are in the area, too, but are seldom caught by anglers. Fifty- to 100-pound tarpon appear at dinner time, to be fed by tourists at the Grand Cayman waterfront in George Town, the capital city; and divers frequently see large tarpon in deeper water off the reefs, but virtually no one fishes for them.

Bonefish are found near all three islands, with the most opportunity existing around Little Cayman and Cayman Brac. They run from 2 to 6 pounds on average and are plentiful. The flats at the sister islands (which are 5 miles from each other and 89 miles northeast of Grand Cayman) are pristine, with turquoise water. The lightly populated islands (with lodges) are remote enough that one is truly away from it all.

Anglers land bonefish year-round in the Caymans, but the better fishing exists in the summer, from May through July, when winds are light; winter months can be good if winds don't drive the fish to slightly deeper water, although big schools are present then, and sight or blind casting with light jigs is likely to be effective. Some fishing from a boat can be had for bonefish in the deeper water of the North Sound at Grand Cayman, but the prime places for flats stalking are at the northwest end of the island, in the South Sound, from Pirate's Lair to Red Bay; in Frank Sound, from Betty Bay Point to Cottage Point; and on the eastern end at Colliers Bay. Some mangrove flats on Grand Cayman have been set aside for protection.

Permit and pompano are also available on the flats but are less frequently encountered. The local record for permit is 36 pounds. Barracuda frequent the shallows and provide good light-tackle sport. Anglers also land them around the reefs.

Reef fishing here is likely to produce Nassau grouper, jack crevalle, mutton snapper, yellowtail snapper, and other species, although it is lightly pursued in favor of flats and offshore action. Some angling visitors combine a trip inshore or offshore with a dive on the reefs.

The Caymans offer many facilities, including well-equipped and experienced charter boats and guides on all three islands.

CEDAR JIG

An old-time saltwater trolling lure used for schooling fish.
See: Trolling Lures, Saltwater.

CELLULAR TELEPHONE

See: Communications.

CENTREPIN REEL

A revolving-spool single-action reel with a large arbor, used in Europe for fishing with a float *(see)*. Also known as a float reel, and similar in appearance to a fly reel, this item always has two handles and a 3- to 4-inch diameter, and a very sensitive and free-spinning spool.

CHAFING GEAR

A wrapping of tape, cloth, canvas, tubing, or other material over line or boat rigging to prevent wear.

CHAIR, FIGHTING/FISHING

See: Fighting Chair; Sportfishing Boat.

CHALK STREAM

See: Limestone Stream.

CHARR

The term charr (or char) is used to describe five members of the genus *Salvelinus*. They are members of the Salmonidae family, which also includes trout, salmon, whitefish, and grayling, all of which are endemic to the temperate and cool regions of

A silvery Arctic charr caught in the ocean along the coast of Victoria Island, Nunavut Territory.

Charr as a group are among the most distinguished-looking and prettiest fish that appear in freshwater. Some are especially colorful, particularly in spawning mode. All have distinctive body markings, although there are great variations depending on their environments. The lake trout found deep in one of the Great Lakes, for example, is rather bland compared to the lake trout caught in more sterile waters of the far north.

Most members of the Salmonidae family are in some way associated with cold, often rushing waters and high oxygen demands. Some, including two of the charr, are also tied to the sea, spending a portion of their lives there. All members of the family spawn in freshwater, and most require cold running water. Members of some of the sea-running species, including at least arctic charr, have become accidentally or deliberately landlocked, living and reproducing successfully entirely in freshwater without ever taking a journey to saltwater.

Some charr species, especially arctic charr and lake trout, are of great historical, cultural, and food significance to native peoples of the Arctic or near-Arctic and to settlers, and they have had—and to some degree still have—both subsistence and commercial value. All native charr have rich, red flesh and are excellent eating, primarily when fresh or smoked. They are all highly valued sportfish, although the limited range or remoteness of arctic charr, Dolly Varden, and bull trout make them less encountered by, and less known to, anglers. The poorly named lake trout and brook trout are

the Northern Hemisphere but have been introduced widely outside their native range.

The charr group includes only one species that is actually called a "charr" in the English language, the arctic charr *(Salvelinus alpinus)*, which is also referred to in some scientific texts as the "*S. alpinus* complex,*"* because in modern times it has come to represent many fish that were previously thought to be separate species or subspecies. The arctic charr's four cousins include two of the most prominent species that are referred to as "trout," the lake trout *(S. namaycush)*, and the brook trout *(S. fontinalis)*, and two less widely known species, the Dolly Varden *(S. malma)*, and the bull trout *(S. confluentus)*.

Charr and other members of the Salmonidae family are primitive fish; their fossil remains date to more than 100 million years ago. Evidence indicates that many of the more advanced or specialized families of modern-day bony fish have ancestral stocks closely resembling these primitive fish.

The most clearly evident primitive feature of the group is the lack of spines in the fins. Most of the soft rays in the fins are branched. The pelvic fins are situated far back on the body—in the "hip" region where the legs of amphibians articulate with the body. This position differs from the location of the pelvic fins in many other species, including largemouth bass *(see: bass, largemouth)* for example, which are so far forward they are almost directly beneath the pectoral fins. Other indications of their primitive nature are an adipose fin and a crude type of air bladder.

A colorful brook trout from the English River, Labrador.

among the most valued North American game species. Both have been extensively cultivated in hatcheries and have been widely planted to supplement existing stocks, to reintroduce the species to waters where natural populations were extirpated, or to introduce them to waters where they did not previously exist.

Like virtually all members of the Salmonidae family, charr have suffered from changes wrought by humans. These include overfishing (especially of lake trout in the largest waters via commercial efforts, and in some remote waters from sportfishing), pollution, habitat alteration, factors that have caused a warming of waters, hatchery impacts, and competition from exotic species.

Some populations of the various charr have declined dramatically, and most are not what they were decades ago, in terms of overall size as well as in number of large individuals. In addition, some landlocked forms with limited distribution (blueback trout, Quebec red, and Sunapee trout) have become extinct, their loss in some cases hastened by stocking of nonnative salmonids. Commercial fishing for lake trout and arctic charr has been stopped or greatly reduced by quotas in many places, although in the far north subsistence netting by native peoples continues at varying levels.

The subject of the proper spelling of this group—charr or char—has generated spirited debate in the scientific community. The original and historical spelling is reportedly Celtic (from *ceara,* meaning blood red), and became charre in seventeenth-century England, then charr. The general public, especially the popular media, today predominantly use "char," and this spelling is recognized in several prominent U.S. authoritarian lists. Many Canadian ichthyologists, who arguably have a greater claim to the group because of their abundance of these species and studies of them, use "charr." At least one pundit has noted that "char" means "to burn," as in char-broiled steak, and is confusing, implying that "charr" is unambiguous. Another has noted that such other accepted words of Celtic derivation, redd and parr, would be inappropriate if the second *d* or *r* was dropped. Usage of the word char, however, will not be the first instance in which the wrong spelling of a word becomes the accepted one through common expression, and it has happened with other fish species.

See: Charr, Arctic; Dolly Varden and Bull Trout; Trout, Brook; Trout, Bull; Trout, Lake.

CHARR, ARCTIC *Salvelinus alpinus.*

Other names for the seagoing fish—char, red charr; Cree: *awanans;* Danish: *fjeldørred;* French: *omble chevalier;* German: *saibling;* Greenlandic: *eqaluk;* Icelandic: *bleikja;* Inuit: *iqalugaq, iqaluk, ilkalupik, ivisaaruq, kisuajuq, majuqtuq, nutiliarjuk, situajuq, situliqtuq, tisuajuq;* Japanese: *iwana;* Norwegian: *arktisk roye, royr;* Russian: *goletz;* Swedish: *röding.*

Other names for the landlocked fish—blueback charr, blueback trout, Sunapee trout, golden trout (Sunapee), Quebec red.

Although the majority of anglers are unfamiliar with arctic charr and have not even been close to catching one, this species is technically among the most widely distributed salmonids, and the most northerly ranging member of the Salmonidae family. It is one of five species that are actually classified as charr *(see),* including the more familiar lake trout *(see: trout, lake)* and brook trout *(see: trout, brook).* The arctic charr varies so greatly in coloration throughout its North American, Asiatic, and European ranges that up to 26 varieties, many thought to be species or subspecies, have heretofore been identified, resulting in a great deal of confusion and a tremendous problem for taxonomists. This confusion extended to anadromous and nonanadromous forms, the latter including three New England charr—the blueback trout, Sunapee trout, and Quebec red trout, which were once separately recognized species but which were all reclassified and folded under the highly inclusive umbrella *S. alpinus* in 1974.

The arctic charr exists in anadromous (migrating annually to the sea) and nonanadromous (landlocked or living entirely in freshwater) forms. Because of plentiful food resources in the ocean,

Arctic Charr (sea-run phase)

Arctic Charr (spawning phase)

the anadromous version tends to be larger than the landlocked one and of more importance to commercial and sport fisheries. The landlocked charr is blocked from the sea by some physical barrier. It is found everywhere that the sea-run charr exists but also occurs in smaller numbers much farther to the south. Thus, the arctic charr is known as a glacial relict in cold, deep lakes as far south as New England, Switzerland, and Britain.

Some anglers consider sea-run arctic charr the equal of Atlantic salmon, because both are strong battlers that make long runs and thrilling aerial jumps when hooked. The charr are perhaps more prone to furious spinning and head-twisting gyrations. Although charr may be caught in river pools like Atlantic salmon, most arctic rivers are more turbulent and swift than salmon rivers, and fishing concentrates at the head of pools and where swift runs empty into open areas. Arctic charr are also schooling fish and are likely to be present in small numbers in a given location.

Arctic charr have long been a staple in the diets of native peoples (and their dogs) in the far north, and in North America they have been an object of commercial fishing since the 1860s off Labrador, as well as commercial interest in Newfoundland and in Nunavut Territory and the Northwest Territories at Rankin Inlet, Cambridge Bay, Pelly Bay, and Nettling (Seal) Lake on Baffin Island. They are primarily taken with gillnets.

The flesh of sea-run charr is deep orange red and an Epicurean delight, although it can spoil quickly. Depending on diet and location, some charr may have lighter colored, or white, flesh.

Arctic charr is marketed mainly fresh and frozen as whole dressed fish and steaks. A small quantity is canned. Red-fleshed fish command the highest price.

Like other salmonids, arctic charr have felt the impact of human encroachment, mainly increased development and overfishing, and some stocks have declined in overall number and average size. Sportfishing has also had some impact in a few places, especially when numbers of the largest specimens were removed, as these are fairly slow-growing fish. Other than humans, the arctic charr has few enemies. Gulls and loons prey on small fish, and a few seagoing charr may succumb to seals and white whales, but the greatest effect may be predation by other fish.

Identification. Like all members of the *Salvelinus* genus, the arctic charr has light-colored spots on its body, including below the lateral line, and the leading edges of all fins on the lower part of the body are milk white. It is a long and slender fish with a small, pointed head, an adipose fin, an axillary process at the base of each pelvic fin, and a slightly forked tail that almost appears squared. It also has very fine scales, so deeply embedded that the skin has a smooth, slippery feel. Unlike the trout, it has teeth only in the central forward part of its mouth.

Coloration is highly variable among seagoing and landlocked forms, and can change even within individual stocks; those migrating to one coastal system may appear different from those migrating to another, as also happens with salmon and trout. In a general sense, however, the arctic charr is silvery in nonspawning individuals, with deep green or blue shading on the back and upper sides, and a white belly. Spawning males exhibit brilliant red or reddish orange coloration on the sides, underparts, and lower fins; their backs are muted, sometimes without the blue or green coloration or possibly with orange to olive hues. Spawning males of some populations develop a kype, and some have a humped back. Spawning females are also colorful, although the red is less intense and present only on the flanks and belly; the back remains bluish or greenish.

The tremendous variation among arctic charr (which leads some scientists to view different stocks as subspecies) makes it almost impossible to make a clearcut identification based on coloration, especially if other charr exist in the same area. Lake trout, Dolly Varden, and bull trout *(see: Dolly Varden and bull trout)*, for example, may overlap with arctic charr, and whereas lake trout are readily discerned due to their bodily patterns, the other species are not. Color, for example, is not a factor that distinguishes the arctic charr from its close relative the Dolly Varden, which is the species most often confused with the arctic charr.

Often it is virtually impossible to distinguish between the two species except by laboratory analysis, and even today there are few scientists who know how to make a positive identification. Much incorrect information has been published concerning the distribution of each species, and consequently anglers and scientists alike have made many false identifications based on the mistaken belief that only arctic charr or only Dolly Varden occurred in a given area, lake, or river (especially in Alaska). An individual who is familiar with both species may be able to make an identification based on the size of the spots, which are larger on the arctic charr. Fish returning from the sea are often silvery with no spots at all, however, making external identification all but impossible. Gill raker counts are helpful. On Canada's Victoria Island, charr have about 25 to 30 gill rakers on the first left gill arch. Dolly Varden have 21 to 22 gill rakers. Arctic charr have 40 to 45 pyloric caeca (wormlike appendages on the pylorus, the section of intestine directly after the stomach), whereas Dolly Varden have about 30.

Size/Age. How large arctic charr can grow is uncertain, but some may live up to 30 years and grow to 3 feet in length. Sea-run charr grow much larger, and the all-tackle world record is a 32-pound, 9-ounce sea-run fish that was caught in 1981 in the Tree River of Canada's Northwest Territories. It has been reported that a 15.4-kilogram (33.8 pounds) charr was caught at Novaya Zemlya in Russia.

In most places sea-run arctic charr range up to 10 pounds and average 7 pounds; landlocked fish normally weigh a few pounds. A sea-run arctic charr weighing more than 15 pounds is a trophy in most waters, although such fish are not uncommon to streams entering Coronation and Queen Maud Gulfs in north-central Canada, and emanating from Victoria Island. These waters are especially notable for arctic charr that range from 15 to 20 pounds, and sometimes higher.

Distribution. As the name suggests, the arctic charr is circumpolar in distribution, occurring in pure and cold rivers and lakes around the globe, from the northeastern United States north and west across northern Canada, Alaska, and the Aleutian Islands, and from northern Russia south to Lake Baikal and Kamchatka, as well as in Iceland, Great Britain, Scandinavia, the Alps, and Spitsbergen, among other places. The most northerly ranging fish, it has been reported above the eightieth parallel from Ellesmere Island's Discovery Harbour, some 800 kilometers below the North Pole.

In North America, they occur from Alaska around the Bering Sea and along the Arctic coast to Baffin Island, along the coastline of Hudson Bay, and from the northern Quebec coast easterly and southerly to Maine and New Hampshire. Except in larger rivers, they seldom range far inland here, although there are a few pockets of landlocked charr. In the Northwest Territories and Nunavut Territory, where they are especially known, charr distribution includes most coastal rivers, some coastal lakes, the streams of the high-Arctic islands, and several islands in Hudson Bay.

Habitat. In their ocean life, arctic charr remain in inshore waters; most do not migrate far. In rivers, they locate in pools and runs. The lakes inhabited by anadromous and landlocked charr are cold year-round, so the fish remain near the surface or in the upper levels and may gather at the mouths of tributaries when food is plentiful.

Life history/Behavior. The charr spawns in September or October in colder regions and later if it lives farther south; a water temperature of around 4°C is preferred. The spawning female seeks out a suitable bed of gravel or broken rock. It will choose a stretch of river or lake bottom deep enough to keep the eggs safe from the winter ice, or it will choose the bottom of a rapid, where ice does not form.

Using her fins, the female scoops out a nest, or redd, in the loose gravel. The nest is little more than a shallow depression about the length and width of the female's body. Here, she releases some of her 3,000 to 7,000 eggs as the male releases milt. Then, the female lightly fans the gravel over the fertilized eggs, usually in the course of digging another nest nearby. This process is repeated until the female is spent.

The eggs hatch sometime in the first week of April, although the timing depends on light and water temperature at the specific location. Temperatures above 8°C at any time will kill the eggs. The alevin remain hidden in the gravel for many weeks, emerging as free-swimming fish or fry only when the food reserves are used up. This occurs around the time of ice breakup, which may be as late as mid-July in the most northerly regions, when their emergence coincides with the renewed growth of plankton.

The anadromous charr lives in its birth river for at least four years and is about 15 to 20 centimeters (6 to 8 inches) long when it migrates to the sea for the first time. Spring comes, the rivers break free of ice, and the four- or five-year-old charr makes its first trip down to the ocean. It will return anywhere between mid-August and late September, before the ice begins to form again. The larger fish return first, even as soon as mid-July in some cases. Unlike other salmonids, all arctic charr leave the sea and overwinter in rivers and lakes, although not all are spawners; some go back and forth several times before they first spawn.

The charr matures sexually around its 10th year in the Arctic, when it has reached a length of about 65 centimeters, although maturity comes a couple of years earlier in Labrador, and at a shorter length. After that, the fish spawns every second or third year. Often it does not migrate to the sea during its reproductive years.

It is not known what mechanisms control migratory behavior, but it is thought that hormonal changes are touched off by changes in light intensity. Once in the sea, it is clearly the availability of food that governs movement. When food is plentiful, the fish tend to remain near the mouth of the river from which they emerged. In times of scarcity, however, they move into offshore waters, sometimes traveling long distances. Tagged charr are frequently recovered 30 to 50 kilometers from their river of origin, and some fish have made recorded journeys of up to 600 kilometers; the record is 1,000 kilometers.

While in the sea, charr from many different rivers meet and mingle, but when the time comes to return upriver, they tend in most cases to separate and return to the parent stream. In some instances, they even return to the exact spawning site of previous years.

The cold northern waters are not conducive to rapid growth. Even with its flexible eating habits and its fine adaptation to a cold environment, the charr grows slowly, which makes it vulnerable to excessive exploitation. At the age of one year, when scale development begins, the charr is often less than 5 centimeters (2 inches) long. Growth rates vary greatly among individual fish within a given habitat. It is usual, however, for a charr to reach full growth at 2.5 to 3 kilograms, or at about age 12.

Nonanadromous or landlocked charr tend to reach maturity when they are smaller and younger. They have the same lifestyle as their anadromous brethren.

Food. Insects, mollusks, and small fish constitute the diet of arctic charr. Ninespine sticklebacks are important forage in some places. The charr often does not eat in winter, when its metabolic rate slows in tune with a cooling environment. Rather, it lives on the fat it has accumulated during the summer, and growth is accordingly limited during the cold months, and greatest when at sea.

Angling. The magnificent coloration of spawning fish, the excellent quality of the flesh, its terrific fighting spirit, and its relative inaccessibility combine to make the arctic charr a highly desirable quarry for those relative few who have the time and means to venture to the far north. They are as royal a fighting fish as is found in freshwater, known for blistering runs and salmonlike leaps, especially in river environs, and great tenacity in swift rivers.

Sea-run arctic charr are the main interest of anglers, although landlocked charr are caught in lakes, usually incidental to fishing for lake trout or when they are the only sportfish present. Most of the better fishing for larger charr occurs far north and in a very limited time window, mainly in mid- to late summer. Some areas have just a six-week season before the weather becomes cold and possibly snowy. The end of this period, however, is usually when the largest and most colorful spawning fish are available, although this varies with location.

Arctic charr angling can be a feast-or-famine affair. Charr sometimes are clustered so thickly that a river seems full of these fish, or they can be scarce. Although the fishing is sometimes fast, with continuous action, these fish are easily spooked; when a school is alarmed (as can happen when one or more of its members are caught), it will move off, and the spot has to be rested for an hour or two.

River fishing is more dependable than lake fishing, with the charr often holding at the head of a pool. Where current drops over a gravel bar and dumps into a deep pool is a particularly good location. In swift, high water it is necessary to use heavy-bodied spoons, which sink below the surface turbulence; a touch of red or orange on the spoons is helpful. Weighted spinners and some plugs may also do the job, and heavily dressed flies on fast-sinking lines are necessary for fly anglers. Fly fishing is better when the water level is lower; many different wet flies and streamers are appropriate, also with some bright color for appeal, and dry flies may catch fish when there is a hatch (often mosquitoes) in progress.

Anglers do very little fishing for charr in the sea or in nearshore ocean waters, because of a lack of suitable boats in far northern locations, because of the dangerously cold temperature of the water, and because enough fish are usually available in nearby rivers. Arctic charr range along coastal shorelines and estuaries in summer prior to migrating upriver, however, and can provide some excellent action. Shore-based anglers usually find it necessary to wade out on extensive, shallow, nearshore flats to make long casts with heavy-bodied spoons into deeper water. Long spinning rods and light line are

A large, colorful Arctic charr from a river on Victoria Island, Nunavut Territory.

well suited to this, and the fish that are caught are chrome-bright, faintly spotted, and very vigorous. It is not possible to sight-cast to these charr, so blind casting is the norm.

In lakes, anglers concentrate on inlets, where the river dumps into a lake. Early in the season, charr in lakes can be seen and caught as they wander along the edges of ice floes that are breaking up; a spoon, jig, or streamer fly will take them.

Light to medium spinning tackle are best for arctic charr, and 6- to 10-pound line is the standard. Fly anglers need a reel with ample backing, and usually fast-sinking or sink-tip 7- to 9-weight outfits.
See: Charr.

CHARTER BOAT

A sportfishing boat available for hire and capable of taking a limited number of anglers aboard on an exclusive basis, nearly always by advance reservation. Most charter boats exist in navigable waters and are piloted by captains certified by the U.S. Coast Guard. Charter boats are primarily found in saltwater and on large lakes and rivers, and are usually craft in the 25- to 50-foot range with broad beams, deep-V hulls, and the ability to run great distances and endure rough conditions if necessary. They typically take four anglers for a day of fishing, but may take between one and six anglers depending on the size of the boat. In some places, primarily in freshwater, 20- to 25-foot cabin or center console boats are also chartered for fishing, taking fewer passengers, and generally angling in less demanding situations. The term charter boat is sometimes erroneously applied to smaller boats for hire, such as 18- to 20-footers that accommodate two anglers and an operator; these are actually guide boats (see), even though the "guide" may have a captain's license.

Charter boats are usually hired for the day, but may be engaged for several consecutive days, a week, or longer. In some places a charter boat may be hired for half a day. In most situations, charter captains are assisted by a mate (perhaps two on the largest offshore big-game sportfishing boats) who is responsible for setting and rigging lines and baits, assisting customers, netting or gaffing fish, cleaning fish, and associated chores. Some smaller charter boats in freshwater do not use a mate, and the captain serves both functions, usually having one of the passengers steer the boat while he takes care of rigging.

Charter boats supply all of the customary fishing equipment unless some specialized angling is preferred. Anglers usually bring only their own food, beverage, and personal comfort items (sunglasses, sunscreen, foul weather gear, etc.), and are expected to wear appropriate footwear (nonscuff boating shoes or sneakers). The majority of people who fish on a charter boat are relatively inexperienced, or at least unaccustomed to the style of fishing or the species pursued by that boat in that location. Many charter boats use fairly heavy tackle to compensate for their customer's lack of experience, particularly in freshwater when fishing for trout, salmon, and muskies. However, some charter boats specialize in certain techniques or species, and market themselves to anglers with specific interests or abilities. An increased interest in light tackle fishing has caused some charter boat operators, particularly in saltwater, to specialize in using light spinning, baitcasting, or fly tackle.

Hiring a charter boat is a great way to set up good odds for a rewarding fishing experience, and it is also one of the best ways to learn more about sportfishing. Although it may be expensive on a per trip outing, it may, in fact, be an economical means of fishing if several people share expenses, and if you are otherwise limited in the number of times that you are able to go fishing. If, for example, you owned your own boat, but could only use it ten times per season for fishing, the cost of equipment, fuel, amortization, insurance, dockage, and other items might annually be greater than it would if you chartered a boat ten times, especially if you pooled the cost with others. Not to mention that you would have to find and catch your own fish instead of being with a professional who does it day in and day out.

On the other hand, chartering is a terrific way of learning about boats, fishing methods, equipment, locations, and other issues, as a prelude to getting your own boat and being your own skipper. Many people have plunged deeply into some facet of sportfishing (and boat and equipment ownership) after having booked a few charters and gotten a yen to run their own boat and find and catch their own fish. So it works both ways.

General Fishing Issues

Taking turns. There is great diversity in the types of fishing and species pursued on charter boats. When jigging or drift fishing, and especially when drifting bait in a chum slick, anglers may hold a rod or be assigned a rod to watch and all or many of the anglers on the boat can be active simultaneously. However, when trolling, which is a primary charter boat activity, there may be many rods in play, only one of which actually gets a hookup, and a fair system has to be worked out to determine who gets to fight the fish. Many customers will ask the mate or captain what to do, but they will usually leave it up to their customers to decide.

One way to do this is to assign each angler to a rod, but since some rods inevitably get more strikes than others, this is the least acceptable and least fair method. After all, the fish are primarily attracted to strike due to the trolling efforts of the captain and mate, not the angler. The angler is there to play the fish and bring it to the boat. Most anglers simply take turns "up," like batters coming to the plate on a baseball team. When a fish strikes, it's somebody's turn, and he catches the fish and then yields to whoever has the next turn, and so on. A variation

Around the world, charter boats are the means for visitors to enjoy a day of offshore fishing.

of this is to establish a time limit on each turn, usually 30 minutes. If there are no strikes in that time, it's the next person's turn. Of course, the timing of a strike has nothing to do with the angler, and this system takes on more of a lottery-like scenario.

The key thing is to establish some order before you actually get fishing; don't wait until a fish strikes and someone—usually the person who is quickest, most eager, or closest—grabs the rod. Drawing straws is a fair way to get turns established. It might happen that with four anglers on the boat, only two fish are caught, and the anglers who have the first two turns are the ones who get to battle them.

Another thing that should be addressed is whether a "turn" is ended if an angler plays and loses a fish without landing it. Time limits make this a moot issue if it is determined that whatever strikes in a given time period occur to the person who has that block of time. If not, does a person who has had an opportunity to play a fish lose his turn if the fish breaks off or otherwise escapes the hook? If they don't lose their turn, what if they play and lose another fish, and another? Some charter groups adopt a three-strikes-and-you're-out attitude, which may rankle some of the people onboard, and which may work for dolphin fishing when there's plenty of action, but not marlin or sailfish when there's relatively few opportunities.

This may seem like nitpicking issues to some, but when you've been part of a group chartering a boat for between $300 and $1,000 for a single day of fishing, you'll appreciate the establishment of a system that is agreed upon and which tries to offer everyone opportunity.

Etiquette. Despite the fact that you're paying someone to take you fishing when hiring a charter boat, you must remember that it's not your boat; it's the captain's or his employer's. The captain is in charge and presumably knows what's best in the maintenance and operation of his craft, as well as the most effective fishing techniques in his backyard.

No matter what your level of fishing expertise, it is rude and presumptuous to flaunt your knowledge or demean that of the captain or crew. There is no better way to get off on the wrong foot and diminish the day's fishing experience than to play "know all" with people who sportfish for a living every day. If you spot a crewman doing something flagrantly wrong, it will not help the mood of the day to point it out to him, especially in an arrogant manner.

Realize that what you're paying for is the crew's superior knowledge of the particular area and species sought, and what it takes to catch fish in their local water. One of the primary reasons for hiring a charter boat is to learn, especially if you have your own boat, and hopefully to take what you learn and apply it yourself. The more varied your charters and locales, the more varied will be your store of techniques. When chartering, just remember that the people you are fishing with are your teachers. If the mate is doing something (like rigging baits) in an unfamiliar manner, watch carefully; it just might be a technique you could learn and use elsewhere. So take their advice and counsel, and ask about the things you do not know.

If you do wish to provide input, do so in a way that's not overbearing and offensive. A pet peeve of charter mates the world over is hearing the comment, "That's not the way we do it back home." Naturally, when they hear this they think, "Then why didn't you stay home?" or "This isn't home." It's not rude to make gentle suggestions, which will be better received than criticism or confrontational demands. An offer of your own equipment that you deem more effective will hardly be turned down. Granted, there are times on charters, especially in Third World countries, where the latest in modern equipment and techniques have not yet arrived or boats cannot run up to adequate lure trolling speed, when you may have little choice but to politely insist on doing things your way.

Occasionally, of course, you may actually know better. For example, if the mate has not sharpened old hooks, why not pull your sharpener from your bag and simply begin sharpening hooks yourself? Any mate worth his salt will instantly pick up the clue and gladly borrow and use your file for the balance of the day; there's no need for you to shout orders to do so. He will usually watch you sharpen the first several hooks and imitate your technique thereafter, or will simply thereafter hand you hooks to sharpen yourself. Most good mates in hot fishing areas know how to earn good tips, and anything that may contribute to lost fish will be avoided.

Many misunderstandings aboard charter boats can be avoided by a friendly discussion as you step aboard, especially if you want to "do your own thing." A quick and early examination of the condition of the natural baits, for example, on an offshore charter boat trip, might prompt you to prefer using artificial lures all day. The time for such a suggestion would be early on, not as a complaint later in the day.

Setting the hook and rod handling. Another thing you need to address is the matter of setting the hook yourself, or allowing the mate or captain to do it. Many anglers will not take a rod and fight a fish if someone else has first set the hook and then attempted to hand them the rod. They feel that it's unfair, and that the person who set the hook should play the fish. If one person sets the hook and then hands the rod to someone else, and the fish turns out to be a world record candidate, that action would be judged unfair and would disqualify the catch from record consideration, according to the rules established by the IGFA. Most big-game anglers are familiar with this but the vast majority of anglers are not.

If you have any concerns or interests regarding establishing a record (see) catch, then no one else should touch your rod. If you feel strongly that it is unfair to have someone set the hook and hand you a rod, then you should not allow it when it's your turn. You may have to make your feelings on this issue known to the captain or mate, or have a discussion about it with them before the moment of truth arrives. In foreign countries, especially those in the Third World, charter boat crews are unfamiliar with the rules for establishing records, and unless they are instructed (politely and pleasantly) about what is expected at the beginning of the day, it is likely that someone from the crew will grab a rod (especially when trolling for billfish) before the angler can get to it.

Many charter boats in saltwater, especially those who fish for big-game species and participate in tournaments, are ever-conscious of records and of following the sportfishing regulations established by the IGFA in regard to the tackle used, and in regard to leader lengths, method of fishing, and manner of landing the fish, so they are well attuned to the issue of who sets the hook and handles the rod. If he is concerned about the abilities of a customer, a captain will allow that customer to set the hook, but then actually aid his efforts by increasing the throttle greatly when the actual hook setting occurs and immediately afterward, in order to help drive the hook into the fish. Should they really be doing that? And who really set the hook? It's a debatable point.

The hook-setting issue is of particular concern on charter boats, because in many situations the mate actually grabs a rod when a fish strikes, then sets the hook. Part of the reason for this is that with some species, it is necessary to do more than just set the hook. The line may have to be paid out under freespool for a short while so that the fish gets a good hold of the bait; then the reel has to be put into strike mode, the hook set, and perhaps the drag adjusted for playing the fish. Anglers unaccustomed to doing this often inadvertently strike too soon, apply too much pressure on the line when the fish is actually swallowing the bait, or do other things that cause the fish to drop the bait or to avoid being hooked. If these missed opportunities happen repeatedly, the mate and captain (and other anglers waiting their turn), may get testy. Charter boat skippers are very concerned with their productivity, which translates into the number of fish actually caught. Fair or not, it's a measure of their ability, a competitive thing amongst the charter fleet, and a means of securing other customers. To ensure that customers actually catch fish (whether they're kept or released), they like to get solid hookups and, if they're worth their charter fees, they know how to do it well.

If you need instructions on the proper manner of setting the hook for the species being pursued or the method being employed, the mate and captain should be able to give you instruction and coach you through this. However, charter boat captains universally agree that many of their customers, especially men, and especially people with some fishing experience, do not listen to their instructions or do not follow them fully, while inexperienced anglers and most women pay greater attention to instructions and to the execution of them, resulting in better success.

If you have no qualms about being handed a rod, and no concerns about records (the chance of catching a record fish is usually slim), then this is a nonissue. Most mates and captains simply want their customers to catch fish, and because they're on the water every day, they are on top of their game while most of the customers are not. The majority of anglers, especially in freshwater, don't have any problem with taking a rod that someone has handed them, but most of them also don't understand the ramifications. In saltwater fishing, especially for big-game species, this is a major issue.

Other Matters

Ownership of the fish. If you have caught and kept fish on a charter boat, who do they belong to? Logic says they belong to the angler who caught them. In freshwater, this is almost always the case. Freshwater sportfish throughout North America are also designated as gamefish and cannot be sold. In saltwater, that is sometimes different; sportfish may not be designated as gamefish in certain places, and may legally be sold. In those places, some charter boat captains seek to sell all or part of the day's catch to enhance their earnings or to subsidize their costs.

Customers may give their catch to the mate or the captain if they don't want them (although there is an ethical question: Why not release them if you didn't want them?), or to other customers. But some saltwater fish have a lot of market value, and in some places they may be sold, with or without a special permit or commercial license. There is special interest in tuna, mako shark, dolphin, swordfish, other billfish, and certain other species, and a good sport catch can have monetary value. Tuna are especially valuable, and giant bluefins can be worth in the tens of thousands of dollars. The cost of fishing on a deluxe charter boat is expensive, especially if a lot of fuel is expended in offshore runs, so some charter boats claim ownership of their catch, or a portion of the catch. Customers should be advised of this up front, in fact prior to making a reservation. If you have a problem with this, you should resolve it before the boat leaves the dock. Many people don't have a problem with this, but should. And some don't become aware of it until they're out fishing or headed back to the dock with the day's catch.

In foreign countries, language barriers or local custom sometimes cause a problem with regard to ownership of the fish, or especially with regard to fish that a customer wants to release immediately unharmed but which the captain or crew expect as food. In these cases, especially in Third World countries, your wish to release all or certain species caught must be established at the start of the day, perhaps by an agreement that you will pay an extra tip for this (representing the amount the crew would probably earn for the fish at the market). This decreases the chance of unpleasant shouting matches when desirable fish are caught. In Third World countries it might help to pay some tip in advance for expected services, provided that you are sure that you can communicate what is expected.

Limits. There's a temptation on charter boats (as there is in other group fishing activities, but especially so on charter boats, perhaps because of expense) for anglers to pool their fish or for more successful anglers to contribute more than their allowable share to the overall pot. Four anglers on a charter boat sometimes may catch the legal limit of a particular species that would apply to six people, figuring in the mate and captain, who did not actually fish but who possess licenses (if licenses are required). Then they divvy the six-limit catch among the four anglers at the end of the day. Except it's illegal. And tough to police.

In most places the legal limit for sport-caught fish applies to one day's catch and to each individual angler, who is responsible for catching those fish himself. One person can give another angler the fish that he caught, but may not catch more than his own legal limit. In other words, if the limit is five fish, you can't legally catch six and give one to someone else. Some charter boats encourage this or look the other way when it happens because they don't want to anger possible repeat customers. On the Great Lakes, you can hear charter boat captains talking all the time on their VHF radio about "filling the box up," which usually means by hook or by crook and by whomever.

While few reputable charter boat skippers will exceed limits in aggregate, sharing like this is fairly common in freshwater and saltwater. Captains should discourage it and work to make sure that people who don't catch as many fish as others get help, but customers need to recognize that this activity is unethical and illegal; if they're caught, there are legal ramifications.

In some waters, there are no limits, or extremely generous limits, on all or certain species of fish, and in the midst of frenzied action some boats have loaded up. The customers have gone home with coolers full of fish, and then they've rotted in the garbage or freezers later on. This has happened on charter boats as well as party boats and private fishing boats, and there really is no justification for it. Many a saltwater angler who has helped plunder fish on great days has later whined about the absence of fish, never associating his own excesses with that absence.

Where there are no limits, a charter boat captain should establish a reasonable boat or per-person limit and cut the anglers off when they've reached it. It's more than shameful to participate in this excess, it's unethical. Customers should keep only those fish that they can eat in a reasonable period of time, and not every fish they catch. The idea of never-ending bounty, irrespective of some days in which the water seems full of fish, was debunked long ago, and some people argue further that anglers should not give their catch away to others, who may not have licenses or in any way contribute to the maintenance of natural resources. Another debatable issue.

Tipping. It is customary to give a cash tip to the mate on a charter boat at the end of the day. This will vary depending upon the activities, the efforts of the mate, and whether there have been some exceptionally good (or bad) things happen. The customary tip for the mate is usually about 10 percent of the cost of the charter, or slightly more to be split between two mates (if the boat has two mates, although it might be split to give more to the primary mate and less to the secondary mate, who is usually someone learning. A lesser tip might be in order if you've had major problems, or a larger tip if the day is truly spectacular or extra services (like a lot of fish cleaning) are rendered. The captain is not generally tipped. It is customary in saltwater big-game fishing to generously reward the mate (and perhaps the captain) when you've caught a record fish, achieved a significant milestone, won a tournament, earned cash from a calcutta pool, and so forth.

Finding and Hiring a Charter Boat

Standard procedures. As with most good products or services, the best advertisement for a good charter boat captain is a happy customer, so if a friend, relative, or acquaintance has a strong recommendation for a charter boat to hire, consider it seriously. Otherwise, you must do some homework, checking out ads, asking people, reading fishing publications, and possibly talking to some references given by the charter boat captain.

Be wary of extreme claims. There cannot be outstanding success or big fish every day. Be wary of captains who guarantee fish, promising a refund if nothing is caught. It's a good-sounding strategy, but some guarantee-fish operators, near the end of a day spent unsuccessfully seeking certain species, will ease out to places where they are sure to find a few nontarget fish that will technically result in a "catch." On the Great Lakes, for example, some skippers will drag the bottom to catch a few lakers (often a sure thing) when they've been unable to get salmon.

Be prepared to pay a deposit in advance to secure your reservation, and to lose it if you don't cancel early enough to allow your date to be filled. Charter boats do have peak seasons and it's not always possible for them to get stand-in customers on short notice, so when they lose parties in prime time, they may not be able to recoup.

If bad weather cancels a booking, the captain should apply your deposit to another date or refund it to you. If bad weather or unusual circumstances adversely affect your day of fishing, some captains will give you a credit or reduction toward another booking. People who book the same charter boat frequently, several or more times a year, usually get a rate break, as well as date preference.

If you can inspect a charter boat before reserving it, that may be helpful; in vacation spots this is often possible. Talking to people at the docks, the marina, or local tackle shops can be very helpful. If you can, get to a dock in the afternoon when the boats come in and talk to customers who have just returned from a day with a charter captain; they'll usually talk freely.

The condition of a charter boat is sometimes an indication of the ability of the skipper and sometimes not. Not every good captain spit-polishes his boat at the end of each day. And not every new and sparkling boat is better than an older weathered one. Do your homework, ask questions, and make sure to tell a prospective captain exactly what you want.

When booking charters in distant places, especially a foreign land, start with a booking agency that specializes in fishing trips, rather than general travel agencies. Such organizations can give advice on numerous destinations and create complete travel packages. The larger and better agencies keep tabs on current fishing conditions all over the world and many have personal experience with both the local areas and the charter boats and crews. Their recommendations are generally reliable.

When planning a trip with a booking agent, it's wise to pose a number of questions in advance of paying a deposit. Things you should know in advance might include many of the issues previously

A lot of factors are involved in selecting a charter boat.

mentioned regarding setting your own hook, releasing fish, the type of tackle supplied and condition (you may wish to bring your own), extra costs, the name and phone number of someone who fished with the charter captain (or camp) the same time last year; if the crew speaks English or there's an interpreter, and other issues germane to visiting a foreign country or a lodge with fishing services. Confirm everything in writing to avoid misunderstandings. And never accept, "No problem," as a satisfactory or complete answer to any of your questions; get details.

Make-up charters. An angler who would like to fish aboard a charter boat but doesn't have the money to hire one alone, or doesn't have enough people to share the expense, sometimes has an alternate option. Many charter boat captains will work up what are commonly referred to as "make-up charters." As the name implies, anglers call and have their names added to a list, and as soon as sufficient anglers are available, usually four to six people on the average-size charter boat, everybody can be accommodated.

There are some operators at major fishing locales who specialize in make-up charters. This is especially true in tourist areas, and often you can talk with the concierge of a hotel adjacent to a fishing area; they will be pleased to work with you to get you aboard a quality boat with a captain and crew capable of putting you into a good day's fishing. Keep in mind that it is often to their benefit to direct you to a professional, qualified captain. In many instances they receive a referral commission, but equally important is that as a result of your being a guest in their establishment, it is in their best interest to provide the best service possible.

Another source of make-up charters is often a local marina, especially those with large fleets of charter boats. Frequently there are boats without regular, full-boat charters, and the captains advise the marina office that they are available. Occasionally you may luck out and get a captain who's anxious to be on the water and who will sail even if he only has two or three anglers, paying only a portion of the regular charter price. While it may seem like a losing proposition on the surface, the income may at least pay for boat costs, and it keeps the captain and his crew active. They also stay with the pulse of the fishing, which is an important consideration in chartering.

What's especially nice about make-up charters is that they bring together a group of people who essentially have the same problem: They want to go fishing, but don't have anyone to go with. You'll usually find that conversation is spontaneous, and many friendships develop, with a camaraderie that is typical among outdoor enthusiasts.

Other matters. Some people have unreasonable expectations with regard to hiring a charter boat, and it's important to remember that this is fishing, not an exact science, and that things can change from day to day. This makes it unpredictable as to whether on a given day you can expect to catch a certain size or number of a particular type of fish. Do not be disappointed if your day doesn't live up to the catch of the previous day, and don't expect to get a break on the charter cost for this unless there have been extenuating circumstances.

You should recognize that although this is a fun outing or vacation day trip for you and your companions, it is also a job for the captain and the mate. Help out where you can if that is feasible, and be grateful for their assistance and for good results. Recognize that the length of the charter doesn't mean the amount of time that you will necessarily be fishing; an eight-hour charter almost always means that you are back at the dock eight hours after you left, even if you had to spend two hours to get to and from the fishing grounds.

Finally, don't be upset with the captain if you move off a place that has been producing good action, such as a reef or wreck. Once you've caught a reasonable amount of fish from a known structure like this, the captain may move to another area to avoid overfishing that spot. This is not unreasonable. Both you and he would like to return to that place again sometime and have good results, but that won't happen if the structure is beaten to death every day.

See: Fishing Lodge; Fishing Regulations; Guide Boat; Party Boat.

CHARTER BOAT CAPTAIN
A licensed skipper of a charter boat (see).

CHART, NAVIGATIONAL
Also called a nautical chart, this is a precise and accurate aid to navigation printed on durable paper and used by mariners. Navigational charts are primarily used in boating applications because they detail water areas, but also have great value to anglers who use them to identify depths, habitats, and underwater features relevant to specific fish species.

See: Maps.

CHART PLOTTER
Electronic navigation equipment featuring maplike or chartlike detail in electronic cartographic form, used in conjunction with GPS.

See: GPS.

CHART RECORDER
Also known as a graph recorder, this is a sonar device using a roll of paper upon which the images of fish, objects, and underwater terrain are displayed.

See: Sonar.

CHILE

Chile has an excellent fishing reputation, yet it is an angling enigma. This 2,650-mile-long country is entirely bounded on the west and south by the Pacific Ocean, but its long coastline is currently not a hotspot for visiting saltwater anglers. The topography of Chile is dominated by the Andes Mountains, and the country is highly regarded for its freshwater trout fisheries. Yet brown and rainbow trout are not native here. The primary angling action for trout occurs in the country's southernmost 1,000 miles. Despite its many lakes and rivers, Chile is not noted for diversity in its freshwater species, although this doesn't bother trout anglers, as it has plenty of diversity in its trout waters.

Because Chile's most popular trout waters are in the Southern Hemisphere, they can be enjoyed when most visiting anglers from the Northern Hemisphere are experiencing cold weather at home. This advantage—coupled with terrific scenery, friendly and hospitable Chileans, and trout that are eager and large on average—makes for an inviting situation.

Bordered on the north by Peru, on the northeast by Bolivia, and on the east by Argentina, Chile has an average width of under 110 miles and is fringed by the Andes along the entire eastern region. The Andes are widest in the north and include broad plateaus and many peaks over 20,000 feet. Northern Chile, which is arid, also features low coastal mountains on the west; between these and the Andes is a plateau region. This area has few freshwater resources, but the northern coast has garnered historical billfishing significance.

In central Chile, which has a Mediterranean climate (somewhat akin to northern California), the plateau region becomes the fertile Central Valley, which is about 600 miles long, between 25 and 50 miles wide, and the most heavily populated area of the country. This is Chile's main agricultural area. The Andes in central Chile are narrower and lower, but they have the most important passes. The central coast has Chile's finest natural harbors.

Southern Chile has a temperate climate (similar to the Pacific Northwest in the United States) and is without an interior valley. The Andes here are mainly under 6,000 feet, and the coastline is markedly indented with fiords. Archipelagoes extend along the southern coast from Chiloé Island to Cape Horn, and are actually the peaks of submerged coastal mountains. These include the Chonos Archipelago, Wellington Island, and the western portion of Tierra del Fuego. The central and southern regions contain the greatest freshwater fishing opportunities, with numerous deep blue lakes and hundreds of rivers and streams that are relatively short and flow from the western slopes of the Andes toward the Pacific Ocean.

Large portions of Chile are considered geologically unstable and are subject to earthquakes and volcanic activity. These events have affected some freshwater resources over the years.

Freshwater

Although it has been visited by intrepid anglers since the late 1940s, and despite its size and abundance of waters, Chile has relatively few fishing camps. Many operators have come and gone over the years, and possibly two dozen in total exist today, perhaps half of which have opened since the early 1990s. That may reflect a new interest and growing popularity in Chilean fishing, but it also implies an abundance of wilderness water that is rarely visited.

For the trout angler, Chile offers wading or drifting in rivers under a backdrop of snowcapped peaks, and dozens of trout daily, all in the 1- to 3-pound range and some that press the 5- to 8-pound mark. The fishing isn't always that good, and some rivers have better-size fish than others, but good numbers of quality fish combined with gorgeous scenery is the reason anglers travel to Chile.

Chilean rivers are relatively short, generally rising in the Andes and flowing west to the Pacific; some originate in Argentina, and most are fed primarily by the perpetual snow cover of the Andes. Brown trout and rainbows are the mainstays, although some brook trout exist as well in certain streams. The browns were introduced from Germany in 1905, while the rainbows and brookies came from the United States.

The "Lake Region" of Chile has gained a lot of attention in the past, and is well known among traveling trout anglers. Situated about 500 miles south of the capital city of Santiago and located in an area extending roughly from Temuco to Puerto Montt (the southern part of Chile's central region), the Lake Region includes Lakes Villarrica, Ranco, Rupanco, Panguipulli, Riñihue, and Llanquihue—all of which are connected to rivers and in the past have supported the bulk of Chilean angling. Among the rivers of note are the Cumilahue, Calcurrupe, Petrohue, Tolten, San Pedro, Trancura, Liucura, Furaleliu, Nilahue, and Carran. Many of the region's larger waters, such as the Petrohue, are floated in drift boats, as well as waded.

The southern region, however, has some of the less-accessible and more undisturbed fishing, with excellent angling for brown and rainbow trout. The arrival of camps in the area has focused increased attention here. The region is sometimes referred to as the Chilean Patagonia, because the Patagonia region of South America once included the southern parts of both Argentina and Chile. Local lakes include Paloma, Yelcho, Pollux, and others, which likewise are amid rivers and generally known for larger trout on average. Significant rivers include the Paloma, Azul, Balboa, Simpson, Desague, Sin Nombre, Nireguao, Futaleufu, Palena, and Cisnes. There are many more, including tributaries, and other lakes. Some are floated as well as waded.

Although trout are the almost exclusive quarry of visiting anglers, steelhead, chinook salmon, and coho salmon also flourish in southern coastal rivers.

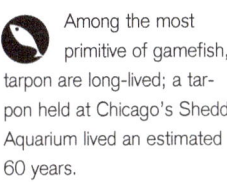

Among the most primitive of gamefish, tarpon are long-lived; a tarpon held at Chicago's Shedd Aquarium lived an estimated 60 years.

These have become established over the years as a result of escapes from pen-rearing farm operations along the coast. Sea trout exist in the southernmost region of Tierra del Fuego *(see: Argentina)*.

Trout fishing in southern Chile consists almost exclusively of fly fishing, primarily because local lodge operators want it that way. Various methods produce, so an assortment of fly-line types are necessary; 6- to 8-weight rods are suitable. Flies vary widely, but it's worth knowing that a common trout food item in many Chilean rivers is a small freshwater crab called the *pancora*. Felt-soled waders are necessary for mossy rocks, and light chest waders are best. Good sunglasses are necessary, especially when sight fishing for trout, which is sometimes possible in low clear waters.

The trout season in southern Chile is the opposite of what visitors from the Northern Hemisphere are accustomed to. Spring and summer extend from October through April, and trout fishing generally takes place from November through early April Some anglers prefer to fish early and late in the season, but in some locations this may have no bearing. Later in the season, however, larger browns often move out of the lakes and into rivers prior to spawning. Early-season fishing can be productive during periods of high cold water due to runoff.

Saltwater

Approximately 3,100 miles of Pacific coastline should offer opportunity for exceptional saltwater fishing, but Chile has not developed this resource; boats, guides, information sources, and the like are almost nonexistent in most areas. Their availability has fluctuated a good deal over time, in part due to offshore current shifts, in part to commercial activities.

Chile has a great number of beaches, coves, bays, fiords, and the like from which to fish, and Chileans primarily fish from the shore or surf for corvina and flounder. Some boat fishing exists near shore for these species, as well as other bottom fish and mackerel, but offshore fishing is nearly nonexistent. The reasons for this are many: Boats and tackle are unavailable or too expensive, the water can be rough, and recreational angling is of minor interest and is not a tradition among Chileans. A host of other factors influences this trend

Perhaps ironically, Chile is engraved in the historical annals of broadbill swordfish angling. This is because the northern coast was once a hotbed for this species. The northern ports of Antofagasta, Tocopilla, Iquique, and Arica, were jumping-off points for offshore expeditions for swordfish, black marlin, striped marlin, dolphin, and tuna, with Iquique being the most prominent site. In the early 1950s, Iquique had a few sportfishing boats, and expeditions here by renowned anglers S. Kip Farrington and Michael Lerner were well chronicled. Many broadbills, and numerous large fish, were caught here, and sight fishing for these bruisers became legendary. The current all-tackle world record—a 1,182-pounder—was registered

There are no crowds to compete for the trout on the Rio Baker.

at Iquique in May of 1953, and, in light of the worldwide depressed state of swordfish, seems like an untouchable accomplishment. Two other record swordfish, 759 and 772 pounds, were also caught during this period.

This great fishery existed thanks to the course of the cold, rich Humboldt Current and its upwelling nature near shore, but the fishery for broadbills and marlin declined as a result of commercial fishing, the vagaries of El Niño, shifts in the Humboldt Current, political changes within the country that made angling forays less likely, and perceived problems related to the collapse of anchovy stocks off Peru. As a result, there was almost no offshore fishing effort for decades, until the mid-1980s. Swordfish of 533 and 657 pounds were caught in the late 1980s at Algarrobo, about 50 miles south of Valparaiso, which is much farther south from Iquique. These established new line-class records and they, as well as other fish caught and observed around the same time, proved that big fish still existed. This did not result in a rush of anglers, however, in part because the entire coast is devoid (or nearly so) of recreational boats, there is no infrastructure for saltwater angling tourism, and hot billfisheries exist elsewhere. Also, with most swordfishing being a sight-and-bait affair, it's necessary to have calm conditions. A preponderance of rough weather here from January through May can mean a lot of down time, not to mention cold-weather fishing.

Nevertheless, the central coast is one that might be viable in the future should a number of conditions change. It could well be the place for catching record swordfish in the future.

CHINA

Covering nearly 3.7 million square miles of Asian territory, China is the third largest country in the world, yet it is virtually anonymous to anglers. With no known history of fishing for sport, with a great dependence on inland and marine fish as protein, and with no infrastructure for angling-related travel, China has been virtually off the world angling radar screen for most of the twentieth century. This is likely to be unchanged in the near future, although the country has enormous water reserves and the world's longest history of fish cultivation and propagation. There are rainbow trout in China as well as a smattering of largemouth bass, plus the mother lode of carp; pelagic species are reportedly caught sporadically off Hong Kong. There are no reports of commendable opportunity, however, although the exotic nature of travel within China is in itself meritorious and compelling.

To comprehend why there is so little opportunity in such a large country with a lot of water, and also why it might have potential in the future, it is helpful to understand the overall nature of the country, its natural resources, and the needs of its people.

China has a diverse landscape, not unlike the United States. Its higher elevations are generally in the west and include some of the world's highest mountain ranges and plateaus; mountains take up more than 40 percent of the country, mountain plateaus more than 25 percent, and basins and plains the remainder. Climate varies from subarctic to tropical, with alpine and desert regions, and there are broad water resources.

China's population of more than 1.4 billion people constitutes more than 20 percent of the world's population. Obviously, fish are an important food resource today, but they have been so for thousands of years. China's Fan Li is believed to be the first person to breed and raise fish (reportedly common carp); this occurred more than 2,400 years ago in the eastern part of the country, at Wushi in Kiangsu Province. Fan Li wrote the first known document on fish culture, a book entitled *Fish Breeding*, in 473 B.C.

The Chinese have almost exclusively viewed fish as an integral part of farming. Fish culture in China exists in ponds, reservoirs, and lakes. Chinese farmers and scientists have become masters of integrated fish farming. They have long utilized cut grasses to feed pond carp, for example, and now use animal manure (treated to kill parasites and bacteria) for fertilizing the ponds where fish are raised.

They have also mastered fish production in rice fields (paddy culture). Rice has always been the number one grain crop in China, and relics unearthed from the mid-Eastern Han Dynasty (A.D. 25–220) have shown that even at that time farmers placed excess carp fry from cultivated ponds in their rice fields. This cultivation practice was evidently reserved for carp until the middle of the twentieth century, but since then has included other species, among them tilapia, catfish, and rainbow trout (in the north). Rice-fish farming has become much more refined in recent decades and is now an important component of the national drive to increase food production.

Commercial sea fishing and inland fish farming have been vitally important to the Chinese, both for national consumption and export. Taken together, these constitute an annual fisheries harvest that has ranked China first among all nations since 1990. Sea harvests have been decreasing, however, particularly in local waters, and aquaculture efforts—especially inland—have intensified with the encouragement of the Chinese government. China has 192 fisheries research institutes with nearly 30,000 specialists. Five fisheries institutes have 9,000 students. Virtually all of this effort is focused on food production and not on fisheries development or management that provides recreation. As a result, China's food-fish harvest since 1985 has increased at roughly 10 times the annual rate of increase in the rest of the world. The production of inland aquaculture ranks first in the world, and 75 percent of it occurs in ponds.

Anglers often cast to the wake of a cruising fish. The wake indicates where the fish has been; you need to determine where the fish is headed and then cast ahead of it.

This success has not been without some problems, including reduced water quality, water needs that exceed supply in some areas, fish diseases, and declining inshore saltwater fishery resources. Concurrent with this are problems with regard to pollution of major rivers and deforestation. The objective of fisheries managers in China in the late 1990s was to increase aquaculture production by 60 percent. This would seem to leave little room for predatory species favored by anglers, given that the benefit and revenue from whatever tourism is so generated would be dwarfed by commercial activities.

The major fish species for inland aquaculture today are grass carp, black carp, silver carp, bighead carp, common carp, crucian carp, Chinese bream, mud carp, and tilapia. Marine aquaculture in China is mostly operated in shallow seas, shoals, and bays, with cultured species including shrimp, oysters, mussels, scallops, various clams, abalones, red porgies, black porgies, grouper, and crabs.

Freshwater Resources

The major rivers, and more than 50 percent of China's watershed, drain to the Pacific. Rivers account for nearly 40 percent of China's water resources. The most well-known rivers include the Yangtze, Yellow, Lujiang, Lancangjiang, Yarlung Zangbo, Heilongjiang, Liaohe, Haihe, Huaihe, Xijiang, Tumenjiang, Yalujiang, Qiantangjiang, Minjiang, and Oujiang. Although these rivers are large, some are nearly or virtually dry at their mouths due to upriver needs and usage, and many are extremely dirty.

Lakes contribute more than 42 percent of China's water resources. The most prominent freshwater lakes are Boyanghu, Dongtinghu, Taihu, Hulunci, Hongzehu, Chaohu, Weishanhu, Xingkai, Qinghai, Dalai, Namucuo, Qilincuo, Nansi, Boshiteng, Aibi, and Zarinanmucuo; reportedly, more than 130 of China's lakes cover more than 100 square kilometers. Large saline lakes include Qinghaihu, Namujiehu, Zhalinghu, and Bositenghu.

The remaining 18 percent of China's water resources are contained in tens of thousands of reservoirs (one source pegged the number at 38,600, although there are conflicting reports), and many tens of thousands of ponds. The majority of reservoirs and ponds are in the east, mostly in the vicinity of the middle and lower reaches of the Yangtze Valley. The overall water area is increasing as the Chinese dam rivers and create new reservoirs and ponds. Many of the reservoirs, and reportedly some of the lakes, are subject to extremes in fluctuation. Bighead carp are the most prominent species in reservoirs, and grass carp the most prominent one in ponds, which are heavily eutrophic.

According to a report by the Food and Agriculture Organization (FAO) of the United Nations in 1977, China has more than 500 species of freshwater fish; these are dominated by cyprinids (carp), and of these some 200 are suitable for table use. According to a 1981 report, China has 709 freshwater fish species and 58 subspecies, excluding 64 species that migrate between sea and inland waters.

The FAO characterized China as "having fewer native species of freshwater fishes than in North America, and many fewer than in South America or Africa. The Asian species are more typically riverine. Thus, the natural or spontaneous fish fauna of lakes and reservoirs does not encompass the variety of feeding habits that is typical of the faunas of most African water bodies. Mollusks, detritus, phytoplankton, and plant feeders, and even zooplankton feeders adapted to open water, are often missing."

There are evidently only a few native predator species in China, and it is unclear what these are, although a couple have been reported to be similar to popular Western species. The evidence, however, is mainly anecdotal. In 1982 some anglers spent several days fishing large Jingpo Lake in southeastern Heilongjiang Province, which is in northeast China. The lake, which covers about 90 square kilometers and is 45 kilometers long, produced a fish locally called *Ao Hua Yu,* or "number one fish," which was described as basslike with tiger marks (striations) on its side. These fish were said to average 7.5 kilograms in the lake and reach up to 15 kilograms, but this has not been verified. However, it may have been a species referred to by the FAO in its 1977 report as mandarin fish *(Siniperca chautsi),* although it appeared to resemble a large white bass in body shape and could be a member of the Percichthyidae family (which includes white bass, yellow bass, and striped bass). The gringos called it a "China tiger bass," although there is no such recognized nomenclature, and its exact taxonomic classification is uncertain. The species was reportedly a game battler, however.

These anglers and their local guide also suggested that the lake, which has depth to 180 feet, held lake trout and muskellunge, but these species were not caught or personally verified. Whether there are lake trout, or a different species of lake-dwelling trout or landlocked char, here or elsewhere is unknown, and the probability of true muskellunge is remote, although the existence of a pike- or muskielike fish (perhaps the so-called pikehead of Southeast Asia) is plausible. The anglers fished from old rowboats, from narrow 30-foot-long motor launches, and also from shore.

A traveler to the middle of mainland China in 1997 reported seeing largemouth bass in a restaurant aquarium, and was told that they existed up to 5 kilograms in one lake in the region. The presence of largemouth bass in China has also been reported by a Canadian fisheries authority and by an independent resource organization, although specific locations and sizes in China have not been confirmed, nor is it known if they exist in any waters that are accessible for public recreation.

It is believed that largemouth bass, and also walleye, have been brought to China for cultivation purposes and to assess their prospects as farmed fish. Reportedly there is a fish similar to the walleye in Chinese waters (it has the similar opaque and reflective eye), although where and how widespread is unknown. Native predator fish have been expunged from natural lakes and reservoirs when local water authorities determined that the body of water should be domesticated and used for food-fish production. If predators are found in existing or created lakes and reservoirs, the body of water is often poisoned to remove the predators and then stocked with filter-feeding species.

The FAO reported just two favored species of predatory fish in China in its 1977 report, which was based on a visit by a professional fisheries team. One was the basslike species previously noted; the other was a snakehead *(Ophiocephalus argus)*, or murrel, which is a bowfinlike species, some of which are barred along the flanks and may be known as striped snakehead or chevron snakehead. Although possibly growing to 2 or more feet in length, this fish would be of little interest to visiting anglers.

Other species, although in unknown quantities and distribution, that have been reported in China's freshwaters—according to an independent resource organization in 1997—include various sturgeon, catfish (including channel catfish in aquaculture and wels catfish), and tilapia; copper and putitor mahseer; barramundi; and white-spotted charr (also known as Siberian charr and which may be the species referred to as salmon in some literature).

While rainbow trout are farmed in the cooler areas of northern China, aquaculture reports from Chinese agencies indicate that salmon (species unidentified) are also produced, but it is unknown if there are any wild or naturally occurring trout or true salmon in this country, with the exception of Tibet. Brown and rainbow trout are known to exist in the high mountain lakes of the Himalayas, and they may exist in some waters of Tibet near the border with Bhutan, Nepal, India, or Pakistan, but this is speculative. Many of the lakes in the Tibetan Plateau of southwestern China are saline, but the headwaters of many major Chinese and south-Asian rivers originate in the mountain and plateau region.

Saltwater
On the east, China borders the Bohai, Yellow, and East China Seas; and on the south it borders the South China Sea. The coastline is 18,000 kilometers long, and the more than 6,500 islands along it form numerous bays.

There are reportedly more than 3,000 marine species in the region, and coastal resources have been pressured for a very long time, especially in more recent times. The economically important species caught commercially in local waters, according to Chinese scientists, are various croaker, chub mackerel, scad, Pacific herring, Spanish mackerel, Chinese herring, pomfrets, flounder, butterfish, porgies, red snapper, cod, sardines, sharks, and anchovies. Cuttlefish, squid, octopuses, mussels, oysters, clams, abalones, and scallops are among the mollusks taken, with shrimp and crabs among the shellfish. Aquaculture is practiced in the tidal inshore areas.

Little, if any, angling takes place, as it is inconceivable to fish for any purpose other than securing food, although reports indicate some sportfishing for pelagic species at several oil platforms 60 to 90 miles offshore from Hong Kong. Small black marlin are said to be available here—plus wahoo, yellowfin tuna, barracuda, and rainbow runners—from April through October. Sailfish were reported in the past but not in recent times. There were reportedly 6,500 pleasure boats in Hong Kong in 1998, but only two were rigged for sportfishing.

Other species, although in unknown quantities and distribution, were reported in China's brackish and marine waters by an independent resource organization in 1997. Among them were various sharks, trevally, tuna (including bigeye and bluefin), snapper, grouper, and flounder; dolphin; barramundi; kawakawa; cod; steelhead; blue marlin; and oxeye or Indo-Pacific tarpon. As with inland species, there is apparently little, if any, sportfishing effort for these species.

Ninety miles from mainland China, the island of Taiwan reportedly has recreational fishing for grouper, snapper, jack crevalle, sea bass, trevally, mackerel, corvina, barracuda, needlefish, and ladyfish, mainly from rocky shores and surf. Swordfish, marlin, sailfish, wahoo, yellowtail, albacore, and dolphin were reported in the late 1980s in offshore waters, mainly some 42 miles southeast of Taiwan at Lanyu (Orchid) Island, although the present status of fisheries there is speculative.
See: Mongolia.

CHINE
The longitudinal strake between the upper portion of a boat above the waterline, and the bottom; the meeting spot of the bottom of a hull and the sides.

The angle of a hard chine is very precise whereas the angle of a soft chine is rounded or curved. A hard chine typically benefits speed but sacrifices comfort in heavy seas; a soft chine does not permit as much speed as a hard chine, but takes big waves more softly. In fiberglass fishing boats, manufacturers may modify these two basic chines to create a style that improves the performance of a particular hull, often with the added objective of producing a dry ride by deflecting spray.
See: Boat.

CHIRONOMID
Insects of the genus *Chironomus*.
See: Midges.

CHOCK

A block or wedgelike object set behind the wheels of a tow vehicle at a launch ramp to keep the vehicle from sliding backward while a boat is being launched or loaded; also a fitting that controls a rigging or mooring line.

CHRISTMAS ISLAND

See: Kiribati.

CHUB

In North America, the term chub is used to describe many unrelated fish, all of which are members of the largest fish family in the world, minnows *(see)*. Although the word minnow is commonly applied to many small fish, to scientists the minnow family is a large and old group of bony fish, Cyprinidae, which includes river chub as well as countless species of shiners *(see)*, dace *(see)*, and carp *(see)*.

Confusion about the chub branch of this family exists nevertheless; this is particularly evident when one sees "smoked chub" on a menu or in a fish market. This is actually a fish-market description for species of whitefish *(see)* or cisco *(see)* from the Great Lakes, which are not cyprinids. True chub are rather bony and do not make admirable table fare.

Species and habitat. Twenty-six minnows merit the name chub and inhabit waters from the Appalachians to the Pacific Coast. The larger, primitive chub of the genus *Gila* inhabit western North America. The most familiar chub may be the creek chub *(see: chub, creek)*, an inhabitant of creeks and lakes throughout eastern and central North America. Also well known are the various river chub, which are members of the genus *Nocomis* and famed architects of the fish world.

River chub are olive-colored minnows with stout bodies, large scales, and light yellow to red orange caudal fins. The seven *Nocomis* species are identified by unique patterns and the size of the tubercle spots on the head and snout of males. Female and young chub lack tubercles.

The largest river chub are bull chub and bigmouth chub, and the largest males range from 12 to 15 inches. Bull chub and bigmouth chub are rivaled in size only by the fallfish *(Semotilus corporalis; see fallfish)*, the largest native eastern minnows. The closely related creek chub *(Semotilus atromaculatus)* rarely reaches 12 inches in length.

River chub are widely distributed in streams of eastern and central North America, although some have restricted distribution: redspot chub in eastern Oklahoma and parts of Kansas, Missouri, and Arkansas; redtail chub in the highland rim of the Cumberland River drainage of southern Kentucky and north-central Tennessee; bigmouth chub in the New River drainage of North Carolina, Virginia, and West Virginia; and bull chub from parts of Virginia and North Carolina.

Other species (hornyhead, river, and bluehead) are more widely distributed. The hornyhead is a common baitfish, often called redtail chub. The wide distribution of chub stems from past geologic events, such as glaciation and changing river courses.

Chub often occur in schools with other minnows, particularly stonerollers, in runs and pools of clear, moderately sloping gravel and rock-bottomed streams and rivers. It is not unusual to see young smallmouth bass swimming and actively feeding near chub. Chub and young bass may be eating the same prey, but older smallmouth bass readily consume chub. Bluehead chub, redspot chub, and redtail chub more commonly inhabit smaller streams, whereas river chub, bull chub, and bigmouth chub are more common in main stems and large tributaries.

Chub are primarily sight feeders, taking small invertebrates from the bottom or from the drift. Although they have small barbels, they may not be useful for feeding, more likely being a trait retained from a primitive ancestor. Chub primarily eat immature insects, although they also eat aquatic worms, crustaceans, mollusks, water mites, small fish, and aquatic plants. Chub prefer to feed in the swifter-flowing sections because more food is available there, but to avoid sapping their energy, they usually stay within 4 inches of the streambed, often behind larger stones.

Spawning. Chub spawn in spring when water temperatures are between 60° and 75°F. During the breeding season, males develop large hornlike tubercles and spectacular coloration—pink, rose, yellow, orange, and blue, depending on the species. The "bluehead" name comes from the intense slate blue head of the spawning male.

Colors and tubercles signal spawning readiness to nearby ripe females. Male river chub, bigmouth chub, bull chub, and bluehead chub in breeding colors also have a swollen head, or "nuptial crest." Female chub do not grow as large as males and lack tubercles, presumably because females play no role in building or defending the nest.

Large body size and tubercles help the male repel other males that invade his territory. Fights can be vicious, and the nuptial crest cushions blows to the head from other males. Tubercles may play a role in stimulating the ripe female, but probably the tubercle patterns help female chub recognize the correct species for breeding.

All species of *Nocomis* chub construct gravel mounds, as do the tongue-tied and cutlips minnows (genus *Exoglossum*). Fallfish and creek chub build a similar, although more ridge-shaped, mound. The gravel nests of chub are truly impressive in size.

The male chub first picks up pebbles with his mouth or pushes them with his head to remove them from the nest site, forming a depression 2 to 4 inches deep. He then fills that depression with pebbles to form a platform, and adds pebbles to the platform to make a circular mound.

Males collect pebbles from areas within 20 feet of the nest, but sometimes they gather material from as far away as 80 feet. The geometric shape of the mound suggests that the architect understands fluid mechanics. The mound actually creates an eddy behind the nest and slows the current in the spawning trough where eggs and sperm are deposited.

Often the male is spooked before an observer encounters a nest, leaving no clues to the builder's identity. As water levels recede, some chub mounds are left "high and dry," resembling castles. Early ichthyologists thought that children or crayfish built the mounds.

Bigmouth and bull chub build the largest mounds, up to 50 inches in diameter and 15 inches high. The usual pebble used in mound construction is 1 to $2^{1}/_{2}$ inches in diameter, which is quite a mouthful, yet some are as large as 4 inches in diameter. The largest stones must be pushed or dragged to the mound. It has been estimated that a male chub spends 20 to 30 hours building his gravel mound and may travel up to 16 miles during his many short forays to collect pebbles.

To indicate readiness to spawn, the male expels pebbles from the spawning trough, positions himself over the trough, and quivers his anal fin and lower body, as if fanning the spot intended for eggs. The female then approaches and swims beneath the male. The male quivers his caudal fin and embraces the female as eggs and milt are shed in the spawning trough. The brief spawning act is repeated dozens of times in rapid succession with one or more females. The male then collects more pebbles to cover the fertilized eggs and repeats the process; he tends the nest for up to two weeks after spawning.

Spawning may be interrupted when male chub from other nests attack the spawning male. Hornyhead chub have been observed diving headfirst into the spawning trough of another male and dislodging some eggs, which are quickly eaten by other chub. After such bold affronts, the fight is on.

Perhaps as a means of sizing up each other, males sometimes align themselves and swim upstream with strong tail swings, head butting, or heads pressed together in a fish version of locking horns. At other times, the nesting male and his challenger swim in a circular pattern over the nest, not unlike wrestlers moving around the ring, planning their next move.

Chub use these displays to avoid fights they can't win. Fights usually occur between similar-size males. In later spring, one might find dying males with head wounds, suggesting the heavy toll of breeding behavior.

Egg-eating predators, which are common in streams, occasionally invade the chub's nesting territory. Male chub charge and head-butt intruding suckers that are easily five times heavier. Sometimes a group of male chub simultaneously attack the intruder, an effective signal for a sucker to move on.

Building a large gravel mound is an enormous undertaking that must be worth the investment or the habit never would have evolved and persisted. The mound protects eggs and larval chub from predators, current, temperature variation, and siltation. The gravel mound also provides greater aeration and water flow.

Community nests. Chub mounds become hotspots for spawning by other minnows as well, often resembling "minnow orgies" as hundreds of minnows in breeding color are attracted to these mounds. It has been reported that at least 13 minnow species have reproduced on a bluehead chub nest. Several species of minnows may spawn on a single chub mound, and the male does not chase the minnows away, even as he continues to spawn. Minnows spawn most often on chub mounds regularly attended by a male chub; abandoned mounds are inferior.

This relationship may be obligatory for some minnows; yellowfin shiners, for example, do not display reproductive colors or behaviors unless spawning bluehead chub are present. Apparently, yellowfin shiners are stimulated by the spawning activity of chub. These and other nest associates benefit from a clean, protected nest site, tended by the diligent male chub. Chub may also benefit from the association because chub embryos and larvae represented only 3 percent of the young reared in these "co-op" mounds. So the more numerous young yellowfin shiners diluted predation on young chub.

As builders and tenders of the spawning habitats for numerous species, river chub are what biologists call "keystone species." In other words, removal of chub from a stream would be more detrimental than the removal of other species. One researcher discovered that chub nests were possibly the only suitable spawning gravel for common and rosyface shiners in a small creek. Chub concentrate gravel that otherwise would be scattered over unsuitable nesting substrates, thereby enhancing minnow reproduction.

Chub watching and angling. Chub nests can often be spotted by the observant angler, beginning when water temperatures first exceed 60°F. Concentrate a search for nests in knee-deep water with noticeable current and patches of gravel. If you're wading, use polarized glasses to reduce surface glare. For a closer view, don a face mask and gradually move through likely areas such as transitions between riffles and pools, where surface turbulence is slight.

The most obvious benefit anglers derive from chub is using them as bait when fishing for such top predators as smallmouth bass, spotted bass, catfish, walleye, and sauger. These fish are all adaptable predators that normally take advantage of locally abundant chub and minnow populations.

Chub do not have a devoted following of anglers and are not considered a gamefish, but some people

 A six-month growth of barnacles on a ship's hull can result in having to burn 40 to 45 percent more fuel to maintain cruising speed.

do angle for them with light tackle; there is plenty of enjoyment to derive from this sport, especially since it is easy to find unfished populations. Small chub can be caught by fly fishing with small nymphs or by drifting a bit of worm. Larger chub are more prone to streamers, standard-size nymphs, and spinners. Chub stay close to the streambed, so it's important to get and keep your offering in the chub's domain.

Threats. Like other stream fish, chub are threatened by large-scale alterations of native habitats. Chub populations have been locally reduced or eliminated by excessive sedimentation, daily flow fluctuations that obliterate mounds, deep-release dams and associated cold tailwaters, gravel mining, and nonnative fish predators. Good land management practices that restore or protect streamside vegetation and natural stream meandering benefit chub and the rest of the fish community. None of the chub in the genus *Nocomis* are federally threatened or endangered. Some are, however, listed as species of special concern due to their limited distribution or recent declines in distribution or abundance.

CHUB, BERMUDA *Kyphosus sectatrix*.
Other names—Bermuda sea chub; French: *calicagère blanche;* Spanish: *chopa blanca*.

A member of the Kyphosidae family of sea chub, the Bermuda chub is a commonly encountered species, although not one that is aggressively sought by anglers. It is often caught in clear-water harbors and around reefs. Most individuals are reportedly good table fare, but their flesh spoils quickly and should be eaten soon after capture.

Identification. The Bermuda chub has an ovate profile with a short head and small mouth. A yellow stripe, bordered in white, runs from the edge of the mouth to the edge of the gill cover. The body is compressed and generally steel or blue gray with muted yellowish stripes. The fins are dusky, the tail forked, and the scales are usually edged with blue. It may occasionally have white spots or blotches. A less common, very similar, but larger-growing relative is the yellow chub *(K. incisor)*.

Size. Bermuda chub commonly weigh $1^1/_2$ to 2 pounds and measure 10 to 12 inches in length. Reported maximum lengths and weights vary widely; the all-tackle world record is a 13-pound, 4-ounce Florida fish.

Distribution. In the western Atlantic, the Bermuda chub occurs from Massachusetts and Bermuda south to Brazil, including the Gulf of Mexico and the Caribbean; in the eastern Atlantic it occurs south of Morocco to the Gulf of Guinea, and rarely in the Mediterranean or off Madeira.

Habitat/Behavior. Like most other sea chub, the Bermuda chub is a schooling species that moves quickly and is often abundant in clear water around tropical reefs, harbors, and small ships.

Food and feeding habits. Bermuda chub mainly feed on benthic algae, and also on small crabs and mollusks. Because of its small mouth, it nibbles food and is regarded by anglers as an accomplished bait stealer.

Angling. Although Bermuda chub are numerous in some areas and very energetic and scrappy fighters, there is no concerted angling effort for them. They are primarily caught in clear-water harbors around docks, and incidentally on reefs. They are not aggressive feeders like most predators, and patient anglers using light tackle catch them on small hooks baited with pieces of shrimp, crab, or cut bait. Because they nibble food, it's necessary to set the hook quickly the instant that one gnaws on the bait.

CHUB, CREEK *Semotilus atromaculatus*.
Other names—horned dace, common chub, brook chub, mud chub.

The creek chub is one of the largest chub and a member of the minnow, or Cyprinidae family, making it a distant relative to carp *(see)*. Occurring in great abundance in North America, it is important forage for sportfish, often competes with those larger predators for food, and, because it is hardy and lively, is also a prominent bait used by anglers.

Identification. The snout of the creek chub is pointed and its mouth large, with a single small barbel in the corner of each jaw, sometimes hidden between the maxillary and the premaxillary. The body is stout, colored olive brown on the back, silvery on the sides with shades of iridescent purple, and whitish on the underside. Both adults and juveniles have a blackish stripe along the back and a black caudal spot, although these become faint or absent on adults. There is a large black spot at the front of the dorsal fin. Breeding males take on an orange hue, also gaining 4 to 8 large, thornlike tubercles (thus the name "horned dace") on their opercles, body scales, and fins. The creek chub may occasionally appear to be speckled with black sand, but this is the result of being heavily covered with the parasite that causes black spot disease (which is harmless to the fish and is not transmittable to humans), and not as a result of natural coloring.

Other characteristics include a complete lateral line with 47 to 65 scales, 8 anal fin rays, 8 dorsal

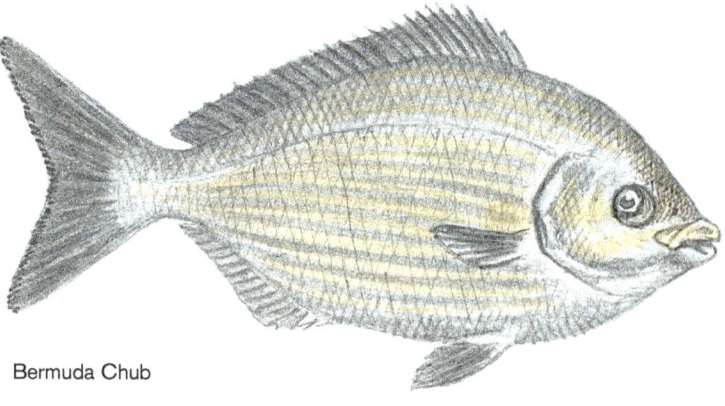

Bermuda Chub

fin rays, and a pharyngeal tooth count formula of 2-5-4-2 (2 teeth in minor rows and 4 or 5 teeth in major rows).

The creek chub can be distinguished from the pearl dace (*Semotilus margarita*, a k a *Margariscus margarita*), by its larger mouth. The fallfish (*Semotilus corporalis; see fallfish*), is a strikingly similar fish to the creek chub, but with larger scales, larger eyes, and without a black spot on the dorsal fin.

Size/Age. The creek chub can attain a maximum length of between 6 and 12 inches, depending on environment; the average 4 to 6 inches long. Adult males grow faster than females, and the largest creek chub are usually male. They can live up to seven years.

Distribution. Creek chub are found from the Maritime Provinces of Canada west to Montana and south to Texas and northern Georgia. Their distribution extends throughout the eastern half of southern Canada and the central and eastern United States. They occur in the Atlantic, Canadian (of New Mexico), Great Lakes, Gulf Coast, Hudson Bay, and Mississippi drainages.

Habitat. These fish prefer cool, clear water in the gravel-bottomed pools and runs of creeks and streams. In dry weather and during low water, they can survive in isolated pools. They are seldom found in lakes. Some ichthyologists refer to the creek chub as "king of the headwaters" because they are often the largest fish found in very small streams. Deeper pools usually contain the largest individuals. Creek chub are tolerant of some pollution and can be abundant in urban streams.

Spawning behavior. Creek chub are pit-ridge spawners that build their gravel nests in runs and the downstream sections of pools. Nest building and spawning occurs between March and June in water temperatures ranging between 12° and 20°C. Creek chub have an interesting spawning ritual, which begins in spring when the male digs a pit in the stream bottom by removing bits of gravel with his mouth. He carefully guards the pit where the spawning occurs and attracts a female. Adult males are territorial during the breeding season and can be observed swimming in parallel, chasing each other, and ramming their tuberculate heads against each other. Some males attempt to spawn over the nests built by other males. Spawning occurs when the male wraps his body around the female and eggs are released over the nest. A single female can produce more than 7,000 eggs, but only a portion of these are released during a single spawning event. Females are often observed floating belly up for a few seconds after spawning. They quickly recover and can spawn again.

Food. Creek chub are omnivores that feed on a variety of foods, including zooplankton, aquatic and terrestrial insects, crayfish, mollusks, frogs, and fish. Adult creek chub have been shown to primarily consume fish, including the young of their own species.

Creek Chub

Angling. Although sometimes caught for recreation, often by stream netting, the creek chub does not support much angling effort; however, most captured fish are used as baits. Although edible, it is usually not eaten due to a multitude of tiny bones.
See: Chub; Minnow.

CHUB, EUROPEAN *Leuciscus cephalus*.
Other names—chub; French: *chevaine*; German: *aitel*; Italian: *cavedano*; Spanish: *cacho*.

The European chub, which is primarily known simply as chub in Europe, is an important coarse fish *(see)* that is widely sought by anglers and the subject of minor commercial interest. It is a member of the large Cyprinidae family, which includes minnows *(see)* and carp *(see)*, and is a darker and larger-growing relative of European dace *(see: dace)*. One of the warier coarse fish, it is pursued with varied baits and some lures, and by stalking as well as by stillfishing.

Identification. European chub have a stocky and somewhat cylindrical body, a blunt snout and large wide mouth, slightly forked tail, and an erect dorsal fin. The scales are dark-edged, which produces a grille-like appearance. The back is dark and the sides golden brown tapering to a white or gray belly; the fins are tinged with pink coloring in young fish and are darker in older fish. Young chub may be confused with dace (*Leuciscus leuciscus*); fin coloration is different, however, as is shape. The chub has convex dorsal and anal fins, whereas those of the dace are concave.

Size/Age. This fish is commonly caught in the 1- to 3-pound class, and any specimen over 5 pounds is a good one. The all-tackle world record is under 6 pounds, but this is not indicative of its potential, as the European chub is reported to attain a maximum of 16 pounds. Chub exceeding 7 pounds are rare, however.

European Chub

Distribution. The European chub is widespread in inland waters from Portugal east to the former Soviet Union and Turkey.

Habitat. Creeks and fast-flowing rivers are the principal domain of this chub, although it also enters brackish water in the eastern Baltic and has been introduced into some lakes. The upper reaches of flowing water are primary habitat, but it may compete in those environs with salmonids and be viewed with disfavor by anglers.

Behavior. During spawning season male chub develop large hornlike tubercles like their smaller North American relatives *(see: chub)*. They spawn in the spring in rocky shallows, and the young form schools, or shoals, and feed eagerly; these schools dissolve by maturity, however. Adult chub are not a school fish, but they are nearly so. There may be a collection of chub in one place, and these may be of similar or disparate sizes, but this is a loose collection rather than a school. Only when alarmed do chub seem to act as one, and otherwise the fish behave singularly.

Food and feeding habits. The omnivorous European chub has a general-purpose appetite, which is one of the reasons why it is an amenable fish for anglers. It consumes aquatic insects, invertebrates, crayfish, snails, assorted small fish, lamprey eel larvae, and other food items, and may feed at all levels of the water column. Its powerful pharyngeal teeth (throat crushers) allow it to cope with various forage, some quite large.

Unlike most other cyprinids, these chub are prone to feeding throughout the day, rather than principally in low-light conditions, and they are not as averse to cold water. In warm water, they are likely to feed aggressively and may then be easily caught. Yet they are also discerning and sometimes take a hooked bait without offering any strike indication.

Angling. Like many other coarse fish, chub are tenacious but not spectacular fighters. Fishing for chub is similar to fishing for other coarse fish, although there may be more of them available in a given spot than of other species.

Most chub fishing is done from the bank or shore, with people fishing river runs that are from within 2 to 6 feet deep. Bottom fishing with assorted baits is the primary tactic, and this involves intensive prebaiting or chumming *(see)*, using groundbait *(see)* and an assortment of prepared, processed, and natural baits. Maggots, corn, worms, cheese, bread, pastes, slugs, and other items are used. Hooked baits may be fished with or without a float. Anglers use rods from 11 to 14 feet in length, line from 3 to 6 pounds in strength, and No. 8 to 20 bait hooks.

Although chub are mostly taken on baits, it is very possible to use other methods, especially fly fishing. Weighted nymphs are especially popular, followed by wet flies, terrestrial imitations, and dry flies dappled on the surface.

Chub are sometimes sought by sight fishing, rather than by angling in known chub-holding runs or pools. This requires spotting fish and using stealth to approach them, as chub spook readily.

CHUB, HORNYHEAD *Nocomis biguttatus.*
Other names—redtail chub.

The hornyhead chub is a member of the large Cyprinidae family, and a fairly common stream and river resident; smaller specimens are used as bait by anglers.

Identification. The body of a hornyhead chub is slender with a rounded snout. The mouth is large, almost terminal, with a small barbel above the jaws, and it has pharyngeal (throat) teeth. Hornyhead chub have dark-edged scales, a complete lateral line, and seven anal rays. Their coloring is bluish olive on the back, yellowish with iridescent green on the sides, and whitish on the underside. On the adult male, there is a bright red dot behind the eye; on the female the dot is brassy colored. Yellow iridescent stripes run along the back and the sides. There is a dark caudal spot, which is darkest on juveniles, around the snout. Breeding males are colored pink with pinkish orange fins and have many tubercles on the head.

The hornyhead chub can be distinguished from a bull chub *(Nocomis raneyi)* by its shorter snout, larger eyes, and red dot behind the eye. The bluehead chub *(Nocomis leptocephalus)*, although strikingly similar, has no red dot behind the eye, and it has a large loop on the right side of its intestine, distinguishing it from the hornyhead.

Size. The average size for a hornyhead chub is 8 inches, although some can grow to up to 10 inches.

Distribution. The hornyhead chub is found from New York west to Wyoming and Colorado and south to northern Arkansas; in its easternmost range in New York, it can be found in the Niagara River and several streams in the Mohawk River system, but it does inhabit the Susquehanna, Delaware, and Hudson Rivers.

Habitat. This species lives in small to medium-size rivers and streams. It prefers warm, clear waters with a moderate to sluggish current, especially with a sandy, gravelly bottom and aquatic vegetation.

Spawning behavior. The spawning season for hornyhead chub is from late May through June, when the male develops tubercles on the head. The male builds a nest from pebbles *(see: chub)*. Other

Hornyhead Chub

kinds of fish use this nest for spawning, but the male hornyhead will ward off other fish of the same species.

Food. The hornyhead chub is omnivorous, feeding primarily on insect larvae but also consuming small crustaceans, earthworms, and algae.

Angling. As with other chub, the hornyhead presents minor sportfishing value, although it is occasionally caught on small jigs, flies, and spinners fished close to the streambed. The greater interest is in smaller specimens as bait for predator species.
See: Chub.

CHUB, SEA
Sea chub are members of the Kyphosidae family, which are distributed in the Atlantic, Indian, and Pacific Oceans. Some 50 species are among this group, and most are usually found near shore. Some are primarily algal feeders, others are primarily carnivorous. Most are medium-size schooling species and are abundant in clear water around tropical reefs, harbors, and ships. The most commonly known member is the Bermuda chub (see: chub, Bermuda).

CHUBSUCKER
Chubsuckers are members of the sucker (see: suckers) family, Catostomidae. They are divided into three separate species: the creek chubsucker (*Erimyzon sucetta*), the lake chubsucker (*Erimyzon oblongus*), and the sharpfin chubsucker (*Erimyzon tenuis*). All species are extremely similar and are interchangeably referred to as "suckers" or "mullet" in different locales.

Chubsuckers are of little importance commercially and are predominately ignored for sportfishing. When taken from cold water, however, chubsuckers have good-flavored, firm flesh. Because of their abundance and their large size, suckers often account for the greatest biomass in streams and lakes, making them important forage for predator species.

Identification. Chubsuckers are characteristically defined by their small, protruding, suckerlike mouths and thick fleshy lips. Creek, lake, and sharpfin chubsuckers are similarly colored a greenish bronze, without a lateral line. There are usually 10 to 12 dorsal rays and 7 anal rays. The scales are dark-edged, and, on the creek chubsucker, accompanied by dark blotches. Young chubsuckers have a concentrated black band from the tip of the snout to the tail, on top of which is a yellow band. Breeding males are dark with a pink orange tint and several tubercles on each side of the snout. The creek chubsucker has a chubby body, whereas the lake and sharpfin chubsuckers are slightly more elongated.

All suckers excepting the chubsucker have a fully developed lateral line.

Size/Age. Chubsuckers can grow to 13 to 15 inches, but they rarely exceed 10 inches in length. The average age for a chubsucker is 5, although one can live up to 8 years.

Lake Chubsucker

Distribution. Creek chubsuckers inhabit waters from the Great Lakes and the Mississippi River drainages south to Georgia and gulf slope waters. Lake and sharpfin chubsuckers inhabit waters similar to those favored by creek chubsuckers, including waters as far west as Oregon and as far south as Florida.

Habitat. Lukewarm, clear waters of creeks, small rivers, lakes, ponds, and swamps, or other waters without turbidity, are favored environments. Chubsuckers are seldom found in streams, favoring the depths of still, calm waters. As bottom dwellers, chubsuckers prefer sand, gravel, or silt bottoms with abundant vegetation.

Life history/Behavior. Spawning occurs in early spring in small tributary waters. Sometimes the male builds a nest, but the eggs are usually scattered randomly over sand, gravel, or vegetation bottom and left to hatch unattended.

Food and feeding habits. Chubsuckers are bottom feeders, consuming insect larvae, aquatic plants, and small crustaceans.

CHUGGER
A term for a popping plug.
See: Surface Lure.

CHUM
Various types of food and attractants used to interest, hold, and concentrate fish. Chum is generally used in quantity, most often for bottom-feeding or pelagic species of fish; it is most frequently employed in conjunction with the use of a hooked bait (hook bait), but may also be used to bring fish into the range of anglers who cast a lure or fly. Chum may include live baitfish; whole dead baitfish; chunks of fish; a ground-up hashlike mixture of fish, various aquatic organisms (including mollusks and crustaceans), worms, or sundry other foods; bread (see: groundbait); grains; and processed foods. Chum may be dispensed by hand or in some type of containment device. It may be made and prepared by anglers or purchased ready-to-use from vendors; some items used as chum (shrimp boat refuse and bycatch, for example) are acquired from commercial fishermen and prepared for angling use.

Anglers who make their own fish-based chum primarily use the carcass of fish that they have kept and removed the meat from, or assorted forage fish that they have caught (usually by netting), perhaps mixed with mollusks or crustaceans, and mash these up using a heavy-duty meat grinder. Freshwater anglers have made creative soupy chums, particularly using worms, with kitchen blenders. Most mashed chum for saltwater fishing is purchased at bait stores, and shark anglers, who are especially likely to use chum, buy this by the bucket-load.

Chum is mostly used when anchored, and sometimes when drifting, but almost never employed for trolling. The use of chum is an integral part of many types of saltwater fishing. It is a small element of most freshwater fishing in North America, but an important one for certain species, in certain locations, and with some presentation methods, and is more popular in other parts of the world. In North America, the use of chum in freshwater is illegal in some localities, and a freshwater angler who wishes to use any type of chum should check on this, as well as what foods or baits are defined by the regulating agency as chum.
See: Chumming.

CHUM BAG
A mesh bag or sack filled with chum and lowered into the water next to a boat to attract fish.
See: Chum; Chumming.

CHUM LINE
The continuous underwater trail of chum and chum particles that is carried away from a boat by tide and or current.
See: Chum; Chumming.

CHUMMING
An effective technique for attracting, holding, and concentrating fish so that they will be available and susceptible to the angler's offerings. In chumming, various foods, called chum *(see)*, are put into the water to draw fish. The chum may include live baitfish; whole dead baitfish; chunks of fish; a ground-up hashlike or souplike mixture of fish, various aquatic organisms (including mollusks and crustaceans), worms, or sundry other foods; bread; grains; and processed foods. In saltwater, the items used for chum are most often endemic to the area, such as anchovies, herring, menhaden, or other forage fish, and are ordinarily favored by the species sought. Giant bluefin tuna, occasionally weighing more than a thousand pounds, will readily circle through a chum line, picking up chunks of herring, a fish they naturally consume. However, chum is not necessarily limited to the food on which fish normally feed. Bread is often an effective chum for some fish, as is whole kernel corn, neither of which exists in the normal food chain. A river carp, weighing just a few pounds, will eat both of these nonnatural items, as well as assorted processed baits. In saltwater, more anglers are experimenting with chum that includes oatmeal, cornmeal, and bread; and some use flavored dog food in bags or containers.

Chumming is most often done from a fixed position, such as an anchored boat, but chum may also be utilized in nearshore areas by a bank-, beach-, or pier-bound angler, and may be used while drifting in a boat. It is not employed when trolling but may be used to attract fish into casting range for both lure and bait presentations, although most chumming is coincidental with the offering of hooked bait.

Nearly every saltwater fish, and many freshwater species, will respond to some type of chum. However, chum is most practical for pelagic, or roaming, species, and for bottom-feeding fish. For sharks, chumming and fishing with bait is the major means of angling *(see: shark)*. It is also more practical for fish that rely on their sense of smell and taste more than vision, especially in freshwater. When one considers the energy expended as fish search for a meal, it's easy to understand why they will readily move toward the source of food, which in many cases is carried along by current. This may ultimately be their undoing, of course, when they encounter a piece of bait with a hook in it drifting or laying with the unhooked chum.

Dispersing chum in the water and then placing a hooked bait among it seems, at first glance, an easy technique and one that would guarantee successful angling, but this is not necessarily the case. There is an art to chumming, as well as to fishing in places where chum has been established. You must plan and work at it to be successful. Although chumming isn't always essential for a good day's catch, sometimes it does make the difference between success and failure. Moreover, chumming is not only used in conjunction with fishing a hooked bait, but often used in conjunction with lure or fly fishing. Saltwater fly anglers, for example, often chum on flats and in offshore waters to draw fish close enough to cast a fly to them.

When chumming, the route to achieving consistent success and minimizing failure is experience. Knowing where to anchor, whether to anchor or drift, how frequently to dispense the chum, when to add weight to your line to take the bait deeper, when to use a float to keep it at the right level, and other issues is possible only with experience. Even then, successful chumming may simply be trial and error. But, since so much of angling is finding and attracting fish, chumming is a technique that deserves consideration by every serious angler.

Saltwater Chumming
Chumming is an important element of catching fish in saltwater, yet this technique varies from area to area and for each species sought. There

are literally scores of variations, and the following sampling is representative of the most popular. Chumming in saltwater should be in every angler's arsenal of options; keep in mind that although most saltwater chumming takes place from boats, it may also be practiced from jetties, beaches, bridges, piers, and bulkheads.

Because saltwater is affected by tides and current (plus wind), chum is dispersed according to the movement of water. It may be dispensed by hand or from some type of container that is lowered into the water, or via a combination of both approaches, plus some innovative spot methods (like sand balls mixed with chum, which disperse as they lower). Putting chum into some type of dispenser is common. Devices used to contain various types of chum include a pot, bucket, mesh bag, wire basket, plastic crate, and an assortment of similar commercial or homemade devices. The overall size of these, and the size of holes or mesh, will vary with the bait used. There are also commercially available chum logs (made of zooplankton and menhaden oil). Most objects are hung from a transom cleat and lay in the surface of the water aft of the boat. Some chum baskets or cages may be lowered to various depths or near to the bottom, with a heavy weight. Long-distance placement of chum is made via quick-release arrangements.

In chumming, the tide or current moves the pieces or particles away from the place where they are dispensed, and they form an underwater trail called a chum line. A visible surface indication of the presence and movement of the chum is called a slick. A chum slick is the oily surface of the water above a chum line, and it is also carried away from the boat and may or may not extend as far back as the underwater trail of chum. Usually the chum particles sink deeper as they are carried away from the initial drop point, and the slick portion of surface water dissipates at some distance from the boat.

Where the current is substantial, the chum line may extend a long distance, and particles may not sink very deep. In slack water, the chum line has much less distant movement and more vertical sinking. Many saltwater species are fish that move in and out of areas or move widely in search of food, so if they are present in the area you chum, they will eventually detect the chum line. However, in some locations, particularly in shallow backwaters and marshes, and on reefs, the fish are more resident and wander less, and may require more concentrated chum rather than a long trail.

Maintaining the chum. To be successful at chumming, you must maintain a delicate balance. You want to attract the fish you're seeking so that they will respond to a baited hook or to an artificial lure that is fished in the chum line or in the area being baited. However, if you chum too heavily, the fish will often settle well back in the slick, gorging on your offering. On the other hand, if you chum too sparingly or fail to maintain a consistent flow of chum, the fish will show little interest and will often move off. Maintaining that perfect balance is something that isn't difficult, but it comes with experience. A good rule of thumb is to drop pieces of chum into the water at regular intervals. When fishing with a group of anglers, and especially aboard a boat, one person should be assigned the responsibility of maintaining the chum line because, in the excitement of catching fish, the chumming is often forgotten, only to be remembered too late, after the fish have moved out of the area.

Offshore, eastern Atlantic canyons. Anglers seeking bigeye tuna, yellowfin tuna, and albacore in the offshore canyons and shelf areas of the eastern Atlantic often use a combination of chunks of fish and ground fish with excellent results. Boats either are anchored or drift along with the wind or current, usually along the edges of the dropoff, where an upwelling of currents causes baitfish to congregate and the larger gamefish to feed.

Forage species, such as butterfish, mackerel, and herring, are cut into pieces, usually about the size of your index finger. Five or 6 pieces from a butterfish, and 8 or 10 from a mackerel or herring, is about right. This is usually done before leaving for the fishing grounds to save the chore of doing it on the water. The chummer tosses three or four chunks into the water and watches as they drift away. When the chum is 30 to 40 feet from the boat, more pieces are tossed over.

Chum needs to be dispensed at a consistent rate to keep a steady stream in the water column, but without providing too much free food.

After a dozen or more chunks have been deposited into the sea, a ladle full of "soup," which is a mixture of ground menhaden, mackerel, or herring and equal parts seawater, is deposited into the ocean. This mixture disperses in a cloud and is carried along with the current. As fish detect the scent of the soup drifting along, they move toward its source, picking up tiny pieces of the ground fish and also the chunks. It's not unusual to attract a school of tuna and see the fish moving ever closer to the boat, as the fish vie for the offering drifting along.

As the chummer goes about the task of attracting the fish, anglers must work their lines so as to present the bait in a natural drift. Terminal rigging is very basic. Some anglers just tie a size 4/0 through 7/0 O'Shaughnessy, beak, or circle style hook directly to the ends of their lines. Because the members of the tuna clan are often line-shy, many anglers use fluorocarbon leaders. The hook is tied directly to the end of a fluorocarbon leader that is 5 or 6 feet long, and the leader is attached to the monofilament line using a Surgeons Knot.

A half or a whole butterfish is an effective bait in the chum line. Some people favor the head section of butterfish because it is more durable, and others prefer the tail section. The choice evolves from experience as to which works for you.

Because squid are abundant in offshore and canyon waters, as are mackerel, some anglers will obtain a live bait and work that in the chum slick with excellent results. A live bait in distress will often immediately attract tuna. If your boat has a livewell (see), you can keep fresh bait in it. Live spots or porgies, 6 to 7 inches long and caught from coastal rivers and bays, also make an effective bait in a chum line.

Once hooked, the bait should be permitted to drift back with the chum unimpeded. Keep no tension on the line, letting it drift along with the chum until it is a hundred or more feet from the boat. Then reel in and repeat the procedure. As a rule, the angler who works at keeping the bait moving along with the chum will catch far more fish than the angler who locks the reel in gear and keeps it in one position. If you let the line hang in a fixed position, the current pushing against the bait will often push it toward the surface and spin it in a manner that is not as attractive to the fish as a drifting bait.

Make sure the hooked bait drifts with the chum; this may require adjustment from time to time. When there is little or no current, the chum will sink directly beneath the boat, as will your bait. With a moderate current, the bait and chum will usually flow together, and this is easily observed in the clear offshore water. If you see the chum settling deep and the current carrying your line near the surface, attach a rubber-cored sinker to your leader about 5 feet from the bait. Select a sinker size that will keep the bait drifting at the proper depth.

At times, even with a light current carrying the chum, the bait may tend to sink too deep. You can counter this by inserting a tiny piece of Styrofoam into the bait to give it a bit of buoyancy.

Another possibility is using a 4-inch block of Styrofoam with a slit cut into it; place your line in the slit, adjusting it so the bait will be suspended at a desired level as you let it drift back in the chum line. This may prove effective at keeping the bait just 10 feet beneath the surface or 50 feet deep. Catching fish beyond the latter depth is generally not a result of fish feeding on the chum, although some anglers do set one or two lines to depths of even 200 feet for the tuna and occasional swordfish feeding at those levels. An inflated toy balloon may also be used as an effective float.

This is an overview of offshore chumming, and elements may be modified as conditions warrant. Some anglers rely especially heavily on the use of chunks of bait, which has come to be called chunking. This term refers to the use of pieces of fish meat, often in 2- to 3-inch cubes, especially for chumming yellowfin and bluefin tuna. The procedure is essentially the same as that described earlier, although heavy pieces sink deeper and faster than smaller chum and particles, so you have to be constantly attentive to the location and condition of your hooked chunk.

In fact, you have to be alert at all times in this type of fishing. As you permit your line to drift in the slick, the fish will move up and inhale your bait and swim off with it in an instant. It will take longer to read this sentence than the reaction time needed to set up on the fish. A good rule is to always keep your rod pointed in the direction the line is drifting, with ever-so-light pressure on the line to keep it from overrunning. As the fish moves off, lock your reel in gear, lift the tip smartly to set the hook, and the fight is on.

Inshore, eastern U.S. Chumming for inshore species, such as bluefish, striped bass, bonito, school bluefin tuna, Spanish mackerel, king mackerel, and little tuna, is similar to offshore chumming. Basically, tackle is scaled down from the 50- to 80-pound outfits used offshore to more appropriate 15- to 30-pound-class tackle. Likewise, hook sizes from 1/0 through 5/0 are more in order. Even the chunks of bait used as chum are smaller—usually about the size of your

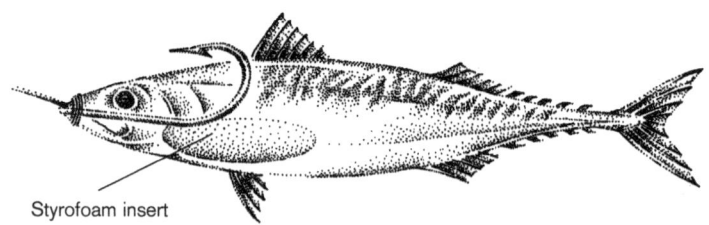

To give a bait the buoyancy that it needs to drift along with chum, insert a piece of Styrofoam into the stomach cavity, forcing it down the mouth; then insert the hook and sew the mouth closed. This method is typically used with whole mackerel or herring when offshore canyons are being fished for various tuna.

thumbnail or slightly larger—as are the baits. Small mullet, spearing, sand eels, and killies are all effective in attracting strikes when drifted back in a chum line, and chunks or strips of butterfish, mackerel, croaker, bluefish, spot, and menhaden are popularly used.

Menhaden is the preferred chum substance; it is commonly purchased in frozen blocks by private and charter boaters. A few operators, including some party boat operators, have large electrical grinders to mince fresh menhaden onboard—an operation that is noisy and messy. Some inshore menhaden chummers will ladle out chum; others like to put the frozen chum in a covered plastic 5-gallon bucket that has been riddled with 1-inch holes, hanging it alongside the boat with a rope that has been run through a hole in the side and the top. Fifty pounds of chum is recommended for a full day of fishing, especially if the water is warm and the currents swift.

Arrive at your designated fishing spot before the top or bottom of the tide, and allow some time to anchor and get the chum line going. Use the frozen material for chumming, but bait up with fresh fish pieces. Fresh bait, which has not been previously frozen, works best and does not become as mushy on the hook. Although at times any piece of bait works well, strips may be more effective in moderate current and chunks in heavier current.

One slight modification in terminal rigging is essential when the targets are bluefish and king mackerel, both of which have extremely sharp teeth. A 6- to 12-inch-long piece of No. 8 or 9 coffee-colored stainless steel leader wire, connecting the hook on one end and a tiny barrel swivel on the other, prevents these fish from biting through the monofilament. If you don't want to use a wire leader, which can be a detriment when the fish are leader shy, try a directly tied long-shanked hook, although now and then when a fish takes the bait deep it will still gain its freedom by biting through the monofilament.

Inshore/offshore, western U.S. Anglers on the West Coast of the U.S. enjoy exciting chumming for a wide variety of species when they're able to obtain live anchovies as chum. Southern California boats that fish the inshore kelp beds, along with long-range boats that head far to sea for albacore and those who head off the Baja Peninsula for yellowfin tuna, rely on the anchovies to bring gamefish within range.

Boats sailing from ports such as San Diego, Long Beach, and Newport Beach take on dipnets, popularly called "scoops," full of anchovies from bait barges anchored in coastal harbors. The anchovies are kept in livewells with circulating seawater to keep them in perfect condition until the fishing grounds are reached.

When inshore fishing at the kelp beds, boats anchor just off from the kelp, which is massive and looks like a willowy tree growing up from the sea

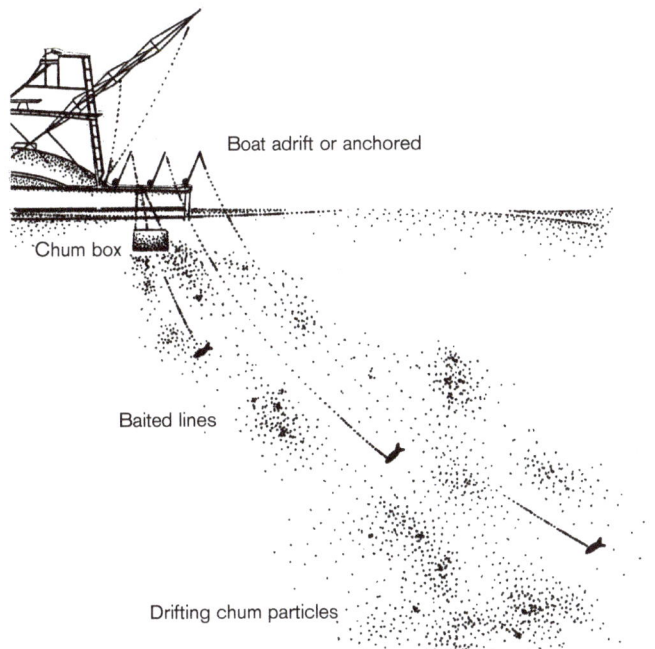

This is a typical ocean chumming scene; chum particles drift with the current, and hooked bait is allowed to drift at different levels amidst the chum.

floor. Its density makes it impenetrable to a boat, but the baitfish seek sanctuary there and gamefish roam nearby, occasionally making sorties into the kelp for a meal.

It takes patience and skill to coax fish from the kelp. A small dipnet is used to remove several anchovies from the livewell, and the chummer tosses these into the air so they land midway between the boat and the kelp. The excited anchovies either seek the sanctuary of the kelp or hurriedly swim back to the boat to seek shelter beneath its stern. Gradually the anchovies get the gamefish excited, and it's not unusual to have yellowtail, white seabass, bonito, barracuda, and kelp bass vying for them.

The most popular technique is to tie a tiny hook, such as a No. 3 or 4 O'Shaughnessy, Beak, or Claw style hook directly to the end of the line. Gently hook a lively anchovy under the gill collar. Anchovies are only 3 to 5 inches long, and too large a hook will restrict the movement of the live baitfish. While the collar-hooking method is most popular, some anglers hook the bait through the lips or the eyes, or place the hook into the back just ahead of the dorsal fin.

The bait is cast away from the boat, using either conventional or spinning tackle, and live-lined. An active anchovy will often swim about excitedly, and when gamefish are plentiful, the strikes come fast and furious. Always keep your rod tip pointed in the direction the line is moving; when a fish picks up the bait and moves off, lock your reel in gear and lift back smartly to set the hook.

Anchovies are also a popular chum on the Pacific's offshore grounds, as are several small species of mackerel and jacks. Long-range boats usually sail with a supply of chum in the tanks but often stop on productive banks where anglers onboard fish to fill the live tanks with a supply of fish that can be used as live or dead chum.

In some cases, boats anchor over productive banks and kelp beds. Albacore anglers often troll until either albacore or bluefin tuna strike the trolled lures; while the trolled fish are being fought, the chumming begins and holds what is usually a school of albacore at the boat. The techniques used with other types of chumming are essentially the same. Maintain a chum line of the anchovies, but don't feed the fish. When done properly, you can actually see the albacore picking the anchovies right off the surface (called a "boil") and being teased ever closer to the boat by an experienced chummer. Keeping the bait drifting back unimpeded is very important.

Tackle and hook size must be tailored to the species sought. When huge 250- to 300-pound yellowfin tuna are targeted by long-range boats, short stand-up outfits are favored, along with fluorocarbon leaders. Tailor the hook size and style to the bait being used, with the smaller bends ideal for anchovies and the larger for mackerel and jacks as hooked baits.

While anchovies are popular Pacific Coast chum, the use of chunk bait has become more popular, following the lead of Atlantic Coast offshore anglers, as mentioned earlier. Some of the largest yellowfin tuna are now caught by chunking, using pieces of mackerel, rainbow runners, jacks, or other common fish, burying the hook inside the pieces so that the point is buried and does not penetrate the skin. The most common hooks for this are 8/0 and 9/0 sizes, usually connected to a 150- to 200-pound-strength fluorocarbon leader, which in turn is connected to the fishing line via a 4/0 to 6/0 black barrel swivel.

Hooked chunks are changed frequently and observed closely as they drift with unhooked bait. Strong current and no current require a little more attention and finessing, the former keeping the bait up and the latter permitting it to sink. When chunks sink for two minutes, they should be retrieved and redropped.

More on chumming with live fish. As West Coast anglers who use live anchovies to chum fish know, there is a lot of merit to chumming with live fish as bait. In many cases, however, this is a specialized affair with several requirements: a means to store and keep the fish lively, the ability to obtain or find copious amounts of the proper baitfish, the ability to catch large numbers of live baitfish in a short time period, and sometimes gamefish that are concentrated or visible.

Livewells or baitwells with ample capacity and constant seawater replacement are standard today on many sportfishing boats, so it is possible to keep many small fish alive and frisky for a day of angling. The baitfish used are generally small and are located in inshore waters. Species will depend on locale but may include herring, anchovies, menhaden, mullet, and pilchards, to name some of the more abundant and popular ones. These are caught by using a net, in most cases a cast net *(see)*, and this method takes energy and effort, and is dependent on finding ample schools of baitfish, usually in fairly shallow water.

In south Florida, charter boat captains developed a technique of using live pilchards for offshore fishing, especially dolphin and sailfish. They start by finding schools of pilchards via sonar in inshore environs. Softball-size balls of sand are readied and tossed in the water where pilchard schools are located, usually within 20 to 30 feet of the surface. When the balls are pitched into the water, they sink and disperse in a cloud, which draws the pilchards. A large cast net is thrown on top of the spot where the ball was pitched; if it sinks fast enough and the schools are large enough, a bunch of pilchards will be captured and quickly deposited into a livewell. This is repeated until at least 100 to 200 baits are garnered. Then the boat runs 15 to 20 miles offshore.

From a tower, the skipper can see cruising sailfish or dolphin that are clustered near weedlines or flotsam. The skipper searches for fish and, upon finding them, idles the boat while the mate pulls out a dipnet of live pilchards and tosses them individually in the vicinity of the dolphin or sailfish. Often this sudden presence of frisky bait gets the dolphin or sailfish to attack; the angler casts a hooked live pilchard amid the activity and in short order is into a fish. This type of live-bait chumming is repeated as long as there are fish around; then the boat moves and looks for more fish elsewhere.

This live-bait chumming is very exciting; it may also be used to draw gamefish close enough to the boat to take a cast offering of an artificial, usually a fly. It is a technique that should work well for some other species, inshore as well as offshore, although its success is hindered by a frequent inability to find ample live baitfish.

Bays, rivers, and estuaries. In protected bays, rivers, and estuaries where striped bass, weakfish, spotted weakfish, and summer flounder reside, you may continue to use essentially the same techniques previously described, selecting as chum the foods most often found in these inshore waters. Common grass shrimp measuring 1 to 2 inches in length are plentiful in inshore waters and constitute a major portion of the diet of these species. Also very plentiful and a major source of food are the many species of crab, most notably the blue crab, calico crab, and sand crab. Both the grass shrimp and various crabs are very effective as chum and hook baits.

Grass shrimp may be obtained using a seine worked in coastal marshes and around pilings and along bulkheads. A couple of quarts are all that are needed to fish a tide. Crabs may also be seined or caught in traps. Since crabs are larger, they are often cut into small pieces. Some anglers prefer eating the crabs and saving the discarded pieces for later use as chum. Both the grass shrimp and crab pieces may be frozen and used as chum as the need arises.

The preferred method of fishing is to anchor along the edge of a channel where these species are known to move with the tide as they search for a meal. The same consistent chumming is all that is needed to attract them to your boat, just dribbling a few shrimp at a time overboard or a nominal amount of crab, or a combination of the two. The crab gills, stomachs, and swim fins offer a great attraction in the chum line; they are small enough that they do not feed the fish but still get them to the hooked baits.

Because the shrimp are so small, No. 1 through 4 Claw or Beak bait holder hooks are preferred. A tiny rubber-cored sinker is often used if the current is swift, sometimes in conjunction with a float, keeping the bait at a desired level. In many bay and river waters, you'll be fishing in depths of just 6 to 12 feet, so the float and sinker combo works well. Just let the bait drift out a hundred feet or so; reel back in and repeat the drift so that the bait moves along with the chum.

The techniques outlined for using grass shrimp and crabs as chum work well when fished from piers, bulkheads, docks, and bridges. In each type of platform, the key is positioning yourself so you can dispense the chum and have it carried away by the current, along with your baited rig. The float and sinker combination often proves deadly. It's not unusual to see the fish move up into the chum line, especially when you are fishing night tides from bridges, piers, and docks that have bright lights.

Chumming for bottom feeders. Bottom-feeding fish, such as winter flounder, sea bass, and porgies, also respond to a chum line, but for these fish the chum must be on the bottom. To accomplish this, anglers use a chum pot. The most popular size chum pot is 4 to 5 inches in diameter by 8 to 10 inches in height. It is made of a lead bottom, hinged metal top, and $1/4$-inch galvanized wire mesh. The pot is filled with ground chum, and the chum pot is then eased to the bottom via a piece of cord. As the chum thaws, it oozes from the pot and is carried along the bottom, and the fish move toward the source of the free meal.

Many kinds of ground chum are effective when used in a chum pot. Ground menhaden, mussels, clams, conch, grass shrimp, and sea worms all have their devotees. A combination of these ingredients often works extremely well. If you have a little spare time, make up several batches of chum and keep them in your freezer. The chum is easy to make and stores well in the freezer, and you will have a supply on hand and ready to go.

After a strong storm, you can often go to the beach and collect a 5-gallon bucket of big sea clams that have been washed up by the storm. Remove all the clam meat from the shell; grind it up with a grinding head that produces pieces small enough to be carried from the chum pot's $1/4$-inch mesh. You can also grind up the meat from sedge, black mussels, and conch. Be attentive to local regulations with regard to shellfish harvest, since some states prohibit collecting shellfish in certain waters.

Once you've ground the ingredients, add an equal quantity of boiled white rice to the same quantity of whole kernel corn. Mix all three ingredients together, and place the chum in paper cups of a size that will fit into the chum pot. Then freeze the cups of chum.

Upon arriving at the fishing grounds—which could be a mud flat or dock for flounder or a reef

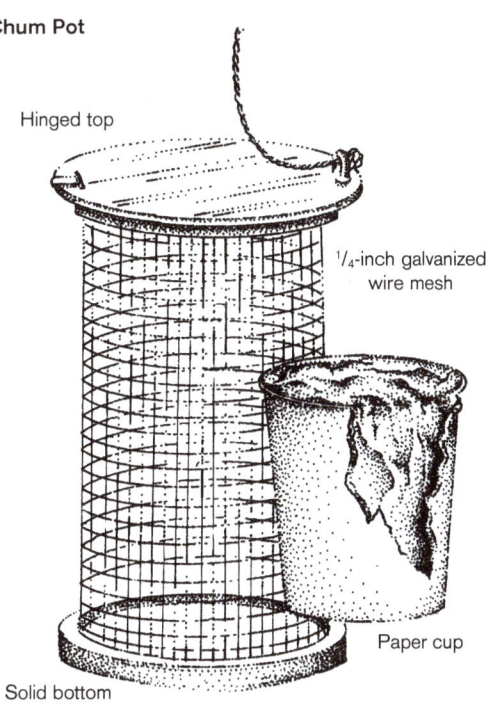

Chum Pot

Tear away the paper cup that contains the pre-frozen chum, place the frozen chum into a mesh pot, and lower it by heavy line into the water.

for sea bass, porgies, and tautog—peel off the paper cup from the frozen chum log and insert it into the chum pot. Ease the pot to the bottom via a piece of cord, and let the current carry the chum to the fish. You can use the same bottom rig for winter flounder that you would use if you were not chumming, usually a pair of No. 8 or 9 Chestertown hooks baited with bits of clams, sandworms, bloodworms, or mussels. In the case of sea bass, porgies, and tautog, a high-low rig, with hook size tailored to the fish in residence, works fine. Sizes 2 to 6 Beak or Claw hooks snelled to 8 to 12 inches of leader material are ideal. Strips of squid and pieces of clam and conch work well with sea bass and porgies; fiddler crabs and pieces of blue or green crabs are perfect for the tautog, popularly called "blackfish" or "white chins" in some areas. Occasionally it pays to give the cord holding the chum pot a good yank, especially if there is little current around slack tide; this will send a cloud of chum streaming from the pot.

Although all these species are fun to catch on light tackle, some anglers often attach a baited rig to the chum pot. This action often gets a couple of bonus fish for the pan and proves that the chum pot attracts them. Further proof of the chum's effectiveness is evident when you clean your catch; whether you've caught tuna in the canyons or flounder in bay waters, they will invariably have chum in their stomachs.

Still another trick to attract winter flounder in particular is to stir up the bottom by using a long pole with a plumber's toilet plunger or a garden cultivator attached to the end of it. Stirring the bottom creates a cloud of mud that is carried off by the current. The mud, in turn, attracts flounder to the area, where they often find sea worms, crabs, and shrimp that have been stirred up out of the mud.

Whole sea clams, conch, and mussels are used by many middle and north Atlantic Coast bottom anglers to attract codfish, pollock, sea bass, porgies, flounder, and a host of other bottom feeders. The clams, conch, and mussels are crushed with a hammer, and the combination of shell and clam meat is dispensed overboard to settle to the bottom around the boat.

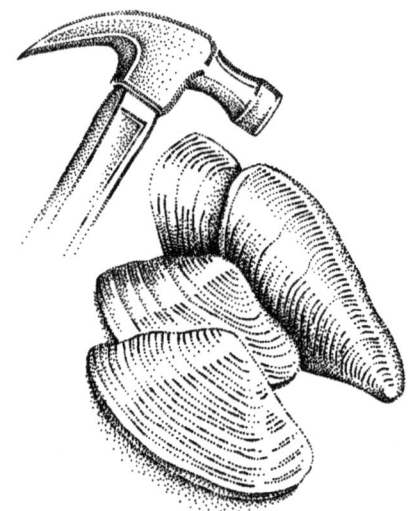

Use a hammer to break up whole clams and mussels; then drop the shells and meat overboard to attract a variety of bottom feeders.

When bottom-feeding fish pick up the scent of the chum, they move to the source and pick away at whatever meat they can obtain from the crushed shells. When they spot a piece of clam on a hook, they're onto it in a flash.

Reefs and wrecks. Chumming is very effective for reef- and wreck-dwelling fish. In Florida and along the Gulf Coast, many party boat captains who fish reefs and wrecks wouldn't think of leaving the dock without a good supply of chum onboard (roughly 5 pounds of chum per half hour of fishing). Their chumming techniques are quite productive and worth noting for the benefit of large- and small-boaters alike.

These skippers find a specific reef and then use sonar to determine where on the reef the fish are located. Then they position the boat and place an anchor in sand bottom just off from the reef, easing back and using sufficient anchor line to place the boat at the edge of the reef.

The act of ladling out chum and selecting appropriate devices and equipment to use for chumming is a big part of this technique. However, it can all go for naught if you are not positioned properly to fish with the chum or if the chum does not get where it needs to be to attract fish. Simply putting chum in the water, even if near an appropriate reef or wreck, does not guarantee that the chum will act like a fish magnet. Whether you anchor or drift, how you position the boat to set up your chum line is very important. The better boat captains may reposition themselves frequently until they get into the right position, since being just off the spot may sometimes make all the difference.

Chumming always takes place with the boat positioned upcurrent of the chummed location. When you are trying to attract fish from a deep location, such as a reef or a wreck, you must assess the flow of the current and the distance to your target area in order to determine where you need to be. A strong current will keep bait up, and a slow current will allow it to sink deeper, so you may need to position the boat farther away when the current is strong than when it is weak.

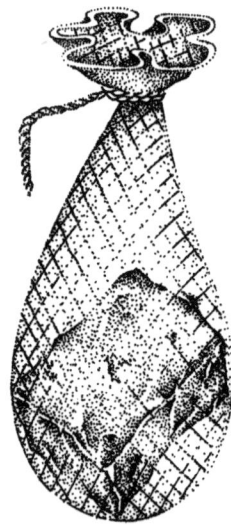

Place a 5-pound block of frozen ground fish chum in a cloth mesh bag, and hang it over the side of the boat so that it gradually thaws and oozes through the bag.

In many areas, and including Florida, reef chumming begins with frozen ground fish chum that is supplied in 5-pound cardboard boxes. The cardboard is pulled away from the frozen block of chum, which is placed in a mesh bag and hung over the side. As the chum thaws, it oozes from the mesh bag.

The deckhands then begin to dispense a separate chum concoction that was previously prepared. It is composed of thawed chum, rolled oats, and play sand in equal parts, with just enough water added to enable the chum to be molded into what are commonly referred to as "meatballs."

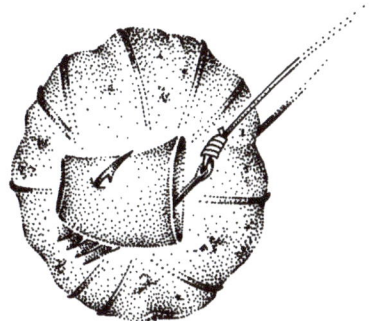

A chum meatball consists of ground chum, rolled oats, and beach sand, with a bait hook placed inside; a leader is wrapped around the meatball to hold it together while it settles to the bottom.

The chum is molded into a meatball the size of a tennis ball and dropped overboard around the boat. The weight of the sand in the chum mixture immediately takes the meatball to the bottom, where it crumbles and is carried along the bottom.

To get bigger pieces of chum to the bottom, "depth charges" are employed. These are made by using two small brown paper lunch bags. A layer of sand is placed in the bottom of one bag and then a layer of cut-up fish. Any fish will do, such as mullet, pilchards, balao, or scraps from fish that have been cleaned. On top of this is added a layer of rolled oats. This bag, which when filled will weigh about 2 pounds or more, is placed inside the second bag so that the package doesn't fall apart on its descent to the bottom. The bags are loosely twisted closed and dropped overboard near the bow of the boat.

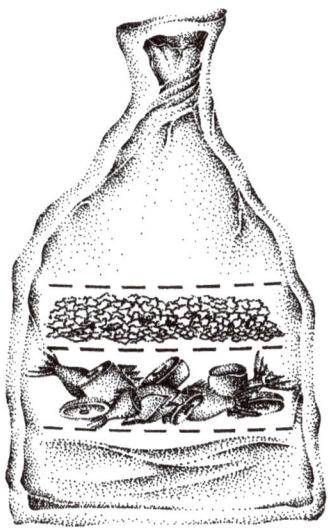

A chum depth charge can be made by placing one paper bag inside another and then layering the interior with sand on the bottom, pieces of bait on top of the sand, and rolled oats on top of the bait pieces. Twist the bag closed.

When the depth charge reaches bottom, the paper bag quickly disintegrates. The oats and pieces of fish are carried along the bottom by the current, attracting the fish from the reef to a point beneath the boat.

Once the chum area has been established via the three sources of chum, fishing begins in earnest. Some anglers fish with a regular bottom rig; others employ a meatball rig to entice strikes.

The favored bottom rig is fairly simple. Slip an egg-shaped sinker of appropriate weight, usually 1 to 4 ounces, onto your line and tie a tiny barrel swivel to the terminal end to secure the sinker. Then tie a 24-inch piece of monofilament leader material to the other eye of the barrel swivel, and a Beak or Claw style hook to the end of the leader. The hook is often 1/0 size but may be smaller if small yellowtail snapper are the only target; the hook could be up to 6/0 size if big black grouper, Nassau grouper, or mutton snapper are in residence. Baited with live shrimp, pieces of squid, chunks of bonito, mullet, or other fish, the rig is lowered to the bottom. Now it's a waiting game until the reef dwellers are attracted by the chum in the depth charges, and eventually find your bait.

The baited meatball rig is another effective method of combining chum and bait. It works in Bermuda, the Bahamas, Florida, the Gulf Coast, and wherever reef dwellers are found. The rig is made up of the same mixture described for meatballs (the consistency should be suitable for forming into balls).

To make it, tie your hook directly to the end of the monofilament line. Leaders are seldom used, unless very heavy grouper or snapper are around. Bait the hook with a pilchard or a piece of cut bait. Mullet, balao, or a piece of bonito are very effective. Bury the bait carefully inside the chum, and make a complete offering that is the size of a tennis ball. Next wrap the monofilament line around this ball, much the same as you would wind up a ball of yarn, making two wraps and then a turn, for a total of about 10 wraps. Then firm up the ball so it stays together.

To fish it, strip off a sufficient length of line to reach the bottom. Toss the meatball away from the boat underhanded so that it lands 10 to 20 feet from the boat; let it settle unimpeded to the bottom. Keep the bail of your spinning reel open, or keep a conventional reel in freespool. While the meatball and bait are settling to the bottom, the meatball begins to disintegrate and creates its own mini-chum slick. In just a minute or so, the meatball will disintegrate and be ravaged by the first fish to reach it. By watching the line, you'll quickly know that the fish has it. As the fish moves off with the bait, keep your rod pointed in the direction of the line and close the bail or engage the spool; lift back smartly, and you're apt to be hooked to anything from a 2-pound yellowtail snapper to a 60-pound black grouper. The key is always having sufficient line stripped from your reel so that the meatball reaches bottom unimpeded. If there is any drag whatsoever, the meatball will disintegrate completely on the way down, leaving the bait at midlevel and losing its effectiveness.

The meatball rig differs from other chumming tactics in that it is a self-contained chum-and-fish arrangement. You might call it in-line chumming. Another way to accomplish the same thing is to tie small bags filled with chum loosely on your line. Cut a paper grocery bag into 5-inch squares, and fill each square with up to a dozen pieces of freshly cut $1/4$-inch chunks of bait. Twist together the ends of the paper square and secure with two half hitches of light line/leader that extends from your bait rig. Bait a hook with the same chunks, and lower the whole thing to the bottom; give a quick jerk on the fishing line and the half hitches unravel, depositing a burst of bait right where your hook is. This technique can be used at mid-depths, too; some swordfish anglers put a baited bag pocket on their rig below a light stick and then yank the line to free the bait at the desired depth.

Other methods of deep chumming are also worth noting. In addition to frozen blocks of chum, options include shrimp bycatch, chunks, and live bait. Usually a mesh bag of chum is hung over the side in conjunction with other types of chum or bait usage. In some places, a bit of fishing effort may produce some species that can be used as fresh cut bait or as live bait; these include balao, bonito, and mackerel.

If the chum in the upper water column draws many small fish, you may want to get down deeper with the chum. Several innovative tactics make this possible. One is to secure a heavy (10 pounds or so) weight on the end of a strong line and place small mesh bags at various spots along the line. To draw fish from deep areas, you might try lowering live bait in a container with a trip line or trip mechanism. The container is heavily weighted, and the opening mechanism is tripped to free the bait. This can be repeated at higher levels in the water column, the object being to draw fish up from the bottom.

When reef and wreck angling, remember that fish may sometimes be found away from the objects. This is especially true with wrecks, where species like yellowtail, barracuda, and bonito may be 50 to 100 yards away on the downcurrent side when that current is strong. You may have to either reposition an anchored boat to approach these fish or strip-line your bait a long way to get to those fish. Also, for some types of fish, it can be advantageous to chum the entire water column, which may require a multiple-method approach to chumming.

Shrimping bycatch. Shrimp trawling is a major business, especially from the Carolinas to Florida and along the Gulf Coast. Shrimpers trawl mostly at night and anchor during the day, culling their catches and tossing overboard huge quantities of refuse, which is referred to as trash or bycatch. The trash consists of literally dozens of species of small fish, squid, crabs, and crushed or broken shrimp. When dropped into the sea, this smorgasbord attracts hordes of gamefish in quantities that sometimes defy description. At times, hundreds of fish gather to feed on this chum line from the shrimp trawlers.

Anglers who know the shrimp trawler owners or captains may get permission to tie up to the stern of the shrimper and take advantage of the chum slick that is established as the trash is shoveled over. Others often pull up to a shrimper and for a few dollars or some horse trading take aboard a couple of containers filled with trash. Some shrimpers retain the trash and sell it when they return to port.

The approach used when chumming with shrimp trash is to cut small fish into several pieces and then dispense them overboard to attract a multitude of species, most notably yellowfin and blackfin tuna, bonito, dolphin, wahoo, amberjack, and even the occasional sailfish and white marlin. The trash chum also accounts for many fine catches of cobia and tarpon along the Gulf Coast. In offshore waters, the trash and cut fish are used essentially as previously described in the section on offshore chumming.

In inshore waters, the shrimp boat trash is regularly used to attract tarpon and permit to hooked baits. There is an extensive fishery for these great gamefish in the waters adjacent to Key West, Florida, for example, where the tarpon and permit follow regular patterns, moving with the tide as they feed. The accepted manner of chumming for them there is to anchor in an area they frequent; the anchor rope is attached to a quick-release floating red buoy so that you can get off the anchor quickly to chase a hooked fish.

Once positioned on anchor, small pieces of trash are dropped overboard and carried away with the tide. Light 20-pound-class tackle is most often employed on these fish, for the permit average 15 to 35 pounds and the tarpon range from 50 to 100 pounds or more. A size 6/0 O'Shaughnessy hook is used by many guides and tied directly to the monofilament leader, which is 50-pound test or stronger. Most baitfish are silvery and because of their reflective qualities are favored for tarpon, although most anything removed from the trash, including crabs, shrimp, or squid, will bring strikes. If permit are the target, a large manta shrimp is an excellent bait choice.

The key, as in all chumming, is keeping the bait moving with the chum. If there is no pressure on the line, the bait will drop deep as it moves along in the swift current with the chum. It's not unusual to pay out 125 feet of line. If a strike isn't received, the bait is reeled back in and the step repeated. Even though both tarpon and permit are big, their strikes are often subtle, and you have to be alert and set back quickly and hard, especially with tarpon because they have bony mouths that are difficult for a hook point to penetrate. Make your hooks needle sharp; sharpness often determines whether a hook penetrates or pulls out of a tarpon's mouth at the time of the strike.

Chumming bonefish on flats. Many anglers feel that the only way to catch bonefish is to hunt for them by observing them tailing and then casting to them. However, wind conditions sometimes make it impossible to pole the flats; also, tidal conditions or a storm can roil the flats and make visual contact virtually impossible. Under such conditions, chumming is an effective way to attract bonefish within range.

Veteran bonefish anglers will stake out their skiffs on a promising flat or thoroughfare that is known to be frequented by bonefish at a particular stage of the tide. They prefer a spot that has a patch or two of open sand bottom within easy casting range of the skiff, usually 25 to 35 feet. They take live shrimp from the livewell and break them into two or three pieces. These pieces are tossed out and targeted to land on the sandy bottom. Then it becomes a waiting game.

Bonefish have fixed patterns of movement as they search for a meal and thus can often be seen approaching the area. They soon get the scent of the shrimp chum resting on the sand. It is then that anglers make their casts, with just a single live shrimp on a size No. 1 or 1/0 Beak or Claw style hook tied directly to the monofilament line. Many anglers have caught their first bonefish using this approach. Once you've mastered casting to these cautious fish, you can advance to casting tiny bucktail jigs to them or even employ a fly rod to present a shrimp fly or crab fly after the bonefish have been coaxed within range using the shrimp chum.

Chumming giant bluefin tuna. Giant bluefin tuna are those weighing in excess of 300 pounds and at times achieving a weight over 1,000 pounds. These world travelers are classified by many as the strongest, hardest-fighting fish in the ocean. A single fish requires huge quantities of food each day to sustain it, so when large schools of giant tuna move into an area, they need an enormous quantity of forage on which to feed. These giants usually roam the sea from June through October from New Jersey north to the Canadian Maritimes, settling into areas where mackerel and herring, their staple foods, are abundant. Although mackerel and herring constitute the bulk of the giant bluefin's diet, tuna are not adverse to feeding on the abundance of squid, bluefish, red hake, and silver hake that are found in the area, along with most any fish they encounter.

This search for food and voracious appetite make tuna a natural for chumming, and the bulk of the summertime fishery is done by private and charter boats who anchor in choice locations and use huge quantities of forage species as chum. A single boat may dispense several hundred pounds of chum overboard in a day.

Catching these giants is a challenge requiring the finest quality tackle and a crew working as a single team. With 130-pound-class tackle, which is the standard for these bruisers, there is no room for error.

Anglers have learned that giant bluefin tuna usually follow a pattern of moving along the coast searching for food. Some feel that a tuna may travel a hundred miles in a day, making a massive sweep of an area. Chummers position their boats by anchoring in known tuna travel spots. Aboard are two plastic trash containers filled with either mackerel, herring, or menhaden, usually obtained directly from a local dragger. Chumming begins by taking a whole fish and cutting it into three or four pieces. If the mackerel or menhaden are small, they may be used whole or in halves.

Some chummers use what is popularly called "cod guts" as both chum and bait. These are the carcasses of fish that have been filleted by commercial fishermen. Sometimes the carcasses are cod, hence the name, but pollock, haddock, hake, bluefish, and other species are used. It's not unusual to have huge tuna swarm into this type of chum, gorging on what were 5- to 10-pound fish, which, even without the fillets, still weigh a couple of pounds with the head, body, and entrails remaining.

As with all chumming, steady maintenance of the chum line is essential. Often these big fish are spotted on sonar. They swim through the chum line, moving in a big circular pattern, picking up pieces as they go. At times when they move near the surface, you can actually toss three or four pieces, at 5-foot intervals, and the fish will draw in each piece of chum as it steadily swims along.

There are many ways to rig the basic 130-pound-class tackle to present a bait in the chum line. The standard approach is to employ 130-pound-test Dacron line, with a 150- to 200-foot-long piece of 250-pound-test monofilament spliced into the Dacron. Some anglers snell or crimp the hook directly to the monofilament. Others use a ball bearing swivel and a 10- or 12-foot-long fluorocarbon leader, to which the hook is snelled or crimped.

A wide range of giant tuna hooks are available, and opinions vary on which is best. Some anglers prefer a size 7/0 or 8/0 forged offset hook, reasoning that the small hook is more easily concealed in the bait; others prefer the extremely strong forged size 12/0 and 14/0 Martu models. Circle hooks have also come into vogue after their successful use in the Hatteras, North Carolina, winter giant tuna fishery.

Tuna anglers often bait up with a whole mackerel or herring, but some use half a fish so that the bait looks like the chum being employed. Fillets from a bluefish also bring strikes. When using dead baits, many anglers insert a small piece of Styrofoam into the bait; the Styrofoam makes the bait more buoyant and it drifts along in the chum much the same as a piece of chum.

New Zealand is noted for its rainbow trout fishing, but rainbows are not a Kiwi native; they were shipped to New Zealand from the United States in 1883.

Live bluefish, which sometimes may be caught on the tuna grounds, are also an excellent bait. Often tuna anglers will bottom fish for silver hake or red hake, popularly called ling, to use as live bait. Live baits are hooked through the fleshy part of the back, just ahead of or behind the dorsal fin.

The most effective way to fish baits in a chum line for giant tuna is to work the bait, paying it out with the chum and then pulling it back in and repeating the procedure. Many people prefer to coil 100 feet of the fishing line in a plastic trash bucket, and pay line out hand over hand into the slick. This keeps the line from getting tangled, but safety should be observed so that your feet don't get hung up in the line as a giant takes the hooked bait and runs off with it.

The normal procedure is to pay out the line by hand with the rod positioned in a rod holder (usually in a fighting chair) and ample line in a bucket. When a strike is received, the fish is struck by hand by the person holding the line; then the line is quickly dropped and permitted to flow from the bucket until the hooked fish takes all the free line and then it is tight to the rod and reel.

For these big fish, it's not unusual to fish with 40 or 45 pounds of drag pressure, using a fighting harness *(see: harness, fighting)* with safety line attached to the chair, to assist in fighting the fish. As soon as the fish is hooked, the boat is released from the anchor line buoy, and the fish is followed by the boat, positioning the angler so maximum pressure may be brought to bear. The objective is to boat the fish as quickly as possible, and some experienced big-game anglers can boat a fish in less than a half-hour, although individual fish may be fought for six hours or more.

During the early 1990s, a large school of medium and giant bluefin tuna were located in the waters adjacent to wrecks off Hatteras, North Carolina. This discovery resulted in the development of an exciting chumming fishery that takes place during January through April. During the day at that time, tuna travel from wreck to wreck or to wherever there are heavy concentrations of forage. Boaters locate them on sonar and then chum with half or whole menhaden, called bunker or mossbunker, as the boat idles along above where the fish are spotted. This provides exciting fishing as the tuna boil to the surface, often snatching the bunker as quickly as they are tossed over.

Once the fish are boiling, the angler gets into the fighting chair, or attaches and hooks up a shoulder and belt harness if using stand-up tackle. As several pieces of chum are tossed, the Circle hook baited with a whole menhaden is tossed over and permitted to settle with the chum. When the fish are actively feeding, two or more tuna may zero in on a single bait.

Federal regulations limit a boat's catch to one medium tuna per day, which keeps down the take. The season on giants over 300 pounds is closed at this time, and the fish are usually brought to boatside quickly and released. The Circle hooks are often lodged in the corner of the tuna's jaw, and release is easily accomplished, especially if using the proper hook remover.

Chumming sharks. Chumming is the primary method of angling for sharks and is discussed in more detail elsewhere *(see: shark)*. However, a few words about shark chumming are appropriate here, whether the purpose is to attract sharks to hooked baits (mostly the case) or to lures, especially streamer flies, that are cast, and particularly because some of the tactics employed primarily for sharks may have merit in other fishing.

It is true that most of the chumming activities previously mentioned will attract sharks, especially smaller sharks, and some techniques—like chunking with large pieces of fish or whole fish in conjunction with an established line—may have merit for the larger and more desirable species. However, sharks are especially sensitive to smell, so the approach is a bit different.

In shark fishing, a long trail of scent may be necessary to attract the shark, and even under favorable conditions this method can take a long time. Some shark veterans use a method referred to as power chumming or super chumming to jump-start the action. They do this by leaving a scent and chum trail along a quarter to half mile of water while en route to the primary fishing destination. The boat slows from cruising speed to trolling speed,

Frozen butterfish are thawed and cut into chunks, to be used for chumming tuna and sharks.

and chum is dispensed continuously in the water. One method is to drag a milk-container crate of chum behind the boat; the crate is closed with mesh netting and is attached to a 40-inch poly ball, which keeps it on the surface. Another method is to use the washdown hose to spray overboard some chunks and pieces from a frozen block or can while the boat is underway at trolling speed; the can or block is placed in the splashwell or by the scuppers to permit quick washing into the water and the formation of a long trail. In both cases, once the preferred site is reached, the boat is anchored or allowed to drift, and the standard method of washing the chum through a mesh bag, perforated bucket, or crate is used.

Most shark chumming is aided by a good current and a slight breeze. When the wind is strong, the amount of chumming should be increased in order to keep the shark chum line in good order. This may require ladling additional chum overboard to supplement the chum that is already in a bucket or bag. It may be necessary to use a sea anchor to slow the boat's drift and to establish a thicker chum line. With the wind heavy, shark anglers may also have to weight the hooked bait (which is usually fished on a float) to get it to the right level, or to fish it unweighted if not using a sea anchor and drifting quickly. Running a live bait under a downwind kite is another tactic for high-wind drifting. When the seas are becalmed and current is slack, the chum sinks; some shark anglers take this time to move under power, slow-trolling and spreading their chum trail higher in the water column. In this case the baited lines must be kept spread apart to avoid tangling.

Casting lures amidst chum. Remember that the main purpose of chum is to attract and concentrate fish. Although much chumming includes fishing with hooked bait, it is entirely possible to use assorted lures—including plugs, spoons, jigs, and flies—for catching fish when a chum line has been well established and fish are abundant and aggressive. Competitiveness seems to draw many fish from the end of the chum line to the front of the chum line and causes them to vigorously pursue tidbits of food; when this happens, there is definitely potential for presenting an artificial lure fairly close to you, and it can be very exciting.

Surface plugs, of course, are one possibility. Plugs that pop or chug usually work best, and it helps if they can spit water out and work quickly to look like bait splashing and being hounded over the surface. These lures should be balanced so that they do not tumble forward and foul the line, especially when being fished fast or in rough water. Spoons are a good choice for some species because they can be cast well, and far if necessary; they sink quickly and roll in the process; and they usually have enough flash when being retrieved to draw attention and look vulnerable. Jigs are a chum line possibility at times, usually when possessing a bucktail hair body but also with a soft plastic body. These jigs can also be cast quickly and far if some action is noticed, and they can be drifted down below in the event that some fish are feeding at the bottom depths of the chum line. Flies are usually streamer versions, although poppers catch some chummed fish; the former can be fished on a sink-tip line when it is necessary to get them away from the boat or deep.

Lures should generally be cast beyond and in front of fish, and retrieved properly in front of them. Ditto for flies, although many anglers will drift a fly back in the current and chum line and then jerk it or strip it in quick bursts, rather than repeatedly casting it. Don't be afraid of fishing blind in the chum with a lure, especially a surface plug or a fly. Blind strikes are not uncommon and are usually quite a surprise, so you'd better be holding your rod tightly.

Another chumming technique, practiced by some inshore anglers who ply the tight areas of mangrove backwaters, is to use copious amounts of small live minnows, obtained from baiting and cast-netting, to trigger gamefish into feeding. They toss live baitfish, often with the aid of a handheld tube-style launcher, to a structure that might hold snook and redfish. When the predators start feeding on the dazed live bait, a hooked bait or streamer fly is cast to the same place.

See: Bait; Baitfish; *and individual species.*

Freshwater Chumming

Chumming in freshwater is not as widely practiced for a range of species as it is in saltwater, although it is a major component of fishing for carp, somewhat of a component for catfish and bullhead fishing, and of minor practice for other species, including panfish and trout. In Europe, however, it is a major component of fishing for coarse species *(see: coarse fish)* such as roach, barbel, tench, rudd, and various carp.

To some extent outside Europe, and especially in North America, chumming is a minor technique

A river angler prepares chum for coarse fishing.

because of traditional attitudes and practices. A general abundance of fish and the relative availability of fish to anglers make it theoretically less necessary to "resort" to the use of feeding or chumming. To some extent, a low reliance on chumming in North America is due to the nature of the fish species or the aquatic conditions; sight-feeding, cover-relating fish like bass and pike, for example, would seem a less desirable target for chumming, although this is not an absolute. To some extent it is also due to attitudes; some freshwater anglers, for example, believe that chumming is either undignified or unfair. The low use of chumming is also due to laws; chumming is illegal in some places in North America. There are no general bans on chumming in Europe, with the exception of certain trout waters that are restricted to the use of artificial lures or flies.

One of the most glaring differences between freshwater fishing in North America and in Europe is the heavy reliance on chum in the Old World, and the general lack of reliance on it in the New World. Several important differences contribute to this. European fisheries are not as diverse as those in North America (or South America), where there are many major species that are aggressive territorial sight feeders and easier to catch. These fish have also not been exploited and pressured for nearly as long as the fish in Europe. This is a bit of an oversimplification, but it is true that many European fish, especially coarse fish, which would not be of significant angling interest in North America, are caught and recaught so often that they are extremely wary and require extensive baiting (chumming), and even pre-baiting (baiting well in advance of actual fishing effort), to concentrate and fool with a hooked offering.

However, as a result of these circumstances, freshwater chumming has been highly refined in Europe. North Americans by comparison have barely scratched the surface of freshwater chumming techniques. They may not have to in the near future if fisheries resources are well maintained; but for some species (especially those that rely heavily on their sense of smell), and in isolated locations where fishing pressure is intense, chumming, if legal, may take on more significance in the angler's bag of options.

Freshwater chumming is much different than saltwater chumming. There are few opportunities to obtain, by purchase or catch, large amounts of fish to use as ground-up chum, so chum availability is an inhibiting factor in many places. However, some rivers and large reservoirs support big populations of alewives, gizzard and threadfin shad, smelt, or herring, which conceivably could be used for chum if they could legally be obtained and retained in necessary quantities. Therefore, partially by default, and partially owing to the nature of some of the species that are most susceptible to chumming, most freshwater chumming is done with foods that are not naturally found in the water, or with commercially prepared attractants. Freshwater chumming as practiced in Europe is greatly different, and far more refined, than it is in North America or in many other parts of the world.

History. For over 500 years, anglers in Europe have been practicing the art of chumming for such species as roach, dace, chub, and bream, all of which are nervous schooling fish that can be spooked by just one scared member in their school. Intense fishing pressure and a century of catching and releasing these species have educated these and other fish to all kinds of chumming, especially on venues that are fished regularly in competitions, which are very popular. Thus, European anglers have long been searching for a magical chum (called groundbait in England) that always catches fish. Every kind of bread, grain, seed, spice, oil, blood, alcohol, and more have been mixed and blended trying to find the infallible chum, and the search continues.

Chums and chumming tactics have taken many forms over the centuries. The most unbelievable fish attractant is attributed to James Chetham who, in his 1681 book *The Angler's Vade Mecum,* recommended a chum that consisted of 1 ounce of human fat (found in the surgeries of London), 1 ounce of feline fat, 3 drams of powdered mummy, 1 dram of cumin seed, 6 drops of anise oil, 6 drops of spike, 4 grains of camphor, and 2 grains of civet. This amazing mixture was to be spread on 8 inches of line directly above the hook! Chetham also had a favorite powder, made from human bones, that was to be sprinkled on the moss where the angler kept his worms.

In his 1653 book *The Compleat Angler,* Izaak Walton noted that the addition of honey to bread paste (dough bait) was irresistible to carp. He also mentioned that tar was a deadly additive to bait that would always catch tench.

North American Indians chummed in at least two ingenious ways. One was to gradually crawl alongside a stream so that grasshoppers would jump away into the flowing water; after the fish became preoccupied with this form of loose feeding, the Indians would carefully place a grasshopper with a hook in front of active fish. Another method was to tie a dead animal in a tree above a stream; within a week flies would lay their eggs and the maggots would simply drop off the carcass, providing free food to fish that lined up downstream. The food concentrated the fish and, after the meat was gone, they could easily be caught.

In Victorian England in the late 1800s, fashionable men and women had gudgeon (a small goby) parties along streams in the summer. These exciting parties began with the men rolling up their trousers and the ladies carefully lifting up their skirts, and both walking around on the gravel runs. This stirred up the mud and all kinds of insects that were hiding there; hundreds of gudgeon would immediately swim into the mud cloud looking for food. The men and women retired to the shoreline and used little red worms with tiny hooks under a very small float to catch many dozens of fish, which they would immediately behead, dress, and quickly fry in butter as a delicacy.

Techniques. As with saltwater chumming, all the elements of freshwater chumming are mastered only after much experience; the angler must know a great deal about the targeted fish, including where it lives throughout the year and its feeding habits. Also like saltwater chumming, freshwater chumming aims to keep fish in the area you're fishing, or attract them to it, and then get them feeding on the bait you have on the hook. After you start catching fish, you have to keep them interested; be careful not to underfeed or, worse, overfeed the fish in that area. This is something that only experience can teach.

After much experience, you will develop an instinct for knowing how much and when to feed; the best advice in this respect is to chum little and often. By chumming modestly at the start, you will not overfeed; the worst thing that can happen when you are chumming is to see your chances ruined by a nearby angler who throws in a lot of chum (like a full can of corn). An abundance of chum discourages the fish from picking up your baited hook.

How you chum depends on whether the fish you seek are sight feeders or smell and/or touch feeders. Sight feeders include such species as bluegill, crappie, perch, bass, trout, walleye, etc. Smell and/or touch feeders include catfish, carp, drum, suckers, etc. Chumming also varies by the type of waterway. Stillwaters and flowing waters are very different environments, and each affects the behavior of fish differently. Flowing-water fish, for example, can be drawn upstream hundreds of yards by scent, or by following particles upstream to where they are being introduced. Even stillwaters (especially larger bodies of water) have gentle current that moves in the opposite direction of any prevailing wind; it is possible that targeted fish could be above, below, or ahead of any chum drift you have created. Furthermore, targeted fish can literally be yards away from your scent trail, so they have no way of sensing that your bait is so close to them, unless they feel (via their lateral line) or hear other fish activity near them, or if the wind changes.

Stillwater chumming. There are two methods of stillwater chumming: loose feeding and throwing in balls of chum, which is called balling.

Loose feeding is simple and inexpensive. Corn, chopped worms, or maggots are thrown into the water by hand for close fishing. For chumming at greater distances, anglers use a flat mesh pouch catapult (a special type of slingshot) to get loose feed 30 to 40 yards away, depending on the wind.

Loose feeding is a highly effective way to fish because the idea is to attract fish with the same chumming bait that is used on the hook. Loose

Competition anglers line a canal in Finland, using groundbait to chum the area being fished.

feeding of maggots is generally the best technique for bluegills, crappie, perch, catfish, carp, and shiners.

The balling method of chumming uses ground dried breadcrumbs, which have been carefully blended with water into a ball. The ball does not contain chunks of chum but is fine and unclogged. The best way to mix this chum is in a large bucket or bowl so that any chunks that form can be broken up and mixed in; the end result should be an evenly mixed, damp, fluffy bowl of breadcrumbs.

The basic chum mixture is rolled into a ball in two ways. One is by gently squeezing a ball of chum with one hand so that it just holds together; when this ball is lobbed gently into stillwater, it will explode and drift downward through the water in a cloud. This cloud is extremely attractive to many species of very small fish. In turn, the activity created by the small fish will attract larger species, such as bluegill, crappie, and others, and begin a literal chain reaction of feeding excitement. Since there is nothing of any substance to fill up the larger fish, they will be excited and looking for food, so a hookbait that is cast into the cloud produces action.

Balls of this chum can be thrown even farther than what is possible using loose feeding and a catapult. Balls can be thrown as far as the angler can reach; if greater distance is needed, special catapults with cup pouches can fire chum up to 80 yards away.

The other way to feed the same stillwater mix of breadcrumbs is to squeeze it into a hard ball. When pitched into the water, the hard ball goes directly to the bottom with very little of it breaking off. Corn, chopped worms or minnows, maggots, or liver can be added to the hard ball of chum and will be carried directly to the bottom. This is a good idea for targeting such species as catfish, carp, buffalo, and drum.

Flowing water chumming. In flowing water, a heavier mix of chum is necessary to get to the bottom quicker. This can be achieved by adding cornmeal and breadcrumbs that are much larger and coarser than stillwater cloud chum.

Mixing chum for flowing water takes more time than it does for stillwater. You must slightly overwet the chum mixture so it is very damp, but it must not clog up. The wet and mixed chum must be left for at least 30 minutes so that all the moisture is absorbed and it is very sticky. When you're ready to make a ball, mix in your chosen hookbait; the addition should never be more than 40 percent of the entire ball, or the ball will break up when it is thrown or when it hits the water. Squeeze the chum into a hard ball, and throw it a couple of yards upstream so it lands directly in front of you on the bottom.

Hundreds of baits and chums are successful for catching catfish and carp. A well-known favorite is Wheaties cereal soaked in strawberry soda; it makes a fantastic dough bait for carp and buffalo. There are dozens of effective stinkbaits that catch catfish, but a favorite when the fishing is really tough because of weather extremes is thin slivers of half-frozen liver; the chum here is the blood that leeches out and is carried downstream to those sensitive barbels of the catfish.

The major ingredients for most commercial chums and mixes made by professional European competition anglers are breadcrumbs, cornmeal, and peanuts, although you can experiment with every other type of grain and seed to find a personal favorite. However, most angling activities (at least in North America) only require different textures of breadcrumbs and cornmeal. In places having a lot of stocked fish (usually trout), ground-up fish pellets will be a very good attractant, because the fish will know the smell.

Only with experience will you learn how to correctly blend, wet, squeeze, and feed the chum in a precise spot.
See: Charter Boat; Drift Fishing; Inshore Fishing; Party Boat; Pier Fishing.

CHUM POT
A galvanized wire mesh basketlike pot with a hinged lid that is filled with ground chum and lowered into the water to attract fish. It is often placed on the bottom to interest bottom-feeding fish.
See: Chum; Chumming.

CHUM SLICK
The oily surface of the water above a chum line. The term chum slick is often used synonymously with chum line *(see)*, but a slick is merely the obvious smooth section of the surface, which is made by oil from the dispensed chum sitting on top of the water. The slick is carried away from the boat by tide and/or current, and it may or may not extend as far back as the underwater trail of chum. Usually the chum particles sink deeper as they are carried away from the initial drop point, and the slick portion of surface water dissipates at some distance from the boat. If chum particles stay close to the surface, some feeding fish may actually be visible as they move near the surface and swim through the slick.
See: Chum; Chumming.

CHUNKING
The use of pieces of fish to chum in offshore fishing, primarily for yellowfin and bluefin tuna. Most chunks are pieces of fish meat, in 2- to 3-inch cubes, that are dispensed piecemeal alone or in conjunction with ground chum. The term originated with Atlantic offshore tuna anglers, primarily in the Northeast.
See: Big-Game Fishing; Chum; Chumming; Tuna.

CIGUATERA
Poisoning caused by eating the flesh of fish toxic to humans. Found in many tropical reef fish, ciguatera is caused by a toxin found in certain algae eaten by reef fish. The poison accumulates when reef fish are eaten by larger fish and then by humans. There is no visual clue identifying a fish that contains the toxin, and any reef fish can carry it.

Ciguatera is unpredictable and causes sickness that may last for days, weeks, or months; it is sometimes fatal. It occurs in the Pacific and Caribbean, and is known in the western Indian Ocean only at Mauritius and Reunion Islands. It is a serious problem in some areas, including Hawaii. Symptoms include weakness; diarrhea; muscle pain and joint aches; numbness and tingling around the mouth, hands, and feet; nausea; chills; itching; headache; sweating; and dizziness.

To avoid ciguatera poisoning, health experts advise that anglers know the most common types of reef fish that carry the poison; know if and where cases of ciguatera fish poisoning have been reported in the areas they fish; clean the fish very well; eat only small portions of large fish that might have the poison; and not eat the roe, liver, head, or viscera because they have higher levels of poison.

If ciguatera fish poisoning is suspected, contact a doctor immediately, as well as health or fisheries authorities; save any uneaten portions of the fish for testing. Barracuda, amberjack, mullet, surgeonfish, and moray eel, as well as some jacks, snapper, and grouper, are all fish that may carry the ciguatera toxin.

CIRCLE HOOK
A pattern of hook popular for use with bait in tuna fishing due to its excellent holding virtue.
See: Hook.

CISCO *Coregonus spp.*
Other names—gray back, tullibee, lake herring, whitefish.

There are a number of similar species under the *Coregonus* genus, which is classified as a member of the Salmonidae family and generally acknowledged as a subfamily of whitefish *(see)*. Whitefish and cisco inhabit many of the same waters, and may be confused, although cisco are generally smaller. One of the most common of these is *Coregonus artedii*, simply referred to as cisco. This species is often portrayed as the only cisco because the differences between species are only minor variations in body or snout shape, depth preference, or number of eggs. However, there are, or were, perhaps as many as 11 species of cisco, some of which were primarily very deep-dwelling fish.

Overfishing by commercial interests, predation, pollution, and habitat degradation have caused some cisco to be listed as endangered or threatened; these include the longjaw cisco *(C. alpenae)* and the kiyi *(C. kiyi)*. The shortnose cisco *(C. reighardi)*, may be extinct. It was the only cisco species that spawned in the spring and was last observed in 1985 in Lake Huron. The deepwater cisco *(C. johannae)* is listed as extinct in Canada.

In the Great Lakes, cisco have evidently suffered from competition with more aggressive plankton feeders (like alewives and smelt), and from predation by salmon and sea lampreys, all of which were nonnative species. The bloater *(C. hoyi)* has suffered the least of the Great Lakes species. Bloaters do not support any sportfishing effort, as they dwell far from shore and have a mouth too small for ordinary baits. They are efficient feeders, however, and grow more on less food than do alewives.

Bloaters, as well as other Great Lakes cisco, are commonly called "chub." The bloater, in fact, is also known as a bloater chub. These small, soft-fleshed, and oily fish are tasty table fare and are popular for commercial smoking, usually bearing the name "smoked chub."

Cisco provide some sportfishing opportunity, especially for ice fishing, and are important forage fish for other species, particularly northern pike, walleye, perch, and rainbow trout. They are especially significant to lake trout.

Identification. Characterized by an adipose dorsal fin and forked tail, cisco have a terminal mouth (lower jaw projecting slightly beyond upper jaw). The body is elongate and slender with less than 100 scales in the lateral line. The pelvic axillary process, or daggerlike progression, is well developed. Its coloring is dusky gray to bluish on the back, silvery on the sides, and white on the underside. All fins are relatively clear, although the anal and pelvic fins may be milky on adults.

As a group, cisco (and whitefish) are quickly differentiated from other species by the presence of an adipose fin. Cisco can be differentiated from lake whitefish *(Coregonus clupeaformis)*, which inhabit the same deeper waters, by their pointed snout, terminal mouth, and lack of teeth; the cisco's mouth is at the end of the head, whereas the whitefish's mouth is behind and under the snout. They are differentiated from lake trout *(Salvelinus*

Cisco

namaycush), by having larger scales, a bigger mouth, and lack of teeth.

Size. Cisco can vary in length from 6 to 25 inches, the average size being between 10 and 14 inches and $1/2$ pound; the all-tackle world record is a Manitoba fish *(C. artedii)* that weighed 7 pounds, 6 ounces. The average life span is eight years. In some lakes, the cisco population may be stunted, and most fish are small.

Distribution. Cisco are primarily inhabitants of Canada, where they range from roughly east of the Mackenzie River through Ontario and north throughout the Northwest Territories, as well as throughout much of Quebec. They inhabit the Great Lakes and its tributaries (including the St. Lawrence River). They are found in some lakes of states bordering the Great Lakes, including the Finger Lakes in New York, and in upper Mississippi River drainages.

Habitat. Coldwater lakes are the favored dwelling places of cisco. They may be near the surface when the water is cold, or at depths of several hundred feet, but they generally remain below the thermocline in lakes where this stratification occurs. They tend to school in midwater and move into shallower areas when the water cools in the fall. Water temperatures ranging above 60°F are lethal to cisco, and as the surface waters warm, these fish move deeper. Many swim close to the surface during the winter, providing opportunities for ice fishing.

Life history/Behavior. Cisco are schooling fish that spawn in large congregations in late fall after moving into shallow water roughly 3 to 10 feet deep, often on reefs, and when the water temperature is about 4° to 5°C. Females can lay up to 30,000 eggs on the lake bottom, usually over gravel or stones. The eggs are given no parental care and hatch within four months. Nearly all cisco reach maturity by their fourth season. Some, such as the least cisco *(C. sardinella)*, are anadromous but do not stray far from river mouths during migration.

Food and feeding habits. Plankton is the main food source of cisco. During early spring, which is their most active (and shallow) feeding season, they may also consume minnows, crustaceans, and mayflies.

Angling. There is some open-water fishing for cisco, but this is generally confined to spring, when the fish are abundant and near the surface, perhaps feeding on mayflies. Use ultralight spoons and

spinners, a tiny jig, and flies, fished on fine line or tippets. Most angling for cisco occurs in winter, through the ice, using tiny jigs and ice flies, perhaps tipped with a mealworm or grub and lowered to a depth of from 10 to 30 feet below the ice with an appropriate-size split shot. Small minnows may work also. Fine line, from 1- to 4-pound test, is necessary, and it's wise to use sonar to search for schools of roving fish.
See: Ice Fishing.

CLASS LINE
See: Line.

CLASS TIPPET
A 15-inch-long tippet on a fly fishing leader that conforms to exact breaking strength standards for world record purposes.
See: Tippet.

CLEANING FISH
See: Fish Preparation—Cleaning/Dressing.

CLEAT, BOAT
A small object, usually aluminum or stainless steel, with projecting ends, primarily used for fastening mooring lines on a boat.

CLEATS, WADING
See: Surf Fishing; Waders.

CLICKER
A term for the click ratchet on fishing reels that is used to signal that line is being taken off the reel. It is also known as the warning click.
See: Big-Game Tackle; Conventional Tackle.

CLINCH KNOT
Also called "cinch" and a precursor to the superior Improved Clinch Knot, this is a fishing knot for terminal connections, and a common term for the popular and widely accepted Improved Clinch.
See: Knots, Fishing.

CLIPPERS
A commonly used small tool for trimming knots and cutting fishing line; these may be fingernail clippers or a similar device.

CLOSED-FACE REEL
A spincasting reel.
See: Spincasting Tackle.

CLOVE HITCH
See: Knots, Boating.

CLUTCH
A component of fishing reels and downriggers.
See: Baitcasting Tackle; Big-Game Tackle; Conventional Tackle; Downrigger; Flycasting Tackle; Spinning Tackle.

COARSE FISH
A British term for freshwater species that are not considered gamefish. This is a vague and loose-fitting term referring to such species as bream (see), roach (see), and tench (see), but it has also been used to include carp (see). It is only partly analogous to the American term "rough fish" (see), since coarse species are regularly sought and appreciated by many European anglers.

Most coarse fishing is done with chum (see), particularly groundbait (see), by using various types of generally small baits, and while fishing from shore.

COASTER
A brook trout (see: trout, brook) that leaves its natal stream and spends part of the year in large, deep clear lakes, cruising close to the shore. This occurs in the Great Lakes, and is akin to the activity of salters (see).

COBIA *Rachycentron canadum*.
Other names—ling, cabio, lemonfish, crab-eater, flathead, black salmon, black kingfish, sergeant fish, runner; French: *mafou*; Japanese: *sugi*; Portuguese: *bijupirá*.

The only member of the Rachycentridae family, and with no known relatives, the cobia is in a class by itself, and a popular food and sportfish for inshore anglers in areas where it is prominent.

Identification. The body of a cobia is elongated with a broad, depressed head. The first dorsal fin consists of 8 to 10 short depressible spines that are not connected by a membrane. Both the second dorsal fin and the anal fin each have one to two spines and 20 to 30 soft rays. The adult cobia is dark brown with a whitish underside and is marked on the sides by silver or bronze lines. Young cobia, possessing alternating black and white stripes and speckled with bronze, orange, and green, are more colorful than adults.

A cobia's shape is comparable to that of a shark, with a powerful tail fin and the elevated anterior portion of the second dorsal fin. It can be distinguished from the similar remora (*Remora remora*), by the absence of a suction pad on the head.

Size/Age. Cobia can grow to a length of 6 feet and a weight of 90 pounds, the average size being 3 feet and 15 pounds. Females are slightly larger than males. They generally live 9 to 10 years, and some reports indicate greater longevity. A 9-year-old fish can weigh close to 100 pounds. Scientific reports say that cobia can reach a maximum weight of 150 pounds, but that has not been the case in U.S. waters. The all-tackle rod-and-reel record cobia weighed 135 pounds, 9 ounces.

Distribution. Found worldwide in tropical and warm temperate waters, cobia inhabit the western Atlantic from Cape Cod to Argentina (being most abundant in the Gulf of Mexico), the eastern Atlantic from the coast of Morocco to South Africa, and Indo-West Pacific waters from Japan to Australia and the East Indies.

Habitat. Adult cobia prefer shallow continental shelf waters, often congregating along reefs and around buoys, pilings, wrecks, anchored boats, and other stationary or floating objects. They are found in a variety of locations over mud, gravel, or sand bottoms, coral reefs and man-made sloughs, and at depths of up to 60 feet.

Life history/Behavior. Although juveniles are sometimes found in schools, adult cobia often swim alone or among small schools of other cobia or sharks. Fish in these schools may vary considerably in size. They are believed to spawn in the offshore waters of the northern Gulf of Mexico during late spring and summer, between April and May, and the larvae migrate shoreward. Males reach sexual maturity when they are two years old and 24 inches long, and females at age 3 and 36 inches in length. An adult female cobia may lay 6 to 7 million eggs at one time. Juveniles are abundant in summer along coastlines after the spawning season.

Cobia migrate from offshore to inshore environs as well as inshore from east to west and vice versa. Little about their movements has been confirmed, although it is known that in winter some fish move from shallow to deeper water, or laterally to warmer areas. A tagged cobia migrated 1,300 nautical miles from west of the Mississippi River to Daytona Beach, Florida, in an eight-month period. In the western Atlantic, cobia migrate as far north as Cape Cod in the summer and then south again to tropical waters in the fall.

Food and feeding habits. Cobia feed mostly on crustaceans, particularly shrimp, squid, and crabs (thus the name "crab eater"), as well as on eels and various small fish found in shallow coastal waters.

Angling. With cobia populations having improved in the Gulf of Mexico and along the South Atlantic coast, this species has become especially favored and hotly pursued from spring through fall by boaters, in part because it often offers sight fishing opportunities, making it a species that anglers can cast lures and baits to, and in part because it is fairly predictably found around such structures as bridges, buoys, channel markers, and oil rigs. Cobia are fairly aggressive a good deal of the time, readily striking plugs, jigs, and flies, and are sometimes caught handily on baits. They are usually not afraid of boats and often come to a boat and mill around. In addition to being good fighters on the line, they are known for thrashing about after being boated, which requires caution.

In the Gulf of Mexico, the greatest cobia action occurs from March through May in shallow near-beach waters, when migrating fish are hunted by cruising anglers. Working from boats, they search for shallow, near-the-surface swimming cobia, sometimes close to the beach but as far as a half mile from it. Anglers use jigs or lures, often on spinning tackle with 12- to 25-pound line (using the heavier strength when really big fish are possible), casting 60 to 80 feet to the brown-backed cobia. Live baits are also cast, although positioning is more of a concern because the baits cannot be cast as accurately for long distances. The same is true for fly fishing, although sometimes live baits are used to draw cobia closer to a boat for fly presentation. These fish move offshore on wrecks and reefs in summer and fall.

Live baits for cobia depend on geographic location and availability, but there's a range of choices. Peeler crabs, spot, and eels are favored in some areas, whereas mullet, pinfish, and grunts are used in others, in addition to pieces of squid. Lures include bucktail jigs, tube lures, and assorted swimming plugs.

Some anglers pursue cobia by trolling and by drifting over deep structure, but many carefully approach buoys, channel markers, and oil rigs, where lone or grouped cobia may be present. The quiet approach is an effort to keep the fish from approaching the boat; many anglers gauge current and wind direction and set up to drift by such places, freelining bait or making repetitive casts.

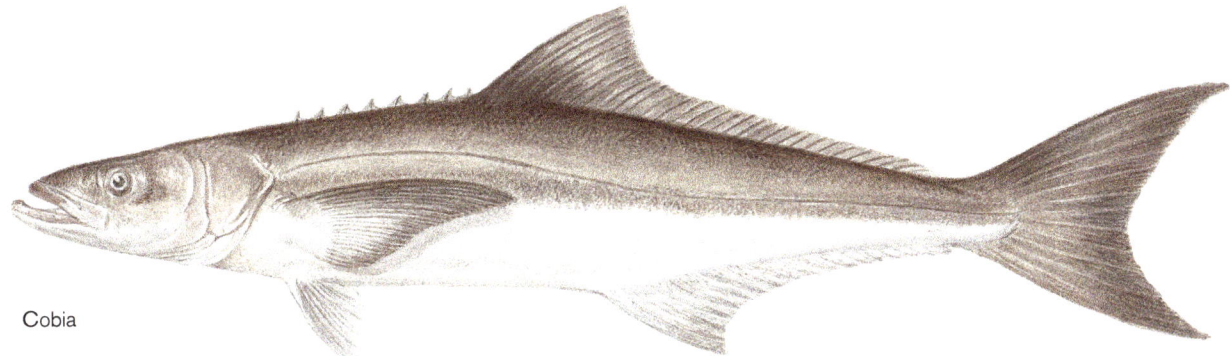

Cobia

COD AND HAKE

The various cod and hake are all members of the Gadidae family of codfish. All codfish live in cold waters of the Northern Hemisphere, some in the Atlantic and some in the Pacific. Most of the species are harvested commercially, although some have been in serious decline.

All members of the cod family have spineless fins. The pelvic or ventral fins are located far forward, commonly ahead of the pectorals. The body is elongated, and there is a single barbel on the chin. Most species have two dorsal fins, some have three, others only one.

Codfish and other pelagic species in the family produce prodigious numbers of eggs. A 20-pound female may lay 4 to 5 million eggs in a season, and a specimen of 75 pounds may produce more than 9 million eggs. Males spread their milt in the sea around the eggs and fertilize them. The eggs float freely, as do the newly hatched fish. The young are about an inch long before they are strong enough to swim well, and the few that survive manage to get into shallow enough water for them to find refuge, feed, and grow. By the time they are three years old, they weigh roughly 5 pounds. Cod are mainly bottom dwellers, feeding on small fish, mollusks, crabs, sea worms, and similar creatures.

Cod have been important in both commercial fishing and sportfishing, although their significance in both areas has diminished markedly. Some cod are sold fresh, but most of the catch is now processed as frozen fillets. In the early days, cod were preserved mainly by salting. Oil from the cod's liver was the main source of vitamin D.

The Atlantic cod (*Gadus morhua*; see: cod, Atlantic) occurs off both the European and North American coasts in cool waters and from near the surface to depths of a thousand feet or more. Smaller fish are generally closer to shore, larger ones remain in deeper water. Cod like cool waters and may sometimes follow cool currents out of their normal range. In winter, for example, they are found as far south as North Carolina.

The Atlantic cod has three dorsal fins and two anal fins. The light lateral line against its dark sides is a distinctive feature. The snout is rounded or cone-shaped on top, the upper jaw projecting slightly beyond the lower. The tail is almost squared or is slightly concave. There are two principal color phases, gray and red; in both, the sides are covered with dark dots.

The Pacific cod (*G. macrocephalus*; see: cod, Pacific) is found on both sides of the Pacific. Off the North American coast, it occurs from Oregon northward, only occasionally straying southward. The Pacific cod is almost identical to the Atlantic cod, differing only in having slightly more pointed fins. It is somewhat smaller on average.

Closely related, and sometimes placed in the genus *Gadus*, is the haddock (*Melanogrammus aeglefinus*; see haddock), found off both the North American and European coasts in the Atlantic. Haddock, like cod, travel in large schools. Today the catch has declined drastically because of overfishing. Most of the catch is filleted and frozen. Some is smoked, which is called finnan haddie. The largest haddock fishery historically has been off the Grand Banks of Newfoundland and in Europe, in the North Sea south of Spitsbergen.

Haddock are bottom feeders, usually found in greatest numbers in water 100 to 500 feet deep. The two most common of the several color variations are grayish green with a dark lateral line and golden brown with a yellow lateral line. Like the cod, the haddock has three dorsal and two anal fins, but it lacks spots on its body. The first rays on the leading dorsal fin are exceptionally long. Just above and behind each pectoral fin is a large, dark blotch.

The pollock (*Pollachius virens*; see: pollock), has been the most popular of the cod family with anglers. Averaging 4 to 10 pounds in weight (but with some catches weighing more than 30 pounds), the pollock is found on both sides of the Atlantic in cool to cold waters, usually close to shore but commonly netted at depths of 400 to 500 feet. The pollock's snout is pointed, the lower jaw projecting beyond the upper; the chin barbel is very small or lacking. The broad caudal fin is forked. Because the back and sides are a greenish brown, another name for the pollock is green cod. There are no spots, however, and the lateral line is white.

Pollock are active feeders, preying mainly on small fish but also taking crabs, mollusks, and other small animals. Anglers catch them principally by trolling, using jigs or spoons, but the smaller fish are known also to take artificial flies along inshore waters. They are strong fighters.

The Atlantic tomcod (*Microgadus tomcod*; see: tomcod, Atlantic) and its close relative, the Pacific tomcod (*M. proximus*; see: tomcod, Pacific), also have three dorsal and two anal fins, which are rounded, as are the long caudal fins. The pelvic fins extend into long filaments that may be sensory in function. These fish are generally olive brown above and lighter below, the sides heavily blotched with black. Tomcod average less than 12 inches in length, and only occasional individuals weigh more than a pound.

Hake differ from cod in having the second and third dorsal fins joined to make one large fin that typically is indented or notched where the two are joined. Directly below is an indentation on the anal fin. The lower jaw projects beyond the upper, and the chin barbel is either very small or absent. The caudal fin is shallowly forked. Hake are predators, feeding on smaller fish and squid. They travel in schools, generally at the edge of the continental shelf or below, down to 2,000 feet. Their eggs contain oil droplets so that they rise to the surface and float in the open sea until they hatch. Compared to cod, the flesh of hake is soft, and thus generally less appealing. Hake have nevertheless been harvested

---

Grayling were once abundant in Michigan's Manistee River and even had a town named after them, but grayling haven't been seen in that state since 1932.

commercially in large quantities.

The South African hake *(Merluccius capensis)* is considered the most valuable commercial fish netted off the African coast. It sometimes reaches a length of 4 feet but averages 2 feet or less. The European hake *(M. merluccius),* which is similar in size, ranges from Norway southward to Africa and occurs also in the Mediterranean.

The common species off the Atlantic coast of North America, from Newfoundland south to the Bahamas, is the silver hake *(M. bilinearis; see: hake, silver),* which is regionally known as whiting and quite popular. In the Pacific, the only representative is the Pacific hake *(M. productus; see: hake, Pacific).*

The white hake *(Urophycis tenuis; see hake, white),* ranging from Newfoundland to North Carolina, is a slender fish that may exceed 3 feet in length and weigh more than 30 pounds. The average is about half this size. As in the hake of the genus *Merluccius,* the second and third dorsal fins are joined. The first ray of the first dorsal is extended into a slim filament, and the caudal fin is rounded. There is a small chin barbel, and the pelvic or ventral fins are reduced to long filaments. The back and sides are reddish, grading into yellowish gray below.

The red hake *(U. chuss; see: hake, red)* occurs in the same general range as the white hake. The filament of its first dorsal fin is much longer, and the sides are mottled. The maximum size of the red hake is 8 pounds; the average is about 2 pounds.

Several other species in the genus *Urophycis* are all about the size of the red hake or smaller. These include the southern hake *(U. floridanus),* which averages a pound in weight. It has dark spots above and behind the eyes and also on the gill covers, and the first ray of the dorsal fin is of normal length. There are round white spots at regular intervals along the black lateral line. The southern hake occurs in the Gulf of Mexico and is sometimes caught on hook and line, particularly in winter.

The spotted hake *(U. regius)* also lacks the long filament on the first dorsal fin, and its scales are larger than in other hakes of the genus *Urophycis.* The slim pectoral fin is exceptionally long, extending to the anal fin. The spotted hake is the most common species in the mid-Atlantic region. It is seldom fished for but is caught accidentally on hook and line. Commercial fishermen also catch these hake from time to time, but the fishery for hake is not large or well developed.

The common species in European waters is *U. blennoides,* which is much more fat-bodied and blenny-like than other species of the genus. About a dozen other rare or commercially unimportant hake and cod inhabit northern waters.

Only one species of the cod family lives exclusively in freshwater—the burbot *(Lota lota; see: burbot),* which is found in deep, cold lakes and streams, sometimes in great abundance, from Alaska southward throughout Canada and in the northern portion of the United States. It occurs also in the cold regions of Europe and Asia. Other common names for the burbot are ling, lawyer, eelpout, and freshwater cod. It is sometimes mistaken for some kind of catfish. Its scales are so small that the burbot appears to be naked, like a catfish, and beneath its chin is a single long barbel. The pelvic fins are located far forward, ahead of the pectorals, directly under the throat. There are two dorsal fins. The first is short, the second long and nearly matched in length by the anal fin below. The caudal fin is small. The burbot is white or yellowish orange, mottled with black, but the coloration depends greatly on the chemistry of the water in which the burbot is living. It is not unusual for the burbot to reach a weight of 5 or 10 pounds and to measure 3 feet in length.

Burbot are active predators. In most places they are considered trash fish that are destructive to populations of more desirable species, but there has been some increased interest in sportfishing for them, particularly among ice anglers.

COD, ATLANTIC *Gadus morhua.*

Other names—cod, codfish, codling, scrod; French: *morue de l'Atlantique;* German: *dorsch, kabeljau;* Italian: *merluzzo bianco;* Japanese: *madara, tara;* Norwegian: *torsk;* Portuguese: *bacalhau;* Spanish: *bacalao del Atlántique.*

The Atlantic cod has historically been one of the world's important natural resources, and the waters of the North Atlantic once teemed with this fish. The Basques fished the Banks off Newfoundland for cod centuries before Columbus discovered America, and cod bones have been found in coastal dwelling sites dating from the Mesolithic period. Overstating the cod's value as a food fish to the New World would be difficult. So important was the cod in colonial America that it even appeared in the state seal of Massachusetts, a reflection of the fact that cod fishing was that colony's first industry and the source of early fortunes.

In earlier times, the cod catch was split, salted, and dried. Salt cod, once a staple food on both sides of the Atlantic, was one of the first export items from American colonies, and it was an important fish during Lent. Today, however, no salted cod is produced in the United States. Improvements in fishing gear, the transition to steam and diesel engines, and technological changes in handling the catch (both at sea and ashore) made it possible to bring the fish to market more rapidly. Quick freezing and filleting resulted in a more popular market form: boneless fillets ready for the pan. Domestic landings now are primarily filleted or steaked and sold fresh or frozen. Most of the fish once used in the production of breaded fish portions and fish sticks was cod, when still in great abundance. The term "scrod," incidentally, is fish market terminology for a small (to 3 pounds) cod with the head on.

Commercial fishing for cod has long been conducted year-round; otter trawls and gillnets have

Atlantic Cod

been the primary gear. Today, the commercial catch of cod is far below its historical levels, and cod are generally in a collapsed or near-collapsed condition, having been overexploited by commercial fishermen even though the U.S. commercial and recreational fisheries for cod are managed under the New England Fishery Management Council's Multispecies Fishery Management Plan. The 1990s experienced record-low commercial catches; older fish have been almost nonexistent, and incoming year classes have been relatively weak. With recruitment extremely poor and spawning stock biomass at unprecedented low levels, there is enormous concern for the future of this species.

Identification. The Atlantic cod has three dark dorsal fins and two dark anal fins, none of which contain any spines. The body is heavy and tapered, with a prominent chin barbel, a large mouth, and many small teeth. Its snout is rounded on top, and the tail is almost squared. There is a characteristic pale lateral line. The coloring is highly variable on the back and sides (ranging from brownish or sandy to gray, yellow, reddish, greenish, or any combination of these colors), gray white on the underside, and with numerous light spots covering the body.

The Atlantic cod can be distinguished from its relative the pollock (see) by its barbel and projecting upper jaw, and from the haddock (see) by its pale lateral line. It can also be distinguished from the Pacific cod (see: cod, Pacific) by the less pointed fins. The tomcod (see) is similar, but the caudal fin is rounded; in the Atlantic cod it is squared.

Size/Age. Young fish ages 2 to 5 generally constitute the bulk of the recreational (and commercial) cod catch, with the average size being from 4 to 15 pounds. Larger sizes in New England are not unusual, some with a length of 30 to 40 inches. When they were more abundant, cod were caught in the 55- to 75-pound range. The largest cod known weighed 211 pounds, 8 ounces, and was taken off the coast of Massachusetts in May of 1895. The all-tackle fishing record is 98 pounds, 12 ounces. Atlantic cod can live up to 22 years.

Distribution. Atlantic cod occur in subarctic and cool temperate waters of the North Atlantic from Greenland to North Carolina, including the Hudson Strait, and from Novaya Zemla, in the former USSR, to the northern reaches of the Bay of Biscay, including the Baltic and North Seas and Iceland. They have generally been most abundant in the Gulf of St. Lawrence, off Newfoundland. In U.S. waters, cod are assessed as two stocks, the first being that of the Gulf of Maine, and the second being that of Georges Bank and southward.

Habitat. These fish are found primarily off the coasts along the continental shelf. They prefer cool water of 30° to 50°F and may reside in depths of up to 200 fathoms. Adults are generally found in water over 60 feet deep, whereas juveniles may be found in shallower water; both move deeper during the summer. Growth rates differ between the two stocks. It has traditionally been slower in the Gulf of Maine than on Georges Bank.

Spawning behavior. The spawning season is during winter and early spring, in December and January off the Mid-Atlantic Bight and from February through April farther north. The transparent eggs hatch, after floating, within 50 days at 32°F, and in 17 days when the surface temperature is 41°F.

Food and feeding habits. Omnivorous feeders, cod are primarily active at dawn and dusk. Many unusual items have been found in the stomachs of adult cod, including an oil can, a rubber doll, finger rings, clothing, and some very rare deep-sea shells that were previously unknown to science; however, their diet is invertebrates and assorted fish. Very young cod feed on copepods and other small crustaceans while at the surface, and, after dropping to the bottom, small worms or shrimp.

Angling. Recreational fishing for cod occurs year-round, although the peak activity is during the late summer in the lower Gulf of Maine, and during late autumn to early spring from Massachusetts southward. A cold winter may cause spring and early summer water closer to shore to be cold, and this may produce cod in shallower waters.

Traditionally, cod fishing was practiced over rough bottoms, but most Atlantic cod fishing today

A group of Atlantic cod, headed for the kitchen.

takes place on wrecks. Those far offshore tend to produce the better fishing and larger specimens. Far offshore, off Georges Bank for example, is the province of long-range party boats, some of which run for five hours to reach desired areas.

In the shallow nearer water, the early fishing—when the cod first show up and are aggressive and abundant—is productive on 10-ounce diamond jigs. This tactic may be useful into the winter if there's plenty of live bait around, but baitfishing is the typical winter strategy. In shallower waters, 8 to 16 ounces of lead are best, as these heavier weights are necessary in the strong tide conditions. Anchoring is possible when there's less current, but most of the time anglers will drift. Skimmer clams are the primary baits, usually fished on high-low rigs and sometimes combined with a tube bait or hooked soft-plastic bait. Jigs are also sometimes combined with a second, upper, lure (plastic or small bucktail), which is especially worth doing when small sand eels are present.

In deeper water, heavier jigs and weights are necessary; live-bait sinkers running up to 32 ounces are the norm, and all fishing is done via drifting. Bottom depths vary from 120 to as much as 200 feet. Fresh baitfish is a necessity. Skimmer clams are the main item, but squid is also used. Bait is provided on party boats, but private boaters must have an ample supply of their own. Some cod anglers will shell a bushel or two of skimmer clams a day before going cod fishing and then salt them in buckets overnight to toughen them so they will stay on the hook.

Because cod are bottom fish, the trick is getting and staying in the right places. The angler must find the weight that will position the rig on the bottom in the given conditions while keeping a little slack in the line. This method enables the angler to detect a strike while the bait is drifting. Jigging does not have to be done right on the bottom, with the jig bouncing off it, but the jig should be fairly close to the bottom. Given the weight of jigs used and the depths attained, many cod aficionados prefer low-stretch lines. Dacron line was favored in the past, but these days the newer thin-diameter microfilaments are popular. Conventional tackle is the standard gear, and 4/0 reels are the norm.
See: Cod and Hake.

COD, MURRAY *Maccullochella peeli.*
Other names—cod, codfish, goodoo, and ponde; also known as *Maccullochella peelii peelii.*

Endemic to Australia, the Murray cod is the largest of that continent's freshwater species, and one of the world's biggest entirely freshwater fish. A member of the Percichthyidae family of temperate bass, it is a fine table fish in its early growth stages, although its flesh becomes coarse and more oily as the fish ages. It is closely related to, and often confused with, the trout cod *(Maccullochella macquariensis),* and the eastern freshwater cod *(Maccullochella ikei).* A small commercial fishery for Murray cod exists in southwestern New South Wales; these fish are for domestic consumption.

Identification. The general body coloring varies from brown or olive green above, and yellow green with a mottling of pale green on the lower sides and fin bases. The belly is white. The caudal fin is convex and may have white margins on the upper and lower tips, as may the soft dorsal fin and the anal fin. The head is broad and depressed, with a rounded snout, and the forehead profile is concave. The upper and lower jaws are usually of equal length.

Size. Reported to grow to more than 1.8 meters and 113 kilograms, the Murray cod commonly reaches 60 to 70 centimeters and up to 5 kilograms when mature, at about five years of age. Anglers fishing waterways such as Lake Mulwala on the Murray River frequently take specimens to 20 kilograms. The average size runs to about 8 kilograms; at that size, they are considered excellent eating. Regulations exist to limit the tackle used as well as the size and number of fish caught and kept.

Distribution. Murray cod were once found throughout the Murray-Darling system from Queensland to South Australia, but wild stocks have declined in recent years and the species is considered rare in many Victoria streams. The decline is largely attributed to the clearing out of underwater cover, and the construction of weirs

Murray Cod

and dams along major rivers. Murray cod are now successfully reared in numerous hatcheries, and their decline has been checked somewhat; stocks have been introduced to many inland streams and impoundments in Victoria, New South Wales, and southern Queensland.

Habitat. The Murray cod, which are found in a wide range of habitats, shows a surprising tolerance to water that ranges from clear to muddy. They favor sheltered areas away from strong currents and like to station themselves on the downstream side of underwater boulders and submerged logs and tree roots, where swirling back eddies carry food to them. In the still waters of impoundments and billabongs, they will establish themselves in areas of weeds, dead trees, and warm backwaters.

Life history/Behavior. Murray cod spawn from spring through early summer (September through October) as water temperatures increase. If spawning coincides with flooding, the larvae will not only have more food available, improving their chances of survival, but the flood waters will also distribute the larvae to feeder streams and billabongs (backwater area or pond connected to a river) downstream.

Spawning takes place when the fish reach 4 years of age. The eggs, which are 3 to 4 millimeters in diameter and demersal, can number to 90,000. They are also adhesive, and stick to hollow logs, rocks, and other hard surfaces. Hatching takes place within 7 to 10 days, and the larvae grow rapidly. They are mature when 4 to 5 years old, at which time they weigh about 5 kilograms. At 15 years of age, they might weigh in excess of 20 kilograms.

Murray cod are territorial and may spend most of their lives within a short (10 kilometers) stretch of a stream.

Food and feeding habits. The huge mouth of the Murray cod enables it to feed on small fish, crayfish, shrimp, freshwater mussels, grubs, worms, frogs, birds, mice, rodents, and any other small creatures that fall into the water. Feeding activity increases during the summer months and is largely nocturnal.

Angling. Although it is one of the largest freshwater fish in the world, the Murray cod is not highly regarded as a sportfish. It is capable of putting up a stubborn fight, but there is nothing spectacular about its struggles when hooked. Complacency, however, can be dangerous when a large specimen takes a bait or lure, as this bulky fish is strong and unlikely to surrender until totally exhausted.

Many anglers using rod and reel, or handlines, resort to such live baits as small fish, yabbies (crayfish), shrimp, worms, and grubs. The most popular grub is the barti grub (the burrowing larva of a large moth), which is extracted from its hole in the ground by a 1-meter length of piano wire with a sharp-pointed corkscrew twisted into one end. The wire is pushed down the hole until the soft body of the grub is felt, screwed into it, and withdrawn.

Bait anglers seek out deep holes away from the main current, or toss their baits into back eddies where the cod rests up. Experienced cod anglers fish along the riverbank, rather than into the main stream, knowing that after dark the cod roams along the sides of the stream seeking out crayfish that burrow in the banks and emerge after nightfall. Anglers favor hook sizes to No. 7/0, and handlines of 15- to 50-kilogram strength.

In those streams where the water runs clear, casting with small diving lures and spinners is highly successful. Where the waters are turbid (common in western streams), rattling lures and large, noisy, bladed spinners take over. Most fishing on impoundments is done from boats, and trolling around, or casting to, patches of dead trees is preferred. Night fishing with surface lures is also worthwhile. Baitcasting and spinning tackle with up to 10-kilogram line are used for trolling and casting. Fly fishing has been successful but is not widely practiced.

COD, PACIFIC *Gadus macrocephalus.*

Other names—cod, gray cod, true cod; French: *morue du Pacifique;* Italian: *merluzzo del Pacifico;* Japanese: *madara;* Portuguese: *bacalau-do-Pacifico;* Spanish: *bacalao del Pacifico.*

Extremely similar to Atlantic cod, and a member of the Gadidae family, the Pacific cod is an excellent food fish and a good sportfish. It is harvested commercially for fish sticks and fillets and is usually sold frozen. In British Columbia, it is the most important trawl-caught bottom fish, with millions of pounds landed there alone.

Identification. Characteristic of the cod family, the Pacific cod has three separate and distinct dorsal fins, two anal fins, and one large barbel under the chin. Its body is heavy and elongated, with small scales, a large mouth, and soft rays. Its coloring ranges from gray to brown on the back, lightening on the sides and belly. Numerous brown spots speckle the sides and back. All the fins are dusky, and the unpaired fins are edged with white on their outer margins.

The Pacific cod can be distinguished from the Atlantic cod, which is almost identical, by its smaller body and the pointedness of its fins.

Size. The average size is less than 3 feet, with a weight of 15 pounds or less. The all-tackle record is 30 pounds.

Distribution. The Pacific cod inhabits waters along the U.S. Pacific coast from Santa Monica,

Pacific Cod

California, to northwestern Alaska; and in Asia from the Chukchi Sea to the Yellow Sea and Lushen (Port Arthur), China. It is common in the U.S. northwest waters of Oregon, Washington, and Alaska.

Habitat. Although primarily a coastal bottom-dwelling fish, the Pacific cod can be found from shallow waters to depths of nearly 800 feet. It prefers rocky, pebbly ground or sandy bottoms in cold water.

Spawning behavior. The spawning season for the Pacific cod is winter and early spring. The eggs are pelagic, or free-floating. It generally lays great quantities of eggs; depending on the size of the fish, a female may release between 1 and 9 million eggs.

Food and feeding habits. The Pacific cod is mainly omnivorous. The adult feeds dominant food organisms, especially herring, capelin, sand eels, sardines, pollock, and other cod. Its habits are similar to those of the Atlantic cod.

Angling. *See: Cod, Atlantic.*
See: Cod and Hake.

COELACANTH *Latimeria chalumnae.*
Other names—latimeria; Afrikaans: *seelakant.*

The coelacanth is not a species of interest to anglers, but it is one of the greatest curiosities of the seas and an important link to the evolutionary past. It is the only known species in its genus and family, Latimeriidae, and is considered an endangered living fossil.

A sensational zoological discovery was made in December 1938 when a coelacanth was netted from the depths of the western Indian Ocean off the Comoro Islands along the coast of South Africa. Before then, coelacanths were known only from fossil records of the Devonian period, considered to be more than 360 million years ago. These fish, ancestors of present-day vertebrates, were believed to have become extinct many millions of years ago. The first specimen captured was sent to a taxidermist, who saved only the skin and not the organs. Scientists considered the decision a disaster. Since then, through a reward program to commercial anglers in the area, other specimens have been made available to scientists and studied in detail.

Coelacanths have been caught in depths of between 75 to 200 fathoms at rocky areas with steep gradients. They evidently also exist in deeper water, but they are bottom fish and cannot be taken easily because ragged rocks prevent commercial fishing nets from reaching them. Very few have been taken by noncommercial fishing methods, although a specially outfitted Japanese expedition caught two specimens, one of 1 meter in length and the other 1.77 meters long (weighing 85 kilograms), in late 1981 using computerized electronic fishing equipment; these were exhibited in February 1982 at the Tokyo Fishing Show.

The maximum size the coelacanth can obtain is not known. They are a slow-moving species, found in caves. They may travel up to 8 kilometers in a night while foraging. They are an ovoviparous fish; that is, the eggs are retained inside the fish, and the young are born alive.

Coelacanth are not handsome fish. They are bulky in form and have shades of brown toward the belly. The scales are large, and the fish is well marked with irregularly shaped whitish or creamy splotches. They are predacious creatures, feeding exclusively on other fish. The fin structure is the coelacanth's most unusual external feature. The second dorsal, pectorals, and pelvics are supported by a stalklike arrangement or lobes—thus the name lobefins (or lobefin fish)—that appear limblike. The fins are supported by their own skeleton and are fortified by an elaborate system of muscles, enabling the coelacanths to move in a wide range of positions.

The value of living coelacanths is their great antiquity; they are by far the oldest vertebrates alive today. Whereas dominant animals such as dinosaurs disappeared from the earth, the coelacanth has remained unchanged throughout the ages. This has been proven by imprints in geological strata and by the paleontologists who reconstructed these fossils before the first coelacanth was taken alive. In addition, coelacanths are the only survivors of the large group of crossopterygians, the focal group from

Coelacanth

which evolved the entire lineage of air-breathing vertebrates up to humans.

The causes for their survival over the ages and their peculiar restriction to the north of the Mozambique Channel between Madagascar and Africa remain a mystery.

COLDWATER FISH

A term for freshwater species whose optimum environment contains cold and well-oxygenated water, usually under 60°F, throughout the season; trout, salmon, grayling, whitefish, and cisco are among this group. They inhabit coldwater streams and generally infertile lakes; in lakes their deep environs must have cold, well-oxygenated water through the summer.

See: Coolwater Fish; Warmwater Fish.

COLLECTING

See: Antique Fishing Tackle; Book Collecting.

COLOMBIA

The only South American country with coasts on both the Caribbean Sea and the Pacific Ocean, Colombia offers fine sportfishing possibilities; unfortunately, these largely hang under a dark cloud of suspicion due to safety concerns. Well-publicized problems with crime exist here for tourists, depending on their nationality and the passport they carry. Although this may not be true for all areas of the country, Colombia's reputation as a dangerous country has largely curtailed sportfishing development and exploration.

In the mid-1980s, developing opportunities in the interior of Colombia—in waters that flow to the Orinoco River—were providing what was at the time arguably the world's best fishing for peacock bass and payara, plus outstanding opportunities for other species. The region in which these fisheries existed was a haven for illicit drug activities, how-ever, and caused travel here to virtually shut down. Although coastal fishing is reputedly less risky, infrastructure remains limited, and interest—especially from North Americans—has been greatly dampened by safety concerns, resulting in little to no recreational angling in many places.

Freshwater

Colombia's principal river is the Magdalena, which flows between mountain ranges from south to north for a distance of 960 miles, emptying into the Caribbean near Barranquilla. A significant tributary to the Magdalena is the Cauca River, which flows for some 200 miles. Sportfishing opportunities and major species in these large waterways have been unreported in recent times. Rainbow trout reportedly existed in the 1960s in mountain waters, and in Lake Tota near Bogota and Lake Cocha near Pasto, although no recent information is available at this writing.

A vast area of eastern Colombia consists of plains, rain forest, and tropical lowlands. It is lightly populated, and traversed by numerous rivers. These flow from the Bolivian Andes to Brazil and Venezuela, contributing respectively to the Amazon and Orinoco Rivers. The many rivers and fish species here are described in the Amazon review under Brazil *(see)*.

Saltwater

Colombia has 1,090 miles of Caribbean coastline and 900 miles of Pacific coastline, the latter between Panama to the north and Ecuador to the south, with many inlet rivers and few harbors. Significant species known to exist along these coasts include sailfish, blue marlin, striped marlin, black marlin, wahoo, amberjack, roosterfish, dolphin (dorado), yellowfin tuna, tarpon, and snook.

Most of these are found on the Pacific side, the species being similar to those found in Panama *(see)* waters. In the mid-1990s, anglers were fishing from Solano Bay on the northwest coast, where deep water is 20 to 50 miles from shore, and fish prowl a series of dropoffs. Fishing for sailfish and striped marlin was reportedly best from April through June, for other marlin from June through August, for tuna from April through July, and for dolphin from December through August. The Cabo Marzo area to the north of this has a good reputation but is difficult to reach. A number of significant rivers in Colombia enter the Pacific, but no information about their fisheries—at the mouth or upriver—is known, although snook are likely found here.

The Caribbean coast is also reported to have sailfish, marlin, tuna, dolphin, wahoo, and the like in offshore environs, as well as tarpon and snook inshore; although here, too, there are no current reports on abundance, seasonal availability, fishing camps, or charter services. The deltaic mouth of the Magdalena River covers a large expanse of lagoons, lakes, and estuarine area; in the past, tarpon were reportedly caught as far up the Magdalena as El Banco, and up the Cauca River to Ayapel.

COLORADO

You would expect a state that covers more than 104,000 square miles and includes 54 peaks that exceed 14,000 feet to have a lot of flowing water and plenty of trout. And, indeed, Colorado does, with approximately 10,000 miles of streams and more than 2,000 natural lakes and reservoirs, which together cause about 750,000 licenses to be sold annually to resident and nonresident anglers. Moreover, it is a headwater state with the unique distinction that every stream within it originates from the Rocky Mountain region.

The Centennial State lies within three geologic areas. The Eastern Plains covers the eastern third of the state from the Front Range to the Kansas-Nebraska line; here, in the southeast, is the state's lowest elevation of 3,500 feet. The Colorado Plateau covers much of the western third, and this includes the Colorado River, which exits midstate into Utah. The Rocky Mountains extend south from Wyoming to New Mexico through the central area, where they are bifurcated in the south by the San Luis Valley.

The central area is responsible for all of the state's water. Here, the Rockies quickly rise from just over 5,000 feet to more than 14,000 feet along and near the Continental Divide. Glaciers formed the present landscape on both sides of the divide and left behind countless small streams fed by alpine lakes and snow melt. These waters contain native species of cutthroat trout: the greenback cutthroat is natural to the East Slope, the Rio Grande cutthroat originates from the Southern Rockies, and the Colorado River cutthroat is indigenous to the Colorado River drainage. The native greenback cutthroat, a species once believed extinct and recovered in the 1990s, is Colorado's state fish.

Although trout are the primary species sought by anglers, the Colorado Division of Wildlife (CDOW) has significantly expanded the number of game species available. In addition to the three native cutthroat trout, anglers have the opportunity to fish for such other coldwater species as Snake River cutthroats, golden trout, brown trout, rainbow trout, brook trout, lake trout, splake, Dolly Varden trout, mountain whitefish, arctic grayling, and arctic charr in coldwater lakes and streams. Anglers also can catch such warmwater denizens as largemouth bass, smallmouth bass, striped bass, hybrid stripers, white bass, northern pike, tiger muskies, walleye, sauger, saugeye, crappie, perch, bluegills, catfish, and bullhead.

The general fishing season runs year-round, although the winter months are limited to fishing tailwaters for trout, and ice fishing for all species. Anglers who prefer to fish streams for trout pursue their sport beginning in March or April. Most rivers below 8,000 feet will be open by then, and pre-runoff angling is often exceptional. Open streams correspond with rainbow spawning, and egglike fly patterns are extremely productive then for rainbows and browns.

The timing of the runoff depends on the snowpack, late-spring storms, and warming temperatures. On average, snow at the middle elevations (7,000 to 9,000 feet) begins to melt in April or May. Lakes and reservoirs at these elevations begin to open, offering excellent angling during the short ice-out period. Runoff normally peaks in early June and begins to subside by mid-June, about the time the high lakes (to 10,000 feet) become ice free. In July the higher elevations (above 11,000 feet) open, although a few alpine lakes may not open until August.

Prime stream fishing follows the runoff. Summer also brings the majority of insect hatches, and excellent angling continues into October. Fly anglers use a variety of patterns to imitate mayflies, caddisflies, stoneflies, midges, and terrestrials, whereas those using other gear are successful with small spinners and spoons, or bait where legal. The fall is often preferred by the more dedicated angler because of decreasing numbers of people. Winter trout fishing on tailwaters is primarily done using flies, mainly very small midge and mayfly or caddisfly nymphs. The most used nymphing rig consists of a leader with a fine tippet, a small amount of weight, and a strike indicator.

On the Eastern Plains, warmwater reservoirs are normally open by March or April. Spring is a prime time to fish these reservoirs because of mild temperatures, cool water that makes the fish more accessible, and increasing fish activity. Summer angling is best early and late in the day.

Colorado was hit hard in the 1990s by whirling disease *(see: diseases and parasites)*, an organism that destroys cartilage in trout fry. The disease is usually fatal to young trout. It affects rainbow trout most severely, and caused a significant reduction in spawning success on some of the state's coldwater rivers. Both hatcheries and streams were infected. In some cases, the loss of rainbow trout was offset by an increase in the brown trout population.

The Colorado Division of Wildlife classifies trout water as Gold Medal and Wild Trout. The Gold Medal designation is given to streams, lakes, and reservoirs that have high-quality aquatic habitat, a high percentage of trout 14 inches or longer, and the potential for trophy trout fishing and angling success. Wild Trout Water designates streams and lakes in which the trout population is self-sustaining without stocking.

Angling behavior and attitudes in Colorado have changed in recent decades, and catch-and-release fishing is more prevalent for both coldwater and warmwater species. Artificial flies and lures have become increasingly popular as anglers attempt to minimize the impact on the state's fisheries. Many anglers in Colorado rate their fishing on the quality and aesthetics of the experience rather than on the total number of fish caught.

Colorado's water is completely allocated. The juggling of a scarce resource requires constant monitoring to meet all of the state's needs and, at the same time, keep water in the rivers. Because most of Colorado's water originates on public lands, the U.S. Forest Service requires that streams on forest lands maintain minimum flows, thereby preventing dewatering of these streams and thus providing fish habitat.

About one-third of Colorado's land is in the public domain and under the jurisdiction of federal and state agencies. Federal lands are administered by the U.S. Forest Service, the Bureau of Land Management, and the National Park Service. State lands include CDOW properties, State Trust properties, and lands administered by the Colorado

A 2,704-pound Russian sturgeon captured in 1924 yielded 541 pounds of caviar, which was worth $300,000 in 1995 market value. Guinness lists this as the world's most valuable fish (commercial).

State Forest Service. This opens many miles of streams and numerous lakes to the public. A majority of the state's high natural lakes are within designated wilderness areas. Access to these waters is restricted to foot and horseback travel. The majority of Colorado's high lakes (above 10,000 feet) were once barren; by planting native (to elsewhere in the state) and exotic species, management agencies made fishing possible, and today they maintain the fishery through periodic stocking of fingerlings.

Despite Colorado's wealth of public land, it has only a small number of legally navigable streams. These waters are rivers can be floated without trespass. Where streams flow through private property, a landowner not only owns the land along the stream, he also owns the stream bottom and can legally prevent access, both for wading and boating. The fish, however, belong to the state. On the navigable-stream sections of the Colorado, Arkansas, Roaring Fork, Gunnison, Animas, and Yampa Rivers, anglers can float and fish through private property as long as they remain in the boat and do not set foot on the private property.

In some cases anglers can fish private property by joining private clubs. A few of these club-managed waters offer angling for better-than-average-size fish, both cold- and warmwater species. Naturally, private waters are available through leasing arrangements to individuals or clubs, and outfitters and guides take clients to excellent waters that may not be accessible to the public.

In addition to the many fishable waters on public land, the Division of Wildlife has developed both coldwater and warmwater fisheries in many Colorado cities. Perhaps every city and town of any size has at least one lake or pond to fish.

Northeast Region
The South Platte River originates near Fairplay, about 100 miles west of Denver. Three reservoirs on the upper river—Antero, Spinney Mountain, and Elevenmile—produce large, fast-growing rainbows, browns, and Snake River cutthroats. The latter two reservoirs also have large northern pike, some of which are taken on flies. Spinney Mountain Reservoir is a designated Gold Medal site. Fifty miles southwest of Denver, the Platte offers world-class tailwater angling in Cheesman Canyon for particularly selective rainbows and browns. The Platte also has close-to-home stream fishing for rainbows and browns in Waterton Canyon.

In the Denver Metro area, Cherry Creek and Chatfield Reservoirs—both contained in state parks—plus Quincy, Aurora, and Bear Creek Reservoirs provide close-in angling for trout, walleye, yellow perch, hybrid striped bass (called wiper), crappie, largemouth bass, and smallmouth bass. Most city-park lakes in the Metro area are stocked with a variety of the same species.

The South Platte River flows northeast from the Denver Metro area to Nebraska. Irrigation reservoirs in the drainage offer a significant and varied warmwater sportfishing resource. The majority of these privately owned reservoirs are open to the public through arrangements with the CDOW. East of Denver along Interstate 76, Barr Lake, Jackson, Prewitt, Sterling, and Jumbo Reservoirs offer angling for bass, crappie, yellow perch, wipers, and walleye. Barr Lake has trout in addition to these species.

The Cache la Poudre River west of Fort Collins, and the Big Thompson River west of Loveland, are both tributaries of the South Platte and offer angling for brown trout, rainbow trout, and whitefish. Between Fort Collins and Denver near the Front Range, some irrigation reservoirs are open through the CDOW and provide fishing for largemouth and smallmouth bass, walleye, wipers, catfish, sunfish, yellow perch, trout, and kokanee salmon. Reservoirs open to angling include Horsetooth, Carter, Boyd, Horseshoe, Boedecker, Lon Hagler, Lonetree, and Boulder. Tiger muskies were stocked in Lon Hagler Reservoir. Along Interstate 25, Barbour Ponds and Big Thompson Ponds State Wildlife Areas offer warmwater fishing.

In and around Colorado Springs are reservoirs that provide fishing for warmwater species. Rainbow trout, Snake River cutthroats, Pikes Peak cutthroats, and mackinaw (lake trout) in the Pikes Peak region are found at Rampart Reservoir and at North and South Catamount Reservoirs. Bison and Skagway Reservoirs are open in state wildlife areas.

Bonny Reservoir, about 15 miles west of the Kansas line on the Republican River, is the only important fishery between the Platte and Arkansas Rivers. Part of the state park system, this large reservoir holds bass, tiger muskies, saugeye, crappie, walleye, wipers, and catfish.

Southeast Region
The Arkansas River originates in Twin Lakes near Leadville. The lakes hold rainbow, cutthroat, and large mackinaw trout. The river is an excellent brown trout fishery, with many miles of public access through Brown's Canyon and the Salida and Granite areas. The river is famous for its Mother's Day caddis hatch.

Downstream, in Pueblo Reservoir, the largemouth and smallmouth bass fishing is so good, tournaments are held there. It also has walleye and wipers. The tailwater below Pueblo Dam has brown trout. The Runyon/Fountain State Wildlife Area in Pueblo offers both warmwater and coldwater angling. East of Pueblo, Lake Meredith, Lake Henry, Horse Creek, Adobe Creek, and John Martin Reservoirs are the primary warmwater fisheries.

North of Lamar, near the southeast corner of the state, Nee So Pah, Nee Gronda, Nee Noshe, and the two Queens Reservoirs are open as state wildlife areas. The lakes have wipers, saugeye, crappie, catfish, and white bass.

Northwest Region

North Park in Jackson County is known for lakes with brook, brown, cutthroat, and rainbow trout. The three Delaney Buttes Lakes, as well as Lake John and the Big Creek Lakes, have good forage, and trophy fish are not unusual. The North Platte River originates here and flows north into Wyoming. Fly fishing in the summer for browns and rainbows is excellent on the North Platte. Other trout streams in North Park include Norris, Roaring, and Grizzly Creeks, the North Fork of the North Platte, and the Michigan and Illinois Rivers.

The Colorado River is fed by every stream heading on the West Slope. It begins in Rocky Mountain National Park, where anglers may catch but not keep brook, brown, and rainbow trout. Shadow Mountain Reservoir and Lake Granby are heavily stocked with these species. Granby also has kokanee salmon and large mackinaws. Anglers sometimes catch fish between the two reservoirs.

Between Granby and Glenwood Springs more than one-third of the Colorado River is open to fishing for browns, rainbow-cutthroat hybrids, and rainbows. Downstream from Gore Canyon near Kremmling, more than 60 miles of the Colorado can be floated, with the opportunity to catch large brown trout. The Fraser, Williams Fork, Blue, Eagle, Roaring Fork, and Fryingpan Rivers are prime fisheries that join the Colorado. The Fryingpan is noted for its July green drake hatch, while a mid-April caddis hatch occurs on the Roaring Fork and Colorado. Between Glenwood Canyon and Rifle, the Colorado is too large to wade, but fishing from the bank or a raft can be good for cutthroat and rainbow trout. From Rifle to the Utah line, the river turns into a warmwater fishery. Endangered species—squawfish, humpback chub, and razorback suckers—could seriously reduce sportfishing opportunities in this section.

Both the North and South Forks of the White River begin in the Flat Tops Wilderness Area. From their headwaters downstream to Buford, where they merge, these waters offer angling for brook, brown, cutthroat, and rainbow trout, plus whitefish in the lower stretches as well as in the White River between Buford and Meeker.

The Yampa River is formed by the confluence of Bear River and Chimney Creek at the town of Yampa. From there, the river runs north into Stagecoach Reservoir, completed in 1989 and containing rainbows and northern pike. From the reservoir, the Yampa is a free-flowing river to its confluence with the Green. Anglers catch northern pike along with trout in the river around Steamboat Springs.

The Taylor and East Rivers merge at Almont in the Central Rockies to form the Gunnison River, 10 miles north of Gunnison. The Taylor has a half-mile stretch of tailwater angling for very large rainbows that are measured in pounds. West of Gunnison, Blue Mesa and Morrow Point

Fishing for trout on a tributary of the Yampa River.

Reservoirs flood much of the river. Both have trout and kokanee, while Blue Mesa also produces large mackinaws. Good rainbow and brown trout fishing on the Gunnison River is available to anglers via rugged foot access in the Black Canyon section of Gunnison National Monument.

The Uncompahgre River joins the Gunnison River at Montrose. About 20 miles south of the town, Ridgeway Reservoir provides trout fishing in the lake and in the tailwater below the dam.

Southwest Region

The Rio Grande begins its long journey to the Gulf of Mexico high in the San Juan Mountains of southwest Colorado. It has good brown and rainbow trout fishing from Rio Grande Reservoir downstream to Del Norte. Fly fishing is best in June and July when stonefly and mayfly hatches dominate the trout's diet. The section from South Fork to Del Norte provides an opportunity to catch trophy brown trout and northern pike. Much of the river is privately owned, but public access is available on state leases.

The San Juan is the main stream in southwest Colorado, collecting the flows of all other southwest Colorado rivers. Because of limited public access, although, the Piedra, Pinos, Florida, and Animas Rivers provide the most stream-fishing opportunities. The Animas offers excellent trophy fishing within the city limits of Durango.

McPhee Reservoir and dam turned the Dolores River from a fair fishery into a very good tailwater that holds brown trout and Snake River cutthroat trout. The reservoir has both coldwater and warmwater species. Below McPhee, about 30 miles of the Dolores is open for wade fishing and float fishing. The San Miguel is the main tributary, although nearly every stream in the region also offers trout fishing.

High-Mountain Lakes and Streams
Throughout the Rockies, countless small streams, some only 3 feet wide, provide angling opportunities primarily for small brook and cutthroat trout. Many of these streams have beaver ponds that hold fish averaging 6 to 10 inches, but they are eager to strike. Favorable conditions can grow 12- to 18-inch trout in the ponds, but this is rare. In most high-mountain lakes, the cutthroats can be temperamental, feeding only when weather conditions and insect activity are optimal. In many cases, headwater streams are rarely visited, offering a combination of solitude and fast fishing.

The Colorado State Forest along the Jackson-Larimer County line offers a rugged landscape with scattered alpine lakes, and at least one has golden trout. The Grand Mesa National Forest in western Colorado is dotted with roughly a hundred small reservoirs, which are maintained by stocking. The Mesa offers angling for rainbow, brook, splake, brown, and cutthroat trout. Most are accessed by road or a short walk.

About 75 percent of Colorado's high lakes are within wilderness areas. This gives the adventurous angler an opportunity to backpack, or use horse or llama to reach remote lakes for extended periods. Those who journey into the backcountry can expect to find less-crowded settings than they would in easily accessible areas. A few high-altitude lakes might be visited by only a dozen anglers in a season. Because of harsh conditions, the fishing season above the timberline (11,500 feet) might be as short as six to eight weeks. Anglers will find an assortment of species including cutthroat, rainbow, brook, golden, and mackinaw trout, and grayling. Wilderness lakes at the higher elevations rarely have conditions conducive to spawning. When this is the case, the state periodically stocks them with fingerlings. Alpine conditions are severe enough to slow growth rates.

Wilderness areas that have consistently good angling include Rocky Mountain National Park; the Comanche Peak and Rawah Wilderness Areas in Roosevelt National Forest; Indian Peaks, Eagles Nest, Never Summer, and Mount Evans in Arapaho NF; Mount Zirkel in Routt NF; Flat Tops, Holy Cross, Maroon Bells, and Hunter-Fryingpan in White River NF; La Garita and West Elk in Gunnison NF; and South San Juan and Weminuche in the San Juan NF.

COLUMNARIS
See: Diseases and Parasites.

COMMERCIAL FISHERMAN
A person who catches fish and shellfish for the purpose of sale. In a general sense, this includes all people who sell their catch, regardless of the capture methods used. It is usually inferred that a commercial fisherman is one who uses harvesting equipment, such as seines and nets, designed to capture numbers or volume; however, this term may include those who capture fish individually on rod and reel, and sell them. Theoretically, a commercial fisherman and a sportfisherman (an angler) are distinguished by methods and intent, but in saltwater the distinguishing line can be blurred in places where anglers who use a rod and reel, and as such are counted as recreational anglers, sell some or all of their rod-and-reel catch. Furthermore, some people harvest fish for their personal consumption without the use of "sporting" equipment; these people are not commercial fishermen or anglers, but they would be considered recreational fishermen because they do not sell their catch.
See: Angler; Recreational Fisherman; Sportfisherman.

COMMERCIAL FISHERY
The entire process of catching and marketing fish and shellfish for sale. This includes fisheries resources, commercial fishermen, and related businesses directly or indirectly involved in harvesting, processing, or sales.
See: Commercial Fisherman.

COMMUNICATIONS
Until the advent of cellular telephones, most electronic voice communications in sportfishing boats were made via fixed-mount or portable VHF (Very High Frequency) radios, and some with fixed-mount CB (Citizen's Band) radios. CB radios are rarely used in boats, in part because there are so few other boaters with these devices, and in part because there is no channel monitoring by marine authorities or channels set aside for marine purposes, particularly the transmission of weather information and contact with the Coast Guard. VHF radios are the standard communications tool on boats, primarily for boat-to-boat communications, although for the sake of a backup and for privacy purposes (anyone with a marine radio can overhear communications if they are tuned into the same frequency and within range), cellular phones have become very popular. Those who can afford them may also use satellite communications devices.

VHF Radio
Very High Frequency (VHF) radios are the standard for marine communications, particularly for communication between boats and for emergency purposes. These radiotelephones are the prescribed method of marine ship-to-ship and ship-to-shore communications; they are limited by law to 25

Legends persist of 100-pound muskellunge, but the largest sport-caught muskie was a controversial St. Lawrence River fish that weighed 1 ounce shy of 70 pounds when taken in 1957.

watts output power and are required to be licensed. Available in fixed-mount and handheld versions, VHF radios are standard equipment on virtually all charter boats and inshore saltwater guide boats. Many private boats possess a VHF radio as well, especially if they navigate waters within the jurisdiction of the Coast Guard, which monitors certain frequencies (channels). Various channels are set aside for specific marine purposes. All distress calls, for example, must be made on channel 16. Receive-only channels are designated for weather broadcasts, which are available on a full-time basis.

Fixed-mount VHFs. Fixed-mount VHF radios are the most common tool for small-boat anglers. VHF radios are used rarely by some anglers and too frequently by others. In some locations, the amount of chatter—most of it mindless—on the radio causes anglers to keep their VHF off except to get a current weather report, call for help, or check in with a friend at pre-arranged times. Some anglers rarely talk on their radios, but leave them on to intercept fishing reports between others in the area. The purpose here is to find out what other anglers are doing (either in terms of success or places they fish) as an aid to their own fishing efforts. This may produce useful information, but it may lead (sometimes deliberately) to a wild goose chase. A great deal of misinformation is passed around on VHF radios by anglers, and the whole psychology of this aspect of fishing is an interesting one, but not worth delving into in this book. Suffice it to say that fishing information obtained or overhead on the radio from anonymous sources is on a caveat emptor basis. However, a group of anglers working together can use the radio (overtly or covertly, usually the latter) to share information that is useful to them all. This usually quid pro quo action pays off for them all over time.

VHF radios range widely in price and features. They are capable of transmitting up to 25 miles on a line-of-sight basis, depending on the height of the transmitting and receiving antennas, but their range is usually less due to other factors. Most VHF radios list their output power as the legal maximum of 25 watts, but many do not actually put out 25 watts when used, which may greatly affect performance. Heat buildup in a VHF causes output to drop unless the unit can dissipate the heat or otherwise overcome the output drop. Radios encased in metal, rather than plastic, have a greater ability to dissipate heat. Output is also related to the voltage level of a battery, which supplies the power. A fully charged battery should produce 25 watts of radio output, but that output lessens when a battery is weaker. Better radios produce more output (although less than 25 watts) than others when the battery voltage is low. Most units are said to be water-resistant, but some are much more so than others. Some are said to be waterproof, but there's a big difference between that and being water-resistant (waterproof means it can be submerged; water-resistant means it can be splashed).

Most of the time, fixed-mount VHF radios are installed inside a console and away from the weather, because even the best models cannot indefinitely survive a constant hosing, especially of saltwater. Often the console is crammed with other electronics, like sonar and navigation gear, and finding a good place that separates these items adequately can be a problem.

More of a problem is the antenna. The best radio is only as good as its antenna, and this is where small-boat anglers have trouble because they like a small antenna that doesn't get in the way of casting. A longer antenna, like a typical 8-footer, provides good range. It can be mounted on the gunwale via a bracket that allows it to lay flat when not in use. But on many of today's more popular rigs, that gunwale is kept open and clear for other uses, so this is acceptable only when you aren't casting. If the antenna is down, however, this means that the unit is off and possibly not being useful. Yet, if it sits atop the console, it is not only in the way of just about everything, especially fly rods, but its close proximity to other electronics (and even the VHF transceiver itself) can create a whole new set of problems.

If the antenna is placed too close to other electronic devices, when you key the mike it produces interference with other devices and may blow fuses. Those who are willing to sacrifice some range to get away from long antennas resort to smaller, more compact antennas, like a 3-foot whip with a short fat loading coil at the base. Generally, however, shorter antennas mean much shorter transmitting range.

If the VHF transceiver and antenna are placed too close together, it can cause feedback, usually in the form of a squeal when the mike is keyed, so you need to separate these by a reasonable distance. A foot should be enough most of the time. No matter how close the unit and the antenna, keep at least 6 feet of coaxial cable between them; it's better to coil up the extra footage than to cut it too short. To get rid of the feedback squeal, disconnect the antenna cable from the back of the VHF, tie a very loose figure-eight knot in it, then reconnect. You might have to change the size and location of that knot a few times to get it right, but this quick fix usually works.

A VHF radio should be separated a greater distance from a GPS receiver, perhaps 10 feet, or when the radio is used it will cause the GPS to lose its satellite signal; it can reacquire that within seconds after the radio is used, but that can be, at the very least, a nuisance, especially if the signal is lost repeatedly in a back-and-forth radio conversation. It may also be necessary to mount some items higher than others for best performance. Some manufacturers recommend putting a GPS receiver 2 feet higher than the VHF radio to avoid interference.

If you don't use your VHF often, you can determine if it's transmitting properly when you do turn it on with a small meter that fits in-line between the VHF and the antenna. It can be mounted inside

the console where you can see it, so when you use the VHF for the first time in months, you can see at a glance if it's working.

Hand held VHFs. There are times when the ability to quickly and easily communicate with another boat is important and would not be possible without hand held VHF radios. These are often relegated to small boaters but may be useful in any size boat when traveling to foreign-language speaking countries, to places where there are no (or few) radios, as a backup for a fixed-mount unit, and for use when away from a larger boat with a fixed-mount unit.

Size and portability is the primary advantage for hand held VHFs, but significantly less range is a primary disadvantage. Hand held units have limited (5-watt) output power and integrated antennas; this combination limits their effective range under the best of conditions to 4 to 5 miles (more or less depending on height). Furthermore, although they are diminutive enough to be easily portable, their small keypad is harder to use, the small speaker inhibits audio quality, and their usefulness is limited to battery life.

Extension antenna. It is possible to considerably extend the range of a fixed-mount or hand held VHF by using any sort of long pole to raise an antenna to an elevation that's 12 or more feet higher. If the antenna disconnects easily from the mounting and the cord is long enough, use the antenna cord usually hooked up to your fixed-mount radio for this. If not, you need a separate antenna. This is also true for hand held radios. Any good 3- to 4- foot sailboat masthead VHF antenna works fine. Using 25 feet of the proper coaxial cable, and the necessary connectors for your VHF, rig the antenna to one end of a long pole. A pushpole is perfect for this. Place the pole in a rod holder or lash it to something that will keep it vertical, connect the cable to the VHF, and go on the air. In many cases you'll more than double your effective range, especially if you're far from land, in a backcountry creek, or other remote area. Keep an emergency antenna stowed in a plastic tube, complete with the necessary coax cable, where it is out of the way but quickly available.

Cellular Telephone

Cellular telephones have become common on sportfishing boats, and may be the best communication tool in an emergency, provided that the user can get a signal and is within range of a transmission tower. Though not a marine radio, the cellular phone is nonetheless a prominent communications device. A cellular telephone has the technical advantages of theoretical access to and from all land-based telephone systems, easy and familiar use, and no licensing requirement. For anglers the biggest advantage is a practical one of privacy; you won't be telling the whole world where you found the fish when you pass that information along to someone else. That is often not the case when using a VHF radio.

A cellular phone, however, is not truly a marine radio, there are charges associated with each transmission, and it does not provide instant marine information. Therefore, cellular telephones are generally used fairly close to population centers for transmission purposes, and as an adjunct to a VHF radio. Usually a cellular phone's working distance over the water is ten times that over land, but it won't do well in the midst of tall trees and other obstacles, as in fishing tidal creeks and inland bays. Sometimes elevation is the cure for that; standing on top of the poling platform or in a tower may make a difference. Moving the boat far from trees or high banks may also be helpful.

Satellite Communications Devices

Although not as widely used as cellular telephones, and far more expensive, satellite communications devices are available, and they offer the ability to communicate anywhere in the world. Some not only offer voice communications, but also fax and data transmissions. The number of satellites servicing these devices has been expanding and will eventually be numerous enough to provide full-time (24-hour) service anywhere in the world. Some systems can be interfaced with GPS, or are part of a combined GPS/communications unit. This aspect of communications will become a more integral part of the big-water boater's equipment.

COMPASS

An instrument used for showing direction, a compass features a free-swinging magnetic needle that points to magnetic north. A compass is marked with points of direction and sometimes degrees of a circle. It is used for navigation *(see)* and is important to many anglers who use boats or visit backcountry waters.

Anglers who boat on large bodies of water, who fish at night, or who may encounter conditions that would obscure their vision (fog or severe weather), should have some type of compass. Boaters using a fixed-mount marine compass should be aware of the need to zero-in the compass for accuracy and to mount it away from metal, magnetic, and electrical influences, which may be difficult in the confined console area of small boats.

Using a compass on a boat for basic purposes is fairly straightforward, especially when there's a clear path of travel from one position to another. It can become more involved when great distances are traveled and navigational charts have to be referenced. Using a compass on land, of course, is very different, and is often done in conjunction with a topographic (topo) map. For backcountry anglers, especially those who seek high-elevation lakes and ponds, a compass may be a very important piece of equipment. For anglers who visit remote areas

(South American rivers, for example, or northern Canada lakes), a compass should be a main or adjunct navigational accompaniment.

In the current age of electronic products, too many people, boaters as well as remote and backcountry land travelers, have a tendency to rely on devices (mainly GPS) that may fail for lack of power (especially small batteries), which can be an obvious impediment to navigation. Therefore, it's important to keep a compass in your pack or emergency kit, and to have a basic understanding of how to use it. If you are ever placed in a survival situation, especially if lost in a remote area, having and using a compass could be critically important; thus, the following information is provided with respect to land-use of a compass (in conjunction with a topographic map), although general principles of use apply for big-water situations.

Compass basics. A compass contains a magnetized steel needle that points toward magnetic north. The end of this needle will be black or red, stamped with the initial N, or shaped like an arrow.

The force that attracts this magnetized needle is the earth's magnetism. The earth is similar to a tremendous magnet, with one pole in the north, the other in the south. Compass needles always point toward magnetic north when at rest. The magnetic North Pole is about 1,400 miles south of the true North Pole. That means that there are two north directions to deal with: true north as is shown on a map, and magnetic north as it is found with the compass.

There are conventional and orienteering compasses. Conventional versions are of watch-case, pin-on, or wristwatch design. Orienteering compasses have a protractor and ruler as well as a magnetic needle, a revolving compass housing, and a transparent base plate. In some situations it is useful to have both, a pin-on model for quick reference and an orienteering compass for cross-country traveling while referencing a map.

A compass and topographic map are not difficult to use. Finding your way with one on land is known as orienteering and is easy to learn. Topo maps contain a wealth of information. Some topos have a scale of 1:24,000, which means that 1 inch on the map equals 24,000 inches (or 2,000 feet) in the field. It may be easier to visualize the area covered by such a map if the scale is translated as $2^5/_8$ inches equals 1 mile.

Topo maps usually show manmade structures, water, vegetation, and elevation. Each is represented in a distinct color. Manmade features include roads, trails, and buildings. All are depicted in black except some major highways, which may be red. Water features are printed in blue, vegetation in green.

Elevation is represented by thin brown contour lines. A contour line is an imaginary line on the ground along which every point is at the same height above sea level. Follow a brown line on the map, and you'll find a number. If the number is 100, for example, everything on that line is 100 feet above sea level. If the line next to it reads 200, then you have a rise of 100 feet and a contour interval of 100 feet (generally, the contour interval is 20 feet). This information is noted at the bottom of topographic maps.

Finding bearings. To find a bearing with an orienteering compass, face the distant point toward which you want to know the direction. Hold the orienteering compass level before you, at waist height, with the direction-of-travel arrowhead pointing straight ahead.

Orient your compass by twisting the housing (without moving the base plate) until the needle lies over the orienting arrow on the inside bottom of the compass housing, with its north part pointing to the letter N on the top of the housing. What you've done is make your compass show actual field directions.

Read the degrees of your desired direction, which is the bearing, on the outside rim of the compass housing at the spot where the direction line, as an index pointer, touches the housing. That's all there is to it.

Following a bearing. Suppose you're standing in a field and decide to travel cross-country to a distant hilltop. Set your orienteering compass for the direction of the hilltop by holding the compass in your hand with the direction-of-travel arrowhead pointing to your destination. Twist the compass housing until the north part of the compass needle points to the letter N on the housing rim. Proceed in the direction in which the direction-of-travel arrowhead points.

If you lose sight of the distant hilltop, hold the compass in front of you, orient it, and sight a nearby landmark in the direction in which the arrowhead points. Walk to that point, then take a similar reading to another landmark, and so on until you reach the destination.

You can forget about degrees and figures when you use an orienteering compass. Your compass is set. Just orient it and proceed.

Returning to original location. Let's suppose that you've reached your destination and want to return to your original location. Your orienteering compass is already set for the return journey.

When you went out, you held the compass with the direction-of-travel arrowhead at the front of the base plate pointing away from you toward your destination. The back of the base plate was in the opposite direction, pointing backward toward the spot from which you came. Make use of this fact.

Hold the compass level in your hand but with the direction-of-travel arrow pointing toward you instead of away from you. Orient the compass by turning your body (don't touch the compass housing) until the north end of the compass needle points to the N on the compass housing. Locate a landmark, and head for your original starting point. Your compass is set—use it backward.

 According to the United Nation's Food and Agricultural Organization, the world's leading fishing nation, as measured in weight of commercial catch, is China.

Using compass and map. The difference or angle between magnetic north and true north is called declination, and it varies according to your geographic location. The degree of declination is indicated on topo maps. Fortunately, magnetic north is also indicated on topo maps, and you can use it to avoid the whole problem of declination and adjusting map bearings.

Instead of compensating for declination, simply draw magnetic-north lines on your topo map. By using these lines instead of the true-north lines of the regular meridians, you make your map speak the same language as your compass. The settings you take on your compass using these lines do not require resetting to compensate for declination—the declination is already taken care of.

To provide your map with magnetic-north lines, draw a line up through the map on an angle to one of the meridian lines corresponding to the degrees of declination given on the map. Then draw other lines parallel to this line, 1 to 2 inches apart.

With your combined knowledge of map and compass, you can now travel from point to point. This is done with three easy steps:

1. On the map, line up your compass with your route. Place the orienteering compass on the map with one long edge of its base plate touching both your starting point and your destination, and with the base plate's direction-of-travel arrow pointing in the direction you want to go. Disregard the compass needle.
2. On the compass, set the housing to the direction of your route. Hold the base plate firmly against the map. With your free hand, turn the compass housing until the orienting arrow on the bottom of the housing lies parallel to the nearest magnetic-north line drawn on your map, with arrow-point to the top. Disregard the compass needle. The compass is now set for the direction to your destination. By using the drawn-in magnetic-north line, you have compensated for any compass declination in the territory covered by your map.
3. In the field, follow the direction set on the compass. Hold the compass in front of you, at waist height, with the direction-of-travel arrow pointing straight ahead. Turn yourself, while watching the compass needle, until the needle lies directly over the orienting arrow on the bottom of the compass housing, with the north end of the needle pointing to the letter N on the housing. The direction-of-travel arrow now points to your destination. Raise your head, pick a landmark, and walk to it. When you've reached it, again check the direction with your compass (be careful not to change the setting). Ahead is another landmark, and still another until you reach your destination. When it's time to return to your starting point, repeat this step, but keep the direction-of-travel arrow pointing toward you. Your compass is already set; simply use it backward to return home.

Applying compass use to high-country fishing situations is not difficult. If you can follow a bearing, you can easily travel across strange terrain to a remote lake you've found on a topo map. When it's time to head back, simply let your compass lead you safely back to camp. With a little practice, you'll be able to travel in unfamiliar territory with complete confidence.

See: GPS; Maps; Navigation; Survival.

COMPETITIVE FISHING

Contests that pit anglers against each other as well as against the fish—called tournaments, derbies, rodeos, or matches—exist for a wide range of species and purposes, with varying importance, prizes, and notoriety, not to mention viewpoints as to their merits and demerits.

More fishing tournaments are held for freshwater bass than any other single species, especially considering all the fishing clubs that hold small-scale competitions for their members. Counting these, the many big-game fishing tournaments, and even the contests run by local sporting goods stores, there are many thousands of events annually in North America alone, plus many more in other countries. In Europe, the primary competitive events are called matches, and match fishing is a specialized, highly competitive activity targeting coarse species.

Competitions focus on the weight of overall catch, on the basis of the largest specimen(s) of a given species, and on whether the effort is an individual accomplishment or that of a team of people (usually two to four). There are many different aspects to the competitions, and they may be one-day or multiple-day events, and sometimes season-long.

Some competitions, especially offshore saltwater events, have large purses and individual prizes.

In the modern era, many prominent fishing competitions are catch-and-release events. This is especially true for bass, and tournaments for these fish have fostered improvements in boat design and livewell construction and performance to help ensure that captured fish (which are usually brought alive to a central weighing point and then released) are returned to the water in good shape, although there is often some level of mortality. (Critics question the delayed mortality, which is when death occurs at a later and unobserved time, of fish that are retained and later released away from their capture sight after boat rides and handling.) Some tournaments, such as those for tarpon and bonefish, are conducted on a point basis for fish that are caught and released immediately at the site of capture. The killing of billfish and sharks in tournaments has been greatly curtailed or has been restricted to fish over a certain size, although some big-game events still result in the death of fish. Many contests on a lesser scale, particularly for stocked species like trout and salmon in the Great Lakes, do not have provisions for the release of any fish entered in the event.

In North America, fishing competitions are lightly regulated by some state fisheries agencies but not at all by others. Few saltwater tournaments have oversight. The level of attention to honesty and sportsmanship in competitions varies widely, although in today's organized events with high entry fees and major purses, and in events run by many well-organized clubs, officials take great steps to ensure that the events are above question. This was not always the case in the past.

Since the 1970s, fishing tournaments have created a new category of people who fish: professional anglers. Technically anyone who pays the entry fee for a fishing tournament and wins something of monetary value is a professional angler, but in common usage this term is attributed to those who fish in competitions as an occupation. This especially applies to bass and walleye tournament competitors, but there are also professional tournament anglers in saltwater, including some who compete in king mackerel events.

Large prizes are at stake in an increasing number of tournaments, including some in the six-figure range for winners of certain events; others feature calcuttas that may double the take-home purse. Many local competitions have modest prizes, perhaps just a trophy or inexpensive fishing merchandise. A lot of competitions are organized to provide funds to charity and even conservation causes.

COMPOSITE ROD

A composite rod is commonly understood to mean one that is constructed of multiple material fibers. This would primarily include a rod that blended fiberglass and graphite, or graphite and boron, in the fabrication of the rod blank. The percentage amounts of the different fibers vary widely, and there is no uniformity among manufacturers; thus, a rod whose fiber materials consisted of 5 percent graphite and 95 percent fiberglass might be marketed as a "graphite" rod, although it would likely be termed a "graphite composite rod."

To some degree, however, all rods, even those made from one material, are composites. Each rod blank consists of a strength or stress element, typically a fiber, and a bonding element, typically a resin. The stress element stores and transmits energy by elastic deformation, and the bonding element both fixes the location of the stress element and prevents the failure of one fiber from directly propagating to another. The material cannot function without being bonded, thus making the rod at the very least a composite of resin and fiber, and subject to evaluation as to percentages of each.

See: Rod, Fishing.

CONEY *Cephalopholis fulva*.

Other names—French: *coné ouatalibi*; Spanish: *canario, cherna cabrilla, corruncha, guativere*.

The coney is a member of the Serranidae family of grouper.

Identification. Because the coney experiences numerous color phases, it is inadvisable to try to identify this fish by color. These phases range from the common phase in which the fish is reddish brown, to a bicolor period in which the upper body is dark and the lower body is pale, to a bright yellow phase. The body is covered with small blue to pale spots, although the spots are uncommon in the bright-yellow phase. There are often two black spots present at the tip of the jaw and two more at the base of the tail, as well as a margin of white around the tail and the soft dorsal fin. The tail is rounded, and there are nine spines in the dorsal fin.

Size. The coney weighs about a pound, although occasionally it can weigh as much as 3 pounds. The average length is 6 to 10 inches, and the maximum length is 16 inches.

Distribution. In the western Atlantic, coney extend from Bermuda and South Carolina to southern Brazil, including the Gulf of Mexico and Atol das Rocas; they are commonly found in the Caribbean and less commonly in southern Florida and the Bahamas.

Coney

Habitat. In the Gulf of Mexico, coney occur in clear deep-water reefs, and in Bermuda and the West Indies they spend the day in caves and under ledges, preferring shallower water the rest of the time. Coney tend to drift immediately above the bottom or rest there in 10- to 60-foot depths, remaining in close proximity to protected areas.

Life history/Behavior. As with many grouper, coney females transform into males, usually when they reach 20 centimeters in length. They are gregarious fish, and the males are territorial.

Food. Coney feed mainly on small fish and crustaceans.

Angling. Like other grouper, anglers primarily catch coney by fishing at the right depth over irregular bottoms.

See: Grouper; Inshore Fishing.

CONNECTICUT

The word "variety" best describes the mix of fishing opportunities in the Nutmeg State. Although small in land area, Connecticut is well endowed with waters ranging from deep tidal rivers to pristine brook trout streams, including man-made impoundments, deep coldwater lakes, boglike ponds, and kettle holes left behind by glaciers. Within Connecticut's borders are an amazing total of 6,000 lakes and ponds and 8,400 miles of rivers and streams, although there are 209 principal lakes, 124 principal rivers, and 169 small streams—ample opportunity for anglers to fish for freshwater species within a short drive from literally anywhere in the state.

Those species include such typical and long-established fish as largemouth and smallmouth bass, chain pickerel, crappie, and assorted panfish, as well as walleye and northern pike. Among coldwater species, brown trout are by far the mainstays, but there are brook trout, rainbow trout, and Atlantic salmon here, in addition to opportunities for shad, sea-run brown trout, and tidewater striped bass.

Six of Connecticut's lakes are classified as bass management areas, and 11 streams as trout management areas (generally using some form management strategy such as no-kill, reduced creel limit, or increased size limit). Eleven rivers, primarily along the coast, are open to fishing year-round. In addition, 26 areas are designated as youth-only fishing, 29 lakes and rivers have handicapped fishing access, and there is a 1,000-foot-long fishing pier in East Lyme that is accessible to the handicapped.

Heavily stocked public fishing ponds are available at the state's Quinebaug Valley Hatchery, and hundreds more small private ponds and lakes can be fished with the permission of landowners. A growing number of private pay-to-fish areas are scattered around the state.

Anglers who like a challenge will enjoy fishing for surplus adult brood-stock Atlantic salmon weighing 4 to 14 pounds on average, occasionally stocked in state waters. And, during the winter and early spring, hearty and reclusive anglers fish a half-dozen coastal rivers that sport remnant populations of sea-run brown trout, some of which reach 8 pounds or more.

Connecticut's saltwater fishery is every bit as compelling as its freshwater opportunities, yet when most anglers from outside southern New England think of great saltwater fishing, the state of Connecticut seldom comes to mind. Even the Dutch, the first Europeans to explore this coast in 1614, passed it by.

Connecticut boasts 253 miles of coastal shoreline, with outstanding opportunities for inshore and coastal species from Byram Point in the west to Pawcatuck Point next to Rhode Island. Connecticut shares this water, of course: half of Long Island Sound with New York, and part of Little Narragansett Bay with Rhode Island. New York and Rhode Island have a border in common, near the entrance to Lords Passage, just off the eastern end of New York's Fishers Island—in effect enclosing Connecticut's marine environs. These aquatic boundary lines hold little meaning for Connecticut anglers, who regularly fish such well-known grounds in New York as Plum Gut, The Race, Fishers Island Sound, and the numerous seaward passages between New York and Rhode Island.

Saltwater angling is an important element of recreational fishing among Connecticut anglers. Nearly one-third of the state's 3.75 million residents live along the coast. At most, it is an hour's drive for the remaining inland anglers bent for the sea. There, the major interests include striped bass, blackfish, flounder, fluke, bluefish, weakfish, mackerel, porgies, and black sea bass.

Freshwater

Ranking 48th in land mass among U.S. states, Connecticut is understandably not noted for big bodies of water. Man-made Lake Candlewood, Connecticut's largest, covers just 5,420 acres, which in most other states would be considered small. Its most significant waterway is the Connecticut River—the longest in New England. Even so, less than one-quarter of it crosses Connecticut en route to Long Island Sound. Inland fishing opportunities, therefore, are best viewed in terms of the Connecticut River and Lake Candlewood, and then by the major species available elsewhere.

The Connecticut River. The Connecticut River, which bisects the state and flows roughly 90 miles from Massachusetts to Long Island Sound, supports the best overall fisheries resource in the state. The river holds tremendous populations of largemouth and smallmouth bass, northern pike, white perch, yellow perch, black crappie, sunfish, white catfish, channel catfish, carp, shad, and striped bass. It even holds Atlantic salmon, produces an occasional walleye, and on rare occasions yields a sturgeon. As mentioned, the Connecticut

Connecticut

Fishing for shad on the Connecticut River.

River is by far the state's biggest, best, most accessible, and most varied fishery resource, and there are numerous shore-based and launch access sites all along the river.

Largemouth and smallmouth bass are especially prominent in the Connecticut River, and although some may disagree, this is likely the state's greatest fishery for those species. Both largemouth and smallmouth bass are caught from Hamburg Cove, which is just 6 miles north of Long Island Sound, all the way to the Massachusetts border in Enfield. Smallmouths are more prevalent north of Hartford and in the deep ledges and narrows around Portland and Middletown. Largemouths tend to dominate the slower-flowing backwater sloughs of the river. Places like Chapman's Pond in East Haddam, and Wethersfield Cove in Wethersfield, are year-round hotspots for bass.

Lake Candlewood. Anglers will find unrivaled lunker trout fishing in Lake Candlewood, located near the western border with New York State. Like many Connecticut lakes, Candlewood has a quality two-story fishery for both bass and trout.

Candlewood is famous for its population of trophy brown trout. Maintained by a huge forage base of landlocked alewives, brown trout in Candlewood gorge themselves to large proportions; 7- to 10-pound brown trout are caught every year. Anglers land most of these large trout by jigging, trolling, deep-fishing with crankbaits or baitfishing in open and deep water around suspended schools of herring, locating them with sonar.

Along the shoreline, anglers will find both largemouth and smallmouth bass in abundance, mixed in with the usual variety of panfish. Largemouth bass fishing is especially productive here, as the lake contains every conceivable type of habitat, from deep rocky ledges to shallow weedbeds. The bass run to good size here, and the lake draws bass anglers from neighboring states, especially early in the season. Candlewood is also known to produce some monstrous white perch of 2 pounds and larger.

Trout waters. For the most part, trout are sustained in Connecticut waters through hatchery plantings. Some of the better waters and those with excellent trout habitat are designated as Trophy Trout Lakes or Trout Management Areas and are subject to special regulations.

The state angling guide issued with licenses lists all of the lakes and streams in Connecticut that are stocked with trout, and the town of their location. Most of the lakes listed in that guide have free public access (and launch) areas. A few of the deeper lakes, such as Gardners Lake in Bozrah, Rogers Lake in Lyme, Beach Pond in Voluntown, East Twin Lake in Salisbury, Lake Waramaug in Kent, and Crystal Lake in Ellington thermally stratify and therefore hold trout throughout the summer, as do some of the other deep-water lakes. Smaller ponds and shallow lakes usually reach the upper limits of the trout's temperature tolerance by June, and therefore do not hold trout through the summer.

Likewise, most of the state's streams do not hold many trout through the summer, although most provide good trout fishing opportunities through mid- to late June. The state's best year-round trout rivers are the upper reaches of the Housatonic River north of Cornwall, and the Farmington River above Burlington, which has cold tributaries and enough summer habitat to hold fish all year.

To the east, anglers will experience great spring, and decent fall, trout action on the Yantic River in Lebanon/Bozrah, the Nachaug River in Chaplin, the Shetucket River from Scotland to Baltic, the Salmon River from Colchester to Haddam, and the Quinebaug River and its major tributaries from Canterbury to the Massachusetts border. The Shetucket and Quinebaug Rivers provide "big water" fishing conditions and some fabulous hatches during the spring and early summer.

Bass waters. The aforementioned Lake Candlewood is probably the state's most noted bass water, in large part due to its size. Another larger lake, by local standards, is Pachaug Pond. At 830 acres this is the largest lake in eastern Connecticut. A shallow, weed-filled, heavily fished body of water, it traditionally exhibits fast-growing largemouths and produces its share of jumbo bass each year.

Connecticut is blessed with many small but productive largemouth bass lakes. Among the more notable of these are Winchester Lake in Winchester, Moodus Lake in Moodus, Lake Zoar in Oxford, Rogers and Uncas Lakes in Lyme, Powers Lake in East Lyme, Lake Waramaug in Kent, Lake Saltonstall in New Haven, and Mashapaug Lake in Union. Mashapaug is the site of Connecticut's state-record 12-pound, 14-ounce largemouth. Moodus Lake is known for its huge bass and has given up more than its share of largemouths of 8 pounds or better.

All of the state's waters that formerly contained only smallmouth bass have been contaminated with largemouths over time, so many waters

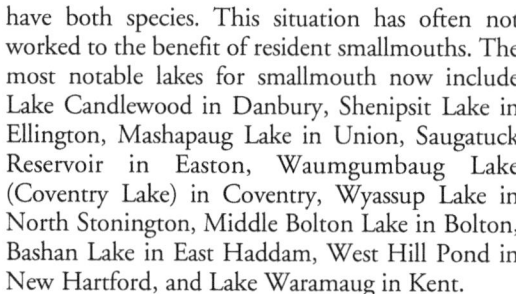

Ever heard of the sweetfish? Growing to 12 inches long, it is abundant and popular in streams in Taiwan and Japan, where it is caught with some very specialized methods.

have both species. This situation has often not worked to the benefit of resident smallmouths. The most notable lakes for smallmouth now include Lake Candlewood in Danbury, Shenipsit Lake in Ellington, Mashapaug Lake in Union, Saugatuck Reservoir in Easton, Waumgumbaug Lake (Coventry Lake) in Coventry, Wyassup Lake in North Stonington, Middle Bolton Lake in Bolton, Bashan Lake in East Haddam, West Hill Pond in New Hartford, and Lake Waramaug in Kent.

Survey work done throughout the state indicates the oldest and largest smallies are found in Wyassup Lake, Middle Bolton Lake, and Shenipsit Lake (site of the state-record $7^{3}/_{4}$-pound smallmouth).

Some good smallmouth bass fishing is available in rivers and streams, including a few of the trout streams that have shriveled up in midsummer. The Housatonic River is regionally famous for smallmouth fishing. The Connecticut, Norwalk, Saugatuck, and Upper Quinnipiac Rivers also sport fishable populations of smallmouth bass. In eastern Connecticut, the Shetucket River is the main big-stream smallmouth bass fishery; however, the Quinebaug, Yantic, Natchaug, Willimantic, and Salmon Rivers all come to life with smallies throughout the summer in a small-stream setting. Most of these little smallmouth rivers can be fished by wading, and are nearly 100 percent fishable with sneakers, shorts, and insect repellent. They are ideal for tiny fly rods and ultralight spinning gear with tiny jigs, spinners, and 2- to 3-inch-long soft-plastic jerkbaits.

Northern pike. The Connecticut River is also the state's best fishery for northern pike, yielding fish up to 15 pounds every year. Bantam Lake in the town of Litchfield runs a close second. A managed fishery, Bantam has been greatly enhanced by pike spawning marshes. The Connecticut River's naturally spawning population of pike is used as a source of juvenile pike, which have been released at Mansfield Hollow Lake in Mansfield/Willimantic. Incidental pike are caught in the Quinebaug River system; these fish drop down from sources in the state of Massachusetts. Aspinook Pond, an impoundment on the Quinebaug River, regularly yields pike each year.

Walleye. Connecticut has also experimentally stocked walleye in four lakes around the state. In the west, bordering on Candlewood Lake, Squantz Pond appears to be producing the largest, most numerous, but hardest to catch walleye in the state. Rogers Lake in Lyme, and Gardners Lake in Bozrah, seem to have fewer, smaller, but more catchable walleye. In addition to walleye, Gardners Lake has excellent fisheries for trout, largemouth and smallmouth bass, and panfish. Walleye have recently been stocked in Lake Saltonstall, a New Haven water-supply reservoir.

Panfish. Connecticut has a small but avid group of anglers who pursue white perch in the Connecticut, Thames, Niantic, and Pawcatuck Rivers each spring. Beginning sometime after ice out, the perch move upriver into spawning areas, where they concentrate in huge schools that provide some of the fastest action of the spring fishing season. Hamburg Cove, Lieutenant River, Salmon River, and Connecticut Yankee's power plant outflow on the Connecticut River are popular and productive spots. However, white perch, mixed with yellow perch, can be caught in any backwater of the river during the late winter and early spring. In the Thames River, Poquetanuck Cove and the Shetucket River above Norwich provide the most consistent white perch catches.

Black crappie, locally known as calico bass, reach their largest proportions in Pachaug Pond and Winchester Lake. Lake Lillinonah in Brookfield, Lake of Isles in North Stonington, Glasgow Pond in Voluntown, Highland Lake in Beach Pond, and the Connecticut River all contain healthy populations of calicos as well. Patagansett Lake in Old Lyme, which produced a 4-pound state-record calico in 1974, is always listed among top waters but has dropped off considerably in productivity over the years.

Shad. The Connecticut River sports one of the premier American shad runs on the East Coast. Shad enter the lower river in early March and begin showing in anglers' creels north of Hartford by late April and early May. The most productive shad spots on the river are the rapids below the Enfield Dam, the mouth of the Farmington River, and the Windsor Locks Bridge. Anglers also pick up shad behind bridge abutments, islands, rocks, and other obstructions. The fish collect in the lee of such objects in order to rest during their upstream migration.

There is a secondary yet productive American shad fishery in the Thames River, located in southeastern Connecticut. The potential of this run is enhanced by a fish-passage facility at the Greenville Dam, which opened during the spring spawning run of 1997.

All the major coastal rivers—the Housatonic, Connecticut, Thames, Niantic, and Mystic—support fishable runs of hickory shad that are often mixed in with schoolie striped bass during the spring. These fish show up sporadically along the coast during the summer and move into coastal estuaries again during the late summer and fall, creating excellent light-tackle opportunities. In the spring, the timing and location of hickory shad is neither as consistent nor as predictable as it is with American shad. The lower Connecticut River appears to develop the largest hickory shad run during both spring and fall fishing periods.

River and winter striped bass. Although technically not a freshwater species, the fabulous spring (and to a lesser degree fall) striped bass runs provide excellent fishing in all major coastal rivers. Action is primarily from school stripers, although fish up to and occasionally exceeding 50 pounds are caught every year. Each spring, as hordes of striped bass migrate through Long Island Sound, they are drawn into the Connecticut, Housatonic, and Thames Rivers by migrating schools of herring, shad, and other forage species. The bass chase bait up to the first major dam or obstruction, where they gorge themselves till the herring runs subside and/or warming waters push them back out to sea, sometime in late May or June.

To a lesser degree the Saugatuck River in Fairfield County; the Hammonassett River in Middlesex County; the Quinnipiac River in New Haven County; and the Pawcatuck, Mystic, and Niantic Rivers in New London County also draw feeding runs of striped bass well upstream from Long Island Sound. Any angling north of Interstate 95 or Route 1, which is the freshwater demarcation line along the Connecticut coast, requires a freshwater license, regardless of species sought.

During the spring striper run, fishing action in these rivers can be exceptional. The novelty lies in the often "trout river" atmosphere in which these fish may be caught. In the shallows of these coastal rivers, anglers can catch striped bass on a variety of gear, including flies and light spinning tackle. For example, in the stretch of the Shetucket River (a major tributary to the Thames) north of Norwich and below Greenville Dam, in the waters below the Derby Dam on the Housatonic, or at Enfield Dam on the Connecticut River, anglers can wade the shallows and catch stripers when the tides are right, or fish for trout, panfish, black bass, and shad when stripers don't cooperate.

The reverse occurs during the fall runs, although at this time stripers do not run as far upstream, nor do they spend as much time in these rivers as they cool down for winter. The prime exception is the Thames River, which, due to its unique fiordlike qualities, draws and holds a huge population of striped bass throughout the winter. The fish tend to settle in the upper third of the Thames, as far north as Norwich Harbor, but move around to some degree in response to rains, snowmelt, and temperature changes throughout the winter. They school very densely, creating fabulous catch-and-release fishing on school fish averaging 14 to 24 inches, although occasional jumbos exceeding 30 pounds are caught throughout the winter.

Salmon. There is a seasonal fishery for discarded brood-stock Atlantic salmon ranging from 2 to 15 pounds or more in the Naugatuck and Shetucket Rivers. In the Naugatuck, salmon are released between Union City and the Thomaston Flood Control Dam, and in the Shetucket between the Scotland and Occum Dams. The salmon are stocked after they've been spawned out in hatcheries in November. They remain in these rivers throughout the winter and spring, but they unfortunately do not tolerate summer temperatures and thus perish. If an angler wishes to keep a salmon, it must be caught on fly fishing tackle; those fish caught incidentally on spinning tackle must be released unharmed.

Anglers fishing the Connecticut River may catch wild sea-run Atlantic salmon while fishing on the main stem or its tributaries. These fish must be released immediately. Efforts to restore Atlantic salmon to the Connecticut River and some tributaries continue but are slow-going. Success is in part dependent on the return of mature adult fish, which can be used by fisheries managers for propagation, and in part upon having large numbers of young salmon (smolts) survive and migrate from the river to the ocean.

A smattering of kokanee (landlocked sockeye) salmon live in three lakes in Salisbury: East Twin Lake, West Hill Pond, and Lake Wononscopomuc. It is unknown how the kokanee got here, but they supported fisheries of varying abundance since at least the 1940s, with a significant population in East Twin and a lesser one at the other lakes, until alewives appeared in East Twin and out-competed the kokanee for food. Brown trout were introduced in order to control the alewives and restore the salmon fishery. At present, there are minor kokanee fisheries on these waters.

Sea-run brown trout. In the 1960s, Connecticut established sea-run brown trout populations in Latimer Brook, the headwaters of Niantic River; Whitford Brook, the headwaters of the Mystic River; Shonnock Brook, a tributary to the Pawcatuck River in North Stonington; and in the Thames River. Historically, anglers caught sea-run trout up to 10 pounds between November and May each year. Stocking of fingerling sea-run browns ended in the late 1970s, but remnant populations of these fish remain in the Niantic, Mystic, and Thames systems. The best fishing is between December and March. Flies and lures are used for these aggressive, hard-fighting, and elusive fish, but most successful anglers employ live killifish.

Hatchery fishing. The Quinebaug Valley Hatchery has ponds open to the public for fishing on a first-come, first-served basis between March and May. Anglers may reserve spots to fish by calling the hatchery prior to fishing, or they can show up and hope there are slots available.

Saltwater

While some anglers catch fish from Connecticut's marine waters throughout the year, for most it's a nine-month season that begins in early March with flounder and ends in late November with blackfish, known locally by the Indian name tautog. Throughout this long season, in addition to these two species, anglers take mackerel, fluke, porgies, black sea bass, striped bass, bluefish, and weakfish.

Connecticut has some great striped bass fishing, and its coastal rivers and inshore reefs produce fish from April through November; many of those stripers are monsters. The existing state-record striped bass, although not accepted by IGFA, is a 75-pound, 6-ounce specimen, which was the third-largest striper caught in the twentieth century on rod and reel. Various world records have been established in Connecticut in the past, including line-class world records for blackfish, weakfish, and striped bass.

Connecticut anglers also have one anadromous species that only a few other Atlantic coastal states offer, American shad. The Connecticut River, which begins almost at the Quebec/New Hampshire border and flows 407 miles south to enter Long Island Sound at Old Saybrook and Old Lyme, is arguably the best shad river on the coast; angling for these fish, however, takes place in the upper reaches of this freshwater flow, not in the salt.

Connecticut's larger freshwater rivers that flow into Long Island Sound are unique in that they have fairly large tidal or brackish sections that provide good habitat for striped bass and flounder. Not as large as the Connecticut River, but also productive, is the lower section of the Housatonic River, which enters Long Island Sound at Stratford; the smaller Quinnipiac River, which enters The Sound near New Haven; the Pawcatuck River; and the rather substantial tidal section of the Thames River at New London.

The lower Housatonic River provides excellent fishing for striped bass, bluefish, flounder, and fluke in season. The town docks in Stratford, Stratford Point, and Milford Point Jetty, provide good, fishable shore-based access to the lower river.

Connecticut's shore along the north side of Long Island Sound differs vastly from that of Long Island, a sandy terminal moraine created 20,000 years ago by glaciers. Instead, it is rocky, highly irregular, and pocked with hundreds of small, rocky islands or outcroppings, all not far from shore. Blackfish and striped bass find such environments just to their liking. The rivers and irregular shore also have created numerous inlets and harbors, and these give anglers great access to Long Island Sound. Their marinas harbor a large armada of recreational craft, and there are nearly a dozen public boat launching ramps.

Some of the best fishing in Long Island Sound is a bit farther out, over numerous reefs and ledges just off the shore. From west to east, these include the Norwalk Islands, the Goose and Falkner islands complex, Madison Reef, Kimberley Reef, Long Sand Shoal, and Hatchett and Bartlett Reefs. A plethora of fishing reefs, shoals, ledges, and islands exist in Fishers Island Sound, and these are shared with New York. There is also a unique geological feature in mid–Long Island Sound, but wholly under the aegis of Connecticut: Stratford Shoal, alias The Middle Grounds. The shoal rises from some of the deepest water in Long Island Sound to depths of 8 to 10 feet. It is capped by a lighthouse on the shallowest part. The shoal extends northeast for a mile and produces some of the summer's best bluefishing.

Because most of the Connecticut shoreline is privately owned, surf fishing spots are few and far between. In Fairfield, anglers can fish the jetty and, in the off-season, the beaches at Sherwood Island State Park. Pennfield Reef, a near-mile-long spit that emerges and sinks with each tide, is one of the premier shore fishing sites in the western half of the Connecticut coast. Access is via a tiny right-of-way at the end of Reef Road in the town of Fairfield.

In Milford, Charles Island State Park is a productive shore fishing location that becomes accessible via a long sand spit that is dry at low tide and covered at high tide. Milford Harbor itself, although small, draws bait, bass, and blues in and out with the tides when in season. Its protected waters also provide habitat for winter flounder, fluke, and snapper bluefish in season.

At New Haven, on the harbor's west side, anglers can wade-fish Sandy Point, a long sand spit that juts into the harbor. To the east, Light House Point Park provides good shore access.

In Madison, Hammonassett State Park provides anglers with a mile-long beach with fishing access jetties at either end. Meggs Point Jetty, at the park's east end, juts into the waters that drain Clinton Harbor, making it one of the most productive shore fishing spots in the middle portions of the Connecticut shoreline.

The lower Connecticut River is one of the state's best marine fisheries resources, but access is limited. Anglers can fish off the Interstate 95 state launch in Saybrook; off the causeway that crosses South Cove; and by walking the rocks (a little more than 1 mile) out to Cornfield Point from Castle Inn, to the west of Saybrook Light House. The best lower-river access is a 1,000-foot anglers' access and observation pier built along the shoreline from the headquarters of the Department of Environmental Protection in Old Lyme to the mouth of the Lieutenant River. The site not only provides good handicapped access to some great waters, it is also an excellent observation point for ospreys that inhabit Great Island. Small-boat anglers can find great striped bass and bluefish action along the shoals at Great Island by launching at the Great Island state launch off Route 156 in Old Lyme.

You'll also find a jetty and beach at Rocky Neck State Park in Old Lyme. This provides seasonally good fishing for striped bass, bluefish, fluke, and winter flounder. West of this location, Hatchett Reef and east Black Point are two top gamefishing spots for those who fish from boats.

Perhaps the best-kept surf fishing secret in the state is Harkness Memorial State Park, in the town of Waterford. This beach has no swimming, so it is open to fishing year-round. Its rocky shoreline and inflowing tidal stream provide excellent habitat for all marine species. Harkness is locally famous for excellent striped bass and bluefish catches, but its rocky shore also harbors blackfish, porgies, fluke, and winter flounder. Bartletts Reef, off the coast and to the west of Harkness, is one of eastern Connecticut's

---

In 1992, a 715-pound bluefin tuna was sold in Tokyo for a then-record price of $67,500, or $94.40 a pound.

best fishing destinations for stripers, bluefish, porgies, and blackfish when these species are present.

In Groton, Bluff Point State Park provides a wide variety of fishing habitat. This mile-long peninsula is bounded by Poquonnock River (a long tidal estuary) to the west and Mumford Cove on the east, with a rocky beach on the seaward side. The cove provides exceptional flounder fishing beginning in midwinter, and attracts striped bass in good numbers throughout the season. Its rock-bound beach is good for stripers, bluefish, and blackfish. Offshore is Seaflower Reef, a locally famous area for fluke.

Access to the Mystic River is mostly over private property, with the exception of the Noank Town access and Six Penny Island. Upriver, where Interstate 95 crosses, is a seasonal shore fishing and small-boat access that is productive for blue crabs, winter flounder, tomcod, and an occasional sea-run brown trout during the late winter and early spring. Off the mouth of Mystic River lies Ram Island and its namesake reef, both sporadically hot striper fishing grounds. To the west of the river mouth, boat anglers can fish the Spindle at Groton Long Point, or move across Fishers Island Sound to the West, Middle, and East Clumps, a series of rocks off Fishers Island, New York, all of which provide excellent rips and currents favored by striped bass.

On the eastern Connecticut border with Rhode Island, inside Little Narragansett Bay and bounded on the seaward side by Sandy Point Island, is Barn Island State Park. The park itself doesn't provide much fishing opportunity, but the launch site at the park is a small-boat owner's best access to fishing the excellent waters of Fishers Island Sound, Fishers Island itself, the southern Rhode Island beaches, and the famous Watch Hill/Fishers Island reef complex.
See: New York; Rhode Island.

CONTESTS
See: Competitive Fishing.

CONTINENTAL SHELF
The shallow area of an ocean that is closest to a continent; it gently slopes near the low-water line and more abruptly slopes around the edge of the continent. The area between the low-water line and the continent margin averages 45 miles in width and deepens as it extends seaward, averaging a depth of about 400 feet. At the shelf break, where the shelf descends sharply to the deeper ocean floor, there is a marked change in fauna, with an abrupt cutoff of species that do not extend past the cliff or slope. Often there are canyons *(see)* that cut deeply into the shelf.

CONTOUR MAP
See: Maps.

CONVENTIONAL TACKLE
Conventional tackle is medium- and heavy-duty fishing equipment characterized by a reel with a revolving spool that turns to both dispense and retrieve line. It is called "conventional" tackle in part because the spool rotates in a normal manner, just like sewing thread, with the line moving perpendicular to the spool axis. It is related in general characteristics to baitcasting tackle *(see)*, which sports a smaller reel that is more limited in its ability to deal with the strongest fish and with situations requiring a lot of line.

Conventional tackle is particularly popular and widely used in saltwater, in part because of the differences in conditions, techniques, and size of fish when compared to freshwater. While conventional gear was once relegated to specific applications, like offshore trolling, bottom fishing, or surf fishing, it now has a wide range of functions, and appropriate versions of conventional tackle can be used in applications ranging from flounder fishing inshore to shark and marlin fishing offshore, and to such in-between uses as deep grouper and cod fishing, casting to tarpon and wahoo, trolling for Great Lakes salmon, and bottom fishing for big catfish and sturgeon. Appropriate models of conventional reels with corresponding rods may be used for casting, trolling, and bottom fishing, but many outfits are best suited to specific tasks, and the factors that go into the selection and use of this or any type of fishing tackle are many and varied.

Reels
The conventional revolving spool reel evolved from the same origins as the baitcasting reel, and the development of both has been intertwined since the nineteenth century. Baitcasting reels originated in Kentucky between 1800 and 1810 at a time when a single-action revolving spool reel was the only reel available for sportfishing, and anglers exclusively used natural bait or artificial flies. The single-action reel was used primarily to store and retrieve line, and had no casting function. To present natural baits at any distance, anglers had to strip an appropriate length of line off a single-action reel and lay the loops down or coil them in the noncasting hand. Using a wooden rod, they made a sideways motion to propel the bait and carry the stripped-off line. This was done because the bait and whatever weights were used could not overcome the inertia of the single-action spool.

In 1810 or sometime during the preceding decade, George Snyder, a Kentucky watchmaker and reputedly president of the Bourbon Angling Club, invented a reel with a delicate spool that would pay out line during the cast, and which revolved several times for each turn of the crank handle. Thus was born the multiple-action reel, to be called the multiplier or multiplying reel, as well as a spool capable of dispensing line during a cast. The line of that day was raw silk, and there were no lures; for decades multiplying reels were small, and because they were exclusively used for tossing natural bait, they became popularly known as baitcasting reels.

For most of the nineteenth century, such reels were made by hand. There were various modifications and improvements, including the addition of a mechanism to distribute line evenly on the spool (called levelwind), better gears, and the addition of external drag. What had developed as a tool for freshwater fishing, primarily for bass, became available in large sizes for situations where greater line capacity and mechanical strength was needed.

Multiplier types of revolving spool reels for saltwater use were being made in the late 1800s, but they lacked an internal drag mechanism. To offset this, anglers applied pressure to the reel spool with their thumbs (which was ineffective for large fish and sometimes painful to the angler) or with a leather thumb pad that was attached to the reel frame.

William C. Boschen, a member of the legendary Catalina Tuna Club of California, is credited with originating the concept for the first internal star drag reel, a handy threaded knob adjustment that internally regulated spool pressure. Reportedly a prototype of a reel with such a device was made for Boschen by Brooklyn, New York, reel manufacturer Julius Vom Hofe, and used by Boschen to catch the first broadbill swordfish (358 pounds) ever taken on sporting rod and reel. That catch was made in the summer of 1913 off Catalina Island, and later versions of the reel were named B-Ocean.

This product was the predecessor of the modern conventional fishing reel. The star drag mechanism provided an internal friction adjustment mechanism (or brake) to help pressure strong fish and slow the rate of line being pulled off the reel. It was incorporated on all types and sizes of revolving spool reels in later years. All products that are today categorized as conventional reels feature a star drag; all baitcasting reels also feature a star drag. Other aspects of these reels evolved and improved over time, particularly drag washer materials, gears, and component materials.

A conventional reel today is essentially a medium- or large-size revolving spool reel, and is usually a product that does not have a levelwind line guiding mechanism (although there are exceptions). In modern marketing parlance, conventional reels are called many things, particularly boat, bay, surf, trolling, bottom fishing, and ocean reels. Categorically they are distinct from baitcasting reels, as well as from big-game or lever drag reels *(see: big-game tackle)*, although there are overlapping features.

Conventional reels are larger than baitcasting reels. They have a star-spoked wheel drag, are likely to be used with heavier lures and weights, and may or may not have a line-leveling mechanism. Some models may be cast, but many are used for bottom fishing and trolling. In saltwater, they are extremely popular for diverse usage; in freshwater, they are mainly used for the most-demanding applications. Conventional reels differ from lever drag reels, which are essentially a big-game fishing tool with a different method of achieving freespool and applying drag tension (using cam rather than threaded adjustment).

Most conventional reels of the modern era are more elementary in design and features than contemporary baitcasting or spinning reels, primarily because they are used for more demanding fish and in more punishing circumstances. Unlike contemporary baitcasting reels, which are primarily used for cast-and-retrieve angling activities (with lures rather than with natural bait), modern conventional reels are less frequently cast.

Many conventional reels are never used for casting, but exclusively used for trolling lures or bait and for fishing at various depths with sinking lures or bait, both of which call for paying line off the reel rather than casting. An ever widening interest in varied methods of fishing, coupled with a need for greater line capacity than even the largest baitcasting reels can provide, has resulted, however, in demands to use some modern conventional reels for casting either lures or natural bait. This requires some models to have features appropriate to the demands of frequent casting and retrieving. Thus, some conventional reels are used for casting as well as other types of fishing, despite their comparatively large size and greater weight.

One of the most distinguishing differences between a conventional reel and a baitcasting reel is that the latter have a level line-winding mechanism and the majority of the former do not. Thus, when using most conventional reels, the angler must manually direct the placement of line on the spool to produce an even line lay.

Manually leveling line on a spool is the biggest drawback to using conventional tackle, and often a problem for inexperienced anglers or those who

Assorted conventional reels and rods are displayed at a sport show.

are unfamiliar with this action. When line is not wound evenly, it bunches and impedes retrieval or dispensing, and contributes to binding of line wraps. Manual line leveling can seem even more burdensome when combined with the fact that conventional reels, which sit on top of the rod facing the angler, are heavy and, for some people, awkward to hold.

Being heavy is a double-edged sword, however. The weight is a result of the size necessary for adequate line capacity, which ranges from about 275 yards in smaller models to over 1,000 yards in the largest models, and a result of the sturdy components necessary for the frame, spool, and gears, which is what makes these reels capable of handling tough fishing.

Line capacity, gears, and drag are the most critical components of conventional reels. One of the problem areas with conventional reels in the past was a drag that became erratic when heavy pressure was intense and sustained or as a result of long-term compression of friction washers during storage. Modern conventional reels have improved, particularly the drag systems, which have become smoother due to modern friction materials, and which better resist compression and the effect of heat.

Conventional reels do have a drag-related drawback where striking and fighting large, powerful fish is concerned. Drag tension is not easily or readily adjustable to known levels. Turning the star wheel adjusts the drag tension, which is usually set to a predetermined level before fishing. If that wheel is deliberately or accidentally turned later, especially while playing a fish, drag tension is changed and may be too little or too great for the circumstances. Once the tension is changed, it cannot be recalibrated with absolute certainty while playing a fish. Furthermore, it may be desirable to deliberately increase or decrease drag tension while playing a fish (usually a very large and powerful one for the tackle), but doing so means making an adjustment to an uncertain level, and being unable to return to that preset level if necessary later on, as well as possibly exceeding the limits of the tackle. This drawback—which is primarily related to big-game fishing *(see)*—is one that lead to the development of the special purpose lever drag big-game reel *(see: big-game tackle)*.

Experienced anglers can make adjustments to the preset tension of a star drag reel and be reasonably close to the tension level necessary for the circumstances. But most anglers cannot do so, and may have a high degree of error when making adjustments by feel under difficult and pressured angling circumstances, which can have harmful results.

This, of course, is most significant when fishing for the biggest and hardest-fighting species, and when using lighter lines. For the majority of angling circumstances involving conventional reels, adjusting the star drag while playing a fish is seldom necessary, and preset tension is maintained throughout the fight.

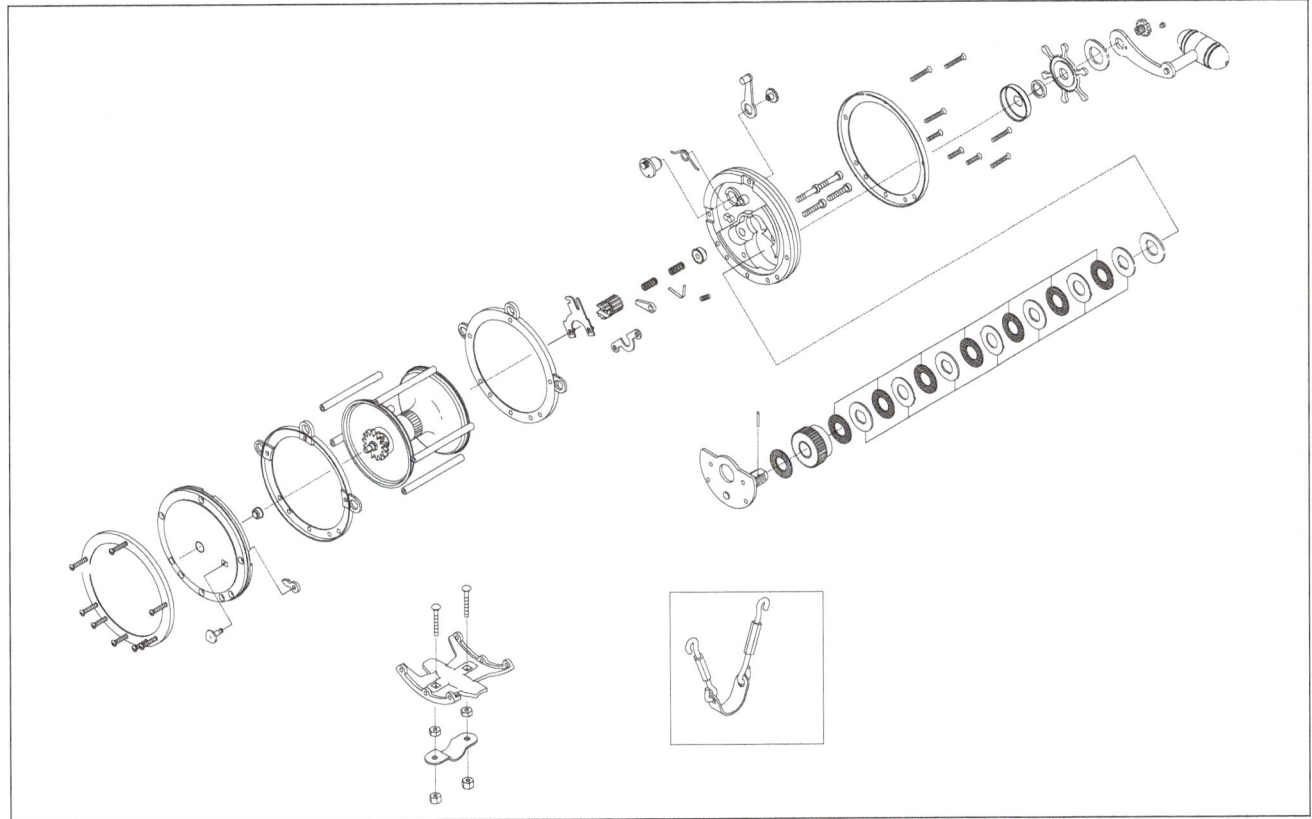

All of the parts of a Penn Senator conventional trolling reel are shown here; this product features a multi-disc star drag system.

General Operation

In the most basic sense, conventional tackle works like all other tackle except flycasting in that a weighted object at the end of the line pulls line from the spool. The spool of a conventional reel revolves during the cast, as line pays out and when line is retrieved, when you turn the handle. When the gears are disengaged and line is dispensed from the reel, a backlash *(see)*, or spool overrun, can occur if the revolving spool turns faster than the line is carried off that spool. Applying light pressure to the spool can prevent this, and it may be accomplished in several ways. One of these is with finger or hand tension, another is with a lever-operated clutch, which can be engaged or disengaged as in a car.

The conventional reel has a lever that activates or deactivates the gears and essentially takes the reel into or out of freespool. In use, with the reel on top of the rod handle and facing toward the angler, the rod-holding hand thumb is placed on the spool to keep the line in check, and the free hand is used to move the gear lever backward, which disengages the gears and puts the reel in freespool. When thumb pressure is relaxed, line flows off the spool and out through the rod guides, carried by the weight of the object at the terminal end of the line. Conventional reels feature a click ratchet, used to signal that line is being taken off the reel; this may be employed when a reel is not held or when it is left unattended.

To retrieve line, the gears are engaged by moving the lever forward, and the spool is turned by rotating the handle, which winds line onto the reel. When line is wound onto the spool, the user generally must level the line manually for even line distribution, although some lighter-duty conventional reels have a levelwind mechanism that automatically distributes the line back and forth across the spool.

Every conventional reel has an adjustable drag mechanism, activated by turning a star wheel on the drive gear. This is located on the sideplate under the handle. The drag tension is set to the desirable level at the beginning of each day's fishing and relaxed when the day is concluded.

These are the basic elements of operating a conventional reel. In some models cast control and anti-reverse features come into play; the size of the spool, the materials used, and the designed application of each product also have relevance to its use.

Line Release/Casting Features

The vast majority of conventional reels, and virtually all large models, are not used for casting. Some smaller-size reels are used for casting as well as for other applications. In all models, controlling the flow of line off the spool is an important element of use.

Freespool. Disengaging gears to enable a reel to freely turn backward and dispense line is known as putting the reel into freespool. This is accomplished in conventional reels by moving the eccentric lever that is located on the sideplate and extends just beyond the edge of the plate. This lever is actually a gear shift lever but may be known as the freespool lever or freespool clutch. It should not be confused with the lever that controls drag tension on a lever drag reel, although they are both in similar locations. A similar mechanism is used on baitcasting reels but is in the form of a button or bar, which is more convenient; a lever is used on conventional reels for positive engagement and strength, and because casting is less prevalent.

Under the sideplate, the pinion gear, which drops down on the spindle and drives it, is cradled in a yoke. When the eccentric lever (clutch) is moved to the freespool position, which is usually backward or toward the holder, it moves a shifter that pushes a ramp in, lifting the pinion off the spindle to disengage it. Now the reel is in freespool mode. In this method of achieving freespool, the gears are still intact but not the drive mechanism; this is different from lever drag reels, where pulling the drag lever back into the freespool position keeps the gears intact but disengages the clutch parts.

This is the basic method used in conventional reels to achieve freespool. Some reels achieve this in a circular fashion, where there is a ramp on either side of the yoke to lift the pinion, although this is more common in smaller reels (and baitcasting products) and necessitated by a smaller area under the sideplate.

This is a very straightforward operational method. Some conventional reels, especially those with a pair of eccentric springs, provide more decisive and forceful shifting in both directions, but all are reasonably fail-safe.

Spool revolution. Before putting the reel into freespool, you must apply finger pressure to the spool to prevent line from paying out prematurely or haphazardly. Without this pressure, and assuming that a lure or weighted bait is tied to the end of the line, the weight of either object causes the spool to turn the moment the reel is placed into the freespool position, which could cause an instant backlash on the spool.

Therefore, it is necessary to place the thumb of the rod-holding hand on the spool so the spool can't turn, and then move the eccentric lever into the freespool position. Now the line can be released by easing the tension or, in some instances, by casting.

When releasing line without casting, thumb pressure is lessened on the spool to pay line out at a controlled rate; the objective is to let a sufficient amount of line out for the fishing circumstances at a rate that doesn't cause the spool to turn so fast that it causes a backlash. This is important because a revolving spool can gather speed quickly, and an uncontrolled spool can lead to a serious backlash in seconds. The backlash not only impedes immediate fishing effort because of the time required to undo it, but can also damage the line. This situation becomes even more acute in those conventional reels that are used for casting applications, because the activity of casting builds up greater spool speed.

Casting requires precise control of the revolving spool. In either application, it is necessary to brake the spool to slow its speed. For more details about the cause and cure of backlash, see: *Baitcasting Tackle*.

Spool braking/control. The majority of conventional reel users employ thumb pressure to brake the spool, because most do not have any other means of controlling spool revolution. Applying thumb pressure is an action learned through trial and error and perfected with experience; it requires the application of different degrees of braking tension for the weights on the line, distances being cast, and types of rods and reels being used.

There are also magnetic and mechanical ways of helping to control revolving spool speed. In function, magnetic spool breaking systems employ a magnetic field to place variable degrees of resistance on the spool. Magnetic spool braking is seldom used on conventional reels and rarely in saltwater applications. It is popular for baitcasting reels used in freshwater and described in more detail in the baitcasting tackle *(see)* entry.

Some conventional reels have a mechanical means of controlling spool braking via centrifugal brakes. Those with it have blocks that must be engaged to effect spool braking. These blocks are usually found on the left side of the reel, and accessed by removing the left sideplate. Underneath the click ratchet and next to the spool flange is a cross pin with a centrifugal brake block on either side. To be employed, these brake blocks must be moved out toward the flange and snapped into a notch. In this position they rub against the flange and, due to centrifugal pressure, exert the greatest force at lightest speeds, and slow down the spool to help avoid a backlash.

This system is common on baitcasting reels but uncommon for conventional reels, although models with this feature are used for specific saltwater casting applications, especially in long-range party boat *(see)* and kingfish angling, and some bluefish and tuna angling. The centrifugal casting system is an extra feature that makes reels so equipped more expensive than comparable models without the feature.

Spool tension control. Some people view the adjustable screw tension mechanism found on most conventional reels as a means of controlling spool braking, although its value in this regard is limited. This device is sometimes the knurled knob or bearing cap on the nonhandle sideplate (usually on the left sideplate, but it may be on the right sideplate), which is adjusted by hand. In some reels it may be a slot that is adjusted with a screwdriver or coin. Tightening this device does put tension on the spindle of the spool, but its real purpose is to control excessive end play, or sideways movement, of the spool.

If the mechanical spool control on a reel is too loose, there is too much movement in the spool and line could get behind it. If the engineering mechanics of a reel are correct, line should not get behind the spool; you should be able to loosen it completely and, though there will be excessive end play, still not be able to pull the flange of the spool out of the centering ring of the sideplate. Even if you lose the adjusting screw, this should not happen.

On conventional reels, a small piece of rubber or a dished spring lies on the sideplate fronting against a brass or bronze wear plate. As the adjustment knob is tightened, the wear plate rubs against the stainless steel spindle. Tightening is usually a clockwise motion, and this should be adjusted so that there is barely any perceptible sideways motion of the spool. One manufacturer recommends that the sideways motion be no more than the thickness of a hair; ascertaining this by sight is dubious, but it provides a clue as to the acceptable level of end play. To see how much play there is, take both thumbs and put them on either side of the spool and press back and forth to see if you can move it. Adjust it to a tight but not immovable tolerance.

Do not fully tighten the spool tension adjustment mechanism; this can damage or cause premature wearing (and failure) of the right and left side bearings. The rubber should provide some cushion for a better range of adjustment, and in the event that something wears out, it will preferably be the wear plate and not the spindle.

In reels that are not employed for casting, the tension control mechanism is seldom used after any sideways movement has been eliminated. Most people don't use this adjustment much. Experienced anglers who cast often with a conventional reel will tighten or loosen the adjustment knob, and employ this level of control in conjunction with an educated thumb. People who are unfamiliar with casting a revolving spool need a tighter adjustment for some assistance with spool braking, however, or they will be picking backlashes out with every cast. This tension should gradually be lightened as they become more proficient with thumb control.

Retrieving/Line Recovery Features

The elements that affect line retrieval with conventional reels are similar to those for all other reels, although because of the applications of these products, those elements are very significant. They especially include gear components, gear ratio, spool diameter and capacity, and the handle.

Line pickup. To be in a position to set the hook and to return line to the spool, some drag tension must be established and the gears must be engaged; the latter is accomplished by moving the eccentric lever from the freespool position to the retrieve position. These positions may or may not be labeled on a given reel, but this is usually accomplished by moving the lever upward or forward (clockwise if looking at a reel from the side). This action drops the pinion gear onto the spindle and engages the drive mechanism.

With the eccentric lever forward, and some drag tension in effect, turning the handle revolves the spool, bringing line onto it. Turning the handle

Dolphin (mahimahi) are an incredibly fast-growing yet short-lived fish; one-year-olds will be about 13 pounds, and soon-to-die four-year-olds 70 to 80 pounds.

without moving the eccentric lever forward does not engage the gears in most conventional reels. The operation of others is more like a baitcasting reel, with the lever moving to the retrieve position automatically when the handle is turned forward. More mechanics are involved in such reels, however, and they are generally less favored for saltwater application.

Left/right retrieve. With a few exceptions, the majority of conventional reels today are only set up for right-handed retrieve and are not convertible. Some conventional reels are made in left-retrieve versions. The left/right retrieve situation with these products is akin to that for baitcasting, and it mostly favors people who are right-handed.

With regard to catching smaller fish and using lighter gear (like baitcasting), it is beneficial for people who are right-handed to reel with their left hand and for lefties to reel with their right hand, so that the dominant hand is the one that holds the rod and is used to play the fish or direct the retrieve. This is especially significant when frequent casting is involved. Because the dominant hand is used to cast the rod, no further action is required after casting to start using the reel; the other hand is immediately placed on the reel handle grip and starts turning the handle. This lack of time delay is important in some fishing situations.

However, because less casting is done with conventional reels, applications are more demanding, the outfits are generally heavy, and most people are right-handed, the right-retrieve aspect of most conventional reels is not the problem that it is in baitcasting products. Large conventional reels especially are used for big fish, and it is common to attach these reels to a harness, which relieves the rod-holding arm. If a person is right-handed, all of the heavy-duty cranking of the reel is done with the stronger hand, which, in theory, is better for anyone who is right-handed, although not as desirable for a lefty.

Left-handed people complain about this to reel manufacturers, and although a few left-handed retrieve conventional reels are available, there aren't enough to suit people who prefer to reel with their dominant left hand. From a manufacturer's perspective, changing retrieve comes down to the gearing. It can be done, but the engineering isn't just a simple matter of reversing things. Conventional reels that feature a levelwind are even more problematic. Completely new tooling, including a new frame or sideplate, is necessary to produce a left-retrieve levelwind product, which is obviously much more expensive.

The problem essentially is one of demand. Manufacturers would make such reels if there were enough demand. There aren't enough left-handed anglers (or not enough of them have complained) to make it worthwhile for manufacturers to undertake the costs necessary to produce two versions of every conventional reel. Finally, from a practical usage standpoint, owning both right- and left-handed retrieve models of conventional reels becomes more gear-intensive than most people would like or can afford. This is especially true for party boat operators, charter captains, or private boat owners, who take customers, friends, and family fishing. It is simply easier to have everything that works the same way (right-retrieve), especially because most people are right handed.

Line winding/Levelwind. Line is wound directly onto the spool of a conventional reel, but most conventional reels do not have a mechanism for leveling or dispersing that line across the spool. For such reels, this leveling must be done manually. The hand that holds the rod must be situated in such a way that the thumb can be used to direct the line back and forth onto the spool as it is retrieved. This means holding the rod at the foregrip ahead of the reel, and extending the thumb to the right to catch the line with both sides of the tip of the thumb, moving it to the left and right to disperse the line. This has to be done whenever the handle of the reel is turned and line is recovered onto the spool.

Failing to disperse the line by hand results in bunching on the spool. If the line bunches severely enough, it may jam at the frame crossbars and prevent retrieval of additional line or inhibit outflow of line when the reel is placed in freespool. It also causes wraps to bind among each other, impeding the free flow of line off the spool. Bunching also makes it more likely to incur a spool overrun; a horrific tangle must be painstakingly picked apart.

Some conventional reels have a mechanism, known as a levelwind, to automatically disperse line evenly across the spool. This does not require any hand or thumb movement to accomplish. Conventional reels that have a levelwind mechanism are the same in every other way as conventional reels without this mechanism.

In conventional reels, the levelwind may be gear-driven by the spool or by the main gear and

A minority of conventional reels have a levelwind feature, and this model also sports a digital line counter.

turn whenever the spool revolves, both forward and backward. The mechanism is located in a carriage that spans both sides of the reel. Inside is a nylon idler gear that turns a worm gear and catches a pawl that moves the line guide back and forth across the spool. This mechanism distributes line evenly on the spool, which avoids line buildup.

Although a minority of conventional reels feature a levelwind, this feature has been growing steadily in popularity among conventional reel users, perhaps as a spillover effect from the freshwater use of baitcasting reels. Virtually all mass-produced baitcasting reels have featured a levelwind mechanism for many years. Only competitive tournament casters are likely to have a small revolving spool reel without a levelwind, and that for distance events.

In this area of conventional reels, there is disagreement among users, especially between saltwater and freshwater anglers. The average saltwater angler looks at a conventional revolving spool with a levelwind as an item for neophytes and views the mechanism as an accident waiting to happen. The average freshwater angler looks at a conventional revolving spool reel that doesn't have a levelwind mechanism and asks why not.

For saltwater anglers who cast with conventional reels, like surf anglers, the levelwind is disliked because it reduces casting distance. How much it reduces distance is debatable, but it does reduce it some because there is friction on the line when it flows off the spool and contacts the line-winding guide during a cast. Achieving distance is often important in surf fishing *(see)*, as well as in other saltwater casting applications.

More important for saltwater anglers is the possibility of the levelwind, which is always exposed to the elements, malfunctioning. This can be caused by the corrosive effect of saltwater or the levelwind trapping sand particles from the line, even when it is carefully cleaned and maintained. Added friction on the line can also cause the loss of really powerful fish. Generally, saltwater anglers like to simplify things because of the corrosive environment they constantly deal with. Enough goes wrong without adding more to worry about, and the levelwind is viewed as another potential point subject to breakage. Furthermore, really big, powerful fish can strip line extremely fast off a reel. The line guide cannot keep up with the swift back and forth movement of the line, necessarily putting friction and more tension on the line, which might cause the levelwind to fail or the line to break. For this reason, no large conventional reels have a levelwind mechanism.

Although veteran saltwater anglers spurn conventional reels that possess a levelwind, the use of these reels in saltwater is increasing, and they are considered essential in freshwater applications. This may be partly due to more people with freshwater fishing experience venturing into saltwater, and partly due to minor improvements in levelwind reliability, but mostly due to application. Levelwind conventional reels are being used more in lighter saltwater applications, such as inshore fishing, bottom fishing for flounder, and casting for bluefish and striped bass. They are being used in all places where there is less likelihood of pressure-related levelwind problems provided that the reel is cleaned properly after every use. Some saltwater charter boat captains are using levelwind reels more because they're tired of having problems with inexperienced angling customers who forget to manually distribute the line on non-levelwind reels.

A few levelwind-style conventional reels have a line counter for determining the amount of line that is off the reel. This is of primary use in freshwater trolling, in drift fishing with bait for suspended fish, or in bottom fishing at specific depths, and may be mechanical or electronic.

Gears. The most basic part of the operation of every reel is the gear set, which, in a conventional reel, is universally heavy-duty and more efficient than that of a stationary or fixed spool reel because the gear set operates on a parallel axis.

In a conventional reel, a large gear, which is the main or drive gear, engages a smaller gear, which is the pinion. The drive gear is linked to the reel handle and the pinion gear connects to the spool. This system provides the multiplying gear ratio for ample line retrieval rates with a small spool and still delivers substantial cranking power. It also allows for the use of heavy lines.

Most better conventional reels have a stainless steel pinion gear and a bronze main gear. In a few reels both are stainless steel, and in some bargain-priced reels both may be brass, but unless one gear is slightly softer than the other, this can cause problems.

In almost any simple gear set one gear material is normally different from the other. This is because use of the same materials tends to cold weld, or "gall" together; dissimilar metals nearly always offer the lowest coefficient of friction. The presence of an oil film helps to reduce friction. The result of using dissimilar metals and an oil film is that gears run smoothly for a longer period.

The best situation is for the main drive gear material to be slightly softer than the pinion gear for wear characteristics, especially in reels that are used often for demanding applications, and where the gear ratio is high. In a multiplier reel, one tooth of the pinion gear contacts its mating teeth on the main gear the same number of times as the gear ratio. That is, in a 5:1 ratio reel, each tooth on the pinion gear is activated five times more often than its counterpart on the main gear. Therefore, it is subject to five times the wear and needs to be harder simply to survive. The predominance of stainless steel pinion gears and bronze main gears in conventional reels produces a hardness differential that favors the smaller diameter pinion gear to provide longer life.

These are low-speed (left) and high-speed gear sets from different conventional reels; both feature a stainless steel pinion gear and bronze alloy main gear.

Gears are made to work in a given way with respect to each other, so there must be a certain distance between the two to match up; otherwise the gears will feel tight. Naturally, it is important that the gear teeth are machined as precisely as possible to assure smooth operation and long life. Some conventional reels, especially those with a higher gear ratio, have helically milled gears. This means that each gear tooth is spiral or curved, rather than straight, on the gear circumference. Helical milling results in increased contact area, resulting in greater strength, thicker cross section, and a high degree of inherent smoothness, particularly for smaller gear teeth. The major benefit is that, unlike straight-milled gears where only a single gear tooth is fully engaged at one time, helical gears allow at least partial engagement of several gear teeth at all times, spreading the load and potential wear. This is mainly an issue where the gear teeth are small, and there is less surface to make contact, as is found on higher ratio models.

The high-stress cranking that is experienced with conventional reels requires a rigid support system, so that under great duress there is no flex to affect the inner workings of the reel. The use of heavy line, and cranking large fish in extreme conditions, can put tremendous stress on all components. Both the material and construction of the frame and shaft supports are what keep the gears precisely located and delivering long life.

Gear ratio. Because the drive gear is linked to the reel handle and the pinion gear is engaged to the spool, the basic numerical ratio of the drive and pinion gears in a conventional reel merely establishes the number of revolutions made by the spool per turn of the handle. That number is determined by counting the gear teeth on the larger drive gear and dividing that by the tooth count of the smaller pinion gear. In a gear set consisting of a 53-tooth drive gear and a 10-tooth pinion gear, the ratio would be calculated at 5.3:1, since the pinion will turn 5.3 times for each full rotation of the drive gear.

Gear ratios are generally categorized as high (fast) or low (slow), but this is relative to the type of reel and application. Furthermore, the size of the spool may be such that a low gear ratio reel actually recovers more line per full turn of the handle than a high ratio reel with a smaller spool. What is high for many conventional reels would be low for nearly all baitcasting reels, if numerical ratio was the only factor of comparison. Typical low gear ratios for conventional reels are 2:1 to 3:1 and typical high gear ratios are 3.5:1 to 5:1, although they range both higher and lower. In a conventional reel, a high gear ratio may be preferable for cast-and-retrieve fishing, but a low gear ratio reel may be preferable for deep bottom fishing. What is gained in retrieve speed is lost in cranking power.

The higher the ratio, the greater the potential for stripping gears under severe strain. On a high gear ratio reel, the individual teeth become narrower because more teeth are fitted into a given area, and they are weaker. An inexperienced angler is more likely to do damage on a high gear ratio reel when he puts the smaller gear teeth under a heavy load. Fishing with a high gear ratio reel requires using the rod a lot, pulling it back and then winding line onto the spool quickly on the down stroke. This is necessary because with high gear ratio reels the smaller tooth configuration does not have sufficient cranking strength. This is a factor in all reels, but obviously of more concern with reels that get a heavy load, such as conventional and lever drag reels.

Cranking power. Gear ratio and cranking power are inextricably linked in all reels, and most affect how easy or difficult it is to retrieve a heavy weight, or an object that offers a lot of resistance. Reels that can easily handle a heavy load are said to have a lot of cranking power. Various factors affect this.

The length of the handle has a bearing because length has to do with the leverage that you can put on the handle. The longer the handle, the more leverage and the easier it is to retrieve a set load. If you make a handle longer, you reduce the force at the knob. It is essentially the same principle as having a long-handled wrench; it's easier to loosen nuts with a long-handled wrench than with a short-handled one. So a longer handle equates to greater power (although your hand and arm must describe a larger circle to operate the reel).

The gear set itself is also a big factor with regard to cranking power. If you have a conventional reel with a gear ratio of 2:1, it's easier to retrieve a load because this is a low gear ratio. If you have a conventional reel with a gear ratio of 5:1, which is high, it's much more difficult to retrieve a load, although you get more speed. If you're retrieving something that offers very little resistance, the high gear ratio is okay. But you need a lower gear ratio for something that offers more resistance. Thus, the lowest gear ratio reels have the greatest cranking power, and the highest gear ratio reels have the least cranking power.

No matter what the gear ratio is, the evaluation of a reel's ability to retrieve line should boil down to something engineers call Inches Per Turn of the handle, or IPT. This is the amount of line recovered per turn of the handle, or, simply, line recovery. That is a better measurement of retrieval ability than gear ratio. Line recovery is determined by spool diameter, which is a key dimension for any reel and which sets the circumference of the line level on the spool and the amount of line wound onto the spool with each turn of the reel handle.

When the level of line on a spool is low, as it might be when a strong fish takes a lot of line, less line is recovered per turn of the handle than would be when all of the line is on the spool. Similarly, the amount of line recovered per turn of the handle of a fully spooled 4:1 ratio reel that has a small spool would be less than the amount of line recovered per turn of the handle of a fully spooled 4:1 ratio reel that has a large spool.

The amount of line recovered is the measurement an angler should be most interested in. Yet anglers cannot quickly determine line recovery when evaluating a reel they might purchase because specifications on the circumference of the spool are seldom provided on the reel or in the packaging materials. While in a 4:1 ratio reel, for example, you know that one revolution of the handle puts four wraps of line on the spool, if you don't know how much line is gained with each complete wrap, you don't know the actual recovery. (In a reel that you own, this can be determined by marking the line and then measuring it.)

For a greater discussion of this subject, *see: Gear Ratio and Line Recovery*. Although most consumers have a notion that gear ratio is of primary importance in retrieval and some think that the higher the ratio the better, other factors are involved, and line recovery is a major one. Remember, however, that reels with a low gear ratio do better under heavier loads, whether those loads are due to the size of the fish or the equipment being used (heavy weights, deep-diving lures, etc.).

This issue is critical in conventional reels because of their basic size, capacity, and applications. Chances are the bigger the reel, the more likely it is that a heavy load will be placed on it. The larger the reel, the more noticeable the effect of a high gear ratio, so you'll feel that load a lot more.

Handle. The length of the handle affects cranking power, so the distance from the center of the handle to the handle knob is a key element in retrieval. A long handle equals power, yet many people have the misconception that a long handle also equals speed, that the longer it is, the faster it can travel. It's just the opposite. The longer the handle, the greater distance the cranking hand has to travel with each turn. The shorter the handle, the quicker it can be turned, but then there's less power, so there's a tradeoff either way. You can't get power and speed simultaneously.

Some conventional reel handles are equipped with two center holes so you can change the distance from the crankshaft connection to the handle knob and thus affect power and speed to best suit the physical build of the angler. For others, it may be possible to purchase a convertible handle as an accessory.

Some conventional reels sport a counterbalanced handle: one handle knob and an opposing counterbalance weight. This is usually found on medium-size reels (up to about 4/0) used in applications where there is a lot of retrieving. The counterbalance gives the reel a more solid feel with a better cadence to the retrieval action, which is important when you're casting frequently and regularly using a quick retrieve. In some situations, like casting plugs for wahoo, you can't retrieve too fast for the likes of the fish. With a bigger reel, you wouldn't feel such rapid retrieving because of the mass of the reel, but then speed of retrieval is seldom an issue on larger reels, which is why they don't have a counterbalanced handle. Power is the main issue with larger reels, and this is consistent with their lower gear ratio.

Nearly all conventional reels have a single handle grip, or knob, which is what you hold onto to turn

The cranking power of conventional reels makes them preferable to some surf anglers, especially for catching large fish.

the handle. This is contrary to baitcasting reels, where nearly all handles have dual grips. While a single handle grip would look out of place on a baitcasting reel, a dual handle grip would look out of place on a conventional reel, where the grips are fairly large and two of them would seem garish. It is worth noting that the way these reel handles are held and turned has some bearing on this design. A baitcasting reel knob is mainly gripped with the fingertips and operated by wrist motion, and is not affected by the presence of a second handle knob. Larger conventional reel knobs are gripped with more of the finger and operated with the arm and elbow, which would be affected by a second knob.

Conventional reels have various styles of grips or knobs, and size is usually commensurate with the size of the reel. Small and medium reels have a soft nonslip handle grip with a large and comfortable surface area. Many reels, particularly larger models, have barrel or torpedo shaped grips, which tend to be grasped by the whole hand rather than just the thumb and index finger.

Ball bearings/Bushings. Bearings and bushings provide a way to minimize friction on rotating shafts. Bushings don't spin as freely as ball or roller bearings, which are typically viewed as durable and reliable and a way to add rotational freeness to the retrieval system. A bushing can deliver as smooth a retrieval as a ball bearing under low load conditions, but under heavy loads, ball bearings are vastly smoother and more durable. Two to four stainless steel ball bearings are used on many conventional reels, primarily on both ends of the spool shaft and on the crankshaft. These are (or should be) of the highest grade, and some manufacturers claim to use aircraft quality stainless steel ball bearings on certain reels. For a more detailed review of ball bearings and bushings, *see: Reel, Fishing.*

Warning click. Primarily known simply as a click or clicker by most anglers, this is a ratchet device that is primarily intended to let an angler know that line is going out. It is generally employed when a rod and reel have been placed in a rod holder (as when surf fishing, trolling, or bait fishing) and is not handheld. In some situations, as when fishing with bait, the reel is placed in freespool with the warning click on so that if a fish picks up the bait, the line is free to move with minimal resistance yet without risking a spool overrun. In other situations, such as when trolling, the gears are engaged and the warning click is employed so that it instantly alerts an angler (or mate or boat captain) to a strike and to the fact that a fish is on and taking line off the reel.

The click itself features a spring-loaded tongue that moves back and forth against ratchet teeth to make this sound. It is activated by moving a small off-center button on the sideplate (usually the left sideplate). The click is intended for part-time rather than full-time use, and the click button should be disengaged when retrieving. Continued use of the click causes premature ratchet wear. Leaving it on is viewed by some people as a sign of an inexperienced angler, although some charter captains like it to be left on because the sound lets them know what a customer's fish is doing; when the clicking sound speeds up, for example, the fish is taking line. Some have even asked manufacturers for different types of sounds in the click (this is especially prevalent in the Great Lakes, where the clicks are always used for trolling).

In older reels, if the click wore out you needed a whole new sideplate, but in newer models the configuration allows for replacing the subassembly but not the whole sideplate. Thus, excessive wear is not as big or costly a problem as in the past.

Drag Features
The purpose of the drag function on any reel is to let line slip from the reel at varying pressures when force is applied to the line. It serves as a sort of clutch, or shock absorber, and is especially important when using light line, when playing large and strong species, and when fish make strong and sudden surges while being landed. If an angler never catches large fish, only uses heavy strength line, and is content to wind fish in, it is conceivable that his drag will never be used. This is not the case with conventional tackle, however, which is expressly meant for catching large fish and dealing with tough conditions.

Nevertheless, catching large fish, which weigh more than the actual breaking strength of the line, or which can apply extreme pressure on the tackle, requires some finesse rather than sheer strength. This means that the drag will come into play, because if it doesn't, the force will exceed the strength of the line and the line will break.

When the drag comes into play, it allows the fish to continue applying force, but at a pressure that is less than the breaking strength of the line, because when the force reaches a certain level (usually a specific percentage of the line's breaking strength), a properly set drag mechanism allows line to slip from the reel under tension by turning the spool. In essence, it means that a fish can run instead of engage in a tug of war, but it has to work for the line that it takes off the reel, which is tiring and helps the angler subdue it.

Many people mistakenly think that they need to set the drag very tight for effective hook setting. Once you have 20 yards of line out and you have rod flex, line stretch, and the dampening effect of the water to contend with, you don't need very much drag force at the reel. You cannot exert the maximum pressure when you set the hook. But when you set the drag pressure at or near maximum force, once the fish is close to the boat and there is less of a contribution made by line stretch, rod flex, and water, having the drag locked down may mean that the line cannot absorb the sudden shock of a quick run, even from a fish whose weight is less than the breaking strength of the line. People

These are stainless steel ball bearings (left) and a series of carbon friction and stainless steel washers, both found on better conventional reels.

are often amazed that a 15-pound fish can break 20-pound line, but that doesn't happen if the drag is set properly and the washers are allowed to slip freely when necessary.

In typical fishing with conventional reels, anglers set the drag at 25 to 30 percent of the breaking strength of their line. This is measured by some people with a short length of line on a straight pull off the reel. It is measured by others with line running through the rod guides and the rod flexed as it would be in fishing circumstances. Most people use the "feels good" method of establishing drag tension by pulling line off the reel and adjusting the star wheel until the tension feels right. The most precise way to measure drag tension is by using a reliable scale and attaching it to the line. No matter what method is used, the objective is to adjust the drag so that the line will not slip until the appropriate amount of tension is applied. Understanding how to use and set drag is one of the most important aspects of sportfishing, and is reviewed in detail elsewhere *(see: drag)*.

The drag mechanism is an especially important characteristic of a conventional reel due to the applications that these reels face. For years manufacturers employed various types, combinations, and numbers of drag washers, which produced mixed results when tested by powerful fish. Better materials, however, have greatly improved the drags of these products, and many contemporary models have very good drag systems. Moreover, because of the nature of revolving spool reels, no twist is imparted to the line when an angler reels at the same time that line slips off the spool via the drag. This is a common problem with spinning and spincasting reels. Twist isn't possible on a conventional reel if the handle is turning and the spool is simultaneously slipping. When the drag mechanism is activated on a conventional reel, the spool rotates and line unwinds in an untwisted manner. There is no line twist unless it comes from lure use or you put it on when the spool is filled.

Drag system. On conventional reels, the drag is located on the main gear and is usually a multi-element system with washers that are keyed together. The main gear is hollowed out, which decreases weight and increases space, and a stack of washers is located ahead of this, with all of these fitting over a threaded gear stud. The washers are alternately stainless steel and friction material, interleaved to increase the working surface area.

Drag tension is increased or decreased by turning a drag star (radial-arm star wheel), which is located under the handle on the sideplate. The drag star threads onto the gear stud or drive gear, which is connected to the handle, so it rotates concurrently with the handle without affecting the setting. Turning the drag star clockwise or forward increases tension; turning it counterclockwise or backward decreases it.

Turning the drag star forward causes it to spiral around the threads of the gear stud and compress a tension spring washer, which compresses the drag washers. The stainless steel washers are keyed separately to the gear shaft and the main gear to prevent slippage; without keying, all washers would slip and there would be no drag since the interleaving would be inoperative. Washers that are alternately keyed off both the shaft and the main gear transmit power from the handle into the gear via the drag material itself by relying on the friction between those oppositely keyed parts to drive the gear. The more pressure on them, the more friction that is applied to the spool.

When spool friction exceeds the tension on the line, the reel handle turns the main gear and the spool, and allows line to be recovered. When tension on the line exceeds friction on the spool, the spool revolves against handle pressure, and line can be pulled off the spool. The handle is prevented from turning backward by a dog and ratchet, which is known as an anti-reverse.

Variation/Force. Variation is an important aspect of drag function. If you set the drag to create 4 pounds of tension on the line, it should stay at 4 pounds. If it varies to 5 and 6 pounds, that is not good. Influencing factors include how fast you pull on the line, and where you set the drag. If you have

30-pound line and you set the drag at 4 pounds, you'll have less variation than if you set it at 10 pounds. With lower force, it is easier to control variation.

Another aspect is maximum drag force. For most fishing, the drag on conventional tackle should be set at 25 to 30 percent of breaking strength. For a 30-pound line, that would be between $7^1/_2$ and 9 pounds. If you could only set it at 6 pounds, it would probably not be enough for some fishing situations, meaning that the maximum tension for that reel is less than what is desirable for ordinary fishing. So you should check the maximum force you can obtain on the reel before using it to make sure that it will be adequate for your needs. With most conventional reels, this is not a problem, and maximum drag force usually exceeds the strength of line for which the reel is rated. But this can be a problem on an older or poorly maintained product.

Some anglers are very interested in being able to readily get maximum force, which locks the reel down and completely prevents the drag from slipping. This is more common for smaller reels used in freshwater. However, this maximum force is seldom beneficial for most fishing activities, including playing large or strong fish, unless you're using very heavy line. Where it is most likely to be useful, however, is when a lure or hook gets snagged and cannot be freed; this situation may require you to lock the reel down, point the rod directly at the snag, and pull back to free the hook or break the line *(see: unsnagging)*. If the drag cannot be locked down completely, line will slip off, and it may be harder to free the hook.

Range. Another important aspect of drag function is range of adjustment, or how many revolutions you can turn the control mechanism on the reel to achieve the desired result. Most star wheels have a lot of latitude in revolutions from the point where the wheel cannot turn backward any further to the point where it cannot turn forward any further.

Range actually starts the moment you've got some drag tension, not from the point where the star wheel is completely backed off. Sometimes you can make two revolutions from the fully backed off position before achieving resistance. This does not affect the drag tension. To avoid this, manufacturers may put a spacer of varying size inside the mechanism to cut down on the turns of the star wheel necessary to produce tension. Although anglers generally dislike making these extra turns, having this provides some leeway for the manufacturers in case the drag materials differ in thickness from the norm. Thicker materials take up more space; if a spacer is placed in the mechanism, it may not be possible to completely back off the drag tension, so this adversely affects range. In a situation requiring ultralight drag tension, it may not be possible to back the drag all the way off to get that light amount of tension.

The wider the area from the point where line slips under no load to where it doesn't slip at all, the finer the tension adjustment. A wider area makes setting drag tension easier, especially for the more experienced angler. For conventional reels, a good range of drag adjustment from initial tension to maximum tension should require one and a half to two revolutions of the star wheel. This is an arguable point, however, and personal preferences vary. The problem with adjustment range comes from conflicting demands. Some anglers want a wide range of adjustment while others want to quickly get to maximum force, or lockdown. Satisfying these differences requires tradeoffs in design elements. There's a point where smoothness and lockdown become incompatible. Nevertheless, how many rotations it takes to get to the lockdown point is important. Ideally, a conventional reel drag should have a wide range of adjustment from initial tension to about 50 percent of the line's breaking strength, and then quickly jump to the maximum point; the lockdown mode is then achieved quickly in case you have to break off, pull on a snag, or have the greatest possible tension for special circumstances.

One factor that contributes to range as well as overall performance is the material of the friction washers; a material with a relatively high coefficient of friction helps a lot. Another factor is the size of the thread on the stud or main gear. If a reel has a post with heavy pitch thread, just half a turn could take you from initial tension to maximum tension. If a reel has a post with very fine pitch thread, it may take three turns to go from initial tension to maximum tension. So a finer thread provides a better range of adjustment no matter what the materials or components are. Having a conical washer with the crown up also provides range as the washer collapses.

Friction washers. The material of friction washers is critical to the operation of any reel, especially conventional reels used for rugged fishing. Ideally, the drag in any reel operates smoothly, without hesitation. In other words, it starts immediately when needed and maintains a constant rate of tension as line flows continuously off, and it keeps the same level of tension as it is periodically called upon during the time it takes to play and land a strong fish. The less variation there is in the performance of the drag, the better. Some of this performance is affected by the capable range of adjustment, as previously noted. Some is affected by the number and material of the friction washers.

One of the problems with friction washers is that they are asked to do something which is very difficult. It is desirable to have a drag that slips freely and yet can create a high amount of pressure. It has to be able to slip, yet also to sustain a high load, perhaps even a complete no-slip lockdown load. Thus, you're looking for two opposite attributes in a friction washer to accomplish these needs.

One of the most unusual artificial reefs was one constructed in the 1950s off Fire Island Inlet, New York, from 14,000 concrete-filled beer cases.

Friction washer materials in conventional reels, like those in other reel types, have evolved over the years. They've been made of many materials in the past, including felt, leather, asbestos, and Teflon. Most contemporary conventional reels use a washer made of woven carbon fiber. Penn Reels, which was the first manufacturer to discover this material and use it in the 1980s, calls their carbon fiber friction washer HT 100, because in their initial test, they ran it under tension for 100 miles and it was as good after that as before, with no appreciable wear on the friction material (although some on the metal washers). This synthetic material was first used to brake F-16 jets.

This woven carbon fiber compresses slightly, and that little bit of give contributes to excellent drag range. A bigger factor, however, is that the carbon fiber doesn't change characteristics when it heats up, because it is, in effect, already "cooked." With other friction materials, as heat builds up, the material changes and there is more friction. Other materials become inconsistent after they are heavily worked. The carbon fiber doesn't build up friction as it heats up.

Heat dissipation is obviously an important element that complements, or constricts, the action of the friction washers. As mentioned previously, the metal washers in the drag stack help disperse heat buildup from the action of the friction washers. The heavy main gear containing the drag acts as a heat sink, and takes out heat for all or part of most initial runs by a fish. However, these cannot dissipate the tremendous heat built up by the lengthy and sustained run of a really huge fish, and it is possible to overheat a reel to where the drag becomes paralyzed. The carbon fiber friction washer resists that type of problem better than other materials.

The carbon fiber is also especially good when applying maximum tension, or deliberately locking down the drag tension as far as it will go. Some friction washers, such as Teflon versions, can't be locked down enough on a conventional reel that is used for large fish; they still slip even when the drag star is turned as tight as possible. Bearing down on a big grouper so you can just pull the fish up out of the structure is a type of situation where you might need real lock-down power. The carbon fiber permits that type of lockdown; by comparison, asbestos and Teflon friction washers are slippery and, when compressed fully, may still give.

Carbon fiber friction washers also resist sustained compression as well as contamination from water, salt, dirt, grease, and oil. Although other materials are used in friction washers, many conventional reels now possess this material.

In most conventional reels, and especially better quality models, carbon fiber friction washers are used with stainless steel washers. The number of combined friction and metal washers in a drag stack varies; some manufacturers have between seven and thirteen elements, the greater number being on bigger reels, in each case alternating friction washers with metal ones. More friction washers increases the total drag surface area. This interleaved stack is topped with a tension spring washer for range and compression purposes, and might also have a spacer and a ball bearing, the latter providing a smooth feel without any load.

If the stainless steel washers are removed for maintenance, care should be taken when replacing them. These are stamped parts, and one side is slightly concave and the other slightly convex. Find out which side has a slight bow (use a straight edge), and put the bow side up. This way, when the drag is tightened, surface contact is made at the very end, and then flattens out and spreads over the full area of the friction washer.

The drag performance of most conventional reels is good to excellent, which it must be for the strenuous applications they endure. A majority of conventional reels sold are used for saltwater use, where the drag is frequently employed and often tested, so it has to be of high quality.

Spool diameter. Due to the normal usage of conventional reels, capacity is an important aspect. Capacity is linked to diameter, and the diameter of the spool at any given moment can also be a factor that affects drag. More line is recovered per turn of the reel handle when the diameter is greater than when it is smaller, so it is easier to retrieve line when the diameter of the spool is high. Where the drag is concerned, as line is pulled off the spool and the diameter decreases, it takes more effort to pull it off. So drag tension increases as the diameter of the spool decreases; it starts out at one level when the spool is full of line, but increases when the diameter of the spool is smaller due to a fish having taken plenty of line. Fortunately, with some lines the increased stretch of the longer length being fished tends to compensate for this.

This is a matter of physics and an unchangeable one, but it's important for anglers to recognize. When spool diameter has decreased and drag tension increased, it is all the more important to have a smooth drag and friction washers that maintain top performance. Because of the dynamics of carbon friction washers, drag tension remains on a more even level with heat buildup, rather than increasing as line is lost; these washers do not make it easier to pull line off when the level of line on a spool decreases, but they do make the drag tension more consistent, meaning that more even drag pressure is maintained.

Anti-Reverse Features

The anti-reverse component of reels is an element that restricts backward movement of the handle. In most conventional reels, it is a dog and ratchet mechanism that provides a variable amount of backward handle movement; this is a multi-stop anti-reverse. The amount of this movement is decided by the number of ratchets for the dog to catch. In some reels, it is a one-way roller bearing that allows no backward movement and is called continuous or infinite anti-reverse.

This aspect of conventional reels is of most significance to cast-and-retrieve applications and to some styles of baitfishing, primarily because it is relative to how the reel operates when the forward-turning motion is stopped. There is a natural tendency to pull up on the handle when not reeling, whether to set the hook or to momentarily stop while retrieving. If there is considerable play in the handle and drive gear when the reel stops, the handle may actually turn backward slightly. This produces a feeling of sloppiness or instability, and if there is too much backward movement of the handle, it may adversely affect hooksetting. Ideally, a conventional reel used for casting should engage instantly and firmly. The few models that have a continuous anti-reverse keep the handle and drive gear from moving even the slightest bit backward.

One thing that governs how quickly the drive gear engages in a reel with multi-stop anti-reverse is the number of ratchets in the system. The ratchets are little stops for a dog; as you turn the handle, this part slides over a ramp, and when the dog stops moving, it slides backward and engages a ratchet. The more ratchets there are, the quicker it engages; if there are ten ratchets, there will be ten stops per turn of the handle. More ratchets also mean finer teeth, which are easier to break or clog. Therefore, the number of ratchets varies on conventional reels depending on their designed usage. Infinite anti-reverse reels use a cam-operated roller and are self cleaning. This property may be more important to some anglers, like surf casters, for example, than any other.

In theory, having more ratchet stops could pose a strength problem, because you're depending on more ratchets with less material backing to stop the force of the hookset. This would seem like it could be a problem when using low-stretch lines and when using line that is overmatched by strength for the reel. However, having few ratchet stops may actually be worse, because that will provide perhaps an extra 4 or 5 inches of rod tip movement when you set the hook before you take up the slack and engage the dog. With a hard hookset using strong low-stretch line and a tight drag, you can develop a lot of force and strip the dog and ratchet system when there is this much room to move.

In a trolling application, where baits or lures are always set out under a fair load, when you have a strike you are already in a position to respond without any backward movement of the handle, no matter how many ratchets there are. So in this application, there is no relevance. In a casting application, where it is undesirable to have backward travel of the handle when you set the hook, more ratchet stops are advantageous for quick hooksets. A one-way roller bearing, which provides continuous anti-reverse, however, is most desirable.

Some conventional reels have an optional anti-reverse feature, which means that the anti-reverse can be disengaged so the handle and the spool can be turned either forward or backward. This is accomplished by moving a small spring-loaded lever on the sideplate (usually the right sideplate or handle sideplate). This may be referred to as a direct drive feature, although it is actually a mechanism for disengaging the anti-reverse.

This is a feature preferred for specific fishing applications, often when anglers want a direct feel of the line for strike detection, as when fishing with bait in the surf, or when they are drift fishing and putting the reel in and out of gear all the time, or when they are live-lining bait and want to let line out frequently to follow the movement of the bait. After casting, engage the main gear by moving the eccentric lever from the freespool position to the retrieve position, and then disengage the anti-reverse. When a fish takes and runs off, flip the anti-reverse lever into the on position and set the hook. If you leave the anti-reverse disengaged, the reel handle is free to move wildly backward as line comes off the spool, which could cause trouble. Make sure to keep your hand on the handle if you have the anti-reverse disengaged, or you'll have a runaway handle.

Other Features

Frame/spool materials. Because conventional reels are predominantly used in saltwater, and because they are susceptible to extreme stresses and fishing conditions, construction and materials must be of the highest caliber, and not only suitable for the marine environment but for withstanding severe usage. This is especially true in the larger models meant for heavy lines. One-piece aluminum frames are especially favored for heavy-duty applications; conventional reels used for light applications may have a multipiece frame. One-piece frames provide superior strength and precision alignment of the spool and other components. These may be of extruded anodized aluminum in top contemporary models and graphite in others (some older reels can be retrofitted with a one-piece frame through a conversion kit). At the present time, a graphite frame on a midsize reel is pushing the limits of graphite for use in saltwater. When newer grades of materials emerge, graphite may be used in heavier reels, which will lower weight and increase corrosion protection (it is essentially corrosion-proof). Graphite does not yet have the strength of properly manufactured aluminum; the newest generation of graphite material has greater strength than previous generations, and is more resistant to flexing, but it is still not up to aluminum. That is why bigger contemporary reels have aluminum frames and the smaller ones, meant for under 50-pound-test line, have graphite.

One of the problems that occurs in using midsize reels with graphite frames is that aggressive

The unheralded, disdained, and toothy gar can trace its genealogy back over 70 million years; the alligator gar species can grow to 300 pounds.

anglers fish them with heavier line than they are rated for, punishing both the spool and frame. A graphite-frame reel that is meant for 30-pound line, when used with 50- or 80-pound line, may break or become deformed.

Conventional reel manufacturers all strive for products with lower weight, but these items still tend to be heavy, and some brands a little heavier than others. The use of various materials has a bearing on weight, of course, but also on strength. There's always a balance. While anglers prefer lightweight equipment, they also need performance for battling bigger fish; doing this requires heavier materials and sturdy construction.

Aluminum spools, for example, are common on most top conventional reels, while a few also have chrome-plated cast bronze spools. You cannot get by with graphite spools on large saltwater conventional reels; they'll be broken left and right, especially when used with heavier line than the reel is intended for. You can use graphite spools on lightweight reels meant for either saltwater or freshwater use, but when these models are heavily used, they may not hold up to extreme pressure.

The manufacturing process for spools (and other components) has improved greatly and is one reason why today's reels are much better than yesterday's. Aluminum spools may be diecast, forged, or machined, which have different strengths and advantages. It is a lot cheaper to diecast, in which the metal is melted down into a mold. In forging, the metal is softened and banged into shape. In pure machining, a form is cut out of a solid block of aluminum; this is more labor intensive and expensive. Different uses and price points of reels dictate what process manufacturers use. The most demanding applications require forging because the molecules are compacted closer together in the forging process, which makes them stronger. However, it is not the process alone that accounts for strength; some aluminum alloys are much stronger than others, reacting differently to these processes.

Other manufacturing features include injection-molded sideplates and stamped stainless steel exposed parts. Sideplates used to be compression-molded, which meant taking the material in a mold and closing it. Most sideplates are now molded by injection methods, which results in superior strength. Environmental concerns have made the multi-step chrome-plating process used for exposed parts less desirable, so stamped stainless steel parts have become more prevalent.

Clamps/Lugs/Braces. Larger conventional reels used in saltwater may have clamps to secure the reel to the rod, lugs for attachment to a harness, and on some versions a brace for additional support.

Older conventional reels used to have metal rod clamps which were fastened around the rod with exposed wing nuts. These could get in the way of grabbing or lead to scratching. They've been replaced by molded synthetic clamps with recessed screws; there is no protrusion to get in the way, and they allow easier handling or even palming.

Reels meant for 30-pound line and up sport harness lugs on the top of the reel because they are often used for bigger fish. The angler is likely to wear a shoulder or kidney harness *(see),* which is attached to these lugs. Forward and rear braces on the biggest models are used to provide torsional stability on rods.

Reel designations. Conventional reels are generally classified by the strength of line that they are designed for and the capacity they hold. Some have long been characterized by an "O" (or ought) designation that was created many years ago, and which has been gradually fading in common parlance. However, some conventional reels for saltwater use have been labeled from 1/0 to 14/0 sizes, the latter meant for 130-pound-test line. The most popular sizes in this categorization system have been the 2/0, 4/0, and 6/0 models, which are respectively meant for 20-, 30- and 50-pound line. It is more likely to see contemporary reels designated by manufacturers according to the product series name, accompanied by some combination of model numbers and letters; these may or may not have an obvious connection to the intended line strength or line capacity.

Ergonomics. Conventional reels are by nature large, generally cumbersome, and often heavy. There are few points to be made about their ergonomic nature other than weight and rod clamps, which have been discussed, and the sideplates and handles. Cosmetics or appearance has nothing to do with function.

A smooth sideplate on the noncranking side of the reel (which is the left side for most conventional reels) is preferable for general comfort and use, especially in smaller versions that may be palmed. Bearings on the sides are not good for gripping; they used to be on the left side of some reels, but have generally been moved to the right, where they are also more secure. Likewise, some conventional reels now have a contoured cutout on the back of the frame for more thumb contact on the spool.

Some people like bigger handles and some smaller, owing to application and interest in power versus speed. Handles can be changed, and aftermarket accessories are available for this. The torpedo shape of many handle grips is still available on some conventional reels, but is dated and likely to disappear altogether on smaller products. Most small and midsize conventional reels have a soft grip handle, which has a large surface area and comfortable nonslip material. Generally, smaller reels have counterbalances and soft grips. Reels from 4/0 on up generally have torpedo grips and no counterbalance, and the largest reels have a barrel knob, because it's necessary to have a bigger grip that can be worked with a full hand.

Rods

Rods that are used with conventional reels may in general terms be called "conventional rods," but this is misleading because a vast array of rods falls under this oversimplified categorization. Some products in that array, in fact, may be called ocean rods, deep sea rods, boat rods, bay rods, pier rods, trolling rods, bottom fishing rods, live-bait rods, wire line rods, saltwater rods, downrigger rods, and so forth.

They are generally stiff, heavy-action products, with longer ones used in pier and bridge fishing and downrigger trolling and shorter ones in such boat work as casting, jigging, and bottom fishing. Special attributes exist with some models for particular applications, such as standup fishing (see).

For the most part, these are workhorse products with long, beefy two-handed handles that securely accommodate either level- or free-winding conventional reels, primarily the latter. Virtually all models have a long cushioned foregrip, large enough for two-handed use, for heavy-duty fish fighting and lifting, and the butt of many handles has a gimbal (sometimes with detachable butt cap) for insertion into a gimbaled rod holder or belt.

Heavy-duty double-foot rod guides are used with such rods and are mounted on top of the rod like the reel. This is because fish fighting is what such tackle does best, and the load of a gamefish on the line applies both a crushing downward force on the guide ring and frame, and a simultaneous tendency to torque or twist the rod, so guides must be of top quality and properly spaced and placed. Some rods feature a full complement of roller guides or tip and butt-end (stripper) roller guides. The guide rings are generally small, because little casting is done with most such rods (although it is done with some versions).

Lengths and materials vary, although fiberglass and composite materials are used with greater frequency in many more such rods than in other types, and few are exclusively made with graphite. Graphite may be used in some reel seats, however, all of which are extremely rugged; a few rods also feature trigger grips.

Unlike reels, many of the issues pertaining to rods used with conventional reels—functions, materials, components, etc.—are similar to those of other rods, and these are more fully detailed elsewhere (see: rod, fishing).

Using Conventional Tackle

Line. Although various line strengths from 6 through 130 pounds can be employed with the appropriate conventional gear, 20- through 80-pound lines are the most commonly used strengths in saltwater, and 12- through 30-pound lines are common in freshwater. Application dictates use, and one of the things that is frequently done by conventional reel users is stepping up to a higher strength line, which may not be what the reel is designed for. Often, anglers use a wider spool version of a particular model to step up in line strength while maintaining capacity. Some reels that are rated for 30-pound line are used by just as many people with 50- and 80-pound line on it as 30; such users may also tighten the drag way down for big bottom fish, and this type of action may be too much for the reel. There are implications to doing this, especially for the reel in terms of the frame and spool material, and drag tension adjustment, and these are discussed earlier in this section.

Fishing line is not pre-spooled onto conventional reels, although when purchased from some tackle retailers it may then be spooled by the dealer with the brand and strength of line you desire using a line winding machine. Because capacity is great, this can be beneficial for first-time conventional reel users, especially since it is important that the line be distributed properly on the reel and with ample tension. When you spool line on yourself, you should use a large bulk filler spool.

Nylon monofilament is the overwhelming choice of line type for conventional reels; there is some use of microfilament line, and on certain models (usually with narrow spool), wire line, lead core, and braided Dacron lines are employed. Because line coiling is not much of an issue on these large-spool reels, suppleness may not be much of a factor; abrasion resistance is a high priority in line for many conventional reel users, especially those

Using a fairly substantial conventional reel and rod equipped with wire line, a fisherman plays his catch with the butt of the rod in a seat gimbal.

who fish on the bottom and around wrecks and reefs. For casting applications, however, there is more of a need for a line with balanced properties, including less stiffness.

Obviously, conventional reels hold a lot of line. The range is from 275 to 1,000 yards with conventional diameter nylon monofilament line, and this is often understated by manufacturers. Using line that has the strength of conventional diameter nylon monofilament but has a thinner diameter allows for greater capacity, and using a heavier strength line with conventional diameter results in less capacity.

Generally, it is best to keep within the recommended line strengths when filling a reel. For the most part, you can take a conventional reel and not have a problem going 10 or 20 percent over the recommendations. Remember that when a manufacturer recommends using 30-pound line with a particular reel, that recommendation is based upon a standard 30-pound line with a conventional diameter. You can probably use conventional diameter 25- and 40-pound line as well, but it would not be worthwhile to use much heavier line. Not only is spool size and capacity an issue, but this reel may not be able to handle the greater stresses that might be generated with much heavier line, as noted previously. So, for example, putting 50-pound line on that reel could be problematic.

However, and this is where things get tricky, there are 50-pound lines that have the diameter of a conventional 30-pound line, so you can get just as much of it on the spool. Nevertheless, it is still line with a 50-pound breaking strength (and may actually break much higher); this may be capable of overpowering the reel frame or spool. If the rod is up to handling a lot of stress, and the line is rated to break at a minimum of 50 (often more) pounds, and the reel is meant for up to 30-pound line, then the forces generated on the reel by maximum pressures could be harmful.

On the other hand, you might use a 30-pound line with the diameter of conventional 17-pound line, and achieve much greater line capacity on the reel at a line strength that the reel is rated for. Or, you could "cheat" a little bit and use 40-pound line that has a diameter of conventional 20-pound line, if that benefited your fishing situation *(see: line)*. This is a grossly misunderstood aspect of reel usage that has largely been brought about by the emergence of thin diameter lines (nylon monofilaments, braids, and microfilaments).

Filling/refilling the spool. The various aspects of properly filling a reel spool are detailed elsewhere *(see: line)*. Putting line on a conventional reel spool is not complicated, but it must be done evenly and under tension. If you are an inexperienced angler or new to the use of conventional reels, the fastest and easiest way to fill a reel is to have it wound on by a linewinder, which is a professional machine. Many tackle dealers offer this service to their customers, although that service is seldom available from a mail order supplier or mass merchant.

In brief, the spooling process entails mounting the reel on the rod and running line from a service spool through the rod guides beginning at the top of the rod. Tie the line to the arbor of the spool, snip off the tag end excess, and reel the line on under tension. It is important to avoid or at least minimize twisting of the line during the spooling process, as detailed elsewhere *(see: line)*. Fill the spool to within no more than $3/16$-inch of the lip.

When the line gets low on the spool, or when it is old and needs replacement, you have the option of completely refilling the spool, or refilling only part of the spool. If a conventional reel holds 450 yards of line, it makes sense economically to refill with just 120 or 180 yards of line rather than the full 450, but that may not be a good practical decision.

When you partially refill the spool, you must tie a line-to-line knot *(see: knots, fishing)*. The weakest portion of a line is usually the knot, so this connection must be a good one to maintain the basic strength of the line, should that knotted section come under pressure. This is especially important when angling for large and strong fish. However, the problem with making a line-to-line knot for most conventional reel filling is that the line used is fairly heavy with a thick diameter, and the line-to-line knot is bulky and obtrusive on the reel spool. Furthermore, it may get caught on a rod guide when departing under extreme tension and cause a breakoff or spool overrun. Depending on your application, this disadvantage may be a deciding factor; most conventional reel users do not tie line-to-line knots on the reel, but spool up with new unknotted fresh line.

Line twist. Line twist is not an inherent problem in conventional reels. With other types of tackle, twist is often caused when the angler turns the handle against a slipping drag. Twist isn't possible on a conventional reel if the handle is turning and the spool is simultaneously slipping. When the drag mechanism is activated on a conventional reel, the spool rotates and line unwinds in an untwisted manner. There is no line twist unless it comes from lure use or is incurred through improper filling of the reel spool.

Matching and selecting. As with any type of fishing tackle, the issue of matching the right reel to the right rod is an important one, but in these times it is a relatively easy one. Conventional reels and rods are usually not packaged in combination, but there are some, and tackle retailers can match rods and reels for you. Most of the time a reel is purchased separately from a rod. Matching these used to be referred to as balancing, and properly paired outfits were referred to as "balanced tackle." This simply meant that the rod and reel felt right when used together; the outfit was not overly butt heavy due to a large reel paired with a lightweight rod, or tip heavy due to a small reel paired to a medium or heavy action rod.

Fishing rods are virtually all labeled by line classifications and by weight of objects to be used, which practically assures that you don't put a light-duty reel, for example, on a medium-heavy rod.

Conventional tackle is often classified by the manufacturers as being in a certain category and for a certain use, such as jigging or bottom fishing or trolling. Reels, for example, might be classified as high speed, or heavy-duty, or casting, as well as levelwind, but the exact definition of some of these categorizations can range from one manufacturer to the next, and in any event is determined by the line capacity, features, and components.

When selecting conventional tackle, as well as matching a rod and reel, you must take into consideration the applications for it. A beginning angler may be unsure what to select without any prior fishing experience. Guidance from a knowledgeable sales person is very helpful; such a person is more likely to be found in a specialized store (a sporting goods dealer or bait and tackle shop); guidance will not be found from a mail order supplier and seldom in a mass merchandise mart. Lacking this, or in addition to it, might be advice from an acquaintance or relative who has experience with this type of equipment and some knowledge of the fishing that a beginner is likely to do.

In a general sense, selecting conventional tackle starts with a determination of the size of fish that you are likely to catch and evaluating the conditions under which you'll be fishing. The larger and stronger the fish, the stronger the tackle necessary for beginners, until you get enough experience to use lighter gear. Fishing where there are a lot of obstructions usually requires medium or heavy grades of tackle; in saltwater, it is often necessary to turn or move a deep- or bottom-dwelling fish soon after it strikes to keep it from getting into cover, and this may take a lot of pressure and tough tackle.

Most selection thus starts with a determination of the line strength necessary for the conditions, and having the rod and reel appropriate for this. You should also give a lot of attention to line capacity so that you have an appropriate amount of line on the reel for the application.

Holding the rod and reel. Few conventional reels come in left-handed retrieve models, so most require left-handed holding and right-handed retrieval. This is akin to the use of baitcasting tackle, and it obviously favors people who are right-handed. Because less casting is done with conventional reels, applications are more demanding, the outfits are generally heavy, and most people are right-handed, however, the right-retrieve aspect of most conventional reels is not the problem that it is in baitcasting products. Large conventional reels especially are used for big fish, and it is common to attach these reels to a harness, which relieves the rod-holding arm. If a person is right-handed, all of the heavy-duty cranking of the reel is done with the stronger hand, which in theory is better for anyone who is right-handed, although not as desirable for a lefty.

Clearly, when casting with conventional tackle, right-handed anglers must keep their thumb on the reel spool and control the spool revolutions, then, after the cast, switch the rod into the left hand to reel with the right hand. Most conventional reels are too large for palming and are not conducive for usage like a baitcasting reel, so they are usually held by putting the left hand on the rod foregrip. This is obviously the hold for placing the butt in a belt gimbal or into a harness; for bait and jig fishing, the butt is tucked into the armpit and between the left arm and body, with the hand on the foregrip and the rod held level or pointed slightly down. Holding the foregrip with the left hand also helps with guiding the line on the spool in a level manner, and with feeling the line by keeping your fingers on it.

Casting technique. The actual method of casting with conventional tackle is similar to that for baitcasting tackle, although the former is heavier and the objects cast are usually much heavier, so the casting motion is more one of throwing than casting, with the exception of conventional tackle used in surf fishing *(see)*.

Setting up the centrifugal casting control is necessary for those reels that possess this component, and the drag should likewise be pre-adjusted. To cast, begin with the reel facing upward and toward you. Adjust the drag for fishing. Hang the lure or weight from 4 to 8 inches below the tip of the rod and place the thumb of the rod-holding hand on the spool so the spool can't turn; then move the eccentric lever into the freespool position.

The vast majority of conventional reel users employ thumb pressure to brake the spool because most do not have any other means of controlling spool revolution. Applying thumb pressure is an

An angler plays a fish on conventional tackle, being careful to use his thumb to evenly lay the line on the reel as it is retrieved.

action learned through trial and error and perfected with experience; it requires the application of different degrees of braking tension for the weights on the line, distances being cast, and types of rod and reel being used.

Keep tension on the line with your thumb; this will be released at the optimum point in the forward motion of the cast. When this tension is released, line flows off the spool and out through the guides, carried by the weight of the object at the terminal end of the line. Applying too much pressure results in a cast that is short, and applying too little pressure results in a backlash.

Accuracy is often not an issue with conventional tackle because anglers do a lot of open-water casting with this equipment; however, it can definitely be an issue when casting bait to visible, quickly moving, or feeding fish. Achieving distance is an issue for some conventional tackle users, especially surf anglers *(see: casting)*.

Setting/checking drag. Before any on-the-water use of a conventional reel, it is vital to set the drag to the proper amount of tension. Issues pertaining to drag in conventional reels were reviewed earlier in this section, and using and setting drag is covered in more detail elsewhere *(see: drag)*.

Briefly, however, in typical fishing with conventional reels, drag tension is increased or decreased by turning a drag star (radial-arm star wheel), which is located under the handle on the sideplate. The drag star threads onto the gear stud or drive gear, which is connected to the handle, so it rotates concurrently with the handle without affecting the setting. Turning the drag star clockwise or forward increases tension; turning it counterclockwise or backward decreases tension.

Anglers set the drag on conventional reels at 25 to 30 percent of the breaking strength of their line. This is measured by some people with a short length of line on a straight pull off the reel. It is measured by others with line running through the rod guides and the rod flexed as it would be in fishing circumstances. Most people use the "feels good" method of establishing drag tension by pulling line off the reel and adjusting the star wheel until the tension feels right. The most precise way to measure drag tension is by using a reliable scale and attaching it to the line. In any method, the objective is to adjust the drag so that the line will not slip until the appropriate amount of tension is applied.

If a reel is used infrequently, it is a good idea at the end of each outing to back the drag tension off to relieve pressure on the drag washers. This is not quite as important for conventional reels with graphite drag washers because they resist compression better than washers made of other friction material; nevertheless, releasing tension is still a good idea. When starting a day of fishing, you should check and adjust the drag tension setting before starting to fish. Many an angler has neglected this and found upon hooking the first fish of the day that the drag was so weak it impaired hook setting, or so tight that it adversely affected fish playing.

Maintenance and repair. Maintenance is an ongoing issue for conventional tackle users, especially saltwater anglers. Rods and reels must be washed down every time they are taken on the water, even if not used, since they are likely to be exposed to salt spray. Use a fine but ample spray of freshwater, rather than a hard stream, to clean the reel and remove salt deposits, and do so as soon as possible after you return to the dock or launch site. Use soap and a scrub brush to remove any hardened matter. Warm water is best if available; make sure not to use a hard stream, which could drive salt deposits into the internal mechanisms. Dry off excess freshwater on the reel and lubricate exposed areas, perhaps with a pressurized spray oil. A light coating of oil with a rag can also be applied to exposed metal parts. Give the reel a chance to dry out completely, and store it in a cool, dry place, not in a bag that is wet or which will promote condensation.

Make sure to periodically examine screws and fittings. If the reel has any loose part, which is most likely to be a sideplate screw, it should be tightened as soon as you notice it.

Many people tend to excessively lubricate conventional reels, which may cause harm if oil or grease gets on parts that don't need, or shouldn't have, the lubrication. That includes graphite drag washers. Over-lubrication can be especially problematic for a reel employed for casting. Some older conventional reels used to have built-in lubrication points with spring loaded balls, which worked great when they were used right, but people had a tendency pump too much oil in there and it got into other parts of the reel. Using the wrong kind of lubrication is also a problem. Follow the manufacturer's recommendations for the type of lubrication, the locations, and the frequency, as this will vary with different brands.

Details on tackle maintenance are discussed elsewhere *(see: tackle care/maintenance/repair)*. Manufacturers recommend that conventional reels be overhauled at least once a season, perhaps more if used vigorously. Periodically oil and grease frictional parts, but don't overdo it. Some reels come with small oil or grease tubes, and these can be purchased from tackle suppliers or obtained from the manufacturer. A thorough cleaning requires disassembling most of the reel, scrubbing or rinsing most of the gunk from the parts, drying, and then relubricating and regreasing. If you are unsure about doing this yourself, have a reel service and repair shop do it, or send it to the manufacturer for servicing.

COOK ISLANDS

The Cook Islands are a group of 24 coral atolls and volcanic islands in the South Pacific Ocean,

flanked on the west by Tonga and Samoa and on the east by Tahiti. The group is about the same distance south of the equator as Hawaii is north of it. Originally a New Zealand protectorate, the Cook Islands became independent in 1965 but exist in free association with New Zealand, which provides considerable assistance to these islands.

Named for the English explorer Captain James Cook, the island group has a total population of approximately 19,000 friendly and good-hearted people of mostly Polynesian descent. Nearly all speak English in addition to Cook Island Maori, and there is little crime.

The capital of the group and site of an international airport is Rarotonga, a high volcanic island and the most developed one in terms of quality accommodation. The main town is Avarua. Light aircraft make regular flights from Rarotonga to most of the other islands in the group, regularity depending on demand.

Currency in the Cook Islands is the New Zealand dollar, supplemented by coins and notes minted for local use that are not negotiable outside the Cook Islands but are sought after by collectors. This is one of the few places in the world where you can get a $3 bill.

Several 28- to 38-foot charter boats work out of Rarotonga, as so several smaller open boats, but they are not of international quality. Serious anglers should bring their own tackle. With little in the way of offshore structures, most boats troll around the edge of Rarotonga or target the fish-attracting device off the airport. Catches are mostly yellowfin and skipjack tuna, wahoo, and mahimahi (dolphin); some marlin, mostly blues and some blacks, are also caught.

Fishing success is a little spotty, with more wahoo from June through September (the cooler, drier winter) and the other species more common from December through March, which is the warmer, wetter time of year, with occasional cyclones (hurricanes), and temperatures from 22°C to 30°C.

Shore fishing centers on several reef passes, Muri lagoon, or the town wharf. Lures or baits are used. All manner of tropical reef species can be caught, with bluefin and giant trevally the most sought-after gamefish.

A popular sportfishing destination in the Cook Islands is the picturesque atoll of Aitutaki (pronounced a-to-tark-ee). One of the most scenic spots in the Cooks, it has 13 islands (called *motus* locally) and a ring reef 45 kilometers in circumference, which encloses a magnificent lagoon.

The atoll is about 8 kilometers long and 4 kilometers wide, and has a population of approximately 2,000 people. An hour by light plane north of Rarotonga, Aitutaki has accommodations that range from full hotel to guest house. There are some enthusiastic anglers here, and visiting anglers are advised to join the local fishing club on arriving.

There are two 30-foot charter boats at Aitutaki, which are probably the best available in the Cook Islands, although isolation makes maintenance difficult. As in Rarotonga, visiting anglers should bring their own tackle. Of the numerous small open boats, some are of dubious quality.

Trolling outside the reef produces barracuda and wahoo in the colder months, and mahimahi, yellowfin tuna, skipjack tuna, and blue marlin during the warmer months. Blue marlin over 200 kilograms have been caught here from small boats. Flying fish are a popular trolling bait and are caught at night under lights.

Deep jigging with metal lures on the reef dropoffs has produced such tough customers as dogtooth tuna and bigeye and black trevally, as well as a wide range of reef fish. Anglers fish the reef by casting inward from a boat or, more interestingly, by wading out to the reef on the lee side. It is plate coral and easy to walk on, but anglers need to beware of any large swells.

During warm months, heavy (15-kilogram) casting tackle and large surface lures or spoons can see giant and bluefin trevally action in the surf breaks. At any time of the year, lighter tackle (4 kilograms) and smaller minnow lures, spoons, and soft-plastic lures can produce a lot of fun around the reef and inside the lagoon. Common species are smaller trevally, longtoms (needlefish or houndfish), queenfish, a wide range of colorful wrasses, reef snapper, and small grouper. Many of these species are adept at diving under coral heads for shelter, so anglers should use abrasion-resistant leaders.

The lagoon itself is extensive and up to 15 meters deep in places. There is excellent fishing inside for a wide variety of fish, including barracuda, bonefish, and several species of trevally.

The bones here average 3 to 4 kilograms and are found in reasonable numbers. As yet, however, no one has located an area that produces classical flats fishing. Most bonefish seem to be located in an area of the lagoon called *vehu*, which roughly translates as "milk water." It appears to be a giant "mud"— an area of bottom disturbed by feeding fish. Unfortunately, it is too deep and dirty for sight fishing, and most bonefish here are taken on bait.

Many of the other islands in the Cook group can be reached by light aircraft from Rarotonga. These include Atiu, Mangaia, Mitiaro, Mauke, Manihiki, Pukapuka, and Penrhyn. All of these have some form of accommodation, be it only in guest houses or private homes.

No formal charter boats exist in these places, but often a local fisherman can be persuaded to take a visiting angler out. In addition, nearly everywhere you go, good sport can be had casting small lures off the shore. Soft plastics and small metal baitfish imitations are best.

These outer islands are ideally suited to the adventurous angler who is prepared to take things as they are; there's no five-star service here. The people are kind and friendly, however, and if this is reciprocated by the visitor, they will often go out of their way to help.

A great many fishing stories have come from the outer Cook Islands. Some of the more reliable ones include the capture of a wahoo in excess of 80 kilograms, and an 11.5-kilogram bonefish speared from a school that included even bigger fish in one remote lagoon. Difficult access to some areas has been the main barrier to further exploration of fishing opportunities in the outer Cook Islands. Nevertheless, this region may have some rewarding angling surprises in store in the future.

As in many Pacific islands, Sunday is a day of rest in the Cook Islands, and Sunday fishing is frowned upon. The intensity of this prohibition varies from island to island, so ask the locals before wetting a line. When interacting with Cook Islanders, visitors should be aware that time means little here, and punctuality is not a strong point. You have to go with the flow. Dress is informal, but revealing clothing should not be worn when visiting towns and villages.

COOLWATER FISH

An occasional term for freshwater species whose optimum environment is water of intermediate temperature, approximately from 60° to 70°F; northern pike, muskellunge, yellow perch, walleye, and smallmouth bass are among this group. They inhabit cool to moderately warm rivers and lakes of moderate fertility, often existing in waters that also accommodate species preferring colder and warmer temperatures.

See: Coldwater Fish; Warmwater Fish.

COPEPODS

Minute crustaceans at the bottom of the food chain *(see)* that consume phytoplankton *(see)*.

CORAL REEF

A coral reef is a complex colony of individual animals called polyps. These produce limestone skeletons cemented together by blue-green algae, resulting in massive but surprisingly fragile formations.

Polyps are filter feeders that trap floating plankton in their tentacles and eat it. As polyps die, new ones expand the reef by growing on their remains. Polyps enjoy a mutually beneficial relationship with algae *(see)* living inside them. This efficient symbiosis makes coral reefs rich with an incredible diversity of animal and fish life. Smaller fish on coral reefs attract larger predators; thus, anglers may find it advantageous to fish near them or along their perimeter.

In the coral reef environment, life has evolved elaborate strategies for exploiting every available niche. The sea's nutrients are extracted and redistributed, and shelter from predators is provided.

Coral reefs have existed for millions of years and are as ancient as rain forests. They grow in tropical waters where sea temperatures are more than 70°F all year. They occur only off the east coasts of the world's continents, seldom farther north or south of the equator than 22°, in clear water with maximum light penetration, and rarely at depths exceeding 200 to 250 feet. Optimum growth occurs within a few yards of the surface.

Boat anchors destroy a lot of coral reef, so they should never be dropped directly on a reef but rather in the sandy patches found between coral formations. (The water over a reef appears dark; sandy areas are light.) Only anchors that will hold in sand should be used, and at least four times as much line as the water depth should be laid out. Boats should navigate slowly and carefully in all reef areas to avoid the possibility of striking projecting reef formations, and should not be navigated through shallow formations.

See: Reef.

CORBINA, CALIFORNIA
Menticirrhus undulatus.

Other names—California whiting, surf fish, sucker.

The California corbina belongs to the family of fish Sciaenidae (croaker and drum) and is a member of the whiting group. But because it lacks a swim bladder, it cannot make the croaking or drumming noises characteristic of the croaker family. This bottom fish is popular with surf and pier anglers, and has excellent table value; it should not be confused with the corvina *(see)*.

Identification. The body of the California corbina is elongated and slightly compressed, with a flattened belly. Its head is long and the mouth is small, the upper jaw scarcely reaching a point below the front of the eye. The first dorsal fin is short and high, the second long and low. Coloring is uniformly gray with incandescent reflections, and with wavy diagonal lines on the sides.

This croaker and the yellowfin croaker *(Umbrina roncador; see croaker, yellowfin)* are the only two of the eight coastal croaker present in California waters that have a barbel on the lower jaw. The California corbina can be distinguished from the yellowfin croaker by the presence of only one weak spine at the front of the anal fin; the yellowfin croaker has two strong spines.

California Corbina

Size. The average corbina weighs 1 pound. The all-tackle record is 6 pounds, 2 ounces, but corbina are reported to grow to 8 pounds.

Distribution. California corbina occur from the Gulf of California in Mexico to Point Conception, California.

Habitat. Preferring sandy beaches and shallow bays, the California corbina is a bottom fish appearing along the coastal surf zone.

Life history/Behavior. Males mature when two years old, at a length of 10 inches; females mature at age 3, at 13 inches long. Spawning occurs from June through September, although it is heaviest in July and August, and takes place offshore. California corbina travel in schools or small groups, although large individuals often solitary.

Food and feeding habits. A fussy feeder, the California corbina primarily consumes sand crabs and spits out bits of clam shells and other foreign matter; they also consume small crustaceans and marine worms. Corbina scoop up mouthfuls of sand and separate the food by sending the sand through their gills. Adults are sometimes seen feeding in the surf, occasionally in water so shallow that their backs are exposed.

Angling. Surf and pier anglers use bottom fishing rigs to catch corbina on small crabs and worms.

CORDAGE
A nautical term for rope or line.

CORK
(1) A cork-bodied float *(see)*.

(2) A common material used for the grip and handle of a fishing rod *(see: rod, fishing)*.

CORVINA
Members of the Sciaenidae family (drum and croaker), corvina inhabit the Pacific Ocean and are known for the noises they make. These fish are often called corbina as well as corvina, and both words appear in the Spanish and Portuguese languages for common names applied to various drum and croaker.

They are typically referred to as croaker by some anglers and as weakfish by others, and inhabit tropical and temperate seas. Almost all are inshore bottom-feeding fish usually found over sandy bottoms, either in schools or in small groups. Corvina are generally Pacific species, primarily inhabiting the Gulf of California and waters south of the gulf; they are likely to inhabit the surf line and to hug the near shoreline, feeding on crustaceans, worms, and small fish. They generally have a silver sandy coloration that blends with this environment. Most if not all are good to eat.

Species that may be encountered include the orangemouth or yellowmouth corvina *(Cynoscion xanthulus)*, which occurs throughout the Gulf of California in Mexico and south to Acapulco, as well as in the Salton Sea in Southern California, and can grow to 36 inches; the Gulf corvina *(Cynoscion othonopterus)*, a resident of the upper Gulf of California that grows to 28 inches; the shortfin corvina *(Cynoscion parvipinnis)*, a surf fish also in the Gulf of California and south to Mazatlán that grows to 20 inches; the yellowfin corvina *(Cynoscion stolzmanni)*, ranging from the Gulf of California to Peru and growing to 35 inches; the striped corvina *(Cynoscion reticulatus)*, ranging from the Gulf of California to Panama and growing to 35 inches; and the totuava or totoaba *(Totoaba macdonaldi)*, a white seabass *(see: seabass, white)* look-alike that was once abundant and is now endangered. It inhabits the middle and upper Gulf of California and once grew to 6 feet and 300 pounds. The totuava is the largest of all croaker and was slaughtered in great numbers in the early 1900s for its air bladder, which was used as a soup base, and then later for its meat.

See: Corbina, California; Croaker; Croaker, Yellowfin; Drum; Queenfish (Croaker); Weakfish.

COSTA RICA
Costa Rica means "rich coast," an appellation bestowed in the sixteenth century by Spanish conquistadors seeking gold. They didn't find that precious metal, but traveling anglers today find a different sort of treasure in this peaceful and scenic country. That treasure has fins, grows large, fights hard, comes in varied denominations, and is plentiful. Offering a stable democratic government, an excellent overall tourism base, an emphasis on ecotourism, a favorable climate, and easy access from the United States, Costa Rica has become one of the most popular destinations for the traveling angler.

Facing the Caribbean on its east coast and the Pacific on the west, Costa Rica can offer exciting action for the premier gamefish swimming in both environs. In particular, anglers land tarpon and snook in the Caribbean, and sailfish and marlin in the Pacific; dolphin, wahoo, cubera snapper, amberjack, jack crevalle, roosterfish, grouper, barracuda, cobia, yellowfin tuna, and a plethora of other species in offshore and inshore waters. And that's just in the oceans. A few lakes and countless miles of inland rivers and estuaries produce rainbow trout, guapote, machaca, and other species.

Orangemouth Corvina

This is indeed a lot for a small country, and there is no lack of lodges and charter operations for visitors. Many camps specifically devoted to angling exist on both coasts. Most have excellent equipment and boats and are easily reached by connecting through the capital city of San José.

Caribbean Coast

Big fish, lots of fish, arm-wrenching action, more fish jumps in one week than most people see in a lifetime, double hookups—these are just some of the reports that regularly filter out of experiences on the Caribbean side of Costa Rica. This is one of the premier places in the world to fish for tarpon and snook. It is *the* place for the angler who prefers relatively light tackle and the resulting muscle-match with fish that are tough and big, but not so big that they require special tackle and tactics. Something on the order, say, of a 20-pound snook or a 70-pound tarpon. You can catch a few other species for diversion as well. Guapote, machaca, mojarra, and mangrove snapper are small but plentiful fish that provide fun in the creeks and tidal rivers. Fishing the coastal rivers, lagoons, and nearshore open water here is sure to delight all but the most jaded angler.

A particularly fine aspect of this fishery is the jungle treks to and from fishing spots. Anglers can enjoy the flora and fauna, which include rich vegetation and plentiful birdlife, not to mention assorted monkeys.

Along Costa Rica's largely unindented Caribbean coast, the main rivers include the Colorado, Parismina, and Tortuguero, each with many tributaries and lots of jungle atmosphere, some in or close to extensive wildlife refuges. Irrespective of tide, the rivers flow well, but during the rainy season they are swollen and muddy, and are not fished. Lodges are located near the mouths of these rivers and can be reached via a short flight from San José.

Other areas of the coast have little access. Some remote waters in the north near the Nicaragua border have been accessed in recent years via a mobile houseboat operation, fishing lagoons, rivers, and nearshore waters in both northern Costa Rica and southeastern Nicaragua. Tarpon and snook headline the fishing here, but great variety of species, especially in the lagoons and including the likes of sharks and huge sawfish, also thrive here.

Tarpon. Tarpon, or *sabalo,* are the premier attraction in Costa Rica's Caribbean waters. Although tarpon grow bigger elsewhere, they are nowhere more numerous or less finicky. Tarpon in the 50- to 100-pound range are caught all along the Caribbean coast. Some bigger fish are possible, and 75-pounders are about average. In the past, much of the angling took place in rivers and at river mouths, but netting and increased boat activity have gradually changed this. Today more action is available in the ocean, off the river inlets, where there are big fish and also schools of them.

A tarpon takes to the air along the Costa Rican coast near the Parismina River.

While in the ocean, the tarpon travel in great schools, then move individually into the freshwater lagoons and rivers that characterize the Caribbean coastline. More a mating rendezvous than spawning grounds, these beautiful jungle rivers and backwaters used to offer the kind of sport people dream about. Not long ago, in the early morning hours one could often see hundreds of tarpon rolling on top. This has not been a staple of recent years, but it could happen again if efforts to prohibit commercial netting near the river mouths hold up.

Thus, the tarpon are mostly sought in the ocean, water conditions permitting. In rough weather, going to sea can be an adventure due to bars at the river mouths. At some camps, however, oceangoing fishing boats have evolved from small jonboats to rugged center-console V-draft fiberglass vessels. This not only increases accessibility, but it also improves the fishing; when the water is rough, angling can be difficult or unproductive in a small boat.

Anglers practice both sight and blind casting for tarpon in the nearshore waters off the river mouths, depending on locale and water clarity. It is easier and more enjoyable to search out and cast to roving pods of fish, the method favored when and where the water is clear and fairly calm. This is the most preferred form of fishing, and under favorable conditions opportunities to cast to pods of fish with flycasting, baitcasting, and spinning gear abound. Flycasters use 12-weight fly rods, fast-sinking lines, and large streamer flies.

This is not flats fishing, and the boats cannot be poled to intercept fish. When the schools are observed, boats attempt to move into position to intercept them, trying to drift where possible, as motor noise will spook the fish. Although spotting and casting are preferred, when storms have dispersed the schools and colored the water, there is likely to be little sight fishing. Then fish can be caught by deep jigging with heavy metal jigs.

Tarpon are available in the Costa Rican Caribbean all year, but the best fishing is usually from mid-January through June, when the heavy rains start. After June the bulk of the tarpon move out; although some fish are around, they are not as concentrated. Action is also good, however, from late August to mid-October, when the ocean flattens and anglers can more readily position themselves outside the river mouths. At that time, offshore adventurers often find schools of jack crevalle, kingfish, tripletail, barracuda, and occasional cobia, sailfish, yellowfin tuna, and wahoo, although the offshore environs and species are usually pursued only by anglers who have caught plenty of tarpon and look to do something different offshore for a day.

Snook. Although tarpon receive a great deal of attention, snook are an equally formidable resource in Costa Rican waters and, unlike tarpon, are found on both coasts. Several species of snook inhabit the Caribbean coast, including the fat snook (locally called *calba*).

The best fishing for snook is from July through October, when the bigger fish are available. During that period it is possible to encounter a surf run of 20-pounders, and even bigger fish have been landed. Among the many world-record snook taken from Costa Rica's Caribbean waters are a 53-pound, 10-ounce fish that holds the 20-pound line-class and all-tackle world records. That fish was caught in October at Parismina, and shows the size potential of these fish. Generally, a big snook from these waters would weigh more than 25 pounds. When small snook are abundant, it is possible to catch dozens in a day. Snook fishing is concentrated both in the rivers and in the frothing surf at the river mouths, with the latter producing the biggest specimens.

When the rain begins in late November and December, the region also gets a run of fat snook that average about 4 pounds, seldom more than 7. Pound-for-pound they fight as well as their big brothers, and catches of dozens or more a day are not uncommon on ultralight tackle.

Pacific Coast

A volcanic mountain landmass separates the eastern and western coasts of Costa Rica, and even though the distance between oceans varies from just 75 to 180 miles, the gap might as well be a lot farther, as the coasts differ greatly from one another. Costa Rica's 275-mile-long Pacific coastline is a narrower lowland region broken by a number of bays and is much more developed. Sportfishing has progressed significantly in the past two decades. From Nicaragua on the north to Panama on the south, there's an incredible number and great variety of fish, an almost year-round season, easy accessibility, and a well-established infrastructure.

For light-tackle offshore anglers in particular, this has been something of a mecca. The world-record books are cluttered with fish caught in these waters, especially Pacific snook.

Sailfish are the mainstays of the fishing here, but blue, black, and striped marlin are all part of the mix, not to mention dolphin (dorado) and yellowfin tuna, and a host of inshore species headlined by roosterfish, cubera snapper, and amberjack.

Well-developed facilities exist at many places along the coast, including Quepos, Flamingo, Guanamar, Tamarindo, Golfito, Ocotal, and Drakes Bay. The hot ports have differed over the years, as billfish availability and water temperature changes have varied. Quepos, which has also become a popular tourism town, is generally regarded as the leading sportfishing port on the southern Pacific coast. In recent years, however, some operators have become more mobile, and mother-ship operations even exist, to take anglers to less accessible or more active areas. This has paid off for some such operators, particularly in the 1990s when El Niño affected billfish areas, making the northerly waters much more active than the southerly ones.

At the centrally located Quepos, the top billfishing time is usually from November through May, when the weather is also at a peak and dry, with seas fairly calm. January through March is peak—a time when the area is crowded with sportfishing boats, requiring arrangements well in advance. It is typical in this region to land between 5 and 10 sailfish on an ordinary day; when conditions are right, several times that number are possible. With plenty of in-season sailfish action, few boats venture farther offshore for attempts at marlin, wahoo, and tuna.

Sailfishing normally takes place within 30 miles of port. Trolling with rigged baits, usually mullet, is standard procedure. The presence of many sails, however, presents light-tackle opportunities, making this area ripe for bait-and-switch strategies, using teasers to draw the fish in for fly presentation.

In normal years the prime sailfish season is a bit different in the waters fished from Flamingo and nearby Guanamar and Tamarindo. May through September has historically been the hot period, when the seas here are calm. Conversely, in the rough-water period, from November through March, the marlin are most likely to be present, although they can be caught at other times. It was just out in front of the Guanamar Sportfishing Resort at Playa Carrillo in May of 1991 that Costa Rica's 13th Annual International Sailfish Tournament posted the highest score in tournament history with a phenomenal 1,691 sails caught and released in four days. May has varied as a good month, however, in years since that event. Traditionally, December through June has been the most productive season, with April and May considered peak.

One of the most productive fishing areas here is Guardian Bank, 120 miles west of Punta Guiones. Rising 1,700 fathoms to 15 or 20 fathoms in the blue water, it has been widely fished by commercial tuna boats. But immense concentrations of bait, particularly squid, make the bank a playground for huge marlin and swordfish, as well as locomotive-size tuna and other species.

The northern Pacific coastal area above Punta Guiones is handicapped by heavy winds that usually blow from late November through March or early April, and some operators in that area move south during the northerlies.

Although the winds and resultant heavy seas don't make for particularly pleasant fishing, it doesn't mean the fish aren't there, and increasingly larger and more seaworthy boats have made it possible to enjoy what is often the best season for big marlin, with a liberal sprinkling of sails, dorado, roosterfish, and tuna at that time.

In the northwest at the long, wide Gulf of Papagayo, anglers run offshore to the deep water or fish around the Bat Islands. These islands have been productive for billfish and other species, as have the grounds offshore at the 100-fathom mark, and off of Catalina Island.

This is a bait-rich area, due in part to the easterly North Equatorial Current, which washes into the gulf in the summer months, drawing small-game species and larger ones. The black marlin, which have averaged 300 pounds in the past but have also been much larger, usually arrive in the gulf in May. Blue and striped marlin follow, although they are not as populous.

Although the emphasis is on billfish along the Pacific, these certainly aren't the only attraction. Dolphin are sometimes a nuisance, bouncing a billfish bait as fast as it hits the water. They are thrillers on light tackle, however, and the long-standing International Game Fish Association (IGFA) all-tackle record dolphin (an 87-pounder) came from Costa Rica.

When the billfishing is slow, or for extra diversity, there is plenty of opportunity for catching varied reef and bottom species by trolling, casting to rocky shorelines, or jigging or baitfishing in inshore water. Roosterfish from 20 to 70 or more pounds are possible, as are similar-size cubera snapper in some locales. The inshore waters have produced numerous world-record cuberas. Amberjack, snapper, grouper, jack crevalle, dogtooth snapper *(pargo)*, and other species are on the menu as well, although species and sizes may vary by locale.

With so much boat fishing for various species, visiting anglers pay little attention to the shoreline. But at least four species of snook frequent the Pacific coast, including the large-growing Pacific black snook. An all-tackle world-record 57-pound, 12-ounce black snook was caught at the mouth of the Río Naranjo, accessed from Quepos. A 69-pounder was caught in the 1960s at the mouth of the Tarcoles River, and a 72-pounder was caught at an unidentified site in 1992.

As with fishing in the Caribbean, most snook are caught at or close to river mouths. They can be caught year-round on this side of the country, but big fish are more likely in December, January, May, and June.

Conservation is a major consideration in Costa Rica, as it is in many Central and South American countries. It must be if the Pacific coastal fishery is to survive. Commercial longliners have been hurting sailfish and other billfish; tuna have been under a lot of pressure; and netting in estuaries and at river mouths has impacted tarpon and snook. The Costa Rican government has had some success with regulating these activities.

Inland

The San Juan River, which flows along the border with Nicaragua and forms the Colorado River, has recently become a more prominent site. Tarpon are said to be up the river nearly all year, but the dry months of March and April are best. Good fishing can also be expected in September and October when the tarpon reach as far upriver as Caño Negro Lagoon, 40 miles south of Lake Nicaragua but within the confines of Costa Rica. The rapids are perhaps the best location on the river, and there are two on the San Juan—one close to El Castillo on the upper river not far from San Carlos, and the other about 10 miles upriver from the confluence with the Río Sarapiquí.

Snook are also available in this region, and October and November are the best months. They move up through the Colorado River into the San Juan and all the way to Lake Nicaragua and the Río Frío in Costa Rica. Fish from 10 to 15 pounds linger around small tributaries to the main river.

Guapote have grown into a popular freshwater prey throughout Costa Rica. Dubbed "rainbow bass" because their iridescent shadings are reminiscent of rainbow trout, they are fished similar to largemouth bass. Also a popular food fish, guapote are extremely strong fighters, seldom breaking the water surface, although they do take surface lures viciously and pounce on trolled lures.

In the rivers, guapote favor deep pools and cuts, and generally calm water. They inhabit all of the rivers draining to the Caribbean or following a northerly course to the San Juan basin (on the Pacific side, guapote are present only in rivers north of Puntarenas).

The favorite guapote site in Costa Rica, however, is Lake Arenal. Guapote became landlocked here when the dam was finished, and they flourished into a great freshwater fishing attraction. Surrounded by lush, green mountains and dairy farms, Arenal provides a high percentage of the nation's hydroelectric power and is a popular overall recreation area. In addition to guapote, the lake also has machaca, a high-jumping silvery fish that readily takes a fly or surface popper. Its acrobatic leaps, scaled sides, and bone-hard mouth have caused locals to refer to the machaca as the little tarpon.

Arenal Volcano stands at one end of the lake and is one of the most active volcanoes in the world, bellowing towers of lava that create an incredible pyrotechnic display at night. Guide service is available locally, a few lodges exist at the lake, and there

 Wild saltwater sportfish with low levels of fat and calories include sea bass, red snapper, and halibut; high levels belong to flounder and mackerel.

are campsites nearby. A number of the rivers that feed Lake Arenal from the high mountaintops have reputedly been stocked with rainbow trout.

Among the many Costa Rican rivers popular among anglers is the Teffaba, in the southern part of the country. It can be waded for more than 50 kilometers of its length, from the Brujo Bridge to Palmar Norte. It is muddy about half the time during the rainy season, but during dry months it is a beautiful stream.

A combination of fast water, deep and shallow ponds, and a broad estuary where the Teffaba flows into the Pacific provide a shot at both freshwater and saltwater species. Snook, red snapper, and occasionally jacks work well up the river, but big snook are found among the hundreds of square kilometers of estuaries that wind through the mangroves.

Rivers flowing east into the Caribbean and north into the Río San Juan offer Costa Rica's best bobo fishing. The bobo is a variety of mullet that occasionally grows to 12 pounds and favors fast water. Most are taken on a variety of natural bait, and some on spinners. The bobo also frequents Panama and Nicaragua, but only in Costa Rica, and among local anglers, are they highly regarded as a sportfish. They head for fast water when hooked, and use the current to good advantage. They are an excellent table fish. These rivers also harbor machaca, croaker, and other species that are great on ultralight tackle.

The San Carlos, Sarapiquí, Reventazón, and Rio Frío are the most popular rivers with local anglers, not only for the fishing but also because of their beauty and clear, clean waters during the dry season. They are muddy during the rainy period, especially in the late afternoons, but even then they usually begin to clear by midmorning, as most of the rain comes in the late afternoon.

Although these streams carry a great volume of water, they can be waded for 75 percent of their length, and most can be reached within a two-hour drive from San José.

COUNCIL
See: Fisheries Management Council.

COUNTERSHADING
A scheme for coloring fishing plugs that contrasts with nature by placing the most visible color on the underside, or belly, of the lure and the least visible color on the top, or back.
See: Lure.

COUNTING DOWN
A method of determining the relative depth to which a lure has sunk by counting each second that it is sinking. The sink rate of a lure varies with its weight, material, and shape. To determine relative depth, start counting every second once the lure enters the water until it strikes bottom and the line goes limp. If you counted to 10, then the next time you let out the lure you know that counting to 5 puts that lure halfway in the water column, and counting to 9 brings it just above the bottom.

By measuring the line, you can be more precise and determine the sink rate. If it took a count of 10 to put the lure on the bottom in 20 feet of water (measured from the surface), the lure falls at a rate of 2 feet per second under existing conditions; therefore, to fish it precisely at 16 feet, count to 8 before engaging the reel and retrieving (or jigging). By knowing the sink rate, you can cast a sinking plug, for example, a long distance away, count it down to a certain level, and then begin retrieving to keep the lure at a specific level. A jig can be fished at a certain level vertically by counting it down from the instant it enters the water by the boat; jig it upward and then count it down to a different level. By repeating this action, you can fish through the water column at known levels, and return to levels where strikes have been received.

COVER
Any natural or man-made object that provides shelter and feeding opportunity to fish, and which fish use as a place from which to ambush prey. Some species, like largemouth and smallmouth bass, northern pike, muskie, walleye, crappie, and sunfish, are largely cover-oriented, whereas salmonid species are not. Shallow cover-oriented species of fish are usually more conducive to casting than to trolling. In saltwater, snook are shallow-water fish that prefer cover, while groupers are deep-water fish that use reef bottoms for cover.
See: Finding Fish.

COWBELLS
Cowbells are a form of attractor featuring multiple in-line blades and used in trolling to simulate a group of baitfish. They usually feature a series of lightweight spoons, or blades, spaced at intervals over a short to medium length of braided-wire line. There are many versions; some feature a rudder at the head, to which the fishing line is attached, and all feature a swivel to prevent line twist. A short leader (6 to 24 inches) and lure is attached to the end of the rig. Usually a spoon or streamer fly is attached to cowbells, but sometimes a shallow-swimming plug or strip of bait is used.

The shape and size of the blades vary widely. Shapes include willowleaf, Colorado, and Indiana; lengths may be $1\frac{1}{2}$ to 5 inches, although only a few anglers use the larger sizes. Blades are predominantly silver, but they can be painted or taped with colors.

Cowbells are used mainly for deep lake trout trolling. A few anglers use them with downriggers, but traditionally they have been fished on wire or

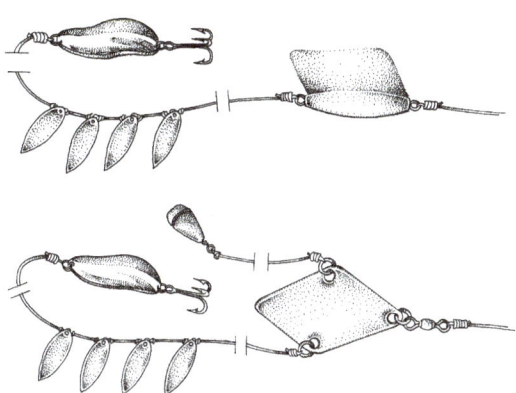

Two versions of cowbell rigs, both with a rudder and a series of spinning blades, are depicted here, each followed by a spoon.

lead core line, or on lines weighted with a heavy sinker. A novel deep fishing presentation is a string of large bladed cowbells snapped to a downrigger weight, with a lure running slightly above and behind them and attached to a line release located on the downrigger cable just above the weight.

CRADLE
Also known as a fish cradle or release cradle, this device is used to land a fish that is intended for release, and which supports the full body of the fish in a horizontal position. The most popular version features two long narrow wood boards that are connected by $1/4$-inch soft-mesh netting that is closed at the ends and which droops into the water to envelop a fish as if it were slipped into a purse. The cradle is kept in the water while the fish is unhooked and then released. Another version, for shorter fish is smaller, with open ends and open-grip handle.
See: Catch-and-Release; Landing Fish.

CRANEFLIES
See: Midges.

CRANKBAIT
A term that has reached popular usage in North America, "crankbait" refers to various small and midsize treble-hooked diving and sinking plugs that have a built-in, vibrating, wiggling, swimming action. The term originated from the fact that the simplest and most practiced way to fish such a lure after casting it is to crank the reel handle steadily to bring it in on a nonstop retrieve. This is not the only way to use this lure, nor is it necessarily the best, but the mere "throw it" nature of this plug has resulted in the name.

Crankbaits are staple lures in bass fishing, and have a following in walleye fishing as well. Although most plugs used for these activities are commonly known as crankbaits, they are, in actuality, plugs and are useful for a wider range of angling activity. For this reason, these lures are covered in greater detail under the plug entry.
See: Plug.

CRAPPIE, BLACK *Pomoxis nigromaculatus.*
Other names—speckled perch, calico bass, grass bass, speckled bass, strawberry bass, oswego bass, sacalait, barfish, crawpie, bachelor perch, papermouth, shiner, moonfish; French: *marigane noire.*

Crappie are like that Chinese dog called a Shih Tzu. Most people don't say the name of that dog in a way that sounds flattering. Ditto for the poor crappie. If its name were pronounced by more folks as if it contained the letter *o* instead of *a,* as in "crop," we would all be better off. No matter how you pronounce the name, both the black crappie and the white crappie *(see: crappie, white)*

Black Crappie

are the most distinctive and largest members of the Centrarchidae family, which includes sunfish and black bass. Both species are considered excellent food fish and sportfish, and have white flaky meat that makes for sweet fillets. In many places crappie are plentiful, and creel limits are liberal, so it does no harm to keep a batch of these fish for the table.

Identification. The black crappie and the white crappie are similar in color—a silvery olive to bronze with dark spots, although on the black crappie the spots are irregularly arranged instead of appearing in seven or eight vertical bands as they do on the white crappie. Both species are laterally compressed and deep-bodied, although the black crappie is somewhat deeper in body, and it has a large mouth that resembles the mouth of a largemouth bass. It also has distinct depressions in its forehead, and large dorsal and anal fins of almost identical size. The gill cover also comes to a sharp point, instead of ending in an earlike flap. The best way to differentiate the two species of crappie is by counting the dorsal fin spines, as the black crappie usually has seven or eight, the white crappie six. The breeding male does not change color noticeably, as it does in the white crappie species.

Size/Age. With lengths of up to 13 inches, the black crappie can weigh up to 5 pounds but usually weighs less than 2 pounds and is commonly caught at a pound or less. It is thought to live to 10 years of age. The all-tackle world record is a 4-pound, 8-ounce fish taken in Virginia in 1981.

Distribution. Black crappie have been so widely introduced in North America that the native range is uncertain, although it appears to start at the Atlantic slope from Virginia to Florida, the Gulf slope west to Texas, and the St. Lawrence–Great Lakes and Mississippi River basins from Quebec to Manitoba, Canada, south to the Gulf of Mexico.

Habitat. Black crappie prefer cooler, deeper, clearer waters with more abundant aquatic vegetation than do white crappie. This includes still backwater lakes, sloughs, creeks, streams, lakes, and ponds. Because they form schools, an angler who comes across one fish is likely to find others nearby. They are especially active in the evening and early morning, and remain active throughout the winter. An abundant species, black crappie occur in smaller concentrations than do white crappie.

Life history/Behavior. Spawning occurs in early spring and summer in water temperatures between 62° to 68°F. These fish spawn over gravel areas or other soft material and nest in colonies. The males excavate the nests, and the females lay the eggs, sometimes in several of these. The eggs incubate for three to five days, and the young mature sometime between their second and fourth years.

Food and feeding habits. Black crappie tend to feed early in the morning on zooplankton, crustaceans, insects, fish, insect larvae, young shad, minnows, and small sunfish. Small minnows form a large part of the diet of adults; in southern reservoirs, gizzard or threadfin shad are major forage, and in northern states, insects are dominant. Crappie also consume the fry of many species of gamefish. They continue to feed during the winter and are very active under the ice.

Crappie are among the panfish species that are especially well suited for young anglers.

Angling. In the spring, when water temperatures reach about 60°F, crappie move shallow to build nests and spawn, and this is a particularly favorite time for angling. Most crappie enthusiasts pursue these fish around some form of wood or brush. The behavior of spawning crappie is reasonably predictable, making them easy to catch. After spawning, they move to deeper water and gather in schools, congregating tightly in sunken weedbeds, dropoffs, offshore brushpiles, river-channel drops, shoreline riprap, flooded timber, and sunken cribbing. Many crappie are caught in 10 to 15 feet of water among tree limbs in standing timber. During the hottest part of the day, they hold on the cool, shaded side of such structures. Other shaded areas that may attract these fish, although not necessarily in large numbers, include bridges, piers, docks, and the bases of old tree stumps. Massive schools of crappie may form at different levels of the lake, and usually are spread horizontally rather than stacking vertically.

In the fall, crappie may move into deeper water to gather around underwater structures such as old channels, rocky ledges, or weedbeds. Although they will move around a bit, they generally remain in deep water until spring. Crappie also offer a prime opportunity for winter fishing, and many northern ice anglers make these fish their number one pursuit.

In many bodies of water without timber, especially large reservoirs, anglers plant brushpiles (where it is legal) to attract and hold crappie, as well as other fish. Where this practice is allowed, anglers may plant many brushpiles, often in places known only to them and sometimes in front of their own docks or boathouses, and will visit them often.

Although some anglers troll for crappie, the vast majority drift or anchor, and either jig or stillfish with minnows. A greater number of crappie are caught using live minnows than on any other baits; other good baits, however, are grasshoppers, crickets, and worms. Unquestionably, the favored artificial crappie catcher is a small, fine-wire jig. Marabou or soft-plastic bodies (grubs especially) are favored. White and yellow are the standard colors, but silver, green, chartreuse, and multicolored tinsel versions are productive. These should be small—the $1/8$-ounce size is perhaps most useful—but slightly lighter or heavier weights are used as depth and wind warrant. A small, single-bladed spinnerbait, with a plastic grub or curl-tail body, is another good crappie taker, as is a small jig tipped with a tiny minnow (hook it from the top of the head through the mouth). Crappie have tender mouths, and strikes are often delicate; the most regularly successful anglers are those who develop a fine jigging motion and a subtle feel.

Crappie don't usually strike a large minnow or lure, although this does happen occasionally, especially where these fish are abundant; $1^{1}/_{2}$- to $2^{1}/_{2}$-inch-long offerings are best for jigs, spinnerbaits, and plugs. Few small crankbaits will dive very deep unaided, although they can be fished deep with the assistance of bottom-walking sinkers. These can be cast or trolled.

These fish are not prone to striking fast-moving baits. You have to get down to their level (usually bottom) and work your offering slowly. Many anglers work lures too quickly for crappie, even though they think they're retrieving at a reasonable speed. Anglers also have a tendency to go too fast when jigging. It's essential to put some effort into maneuvering the boat properly over crappie structures and fishing carefully. Rather than fight wind, many anglers tie off to brush or stumps, or they simply drift. A moderate wind will move a boat along at a speed conducive to drifting, especially when an electric motor is used to control location and rate of drift. With the right wind speed and direction, you can drift slowly over deep-water channels, weedbeds, or dropoffs, or through timber, using a slow lift-and-drop method with jigs, spinnerbaits, or plug-and-sinker combinations.

Crappie anglers primarily use ultralight spinning or spincasting reels equipped with 4- or 6-pound-test line and 5- to $5^{1}/_{2}$-foot-long rods. Fly rods, telescoping fiberglass rods, and cane poles are popular as well. Cane poles or telescoping glass rods play a large, traditional role in crappie fishing. Boat anglers favor 8- to 12-foot poles, but bank anglers prefer 16- to 20-footers. The line is seldom longer than the length of the pole. Live baits are used, and dabbled in place after place.

See: Panfish.

CRAPPIE, WHITE *Pomoxis annularus.*
Other names—crappie, speckled perch, speckled bass, calico bass, sacalaitt, papermouth, bachelor perch; French: *crapet calicot.*

Members of the Centrarchidae family, which includes sunfish and black bass, white crappie are usually thought of in the same breath as black crappie. Both species are considered excellent food fish and sportfish, and have white flaky meat that makes for sweet fillets. In many places, crappie are plentiful, and creel limits are liberal, so it does no harm to keep a batch of these fish for the table.

White Crappie

Identification. The white crappie and black crappie are essentially the same color, a silvery olive to bronze with dark spots, although the white crappie is somewhat paler; in the white crappie the spots are arranged in seven or eight vertical bands on its sides, whereas in the black crappie the spots are scattered. Deep-bodied and laterally compressed, the white crappie has a large mouth, an upper jaw that extends under the eye, and a lower jaw that seems to protrude. It also has distinct depressions in its forehead, and large dorsal and anal fins of almost identical size. The best way to differentiate these fish is by counting dorsal fin spines, as the white crappie has six, and the black crappie usually has seven or eight. The white crappie is also the only sunfish with the same number of spines in both the dorsal and anal fins. The breeding male grows darker in color and is often mistaken for the black crappie.

Size/Age. The white crappie can reach a weight of 5 pounds but usually weighs less than 2 pounds and is commonly caught at a pound or less. The all-tackle world record is a 5-pound, 3-ounce fish taken in Mississippi in 1957. White crappie live for a maximum of 10 years.

Distribution. Widespread in North America, white crappie are found in the Great Lakes, Hudson Bay, the Mississippi River basins from New York and Ontario west to Minnesota and South Dakota and south to the Gulf of Mexico; they also inhabit the Gulf of Mexico drainages from Mobile Bay in Georgia and Alabama to the Wueces River in Texas. They have been introduced widely elsewhere.

Habitat. White crappie occur in creek backwaters, slow-flowing streams, sand- and mud-bottomed pools, small to large rivers, and lakes and ponds. They prefer shallower water than do the black crappie and can tolerate warmer, more turbid, and slightly alkaline waters. They are usually found near dropoffs, standing timber, brushy cover, or other artificial cover. Because white crappie school in loose groups, when an angler catches one, others are likely to be around. They are especially active in the evening and early morning, and remain active throughout the winter.

Spawning behavior. Spawning occurs in early spring and summer in water temperatures between 62° and 68°F, and during that time the male grows dark on the sides of its head, lower jaw, and breast. Spawning takes place in sandy, muddy, and weedy areas, and the fish nest in colonies. In moderately deep water, males brush away sediment to form a shallow nest and guard the 27,000 to more than 68,000 eggs. The eggs incubate for two to four days, and the young white crappie mature in two to four years.

Food and feeding habits. White crappie feed on small crustaceans, zooplankton, insects and insect larvae, minnows, young shad, small sunfish, and other small fish. Small minnows of many species are probably the most common food item for adults.

Angling. *See: Crappie, Black; Panfish.*

CRAWLER

A nightcrawler.
See: **Natural Bait.**

CRAYFISH

Freshwater crayfish are common stream and lake inhabitants of the order Decapoda and in the Astacidae or Cambaridae families. Over 200 species occur in North America, most of which live for approximately two years, although certain species may live up to six or seven years. They often hide under rocks by day, and forage on stream or lake bottoms at night.

Resembling lobsters and also known as crawfish, crayfish grow by molting, or shedding their shell. After shedding their hard covering, they have a very soft shell, and they hide from predators while waiting for it to harden. They may grow to 6 inches, have five pairs of walking legs, including two large claws, and possess eyes that stand out from the body. They are usually red, orange, brown, or dark in color.

A favorite food of many gamefish, crayfish are widely imitated with hard and soft lures, as well as flies, and are fished in both hard- and soft-shelled forms as live bait. Crayfish tails or pieces of tail meat are used to tip some lures.

CREEL

(1) A basket, bag, or pouch for holding a mobile angler's fish. The traditional creel was a well ventilated wicker basket, which was lined with moist grasses or ferns, and primarily used by bank or wading stream trout anglers, the latter of whom carried it around the back via a strap. Such creels are very rarely used today, in part because of greater emphasis on catch-and-release *(see)*, and in part because other devices made of modern and easy to clean materials (some with insulating properties) are available. Pouches to retain fish are also incorporated into many fishing vests or can be added to them.

(2) To keep or retain a fish for personal use instead of releasing it upon capture, regardless of the method of retaining the fish.
See: **Creel Limit; Creel Survey.**

CREEL LIMIT

Synonymous with bag limit, creel limit means the quantity or number of fish of a species or group of species that may be taken, caught, or killed during a specified period. That period is usually one day, from 12:01 A.M. to midnight, and it may be identified as a "daily creel limit" or simply as a "daily limit." Creel limits may apply universally to many waters or may be site-specific. A creel limit is a legal game regulation established by the fisheries agency having jurisdiction over the location being fished, and enforced by fish and wildlife conservation officers.
See: Fisheries Management; Regulations.

CREEL SURVEY

A fisheries management tool for estimating anglers' catches, usually by a sampling program involving interviews and inspection of individual catches. Creel surveys may be conducted wherever anglers are found (on the water, at access points, at fish cleaning stations, etc.) and are not necessarily dependent upon fish actually being creeled, or physically possessed, by anglers.
See: Fisheries Management.

CREEPERS

Spiked-soled footwear used for walking on jetties.
See: Jetty; Surf Fishing.

CRIMPING PLIERS

A pair of heavy-duty pliers designed for crimping metal sleeves.
See: Leader.

CROAKER

Members of the Sciaenidae family (drum and croaker). The common name "croaker" is derived from the voluntary deep croaking noises made when the fish raps a muscle against its swim bladder. The sound resonates and is amplified, and the resulting drumming noise can be heard from a far distance. These fish are generally good to excellent table fare, mostly of smaller sizes, and common along the Atlantic and Pacific coasts.
See: Croaker, Atlantic; Croaker, Spotfin; Croaker, White; Croaker, Yellowfin; Drum; Queenfish (Croaker); Spot.

CROAKER, ATLANTIC
Micropogonias undulatus.
Other names—croaker, crocus, golden cracker, hardhead, king billy; Japanese: *ishimoki;* Portuguese: *corvina;* Spanish: *corbina, corvinón brasileño.*

The Atlantic croaker is a member of the Sciaenidae family (drum and croaker). The com-

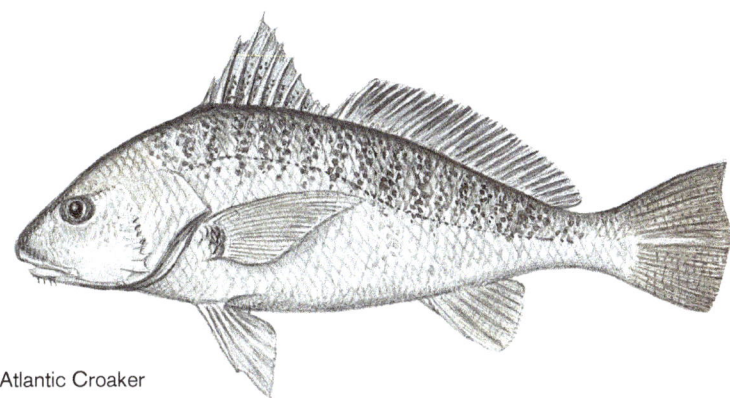
Atlantic Croaker

mon name "croaker" is derived from the voluntary deep croaking noises made when the fish raps a muscle against its swim bladder. The sound resonates and is amplified, and the drumming noise can be heard from a far distance.

The sciaenids as a group are among the most important food fish in the world because nearly all species are good to eat and are harvested commercially. The Atlantic croaker, a bottom fish, is one of the most frequently caught estuarine and near-shore marine fish along the eastern coast of the United States, although in recent years stocks have dwindled in the northern part of its range. It is a good table fish, having lean white meat with a firm texture, often substituted for pompano or mullet in dishes. Commercially, the croaker is sold whole or in fillets.

Identification. The Atlantic croaker has a small, elongated body with a short, high first dorsal fin and a long, low second dorsal fin. There are 6 to 10 tiny barbels on the chin and 64 to 72 scales along the lateral line, and the preopercular margin has three to five spines. The middle rays of the caudal fins are longer than those above and below, creating a wedgelike appearance. Its coloring is greenish above and white below, with brownish black spots and a silver iridescence covering the body. There are dark, wavy lines on the sides. During spawning, the Atlantic croaker takes on a bronze hue (thus the nickname "golden cracker"), and its pelvic fins turn yellow.

It can be distinguished from its cousin the spot *(Leiostomus xanthurus; see:* spot) by its convex tail, which is unlike the spot's concave caudal tail. Its unique coloring and spotted patterns also help distinguish the Atlantic croaker from its other relatives.

Size/Age. The average fish is 12 inches long and weighs $1^{1}/_{2}$ pounds, although the species may grow to 20 inches. The all-tackle record weighed 3 pounds, 12 ounces. The Atlantic croaker, like most fish in its family, can live up to five years.

Distribution. The Atlantic croaker is found along the Atlantic coast from Cape Cod to the Bay of Campeche. While it is abundant off the entire coast of the Gulf of Mexico, the croaker periodically becomes most common in Louisiana and

Mississippi waters; it may also be found in southern Brazil and Argentina.

Habitat. Atlantic croaker are a bottom-dwelling, estuarine-dependent fish that become oceanic during spawning. They prefer mud, sand, and shell bottoms; areas around rocks; waters near jetties, piers, and bridges; and surf. Juveniles in-habit both open and vegetated shallow marsh areas. Adult croaker can occupy a wide range of salinities, from 20 to 75 parts per thousand, and temperatures of 50° to 96°F. Large fish are not found at temperatures below 50°F. Larvae and juveniles, however, are more tolerant of lower temperatures and can be found in waters ranging from 33° to 96°F.

Life history/Behavior. Spawning occurs at sea in winter and spring (the peak month is November), when the Atlantic croaker migrates to deeper, warmer water. In the southerly range, it is assumed that all croaker spawn in the open Gulf of Mexico, near the mouths of various passes that lead into shallow bays and lagoons. Large females may release up to 180,000 eggs, which will drift shoreward after hatching. Croaker larvae are abundant on soft bottoms with large quantities of detritus.

Atlantic croaker grow rapidly at approximately 6 inches per year. Males reach maturity at the end of their second year (10 inches), and females at the end of their third (14 inches). Adults migrate in schools or small groups to the bays in the spring and leave the marsh in the fall to enter deep gulf waters. To the north in the Chesapeake Bay area, the post-larval and juvenile fish migrate into the estuaries and return to the ocean as yearlings.

Food and feeding habits. Larval and post-larval fish subsist mostly on zooplankton; detritus is a major part of their diet as they grow. Adults feed on detritus as well, but they also consume larger invertebrates and fish. Sensory barbels allow the Atlantic croaker to find food on the bottom.

Angling. Atlantic croaker are caught in large numbers from March through October on such natural baits as shrimp, soft-shell or shedder crabs, clams, worms, and cut fish, and with artificial lures such as small jigs and weighted bucktails. Light tackle and small hooks are best, and although some fish are caught during the day, angling after dark is often better. Fishing is also often best just before, or right after, a hide tide in channels or deep holes.

CROAKER, SPOTFIN *Roncador stearnsii.*
Other names—spotty, spot, golden croaker.

A member of the Sciaenidae (drum and croaker) family, the spotfin croaker is a small North American Pacific Coast fish caught by bay, surf, and pier anglers and highly valued as table far. The common name "croaker" is derived from the voluntary deep croaking noises when the fish raps a muscle against its swim bladder, which acts as an amplifier.

Identification. The body of the spotfin croaker is elongate but heavy forward. The upper pro-

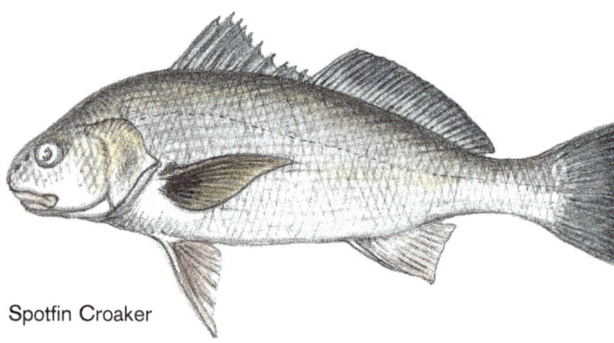

Spotfin Croaker

file of the head is steep and slightly curved, and abruptly rounded at the very blunt snout. The mouth is subterminal, being underneath the head. The color is silvery gray with a bluish luster above and white below. There are dark wavy lines on the sides, and a large black spot at the base of the pectoral fin.

The pectoral fin spot, subterminal mouth, and absence of a fleshy barbel distinguish the spotfin croaker from other California croaker. Small specimens may be confused with small white croaker *(see: croaker, white),* although dorsal fin counts differ. The spotfin has 11 or fewer (usually 10) dorsal fin spines; the white croaker has 12 to 15. Large male spotfins in breeding colors are known as "golden croaker."

Size. The average spotfin croaker is small to medium in size, and most weigh roughly a pound. The largest caught on rod and reel in California was 27 inches long and weighed $10^1/_2$ pounds.

Distribution. Spotfin croaker range from Mazatlán, Mexico, to Point Conception, California, including the Gulf of California; in California they are most abundant south of Los Angeles.

Habitat. Spotfins are found along beaches and in bays over bottoms that vary from coarse sand to heavy mud and at depths varying from 4 to 50 or more feet. They prefer depressions and holes near shore.

Life history/Behavior. Spotfin croaker travel considerably but with no definite pattern, moving extensively from bay to bay, usually in small groups but sometimes in groups numbering up to four dozen. Males are sexually mature at 9 inches in length and about two years of age; most females mature at three years and about $12^1/_2$ inches in length. Their spawning season is from June through September, and spawning evidently takes place offshore, as no ripe fish are caught in the surf, although 1-inch juveniles do appear in the surf in the fall.

Food and feeding habits. Spotfin croaker have large pharyngeal teeth that are well suited to crushing clams, which make up a major portion of their diet; crustaceans and worms are also eaten extensively.

Angling. Although some spotfins are caught throughout the year, the better angling period is late summer, after the fish have spawned and return to the surf line. When a large number of fish have moved into an area (called "running"), there is generally good activity in the bays, and at piers and beaches. Clams and worms are the main natural baits, fished on bottom rigs; relatively light tackle is best for sporting value.

CROAKER, WHITE *Genyonemus lineatus.*
Other names—kingfish, king-fish, king croaker, shiner, Pasadena trout, tommy croaker, little bass; Japanese: *shiroguchi.*

A member of the Sciaenidae family, the white croaker is a small North American Pacific Coast fish. The common name "croaker" is derived from the voluntary deep croaking noises made when the fish raps a muscle against the swim bladder, which acts as an amplifier. The resultant distinctive drumming noise can be heard from a far distance.

Although the flesh is edible, the white croaker is considered a nuisance, being easily hooked on most any type of live bait. Like its cousin the queenfish (*Seriphus politus;* see: queenfish), many white croaker are caught accidentally by anglers.

Identification. The body of the white croaker is elongate and compressed. Its head is oblong and bluntly rounded, and its mouth is somewhat underneath the head. A deep notch separates the two dorsal fins. Its coloring is iridescent brown to yellowish on the back, becoming silvery below. Faint, wavy lines appear over the silvery parts. The fins are yellow to white.

The white croaker is one of five California croaker that have subterminal mouths. They can be distinguished from the California corbina (*Menticirrhus undulatus;* see: corbina, California) and the yellowfin croaker (*Umbrina roncador;* see: croaker, yellowfin) by the absence of a barbel. The 12 to 15 spines in the first dorsal fin serve to distinguish white croaker from all the other croaker with subterminal mouths, as none of these has more than 11 spines in this fin.

Size/Age. The average weight is 1 pound. It is believed the white croaker can live up to 15 years, although most live far fewer years.

Distribution. White croaker range from Magdalena Bay, Baja California, to Vancouver Island, British Columbia, but are not abundant north of San Francisco.

Habitat. Preferring sandy bottoms, white croaker inhabit quiet surf zones, shallow bays, and lagoons. Most of the time they are found in offshore areas at depths of 10 to 100 feet. On rare occasions, they are abundant at depths as great as 600 feet.

Food and feeding habits. White croaker consume a variety of fish, squid, shrimp, octopus, worms, small crabs, clams, and other items, living or dead.

Angling. Easily hooked and caught on almost any type of live baits, white croaker provide little angling excitement. Fishing is good for this species throughout the year from piers or jetties in sandy or muddy areas.

White Croaker

CROAKER, YELLOWFIN *Umbrina roncador.*
Other names—Catalina croaker, yellowtailed croaker, golden croaker, yellowfin drum.

The yellowfin croaker is a member of the family Sciaenidae (drum and croaker), known for the drumlike noises they make when they rap a muscle against their swim bladder. The resulting distinctive drumming sound is amplified by the swim bladder and can be heard at some distance.

The sciaenids are one of the most important food fish in the world because nearly all species are good to eat and are harvested commercially. Found along the Pacific coast, the yellowfin croaker is a popular catch for light-tackle surf anglers.

Identification. The body of the yellowfin croaker is elliptical-elongate; the back is somewhat arched and the head blunt. Its coloring is iridescent blue to gray with brassy reflections on the back diffusing to silvery white below. Dark wavy lines streak the sides. The fins are yellowish except for the dark dorsal fins. It has a small barbel on the chin tip and two strong anal spines; the barbel and heavy anal spines distinguish the yellowfin from other California croaker.

Size. The average weight for a yellowfin croaker is less than 1 pound. The all-tackle record is 2 pounds, 11 ounces.

Distribution. The yellowfin croaker is found from the Gulf of California, Mexico, to Point Conception, California.

Habitat. These fish inhabit shallow parts of bays, channels, harbors, and other nearshore waters over sandy bottoms.

Life history/Behavior. Yellowfin croaker are sexually mature at 9 inches in length. Their spawning season is in summer, when this species is most

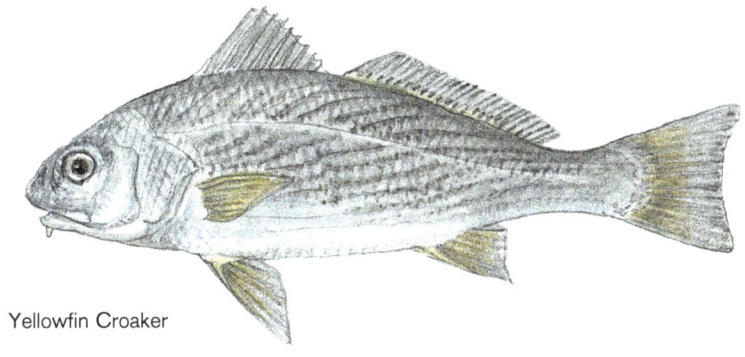
Yellowfin Croaker

common along sandy beaches. They move into deeper waters in winter, traveling in schools or small groups.

Food and feeding habits. Although the yellowfin croaker primarily consumes small fish and fish fry, it also feeds on small crustaceans, worms, and mollusks.

Angling. These fish are mostly caught in shallow sandy areas by surf anglers. Sand crabs, mussels, clams, cut pieces of fish, and worms are used as baits, preferably on small hooks and light tackle.

CRT

A recorder with a cathode-ray tube.
See: Sonar.

CRUSTACEAN

A group of freshwater and saltwater animals having no backbone, with jointed legs and a hard shell made of chitin. In saltwater this group includes shrimp, crabs, lobsters, and crayfish, all of which may be used as bait when angling but are not targeted by anglers or deliberately sought with sporting equipment. Freshwater crustaceans also include crayfish, as well as scuds (see), sowbugs (see), and shrimp.

CUBA

Surrounded by the Gulf of Mexico, the Atlantic Ocean, and the Caribbean Sea, Cuba is the largest island in the West Indies and a location coveted for both freshwater and saltwater fishing. Nevertheless, little of Cuba's fishery is currently known to many anglers. Once a playground for American travelers, Cuba was considered a hunting and fishing paradise in the 1950s; it was famous for blue marlin in the Gulf Stream off the north coast near Havana, bonefish off the south coast on the flats at Isle of Pines, and largemouth bass inland at Treasure Lake. Since 1960, however, American anglers, among the most voracious in the world, have looked upon Cuba as the forbidden fruit.

Although travel to this country for nearby Americans was temporarily relaxed in the late 1970s and early 1980s—allowing numerous expeditions inland for bass fishing and modest saltwater efforts—Cuba's waters have been lightly sportfished for decades, except by a modest number of Canadian anglers and very few Europeans, although some Americans have fished its coastal waters for big-game species. The island lacks a developed tourism infrastructure, reliable and modern equipment, and the means to mount sustained expeditions to explore coastal regions along its 2,500 miles of coastline. Consequently, reports on angling are few, but some have been positively glowing for inshore and bass fishing. It is generally accepted that Cuba has some of the best largemouth bass fishing, and some of the biggest specimens, to be found anywhere; likewise, it is still considered a utopia for light-tackle flats fishing for various species, especially bonefish and small tarpon.

As is common in poor, underdeveloped countries, pollution, commercial fishing, and subsistence fishing have lessened the quality of some of the formerly stupendous fisheries. It remains unclear, however, to what extent these have been affected, as well as which areas may not be affected.

Given Cuba's proximity to the United States, if normal travel becomes a reality, and outside investors provide the means to comfortably fish the varied nooks and crannies of Cuba, a rush to explore its fertile flats, canals, keys, and lakes will ensue, and much will be written about the opportunities. In saltwater, this will be especially likely if private boats are allowed in. If not, visitors may find themselves in mother-ship operations in Cuba's distant backwaters.

Saltwater
Offshore. Cuba's offshore environment is not particularly far from land, especially along the northeast coast. It has been said that you can virtually cast from Cuba's northern shore and wet your hook in the Gulf Stream. Not quite, but the Great Blue River, as Ernest Hemingway called it, does pass surprisingly close to the walls of the now run-down Malecón in Havana, where the water is 100 fathoms deep within 100 yards of land, and the 1,000-fathom curve lies just a short distance beyond.

Today that once beautiful seaside boulevard features local anglers casting for bottom fish with handlines, with the line wrapped around a circular *carrete* and using old spark plugs for weights and a chunk of meat for bait. They fare pretty well, too. But then, so did the Old Man.

Not much in this Caribbean country is as it was in 1960, not long before Papa rode the *Pilar* out to the edges of the blue for the last time. The Stream still flows easterly, however, as it has for thousands of years, coursing through the Yucatan Channel into the Florida Straits, curving around Cabo San Antonio and hugging the shoreline past Havana, then past the small fishing village of Cojímar, which provided the setting for what is arguably the greatest story of the sea ever written.

Each hour the Stream brings with it some 10 cubic miles of tropical water. Hemingway, who considered this the greatest fishing stream in the world, made Havana a port with big-game status through his pioneering exploits here, and there is a museum dedicated to him at San Francisco de Paula, his old estate, where the *Pilar* rests. In tribute to Papa, each year anglers go forth in the spring to ply the edge of the Stream in the Hemingway Tournament, an event that was a national competition for many years but has had some measure of international participation over the past several decades. One of the early winners of that contest, incidentally, was Fidel Castro. In 1960 Castro personally boated three marlin to capture the silver cup by virtue of overall weight.

Indeed, the edge of the Gulf Stream on the north shore does attract billfish, although the tournament seldom produces earthshaking results. Certainly, these are lightly fished waters, and with travel restrictions on many would-be visitors (primarily Americans), meager local tackle and big-game fishing skills, and the likely adverse effect of localized commercial fishing operations, this fishery remains a question mark. Despite the proliferation in angling communication in recent times, and despite the extensive search for new grounds by many anglers, Cuba's blue-water fishing remains an enigma. This is true on the north and south coasts as well as at the extreme ends of the island.

In the past, the best marlin grounds were deemed to be on the north coast, with most effort concentrated at Bahía de Cabañas, 40 miles west of Havana, in front of Havana itself, and 60 miles east at Matanzas. Blue marlin were caught from July into October, with the best fishing for this species, locally called "Cuban black marlin," in August and September. White marlin were present from April through August, and sailfish were reportedly available year-round. Wahoo, tuna, and large dolphin were also caught.

Inshore. Even more enigmatic than the blue-water fishing is Cuba's virtually untapped and even less heralded inshore light-tackle fishing. Although this is believed to exist predominantly on the south side of the island, particularly at the eastern end, Cuba's irregular shoreline is indented by numerous gulf and bays (reportedly 200 bays of varying size), with a vast amount of wetlands and mangroves. Bonefish and tarpon headline the species found in some of these places, and they probably exist in more areas than is generally realized outside Cuba. In fact, Cuba's inshore waters may be one of the few remaining fishing frontiers, even though it is likely that records for weight will probably not be threatened if and when modern exploration resumes.

Very few tourists have visited much of the inshore coast in decades, although in bonefishing circles the flats around Isle of Pines are remembered for their renowned bonefish, which roamed in great schools. Isle of Pines, which was also infamous for its penal colony, has since been renamed Isle of Youth. Reports suggest that commercial fishing around the island has wiped out the bonefish (*macabi* here), although this is uncertain. Few if any anglers have fished the waters nearby, but numerous expeditions have been made to flats and keys some 250 miles to the east, where even today the bonefish are sometimes clustered in schools measuring in the hundreds.

These are small fish, for the most part ranging between 2 and 5 pounds. These weights are characteristic of Cuba's population of this species. Bigger bones do not group like this and appear to be scarce; modern reports of sightings of 10-pound bonefish exist, and the Cuban national bonefish record pre-1960 was reportedly 14 pounds.

Those anglers who have encountered massive bonefish schools have been able to hook scores of them per day, making this a tremendous place for light tackle and for anglers new to bonefishing. Although bonefish have the reputation of being wary and difficult to stalk, it is possible to take several from a single large school on the Cuban flats, to have several bones rush to your offering, and even to allow a hooked fish to swim back and rejoin the school. These are all unusual occurrences and seldom happen in well-trafficked waters. The best time for bonefishing is said to be from November through February, but this is uncertain.

One area that has seen occasional fishing—via bargelike shrimp boats converted into floating hotels and towing small skiffs—is near the province of Ciego de Avila. There is an archipelago known as Garden of the Queens on maps but commonly referred to as Last Paradise Keys, which also attracts divers for its black coral, dropoffs, and walls with diverse life. Huge numbers of bonefish have been landed here, and small tarpon are abundant.

In fact, these waters are rich in many forms of aquatic life. Barracuda, permit, red snapper, jack crevalle, and yellowtail snapper are some of the inshore species, with the likes of amberjack, grouper, and other fish in deeper water off the edge of the flats. Locals talk of 25-pound permit *(palometa)* and 30-pound barracuda *(picua),* although this hasn't been proven. Snook are believed to be along this coast and in some of the lower rivers; snook from 20 to 30 pounds have been reportedly caught in one of the rivers here.

Tarpon in this region are all small, running from 10 to 25 pounds and occasionally to 50 pounds, but they are numerous, and some anglers have jumped several score in a day. Some tarpon *(sabalo)* have reportedly been seen to 100 pounds. The tarpon are said to be present year-round, either in the canals and among the mangrove keys, or out in deeper water, with only the smaller fish reportedly up in the turtle-grass-covered shallows.

Tarpon up to at least 70 pounds roam the freshwater confines of Treasure Lake, once a renowned largemouth bass environment in the Zapata Swamp, not far from the infamous Bay of Pigs. How the tarpon got there remains a mystery, although some locals allege that an underwater passage exists from lake to salty flat. Whatever the explanation, it is quite likely that large tarpon do exist in Cuban waters.

Big tarpon were reported in some of Cuba's larger bays in the 1950s, including those at Havana and Matanzas, and smaller tarpon were known along the north coast, even in some of the rivers that empty into the Atlantic there. Little had been confirmed about modern tarpon fisheries along that coast, although the extensive Sabana Archipelago east of Cárdenas Bay seems worthy of

The deep-dwelling tilefish of the Atlantic was first discovered and named in 1879; it was nearly exterminated in 1882 by a Gulf Stream shift that exposed these fish to excessively cold water.

exploration. It is rumored that large bonefish are in this area, and that snook roam these waters as well.

Freshwater
About a quarter of Cuba's landmass is mountainous or hilly and the rest is flat or rolling terrain, with low-lying coastal areas. Its rivers are relatively short, but there are more than 100 significant lakes (many of them man-made) and many hundreds of small lakes. The latter are mostly of fairly recent construction. They range from shallow mangrove swamp lakes to deep high-mountain lakes.

Largemouth bass exist throughout the country and have been widely transplanted. Their numbers exploded in many of the newly constructed lakes, as often happens, but the overall size of Cuban bass was exceptional in the early 1980s.

Many lakes produced extraordinary numbers of 8- to 10-pounders in the late 1970s and early 1980s. Anglers have landed quantities of fish from 12 to 15 pounds, and some in the 18- to 20-pound class have been verified. Reports indicate that some bass over 22 pounds have been caught illegally, and the possibility certainly exists that a new all-tackle world record could be landed in one of a number of Cuban lakes in the future. Lake Redonda yielded a sport-caught 21-pounder some years ago, and Lake Buffalo a 20-pounder more recently. Lake Hanabanilla, a mountain lake fished extensively in the early 1980s and known for trophy fish, reportedly produced an 18-pound fish in 1996.

The premier lake of old in Cuba was swampy Treasure Lake, which was turned into a popular vacation resort by the time visiting anglers first fished it in 1977. It is no longer fished, but a succession of lakes, including Zaza, Hanabanilla, Redonda, and others, were fished into the early 1980s. Sportfishing was severely limited after that, with sporadic angling at a number of newer waters.

In the late 1990s, Cuba enacted regulations protecting bass lakes for sportfishing, and various lakes are expected to be fished on a rotational plan, all on a catch-and-release basis. A limited number of anglers, including Americans who were visiting to bring humanitarian supplies, have fished some lakes in the latter 1990s. Among the more recently opened bass lakes are Guananeo, Cubano Bulgaria, Porvenir, Granizo, Chambas, Calbario, Versalles, Laguna de la Leche, and Munoz. Bass are also present on lakes on the Isle of Youth.

CULLING
The replacement of a fish that has been caught or confined (in a basket, in a livewell, on a stringer) with a freshly caught fish. A fish that is culled is taken from confinement and returned to the water, usually in order to comply with regulations pertaining to the maximum number of fish that may be kept.

In many locations, once a fish has been reduced to possession, it may not be culled; returning it to the water is illegal. In some locations culling is not illegal, and in others, special allowances let participants in fishing tournaments cull fish that have been kept in a properly aerated livewell. In some locations, once a legal limit of fish has been kept, it is illegal to continue fishing.

Tournaments notwithstanding, anglers should not cull unless they are keeping an injured fish and releasing a healthy one. Fish that have been kept in confinement, especially on a stringer, are usually highly stressed and more likely to experience delayed mortality than fish that are released immediately after unhooking. Fish that have been kept in properly aerated livewells, where the water temperature is appropriate for the fish and the water has been treated with stabilizing chemicals, have the best chance of surviving when culled.

See: Catch-and-Release.

CUNNER *Tautogolabrus adspersus*.
A member of the Labridae family of wrasses *(see)* the cunner is related to, and occurs even farther north than, the tautog *(see)*, ranging from Chesapeake Bay to Newfoundland. Where their ranges overlap, the two species are often found together. They are similar in general body shape, but the cunner is slimmer and has a much lower head profile. Further, the cunner has scales on its gill covers and only about 40 scales in a count along its lateral line.

A big largemouth bass comes to the net at Lake Hanabanilla.

Cunner are smaller fish, averaging only about a quarter of a pound and only rarely exceeding 2 pounds. Anglers catch cunner more by accident than by choice. The fish is a superb bait stealer, but if one is hooked, its spiny fins make it a formidable creature to take off a hook. On very light tackle, this species can be sporting, however, and is generally considered a good table fish.

CURRENTS

Defined as horizontal movements of water, currents are an everyday part of fishing for virtually all saltwater anglers, for freshwater anglers who fish in rivers or streams, and for some freshwater anglers who fish in large lakes with major sources of inflow and outflow.

Anglers in the Straits of Georgia in British Columbia fish for salmon among some of the swiftest currents in the world.

The most visually obvious influence of current is in rivers and streams, whose character and aquatic life are molded by the velocity of water, from trickling runoff in the headwaters to the silted and expansive delta. The types, sizes, and even shapes of fish and aquatic life vary greatly from small, shallow, fast waters in the hills to wider, deeper, and slower waters downstream, possibly even affected by tides (see) in the most downstream reaches. Within the different sections, there are variations in current; narrow, constricted areas cause a swifter flow than wider and deeper areas. Nevertheless, currents flow slower near the banks than in the center of the river, except along the outside bank of a sharp bend.

Currents may exist in large lakes and impoundments but are usually less visually obvious. In some impoundments, when there is high and regular demand for water, usually in summer for power generation, the drawdown of water creates a current that astute anglers can observe around points, around bridge and roadway supports, and along some shores. Since it is intermittent, it is less likely to be a major influence on the composition of aquatic life, although it may influence the behavior, especially feeding, of some species, particularly striped bass. Continual current, which may exist at subsurface levels in some of the Great Lakes, is unlikely to affect fish behavior, but it can affect the behavior of lures and influence fishing patterns when strong, although many anglers are unaware of its existence.

Tides and major oceanic currents are, of course, very well known and observed. Most anglers and boaters in coastal areas are affected by tidal currents, and the world is well acquainted with surface ocean currents, which circle the ocean basins on either side of the equator. These are vastly different natural elements than currents in freshwater.

Surface circulation in the oceans is caused by wind patterns that sweep across the earth in different latitude zones. The general pattern of surface currents is modified by physical factors and the effects of friction, gravity, the sun's heat, the shape of land masses, local winds, and the earth's rotation. Several factors may interact to complicate the general flow. For example, the earth's rotation helps form huge circular water masses that move clockwise in the Northern Hemisphere and counterclockwise in the Southern Hemisphere (known as the Coriolis force). As the sun heats the ocean surface in the tropics, the warmed water tends to flow toward the poles to displace colder, heavier water that, in turn, flows toward the equator in subsurface currents.

These great ocean currents are known as "rivers of the sea," and the ones of greatest interest in North America are the Gulf Stream (see) of the Atlantic, and the California Current (see) of the Pacific. South of the equator in the Pacific, the Humboldt Current, which moves along the west coast of South America, is one of the richest fish-producing currents in the world, and it is this current that is disturbed by the periodic El Niño (see) phenomenon.

There are also subsurface currents in the ocean, although these are generally very slow and the result of deep-water circulation. This is a vertical movement that is the result of cold water from the polar regions sinking. Another vertical movement of ocean water is an upwelling (see), which occurs when deep current meets the shelving bottom or submerged banks. A persistent blow of wind can also bring about a form of upwelling by pushing surface waters outward and turning colder deep waters toward the surface.

Tidal currents exist in all the oceans and are mostly observed in coastal areas as water flows into and out of bays, increasing and decreasing in speed; dangerous, turbulent currents may form where rivers meet the sea, and several currents mix. Tidal currents also exist in offshore waters, usually observed with little change in speed, but slowly and steadily changing direction. Lastly, local currents may also be set up by wave action along the shore or beach, creating undertows as water rushes back into the sea from the beach.

Currents are an obvious influence—and sometimes hazard—to boating, and are clearly a factor in the presence of fish and in fishing efforts.
See: Boat; Finding Fish.

CURVE CAST
An in-air technique for presenting a fly or mending a fly line.
See: Mending.

CUSK
(1) A term for burbot *(see)*.

(2) *Brosme brosme.*

The saltwater cusk (also known as tusk) is a deepwater relative of cod in the Lotidae family. It is found in rocky, hard-bottom areas in a temperature range of 0° to 10°C, and is generally solitary or travels in small groups. It occurs in the western Atlantic from New Jersey to Newfoundland and in the eastern Atlantic off Iceland, in the northern North Sea, and along the Scandinavian coasts to the Murmansk coast. In its western range, it prefers waters between 150 and 450 meters deep, and between 18 and 550 meters in its eastern range.

Relatively slow growing and late maturing, the cusk is a highly commercial species caught by trawlers and longliners; it is an incidental catch for anglers. It can attain a maximum size of 47 inches and 65 pounds, but grows to 35 inches and 20 pounds in the western Atlantic, where it is believed to be overexploited.

CUT BAIT
A chunk, slice, or other piece of fish used as bait.

CUTLASSFISH
Other names—cutlass fish, ribbonfish, Atlantic cutlassfish, Pacific cutlassfish, largehead hairtail; Japanese: *tachinouo, tachiuo, tachuo*; Portuguese: *lírio, peixe-espada*; Spanish: *espada, pez sable, sable, savola.*

Cutlassfish are members of the family Trichiuridae, encompassing nearly 20 species. They are swift swimmers that generally dwell on the bottom. Used as baits for larger gamefish in the United States, cutlassfish are a valued food and commercial species in many other countries, especially Japan, where they may be used for sashimi. They are also marketed salted/dried and frozen.

Identification. Characterized by their long, compressed bodies that taper to a pointed tail, cutlassfish are also commonly known as ribbonfish. The head is spear-shaped, and the fish has sharp arrowlike teeth in a large mouth. Its coloring is silvery, the jaws edged with black.

Size/Age. Cutlassfish can reach up to 5 feet in length and 2 pounds in weight. The average length is 3 feet. The all-tackle record for Atlantic cutlassfish *(Trichiurus lepturus)* is a 7-pound fish caught in South Africa in 1995.

Distribution. These fish are found in the Atlantic, Indian, and western Pacific Oceans. In North America, the Atlantic cutlassfish commonly ranges from Massachusetts to Argentina and throughout the Gulf of Mexico, especially Texas. In the Pacific, cutlassfish inhabit waters from Southern California to northern Peru.

Habitat. Preferring muddy bottoms in shallow water, cutlassfish gather large numbers in bays, estuaries, and shallow coastal areas.

Food and feeding habits. Cutlassfish feed on anchovies, sardines, squid, and crustaceans. Adults usually feed on pelagic prey near the surface during the daytime and migrate to the bottom at night. Adults and small juveniles do the opposite.

Angling. Although occasionally encountered by anglers and used as baits, cutlassfish are not considered sportfish and there is no genuine angling effort for them.

CUTPLUG
A wooden or plastic trolling plug *(see)* with a large scooped out face, lipless head, and body that tapers to a point at the tail. Primarily used in salmon fishing, it is so named because it's similar in appearance to the cut herring natural bait rig commonly employed in mooching *(see)*. Cutplugs have an erratic swimming and darting motion, and are primarily fished deep with weights or downriggers.

CUTTYHUNK LINE
A handlaid, twisted linen fishing line formerly used by saltwater anglers.
See: Line; Linen Line.

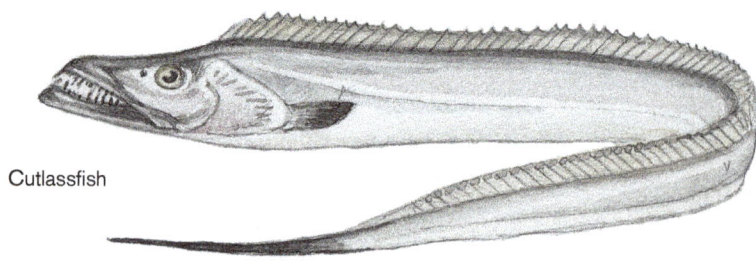

Cutlassfish

DABBLING
A term for flipping *(see)* and pitching *(see)*.

DACE
Dace belong to the largest family of freshwater fish, Cyprinidae, which includes assorted minnows *(see)* and carp *(see)*. These are small and extremely hardy fish. Some dace species in North America are not pursued by anglers, and a prominent variety exists in Europe and Asia that is the source of much angling effort despite its small size.

(1) In North America, dace are distributed widely in small streams, lakes, and ponds, providing an important food source for many species sought by anglers. They inhabit colder, moving, clear water that runs over gravel or pebbles. Adults generally inhabit deep water, and juveniles hold in shallow water closer to shore.

Commonly referred to in North America by the all-encompassing generic term "minnows," dace are small (2 to 3 inches in length) and have slender bodies. Most dace species have terminal barbels. On the pearl dace (*Semotilus margarita margarita*), the barbel is sometimes hidden or even absent. The *Clinostomus* species has no barbels.

Dace are greatly valued as baits for larger gamefish; the blacknose dace (*Rhinichthys atratulus; see: dace, blacknose*) is preferred for trout and salmon, whereas the longnose dace (*R. cataractae; see: dace, longnose*) is highly popular for bass. Dace can survive in very crowded or stagnant waters, like any other member of the minnow family, due to low oxygen demand, so anglers who want lively and sturdy baits value this kind of resilience. Some dace are also valuable for insect population control. The longnose dace, for example, primarily consumes blackfly larvae and is a major factor in the control of the blackfly population.

Identifying and distinguishing between the different species of dace is difficult. Although not all dace are identical, the variations are minor, such as a slightly longer snout. The coloring is extremely similar on all dace: olive green fading to white on the belly, with silvery overtones. The small scales are pronounced and have dark patterns that can change not only from species to species, but also among individual fish. The best way to identify the different dace species from each other, and from other similar fish like chubs or minnows, is by their breeding attributes. *Rhinichthys* dace acquire a rusty tinge on their fins during breeding season, whereas *Clinostomus* dace turn iridescent pink. The pearl dace develops bright-red flanks. All dace, especially males, have well-developed tubercles on the body, primarily around the head and snout. These tubercles, also called pearl organs, are used for nest building, in fighting and courtship rituals, and for maintaining contact with the opposite sex during spawning.

Eggs are given little or no parental care after spawning, and the young feed on zooplankton and phytoplankton for the first several months of life. Adults feed on insect larvae, worms, and algae.

(2) *Leuciscus leuciscus*.
Other names—common dace, Eurasian dace; French: *vandoise*; German: *hasel, hasile*.

The Eurasian dace is one of the smallest coarse fish *(see)* sought by anglers. It is a silvery, slim-bodied fish with concave dorsal and anal fins and a moderately forked tail, commonly caught at 6 to 8 ounces in weight and growing to a maximum of little more than twice that size.

Eurasian dace are widespread throughout northern Europe and northern Asia but are not found below the Alps or Pyrenees. They have been introduced in Ireland. These dace are common in the upper reaches of moderate-flowing rivers and in clean, cold lakes but reportedly enter brackish water in the eastern Baltic. They feed on crustaceans, insects, and plants, and are caught on small bits of natural or processed baits, as well as on flies. Anglers land them at all depths and often throughout the day.

DACE, BLACKNOSE *Rhinichthys atratulus*.
Other names—eastern blacknose dace, brook minnow, potbelly, redfin dace, chub.

A member of the Cyprinidae family of minnows *(see)* and carp *(see)*, the blacknose dace makes excellent bait due to its small size and hardiness, and, like many small minnows, provides excellent forage

Blacknose Dace

for predator fish, especially bass and trout. It is not sought by anglers but may be netted for use as bait.

Identification. The blacknose dace has a long slim body with a slightly protruding snout. The barbels, which are characteristic of most minnows, corner both sides of the mouth. The coloring is silvery, with dark olive gray fading to white on the belly. A dark lateral line runs along either side onto the head. It can be distinguished from the longnose dace *(Rhinichthys cataractae)* by its shorter snout.

Size/Age. Blacknose dace generally live two to three years, and have an average size of 2 to 3 inches.

Distribution. The range of the blacknose dace spans from North Dakota to the St. Lawrence drainage and south to Nebraska and North Carolina.

Habitat. These fish are commonly found in rapid, clear streams, and the rocky runs and pools of small rivers; they can survive in stagnant summer waters and tolerate crowded conditions.

Spawning behavior. Blacknose dace spawn in spring, starting in late May or early June. They build no nest; the fertilized eggs are dropped over the gravel bottom. The male, however, is known to defend spawning territories. Females release approximately 750 eggs, and little or no parental care is given to them.

Food and feeding habits. Blacknose dace feed on insect larvae, small crustaceans, small worms, and plant material.

See: Dace.

DACE, LONGNOSE *Rhinichthys cataractae.*
Other names—dace; French: *naseux de rapide.*

A member of the Cyprinidae family of minnows *(see)* and carp *(see),* the longnose dace has many valuable functions. Easily obtainable, small, and extremely hardy, it is prized as exceptional bait and is especially significant for bass fishing. Primarily feeding on blackfly larvae, it is also valued for its control of the blackfly population. And, like many small minnows, it provides excellent forage for predator fish, especially bass and trout. It is not sought by anglers, but may be netted for use as bait.

Identification. The longnose dace is a distinctive minnow with a long fleshy snout, a subterminal mouth, and a deep caudal peduncle. The head and nape slope downward from its cylindrical body, giving this minnow a streamlined appearance. Pigmentation is widely variable; the dorsum can be greenish, brown, or reddish purple, and the lower sides and venter may be silvery, white, or yellow. The sides are sometimes marked by darkened scales, a lateral stripe, and a blotch near the tail. The longnose dace can quickly be distinguished from most other minnows by the presence of a frenum, a small fleshy bridge between the snout and the upper jaw. It can be distinguished from other species of *Rhinichthys* by its long snout. Other characteristics of the longnose dace are small barbels in the corner of the mouth, small scales, a complete lateral line with 48 to 76 scales, and eyes that are situated near the top of the head. Breeding males have red coloration on the head and fins, and develop small tubercles on the head, body, and ventral fins.

Size/Age. Adults can reach lengths exceeding 6 inches, but most are less than 4 inches long. They have been known to live up to five years.

Distribution. The longnose dace has the widest distribution of any minnow in North America and is an important forage species where it is abundant. Several subspecies are recognized, but further study may reveal the occurrence of unique populations or additional subspecies. The distribution of the longnose dace spans the entire continent, ranging throughout the southern half of Canada and the northern United States. It extends southward to Georgia within the southern Appalachian Mountains and into northern Mexico through the Rocky Mountains. Its northern limit is the Mackenzie River drainage, Canada, which lies within the Arctic Circle.

Habitat. Longnose dace occur in a wide variety of habitats. They are found in the riffles, runs, and pools of creeks, streams, and rivers. Within lakes, they are usually prefer areas around rocky shorelines. These streamlined fish are well adapted to fast-moving waters. Their species name, *cataractae,* means "of cataracts" and is appropriately descriptive of the habitat longnose dace often prefer.

Spawning behavior. Longnose dace mature within two years but may live up to five years. Females often grow larger and live longer than do males. Reproduction occurs between late spring and early summer. Interestingly, an eastern subspecies spawns during the day, whereas a western subspecies spawns at night. Longnose dace are categorized as broadcast spawners, scattering their eggs in shallow, fast-flowing areas and over chub nests. Males aggressively defend spawning areas, but more than one male may line up next to the female during spawning. Spawning occurs on the stream bottom and may result in the burial of eggs within the substrate. The female deposits between 200 and 1,200 eggs during spawning.

Food and feeding habits. Longnose dace feed on aquatic insects (especially midges and blackfly larvae), worms, small crustaceans, mites, algae, and plants. They have taste buds on their ventral fins, lower head, lips, and snout, which may enable them to find food along the stream bottom.

See: Dace.

Longnose Dace

DACRON LINE
See: Line.

DAISY CHAIN
(1) A combination of natural or artificial teasers rigged together in-line and used in offshore fishing, especially for marlin and tuna.

(2) The observed behavior of schools of tarpon swimming near the coast in a circular, rotating motion, prior to their departure for offshore spawning grounds.
See: Tarpon; Trolling Lures, Saltwater.

DAM
See: Lowhead Dam; Tailrace; Wingdam.

DAMSELFLIES
See: Dragonflies and Damselflies.

DANFORTH
A steel or aluminum anchor with two long, flat, and pointed flukes, also known as a lightweight burying anchor, or a fluke anchor.
See: Anchor.

DAPHNIA
A freshwater crustacean that moves along the water's surface with sudden leaps; also called water flea.

DAPPING
Dancing a dry fly on the surface of the water with leader and line held out of the water. The oldest form of fly fishing, dapping can be very tantalizing to fish, especially trout; the term was coined by Izaak Walton.

In general, dapping can be done with any rod to which a light monofilament line is tied and attached at the terminal end to a dry fly; this includes a cane pole, standard-length fly rod, or extra-long fly rod or pole. The shorter the rod or pole, however, the closer the fly must be fished to the angler, and the less likely a fish is to strike, since the fish is likely to see the angler or the boat (if there is one).

In a small, brush-lined creek, where making casts is very difficult, an angler can use a conventional fly rod, kneel behind or beside a streamside bush, extend the rod over the water, and dap the fly over the surface as if it were a natural insect depositing eggs in the water or struggling to stay out of the water.

Dapping is most practical, however, in open areas with the use of long poles. Irish and Scottish anglers dap for trout from boats, using poles that are 14 feet long or longer. In England, dapping poles range from 20 to 30 feet long. The long pole not only provides outward reach in open areas but also allows for a good length of line from the pole to fly. The long line is able to catch any breeze and move the fly around in a manner that cannot be replicated with conventional casting and recasting; the surface of the water remains undisturbed, except when a fish fiercely strikes the fly. When a strike occurs, the angler pauses for a moment to let the fish turn away with the fly and then lifts up the rod to set the hook.

British anglers use a length of silk floss (untwisted silk thread) above a fine tippet to catch the breeze, with a shorter length for breezier conditions and a longer length for calmer conditions. Heavily hackled flies are good for getting the attention of fish. The technique works on small waters in either a strong or a light breeze, but it can be frustrating in places where shoreside cover or trees tend to snag an errant fly or line. In a boat, an angler can avoid shoreside snags and can dap while at anchor or while drifting.

DARTERS
Darters are an incredibly diverse and colorful group of freshwater fish that rival saltwater fish in brilliance. They are actually small representatives of the perch family (Percidae) and are closely related to yellow perch and walleye. The darter group is comprised of approximately 160 species, all of which are restricted to North America. As such, they represent 20 percent of all fish in the United States.

Distribution. Darters range from northern Mexico into Canada and from the eastern coastal plains west to the Continental Divide. Only one species, the Mexican darter *(Etheostoma pottsi),* occurs west of the Continental Divide, in northern Mexico. Darters are most diverse in the southern Appalachian Mountains of Tennessee and Virginia and the Ozark plateau of northern Arkansas. The johnny darter *(Etheostoma nigrum)* is the most widely distributed, followed by the orangethroat darter *(Etheostoma spectabile)* and perhaps the logperch darter *(Percina caprodes).*

Identification. Three genera of darters are recognized: *Percina*, which includes roughly 40 species; *Etheostoma*, which includes roughly 112 species, and *Ammocrypta*, with 7 species. The genus *Percina* contains the largest darters. Most are rather drab and cryptic in coloration, although the males of some species exhibit impressive spawning coloration. The genus *Etheostoma* is diverse in the shape and coloration of its representatives. The

Johnny Darter

bodies and fins of many of these darters are painted with shades of red, blue, yellow, green, and orange interspersed with black blotches. Members of the genus *Ammocrypta* are dull and sand-colored. This camouflages them from predators in the large, sand-bottomed rivers they inhabit.

Darters can reach a length of 12 inches (*Percina lenticula*, the freckled darter), although most are only a few inches long, even as adults. The smallest is the fountain darter (*Etheostoma fonticola*), which reaches an adult size of only $1\frac{1}{2}$ inches. Darters have two dorsal fins, the front with hard spines and the rear with soft rays. The caudal fin is usually rounded or emarginate. Many darters are sexually dimorphic, and the males are usually larger and brightly colored. Males also develop thickened body tissues, fleshy knobs on the dorsal fin rays and spines, and breeding tubercles during spawning. The showy appearance of courting males is thought to attract females during spawning and accounts for the large amount of angling interest in this group.

Habitat. Darters are found in all types of freshwater habitat. They may inhabit small streams, large rivers, spring seeps, ponds, lakes, or reservoirs. They are most frequently found in fast-moving water, however.

Life history/Behavior. As a group, darters are well adapted to life in fast water and on the stream bottom. Their rounded bodies and slightly flattened head regions are especially hydrodynamic. In addition, most members of the group have completely absent, or poorly developed, swim bladders. They use their enlarged pectoral fins to perch on rocks, allowing them to remain on the stream bottom out of the current. Their body style is suited to the unique swimming manner for which this group as a whole is named. Darters do not swim in the same way that most fish do; instead, they leap from one spot to another with short jumps or "darts."

Darters display much variability in reproductive strategies. Most produce few, relatively large eggs and provide some degree of parental care. Most members of the genus *Etheostoma* are cavity spawners and lay adhesive eggs on the underside of medium-size rocks, usually in fast water. Males of this genus are often brightly colored to attract females to nest sites that they have prepared for egg laying. Members of the genera *Percina* and *Ammocrypta* spawn in a simpler manner. Two or more individuals group together in fast-water areas over sand between larger rocks. Males and females align their bodies next to each other, then simultaneously release sperm and eggs into the substrate and bury them. This protects the eggs from predation and floods.

Most darters spawn in spring to early summer. Several species are believed to spawn multiple times per year. Darters are not a long-lived group. Most species live less than five years. Sexual maturity is usually attained between one and three years.

Food and feeding habits. Darters primarily feed on bottom-dwelling organisms, mostly small insects, worms, and snails. However, as a group they exhibit a diversity of feeding strategies that correspond to morphological differences. Large darters feed on insects on top of rocks or pick them out of sand and gravel. Shorter, more flexible darters often feed on clinging insects between and underneath rocks. As a result of these different feeding strategies, several darter species can coexist in the same area of a stream.

Darters as bait. Although darters are not a sportfish group because of their small size, they may be taken incidentally by anglers fishing for other species. Incidental landings are not common because these fish primarily inhabit fast riffles, that is, areas not frequently fished by anglers. Darters are often used as baits, however, most often when anglers collect their own baitfish with minnow seines or other less-discriminating gear. Their effectiveness as baits is likely related to their role as prey for piscivorous gamefish. Many fly fishing streamer patterns and some small jigs imitate darter species, and anglers would be wise to remember the movements of these fish when trying to imitate them.

Darter watching. Darter watching requires careful observation. Because they are small, hide under rocks, and move about quickly, darters are hard to follow and not commonly observed by anglers. Because of their striking coloration and impressive diversity, however, darters are often watched by snorkelers in warmwater streams. The majority of darter species are most colorful during spawning in late spring and early summer, so this is the best time to observe them.

Threats. Most darters survive best in clean and clear water. Because of this, they are good indicators of water and habitat quality. Due to the specific habitat requirements of many darters, the nature of impacts on aquatic systems can be judged by which darters are impacted.

Many darters are declining or are already threatened or endangered. Declines are due to a number of factors, including habitat alteration, pollution, and the introduction of additional competitors and predators. Because many darters require clean substrate for spawning, sedimentation from poor land-use practices can negatively affect their reproduction. Alteration of a stream channel as a result of such disturbances can also eliminate adult and rearing habitats. Because many darters have naturally small populations, one impact can wipe out a whole species. Because of this, anglers who collect baitfish should take care to not remove many darters from a single area. They should also inform themselves of any endangered or threatened species that may be present in areas where they are collecting bait.

DAYBEACON

An unlighted aid to navigation that is a fixed structure on shore or in the water close to shore, used for shallow water and channel marking.

DAY BOAT
A term for party boat *(see)*.

DEAD BAIT
Whole dead fish or other natural organisms used to catch predatory fish, especially bottom scroungers. This term is also spelled as "deadbait."
See: Bait; Chumming; Natural Bait.

DEAD DRIFT
Another term for drag-free drift *(see)*.
See: Mending.

DEAD RECKONING
Dead reckoning is a nonelectronic method of calculating a boat's position, especially on a navigational chart *(see)*, using speed through the water, course steered, and time traveled from a known location. A dead reckoning is done without any adjustment for current, wind, waves, or steering error. It has nothing to do with visual observation of landmarks.
See: Navigation.

DEBONER
A tubelike tool for removing the backbone of a moderate-sized fish that will be used as offshore trolling bait. The tube cuts around and extracts the backbone out of an otherwise intact fish, making it more pliable for better trolling action when properly rigged.

DEBONING
See: Fish Preparation—Cleaning/Dressing.

DECALS, BOAT
A relatively new concept, boat decals are adhesive-backed imitations of small baitfish and squid that are applied to the entire hull of a boat to look like a school or ball of forage and to attract gamefish.

DECOY
Fish-shaped objects used under the ice to lure large species to a baited hook or, more often, within range of a spear. Decoys are not commonly used in standard ice fishing today. Antique ice fishing decoys are collectibles.
See: Antique Fishing Tackle; Spearing.

DEEP-SCATTERING LAYER
A layer of marine organisms in the open ocean at depths greater than 660 feet that produces a scattering effect detectable by sonar. The sonic difference results from an echo produced by gas bubbles within the animals in the layer. More than one deep-scattering layer may be present at any particular place, with the layers moving up in daylight or bright moonlight and descending at night or on heavily overcast days. The movement follows that of schools of small fish, squid, and larger crustaceans.

DEEP-SEA FISHING
A term widely used to refer to ocean fishing. Commonly used by tourism interests, deep-sea fishing usually refers to angling on charter and party boats, especially for bottom-dwelling species, and is distinguished from fishing in shallow waters near or close to shore, or fishing from smaller boats, such as skiffs or guide boats.
See: Inshore Fishing; Offshore Fishing.

DELAWARE
A small state with no large lakes or large rivers, Delaware nevertheless holds its own in sportfishing opportunities. Much of that is in the salt because the Delmarva Peninsula constitutes nearly 95 percent of the state and offers 381 miles of tidal shoreline. The western and southern fringes of this South Atlantic state drain west toward Chesapeake Bay, while the others flow to the Delaware River, Delaware Bay, or the Atlantic Ocean.

In the salt chuck, the First State boasts excellent bottom fishing for weakfish, flounder, and croaker, as well as sea bass and tautog on offshore wrecks; big bluefish, tuna, dolphin, king mackerel, blue marlin, and white marlin; and striped bass, bluefish, weakfish, king whiting, and flounder for surf and jetty anglers. The interior offers impressive smallmouth bass fishing in the northern part of the state; big largemouths in the old millponds and tidal rivers below the Chesapeake and Delaware Canal (also known as the C & D Canal); and good action in various waters for catfish, carp, pickerel, crappie, and sunfish. This isn't too shabby for a state that is smaller than some Texas counties.

Freshwater
New Castle County. In the early part of the eighteenth century, the DuPonts were attracted to Brandywine River and harnessed its power to turn their mills. The mills are long gone, but this waterway is still beautiful and provides excellent light-tackle smallmouth bass fishing.

One of the more enjoyable ways to fish the Brandywine, which has shallow water and moderate current flow, is from a canoe. Anglers launch from the bank near the Delaware-Pennsylvania line and paddle downstream to Rockland. The dam left over from an old paper mill at this location requires a portage before heading downstream again. Another dam, Hagley, at the site of DuPont's first gunpowder plant, marks the end of the line for fishing from a canoe. Smallmouths are pursued in the rocky waters below this point from shore or by wading.

Largemouth bass also thrive in the Brandywine, but they are larger and more common in the ponds of the southern part of this county. Lums Pond, which is the largest impoundment in New Castle County, is one such site; it's located between Routes 896 and 301 just north of the C & D Canal. Another is Becks Pond. This small waterway produces big bass and is located between Route 72 and Salem Church Road.

Delaware doesn't have a population of native trout, but each spring the Department of Natural Resources (DNR) stocks several streams in New Castle County with rainbows. White Clay Creek holds most of these and receives most of the angling pressure. Located near Newark, this stream has a fly-fishing-only section at the north end, but assorted baits are favored along the rest of the waterway.

Tidal streams and the C & D Canal provide good catfish angling. The canal has several fishing piers with easy, safe access. In the tidal streams, bank anglers typically favor the waters around bridges. Augustine Beach has a boat ramp and beach fishing access.

Kent County. Delaware's middle county has a network of small streams and ponds. The streams hold little angling interest, but the ponds offer excellent fishing opportunities for bass, bluegills, crappie, and pickerel.

Many large bass have been landed in the so-called Milford chain, three ponds located near Milford in the southern part of the county. Blairs Pond, Silver Lake, and Haven Lake in the chain produce big bass on a regular basis. Those who expect big bass to live in big water will be surprised to find that these ponds cover a small area. They are old millponds, as are most of the freshwater impoundments in Delaware, and were built on the headwaters of the Mispillion River.

These ponds would have filled in over the years, but the DNR has managed them for the benefit of anglers. Delaware's pond-management program is a model for similar programs in other states. All three are accessible from shore; Silver and Haven Lakes offer boat ramps.

Another noteworthy pond in the county is Killen, which has bass, catfish, sunfish, and pickerel. Located in Killen Pond State Park, it has a boat ramp and camping area and is located close to other good fishing sites in Kent and Sussex Counties.

Sussex County. The overwhelming favorites of freshwater anglers in this part of Delaware are Nanticoke River and Broad Creek. The two waterways join at Phillips Landing, where there is an excellent boat ramp. Largemouth bass are the primary target, but pickerel and stripers are fished here as well.

This is tidal water, so the bass do not grow to exceptional size, yet they strike and fight harder than their larger local pond cousins. The environment here is hard on bass, which must be on the move to overcome tidal currents and keep away from a wider array of predators than are found in sheltered waters.

Fishing on the Nanticoke River and Broad Creek requires working with the tides. As a general rule it's best to start downriver at the Delaware-Maryland line and work upriver toward Seaford or Laurel on a falling tide. As the water washes out of the tidal marshes and creeks, bass set up ambush sites to intercept the baitfish. Anglers cast toward and around shore cover with spinnerbaits, crankbaits, and plastic worms.

Elsewhere in the county, Trap Pond State Park has a unique setting as well as good fishing. Trap Pond drains into Cypress Swamp, the only cypress grove north of the Mason-Dixon line. Here, anglers fish from canoes for bass and pickerel, amid beautiful scenery.

Saltwater

New Castle County. Saltwater fishing in this county is restricted to the southern sector, except during dry spells in late summer, when saltwater intrusion works as far north as the Delaware Memorial Bridge. The jumping-off place for upper Delaware Bay and the lower Delaware River is Augustine Beach off of Route 9, just south of the C & D Canal. A boat ramp is available, and it is also possible to fish from the beach.

Anglers catch small blues and weakfish here in the summer, and striped bass in the spring and fall. Small bucktails tipped with peeler crabs, shrimp, or squid work well on the weakfish and blues. Bucktails are also effective on striped bass, but bloodworms are the first choice for these fish.

Structure, like that found near Reedy and Pea Patch Islands or around the wrecks and lighthouses, holds the best angling potential. On occasion, schools of bluefish or striped bass chase baits to the surface, where diving gulls will mark the location. This activity is more likely to occur early or late in the day.

Kent County. Kent County contains the entire 28 miles of Delaware's Atlantic coastline, plus access to both the upper and lower regions of Delaware Bay.

Fishing upper Delaware Bay out of Woodland Beach produces more consistently than does working the waters near Augustine Beach. The bottom close to shore is covered with the remains of old oyster beds and holds a variety of baitfish and gamefish. Farther out, the edge of the channel provides deeper water where weakfish, flounder, and bluefish stage, particularly at low tide. Bottom fishing with peeler crabs and squid is the most popular technique here, but anglers also find success casting bucktails and plastic grubs. The best bite is almost always at dawn and dusk.

Port Mahon is another launch site for anglers who fish the upper bay. Bowers Beach has a launch ramp and a fleet of charter and head boats; this fleet specializes in bottom fishing for weakfish, flounder, blues, and croaker. There's nothing fancy to this activity, which mainly involves soaking baits, but the action can be fast when schools of fish frequent the shoals or deeper sloughs.

Slaughters Beach is the site of the most impressive run of big weakfish ever recorded during the 1980s, but this might not be seen again. Weakfish are still the most important species here, but they now average less than 5 pounds rather than 15. Brandywine Light, 14 Foot Shoal, and the Coral Beds drew anglers from all over during the banner years, and they still hold good numbers of weaks, plus flounder, bluefish, and croaker. Cut squid, peeler crabs, and live minnows are favored bait offerings, with bucktails and grubs employed by lure users.

Roosevelt Inlet, in Lewes, empties into the lower Delaware Bay, with access to the Atlantic Ocean. Charter and head boats running from this port fish for everything from croaker and weakfish to tuna and marlin. A public launch ramp in town provides access for the private boater. The Lewes Breakwater, a long rock jetty near Cape Henlopen, provides excellent fishing for tautog. Spring and fall are prime, and most fish are taken on fresh-cut crabs.

Surf fishing in the fall is especially good along the beach from Cape Henlopen down to Navy Beach. Big blues and striped bass are the primary targets, with king whiting and weakfish mixed in the catch.

Indian River Inlet, south of Rehoboth, is home to a large fleet of private and charter boats that work the inshore and offshore waters of the Atlantic Ocean. Anglers travel 70 to 80 miles or more from this site to the canyons in search of dolphin, tuna, wahoo, and marlin. Closer to shore, the wrecks provide good fishing for sea bass and tautog. Trollers working over wrecks and seamounts catch big blues, little tunny, king mackerel, and bluefin tuna.

Behind the inlet, Indian River and Rehoboth Bays host hoards of small boaters who target summer flounder, weakfish, and blues. The shallow, sheltered waters of these bays are ideal for family excursions, and pontoon boats are popular craft.

The surf from Rehoboth to Fenwick Island is open to fishing and supports a large number of anglers and their beach buggies. Fishing is best in spring and fall, but summer action can sometimes be good early or late in the day, perhaps depending on tide stage.

DELAYED MORTALITY

A term for the instance when a fish that was caught by an angler and released alive dies at some later time, usually because of injury or stress.
See: Catch-and-Release.

DELTA

A fan-shaped, low-lying plain at the mouth of a river, created by deposited sediment. Formation of a delta depends on the rate of sedimentation, volume of river flow, and the currents of the sea; a strong sea current can prevent formation of, or can erode, an existing delta. The local coastline in a delta is constantly changing as sediment is moved and rearranged.

Deltas are often rich in aquatic life and are especially likely to host nearshore species of gamefish that utilize or tolerate lower levels of salinity. Such species as snook and tarpon are common inhabitants of warm deltas.

DEMERSAL

A term used for fish or animals that live on or near the seabed or water bottom. Examples include flounder and croaker. Demersal is often used synonymously with groundfish.

DENMARK

Situated in northwestern Europe, Denmark is the southernmost Scandinavian country. It is a low-lying nation best known in angling circles for its exceptional sea trout (sea-run brown trout) fishing. Bordered on the south by Germany, Denmark's mainland, known as Jutland (Jylland), is a 400-kilometer-long peninsula bounded on the west and north by the North Sea, and on the east by the Baltic Sea. The country includes more than 500 islands, 100 of which are populated; most of these lie to the east, directly in the outlet of the Baltic.

The largest Danish island is Zealand (Sjaelland), which contains the capital city of Copenhagen. The second largest is Funen (Fyn). Denmark also contains the Faeroe Islands, located almost midway between the Shetland Islands and Iceland in the North Atlantic.

Though small in area at 43,000 square kilometers, Denmark has good fishing opportunities in the ocean, brackish water, and freshwater. Some of the Atlantic's best cod fishing takes place here; sea trout fishing is well developed along much of the coastline; pike and perch fishing is good along the brackish inner islands; rivers contain resident and sea-run populations of trout; and small interior waters hold good fishing for coarse species.

Freshwater

Freshwater fishing in Denmark's rivers for brown trout, sea trout, grayling, hatchery-escaped rainbows, and a few salmon is the favored pursuit among anglers. All of the important rivers are on the Jylland peninsula. A lowland area (the average elevation is about 30 meters), it has no falls or rapids, and the rivers run with good speed.

Only a handful of Danish rivers originally held

Dr. James Henshall is noted for his classic 1881 book on bass fishing, but he also developed fishing tackle and, while in Montana, was the first to breed grayling artificially.

Trout fishing on the Gudenå in Denmark.

salmon. Except for the easterly flowing Gudenå, all the salmon rivers enter the North Sea. They are the Storåen, Skjernå, Snerumå, Vardeå, Kongeåen, Ribeå, and Vidåen. Some of these rivers, especially the Skjernå, once had excellent populations of big salmon. A 60-pounder was caught in the Skjernå in 1956. Agricultural pollution, habitat alteration, and dams wiped out the salmon, however. Today, significant effort and money is being expended to increase or to reintroduce them.

Almost all Danish rivers, from the largest rivers in Jylland to the smallest brooks on Bornholm Island, have runs of sea trout. Quite a few of these, mainly the smallest streams, still contain original strains of wild fish.

Among the better sea trout rivers are the Karupå, Kongeåen, Ribeå, Gelså, Vejleå, and Kolding. The most prolific sea trout river is the Karupå, where the spring run begins as early as the end of April. The largest Danish sea trout was taken in the Karupå and weighed 14.6 kilograms; it was also the world record for many years.

Fresh sea trout enter the Karupå until spawning occurs in November and December. In many of the medium-size rivers, the first fresh trout enter in July and August. In the smaller rivers, fish enter when a good autumn rain facilitates upstream movement. From January through April, rivers experience another popular season, with a run of mainly sexually immature sea trout weighing between .5 kilogram to 1.5 kilograms.

Brown trout thrive in all suitable rivers and streams. They are commonly caught to 1 kilogram, and the summer months of June through August have the best hatches. Grayling inhabit a few rivers, all of them on the west coast of Jylland and in the Gudenå on the east. The official open-river season is from mid-January through mid-November, but in many rivers the season is shorter.

In addition to salmonids, most rivers also support populations of pike, perch, eels, whitefish, and other species in their lower reaches. Some rivers hold large perch—of 1 to 2 kilograms—that enter from the sea to spawn. The most well known is the Tryggevaeldeå, which is 40 kilometers from Copenhagen.

Pike, perch, zander, bream, rudd, tench, whitefish, eels, roach, and carp inhabit most larger lakes. A few lakes hold brown trout, whitefish, and burbot. Apart from this natural fishing, several hundred small put-and-take lakes or ponds dot the country. These are regularly stocked, mainly with rainbow trout from 1 to 10 kilograms, but they also have brown trout, brook trout, salmon, and hybrid trout.

No professional fishing guides are available, but tackle shops can provide assistance, and most Danes speak English. Day tickets can be bought for particular stretches on most rivers.

Anglers require a state-issued license to fish in natural waters in and around Denmark and can obtain one at any post office. Short-term tourist licenses are available. Fishing rights on natural lakes, rivers, and streams are nearly always private, but they are often leased to local angling clubs. These clubs issue daily or weekly permits, which are available from tourist offices. In some locations anglers can rent a boat with fishing rights included.

Saltwater

In addition to facing the North Sea on its west, Denmark is bounded on the north by the Skagerrak, which is an arm of the North Sea, and on the east by the Kattegat Sea and the Øresund Strait, which links Kattegat to the Baltic Sea. On the south it is bounded by the Baltic Sea and Fehmarn Strait.

Because the Baltic Sea is the largest brackish water in the world, most inner and southern islands in Denmark are surrounded by water that holds both freshwater fish like pike and perch and saltwater species like cod. Above the narrow channels where most of the islands are located, the water turns more saline until reaching full salinity at the Kattegat Sea.

The influence of the tides is minimal around most of Denmark. At the most southern part of the west coast of Jylland, the maximum fluctuation is 2 meters. In the channels, the tides range between 12 and 15 centimeters; around the island of Bornholm in the lower part of the Baltic Sea, the difference is visible only when there is no wind.

With more than 7,500 kilometers of coastline in Denmark, saltwater fishing is the country's largest angling resource. All fishing in saltwater is public; and all that is necessary to enjoy the resource is an inexpensive state license. Fishing from the shore or wading in the surf are favored pursuits. The shallow, and in many places well-sheltered, coastline offers excellent fishing for sea trout. A large food supply is available here, as is good shelter for smaller fish.

Thanks to a temperate maritime climate, saltwater fishing for sea trout is a year-round enterprise in Denmark, except for the rare winters when the sea freezes. The main months are March, April, and October, when the fish are moving to and from the rivers. The summers mainly offer night fishing along the open coast; winter fishing occurs predominantly in sheltered bays, where the water is less saline, and on the open coast south of channels, where the water is more brackish. The average sea trout weighs between 1 and 2.5 kilograms; a few are larger, and every year a number of trophy fish are in the 7- to 10-kilogram range.

The main technique for sea trout fishing does not change much throughout the year. Most anglers prefer spinning tackle, using 8- to 10-foot-long rods, light line, and long-casting spoons or plugs. Because 90 percent of the fishing occurs in 1 to 3 meters of water, and long casts are essential, the typical Danish coastal trout lure is not a fast sinker. Shore anglers often wear waders. The technique is simply to cover water by moving between each cast, using casting distances of between 45 and 80 meters. Reefs and areas with tidal current are fished more intensely. A bubble float used with a fly or a bait is also highly effective.

Fly fishing for coastal sea trout is popular, too. Fly anglers use 7- to 10-weight floating weight-forward or shooting-head lines and a 9- to $9^1/_2$-foot-long rod. There's a great variety of food available for the trout, so the fish are normally not picky. Most flies are streamers or shrimp patterns.

Other species commonly encountered from the shore or surf include cod, flounder, and eels; in season, garfish, herring, mullet, and mackerel are pursued. South of the channels, the fiords might hold perch and pike.

Fishing on the open waters is popular and offers a great variety of fish. Winter fishing for big spawning cod in Øresund Strait between Sweden and Denmark is a particularly popular fishery. In winter, large cod gather in this area to spawn. Big specimens are fish over 10 kilograms; individual catches may exceed 20 kilograms. This is one of the best places in Europe for large cod, especially from January through March. In the 1960s it was also a prime place for bluefin tuna.

Most of the year, ocean fishing charter boats pursue cod, flounder, garfish, mackerel, and other common saltwater species, but they might get into 2- to 5-kilogram sea trout. In Kattegat and the North Sea, the list of fish is much longer, and includes catfish, haddock, conger eels, tope, and many more species. Bottom fishing is the primary angling method.

Trolling is a relatively new saltwater tactic in Denmark. Since the early 1990s, a hidden potential has been found by trollers; many larger sea trout feed mostly off the coastline and out of reach of shore-based casters, but trolling can produce these fish. Around Bornholm in the Baltic Sea, a developing trolling sportfishery for Atlantic salmon is underway. The best season is spring, and salmon are in the 7- to 12-kilogram range. In the spring of 1998 the record was broken twice, first with a fish of 19.65 kilograms, then a few weeks later with one of 20.74 kilograms.

Faeroe Islands
Located in the North Atlantic, between Iceland, Norway, and Scotland, are 18 small, beautiful, rugged and windy islands covering just 1,373 square kilometers, populated by 45,000 people and 100,000 sheep. A self-governed territory of Denmark, the Faeroe Islands are accessed via daily flights from Copenhagen, or twice-weekly flights from Iceland. During the summer a weekly ferry crosses from Iceland and Denmark.

There is no reliable river angling here, as only after a good rain will fish be able to swim upriver. Sea trout can be fished outside all streams when there is just a slight chance that they might be able to swim upriver. When it does rain, rivers that contain lakes along their system usually have excellent sea trout fishing. An example is Sandsvatn on Sandoy Island.

Salmon also inhabit the Faeroes but are more plentiful in lakes, such as Saksun and Leynarvatn on Streymoy Island and Skálabotnur on Eystoroy Island. Salmon normally range from 2 to 5 kilograms, and sea trout from 1 to 3 kilograms.

All Faeroe lakes—from the largest, which is Sørvágsvatn at 7 kilometers long, to the tiniest little ponds in the mountains—hold small brown trout. Only a few hold larger fish. The most southern island, Suderoy, has the most lakes. A few lakes offer arctic charr in the 1- to 3-kilogram range. Lowland lakes with sea access might offer good fishing for eels.

All around the islands—that is, anywhere the steep and indented coast permits access—anglers can pursue pollock, flatfish, and red cod. Escaped salmon and rainbow trout are sought after near fish farms. There is potentially good offshore bottom fishing for the likes of cod, pollock, and halibut, but the wind-whipped sea is often rough, making it difficult to find a charter.

No permit is required for saltwater fishing. Freshwater fishing requires a permit or permission from the landowner.

DENTEX *Dentex dentex.*
Other names—common dentex, dentice, denton, dente; French: *denté commun*; Spanish: *dentón*.

A member of the Sparidae family, the dentex is a popular eastern Atlantic gamefish and an esteemed table fish.

Identification. Dentex have an oval, deep body with a smoothly rounded head. Exceptionally large individuals have a profile with a slight frontal hump. Both jaws have well-developed caninelike teeth, plus several rows of smaller teeth of similar shape. The dorsal fin has 11 spines and 11 or 12 soft rays, the spines increasing in length from the first to the fourth or fifth then subequal. The lateral

Dentex

line has 62 to 68 scales. Their coloration is variable, but young dentex are grayish, spotted with black on the back and upper sides, becoming pinkish with sexual maturity. Older individuals are grayish blue with spots becoming more or less diffuse with age. Some have a yellow tinge behind the mouth and on the gill cover.

Its dark spots can distinguish the dentex from other similar species, as can the several rows of canine-like teeth. Other species have more than one type of teeth, or incisor-like teeth.

Size. The all-tackle record is 21 pounds, 11 ounces, which was caught in Italy in 1993, but dentex reportedly grow to 33 pounds.

Distribution. The dentex occurs in the Mediterranean Sea and the Atlantic Ocean from the Bay of Biscay to West Africa north of Cape Blanc, Mauritania, and Madeira. Occasionally, the dentex ranges as far north as the British Isles and as far south as Senegal.

Habitat. Although they inhabit hard bottoms (rock or rubble) down to 650 feet, dentex are more commonly found between 50 and 165 feet.

Life history/Behavior. In summer dentex approach the shore, but in winter they migrate to deeper water. Adults are generally solitary, and juveniles travel in schools.

Food and feeding habits. Dentex are active, predatory fish that feed on fish, mollusks, and cephalopods (octopuses, cuttlefish, squid).

Angling. Fishing methods include trolling with bait and lures, generally in water from 35 to 165 feet, and bottom fishing in these and greater depths with live or dead baits. Angling prerequisites for the canny dentex include light leaders and small hooks.

DEPTHFINDER
See: Sonar.

DEPTH SOUNDER
See: Sonar.

DERBY
A fishing contest, usually open to the general public, and usually one in which a nominal entry fee is charged. Derbies are often associated with events for children or families, and where there is a high number of participants.
See: Competitive Fishing.

DESIGNATED WATER
A term used in some Canadian provinces for waters where Atlantic salmon are considered the primary species pursued by anglers as of a specified date, and where nonresidents must be accompanied by a guide, regardless of target species. Most such waters are also scheduled *(see)*.

DETRITUS
Waste from decomposing organisms, which provides food for many other organisms.

DGPS
An acronym for Differential GPS.
See: GPS.

DIADROMOUS
Fish that migrate between freshwater and saltwater.
See: Anadromous; Catadromous.

DIAMOND JIG
A metal lure with four sides, wide at the middle and tapered to a point at either end. A diamond jig is a common lure in saltwater for bottom fishing and vertical jigging, and it is used on bluefish, striped bass, cod, pollock, and many other species. It is not a jig in the sense of leadheads, but since it has no inherent built-in action, it must be manipulated in a jigging manner to be effective and is actually a type of jigging spoon. Diamond jigs come in various weights and lengths and with single or treble hooks, which are attached to the base of the lure with a sturdy O-ring.
See: Inshore Fishing; Jig; Jigging; Spoon.

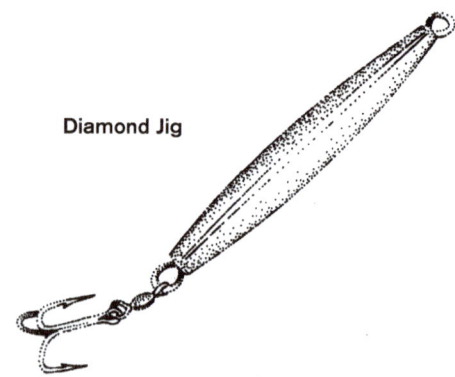

Diamond Jig

DINGELL JOHNSON ACT
See: Federal Aid in Sport Fish Restoration Act.

DINOFLAGELLATE
Unicellular microscopic organisms, classified as plants or animals depending on the presence of chlorophyll or the ingestion of food, respectively. Found in two main groups, armored and naked, dinoflagellates have flagella (whiplike extensions) that provide locomotion, and move vertically in response to light. Many dinoflagellates are phosphorescent, and some greatly increase in number periodically, occasionally resulting in toxic red tides *(see)*. Some dinoflagellate blooms are toxic to shellfish and can cause gastroenteritis in the organisms that feed on them, including humans. As a component of phytoplankton (microscopic organisms that photosynthesize), dinoflagellates are an important basis for marine life.

DIPNET
Any small handheld net, with rigid support about the mouth, used for landing fish. Generally, dipnet refers to a small-mesh net that is used for hand-gathering baitfish and/or some nongamefish species and that is subject to specific regulations. A small net used to land gamefish, such as trout or bass, is also referred to as a dipnet, but it should not be confused with the act of dip-netting baitfish or nongamefish.
See: Landing Net.

DIRECT DRIVE
A term for fishing reels without a gear set, in which one revolution of the reel handle produces one revolution of the reel spool, meaning that there is a 1:1 ratio in line retrieval. This is the simplest and most powerful reel, but also one with slow line recovery, especially when the level of line on the spool is reduced.
See: Big-Game Tackle; Conventional Tackle; Flycasting Tackle; Gear Ratio.

DISC DRAG
A term for reels with disc drag systems; also the disc-shaped washers that are used in reel drags.
See: Baitcasting Tackle; Big-Game Tackle; Conventional Tackle; Flycasting Tackle; Spincasting Tackle; Spinning Tackle.

DISEASES AND PARASITES
Like all other living creatures, fish are capable of harboring parasites or contracting diseases. From a consumption standpoint, these are usually more damaging to the angler's sense of aesthetics than they are to the fish itself, although certain parasites can be harmful to humans, and many diseases are harmful to fish. With proper preparation, most infected fish can be eaten without concern.

Diseases are fairly commonplace in fish populations. Parasites and bacteria are a natural part of the ecosystem in which fish live. Lake fish are especially susceptible because of warmer water temperatures and the abundance of other organisms through which disease may be transmitted. Saltwater fish are not immune, however.

Most parasites spend only part of their lives in fish. Birds, snails, plankton, and even mammals may host a parasite at different stages of its life. Parasites go through as many as six different stages from egg to adult.

Anglers may notice that some symptoms follow seasonal patterns or other cycles. This situation is especially noticeable when parasites are passed to fish through migrating birds.

Most fish disorders are classified as parasitic, bacterial, or viral. Anglers are more likely to come into contact with fish affected by parasites or bacteria than by viruses. Viral infections are usually detected at hatcheries while fish are at the fry stage. Wild or stocked fish with viral infections are generally small, weak, and unlikely to strike at anglers' offerings; natural predators usually catch these fish before anglers do.

Evidence of parasites or infection in an occasional gamefish doesn't automatically point to an unhealthy environment or poor water quality. It also doesn't mean that every fish in the area will be affected the same way. However, some diseases are more insidious than others, and result in the death of significant numbers of fish. Whirling Disease *(see)*, a parasitic infection that attacks the cartilage of young trout and salmon, is such a case. Pfiesteria *(see)*, which is a toxic algal bloom (though many people think of it as a disease), is a mass killer.

Internal Parasites
Internal parasites are found in the muscle tissue, eye, under the skin, and in or around the internal organs. Some of the more common ones include the following.

Yellow grub *(Clinostomum marginatum)*. One of the most common North American fish parasites, yellow grub infests a variety of freshwater fish, though it is rarely found in trout species. The $1/4$-inch-long grub is flat and encased in a cyst just under the skin in the muscle where it forms a wartlike bump. These bumps are often visible at the base of the fins and tail, or may be found on the gills.

Black spot or black grub *(Uvulifer ambloplitis)*. Larvae of black grubs are most noticeable in fillets of fish that have white meat. Infection from the larvae creates small, raised black spots, which look like pepper in the skin and flesh. The tiny larvae are white, but the fish produces a black pigment that surrounds the thick-walled cysts. Skinning an infected fish will remove most grubs, since the majority of cysts occur in the skin.

Eye fluke *(Diplostomum spathaceum)*. Eye flukes seem to be most abundant in rainbow trout but also occur in other species of trout and in bass, bluegills, and other warmwater species. The fluke occurs in the lens and fluid portion of the fish's eye. A popeyed effect is sometimes created from accumulation of fluids in the eyeball. In advanced cases, the eye becomes opaque white and the fish becomes partially or totally blind.

Bass tapeworm (*Proteocephalus ambloplitis*). The bass tapeworm can be very damaging to freshwater fish but is not transmissible to humans. Largemouth, smallmouth, and rock bass are the most susceptible species. Although the adult tapeworm looks serious, with lengths up to $2^1/_2$ feet, the larvae actually do the most damage to the fish. Larvae invade reproductive organs and can cause sterility in the fish. Bass tapeworms are most evident in the fish's intestine. In heavy infestations, internal adhesions may be so great that the intestines, liver, spleen, and reproductive organs are bound into a single mass by a mat of connective tissue.

Trout tapeworm (*Diphyllobothrium spp.*). The larvae of this tapeworm appear as white cysts in the abdominal organs and body cavity of trout. When heavily infested, the trout becomes listless and swims lazily near the surface. Only fish host the larvae of this parasite. Adult trout tapeworms are found in birds, dogs, cats, and bears. Several species are infectious to people.

Seatrout tapeworm (*Poecilancistrium caryophyllum*). This tapeworm and a similar one in black drum are known as spaghetti worms. They are white, 1 to 3 inches long, and are parasitic tapeworms of sharks, which use the trout and drum as an intermediate host. Usually one to two worms exist in a fish, and they are harmless to humans.

Spiny-headed worm (*Acanthocephala*). Various species of these small worms are found in just about all freshwater fish. Spiny-headed worms, usually no longer than $3/_8$ inch, are most often found imbedded in the fish's intestine. These worms are easily identified by their round bodies. They can be white or pale yellow but are often a bright orange color. Their tubelike snout is covered with spines, which are used to attach to the fish.

Roundworm (*Nematode*). Roundworms can be identified by their round elongated bodies and lack of segmentation or suckers. Most roundworms pose little danger to humans, but the kidney roundworm, found in bullhead and northern pike, may be transmitted to humans, as may the herring worm (*Anisakis simplex*) and cod or seal worm (*Pseudoterranova decipiens*), which are marine nematodes. The latter nematodes can be found in all marine fish, not just herring or cod, as their common names suggest. Researchers have found these worms in cod, herring, tuna, mackerel, flatfish, anchovy, pollock, rockfish, salmon, halibut, and squid, to name just a few. Thorough freezing and/or cooking will greatly reduce the possibility of parasite transmission; not doing this, however, poses a serious risk for humans of getting an intestinal disease known as Anisakiasis. Commercial processors candle white-fleshed fish (by illuminating fish portions over a bright backlit table) to see and remove this parasite from the muscle tissue.

Red roundworm (*Eustronglydes sp.*). Red roundworm is one of the most common nematodes, or roundworms. This parasite is found in many species of fish, including largemouth and smallmouth bass, walleye, sunfish, rock bass, crappie, yellow perch, pickerel, and eels. Redworm larvae are found in the fish's flesh and internal organs and are easily recognized by their deep red color. Occasionally, their infestation is so great the fish can't be salvaged to eat. They are infectious to people.

White roundworm (*Philonema sp.*). These small, white, threadlike worms are 1 to $1^1/_2$ inches long. White roundworms are found in the air bladder or free in the body cavity of various trout species.

External Parasites

External parasites are most often found attached to the outside of the skin, fin, or gills of fish. Copepods, which are part of a large group of tiny aquatic crustaceans, are common external parasites that are abundant in both freshwater and saltwater and form an important part of the food chain for fish and plankton-eating marine animals. However, some copepods have turned the tables and adapted to life as parasites. Two of the most commonly seen parasitic copepods are fish lice and anchor worms.

Fish lice (*Argulus spp.*). The 17 known species of fish lice have been found in almost all warm-water and anadromous fish. At first glance, fish lice look somewhat like scales, but they are actually saucer-shaped. The lice sometimes have jointed legs and two disk-shaped suckers, which are sometimes mistaken for eyes. The lice, usually $1/_8$- to $1/_4$-inch long, can creep over the surface of the fish and are found attached to the skin, fin, or gills.

Anchor worm (*Lernea spp.*). When anglers complain of "wormy-" or "grubby-looking" fish, they're often referring to an infestation of anchor

Sea lice, shown here on a pink salmon, are one of the most common and harmless fish parasites.

worm. The parasite is about the size of a grain of rice, is yellowish white, and is found primarily in the gills, mouth, or fins of trout. The head of this copepod is buried in the flesh, with the remainder of the worm hanging from the wound. When the copepod dies and falls off, an inflamed wound may be left.

Other external parasites include the following.

Leeches *(Hirudinea spp.)*. Leeches are sometimes found attached to freshwater fish. They somewhat resemble flukes but are actually segmented and have suckers at the head and tail. Leeches have no effect on the quality of the meat.

Ich *(Ichthyophthirius multifilis)*. Ich is most common among warmwater species but can be found on salmon and trout. Pinpoint grayish-white swellings or elevations on the body and fins are prominent signs of ich infection. The swellings are usually well defined but in cases of heavy infection may appear as irregular, light-colored patches. Similar lesions may occur on the gills, but these are harder to see.

Fungal Diseases

Fish fungi *(Saprolegnia sp.)*. Physical injury or infection stemming from invasion of other parasites usually provides the initial foothold for this fungus. The fungi appear as cottony patches, $1/3$ inch or longer, white or off-white in color, growing on or out of the fish. Threads of the fungus may appear gray or brown if the water is muddy. Fish fungus can occur both internally and externally, usually growing in small patches but spreading in later stages.

Bacterial Diseases

In most bacterial infections, affected areas can be cut away and the rest of the fish eaten after thorough cooking or freezing. However, if the infection is extensive or the fish has a puffy body and swollen eyes (dropsy), the meat should not be eaten.

Furunculosis. In 1894, furunculosis became the first bacterial disease of fish to be scientifically described. The bacteria attack salmonids, with brown and brook trout particularly susceptible. The most common symptoms of furunculosis are ulcers and boils around the dorsal fin. The ulcers may be tinged with blood, and larger ones may contain a sticky, dark-reddish pus. Hemorrhages may also be seen in the eyes and on the fins. Gills may be white or pale pink, and occasionally soft, blisterlike lesions filled with blood form just beneath the skin. Internally, there may be bloody fluid or inflammation around the heart, and red spots in the body cavity.

Columnaris. Columnaris is widespread among freshwater fish, affecting spiny ray species and catfish as well as trout. Outbreaks occur most often when water temperatures are above 55°F. The disease shows up as gray-white spots on the head and fins, although gills and sides of the body may also be affected. As the disease progresses, the spots grow into small circular lesions and the fins become frayed. Yellowish slime may cover tissue exposed by the lesions.

Precautions for Consumption

Most common North American fish parasites are not harmful to humans, but there are a few parasites, including some tapeworms, flukes, and roundworms, that can be troublesome. It never hurts to wear gloves when cleaning fish, or at least protect any cuts, and wash your hands thoroughly after handling fish. Extra care should always be taken when handling fish that have a disease or parasite. In all but the most severe cases, proper freezing and/or cooking will make the catch safe to eat.

Completely remove all viscera and wash the body cavity, taking care to remove all visible parasites. Most importantly, thoroughly cook or freeze your catch before you eat it.

Freezing. Commercial fish-processing procedures, such as canning and freezing, inactivate parasites. As a result, illness from consuming commercially caught fish containing live parasites is very low in the United States.

Although freezing will kill parasites, it is necessary to reduce the product temperature to −35°C (−31°F) and hold it there for 15 hours, or −18°C (0°F) for 24 hours, to kill such parasites as herring worm and cod worm. According to experiments conducted by the Food and Drug Association, five days in a home freezer set at −4°F killed roundworms in rockfish. Home freezers often do not freeze fish as low as −4°F. For these freezers, it is recommended that fish be frozen for five to seven days to kill the parasites. When the fish is wrapped well and frozen while still fresh, the quality of the meat won't suffer.

Freezing alone isn't an absolute guarantee that all forms of parasites will be killed. However, when used in conjunction with cooking, hot smoking, salting, kippering, or marinating, chances of parasite survival are greatly reduced.

Cooking/smoking/salting. Cook the fish until all translucency is gone and the fish flakes completely. This method is not necessarily the best way to cook fish, but using previously frozen fish will alleviate worries about fish on the rare side.

Contrary to popular opinion, smoking does not preserve fish. "Light-smoked" fish can carry the same risks as raw fish. However, most parasite larvae and bacteria are destroyed when the internal temperature throughout the meat reaches 180°F. The meat must be 140°F throughout the fish, particularly the thicker portions, to kill parasites and must reach 180°F to kill any bacteria. You can still light-smoke fish safely if the fish has been frozen first at −4°F for seven days.

You can't count on the safety of salted or marinated fish unless the meat has been frozen first. Use previously frozen fish in raw and marinated fish recipes.

If the meat smells bad or if the flesh is obviously affected throughout, don't take a chance. Dispose of the fish, and be sure that the carcass will be secure from scavenging pets or wildlife.
See: Fish Preparation—Care.

DISPLACEMENT HULL
One of two broad categories of boat hulls that includes canoes, jonboats, and flat-bottomed dories or skiffs. Displacement hulls are noted for slow speed; they push through the water rather than ride on top of it.
See: Boat.

DISTRESS SIGNALS
The boating community has devised many recognized ways of communicating the fact that a vessel is in distress. On large boats, recognized distress signals include radiotelephone communication, marine radio communication (especially the well-known expression of "mayday" for a boat that is in imminent danger, particularly of sinking), activation of an EPIRB, firing of a flare, and continuous sounding of a horn. Smaller boats may be equipped with a horn or spotlight to signal for help. A person who holds his or her arms out to the side and repeatedly raises and lowers them is signaling for help. Continuous noise-making, be that blowing a whistle or horn, is an accepted means of signaling for help, and any action will do in a life-threatening situation.

DIVING PLANER
See: Planer, Diving.

DOBSONFLIES, FISHFLIES, AND ALDERFLIES
These three groups of insects are members of the scientific order Megaloptera, a term derived from *megalo*, meaning large, and *ptera*, meaning wing, owing to the large wings of these species. Their life cycle consists of egg, larva, pupa, and adult stages, with most of this being in the larva stage.

The larvae of dobsonflies, fishflies, and alderflies are aquatic and carnivorous and may bite if handled. The larval stage generally lasts less than a year but may last up to three years. Larvae leave the water and pupate on shore for several weeks, after which the adult insect emerges. The adult dobsonfly has four large wings that are folded back tentlike over the abdomen. They, and fishflies, are most active at dusk or night; alderflies are active during the day. All become abundant in and around the shoreline.

The larvae of these insects are all found in streams and rivers, and they have common traits that distinguish them from other insect larvae. All have three pairs of segmented legs (six legs total) on the middle section of the body, with tiny pin-

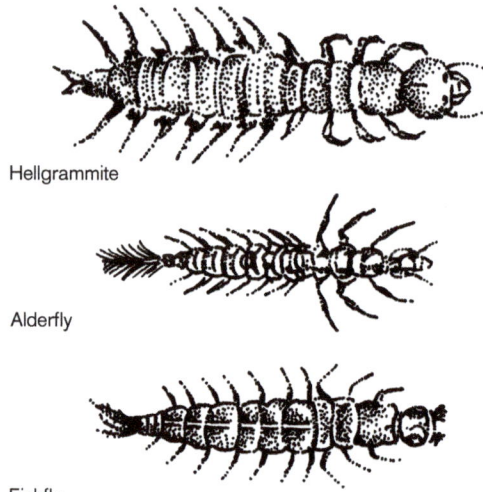

Dobsonfly, Alderfly, and Fishfly Larvae

Hellgrammite

Alderfly

Fishfly

cers at the end of each. The abdominal segments have many fleshy, filamentous (strandlike) appendages extending from each side, and they have large, chewing pincerlike mouthparts.

Dobsonfly larvae are known as hellgrammites and belong to the Corydalidae family. They have paired, cottonlike or filamentous gill tufts under their abdominal appendages; the back end is forked with two short fleshy tails, and two hooks on each tail; they are usually 1 to 4 inches long, and are dark brown to black in color. Although eaten by various fish, they are a preferred live bait (or artificial imitation) for smallmouth bass, and they in turn consume the larvae of smaller aquatic insects, including caddisflies *(see)*.

Fishfly larvae belong to the Corydalidae family as well. They have a smooth abdomen (no gill tufts); the back end is forked with two short fleshy tails and two hooks on each tail; they may be light colored; and their breathing tubes, which may be retracted and not visible, extend from the top of the abdominal surface.

Alderfly larvae are members of the Sialidae family. They have a smooth abdomen (no gill tufts), have a single branched tail filament extending straight back, and may be light colored. Both alderfly and fishfly larvae are much smaller than hellgrammites.

A few species of beetle larvae (especially whirligigs) are sometimes confused with dobsonfly, fishfly, or alderfly larvae because they may have similar fleshy filaments along the sides of the abdomen and also may have four hooks at the back end. On beetle larvae with these characteristics, the four hooks come from a single short projection (point) rather than having a pair of hooks on each of two fleshy extensions like fishfly and dobsonfly larvae. In addition, beetle larvae do not have a single filamentous tail like alderflies.

Caddisfly *(see)* larvae are sometimes mistaken for dobsonfly, fishfly, or alderfly larvae, but caddisfly

larvae do not have fleshy filaments (which look like spikes) extending out from the sides of their abdomen and have only two abdominal hooks.
See: Aquatic Insects.

DODGER/FLASHER

These devices are attractors used exclusively in trolling and primarily in freshwater to get the attention of deep fish (especially trout and salmon species).

Both dodgers and flashers are thin metal objects, oblong and rounded at the ends, usually 2 to 3 inches wide and 5 to 10 inches long. Dodgers sway from side to side and do not rotate unless they are being run too fast; flashers rotate but don't sway. Both have swivels at each end, come in various sizes and colors, and can be altered in appearance with the application of prism tape. Dodgers are more widely trolled than flashers.

Plugs, spoons, flies, and imitation squid are fished behind dodgers and flashers. Flies and squid

Typical dodger (top) and flasher (bottom) trolling rigs.

are the most popular trailing lures, particularly for steelhead and coho salmon, and are run 12 to 18 inches behind the attractor. Plugs (primarily cut plugs) and spoons are run 18 to 30 inches back. There is no need to use long leads; short leads make netting fish easier.

These attractors don't have any built-in weight, so they are usually fished behind a downrigger, but they also are used in conjunction with diving planers and heavy sinkers. The distance from the planer or sinker to the attractor is 2 to 6 feet; a short lead improves its action. When attractors are trolled with a downrigger, it's important to have a moderately tight tension setting on the line release because attractors pull fairly hard and may pull the line out of a lightly set release.
See: Trolling.

DOGFISH, SPINY *Squalus acanthias.*
Other names—dogfish, dog shark, grayfish, Pacific grayfish, Pacific dogfish, spinarola, California dogfish, blue dog, common spiny fish, spiny dogfish, picked fish, spiky dog, spotted spiny, spurdog, white-spotted dogfish, Victorian spotted dogfish; French: *aiguillat;* Italian: *spinarolo;* Japanese: *abura-tsunozame;* Portuguese: *galhudo;* Russian: *katran;* Spanish: *galludo.*

The spiny dogfish may hold the record for most English-language aliases among saltwater fish. It is the most prominent member of the Squalidae family of dogfish sharks, which includes 18 genera and 72 species, among them the smallest sharks in the world. Dogfish sharks are widely distributed in the Atlantic, Pacific, and Indian Oceans. Some live in relatively shallow water close to shore, and others inhabit great depths. They vary widely in length, and one of their chief anatomical characteristics is the lack of an anal fin.

The spiny dogfish is possibly the most abundant living shark. Commercial fishermen view these fish with mixed feelings (when large schools invade fishing grounds, they mutilate other species caught in nets or by hooks), and anglers generally consider them a nuisance. Most anglers catch this species incidentally (and release it) while fishing for other bottom dwellers. Commercial fishermen principally use otter trawls and gillnets to land dogfish. Although they are frequently taken as bycatch and are discarded during groundfish operations in some waters, spiny dogfish are of moderate importance in other fisheries where a good market for this species exists. They are used for human consumption, liver oil, leather, fertilizer, and other purposes.

The U.S. commercial fishery for spiny dogfish is similar to that of European fisheries in its selection of only large individuals (exceeding 5 pounds and 33 inches), which are mainly mature females, to meet processing and marketing requirements. Smaller individuals, however, consisting of both mature and immature males as well as immature females, are also taken as bycatch and discarded. In the Atlantic, these stocks are fully exploited.

Identification. The body of the spiny dogfish is elongate and slender. The head is pointed. The color is slate gray to brownish on top, sometimes with white spots, and fading to white below. It has spines at the beginning of both dorsal fins; these spines are mildly poisonous and provide a defense for the spiny dogfish.

Size/Age. Spiny dogfish are common at 2 to 3 feet in length; the maximum size is about 63 inches and 20 pounds. In California waters, a large fat female will be roughly 4 feet long and weigh 15 pounds. In the northwestern Atlantic, maximum ages reported for males and females are 35 and 40 years respectively.

Distribution. Spiny dogfish occur in temperate and subtropical waters. In the western Atlantic, they range from Greenland to Argentina; in the eastern Atlantic, they range from Iceland and the Murmansk coast of Russia to South Africa, including the Mediterranean and Baltic Seas. In the western Pacific, they range from the Bering Sea to

Spiny Dogfish

New Zealand, and in the eastern Pacific they range from the Bering Sea to Chile.

Habitat. This species is common in near-shore waters along some coasts and may be found in enclosed bays and estuaries; it generally inhabits waters up to 1,200 feet deep, although spiny dogfish have been taken at depths of 2,400 feet. It reportedly enters freshwater but cannot survive there for more than a few hours. It typically favors the bottom. In temperate waters during spring and fall, spiny dogfish can range into coastal waters, heading more northerly in summer. In winter, they are distributed primarily in deeper waters along the edge of the continental shelf.

Life history. Spiny dogfish tend to school by size and, for large mature individuals, by sex. Females are larger than males and produce from 3 to 14 young at a time in alternate years. The species bears live young, and has a gestation period of about 18 to 22 months. Spiny dogfish are long lived and nonmigratory; heavy commercial fishing pressure in a given area will rapidly lower populations of this slow-growing, low-reproductive species.

Food and feeding habits. The spiny dogfish is voracious and feeds on practically all smaller fish, including herring, sardines, anchovies, smelts, and even small spiny dogfish and crabs. They have been known to attack schools of herring and mackerel, as well as concentrations of haddock, cod, sand lance, and other species.

Angling. Assorted baits fished on bottom rigs will catch spiny dogfish. When present in abundance and striking baits meant for other species as soon as those baits reach the bottom, they can be extremely disruptive to angling efforts. This behavior can make it impossible to catch such desirable fish as cod, pollock, and flounder.

Spiny dogfish squirm greatly when captured, and it's necessary to take great care in handling them, as they often stab human flesh with their spines. The mild toxin that is released with the stabbing can cause infections, and the wounds are slow to heal.

DOLLY VARDEN *Salvelinus malma.*
AND BULL TROUT *Salvelinus confluentus.*
Other names for Dolly Varden—Dolly.
Other names for bull trout—bull charr, western brook trout, Rocky Mountain trout, red spotted salmon-trout, red spotted charr.

The Dolly Varden and bull trout are members of the charr *(see)* group of the Salmonidae family and close relatives of arctic charr *(see: charr, arctic)*. Early studies described these two fish as a variant of the arctic charr and as one distinct species, and for a long time the bull trout was considered just a localized version of the Dolly Varden. Today many fisheries scientists believe that Dolly Varden and bull trout are two distinct species that look amazingly similar. As a result of this early confusion, much of the scientific literature on the Dolly Varden is based in part or in whole on the bull trout.

Found in lakes, rivers, and small headwater streams, sometimes migrating back and forth between freshwater and saltwater, and sometimes not, these fish have puzzled fisheries biologists and ichthyologists since they were first discovered. About the only thing everyone agreed on was that they were charr, although somehow the incorrect name "trout" stayed with the bull trout, when the species should have been called bull charr.

Why it is called bull, in fact, is unclear. The Dolly Varden, according to legend, received its moniker because its unique coloration was associated with the colorful clothing of a character in the Charles Dickens novel *Barnaby Rudge*.

Like the arctic charr, the Dolly Varden is an anadromous species, although some populations are landlocked. Its Arctic coastal range overlaps with that of the arctic charr, and its Pacific coastal range overlaps with the bull trout's, which is generally described as a strictly freshwater-dwelling species, although Washington State biologists have found bull trout in Puget Sound.

As gamefish, the bull trout and the Dolly Varden are not as highly rated as most other salmonids, but they do have considerable sporting and food value and are gaining esteem. It was once

Dolly Varden

thought that their predatory nature posed a threat to other salmonids; people attempted to eradicate them, and loggers even dynamited pools where bull trout and/or Dolly Varden congregated. The state of Alaska once offered a bounty on them. Of course, salmon and steelhead managed to survive for thousands of years despite the predatory habits of the bull trout and Dolly Varden.

Not all populations of these species have managed to survive, however; some runs are now extinct, and populations of both species have been steadily declining in much of their range, especially in western lower 48 states, and the bull trout there is generally, although unofficially, considered endangered. Habitat loss, overfishing, rising stream temperatures, stream siltation, and hybridizing with (nonnative) brook trout have all contributed to this decline. Historically, sportfishing regulations were liberal for bull trout and Dolly Varden, but in recent years more restrictive regulations have been imposed.

The flesh of both species is pink and firm and good to eat, and there has been some commercial value for Dolly Varden in parts of its range.

Identification. These two charr, as well as the arctic charr, are difficult to distinguish from external characteristics alone, even for specialists. Due to past misidentification of species in various locales and lack of scientific knowledge, much of the available literature on these species is either misleading or incorrect, and some disagreement as to their distribution still exists among scientists.

In general, the Dolly Varden and the bull trout can be distinguished by their size and habitat. The Dolly Varden is usually a coastal species, whereas the larger bull trout inhabits inland waters, namely large, cold rivers and lakes draining high, mountainous areas. Although both can grow large, they seldom do. Dollies are typically smaller and tend to have a more rounded body shape. Bull trout have a larger, flattened head and a more pronounced hook in the lower jaw.

The color of both varies with habitat and locality, but the body is generally olive green, the back being darker than the pale sides; cream to pale yellow spots (slightly smaller than the pupil of the eye) cover the back, and red or orange spots cover the sides; and the pectoral, pelvic, and anal fins have white or cream-colored margins. The male in full fall spawning dress sports a dark olive back, sometimes bordering on black, an orange red belly, bright-red spots, and fluorescent white fin edges, rivaling fall's spectacular colors. Sea-run Dollies are silvery, and the spots can be very faint.

Bull trout and Dolly Varden can be distinguished from the eastern brook trout (also a charr) by the absence of vermiculations on their back. In addition, the eastern brook trout's red spots are surrounded by blue halos. Bull trout and brook trout have been known to spawn together, and their hybrid offspring can have features of both parents. (Hybridization can be a serious problem in some areas, resulting in the dilution or destruction of the gene pool of the native bull trout.)

Bull Trout

A much greater problem arises in trying to distinguish the Dolly Varden from the arctic charr. Much published information on the distribution of these species is incorrect, and it often presupposed that only one species or the other occurred in areas or rivers where it is now believed both species may occur. The two are outwardly almost identical in every respect, and to complicate matters, significant variations occur in both species. The spots on the Dolly Varden are usually smaller than the pupil of the eye, whereas on the arctic charr they are larger than the pupil. When returning from the sea, both species are silvery and lack spots. Arctic charr on the average have more gill rakers on the first left gill arch (25 to 30 as opposed to 21 to 22 in the Dolly Varden) and more pyloric caeca (40 to 45 as opposed to roughly 30 in the Dolly Varden), but fish with intermediate counts are not uncommon in either species.

Fish that don't clearly "fit the pattern" will almost certainly have to be examined in a laboratory to determine their identity, a matter that is of real concern only if a large and possibly record-setting specimen is caught. Because the problem of identification was only very recently diagnosed, at present very few scientists are qualified to make a positive identification on an unusual specimen.

Size. Sea-run Dolly Vardens generally range from 1 to 3 pounds, and freshwater specimens seldom weigh more than 8 pounds. The all-tackle world record is an 19-pound, 4-ounce Alaskan fish. Bull trout are larger growing than Dollies, although the typical fish weighs between 2 and 5 pounds. The all-tackle world record is a 32-pounder that was $40^1/_2$ inches long and was caught in Lake Pend Orielle, Idaho, in 1949.

Distribution. Varden occur from the Sea of Japan, throughout the Kuril Islands to Russia's Kamchatka Peninsula, throughout the Aleutian Islands, and around Alaska and the Yukon Territory to the Northwest Territory, as well as in the northwestern United States. In North America, they are especially abundant in Alaska and parts of British Columbia.

The bull trout is endemic to the Pacific Northwest and inhabits most of the significant drainages on both sides of the Continental Divide. It seems to prefer large, cold rivers and lakes draining high mountainous areas, and tends to frequent the bottoms of deep pools. It has been recorded in northern California, Oregon, Washington, northern Nevada, Idaho, western Montana, Alberta, and British Columbia.

Habitat/Life history. Bull trout and Dolly Varden prefer deep pools of cold rivers, lakes, and reservoirs. Streams with abundant cover (cut banks, root wads, and other woody debris) and clean gravel and cobble beds provide the best habitat. Their favored summer water temperature is generally less than 55°F, but they nevertheless tolerate temperatures less than 40°F. Spawning during fall usually starts when water temperatures drop to the mid- to low 40s. Cold, clear water is required for successful reproduction.

Bull trout and Dolly Varden have complex but similar life histories. Anadromous (seagoing) and migratory resident populations (for example, lake-dwelling stocks and main-stem rearing stocks) often journey long distances in summer and fall to spawn, migrating to the small headwater streams where they hatched. Mature adults with these characteristics are generally four to seven years old and 18 to 22 inches in length when they make their first spawning run, although they may be older in some populations.

The adults can undergo some impressive journeys on their spawning runs. Fish in Washington's Skagit River system may travel more than 115 miles from the river mouth and ascend to an elevation of more than 3,000 feet. The spawning area may be upstream of areas used by other anadromous species.

Logjams, cascades, and falls that are barriers to the chinook's brute strength and the steelhead's acrobatic abilities may be only minor obstacles to the cunning and guile of Dolly Varden and bull trout. Although these charr can jump remarkably well for fish their size, as much as 7 or 8 vertical feet under good conditions, they are just as likely to maneuver around a difficult spot. At a potential barrier, they sometimes seem to be actively seeking alternative ways around it.

Bull trout and Dolly Varden use headwater areas that typically are in pristine environments. Spawning begins in late August, peaks in September and October, and ends in November. Fish in a given stream spawn over a short period of time, two weeks or less, making redds in clean gravel.

Almost immediately after spawning, adults begin to work their way back to the main-stem rivers, lakes, or reservoirs to overwinter. Some of these fish stay put, others move on to saltwater in the spring, evidently not wandering far. Some survive the perils of the river to spawn a second or even a third time. Kelts (spawned-out fish) feed aggressively to recover from the stress of spawning. In parts of their range where steelhead are also present, this also happens to be when many anglers are searching the river for winter steelhead. Steelhead anglers must learn how to identify these charr and safely release them.

Newly hatched fish emerge from the gravel the following spring. Those that migrate down to the main rivers, reservoirs, and saltwater normally leave the headwater areas as two-year-olds. But further complicating the picture are resident stream populations that exhibit limited movements, living their entire lives in the same stretch of headwater stream. These fish may not mature until they are age 7 to 8, and rarely exceed 14 inches in length. Biologists have observed these local residents spawning side by side with their much larger anadromous kin.

Food. Bull trout and Dolly Varden are opportunistic feeders, eating aquatic insects, shrimp, snails, leeches, fish eggs, and fish.

Angling. Both species are fairly easy to catch and do not display the leaping tendencies of more admired salmonids like arctic charr or steelhead *(see)*. Anglers cast spoons, spinners, and flies to Dollies and bull trout in river pools. Some troll deep in lakes, as they do for arctic charr and various salmon.

DOLPHIN, COMMON *Coryphaena hippurus*.

Other names—dolphinfish, common dolphinfish, mahimahi, mahi mahi, dorado; Chinese: *fei niau fu, ngau tau yue;* French: *coryphéne commune;* Italian: *lampuga;* Japanese: *shiira, toohyaku;* Portuguese: *doirado, dourado;* Spanish: *dorado, dorado común, lampuga.*

The common dolphin is the larger of the two extremely similar species in the family Coryphaenidae, both of which are cosmopolitan in warm seas. This fish is one of the top offshore gamefish among anglers, as it is an excellent, hard-fighting species that puts on an acrobatic show once hooked. It routinely leaps or tail-walks over the surface, darting first in one direction, then another. This fish is a superb light-tackle quarry, although it is frequently caught on heavier gear meant for larger offshore species.

The flesh of the common dolphin is considered gourmet fare, and it is prepared in a variety of ways. It is usually presented in fish markets and restaurants under its Hawaiian name, *mahimahi*. The common dolphin is often referred to as the "dolphinfish," to distinguish it from the so-called dolphin of the porpoise family, which is an unrelated mammal and not sought by anglers.

Identification. The body is slender and streamlined, tapering sharply from head to tail. Large males, called bulls, have high, vertical foreheads, whereas the females' foreheads are rounded. The anal fin has 25 to 31 soft rays and is long, stretching over half of the length of the body. The dorsal fin has 55 to 66 soft rays. Its caudal fin is deeply forked, there are no spines in any of the fins, and the mouth has bands of fine teeth.

Its coloring is variable and defies an accurate, simple description. Generally, when the fish is alive in the water, the common dolphin is a rich iridescent blue or blue green dorsally; gold, bluish gold, or silvery gold on the lower flanks; and silvery white or yellow on the belly. The sides are sprinkled

Dolphin, Common

Common Dolphin

with a mixture of dark and light spots, ranging from black or blue to golden. The dorsal fin is a rich blue, and the anal fin is golden or silvery. The other fins are generally golden yellow, edged with blue. Dark vertical bands sometimes appear when the fish is attacking prey. The color description of dolphin is difficult because the fish undergoes sudden changes in color, which occur in an instant, often when it is excited.

When removed from the water, however, the colors fluctuate between blue, green, and yellow; the brilliant colors apparent when in the water fade quickly. After death, the fish usually turns a uniform yellow or silvery gray.

The common dolphin is so distinctive in body color and shape that it cannot be mistaken for any other fish. The pompano dolphin (see: dolphin, pompano) is the only related species and is considerably smaller and lacks a high forehead. Female and young dolphin are often confused with pompano dolphin.

Size/Age. The average size is 5 to 15 pounds, although larger catches up to 50 pounds are not uncommon. The all-tackle world record is an 87-pounder caught in Costa Rica in 1976, and it has been rumored that fish up to 100 pounds have been caught by commercial longliners. The maximum length is reportedly 82 inches.

Dolphin are fast growing and short lived. Few common dolphin live longer than four years, and most live just three years. Males grow larger than females and are capable of growing to 60 pounds in just two years, although this rate of growth would be exceptional and the result of consistently favorable warm temperatures and abundant food.

Distribution. The common dolphin is found worldwide in tropical and subtropical waters of the Atlantic, Indian, and Pacific Oceans. The greatest concentrations are believed to be in the Indian Ocean and the western Pacific. In the western Atlantic, it occurs in areas influenced by the warm waters of the Gulf Stream, and has been caught as far north as Prince Edward Island and as far south as Río de Janeiro; in the eastern Atlantic it is known from the Canary Islands to Angola. In the eastern Pacific, it ranges from Peru to Oregon.

Habitat. Common dolphin are a warmwater pelagic fish, occurring in the open ocean and usually found close to the surface, although in waters of great depth. They sometimes inhabit coastal waters and occasionally areas near piers, but in the open ocean they often concentrate around floating objects, especially buoys, driftwood, and seaweed lines or clusters. The young commonly frequent warm nearshore waters in sargassum beds or other flotsam. In developing countries, commercial fishermen may place floating bundles of bamboo reeds, cork planks, and the like in the water to concentrate dolphin before seining or gillnetting commences.

Life history/Behavior. The common dolphin is a prolific spawner and grows rapidly, meaning that it must by nature be an eating machine.

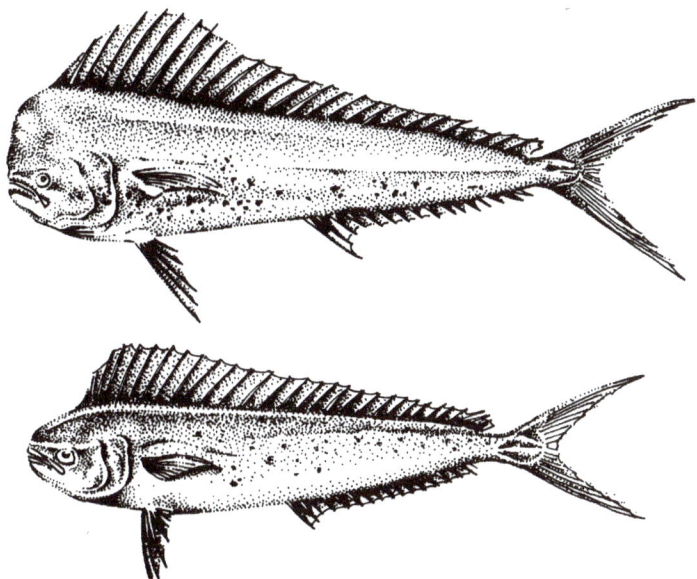

Although both male (top) and female (bottom) common dolphin have a streamlined, tapered body, the male, or bull, is distinguished by a high, vertical forehead.

Spawning season begins primarily in spring or early summer and lasts several months in warmer waters. Dolphin reach sexual maturity in the first year of life and produce a large volume of eggs.

Dolphin are a schooling fish and often congregate in large numbers, sometimes in the thousands. They are almost always between the surface and 100-foot depths, but anglers encounter them on or just under the surface. They are probably the most surface oriented of all big-game fish. This characteristic, as well as their propensity for feeding by sight and thus primarily foraging in daylight, helps endear them to anglers. Offshore enthusiasts frequently encounter packs of dolphin and are able to elicit strikes from several fish in quick order.

These fish are evidently also migratory. It is believed that dolphin in both hemispheres migrate away from the equator in the spring and summer and toward the equator in fall and winter.

Food. Common dolphin are extremely fast swimmers and feed aggressively in pairs, small packs, and schools, extensively consuming whatever forage fish are most abundant. Flyingfish and squid are prominent food in areas where these fish exist, and small fish and crustaceans around floating sargassum weed are commonly part of their diet, especially among smaller dolphin.

Angling. Dolphin inhabit blue-water environs and, although they roam the unobstructed near-surface waters of the open ocean, are commonly found around objects. Floating debris, buoys, weeds, and even boats can attract and hold these fish, and such objects are searched by anglers specifically looking for dolphin.

Dolphin up to 8 or so pounds, which are called chicken or peanut dolphin, are especially found around floating debris, which offers both protection and feeding opportunity. Fish from 8 to 20 pounds or so gather in schools, often segregated by size and/or sex, and they may also be found around debris, especially extensive lines of weeds and tidal rips. Larger dolphin, called slammers by many charter boat captains, are more likely to travel in small packs, usually with one or two bulls and a few cows. These fish are more likely to be ocean roamers rather than object ambushers. They are consequently harder to deliberately target.

Most dolphin are located by trolling, usually by anglers fishing for other blue-water species, primarily marlin and sailfish. Rigged trolling baits on large hooks are usually used, and flyingfish, squid, mullet, and balao are the common offerings. Offshore trolling plugs and feathers are popular as well. Because dolphin are very fast swimmers, a quick trolling speed is optimal. Primarily because it is necessary for larger quarry, heavy big-game tackle is the norm. Although big dolphin fight well even on this tackle, anglers will enjoy the fight much better when pursuing these fish on light big-game outfits or spinning or flycasting equipment.

Trollers often keep spinning and fly tackle handy in case they encounter a school of dolphin while trolling. When this happens, they stop and cast to the fish, using surface or diving plugs, bucktail jigs, spoons, and streamer flies. Live baits are also used. Dolphin run hard and leap often and rather spectacularly, sometimes tail-walking across the surface. This fight is especially enjoyable when a fish has been caught on light tackle and played from a drifting boat. A 7-foot spinning rod and 6- to 12-pound line is ideal, as most of these fish don't weigh more than 20 pounds. The strike, when casting or trolling, is usually savage.

Sometimes anglers keep a hooked dolphin on the line near the boat to encourage a group to stay around, and this may result in catching several or all of the fish out of a group. To keep the fish in the vicinity, some anglers chum once they've found a school, or they use sand chum balls to attract deeper fish to hooked baits.

In some areas, anglers deliberately fishing for dolphin, and casting to them either with live natural baits or lures or flies, cruise offshore areas as the captain searches the waters from the tower and heads toward debris, observed schools, birds, and the like. When the boat gets in casting range of observed fish, the captain instructs the mate and anglers as to their position. Unhooked live baits are thrown to tease the fish close to the boat, and then hooked baits, lures, or flies are cast to the school of dolphin as individuals come close and weave in and out. It is not uncommon for several anglers to hook up at the same time, causing an epic melee of jumping fish, crossed lines, and scrambling anglers.

Not all fishing for dolphins is fast and easy. Sometimes, the friskiest live pilchards, mullet, menhaden, and others don't do the job, and it's necessary to switch to the type of fish the dolphin are preying on around the weedlines. Or, it may be necessary to change tactics entirely, offering other lures or other types and colors of lures, or fishing deeper.

See: Big-Game Fishing; Offshore Fishing.

A big bull dolphin caught offshore from Islamorada, Florida.

Pompano Dolphin

DOLPHIN, POMPANO *Coryphaena equiselis.*
Other names—mahimahi, blue dolphin, small dolphin, dolphinfish, pompano dolphinfish; French: *coryphène dauphin;* Japanese: *ebisu-shiira;* Portuguese: *dourado;* Spanish: *dorado.*

The pompano dolphin is the smaller of the two Coryphaenidae family species and is often confused with the females and young of its larger relative the common dolphin *(C. hippurus;* see: *dolphin, common).* Like its relative, it is caught commercially and by anglers, and it is an excellent food fish. The pompano dolphin is usually presented in fish markets and restaurants under its Hawaiian name *mahimahi.* This species, and its relative, are often referred to as "dolphinfish" to distinguish them from the so-called dolphin of the porpoise family, which is an unrelated mammal and not sought by anglers.

Identification. This species is almost identical to the common dolphin in coloring and general shape, although it has greater body depth behind the head than the common dolphin, and a squarish rather than rounded tooth patch on the tongue. There are fewer dorsal rays on the pompano dolphin—48 to 55 versus the common dolphin's 55 to 65.

Size. The average size is 20 to 24 inches and 4 to 5 pounds, although it reportedly grows to 50 inches.

Distribution/Habitat. The pompano dolphin is found worldwide in tropical seas; in the United States it is most commonly encountered in Hawaii. The pompano dolphin reportedly prefers surface temperatures above 75°F. It is considered more oceanic than the common dolphin but may enter coastal waters.

Life history/Behavior. Little is known of the life history of the pompano dolphin, other than that it is a schooling tropical water species, prone to near-surface feeding and attracted to objects. This fish is similar to common dolphin in most behavioral respects.

Food. The pompano dolphin's diet consists of small fish and squid.

Angling. See: *Dolphin, Common; Offshore Fishing.*

DOODLESOCKING
Doodlesocking, also called yo-yoing, is the activity of repeatedly raising and lowering a jig or worm in an opening made in heavy cover. Using a pole or paddle, the angler makes a small clearing in a clump of thick moss, milfoil, or other grass and drops in a jig or worm to fish for largemouth bass, crappie, and/or panfish.

DORADO
(1) The Spanish word for "dolphin" *(see: dolphin, common).*

(2) *Salminus maxillosus.*
Other names—South American salmon; Portuguese: *dourado;* Spanish: *dorado, dourado, picudo.*

A member of the Characidae family and a relative of the piranha and the tigerfish, the dorado is one of the finest freshwater gamefish, yet it is little known to most anglers. This is due in part to its limited mid–South American range. There are reportedly four species of fish within the genus *Salminus,* but information about the other species is scant, and the taxonomic classification of all four is uncertain. They are believed to be among the most primitive of characins. A related "salmon" of the genus *Catabasis* has been identified from a specimen captured in 1900 but is believed extinct. Smaller dorado may be confused in Brazil with a similar-looking species, pirapuntanga *(Brycon orbygnianus),* a fish that grows to 3 kilograms.

Large and strong, the dorado is an aggressive fish known for hard strikes, frequent aerial displays, and bulldog tenacity, but its population has suffered through habitat alteration. It has long been an important food fish within its native range, where it is held in great esteem; dorado festivals have been held in various river communities, especially in northern Argentina, in celebration of this species.

Identification. In overall body shape, the dorado somewhat resembles a salmon, although it is unrelated. The fins have the same position and shape

Dorado

as those of salmon. There is an adipose fin after the dorsal fin, an axillary process, and the tail is somewhat scalloped. The head is tapered and streamlined, predominantly gold with bluish or dark highlights. The powerful lower jaw, which is stout and strong, contains a double row of teeth, the outer row consisting of strong canines. True to the meaning of its name (golden), the dorado has a golden body, with blue, orange, and yellow overtones or highlights, and a dark splotch or strip in the center of the tail. The fish change colors, turning bright golden with a dark back in clear waters when they spawn in swamps, or into a hazy gold with a greenish back when in tea-colored waters. In all cases their fins are orange red.

Size. The all-tackle world record for dorado is 51 pounds, 5 ounces. Dorado of 60 to 75 pounds and up to 40 inches in length have been reported by anglers in the past. A dorado in excess of 30 pounds is presently an exceptional fish, and fewer such specimens have been reported in recent years.

Distribution. Found solely in South America, the dorado occurs in Brazil, Paraguay, Uruguay, and Argentina, essentially in connected watersheds that flow southward through these countries. Small specimens have been reported by anglers in the Magdalena River system of Colombia, but modern evidence of dorado there has been lacking, and species identification remains unclear.

The native range of dorado has been the Plate River basin, largely made up of the Paraná and Paraguay Rivers and their many tributaries. The main course of the Paraná from southeastern Brazil to Argentina has been impounded for hydroelectric purposes in several places, which has altered native fish species, including dorado.

The native range also includes the São Francisco River basin of southern and eastern Brazil; this system has many tributaries, originates and stays within Brazil, is clear in the headwaters but sediment laden downstream, and also has a number of hydroelectric impoundments.

Neither the Plate nor the São Francisco systems flow into the Amazon River. Dorado have been widely reported from the Amazon and Orinoco basins, but this has not been observed in recent times, and the capture of one from either of these watersheds would be rare.

Habitat. The dorado is primarily a fish of rivers and fast-moving runs. It also occurs in slower tributary waters and in backwater swamps, although larger dorado do not move into tributaries until spawning time. The dorado is often present in groups and moves frequently in search of food; whether this is a migration or not is uncertain, although the dorado do migrate into spawning tributaries. In spite of a similarity in behavior to salmon, the dorado is not an anadromous species and are seldom found in the brackish waters of the Río de la Plata estuary between Argentina and Uruguay.

Food and feeding habits. Dorado feed on other fish and are aggressive predators. Small sábalo, a schooling species, is a significant food item, and dorado follow this bait. They are likely to occur where a quick ambush is possible, including along banks, but especially in the swift runs of rivers and ahead of rocks and other structures.

Angling. Several characteristics of dorado fishing especially endear them to the relatively small number of anglers who have caught this species. The first is that they strike with exceptional speed and savagery. Another is that they not only fight long and with great vigor (often running wildly downstream), but they also repeatedly leap high out of the water, perhaps 8 to 10 times during a battle, and thrash wildly in an effort to throw the hook. Their strength also applies to the viselike gripping power of their jaws, which can crush some lures and mangle hooks.

Big spoons, spinners, and swimming or diving plugs—lures normally associated with striped bass and muskie, and equipped with the best hooks and hardware—are the artificials of choice, especially for large specimens. Trolling is the most common method of fishing in many rivers, usually running at fast speeds, but dorado are also caught by anglers casting lures and drifting with live baits. Most fish are taken on or near the bottom, especially in large rivers. Medium- and heavy-duty baitcasting tackle is the best overall equipment for this species, using lines from 14 to 25 pounds. Fly fishing and lighter tackle are possible in certain situations, especially in smaller rivers, although it is usually important to still use lures or flies with a large body size.

Clear-water environments are best for the largely sight-feeding dorado; silted and roiled waters do not produce as well. Fluctuating water levels and changed water conditions, therefore, can adversely affect success. A heavy rainfall can hurt the fishing, and variable increased releases from upstream reservoirs can also be detrimental. If silt isn't the problem, then scattered baitfish due to increased water area is likely to also disperse the dorado.

In major rivers, dorado are particularly found near sandbars and rocks. They prefer fast water and strong current. Sometimes a school will chase baitfish into the air.

See: Argentina; Paraguay.

DORSAL FIN

A median fin along the back, which is supported by rays. There may be two or more dorsal fins, in which case they are numbered with the fin closest to the head called the first dorsal fin.

See: Anatomy; Fish.

DOUBLE

(1) Two anglers who simultaneously each hook a fish, a feat not uncommon when schools of certain species are encountered or when there is a lot of action in a specific place. In some cases, a triple is possible.

(2) Two fish simultaneously caught on one lure. This occurs when the fish are impaled on the front and rear hooks, respectively, of a given lure, as a result either of both attacking the lures simultaneously or of one trying to take it from the other. This kind of double usually occurs only with very aggressive fish; it is more likely with largemouth bass, smallmouth bass, and peacock bass than with such species as trout or salmon.

DOUBLE ENDER

A canoe with a pointed bow and stern. Double enders are easier to paddle than square stern canoes, which have a square stern for the attachment of a small motor.

See: Canoe.

DOUBLE-FOOT GUIDE

A guide with upper and lower attachment points to the blank of a fishing rod. A double-foot guide is advantageous for fish fighting, and is primarily found on baitcasting and conventional rods, where it is placed on the top of the rod.

See: Rod, Fishing.

DOUBLE HAUL

An element of flycasting in which the line is accelerated on backward and forward casts for better control or greater distance.

See: Flycasting Tackle.

DOUBLE HOOK

A hook with two points.

See: Hook.

DOUBLE LINE

The terminal section of a fishing line that is doubled for extra strength and abrasion resistance. A double line is most commonly used in saltwater by big-game anglers fishing for very large and strong species, but it may be used in any circumstance where the target fish are large compared with the lighter line being used and/or where the conditions (especially an abrasive bottom or fish with sharp teeth or abrasive skin) dictate having the extra insurance that a double length of line can provide.

The doubled section is made from the actual fishing line that comes off the reel, and a Bimini Twist or Spider Hitch Knot is used to convert a certain length from one strand into two strands of equal length. Although a double line may be any desired length, for practical reasons it must be short enough to stay off the reel when used in casting applications, yet not so long for trolling or bottom fishing that it affects the action of the lure or bait. To qualify for world records, international standards established by the International Game Fish Association (IGFA) mandate that a double line in freshwater can be no longer than 6 feet for any type of tackle; in saltwater it can be no longer than 15 feet when used with up to 10-kilogram tackle, and no longer than 30 feet when used with tackle over 10 kilograms. In some circumstances, a leader may be attached to the doubled line; for records, the length of this leader must also conform to certain length standards.

See: Knots, Fishing; Line.

DOUBLE TAPER LINE

A fly line that has the same taper at both ends and a section of level line in the middle.

See: Flycasting Tackle.

DOUGH BALL

A popular fishing bait for carp *(see)* and sometimes catfish *(see)*, these homemade concoctions are prepared from cornmeal, flour, syrup, anise oil, vanilla extract, etc., and rolled into a ball. Carp devotees prepare various flavored dough balls, and many recipes exist for their preparation. For carp, some sweet and flavorful product is almost always an ingredient; for catfish, the concoctions might be sweet, or might be rather vile. Their purpose is to produce a lot of scent and attract roaming fish, and they are fished both on single and treble hooks, although single hooks in general are better.

DOURADA

A South American catfish, also known as golden catfish.

See: Catfish.

DOWNRIGGER

A downrigger is a device that is used primarily for trolling (and sometimes for deep fishing with live or dead bait) and that offers controlled depth presentation of a lure, bait, or fly. This device originated on the Great Lakes for trout and salmon fishing, and then spread inland for muskies, stripers, and walleye, and later to saltwater.

Downriggers are among the best gear ever to have hit the trolling scene. They've revolutionized deep trolling since the early 1960s by making it more sporting and fruitful. In the pre-downrigger age, deep trolling consisted of assorted methods that suffered from imprecise depth control—anglers often were unsure exactly how deep they were fishing—or the use of extremely long lines and tackle heavy enough to tow a submarine. Until the creation of downriggers, getting deep nearly always required deep trollers to use lead weights, weighted lines, or diving planers, all of which were fastened directly to the fishing line.

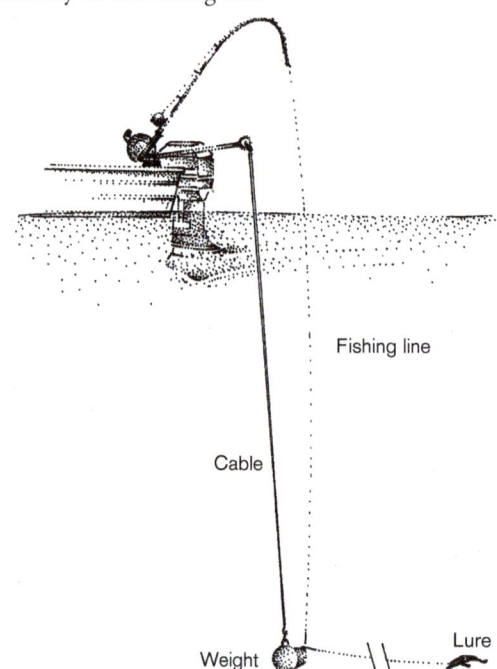

The general concept of fishing with a downrigger is very simple. Fishing line is attached via a release clip (not shown) to a weight, which in turn is attached to a heavy cable. When a fish takes the lure that is on the fishing line, the line is released by the clip.

Downriggers take the burden of getting a line to a specific depth away from the fishing line and put it on an accessory product, meaning that they can be used with light and ultralight tackle that tests angling skills and provides extra enjoyment.

A downrigger is not a complicated device. Components include a reel, cranking handle with clutch, boom, cable, and pulley. A heavy lead weight attaches to the end of the downrigger cable, and a line-release mechanism is located on or near the weight or at any other place along the cable.

A lure attached to your fishing line is placed in the water and set at whatever distance you want it to run behind your boat. The fishing line is placed in the release attached to the downrigger cable. The downrigger weight is then lowered to the depth you want to fish. When a fish strikes the lure, the fishing line pops out of the release and the fish is played on your fishing line, unencumbered by a heavy weight or strong cable.

Downriggers are made in manual and electric models. Manual downriggers include small versions that clamp onto the transom or gunwale, or fit into the oarlock; larger versions can be mounted permanently. Some are available in either right- or left-crank versions. Manual downriggers are always hand-cranked up; some older manual models are cranked down, too, though for most you can release clutch tension to lower the weight. Many small-boat owners use manual downriggers because they are less costly.

Electric downriggers are raised and lowered by flicking a switch. They're generally made for permanent and sturdy mounting locations. Electrics are considerably more expensive than manual downriggers and require power hookups, often through an auxiliary battery. Because they can be easily retrieved through an automatic "up" switch, electric downriggers are invariably preferred by busy veteran trollers.

The length of the boom, or arm, which carries the cable from the spool to a pulley, can vary from 1 foot to 8 feet, depending on the boom's location on the boat and the need to spread out weights over the greatest possible horizontal range of water. The length of the boom also depends on the size of your boat and your ability to move freely around in it to rig lines and set weights. The length of the boom on some downriggers can be changed, and some allow an extension to be bolted on.

As a rule, as boat size increases and the vertical distance from gunwale to water surface increases, the length of the downrigger arm increases. On 12- to 17-foot craft, it is most common to use just two short-armed downriggers. On large boats, such as those with an 8- to 10-foot beam, as many as four 2- or 3-foot-boom downriggers may be spaced equally across the transom, with two longer-boomed downriggers on the gunwales.

In boats with adequate room, the arms can be swiveled in to retrieve the weight or line release and

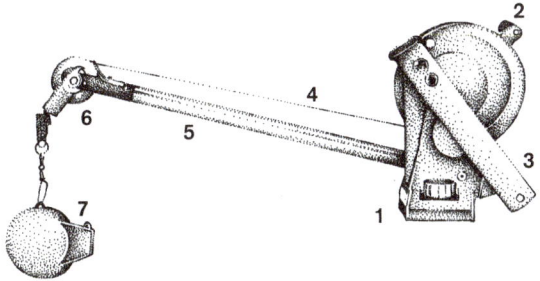

Components of a manual downrigger are: base (1), handle (2), rod holder (3), cable (4), boom (5), pulley (6), and weight (7). Not shown but also near the handle is a counter that indicates the depth of the weight by virtue of the amount of cable in the water.

to set the fishing line in the release. Preferably, the cable can be pulled inward via a free-sliding pulley on the cable that is attached to a lanyard.

At the outer end of a downrigger boom is a pulley that guides the cable downward to the water. This pulley should pivot from side to side because the cable usually extends back rather than down when the boat is moving forward. Some type of cable guard should be mounted on the pulley to prevent the cable from jumping off. Some downriggers sport a hook on the underside of the spool frame, which is convenient for hanging the downrigger weight or a just a snap at the end of the cable, which is useful for in-transit storage. If you are moving from place to place and have the weight stored this way, you can simply unhook it and drop it in the water instead of having to reattach the weight to the snap.

Downriggers utilize 150- to 200-pound strength braided steel cable that does not stretch; the depth on the line counter will conform exactly to the length of cable let out. Spools are filled with approximately 200 feet of cable, though more can be used provided it is unspliced. Cable has a tendency to coil or kink and can be weakened when it does. It can also be weakened in places where line releases have been set repeatedly or where the cable has been nicked because of collision with some object.

It's a good idea to check the cable periodically for signs of fraying or crimping and to cut off the affected length so that you don't lose a downrigger weight and terminal hardware. Be sure to carry tools in your boat or tackle box to remake connections. Keep a supply of connector sleeves, snubbers, large (No. 10) stainless steel snap swivels, and U-shaped cable supports with you. A pair of crimping pliers will help secure the sleeves tightly.

If you lose a weight and terminal hardware and don't have replacement materials, you can still jury-rig an arrangement by running the cable through a heavy-duty snap swivel (or directly to the weight if you don't have a snap; however, you can't take the weight off readily when you do this) and tying a series of jam knots in the cable. Test the holding strength of this arrangement, be careful not to hang the weight on bottom, and re-rig properly at the first opportunity. To minimize fraying and stress at the end of the cable, you can use a rubber snubber that fits over the wire.

Downriggers have a line counter to measure the length of cable that comes off the spool. It's important to account for the length of cable between the pulley and the surface of the water; the counter should read zero when the weight is just below the water surface. If you don't adjust it in this fashion, the weight will run 1 to 3 feet shallower than the counter shows.

The size of lead weight used in downrigging varies, although 10- to 12-pound weights are the norm. Heavy weights are needed to keep the cable directly below the boat, or as close to it as possible, for precise depth determination. This is especially important when you're using a wide-angle sonar transducer (so you can see the weights on your screen or gauge), when there is current, and when you are trolling fast. Heavy weights are also necessary for fishing in very deep water (50 feet or more). In relatively shallow water (20 feet or more), in places where there is no current, and when you are trolling slowly, you can use a 7- or 8-pound weight. A 2-pound weight is used on some small downriggers, but it can be difficult to calculate the actual running depth of a light weight.

Weights are often referred to as cannonballs because the earliest models, and many current ones, are shaped like a round ball. A round ball with a stabilizing fin on the back is the most popular shape, although there are various configurations. Weights shaped like a fish or a torpedo are fairly popular; a favorite with some anglers is a "pancake" weight with a slender head and a broad fin.

Some weights have a thick rubber or vinyl coating. Coated weights don't mar your boat when they hit the side or when they're dropped on

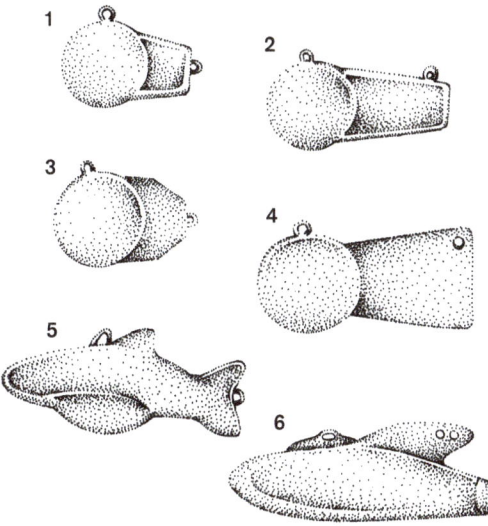

Common styles of downrigger weights include: cannonballs (1, 2, and 3), pancake (4), fish (5), and torpedo (6).

the gunwale or deck, and they're easy to handle. They are no more efficient than uncoated weights, however, although their coloring lasts indefinitely; painted lead weights lose their color over time. Manufacturer-supplied weights are available in white, black, chartreuse, green, orange, and red. Fish are often attracted to the trolled downrigger weight, possibly because of the color but most likely because of the vibration.

Rod holders *(see)* are critical to downrigging, and some downriggers come with integral holders or can be fitted with them as accessories. Mount one or two rod holders on the downrigger itself or locate them nearby. Place rod holders strategically and allow for more holders than you expect to need when fishing—the extra holders come in handy to store rods out of the way when landing fish, rigging, running, and so forth.

Line release. A line release mechanism is also critical to the downrigging system and presents a lot of room for experimentation, as well as problems. The line release must free the fishing line when a fish strikes or when the angler chooses to detach the line in order to retrieve it (otherwise, the weight must be brought in to manually release the line).

Line releases can be attached to the weight, to the downrigger cable at the weight, and to the cable at any location above the weight. In all line releases, the fishing line is clamped into it under variable pressure. Some feature a trigger that pops open and that can be set to release under greater or lesser tension. Some feature spring-loaded jaws capped with rubber pads; how far into the pads you set the fishing line determines the tension.

If the line has been placed properly, when a fish strikes, the line immediately pulls free of the release, which remains attached to the weight or cable. To free a fishing line from the boat, take the rod out of its holder, point the rod tip toward the water, and reel up slack; then pop the rod tip upward as if setting the hook. If this procedure doesn't free the fishing line, it was not properly set in the release or the tension on the release was set too high.

Easily adjustable tension settings are important in line releases, and setting the right tension is critical for catching fish. Most fish that take a lure trolled behind a downrigger weight impale themselves with the hook(s) of that lure when they strike it and pull the fishing line out of the release. A release set too loosely will provide little resistance to help set the hook; if it is set too tight, a small fish may strike the lure and not pop the line out of the release, causing the fish to be dragged for some distance before the problem is discovered. Also, a tight release often cannot be freed by an angler while in the boat when the angler wants to change lures.

There is a proper middle ground that varies, depending upon the strength of the fishing line used and the type of lure trolled. When using light line, you have to set release tension fairly light so that the line isn't broken if a big fish strikes the lure. When using lures that are heavy or that create a lot of resistance when pulled through the water, such as large deep-diving plugs or a dodger *(see)*, you must set the release tension high enough that the fishing line stays in the release and doesn't pop out without a fish striking, especially in rough water.

If you frequently lose fish, either because the hooks pull out or the fish strike the lure and pop the release but fail to get hooked, try tightening the tension on the release and shortening the length of line between the lure and the release. Missed strikes can occur when fish are slapping at the lure or when the release is set too light.

If you want to get technical, conduct the following experiment on dry land: Take a top-quality spring scale and attach it to the end of a fishing line. Set the line in your release, using a tension setting that you judge to be just right. Have someone watch the release and holler at the moment the line snaps out of the release. Watch the scale as you pull on the line to see the weight indicated at the moment your companion hollers. By doing this, you'll get a relative idea of how much pressure it takes to free the release at your chosen setting. Conduct the same experiment with different tension settings, with different lengths of fishing line between the scale and releases, and with different strengths of line. Although this is not quite the same as using line in the water (because stretch and breaking strength of wet line differ), it is a reasonable comparison and may lead you to a better understanding of the tension settings that increase your strike-to-hook ratio.

For some releases, you should twist the fishing line before putting it into the release. Twisting is necessary because the line will slip freely through the release if it is merely snapped into place. If this happens, (1) the lure might swim up to the weight and stay right behind the weight when you set the weight down; (2) a fish may not have enough

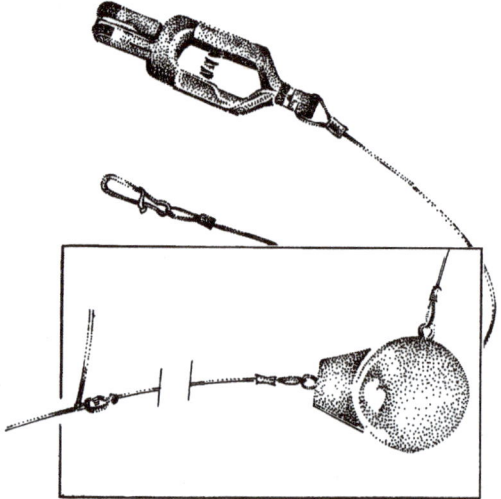

Depicted is a spring-tension release attached to a downrigger weight by a short cable (inset); fishing line is placed inside the forward pad of the release.

resistance at the release to trip it properly, which could mean you'll lose the fish; and (3) you can't trip the release from above because the line might simply slide through the release. To avoid these problems, take the fishing line and make six or seven twists with it after the lure has been set back, and then insert the twisted line or the loop into the release. Although a few anglers complain that twisting weakens fishing line, this practice is generally effective.

Some anglers don't use commercial releases at all but employ rubber bands for this purpose. No. 14 or 16 rubber bands (available in quantity at office supply stores) are preferred by many. These are attached to fishing line via a half hitch and then connected to a large snap affixed to the downrigger weight.

When a fish strikes a line that is attached to a rubber-band release, it must stretch the rubber band to its breaking point to disconnect the fishing line and downrigger cable. Occasionally you'll catch a fish that is small and can't break the band, and the fish will be inadvertently trolled for a long time. Sometimes it will be hard to snap the rubber band from above to retrieve the lure; at other times you'll get broken pieces of rubber band wrapped in your fishing reel, which can be messy when they melt or adhere to the line. Rubber bands left in the sun will lose their strength. A drawback to using even fresh rubber bands is that they may have inconsistent breaking strength.

Setting lines. To use a downrigger and set out a trolled line, begin by opening the bail or pushing the freespool button on the reel and letting the lure out to whatever distance you think it should be swimming behind the downrigger weight. Keep the reel in freespool—with the clicker on if it's a levelwind reel—and either loosen the drag or keep the bail open with a spinning reel. Bring the downrigger weight and line release close to the boat so that you can reach them without stretching far overboard. Grab the fishing line at the top of the rod and place it in the release, twisting the line first if necessary. Set the weight back overboard or swing the boom arm back to its outboard position so that the weight can be lowered. Take the rod in one hand, and make sure that the line is not fouled at the tip and that it will freely come off the reel spool. Use your other hand to lower the weight, either by depressing the down switch on an electric downrigger, by releasing clutch tension lightly, or by back reeling a manual downrigger. Stop the weight when it reaches the depth you want, as indicated on the line counter. Set the rod in a holder, and reel up slack so that the rod tip is bowed in a sharp C position.

Other than changing the length of line between release and lure or altering the depth to fish, you will go through this same procedure every time you set out a lure with a downrigger.

Because you lose touch with how your lures are working once you have lowered them on a

An angler attaches fishing line to a release on the downrigger weight.

downrigger weight, it's important to put them in the water and watch them swim before you set them out and before you attach the line to the downrigger release. Also, don't cast a lure out from the boat—it may become fouled. Place the lure in the water next to the boat so that you know it's working right, and then strip out the correct length of line. If there is a lot of surface debris, don't let the lure snag on debris before it is lowered with the weight.

Acquire the habit of scanning your downrigger rods and watching for signs of action; you'll often see a rod straighten the moment a fish strikes and pulls the line out of the release. When this happens, you should get to the rod fast to set the hook and play the fish. You'll also know when a fish has hit the lure but hasn't been hooked by noting how the rod suddenly dips without springing up. If the rod tip surges, it may be an indication that there is a small fish (baitfish or gamefish) on, even though the release hasn't tripped.

See: Downrigger Fishing; Trolling.

DOWNRIGGER FISHING

Fishing with downriggers is all about making a controlled presentation, whether in deep water, as is usually the case, or in shallow water. With downriggers, you can be versatile enough to cover a broad range of trolling situations, including river fishing, drifting, and live-bait fishing. Proper employment of downriggers begins with their installation on a boat.

Downrigger Placement

Downriggers are primarily located on and across the transom, or near the transom on the gunwales. Transom-mounted downriggers extend straight back, perpendicular to the stern. The booms should be long enough to clear any trim tabs or swim platform and to enable the cable to clear the propeller (especially for an auxiliary outboard) when seas

With two lines attached to the downrigger behind him, a troller watches his sonar to avoid running the weight too deep.

are rough or when tight turns are made. A four-downrigger setup would have one unit on each corner, perpendicular to the gunwale, and one on each side of the motor, facing aft, to give a good horizontal spread to the weights and trolling lines. A six-downrigger setup would have a unit on each gunwale a few feet ahead of the stern, perpendicular to the gunwale, and four properly spaced downriggers on the transom (including two on the corners), all of which would face aft. Long booms would be used on the gunwale riggers to increase horizontal spacing.

On small boats, downriggers can be located wherever they are most convenient, especially if only one or two are used and it is easy to get to them. Place them as close to the stern as possible. If downriggers are mounted amidship and used for shallow fishing, the trailing line may be cut by the propeller in tight turns.

Whether you use pedestal mounts, swivel bases, trolling boards, or the like depends on the interior arrangement of your boat, the amount of freeboard it has, your budget, and your personal taste. On small boats, and on some midsize and larger vessels as well, a cross-transom trolling board is a great way to go. On small boats, it offers versatility and portability for other types of fishing. Swivel bases are handy for gunwale-mount and long-boom downriggers, since the swivel lets you turn the boom inward for docking and trailering as well as for setting lines.

Some downriggers can be mounted in flush-mount rod holders and on rails, but look at such options carefully; some of these don't have the strength to support a downrigger. You could be inviting trouble when trolling in big seas, when using the heaviest weights, or when a weight hangs on the bottom. A handrail would not provide enough support, for instance, and a thin gunwale may not be adequate, even for small, clamp-on downriggers. However, you can reinforce a thin aluminum gunwale with a long, strong piece of metal or wood.

Boaters who use their vessels for many types of fishing, including conventional casting or stillfishing, might want to use downriggers or rod holders for occasional trolling but wouldn't want permanent mountings or drilled holes in a boat that they might not keep more than a few seasons. By fastening downrigger plates to the appropriate transom areas, you can take them on and off with ease. However, a trolling board *(see)* system might be better.

Fishing Depth

The depth that is trolled with downriggers can vary from just below the surface to as deep as the cable on your spool will allow. Determine desired fishing depth by checking temperature levels to see where the thermocline *(see)* or preferred temperature of your quarry, or its bottom habitat, can be found. You can also pick what seems like an appropriate depth temporarily and wait until you find fish on sonar *(see)* before making changes.

Sonar equipment is essential for downrigger fishing. Use it to find baitfish or gamefish and the levels at which they are located, as well as to determine the depth at the lake bottom or ocean floor and other aspects of the underwater terrain. Without sonar, you're just guessing, and you also run the risk of hanging up your weight if the depth gets shallower.

Many downrigger anglers like to use a wide-angle (32 to 50 degrees) transducer to see their weights on sonar screens. This wide-angle view can be valuable, but it can also give false impressions. The angle of view is very large at deeper levels, and sometimes the fish you see with a wide-angle transducer may not be directly below your boat. Nonetheless, a wide-angle display allows you to see more of what is around you.

Be aware that just because your downrigger line counter reads 50 feet, your lures may not be running at exactly 50 feet for several reasons. One of these is swayback.

Cable swayback is the tendency of downrigger cable to angle toward the stern of the boat. It becomes more pronounced if you increase boat speed, encounter underwater current, or fish in fast-flowing rivers. Astute big-lake trollers can tell when they've encountered underwater currents by the increased angle of the cable as it enters the water. With swayback, the weight is not running directly below the boat or at the level indicated by the depth counter, and you must allow for this.

Downrigger Fishing

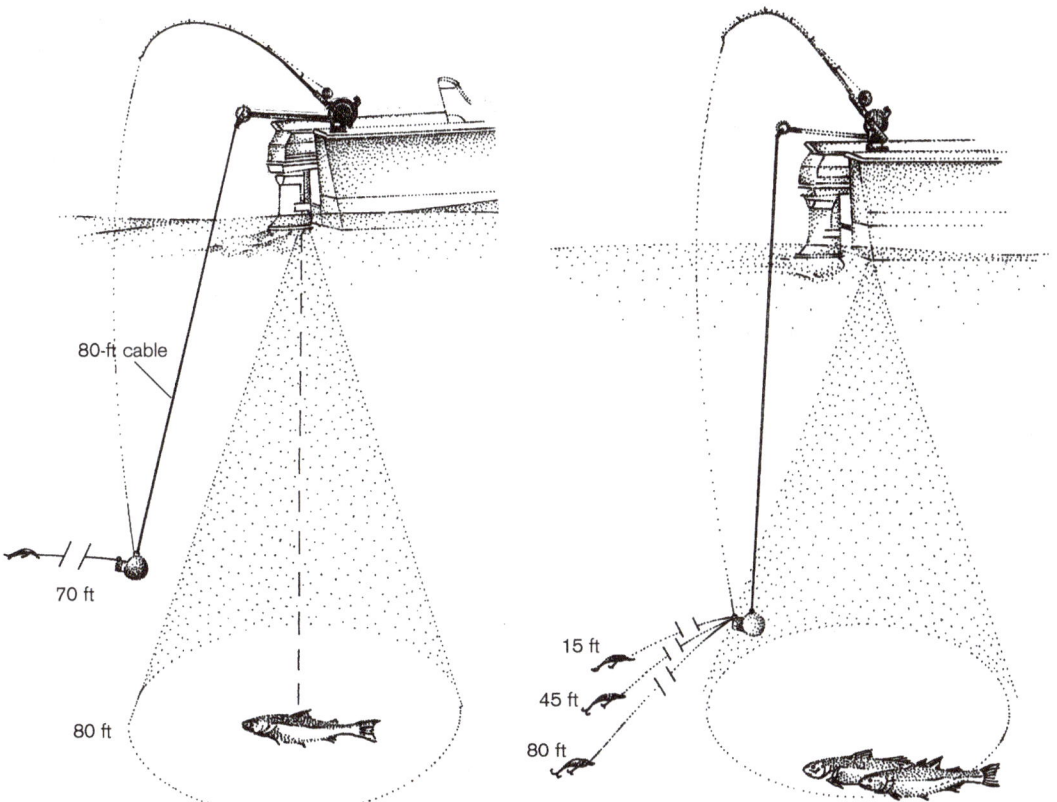

Because of certain conditions, a downrigger weight may not be at the vertical depth indicated on the cable counter. For example, if you set out 80 feet of cable to reach a fish that is 80 feet deep, the effects of swayback may cause the weight to be at the 70-foot level instead. Swayback has to be figured in setting the weight properly to put the lure in front of fish. This means letting out more cable, especially if the lure runs at the same depth as the weight.

Many anglers attach temperature- and speed-sensing probes to downrigger cables. These are usually part of lightweight, torpedo-shaped tubes set just above the weight. Such devices can present more drag and increase swayback; using heavy, 12-pound weights can help minimize this. Such devices also make sonar readings a little confusing because, in concert with the weight directly below them, they make a formidable streak across the screen that can obliterate fish or bait marks that may be at the same level. You can adjust the sensitivity of your sonar unit to reduce this problem, however.

As with swayback, you must account for the extra depth achieved by diving plugs when you troll them behind a downrigger weight. If, for example, you want your lure to run at 20 feet and you set a diving plug at the 20-foot level as indicated on the counter attached to the downrigger, that lure will be below the indicated level and will probably not be successful. If a diving plug runs 5 to 6 feet deep at a given speed and at the distance you have set it behind the downrigger weight, you must set the weight until the line counter reads 13 or 14 feet, no more.

Lures should swim just above fish rather than below them or far above because most fish attack prey from below. When you are trolling a diving plug behind a downrigger weight, the depth at which the lure will run actually depends on the distance it is set behind the weight as well as the design of the lure's lip. Thus, when you detect fish on sonar, the placement of the downrigger weight should take into account the diving ability of the lure.

Lure Distance/Setback

How far back from the weight to set your lures varies from a few feet to 200 feet, depending on the depth being fished and the species being pursued. As a general rule, the deeper you fish, the less distance you need to have between weight and lure; the shallower you set the weights, the farther back you put the lines. This is only a general guideline, because at times some fish can be caught shallow on short lines. Determining the proper setback requires experimentation and analysis of different conditions. It is advantageous, though not always effective, to fish with the shortest setback possible (depending on water clarity, species, depth, and so forth), because a shorter line increases hooksetting efficiency, minimizes possible conflicts with other boats in heavy traffic areas, and makes boat maneuvering easier.

To determine the length of line paid out, you can use one of several systems. With levelwind reels, you can count the number of "passes" that the levelwind guide makes across the top of the reel. Measure the amount of line that comes off the spool for one pass; then multiply that amount by the number of passes to arrive at an approximate setback distance. Some reels have built-in line counters that calculate distance; these are preferred by many charter boat captains and big-water boaters.

Another method, used with levelwind reels possessing a line guide that locks in an open position, and with spinning and fly reels, is to count "pulls." Start with the lure or fly in the water, hold the rod in one hand, and grab the line just ahead of the reel with your other hand. Pull off line in set increments, either as far as your arm will reach or in 1- or 2-foot strips. Count the number of pulls to arrive at setback length.

A third method is to "sweep" by putting the lure in the water, pointing the tip at the lure, and sweeping the rod toward the bow of the boat for a measured length. As the boat moves ahead, bring the rod tip back and then sweep forward again. If your sweep is 6 feet, multiply that by the number of sweeps you make to approximate setback length. Sweeping is a bit less accurate than using pulls or passes.

You can estimate setback distance by sight when surface lures are fished. But rough water, glare, and hard-to-see lures make this tough, and sometimes inaccurate. Many people are not good at judging even short distances, however, and often grossly overestimate the distance that they have set a lure behind the boat; this misjudgment can sometimes be detrimental to angling success.

Line-Setting Patterns

The way you mount downriggers and the number you use determine the horizontal spread that can be achieved with lures presented on downriggers. If you troll with only two downriggers, you needn't be too concerned with line-setting systems other than to keep the weights at different levels; also, try to vary setback lengths and to maximize your opportunities per line or per downrigger. The more 'riggers you employ, however, the more you should employ patterns or systems of operation, not only to cover the water well horizontally and vertically but also to facilitate landing fish, to minimize line crossing and tangling, and to make a better appeal to the fish.

Boaters who fish large open waters with four to six downriggers can employ some variation of V patterns in terms of the depth of the weight and lure setback; such patterns will help prevent inconsistent, possibly confusing, and perhaps troublesome lure and line placement.

Regarding depth, a V-down pattern will have the inner weights set deepest, the weights adjacent to them set shallower, and the outside weights set shallowest. A V-up pattern is just the reverse. An equal-depth pattern will have all the weights set at the same level.

Regarding line-to-lure setback, a V-in pattern will set the inner lures closest to the weight, the lures next to them farther back, and the outside lures farthest back. A V-out pattern is the reverse. An equal-length setback will have all lures set at the same distance behind the downrigger weight.

V-down

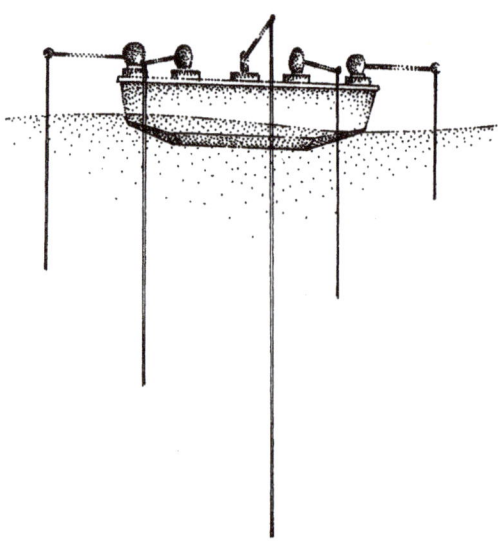

V-up

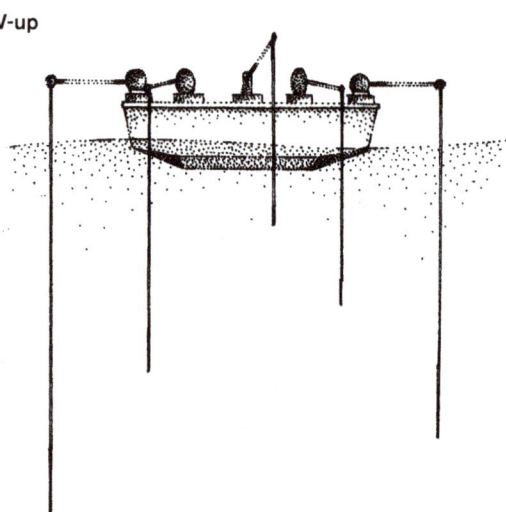

When using many downriggers on a large boat, set the weights in a pattern in order to scour different depths and help minimize tangling. In a V-down pattern, the deepest weights are set in the middle; in a V-up pattern, the deepest weights are set on the outside.

A V-down depth system is preferred by many trollers because the deepest lines are directly below the boat; shallower lines are out of the boat's direct path, perhaps where fish that are spooked by the boat or the inner downriggers may have moved. The V-up system might be the best approach when you're after fish that are attracted to boat noise or prop wash. An equal-depth presentation may be useful when fish are being caught only at a specific level—such as when they occupy a narrow band near the thermocline—or when you don't need to scour all depth levels.

Regarding setback lengths, there is seldom much reason to use a V-out setback. The V-in pattern is favored for the different downrigger depth settings and also for flatlining *(see)* and planer-board trolling *(see)*. When fish are falling regularly to lures trolled at a fairly specific midrange distance behind downrigger weights (especially when depths are nearly the same), there is little reason to stagger them much, so equal-length setbacks can be used. With the V-in system, the inner lures will run under the outer ones in turns, and fish directly below the boat may move up and out toward the lures set farther back. When used in combination with either the V-down or V-up depth settings, this setback system helps avoid line tangling when a fish strikes and pulls a deep line from the release.

Naturally, you have to experiment with these patterns and see which is best for your type of fishing and boat. (When you fish only one or two downriggers, this is all academic.) Such patterns are most useful when fishing in mid- to large-size boats; the most common pattern is a V-down/V-in combination.

Keep in mind that depth and setback distances are relative. A V-down system could set the shallowest depth trolled at 12 feet, the intermediate depth at 18, and the greatest depth at 24, which are not significant variations, or it could set the same progression at 20, 40, and 60 feet. The same is true for setbacks. There are no limitations.

The reason to use some type of pattern is to always know relatively where your weights and lures are, and the more rigs you troll, the harder it is to keep track of things. When a good fish strikes and lines are cleared, you can easily forget which weight the successful lure was on, how deep that weight was, and how far the lure was set behind the release. When you use a pattern, you know these facts, and you can re-rig immediately in a similar fashion. To fish with downriggers at various depths and setback lengths and to change them while trolling invites haphazardness; you won't have adequate control, and you may spend unnecessary time fixing problems.

Because outside lures speed up and inside lures slow down on a turn—and because the effects vary with the type of lure used (floating plugs rise while spoons and sinking plugs descend)—it is important to minimize the possibility of lines crossing and tangling. Some anglers troll for hours without checking their lures, only to find that they've been dragging a tangle for who-knows-how-long. This happens not only when downriggers are used but also when flatlines are trolled. The potential for problems is magnified by the effects of tide and current. To avoid tangling lines, you can employ two other solutions: never turn, or make only very slow, wide turns. Unfortunately, both are impractical and often fail to stimulate fish.

When setting out lines, try to keep the boat running straight, even if you're temporarily headed in a direction you don't want to go. A straight course while rigging minimizes line crossing and tangles.

More than one fishing line can be used with a single downrigger cable and weight, with the second or third lines set at various distances above the weight. This process is called stacking *(see)* and is particularly useful for covering different depths when you're unsure how deep to troll. Another way to cover different depths is to use a slider rig *(see)*, which lets you fish with more than one lure on a trolled line.

Boat Manipulation and Lure Behavior

Unlike casting, where a lure is retrieved by the angler, trolling is a matter of using the boat to work the lures; and in downrigger fishing, once you get the lures set where you want them, you have to make sure that they cross paths with fish and stimulate them. This is not just an issue of locating fish and driving the boat straight ahead, although that does work many times. Unfortunately, it doesn't work all the time, and some fish are not as aggressive as others, meaning that you must try to make the trolled offerings more appealing.

Line placement, lure presentation, and boat control are absolutely critical for sustained trolling success, and they work together. Downrigger fishing is usually combined with sonar use to locate fish or suitable habitat, primarily the former. Many of the fish caught by downrigger trollers have not been spotted first on sonar, which means that the fish were out of the boat's path of travel and that the fish came to the lures, instead of the lures being swum past their noses.

Creative and intelligent boat maneuvering can bring lures into the range of fish that are out of the boat's path. To regularly alter the lure's course of travel, you can turn the boat, steer in an S-shaped pattern or other irregular way, or change the boat speed. A good tactic is to sweep in and out from shore and to plan strategic approaches to points, sandbars, islands, shoals, channels, and the like. To be successful in some situations, you must cover a lot of territory and make versatile presentations; in other situations, you need to keep covering the same area or keep following the fish.

One reason why maneuvering in irregular patterns is a good tactic for trollers is because it imparts varying actions to lures, and these changes in a lure's behavior can precipitate a strike. Do whatever you can to make your offerings more attractive. Turning and altering speed are two basic activities and are aspects of successful trolling that are overlooked. Both alter lure behavior.

When you turn, some lures sink, some rise, some stay at the same level, some slow down, and some speed up, depending on the kind of lure and which side of the boat they are used on. Outside lures tend to speed up, and inside lures to slow down, depending on the sharpness of the turn. When lures are set a short distance behind downrigger weights, it's possible to make very sharp turns; wider turns are necessary when many lures are

Until the politically correct mid-1990s, the state fish of Colorado was the nonnative rainbow trout; it is now the rare but native greenback cutthroat trout.

A 468-pound sturgeon, caught at Benicia, California, in July 1983, is the largest world-record freshwater fish caught by an angler in North America.

trolled and when they are set further back, primarily to prevent them from tangling with each other.

Changing boat speed is a tactic to try when you locate fish but don't catch them, or when you are pursuing species that are known to be curious (lake trout, for example, may follow a lure for great distances before striking or swimming away). Speeding up is often more effective than slowing down, perhaps because it gives the impression of prey trying to flee.

Another way to alter a lure's behavior is by raising and lowering the weight periodically. Some electric downriggers can be programmed to oscillate automatically. It's worth doing this on your own, however, when fishing is slow and you want to trigger a strike from a fish that you've just spotted on sonar. Simply raise or lower the downrigger weight quickly to just above the level of the fish. If that doesn't work, wait a few moments for the lure to pass the fish; then take the rod out of its holder and pop the fishing line out of the release. Let the lure flutter down for a few seconds; then jig it once or twice. If nothing happens, retrieve the lure and reset the line. Often you'll catch fish in some stage of this operation.

Clearing Lines

You've got a whole bunch of lines set and you hook a fish. Do you keep moving? Do you pull in all the lines and raise all the weights?

Many big-boat trollers, particularly charter boat captains who fish a lot of lines, do not stop—they may slow down, but they don't really want to re-rig everything and they hope to catch another fish in the same area. They try to maneuver the boat to land the fish without crossing lines, messing up the rigging pattern, and pulling everything in and resetting. Small-boat trollers with only a few lines out don't have that problem and can usually pull in without too much trouble. Most anglers interested in sport don't like to keep moving, especially for good-size fish. After determining how large the fish is, they may clear everything, or may clear just one side of the boat and work the fish to that side for netting. This depends on the boat handler's skills, the angler's fish-playing abilities, the size of the fish, and the amount of gear in use. With big fish, it's usually best to clear everything, put the boat in neutral, and maneuver the boat as necessary to maintain a desirable position on the fish. There is no question that you get more sport and satisfaction out of playing a fish from a still boat than from dragging it in while the boat is moving.

Rods and Reels

A long rod, preferably having a long handle for insertion in a rod holder and an action that is not overly stiff, is optimum for downrigger use. This primarily means 8- to 10-foot rods, although you can use shorter ones. The stiffer the rod, the harder it is to get a bow into it when rigging and the more likely the tip will be unforgiving in rough water; a stiff rod will often cause a false release when the boat does a lot of rocking and rolling. Longer rods, including the 12-foot and greater noodle rods *(see)* preferred by some ultralight-tackle anglers, can be used with downriggers. Long rods used in steelhead fishing can be adapted for downrigger use but aren't quite as accommodating as more "parabolic" action downrigger rods.

Reels used in downrigger fishing run a wide gamut, but, in general, when fishing deep water, using long setbacks, or fighting strong fish capable of stripping off a lot of line, you need a reel with plenty of line capacity and a good drag. Levelwind products are more functional for downrigger fishing (and all trolling) if they have a clicker.

When you place the downrigger-set rod in a rod holder, it's important to do several things. Reel in all the slack; then pull on the line near the first rod guide while you turn the reel handle to bring the line as tight as possible, without pulling it out of the release. The rod should be well arched if properly set. Also check the reel drag for proper setting. The clicker should be on, so that if a fish strikes and takes line before someone spots the rod tip bouncing, the clicker will alert you that a fish is on and taking line off the reel.

See: Downrigger; Stacking; Trolling.

DOWNRUNNER

A term for shad that have spawned and are migrating downriver to return to the sea. Unlike pre-spawn shad, downrunners do feed and can be caught because of their hunger; however, they are less energetic than pre-spawn shad.

See: Shad, American.

DOWNSTREAM FISHING

Facing, casting, and fishing downstream in flowing water. This is the opposite of most river and stream fishing activities for fly anglers who wade and fish dry flies, since it is normally advantageous to face upstream and cast up, or up and across. However, some situations don't permit an upstream presentation. For lure users and fly anglers fishing wet flies and streamers, downstream fishing is less problematic and is standard procedure; dry fly anglers must mend line to get a proper drift or must be content with a very short drift, which requires an accurate cast to the right spot to start with.

See: Upstream Fishing.

DRAFT

The depth of water required to float a boat, often referred to as the amount of water that a boat "draws," and determined by the vertical distance from the waterline to keel, or from the waterline to the lowest point on the boat (including propeller, skeg, etc.).

DRAG

(1) Drag is basically an adjustable friction clutch that allows line to slip outward from a reel spool when a strong fish cannot be readily hauled in and swims the other way. Without drag, the line may break, the hook may straighten or rip out, or other bad events may occur. The drag essentially allows an angler to wear down and land a fish whose overall weight and strength outmatch the breaking strength of the line. It's an important function of a fishing reel, especially when light line is being used, when large and strong fish are being played, and when fish make strong and sudden surges while being landed.

The drag mechanism on a fishing reel allows line to slip outward by turning or revolving the spool, and it is controlled by the amount of friction applied, primarily by drag washers, to the spool. The amount of friction, or drag tension, is increased or decreased by turning a knob or wheel.

Drag tension ideally should be set before fishing and should not be adjusted during a fight—unless it has been improperly set to start with—because most anglers can't tell by a quick feel whether too little or too much tension has been applied, and the wrong decision is likely to hinder efforts to land a fish.

Most people set the drag via the "feels good" method—pull a little line off the reel, fiddle with the drag adjustment, and pull a little more until it feels "about right." The most precise way to set drag tension is to use a calibrated scale and measure the tension. The drag should be adjusted to the point where it slips at between 30 and 50 percent of the wet breaking strength of the line. That would be 3 to 5 pounds of tension for a 10-pound line. Most people are better off in the 30 to 35 percent range.

There are two methods to measure drag tension, both using a line that is run through the rod guides and tied to a calibrated scale (a good spring scale will do). One way is to hold the rod parallel to the ground and pointed directly at the scale, pulling on the scale so that there is no tension on the rod; adjust drag tension until it takes 30 percent of the line's breaking strength to make the drag slip. This is the least amount of pressure you can apply when fighting a fish, assuming that when a big fish steams off you point the rod directly at it until it stops running and then raise the rod up again to fight it.

In the other method, hold the rod at a 45- to 60-degree angle as if you were fighting a fish, and use the scale to pull on the line so that tension is applied to the rod as it would be in many fishing situations. Adjust drag tension until it takes 30 percent of the line's breaking strength to make the drag slip. In either case, you can apply judicious supplemental tension by placing your palm or fingers on the spool.

Once you have set drag tension in either manner, you'll readily appreciate the difficulty of getting a precise setting by the "feels good" method and, more important, the inadvisability of changing tension in the midst of battle. If you unintentionally up the ante to 70 percent of breaking strength, for example, you're flirting with disaster. If you don't think so, just set the tension at 50, 65, or 80 percent, walk off about 30 feet, and try pulling on the line attached to a scale.

How well the drag operates when it's needed most is the real issue, and that encompasses the following considerations:

- **Variation.** Does it retain its original setting, or does it stray from that setting? Straying is bad.
- **Maximum drag force.** Can the drag be set so that it doesn't slip at all (lockdown), should that be necessary? This is useful but not critical to many situations.
- **Range of adjustment.** How many revolutions can you obtain by turning the control mechanism on the reel? Ideally you should be able to get up to that 30 percent number with just a short adjustment, then have a lot of adjustment from 30 to 50 percent, and finally ramp up very quickly to full lockdown. The force required to start up the drag is an element of this as well, and it can be hampered by a drag that has been tightened and left to sit for several days, which puts a "set" in the drag washers. For this reason, you should relax the drag tension after every trip.
- **Drag washer size.** Are the drag washers large enough for the most severe tests? The most efficient drag washers are those with a large inside diameter as well as a large outside diameter to best cope with heat dissipation.

Much more can be said about the technical aspects of reel drag; these aspects are reviewed under the respective tackle categories.
See: Baitcasting Tackle; Big-Game Tackle; Conventional Tackle; Flycasting Tackle; Lever Drag Reel; Spincasting Tackle; Spinning Tackle.

(2) Drag is the influence of current on a fly, inhibiting the fly from drifting freely. The movement of some flies (mainly dry flies and nymphs) as a result of current is unnatural and is likely to make them unattractive to fish; to counter this, accurate casts *(see: flycasting tackle)* and mending *(see)* of the fly line is necessary.

DRAG-FREE DRIFT

Presenting a fly in current so that it drifts naturally and without the movement that is created by fly line.
See: Mending.

DRAGONFLIES AND DAMSELFLIES

These two groups of insects are members of the scientific order Odonata, a term derived from *odus*, meaning tooth and owing to the large mandibles of these species. They are common inhabitants of silty areas of aquatic environments and usually have a generation time of one year, but many may have life cycles up to four years. Their life cycle consists of egg, nymph, and adult stages, with most of this being in the nymph stage, which is also the stage that is of significance as fish prey. The adults are

Dragonfly and Damselfly Nymphs

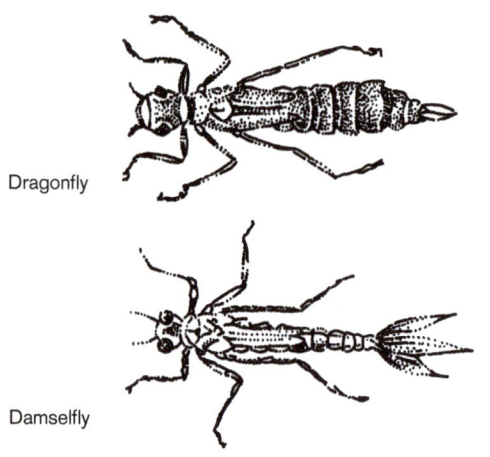

Dragonfly

Damselfly

readily observed along the shore but are not significant food for fish.

Dragonfly and damselfly nymphs are large and highly predacious insects who favor hiding and feeding among algae or aquatic plants, especially in lakes. They are 1 to 2 inches long, and have large eyes, three pairs of long segmented legs on the upper middle section (thorax) of the body, and a large scooplike lower lip that covers the bottom of the mouth. There are no gills on the sides or underneath the abdomen.

Damselfly larvae have a narrow body with three oar-shaped tails (gills) extending in a tripod formation. Their legs are long and spindly, and the body is thin and narrow. Dragonfly larvae have a wide oval or round abdomen that may end in three wedge-shaped extensions. They both capture other insects and small crustaceans with a double-hinged lower lip that is armed with spines.

Damselflies may be mistaken for mayflies *(see)* because of the presence of three tails, but the tails of damselflies are broad and fan shaped and extend from the body in a tripod formation. Mayfly larvae have three (sometimes two) filamentous tails extending from the body parallel to the ground. In addition, mayfly larvae have platelike or feathery gills extending from the sides of their abdomen. Dragonfly larvae are easily distinguished by their wide oval or round (sometimes flattened) abdomen and their large bulbous eyes.

See: Aquatic Insects.

DRAINAGE
The region or area drained, usually by a river.
See: Basin; Watershed.

DRAWDOWN
The deliberate lowering of water in an impoundment, usually as a result of hydroelectric or irrigation needs. This may cause a current to exist in a body of water that is usually without significant current and, if large enough, may quickly change the nature of the shallows of the affected impoundment. Severe drawdowns can affect gamefish behavior and location (sending some species to the security of deeper water where they are harder to locate and catch) and may create navigational hazards.

DRESSED WEIGHT
The weight of a fish after the viscera (or entrails), and sometimes the head and other body parts, have been removed.

DRESSING
(1) The coating or treatment that is used to help float a dry fly or fishing line, or to clean a fly line.

(2) The materials that, when tied on a hook, form the appearance, or pattern, of an artificial fly.
See: Fly.

(3) A term for cleaning fish, especially the act of scaling and eviscerating.
See: Fish Preparation—Cleaning/Dressing.

DRESSING FISH
See: Fish Preparation—Cleaning/Dressing.

DRIFT BOAT
(1) A term for party boat *(see)*, primarily used in saltwater.

(2) A particular type of manually propelled flat-bottomed boat used for floating rivers bow-first; it draws very little water and is extremely stable and maneuverable. Drift boats are especially employed by trout, salmon, and steelhead fishing guides.

Design and components. Drift boats are designed after the East Coast ocean dory, with two obvious differences: They are keel-less, and they have a wide flat bottom to create minimum draft while providing maximum stability and maneuverability. Both the bow and the stern are sharply upswept; the bow comes to a point and faces downstream when the boat is rowed, whereas the stern is usually slightly squared, primarily as an anchor support, and faces upstream when the boat is rowed. The oars are located in the center of the craft, making it easy to pivot from the rowing seat. The gunwales vary from about 10 to 20 inches in height depending on the turbulence of the water that the boat will be used in. The bottom is disproportionately wide compared with the length. A typical 16-foot drift boat, for example, will have a 54- to 60-inch-wide bottom, while a 20-foot boat will have a 60-, 66-, or even a 72-inch-wide bottom, making these craft uniquely stable.

Seating arrangements vary depending on the intended use on any given waterway. The rowing seat, which generally is made out of braided rope or nylon straps (somewhat like a lawn chair), often has no back for several reasons. On most waters, the operator doesn't have to overexert while rowing a drift boat, since drift boats, when properly balanced, row quite easily. However, in rough current with obstacles such as rocks and overhanging limbs, the operator may need to really put some backbone into the rowing and pivoting process. Not having a back on the rowing seat facilitates hard rowing; a back to the seat would get in the way. Most drift boat users choose a rowing seat without a back to make it easier to move from one end of the boat to the other.

The rowing seat is generally attached to a bench that is connected to both gunwales. A popular option is for the bench to have a lift-up lid for stowing gear. Passenger seats are typically mounted to another storage-type bench on a sliding track and are located in front of the rower. The reason for the sliding track is to allow the passengers' weight to be balanced. It is of paramount importance that a drift boat be balanced port to starboard, or the rower will have a most difficult time of rowing and maneuvering the craft.

Another popular seating arrangement, especially for fly anglers, is to have two pedestal seats, one fore and one aft. This gives both anglers the most casting room. This seating arrangement usually incorporates a leg brace located in front of both seats so that when anglers stand up they can secure their legs in the braces. With the braces, the anglers can stay balanced while casting when the boat is drifting through rough water.

Most commercially made drift boats are constructed of either aluminum or fiberglass. However, a few companies still make wooden boats. Wooden boats are most popular among the do-it-yourself crowd, and numerous designers and manufacturers sell blueprints for those that are so inclined. All three materials have pros and cons when it comes to use. Fiberglass is generally the most buoyant; aluminum is most durable; and wood, without doubt, has the most eye appeal.

Operation. Since drift boats draft very little water (draft is the amount of water that a boat needs to float), usually not more than a few inches, they offer excellent river fishing opportunities and have an equal ability to navigate deep or shallow environs. The wide, flat bottom of a drift boat also offers excellent stability in rough whitewater.

A typical 16-foot drift boat has 8-foot-long oars made of wood, fiberglass, or a combination of plastic and metal. Some rowers prefer even longer oars, up to 10 feet in length. Located amidship, the oars make it possible to turn a drift boat on a dime, so to speak. This excellent maneuverability not only allows the rower to position anglers in the best fishing water, but also makes it possible to quickly avoid potential hazards.

When rowing a drift boat, remember that these water craft, unlike other boats, are designed to be rowed forward by pushing on the oars, or backward by pulling on the oars; in other words, with the bow pointed downstream, which is the same direction that the rower faces, when the rower pulls backward on the oars, the stern of the boat heads upstream. The human physique allows the rower to put more strength into pulling oars than into pushing them, so the most critical maneuvering is done by pulling on the oars to position the boat. When approaching a bend in a river, or any other potentially dangerous rowing situation, always point the stern away from the potential hazard so that the rower can pull hard with the oars, backing away from the hazard.

When the boat is running whitewater, the rower must be vigilant and ready to respond on a moment's notice. Despite the apparent stability of a drift boat, it is still possible to upset and sink one. Interestingly, most drift boats do not have any built-in flotation. Therefore, if you sink one, it's going to the bottom.

When rowing downstream, the rower should always keep the boat parallel with the current; getting sideways and hitting a rock is the surest way of sinking a drift boat. A good rule of thumb that drift boat operators live by is: If you have to hit a rock, hit it straight on and hit it hard. Generally, if you hit a rock straight and hard, the drift boat will slide

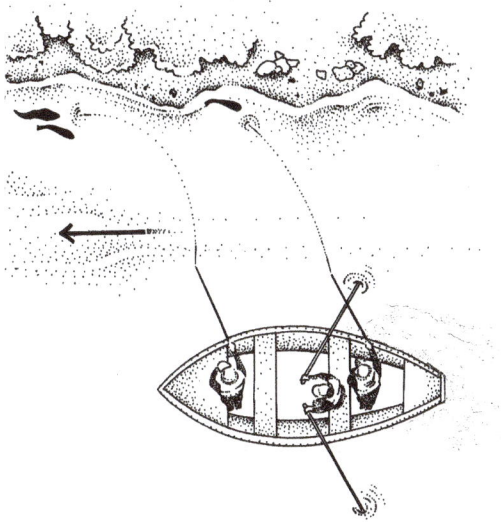

With bow facing downstream, a drift boat operator rows upstream to slow the drift or maintain position, while bow and stern anglers cast to likely fish lies.

over the rock. Fiberglass drift boats tend to slide easily over rocks and gravel, whereas wood and aluminum boats tend to hang up. Therefore, most drift boaters cover the bottom of a wood or aluminum boat with a thin $1/4$-inch sheet of plastic, or they apply several coats of marine epoxy to the bottom, in an effort to both protect the bottom and ease the boat's passage over objects.

One downside to the keel-less, flat-bottomed, and high-sided design of drift boats is that they can catch a lot of wind. They can be difficult to control on big open water like a lake or bay. Installing a stern-end anchor is helpful for times when a boat has to be kept in a specific position; without the anchor, the rower would have to constantly keep rowing to maintain position, which is either tiring or impossible in swift current. Many anchors can be raised and lowered from the operator's midboat position.

Fishing from a drift boat. Fishing from a drift boat offers many unique opportunities, as well as sometimes challenging circumstances. For example, anglers accustomed to wading in a river generally cast upstream to virgin water. In a drift boat, however, the virgin water lays ahead of the angler downstream. And, unless the boat is anchored, or the rower is holding the boat still, the angler and the water are constantly moving, which can create one of several interesting casting scenarios. Depending on the position of the boat in relation to the current, and the position of the water where you want to cast, you will be moving at the same speed as the water, moving slower than the water, or moving faster than the water. Each of these situations can feel quite foreign and awkward to the inexperienced drift boat angler.

When the boat is moving faster than, or at the same speed as, the current, you should cast downstream approximately at a 45-degree angle. If the boat is moving slower than the current, you should cast perpendicularly to the boat. When the boat is anchored, cast upstream, as you would do when wading.

When you are casting flies from a drift boat, it is important to get the most out of each cast and drift, rather than trying to achieve constant accurate casts. A lot of mending (see) can be done to keep a fly in the right position. Leave it in the right position until the fly, or strike indicator, starts to drag and then mend the line. Keep mending until you cannot do so any longer; then cast again. The longer you have to cast, the more the belly of the line is swept up in the current, and the faster the flow, the more frequently you may have to mend line. A good drift boat operator will work the boat into such a position as to keep casting distances down and help even novice anglers get a good drift from each cast. Some circumstances allow a drift boat to get fairly close to the desirable fishing areas, but others do not.

With fly anglers casting from both ends of a drift boat, there are many opportunities for lines to get fouled during casting. To avoid this, the stern angler should be especially mindful of the activities of the bow angler and should try to develop an alternating rhythm to casting; this can be done by casting after the bow angler has cast and laid line on the water and also by either or both anglers saying "casting" when they are about to pick their fly lines off the water. An equitable solution may be to alternate positions.

Both anglers—especially the bow angler—should always be mindful of where the boat is headed and what aspects or features of the river are about to come up, so that they are ready to make a presentation to an especially likely spot. Upcoming objects, current seams, and rising fish may provide a good opportunity, and your offering should be in the water and drifting or swimming properly before you come upon the site, rather than as you draw even with it. Casting back at a site that you are floating by is rarely productive. Obviously the rower is instrumental in positioning and presentation, and the speed of the current is also a critical factor.

Although drift boats can cover a lot of territory, some of which may not be otherwise accessible or often fished, it may be advantageous in some situations to beach the boat temporarily and fish a particular area thoroughly by wading. Trespass considerations may have to be taken into account, however, and in some waters you can fish and float through in a boat but not get out of the boat. A guide should know what is legal in the particular waterway.

Because drift boat anglers, unlike wading anglers, have miles of river at their disposal, it is very important to remember stream etiquette and give wading anglers a wide berth when passing through their area, even though this is sometimes difficult. It may, in fact, be preferable to go behind a wading angler in the area that is not being fished, rather than float through and disturb the area that is being fished. Some wading anglers do not understand that you are doing them a favor by coming behind them, so be courteous and ask for their preference before you float by.

It is also proper etiquette to give other drift boats a wide berth. When approaching another boat in a tight spot, yell ahead to the other boaters, letting them know that you are coming through. If possible, pass them on the side that they request you to pass on.

See: Backtrolling.

DRIFT FISHING

Who hasn't seen television commercials showing an angler sitting in a boat with feet propped up and a line dangling over the side, waiting to get lucky. Although some anglers are indeed like this, others who look laid-back will fool you. These anglers seem to be doing little or nothing, yet they often have an uncanny knack for achieving success. Drift fishing from a boat appears to be about as lazy a fishing method as you can find, but there is more

---

Bronze, blue, nickel, and gold hooks begin to corrode after 3 to 4 days in freshwater and within 36 hours in saltwater; they'll take 2 to 3 weeks to break down in freshwater and 2 days in saltwater.

to it than meets the eye. In fact, drifting with bait or lures is sometimes more advantageous than moving under electric or outboard motor power; for example, when the fish appear to be spooked by motor noise, drift fishing is actually a smart strategy.

Drift fishing can be either haphazard or calculated. The haphazard drifters, who pay little regard to how deep they are fishing, where they are headed, and what they are using, are not likely to be as effective as those drifters who use carefully selected tackle and make calculated approaches that take into account careful boat positioning.

One of the keys to calculated drifting—delib-

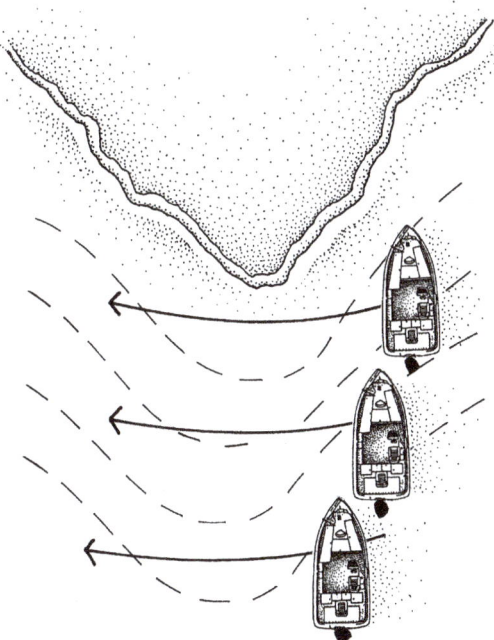

This fishing boat is using the wind to drift across an extended underwater point (note angle of motor to aid drift); several drifts are made to cover the water from shallow to deep.

erately drifting over a specific location—is setting up your boat for it. Because of its design, the weight inside, the hull configuration, and a variety of factors, every boat has a tendency to move off a straight line even though wind direction would seem to dictate a certain path as long as you start at the right spot. To determine how your boat drifts, do it in a controlled situation with the outboard motor in the water and aligned straight with the keel. To counter the tendency to move off a straight line, turn the motor in the direction that the boat wants to head; the motor will act like a rudder and keep the boat in a proper attitude with the wind.

Freshwater

Drifting in freshwater occurs in both lakes and rivers; it is usually a deliberate activity but sometimes can be forced upon anglers. Anglers on a lake may have to drift if the wind is too severe or if their source of power is lost (especially a dead battery on an electric motor). Really strong blows make it impossible for bass anglers to control their actions unless they drift, and anglers in small to midsize boats may be unable to troll without being bounced around.

Whether drifting is forced upon you or deliberately chosen, certain factors affect success and make drifting less likely to be an aimless hit-or-miss activity.

When drift fishing with bait, for example, pay attention to the type of bait rig that you use and to the weight *(see)*, or sinker. Bank, dipsey, pencil lead, and split shot sinkers are commonly used in bait drifting. Split shot are often used for suspending bait at specific depths; the others are essentially used for keeping contact with the bottom and are good in deep water and cast well. Split shot are preferred for light tackle. Dipsey sinkers are also used with light to medium tackle and where bait is suspended off the bottom above the sinker.

A very popular freshwater baitfishing rig, used for drifting as well as for trolling, is a spinner rig, which features a small spinner ahead of a worm, with a fixed sinker or sliding sinker above it; a spinner rig is especially useful for perch, walleye, and bass. Another popular bottom-drifting bait rig features a three-way swivel with one lead going to a sinker and the other to a bait hook.

Bass anglers will find that a Carolina rig *(see)* is a very good worm rig for bottom drifting. You need the right size weight to keep the worm down, of course, which will depend on wind and depth.

Some anglers who cast lures use a wind-aided drift to their advantage, in combination with occasional electric motor use, to help maintain a desired position. In fishing for bass, for instance, anglers can successfully work an open weedy area this way with a variety of lures. Plastic worms are especially good for some slow drifting work and can be fished on a slow retrieve that is combined with a drift. Crankbaits are a good drifting lure because they stay down and generally swim well at varied speeds of retrieval. Generally, however, the best lure to use when drifting is a jig, either with a soft-plastic attachment or with a strip of live or dead bait.

If you cast while drifting, you should cast ahead of the boat to cover the area you are approaching, especially when drifting over weeds. However, a fast wind-aided drift does not allow for proper retrieval of some lures that are cast downwind and retrieved upwind, and some strikes are missed because of decreased sensitivity. When jigging and worm fishing, you are better off fishing on the upwind side of the boat, letting the lures cover ground at the same pace as the boat. It is hard to fish jigs that drift underneath the boat, as they would when fished on the downwind side of the boat. This is especially necessary in deep water. If the wind is pushing you at such a clip that you cannot maintain contact with the bottom, you may need to use a heavier weight, or periodically reel in and lower the jig or worm right beside the boat until it hits bottom. Another option is to cast it to the side and slightly ahead of the boat; this action gives the lure (or bait) the opportunity to reach the bottom by the time the boat is directly overhead, increasing the effective time that it stays in the likely area before swinging upward and having to be retrieved.

To properly drift over a particular stretch of water, you must plan the approach properly, taking wind and current into consideration. Preferably the boat is broadside to the wind, but this is not possible with some boats, although on smaller craft the use of a sea anchor *(see)* can assure this. Note where you start a drift and have success so that you can return and redrift over productive stretches; also drift to the sides in order to cover all of a particular area. The longer you drift and the more the wind shifts, the harder it will be, especially in open water environs, to return to the proper place or to achieve the desirable drift.

When making a long drift, you'll usually find that fish are caught sporadically rather than in one tight spot, but this may depend upon the species. Repeat this drift and focus on adjacent waters for similar drifts. Although the places to drift vary with species pursued, points are a universal possibility. Submerged weeds are good drifting locations for bass and pike, provided the weeds have enough depth and density.

If you have an electric motor, use it sparingly to keep you in the right position or to slow the drift speed. One of the benefits of drifting, especially in shallow water and near shore, is that you are not creating noise, so try to use the motor sparingly.

River drift fishing is popular, too, and there is little that is haphazard about this. Using electric motors, outboard motors, or oars, boaters try to effect a downstream boat movement at a pace much slower than the speed of the current. The slowed movement allows them to cast lures and baits and work them better or longer (or present them more often) in likely places. This drifting method is especially effective for salmon, steelhead, trout, bass, and walleye.

The most critical aspect of river drift fishing is proper bait or lure presentation through boat control. Slipping, which is a form of backtrolling *(see),* is the best way to achieve success in river drift fishing. It entails moving slowly backward downstream while in complete control of your craft, in such a way that you and the passengers can fish at ease. To do this, point the bow of your boat upstream and accelerate the outboard motor in forward gear. With the bow placed into the current, throttle down the motor to a point where your boat has begun to move backward downstream. The thrust of the motor is not enough to keep you going forward, and your boat slowly drifts backward, stern first. The boat moves very slowly, sometimes almost imperceptibly, and you have precise control over your position and rate of descent.

With the motor at a steady forward thrust, the boat backs downstream with ease as you cast and retrieve. Cast upstream and retrieve slowly downstream. Upstream casting allows you to present lures in a manner similar to the movement of natural bait in current. The bow of the boat is always pointed into the current. It is a position easily held, providing you don't allow eddies and backwaters to entrap your boat, and you can readily move across current as necessary.

A similar outcome can be produced in moderate- to slow-flowing rivers by using an electric motor to position the boat face into the current and wind, and then by drifting with bait or jigs. Maintaining pace with the current allows for a vertical presentation that aids hooksetting and gives the fish less of a chance to detect the offering. It also permits the use of lighter jigs, which are often more likely to be taken than a heavier product.

Most river anglers who fish from shore are drift fishing. The standard procedure for casting to nearly every river species, regardless of whether you're using lure, fly, or bait, is to cast across and upstream and then allow the offering to drift or swim naturally in the current.

Saltwater

Drift fishing in saltwater takes place in coastal bays, tidal rivers, and the open ocean, with movement caused by tide and wind. Because of tide, these

Controlling the path and speed of a drift, as these walleye anglers are doing, is usually essential to success.

places can be completely devoid of fish or activity at one stage of the tide, yet provide sterling action just hours later. Thus, it's important to study each place you plan to fish, and determine how different wind and tide conditions affect the area. Above all, study coastal charts of the area, so you know the bottom conformation.

Canal drifting. Canals are a favorite drifting spot because they are usually narrow, clearly defined, and rather restricted, with extremely swift currents, especially during moon tides. Their bottoms may be irregular, including flat areas, shallow spots, sandy areas, rocky areas, and deep holes. The water may run swift and silent in some spots or noisily with large waves in others. Each hour presents a different set of circumstances; by carefully studying the conditions, you can quickly adjust to the changing conditions, movements, and feeding habits of the fish, which can include a wide variety of species. Incidentally, many canals are best fished at night because of daytime boat traffic; dusk and daybreak when the tides are right are also good.

A light popping or spinning outfit is ideal for this type of waterway. Monofilament line in the 10- to 15-pound-test range is preferred, because it is fine enough for employing a variety of terminal rigs and lures, yet sufficiently heavy if you have to pull off an obstruction or shell beds.

If the canal has swift current, flounder will bury themselves in the sand bottom sections; as the current slows, they begin to move about searching for food. They are most active from an hour before the change in tide to an hour after and readily take a bait drifted along the bottom. A good bait rig for flatfish uses a three-way swivel with one arm sporting a short piece of 8- or 10-pound-test monofilament with a loop in the end, which is used for attaching a 1/2- to 1-ounce dipsey sinker. The light mono-to-sinker connection permits you to easily break free if the sinker fouls bottom, and the lightweight sinker doesn't drag bottom but stays down and bounces along while drifting. The rig is completed with 18 inches of 10-pound line and a No. 8 or 9 hook. Next tie a dropper loop into the leader, and tie in a 6-inch leader with a second hook. Bait up with a 3-inch-long piece of sandworm, bloodworm, clam, or mussel, and focus your drifting efforts on either side of slack water.

Another place to catch flounder, especially summer flounder or fluke, is where the canal meets with a bay. The current carries plenty of food; on the flood tide it flows toward the bay, and fishing is productive where the waterway widens and empties into the bay. A three-way drift rig is very effective here, and small live bait, like mummichog, hooked through the lips, are good. You can also add a thin strip of squid to the hook, which flutters when the bait swims. Wait a second or two after feeling the strike, and lower the rod tip to give the fish slack and time to mouth the bait. When you feel a firm pull, slowly reel; this often causes the fluke to bite down securely on the bait, resulting in a hookup. This technique works better than striking quickly at the first sign of a pickup.

If a canal has bulkheads, you may find species like sea bass, blackfish, and porgies close to the bulkheads, feeding on grass shrimp and mussels. Drifting a sinker along close to the bottom often results in snagging on debris, especially in the rocky bottom areas, so use a float rig that keeps the hooked bait just off the bottom yet within range of feeding fish.

Check your sonar to determine the depth of the water where you'll be drifting. Tie a knot in your line at a distance a foot shorter than the water depth. Slip a bead or button onto the line, and then slip a plastic float with a hole in the middle onto the line so that it slides freely. Tie on a No. 4 or 5 Claw or Beak style hook, and finish off the rig by placing a small rubber-core sinker onto the line, about a foot from the hook. The sinker helps hold the entire rig perpendicular to the bottom as you drift along. Live grass shrimp are a good bait to use, but a tiny fiddler crab, small piece of clam or mussel, bloodworm, or sandworm, all work well.

This rig enables you to reel to the sinker, with the plastic float sliding on the line. As you let it back out, the sinker takes the baited hook to the desired depth just a foot or so off the bottom, and the bead and float slide up the line, stopped by the knot, which holds the rig in just the right position. Because the fish stay close to the bulkhead, the best tactic is to drift close to the bulkhead, holding your rod tip as close to it as possible.

Keep in mind that some species (like stripers and weakfish) avoid swift tidal flow and may stack up in deep holes. As the tide slows, usually an hour before, during, and after the change, they fan out searching for food. Live bait is good for these fish

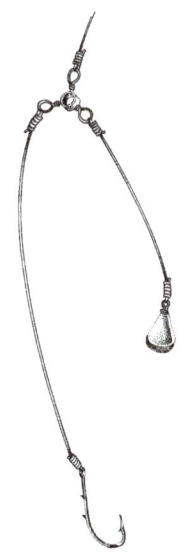

This is a common bait rig for drift fishing.

and is often very effective when drifting.

To rig up with live bait for drifting, tie a 2-foot-long loop in the end of your line using either a Bimini Twist or a double Surgeon's Knot. Then use a double Surgeon to tie a 36-inch-long monofilament leader material to your double line. Tie your hook to the leader. Bait up with sandworms for stripers and weakfish, using No. 1, 1/0, or 2/0 Beak-style hooks with a baitholder shank. Slip the hook point into the worm's mouth, and bring it out about $3/4$ inch from the head. The baitholder shank holds the worm securely, and it will swim enticingly as you drift along. For larger baits like live eels, herring, spot, or other small baitfish, a 4/0 through 6/0 hook is more appropriate.

With live bait, drift along with the current, paying out 40 to 50 feet of line. When the current is running fast, you may have to add a rubber-core sinker to the line to take the bait down, but as the tide slackens no weight is needed. Fish the reel in freespool; as a fish picks up the bait, let the fish move off to ensure that the bait is well within the fish's mouth.

Open ocean. Drift fishing on the open expanse of ocean is totally different from that experienced in a confined area like a canal. On the surface the water is all the same as far as the eye can see. There is a difference on the bottom, however, because depressions, peaks, ridges, rocks, and reefs contribute to where bait will congregate. Where the bait congregates is where you'll find larger game, so it's important to know the bottom conformation and the direction that your boat will drift, whether as a result of wind or tide. Through careful planning, your boat will drift over the area most likely to be populated by feeding fish.

Sharks are a common drift fishing catch, and the best way to score with them is while chumming and drifting, which is reviewed elsewhere *(see: sharks)*. Anglers should position their drift so that tide or wind carries them across known wrecks, reefs, or irregular bottom conformations where fish known to attract feeding sharks are found. If you're well positioned, the drift can carry you several miles, with the chum leaving a shark-attracting trail behind the boat. It may take minutes or hours, but if you cover the grounds, chum correctly, and have your baits set at various depths, you'll have a great chance to score.

Bottom-feeding fish like snapper and grouper are also a common drift fishing catch, located over rock and coral bottom. At intermediate depths around reefs and rocks, you may catch dolphin, king mackerel, Spanish mackerel, barracuda, wahoo, and little tunny. This combination is ideally suited to deep jigging from a drifting boat. Favored jigs are leadheads with either bucktail or plastic bodies. Depending on the depth of the reef and the swiftness of wind or current, use hook sizes ranging from 4/0 through 7/0, with heads weighing from $1/2$ ounce through 3 ounces, the latter where swift currents or 100-foot depths dictate.

The key to successful deep jigging is being intimately familiar with the bottom conformation. This can be accomplished by carefully studying charts of the area and then using sonar to view the reef, wreck, or ridge. The sonar lets you determine where the peaks and valleys exist and where the fish are holding. Then it's a matter of determining the direction of drift. If wind is lacking, you'll be moved by the tidal flow; if wind is present, it may overpower you and move you against the current.

Once you've made this determination, move to the high bottom spot and drop a marker buoy, moving farther away from the marker on each succeeding drift. The buoy allows you to bracket the area and also alerts you to avoid drifting from deep water into the peaks of the reef—where the line may snag and where a hooked fish may escape by diving into the coral and breaking off.

The most effective method is to move up to the marker buoy and shut down the motor. Allow the jig to settle all the way to the bottom. As soon as it touches down, lock the reel in gear promptly, lift back smartly with your rod tip, and begin reeling. Grouper and snapper cruising along the bottom often view the plummeting jig and then excitedly charge it as it leaps off the bottom and heads to the surface.

While retrieving, you can jig with your rod tip, smartly lifting it, which causes the jig to dart upward and then falter; keep repeating this until the jig reaches the surface. Many bottom feeders often strike the jig deep; intermediate cruisers will strike at midlevel, sometimes just as you're about to lift the jig from the water.

When you receive a strike, set back firmly and quickly attempt to get a few turns on the reel, lifting back smartly to get the fish away from the sharp coral. If you've positioned the drift properly, the movement of the boat away from the peaks of the reef will help put more distance between the fish and the bottom. In shallow water the positioning of your drift isn't as critical as it is when fishing offshore reefs.

Still another type of open-water drift fishing that enjoys tremendous popularity is fishing for the various members of the flatfish clan, which typically inhabit a sandy, soft, or mud bottom. Flatfish spend a lot of time almost completely buried, using their fins to flip sand or mud over their backs, with just their eyes exposed. They will do this when storms occur, roiling the water, and particularly when there is a quick drop in water temperature. Sometimes they use this vantage to wait for unsuspecting food to be carried by with the current. When water clarity and temperature are to their liking, they vacate the sand bottom and move about aggressively searching for a meal.

As flatfish move about, they may move along the perimeter of rocky bottom, or where wrecks or artificial reefs litter the bottom. They'll often move to a broad expanse of relatively flat bottom, punctuated by a series of hills or lumps that rise to the surface,

A black marlin tagged at Australia's Great Barrier Reef was recaptured two and one-half years later off New Zealand, some 2,000 miles away.

because forage is most plentiful here. A similar rig to that used in shallow canal or bay waters is used, although heavier weight is necessary to hold bottom. This may be a 6- or 8-ounce bank sinker, or even much heavier if the drift is fast and the depth greater. Using heavier sinkers is often better than using lighter ones, since a fast drift makes it hard to stay on the bottom with lighter sinkers. It may be necessary to keep adjusting by replacing a light sinker with a heavier one to stay on the bottom.

Open-water drift fishing opportunities exist in many bays, rivers, and creeks, where weedbeds can be fished for seatrout. This can be fine light-tackle sport, using a light popping rod or a spinning outfit with 10-pound line. Natural baits and artificials are both effective.

Perhaps the most relaxing tactic is using the time-tested popping cork and shrimp bait combination, which is designed to float a bait just off the bottom or above the weedbeds, or occasionally at intermediate levels. As such, you must know the prevailing depths over which you'll be drifting. A popping cork is slipped onto the line and held in position with a stopper that slides into the bottom of the cork. The popping cork is tapered at the bottom end, and is blunt and hollowed out at the other end, which is positioned facing the rod. Thus, when you pull back smartly, the cork gurgles and pops; the seatrout is attracted to the area, at which time it observes and takes the bait, which can be any variety of live or dead shrimp, as well as a sandworm, or live spot. Casting and retrieving lures, especially jigs with plastic shrimplike tails, is also a possibility.

Leisurely drifting and chumming on a broad expanse of offshore water may bring great rewards. With modern electronics you can cruise known haunts of pelagic species. Once a favorable temperature break is located, you'll often see schools of squid, mackerel, herring, and other types of forage. This can be exploited by shutting the motor, drifting, and establishing a chum line to attract the targeted species. Fishing may include jigging, fishing with live bait, or drifting dead bait or strips in the chum.

While you're drifting along, if you stream a bait out 100 feet or more, the current will push it toward the surface; adding a rubber-core sinker to the leader will keep the hooked bait drifting along at the same depth as the chum. Conversely, in minimal current or wind, you may have to add an inflated balloon, cork, or Styrofoam float to the line to suspend the bait at the desired level. Otherwise, it might sink directly to the bottom while the light, partially suspended chum particles drift off at intermediate levels.

The suspense and excitement generated in far offshore waters comes as a result of not knowing just which of the world's greatest gamefish will strike your bait. It may be a small yellowfin tuna or a blue marlin that normally dines on small tuna.
See: Bait Rig; Bottom Fishing; Drift Boat; Inshore Fishing; Jigging; Party Boat.

DRIFTING
(1) A manner of fly fishing in moving water, especially using nymphs, and resulting in a drag-free presentation.
See: Mending.

(2) A manner of fishing from boats, using current or wind.
See: Drift Boat; Drift Fishing.

DRIFT NET
A long net that is set in the sea (or a large inland lake) by commercial fishermen *(see)* and that passively catches anything swimming into it.

DROPBACK
A tactic used in offshore fishing, especially for marlin and tuna, in which a lure or natural bait, usually the latter, is fed to an interested fish that has been raised into a spread of trolled lures or baits, or that is following or attacking a teaser in the spread. The dropback is simply a maneuver in which the rod is held high above and behind the angler's head with a firm two-handed grip. When the fish grabs the bait or lure, the rod tip is instantly lowered to a position pointing at the fish, thus feeding the bait into its mouth. Then, the rod tip is immediately raised hard several times in a stabbing motion to set the hook. If the hook pulls free, the lure is rapidly reeled back to the surface and the procedure is repeated.
See: Big-Game Fishing; Trolling Lures, Saltwater.

DROPOFF
A place where the bottom of a body of water changes abruptly downward and the depth is significantly greater. Dropoffs are often places to locate gamefish, both in freshwater and in saltwater. In the latter, offshore canyons, seamounts, and shelves have the most extreme dropoffs, which actually cause an upwelling *(see)* of water toward the surface because of current action; there are often dropoffs along the edges of banks, islands, reefs, and the like. In freshwater, natural lakes and impoundments have dropoffs at various places and levels, especially where old channels or river beds once existed or where there are steep underwater ledges or cliffs.

Dropoffs are usually precisely located by observing sonar but may be generally located by reviewing detailed nautical charts or underwater contour maps. Depending on depth, species, and presence or absence of other underwater features, dropoffs may be good places to fish, especially during warm weather.
See: Breakline.

DROPPER FLY

An auxiliary fly, attached on its own tippet, to a fly fishing leader ahead of the principal fly. Droppers can be used in nymph, wet fly, and streamer fishing, and in combination with dry flies. A dropper can be affixed to the leader simply by leaving a few inches of overlap hanging down from the Blood or Uni Knot used to connect different strengths of leader material. Tie a dropper fly to the protruding tippet, and the main fly to the end of the leader. The accompanying illustration shows how this is done by using a dropper on a short tippet.

Although two different patterns of the same fly type can be fished simultaneously, like two wet flies or two streamers, it is common to use a nymph on the dropper in conjunction with a dry as the main fly. In some cases, the dry fly acts as a strike indicator for

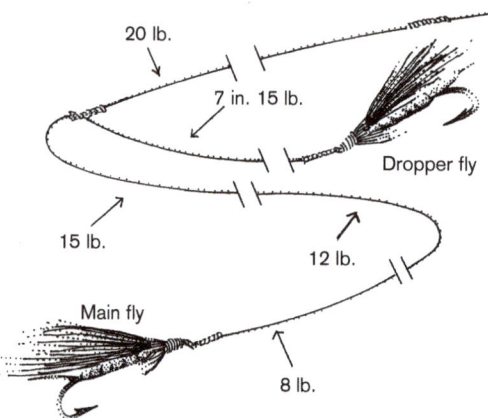

Shown are the latter stages of a knotted tapered leader, with a short length of line extending from one knot to a dropper fly.

the nymph. This is often a good ploy when prospecting and when there is no visible insect activity, or before a hatch occurs. If two fish in a row strike the dry fly, it's a simple matter to clip off the nymph. A dropper fly can also be fished with a lure, incidentally, especially a small spoon or spinner.

Fishing two flies is also possible when the flies are not technically droppers in that the auxiliary fly is fished behind the main fly instead of ahead of it. More of a tandem arrangement, this is accomplished via a short leader attached to the eye of the

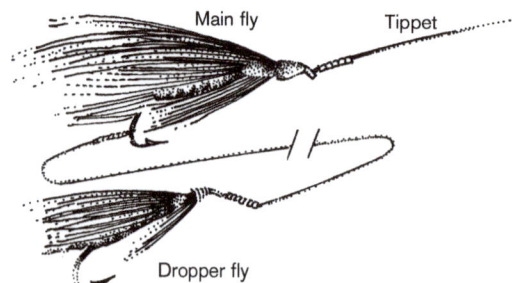

One method of using a dropper fly (in effect a second fly) is to tie it via a short length of line to the main fly.

main fly hook, or to the bend in the main fly hook. Tying to the eye is generally better for nymphs, and tying to the hook is better for streamers, provided the main hook has a definitive barb. These placements have the advantage of less tangling than if a dropper setup were used.

DROPPER LOOP RIG

A bottom fishing rig used for drifting with live or cut bait. Primarily employed in saltwater, a dropper loop rig features a bank sinker that is just heavy enough to touch bottom and one or two baits fished 18 to 35 inches apart. The baits are attached to the main line with 6- to 12-inch-long dropper loops, the lower of which is at least a foot above the sinker. This can be fished with one or two loops (baits) and minimizes the chances of hanging up with the hooks while drifting along the bottom. In obstructed waters where the sinker may get hung, a breakaway leader can be employed, attached via a swivel to the main (heavier) fishing line.

See: Inshore Fishing.

DRUM

Members of the Sciaenidae family (drum and

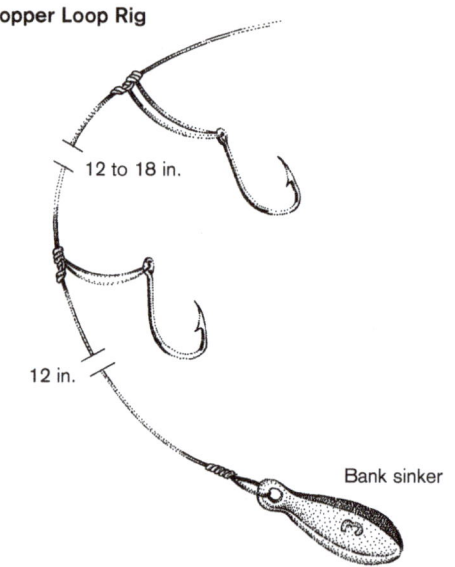

croaker), these fish are known for the noises they make. Most drum have a muscle close to the swim bladder, and when that muscle is vibrated, the bladder acts as a resonator and amplifier for the sound. These noises can sometimes be heard from a far distance. In some species, only the male can make a noise; in others, both sexes can drum or croak. A few do not have a swim bladder and make no noise.

Drum of about 200 species inhabit tropical and temperate seas. Almost all are inshore fish usually found over sandy bottoms, either in schools or in small groups. Only one species, the freshwater drum, inhabits freshwater. Most if not all are good to eat, and some grow to large sizes.

See: Corvina; Croaker; Drum, Black; Drum, Freshwater; Drum, Red; Meagre; Perch, Silver; Seabass, White; Seatrout, Sand; Seatrout, Silver; Seatrout, Spotted; Totuava; Weakfish; Weakfish, Acoupa.

DRUM, BLACK *Pogonias cromis.*
Other names—drum, sea drum, common drum, banded drum, butterfly drum, gray drum, striped drum, sea drum, oyster drum, oyster cracker; French: *grand tambour;* Japanese: *guchi, ishimochi, nibe;* Portuguese: *corvina;* Spanish: *corvinón negro, corbina, corvina negro, corvina, roncador.*

The black drum is the largest member of the Sciaenidae family (drum and croaker). The common term "drum" refers to the loud and distinctive "drumming" noise that occurs when the fish raps a muscle against the swim bladder. The noise is voluntary and is assumed to be associated with locating and attracting mates, and it can sometimes be heard from a good distance, even by people above the water.

The black drum is a popular sportfish in much of its range, and a common market fish that has been in greater demand since tighter restrictions were placed on the commercial catch of red drum. They are bottom feeders, with a strong liking for oysters and an equally strong propensity for destroying oyster beds. Larger fish are typically caught by anglers who bottom fish in surf and bay areas.

Small drum, between 10 and 15 pounds, are good eating, but they are frequently infested with parasites. Infected areas are circular and milky. The parasites are not harmful to humans and can be eliminated by cooking, but they detract from the fish's appeal. Larger black drum are likely to have a greater concentration of parasites. The flesh is coarse, but tender and delicately flavored. Black drum roe is a highly prized delicacy. The large, silvery scales, which are hard and difficult to remove, are often used in fish jewelry.

Identification. The black drum has a short, deep, and stocky body with a high arched back and a slightly concave tail. The lower jaw sports numerous barbels, or short whiskers. There are large pavementlike teeth in the throat, and the mouth is low. The dorsal fins have 11 spines, 20 to 22 dorsal rays, and 41 to 45 scales along the lateral line, which runs all the way to the end of the tail. There are 14 to 16 gill rakers on the lower limb of the first arch. Its coloring is silvery with a brassy sheen and blackish fins, turning to dark gray after death. Juveniles have four or five broad, dark, vertical bars on the body.

The black drum can be distinguished from the red drum *(see: drum, red)* by the absence of a dark spot on the tail base, by the lack of dark streaks along the scale row, and by the presence of chin

Black Drum

barbels. An unusually large spine in the anal fin and many barbels set the black drum apart from other similar species.

Size/Age. Average small drum weigh 5 to 10 pounds, whereas large specimens commonly weigh 20 to 40 pounds; in Delaware Bay between New Jersey and Delaware, fish from 40 to 70 pounds are fairly common in the spring. The all-tackle record is a fish that weighed 113 pounds, 1 ounce. It was caught in Delaware in 1975. Black drum live up to 35 years, although most of the fish caught are 10 years old or younger.

Distribution. Black drum are found in the western Atlantic Ocean, from Massachusetts to southern Florida and across the Gulf of Mexico to northern Mexico. They rarely occur north of New Jersey in this region. They also inhabit South America, ranging from southern Brazil to Argentina.

Habitat. An inshore bottom fish, the black drum prefers sandy bottoms in salt or brackish waters near jetties, breakwaters, bridge and pier pilings, clam and oyster beds, channels, estuaries, bays, high marsh areas, and shorelines. Juveniles are commonly found over muddy bottoms in estuaries. Larger fish often favor shoal areas and channels.

Black drum can survive wide ranges of salinity and temperature. The small fish inhabit brackish and freshwater habitats; the adults usually prefer estuaries in which salinity ranges from 9 to 26 parts per thousand and the temperature ranges from 53° to 91°F. They are susceptible to low temperatures and do not survive long at temperatures below 37°F.

Life history/Behavior. Black drum reach sexual maturity at the end of their second year at 14 inches in length. Adults form schools and migrate in the spring to bay and river mouths for the spawning season; in the Gulf of Mexico this is from February to May. A female can lay up to 6 million eggs; the larger the fish, the more eggs it will lay. Larval black drum remain in shallow muddy waters until they are 4 to 5 inches long; then they move near shore.

The drumming noise characteristic of the drum family is largely associated with spawning behavior. It is used to locate and attract a member of the opposite sex. The drumming of the males is particularly loud, and that of the females is softer.

Food and feeding habits. Larval black drum feed on zooplankton, and young drum feed on small crustaceans and marine annelids. Adult black drum feed on crustaceans and mollusks with a preference for blue crabs, shedder crabs, shrimp, oysters, and squid. They locate food with their chin barbels and crush and grind shells with their pharyngeal teeth.

Angling. Fishing for black drum is a different proposition than fishing for red drum. Most larger fish are caught by standard bottom fishing methods used in surf fishing (see) and inshore fishing (see). In the mid-Atlantic, where the greatest number of larger black drum are encountered (40- to 80-pounders), bottom rigs with baits—especially clams—are the predominant offering. This method is often combined with chumming (see), typically with a clam and crab chum mix. Shrimp, crabs, squid, and cut fish are the most common natural baits in the Gulf of Mexico, where some fish are also caught on spoons and jigs. Spoons, plugs, and flies can produce in conditions favorable to artificials.

Black drum mouth a bait, so anglers need to wait a few seconds before setting the hook when using natural baits. These fish are strong battlers and require stout tackle; bigger blacks are fished with 30- to 40-pound line and heavy terminal gear. They are caught throughout the year along the Gulf coast but are most common along Texas and Louisiana; in the mid-Atlantic, there is a strong bay fishery for large black drum in the spring, but fish are caught all year. The region from southern New Jersey to North Carolina provides the most opportunity.

DRUM, FRESHWATER *Aplodinotus grunniens.*
Other names—sheepshead, croaker, grunt, drum, silver bass, thunder pumper; French: *malachigan.*

The freshwater drum is the only North American freshwater representative of the Sciaenidae family, which includes the croaker, drum, corbina, and seatrout, among others. It also has the greatest range of any North American freshwater fish, is

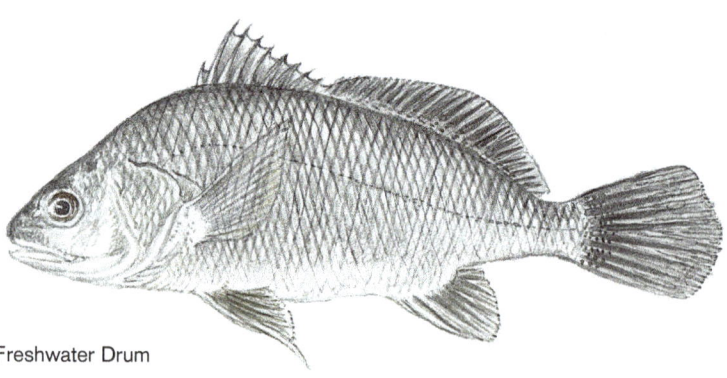

Freshwater Drum

A large freshwater drum from Lake Winnipeg, Manitoba.

highly adaptable, and is an excellent battler on light tackle, although it is extremely underrated and underutilized as a sportfish.

A unique feature of the freshwater drum is its oversize otolith—a flat, egg-shaped "ear bone" used for hearing and balance. It is surrounded by fluid and has a white, enameled surface with alternating light and dark bands that can be used to determine the age of the fish. They are often kept as good luck charms or made into jewelry. Excavated from Indian village sites, huge otoliths from freshwater drum indicate that at one time they grew as large as 200 pounds.

Although a strong fighter with some commercial value, the freshwater drum is not generally highly sought as either a sport or a food fish. It is deliberately sought by some anglers in the southern and midwestern regions of the United States, although it is mostly caught accidentally by anglers. The freshwater drum is often confused with carp in both appearance and taste, although on close examination it does not look like a carp. The drum's flesh is white with large, coarse flakes. It has been described by some as being of low quality, but this determination is inaccurate. Often found in clear waters, it is a relative of saltwater drum and croaker, which are highly valued as food. The freshwater drum, too, is fine table fare. Perhaps 5 to 10 million pounds are taken annually for commercial purposes, mostly from Lake Erie, and mostly for animal feed.

Identification. The body is deep with a

humped back, a blunt snout, and a subterminal mouth adapted for bottom feeding. A set of powerful teeth are in the pharynx. It has two dorsal fins, the first having eight to nine spines. The anal fin has two spines, the second of which is long and extremely stout. The caudal fin is bluntly pointed. Its coloring is green to gray on back with silvery overtones and a white belly. The large, silvery scales are rough to the touch.

The freshwater drum's two dorsal fins and rounded tail distinguish it from the carp and the buffalo. Also, the first dorsal fin of the freshwater drum is composed of eight to nine spines, whereas the carp has only one spine at the beginning of its single soft-rayed dorsal fin, and the buffalo has no spines at all. The freshwater drum can be distinguished from all other freshwater fish by the lateral line, which extends to the tip of the tail and is characteristic of sciaenids.

Size/Age. The average size of a freshwater drum is 15 inches and 3 pounds, although they can grow to 50 pounds. The average commercial catch usually weighs 1 to 5 pounds. The all-tackle record is 53 pounds, 8 ounces. They can live up to 20 years.

Distribution. The freshwater drum occurs over much of the U.S., between the Rockies and the Appalachians southward throughout eastern Mexico to Guatemala's Río Usumacinta system and northward through Manitoba, Canada, all the way to Hudson Bay. It also occurs in some areas of Ontario, Quebec, and Saskatchewan.

Habitat. Although it prefers clear waters, the freshwater drum is adaptable and can withstand turbid water better than many other species. It is commonly found in large lakes and in the deep pools of rivers. It favors deep water, staying at the bottom but moving shoreward at dusk. The drum is rarely found in small streams or small lakes.

Spawning. The freshwater drum spawns in spring when the water temperature reaches 65° to 70°F. The eggs are released over shallow gravel and sandy stretches near shore. They stick to pebbles or stones on the bottom and hatch within two weeks. Neither the eggs nor the young receive parental care.

Food and feeding habits. Young drum feed on minute crustaceans. Adults consume mollusks, insects, and fish. Using their snout, they slowly move small rocks and other bottom materials to find food. Their pharyngeal teeth crush snail or clam shells, and they spit out the shell and swallow the soft body.

Angling. Freshwater drum, or sheepshead as they are commonly known, can be taken on artificial lures or live baits, almost always fished near the bottom. Earthworms fished on bottom rigs or simply with enough split-shot weight to get to the bottom are effective, and small crayfish may also be used. Although small spinners, spoons, and sometimes plugs can catch drum where they are plentiful, jigs are the most reliable lures. Small marabou jigs or leadheads with plastic trailers are generally best, and they can be tipped with a piece of bait as well.

Sheepshead are generally easier to target in rivers than in lakes. In rivers, freshwater drum favor deep holes, tailrace pools below dams, eddies, deep riprap areas, the area outside bends, and similar places. In lakes, they are likely to be around rocky areas, including boulder and riprap banks, but they are not found where there is vegetation.

As with other drum, the flesh of the sheepshead can deteriorate quickly, so it is best to eat it soon after capture, rather than to store it for a long time. This fish can be prepared in many ways.

DRUM, RED *Sciaenops ocellatus*.

Other names—channel bass, redfish, rat red (schooling juveniles less than 2 pounds), bull red (more than 10 pounds), puppy drum (under 18 inches), drum, spottail bass, red bass, red horse, school drum; French: *tambour rouge*; Spanish: *corvinón ocelado, pez rojo, corvina roja, pescado colorado*.

Commonly known as a channel bass and redfish, the red drum is second only to black drum *(see: drum, black)* in size among members of the

Red Drum

drum family, Sciaenidae, but probably first in the hearts of anglers. The common term "drum" refers to the loud and distinctive "drumming" noise that occurs when the fish raps a muscle against the swim bladder. The noise is voluntary and is assumed to be associated with locating and attracting mates, and it can sometimes be heard from a good distance, sometimes even by people above the water.

Red drum have been in great demand in recent decades. They were intensely harvested by commercial fishermen until fishing restrictions or outright bans were enacted, and the great popularity of blackened redfish as a restaurant menu and fish market item was a significant factor in the collapse of redfish populations, especially due to netting in the Gulf of Mexico. A ban on netting, however, resulted in a dramatic comeback of gulf populations and caused exceptional growth in light-tackle inshore fishing. Today the red drum is one of the most popular coastal species in the U.S.

The management of redfish is complicated by the biology of the fish. The younger fish are found in state waters and thus are subject to state regulations, whereas the larger fish and schools are found either in offshore state waters (from shore to 3 miles out) or federal waters (from 3 to 200 miles offshore). Most coastal states have length and bag limits for red drum.

As mentioned, red drum are excellent food fish—one of the most desirable in the Gulf of Mexico. It is still commonly used in the popular dish known as blackened redfish. Larger specimens can be coarse and stringy, but smaller fish are quite good. The flesh is white, heavy, and moist, with a fine texture and mild flavor.

The red drum is also a popular surf fish, often caught under classic surf conditions. Although it isn't a flashy fighter, it is stubborn and determined, persistent on heading for the bottom. Large red drum, which are primarily found in the mid-Atlantic states, are powerful, premier coastal sportfish.

Identification. The red drum is similar in appearance to the black drum, although its maximum size is smaller and it is more streamlined. The body is elongate with a subterminal mouth and blunt nose. On adults the tail is squared, and on juveniles it is rounded. There are no chin barbels, which also distinguishes it from the black drum. Its coloring is coppery red to bronze on the back, and silver and white on the sides and belly. One black dot (also called an eyespot), or many, are found at the base of the tail.

Size/Age. The average adult red drum is 28 inches long and weighs roughly 15 pounds. Although red drum can attain enormous sizes, they seldom do so. A 30-pounder is generally rare south of the Carolinas or in the Gulf of Mexico, although fish weighing up to 60 pounds are caught in offshore locations. Thirty- to 50-pound fish are most prominent in the mid-Atlantic, principally in North Carolina and Virginia; these sizes are considered trophies.

Red drum can live 50 or more years. They are reported to live to at least 40 years in the Gulf of Mexico, and the all-tackle record, a North Carolina fish of 94 pounds, 2 ounces, was reportedly 53 years old.

Distribution. Red drum are found in the western Atlantic Ocean from the Gulf of Maine to the Florida Keys, although they are rare north of Maryland, and all along the Gulf coast to northern Mexico.

Habitat. An estuarine-dependent fish that becomes oceanic later in life, the red drum is found in brackish water and saltwater on sand, mud, and grass bottoms of inlets, shallow bays, tidal passes, bayous, and estuaries. The red drum also tolerates freshwater, in which some have been known to dwell permanently. Larger red drum prefer deeper waters of lower estuaries and tidal passes, whereas smaller drum remain in shallow waters near piers and jetties and on grassy flats.

Red drum can survive wide ranges of salinity and temperature. Smaller drum prefer lower salinity levels than do larger ones. Optimum salinity levels range from 5 to 30 parts per thousand, optimum temperatures from 40° to 90°F.

More big reds and fewer small ones exist in a fairly short stretch of the mid-Atlantic because of the rich feeding opportunities. This is said to keep the fish from migrating southward each fall, as they

A large red drum from Cape Hatteras, North Carolina.

An unusual redfish, with four spots, from Aransas Bay, Texas.

prefer to move offshore to warmer continental shelf waters until spring.

Life history/Behavior. Males are mature by four years of age at 30 inches and 15 pounds, females by five years at 35 inches and 18 pounds. The spawning season is during the fall, although it may begin as early as August and end as late as November. Spawning takes place at dusk in the coastal waters of the northern Gulf of Mexico, near passes, inlets, and bays, and is often tied to new- or full-moon phases. Right before spawning, males change color and become dark red or bright bluish gray above the lateral line. Both males and females, hours before mating, chase and butt each other, drumming loudly. Females may release up to $4^1/_2$ million eggs, although very few survive to adulthood. Currents and winds carry the larvae into estuarine nursery areas.

Adult red drum form large schools in coastal waters, an activity presumably associated with spawning, although it occurs throughout the year. Anglers often see them at the surface or moving under schools of blue runner and little tunny. Sight casting to schools is a favored activity.

Drum are known generally to remain in the waters where they were hatched, although some populations migrate seasonally, and large reds may move offshore as previously noted.

Food and feeding habits. As a bottom fish, this species uses its senses of sight and touch, and its downturned mouth, to locate forage on the bottom through vacuuming or biting the bottom. Juveniles consume copepods, amphipods, and tiny shrimp. In summer and fall, adults feed on crabs, shrimp, and sand dollars. Fish such as menhaden, mullet, pinfish, sea robin, lizardfish, spot, Atlantic croaker, and flounder are the primary foods consumed during winter and spring. In shallow water, red drum are often seen browsing head-down with their tails slightly out of the water, a behavior called "tailing."

Angling. Red drum are a democratic fish in that they are susceptible to a variety of methods, lures, and baits, in clear as well as turbid waters, and along beaches, at inlets, on grassflats, in marshes, in deep channels, and around shoals. Sight casting with lures or flies, bottom fishing with baits, and surf fishing are popularly enjoyed in various locations. They can be very easy to catch at times, and spooky and difficult at others.

Sight casting is probably the most favored method, and takes the form of spotting nearshore roving schools along beaches, or stalking shallow-water tailers as the feed. The former is more likely along the Atlantic coast, and the latter in gulf marshes. Shallow-water stalking is especially conducive to fly fishing, using Clouser Minnows, Deceiver patterns, and crab or bunker imitations. Eight- to 10-weight fly rods are fine for quiet backcountry conditions, but 10- to 12-weight outfits are necessary for the bigger fish found in surf and beach conditions.

When fishing for larger schools, anglers in boats try to get a high vantage point and cruise along beaches and inlets looking for dark masses of fish just under the surface in water that varies from a few feet to 20 feet deep. Sunny conditions are generally necessary for this, and the clear water of spring makes for the best visibility.

Blind casting along the edges of marshes on an outgoing tide is a standard practice. It is likely to produce generally smaller fish but is excellent for light-tackle and small-boat anglers.

Red drum are more likely to take lures than are black drum, and casting spoons, surface plugs, swimming plugs, and jigs are productive for these fish. The smaller fish of gulf waters are commonly caught on leadhead jigs fished with soft trailers. When the water is off-colored or turbid, rattling plugs and poppers can be effective. Smaller fish in estuaries and flats are suited to many of the same lures that catch largemouth bass in freshwater, as well as similar fishing tackle, namely, medium to light spinning and baitcasting outfits. Ten- to 15-pound lines are generally adequate. Live bait such as crab, shrimp, and finger mullet are effective but often unnecessary where the population of reds is good.

The bigger red drum of the Atlantic surf are a different story, however, and they generally require sturdier tackle, bigger lures, and heavier line. Bait is often preferred, with cut mullet being especially favored, although various other bait works also. Red drum frequently mouth a bait before running

off with it, so you need to adapt accordingly.
See: Surf Fishing.

DRY FLY
A floating artificial fly that represents an aquatic or terrestrial insect in freshwater.
See: Fly.

DUN
A post-nymphal but immature aquatic insect or fly (subimago); also, a grayish artificial fly that imitates this.

DUNCAN LOOP KNOT
A loop-type terminal fishing knot, inferior to a Non-Slip Loop Knot.
See: Knots, Fishing.

EARTHWORM

A worm that lives and burrows in the ground. It is estimated that 5,000 species of earthworms inhabit the world, living in all environs except the desert and continually frozen tundra. The most common forms of earthworm are the nightcrawler, which is usually 6 to 8 inches long, and the redworm, which is usually 3 to 4 inches long. Worms are highly popular and effective freshwater bait.
See: Natural Bait.

EBB TIDE

Outgoing, or falling, tide.
See: Tides.

ECHO SOUNDER

See: Sonar.

ECOLOGY

The study of living organisms in relation to each other and their environment; the entire network of associations between living organisms and their environment.
See: Ecosystem.

ECONOMIC VALUE (Sportfishing)

Although sportfishing is a traditional pastime, it has an important economic value, especially in North America and particularly in the United States. Many local and regional surveys of the economic benefits of sportfishing have been done, and in some cases they have been instrumental in increasing or adjusting governmental or private tourism expenditures, increasing or adjusting wildlife resource agency expenditures, affecting the buyout of commercial fishing operators, and otherwise reflecting the importance of healthy aquatic resources.

In the United States, the only national measure of the total economic impact of sportfishing comes from a national survey conducted every five years by the U.S. Fish and Wildlife Service (see). The most recent survey, conducted in 1996, determined that recreational anglers (35.2 million aged 16 or older) in the United States spent $38 billion directly on freshwater and saltwater angling activities and equipment. According to an analysis by the American Sportfishing Association, the $38 billion spent at the retail level had an overall ripple-through economic effect of $108 billion. Comparable figures for other countries are not available.

ECOSYSTEM

An intricate community of interaction among animals (including humans), plants, microorganisms, and the physical and chemical environment in which they live. Ecosystems are everywhere—from exotic tropical rain forests to small urban parks, and from oceans to farm ponds—and, obviously, the earth is the largest ecosystem. A lake or pond is an ecosystem. Every river has its own ecosystem. And all of these are subsystems of larger ecosystems (a lake drains into a stream, which flows to a river, which flows to an estuary, which meets with the ocean), which means that an impact on any given element may influence other elements.

ECUADOR

One of the smaller South American countries, the equator-straddling Ecuador is on the northwestern coast of that continent, bordering Peru, Colombia, and the Pacific Ocean. About one-fourth of the country is coastal plain, one-fourth takes in two ranges of the Andes Mountains, and one-half (the eastern region) is rain forest.

A boat trolls for roosterfish off Punta Elena.

Saltwater

The fertile waters off Ecuador's brief coastline offer among the finest offshore fishing opportunities available worldwide. Most of this originates at the seaside resort town of Salinas, only a two-hour drive through desert flats from the airport arrival city of Guayaquil. Salinas is not far from the once revered black marlin grounds of northern Peru, and just $2^1/_2°$ south of the equator. At Salinas, vacationing city dwellers and villagers from the higher elevations to the east come to enjoy the cool waters of the Pacific and the long, narrow beaches. Here, too, is a fleet of fishing boats available for charter, and thus the opportunity to experience one of Ecuador's major overlooked attractions.

Salinas (and Manta, about 45 miles to the north) is strategically located to benefit from a mix of formidable ocean currents. Just a few miles offshore from the beaches of Salinas and the tall condominiums nearby, an eddy of the cold Antarctic Humboldt Current sweeps by, bringing with it acres and acres of baitfish and a host of predatory species, particularly black marlin, Pacific blue marlin, bigeye tuna, and striped marlin. Stripes are the foremost attraction to the many anglers who come here annually. It isn't the record potential that does it (although Salinas was the site of two long-standing fly rod records for striped marlin). It is the sheer number of fish to be encountered, and the excitement of stalking and baiting them, that turns everyone on.

A typical day begins with a short ride by dinghy from the beach to nearby charter boats. The run offshore travels by Punta Elena, a tall, rocky promontory that serves as a shoreside reference point during the day's fishing. Within an hour, lines are dropped into the water and all eyes are scanning the sea for marlin tails. This is a unique method of fishing for marlin: Here you usually see your quarry before the strike.

Observing and stalking the quarry sounds like hunting, or like fishing on tidal flats for bonefish—not like something you would do in the wide-open ocean over deep, indigo water. In the offshore salt, this would be rather dull if there were very little to see. But because there's a lot to see in the Pacific off Salinas, this pastime is not only exciting, it has transformed the area into one of the world's most renowned spots for big-game fishing.

Salinas is one of few places where anglers deliberately and continuously sight-fish for marlin. Although skirted ballyhoo baits are trolled behind the boat at all times, most fish are first sighted and then deliberately baited. The captain races the engines and maneuvers the boat ahead of the fish to present the baits within its field of view. Often two, or four, or even up to a dozen tails are sighted at once. Pods of marlin are often seen surfing down the long, rolling Pacific swells, and when such a bonanza occurs, the odds for a hookup or two greatly increase.

A minority of striped marlin actually charge one of the baits. Some move off immediately, whereas others look over the various *baits* and follow for several minutes before drifting off. The watching, waiting, and anticipating make for some anxious but enjoyable moments in themselves, especially because up to 20 fish might be spotted in the course of a day. Although great-size blue and black marlin are occasionally seen, their tails visible above the surface of the water, these larger fish usually crash the bait or lure from below without warning. It's hard to say which is more exciting, a blind strike or an anticipated one from a tailing fish, but either way, a marlin strike is for many the experience of a lifetime.

The boats off Ecuador's coast have at times averaged a billfish a day year-round, so even the novice can expect a good chance to tangle with one or more of these magnificent gamefish. This makes Ecuador a superb place for the novice big-game angler to hook that first billfish. Striped marlin are not only abundant, they average 100 to 150 pounds and tire themselves through spectacular greyhounding performances across the ocean surface.

Black and blue marlin in this area, of course, average considerably larger than striped marlin—500-pounders not uncommon. A former world record Pacific blue marlin weighing 1,014 pounds was taken in 1985 off Manta, about 45 miles by boat from Salinas. La Plata Island, between Salinas and Manta, has become a hotspot for blue marlin. The record-size fish swimming in these waters contribute in no small part to Ecuador's angling fame; giant bigeye tuna and blue marlin, in particular, feed offshore from Salinas and nearby Manta, and the constant anticipation of encountering such monsters simply adds to the experience.

Ecuador is blessed with such activity in part because of the interaction of the powerful currents mentioned earlier. The most prominent current along the western coast of South America is the Humboldt Current, a cold northerly flowing stream of water that moves toward the west as it nears the equator. The Equatorial Current at the equator produces eddies that spin off and head back toward Ecuador's coast. These eddies of warm tropical water force the colder Humboldt waters offshore, and they contain baitfish and gamefish species. Additionally, some 10 to 12 miles offshore there's a sharp drop in the ocean floor, which rises back again before plunging into great depths. An abundance of baitfish in this area causes the striped marlin to skim the surface waters, and accounts for all the sightings.

Of course, other marlin are present here, too, perhaps not in the same numbers as stripes but with no less interest from anglers. Black marlin are more prevalent inshore than striped marlin, whereas blue marlin are likely to be farther out over deeper water.

The billfish here are sometimes thrown a whammy by El Niño, creating great concern for

---

Daniel Butler Fearing collected 12,000 books and pamphlets on angling in 20 languages; his collection was donated to the Harvard Library in 1914.

the commercial longline fishery. Yet, monster blue marlin have been taken by anglers (longliners have reportedly taken numerous granders). In May 1985, an International Game Fish Association (IGFA) 80-pound line-class world record Pacific blue marlin of 1,014 pounds was caught off Manta, and several 800- to 900-pound fish followed in later years.

Black marlin aren't typically that large, although 500- to 700-pounders have been hooked. These fish are on average in the 350-pound class, and the median weight for blues is about 400 pounds.

That's good, especially because the blue marlin are available year-round. May through January is the better period. The optimal time for blacks is April and May and again in the fall. Prime time for striped marlin is usually October through January, although El Niños can foul up that timetable; many anglers like variety and opt for September through November, when the overall options are at their best.

Bigeye tuna represent another notable fishery here. These fish average in the heavyweight division, and several records have been set in Ecuadorian waters, including a 341-pounder on 80-pound-test line. Off Ecuador, January through March is a peak time for these bruisers.

Numerous other species inhabit these waters, including swordfish. Anglers seldom attempt to land swordfish, however, which are longlined in fair numbers here and are occasionally seen on the surface. During the late 1970s anglers did put some effort into baiting swordfish. These were spotted fairly regularly on the surface about 30 miles south of Salinas.

Trollers encounter sailfish and dolphin (dorado) here too. Dolphin used to be so abundant that boats ran from them in pursuit of striped marlin. The capture of at least one dolphin for lunch was a sure thing. Dolphin species have been heavily impacted by longlining, however, which started in the 1980s.

Sailfish are a common year-round trolling catch. They often build up in the Ecuadorian winter (July through September) and usually average more than 100 pounds. When an occasional current shift alters the water temperature and turns the billfish bite off, which happens periodically, the do-or-die angler can opt to try casting or trolling coastal rocks for the feisty roosterfish or corvina, or troll a nearby close-to-shore seamount for wahoo.

The commercial fleet that operates here has long raised conservation concerns among sporting anglers, as longliners and gillnetters have been abundant. Even among sportfishing boats in the past, the catch belonged to the crew, and was often sold to local Ecuadorians, for whom the fish is an important food source. Increasing numbers of anglers interested in catch-and-release have helped conservation efforts.

Most anglers need not bring fishing tackle to experience the billfish action, as the seasoned offshore fleet here have first-rate 50- and 80-pound-class tackle. Costs for a one-day charter run less than the fee for a day's big-game fishing at most of the world's angling hotspots.

Galápagos Islands

This fabled group of islands (13 major, 6 minor, and 42 islets with names plus many unnamed rocks and islets) is owned by Ecuador but located about 600 miles off the coast and serviced by flights from Guayaquil into the islands of Baltra and San Cristóbal, as well as by cruise ships. It was here that Darwin formulated his theory of evolution during the famous 1835 journey of H.M.S. *Beagle*.

The only element common to all the Galápagos, a strictly controlled national park, is the friendly nature of its animals and birds, which have lived largely free from predation. Otherwise, the islands, which are spread over about 800 square miles, range from desolate and volcanic to lush, and from cool to semitropical. Although the equator passes through the islands, the Humboldt Current has a cooling influence.

Fishing possibilities are unlimited but have been sampled primarily by large private boats. At this writing, attempts are underway to set up charter operations. An exceptional striped marlin fishery has been discovered on the Cristóbal Banks, north of San Cristóbal. The all-tackle world record Pacific sailfish was caught off Santa Cruz Island on February 1947, but no one has located other such outsize sails since.

Unlike the reptiles and resident birds, which are almost all unique to the Galápagos, fish found around the islands are familiar game and food species, including yellowfin tuna, cubera and mullet snapper, bonito, black skipjacks, dolphin, grouper, wahoo, amberjack, California sheepshead, and many types of sharks. The colorful leather bass isn't a common species in the eastern Pacific but is found around other offshore islands. Most surprising is the abundance of snook in Tortuga Negra Cove on Santa Cruz, opposite the airfield at Balta.

Freshwater

Ecuador has traditionally offered few freshwater fishing opportunities for traveling anglers, but waters in the highlands reportedly have been stocked with trout, and largemouth bass have been stocked in the lagoon at Otavalo. Good fishing for trout reportedly existed in high-mountain waters, at altitudes over 10,000 feet, in the late 1970s and early 1980s, but recent news of this has been scant.

The steep mountains of Ecuador produce many streams; those that flow west from the Andes in Ecuador are relatively short and might be accessible from Quito. The Rio Napo, which originates in the north-central mountains, is the country's major river, but many others flow westerly into Peru and then to the Amazon River. Some of the rivers and fishing possibilities in Ecuador are described in the Amazon review under Brazil *(see)*.

EDDY

A counter current forming on the side of or within a main current. Eddies occur in air and water, are markedly different from the general movement of a large mass of the main current, and usually move in a circular path. They develop where main currents encounter obstacles or where two currents flow past one another. The number and velocity of eddies increase as the velocity of the surrounding mass (air or water) increases. More eddies and faster-moving ones spin off in rapidly moving water than in a more sluggish stream. If water moves around an obstacle, an eddy may form at some critical velocity (this depends on the nature of the obstacle) on the leeward side of the obstacle because the pressure of the fluid is reduced at that point by the rapid movement of the flow. If the velocity of the main current is great enough, a vortex or whirlpool will form. Whirlpools are permanent eddies.

In freshwater, eddies appear in rivers and occasionally in streams or creeks, varying in size and velocity. Many eddies are along the edges of a flowage but may be present where there are large rocks and bridge pilings. Because food, including insects and fish, may utilize or be swept into eddies, predatory fish will use them for feeding opportunities, sometimes stationing themselves in the eddy facing downstream (which is actually facing into the upstream-flowing portion of the eddy), or in the confused water of the seam where the main current and the eddy meet. Eddies of sufficient speed can create tricky casting and presentation situations.

Eddies seldom occur in lakes, although in large inland bodies of water they may be present in a grand and slow-moving scale where there is sufficient current. Eddies are present in the oceans, where they are spun off wind activity, upwellings, or waves encountering an obstacle, and also by the convergence of large current systems. In the latter case, they may be enormous sections of water that do not provide visible clues to direction, although a drifting boat with navigational devices will be able to detect movement that is related to eddies and not wind or wave action. The edges of these eddies may trap minute food organisms and thus attract pelagic baitfish and, in turn, larger predators. The Gulf Stream is a prime example of an eddy-creating ocean system.

EELS

More than 20 families form a large group, or order—Anguilliformes—of jawed fish called eels. They share a number of features that make them unique among fish. All have spineless fins and long, slim, snakelike bodies that lack ventral fins. In most, the dorsal, caudal, and anal fins are joined to form one continuous fin over the rear of the body. Except in a few species, there are no visible scales, although microscopic examination will reveal numerous very tiny scales—100 or more to the square inch. Most eels are palindromic, that is, they have the unusual ability to move equally well forward or backward forcefully. This serves them well not only for burrowing purposes, but for pulling, twisting, and spinning when tearing apart prey that is too large to be consumed whole.

All the different families of eels are marine except the family Anguillidae. Some eels have important commercial significance and are valued food fish; a few are caught by anglers. Not to be confused with eels are the eel-like lampreys (see), which do not have jaws or pectoral fins, and are commonly but erroneously called "lamprey eels."

Freshwater Eels
The Anguillidae family of freshwater eels includes such better known species as the American eel *(Anguilla rostrata)*, European eel *(A. anguilla)*, Japanese eel *(A. japonica)*, Indian eel *(Phisodnopsis boro)*, and about a dozen other species that live in the Indo-Pacific region. Freshwater eels are curiously absent from the eastern Pacific and South Atlantic, presumably due to their higher salinity.

These eels have been prized as food since ancient times and have been caught in eel traps or pots, in nets, or on hook and line. Little was known about their life history until the late 1800s. All sorts of stories were told about how eels came into being, including a persistent tale that they came from horse hairs that fell into the water and somehow came to life. A Danish scientist finally unraveled the strange true story.

The American eel and the European eel both spawn in the same area of the Atlantic Ocean, in deep water at the northern edge of the Sargasso Sea. There, each female lays as many as 10 to 20 million eggs, which the males fertilize. The adults then die. The eggs float slowly to the surface and soon hatch into slim, transparent leptocephali, or larvae, commonly called glass fish.

The baby eels begin drifting and swimming in the ocean currents. Their swimming motions help keep them directed toward their ultimate home waters. Baby American eels travel toward North America, and baby European eels swim toward Europe. How they know which way to go when neither has ever seen its "home" is unknown. For the American eels, the trip is about 1,000 miles; the journey requires about a year. European eels travel 3,000 miles or more, their trip taking nearly three years. It is equally astonishing that the growth rate of each type differs, so that each has developed to about the same size when it reaches its destination. By this time they have metamorphosed from the leaflike leptocephalus stage and have become thick-bodied little eels (also called elvers).

Male eels stay near the mouths of rivers, but the more venturesome females continue to swim upstream into the headwaters. Or sometimes they slither through dewy grass to move from one body of water to another. Eventually they find a place that suits their needs and settle there to feed and grow. The female may reach a length of 3 feet; males rarely grow more than a foot long. After several years, the females lose their greenish color, becoming almost black. They begin their downstream journey to the sea, where they are joined by the mature males, who swim with them to the spawning area. Eels that have established themselves in ponds or lakes without tributary streams do not move out even after maturing. They remain landlocked, living in these waters for 50 years or longer and never spawning.

The adult American eel and the adult European eel are so similar in appearance that they can be distinguished only by counting their vertebrae. An American eel has 103 to 111 vertebrae; the European, 110 to 119. Both have sharp snouts and numerous teeth. Some scientists believe the two are really one and the same species.

In Europe and Japan these eels rank as delicacies. They are less favored in America, even though they're delicious when fried, grilled, roasted, smoked, or pickled. In sportfishing, eel skins and whole live eels are used as bait for striped bass and other marine fish, and artificial eels made of soft plastic and other substances are commonly used.

See: Eel, American; Eel, European.

Moray Eels

The Muraenidae family of morays is the most infamous group within the order Anguilliformes. They constitute a family of more than 80 species occurring in greatest abundance in tropical and subtropical waters, but with a few species straying into waters of temperate regions during warm months.

Morays live primarily in coral reefs or in similar rocky areas. The typical moray's body is flattened from side to side, pectoral fins are lacking, and the scaleless skin is thick and leathery. The dorsal and anal fins are low, sometimes almost hidden by the wrinkled skin around them. The gill opening is small and round, and the teeth are large. Most morays are large, reaching a length of 5 to 6 feet. Some are as much as 10 feet long; a few are less than 6 inches long.

A moray will anchor the rear half of its body in coral and rocks, allowing the front of its body to sway with the current. In this position, with its mouth agape, it is ready to grasp any prey that comes close. This gaping stance appears menacing, but it is an adaptation suited not only to foraging but also to respiration, allowing the eel to pump water across its gills. Morays have vicious tempers, as divers will attest, and it is unwise to torment them. This temper is shown when provoked; spearing morays or reaching blindly into holes where they live can cause an attack. Their bites are not poisonous, as many believe, but a large moray can make multiple deep wounds that not uncommonly become infected and are slow to heal. Deaths have resulted from encounters with morays. Normally, morays are nocturnal, but they never miss an opportunity to appear from their rocky lairs when a meal is in the offing. They feed on small fish, octopus, crustaceans, and mollusks.

Morays themselves are captured and eaten in many parts of the world and have been esteemed food since Roman times. However, the flesh of some morays is reputed to cause debilitating ciguatera *(see)* poisoning.

Green Moray Eel

Many morays are attractively colored. The green moray *(Gymnothorax funebris)*, which lives in tropical and subtropical waters of both North and South America, is an unusual brownish green due to a yellow slime that covers the eel's blue body. Although most green morays are less than 5 feet long, occasional reports of 10-footers exist. The green moray inhabits coral reefs, sometimes going into deep water to prowl for food.

The spotted moray *(G. moringa)* occurs in the same range as the green moray. Smaller, it almost never exceeds 3 feet in length, and it has prominent dark spots or a chainlike pattern of dark lines on its usually yellowish body. The basic body color commonly matches the eel's surroundings, however, and may vary from white to dark brown.

Off the Pacific coast, the California moray *(G. mordax)* is similar in appearance and habits to the spotted moray; it grows to a length of 5 feet. It is found in waters between 2 and 65 feet deep and may live more than 30 years. The blackedge moray *(G. nigromarginatus)*, prevalent in the subtropical Atlantic, the Caribbean, and the Gulf of Mexico, is of similar size, but the black pattern is more pronounced, with black margins on the dorsal and anal fins.

The puhi-paka *(G. flavimarginatus)*, which grows to 4 feet long, is common in Hawaiian waters and elsewhere in the western Pacific. Its fins are bordered with bright green. Also prevalent in the same area is *G. eurostus*, growing to 2 feet long.

Morays of the genus *Echidna*, most abundant in Indo-Pacific waters, are among the most striking eels in their bright colors and patterns. The zebra moray *(E. zebra)* is marked with vertical bands or rings of white the full length of its dark, brownish yellow body. The chain moray *(E. catenata)*, found in the warm Atlantic from Florida to South America, is marked with a black chainlike pattern over a yellowish background. Many of the Indo-Pacific morays of this genus have flattened molars for crushing the shells of mollusks and the hard outer skeletons of sea urchins, crabs, and other sea creatures.

The dragon moray *(Muraena pardalis)* of the western Pacific, is one of several attractive species in its genus, distinguished by its curiously elongated, tubelike nostrils, the posterior pair of which is located far back on the head, just in front of the eyes. In some species, the nostrils are large and leaflike. The dragon moray has irregularly shaped red and white spots on a dark background.

Among the smallest of the morays are *Anarchis* species, including the pygmy moray *(A. yoshiae)* of the Atlantic coast of North America, all measuring less than 8 inches in length.

Another widely distributed species in the Indo-Pacific region is the 1½-foot *Lycodontis petelli*, marked with alternating, broad light and dark bands.

Conger Eels

The small Congridae family of conger eels are marine eels distinguished from the morays by having pectoral fins and by the black margin on their dorsal and anal fins. Conger eels inhabit temperate as well as tropical seas and sometimes shallow inshore waters, where they may be mistaken for the American or the European eel. Conger eels are scaleless, however, and the dorsal fin originates over the tips of the pectorals. Some conger eels live only in deep water. Nine species are found off North America's coasts, eight in the Atlantic and one in the Pacific.

The best-known species are the European conger eel *(Conger conger)* and the American conger eel *(Conger oceanicus)*, which are respectively widely distributed in European and North American waters. The former can reach 10 feet in length and more than 140 pounds. The most common species in Japanese waters is *Astroconger myriaster*. The Catalina conger *(Gnathopis catalinensis)* is a small species, growing to 16 inches and possessing a large pectoral fin; it is found from Southern California to the Gulf of California in Mexico.

Snake Eels

The Ophichthidae family of snake eels have long, cylindrical, snakelike bodies and can move backward extremely effectively. The tail is stiff and sharp rather than broad and flat, as it is in morays. It is used like an awl to burrow tail-first into sand or mud. The nostrils are located in two short, stout barbels on top of the nose, which the eels use to probe into crevices and cavities as they search for food. Compared to morays and most other eels, snake eels are docile creatures, commonly seen crawling over the bottom like snakes.

In most snake eels, the dorsal fin extends almost the full length of the body, beginning just behind the head but stopping short of the tip of the tail. The anal fin is only about half as long, also stopping before the tip of the tail. Pectoral fins are lacking or very small. Only a few of the profuse species reach a length exceeding 3 feet; most of them are less than a foot long. They are typically brightly colored and are generally strikingly marked with bands, spots, or both. Snake eels are found throughout the world in subtropical and tropical seas, a few ranging into temperate waters.

One of the several dozen species in the Atlantic and Caribbean is the spotted snake eel *(Ophichtus ophis)*, averaging 2 feet in length and occasionally growing to 4 feet. Its yellowish body is covered with large brown spots. The yellow snake eel *(O. zophochir)* is a similar species that lives in the Pacific.

Another genus represented by numerous species is *Myrichthys*, which includes the sharptail eel *(M. acuminatus)*, in the Atlantic, and the tiger snake eel *(M. tigrinus)*, in the Pacific. In Indo-Pacific waters, *M. maculosus* is marked attractively with dark bands that bracket round spots.

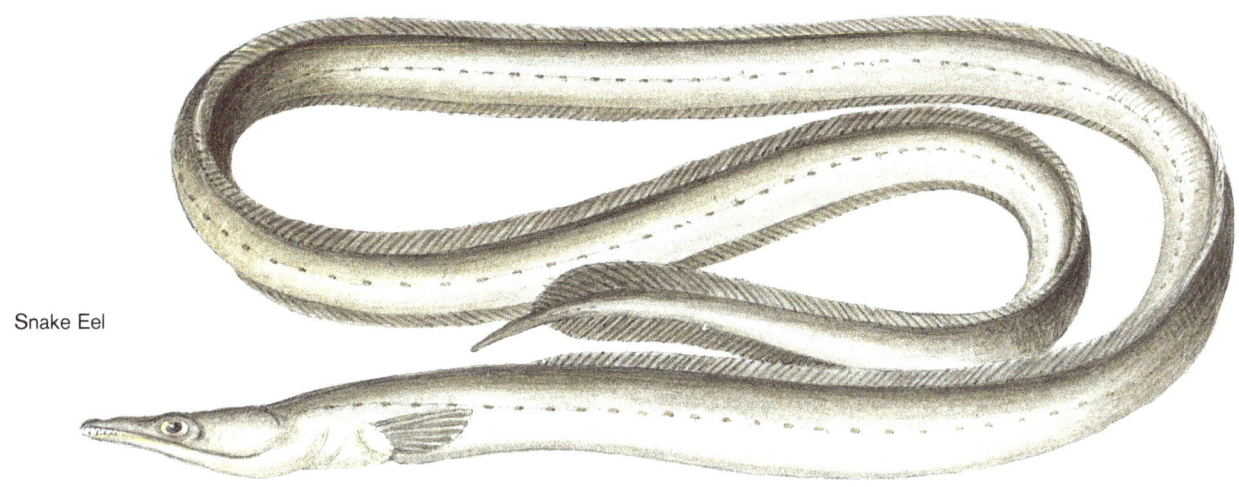

Snake Eel

EEL, AMERICAN *Anguilla rostrata.*
EEL, EUROPEAN *Anguilla anguilla.*

Other names for American eel—silver eel, Atlantic eel, common eel, yellow-bellied eel, freshwater eel, bronze eel, water snake, whip; Dutch: *amerikaanse aal;* Finnish: *amerikanankerias;* French: *anguille d'Amerique;* Italian: *anguilla americana;* Japanese: *unagi;* Portuguese: *enguia-americana;* Spanish: *anguila, anguila americana;* Swedish: *amerikansk ål.*

Other names for European eel—silver eel, common eel, yellow eel, freshwater eel; Dutch: *aal;* Finnish: *ankerias;* French: *anguille, anguille d'Europe;* Italian: *anguilla;* Japanese: *unagi;* Portuguese: *eiró, enguia;* Russian: *retschnoi ugor;* Spanish: *anguila, anguila europea;* Swedish: *ål.*

American and European eels are members of the Anguillidae family of freshwater eels. They are common and have been the object of many wild tales speculating on the nature of their existence. Aristotle was convinced they rose spontaneously from mud, whereas Roman scholar Pliny the Elder believed young eels came from bits of skin that adult eels rubbed off on rocks. Italian anglers believed that eels mated with water snakes. The most common hypothesis was that eels arose spontaneously from horse hairs that fell into the water. These many ancient theories likely occurred because of the mystery and complexity surrounding both fish; their spawning habits and many diverse growth changes are among the most unique among freshwater fish.

These eels are preyed upon by many species at different stages of their existence. They are important forage for such larger offshore predators as sharks, haddock, and swordfish; for inshore species like striped bass; and for many species of birds, including bald eagles and various gulls. Their greatest predators, however, are likely humans.

American and European eels have been prized as food since ancient times and are caught in eel traps and nets, as well as by hook and line and spearing. They are intensively sought commercially in many places and considered a delicacy, especially in Europe and Japan. Eels of all sizes are desirable for consumption, although larger individuals, having spent many years on the bottom of lakes and rivers and being high in fat content, may be especially susceptible to elevated levels of contaminants in areas that are highly polluted.

Larger individuals (10 to 16 inches or so) are used as bait by anglers, especially those seeking big striped bass, and they may be sold as bait in coastal shops. Smaller individuals are also sold by commercial interests for consumption and have been known to fetch many hundreds of dollars per pound. Increased coastal netting of small eels (elvers) due to rising market demands has raised concerns about the exploitation of these fish. European and Asian stocks have been especially diminished, and North American stocks have likewise been under severe pressure. Elvers have been harvested for use in pond culture and aquaculture operations. They have also been caught and transplanted to inland waters to boost or establish eel stocks.

Identification. The body is elongate and snakelike with a pointed head and many teeth. It is covered with thick mucus, hence the phrase "slippery as an eel." The large mouth extends as far back as the midpoint of the eye or past it. There is a single gill opening just in front of the pectoral fins. There are no pelvic fins, and the soft-rayed dorsal, anal, and caudal fins form one continuous fin. There are no visible scales. Coloring changes with maturity, as described later in this text.

The American eel and the European eel are almost identical; they can be distinguished only by counting vertebrae. The adult American eel has 103 to 111 vertebrae, whereas the European has 110 to 119 vertebrae.

Size/Age. American eels grow to 50 inches and 16 pounds. The average size for adult females is about 3 feet, whereas adult males are considerably smaller, rarely growing more than a foot long. They

Eel, American and European

American Eel

can live longer than 9 years in rivers, streams, and lakes. European eels can achieve similar size and age but are usually smaller on average.

Distribution. The American eel occurs from southwest Greenland to Labrador, south along the North American coast to Bermuda, the Gulf of Mexico, Panama, and the Caribbean islands. Within this region, inland it occurs from the Mississippi River drainage east, and northeast to the Great Lakes and to the Atlantic Ocean.

The European eel occurs in drainages feeding the North Atlantic, Baltic, and Mediterranean Seas, and along the east coast of Europe from the Black Sea to the White Sea. It has been introduced to Asia and South and Central America but has not reproduced.

Habitat. These eels are catadromous, spending the majority of their life in freshwater and returning to saltwater to spawn. They prefer to dwell in heavy vegetation or to burrow in the sandy bottom. Their physical structure is such that they can easily swim backward and dig tail first into soft bottom sediments.

Life history/Behavior. When it comes time to spawn, the males and females stop feeding, change in color from olive to black, and move out to sea. Both the American eel and the European eel spawn in the same area of the Atlantic Ocean, in deep water at the north edge of the Sargasso Sea. There each female lays as many as 10 to 20 million eggs, and both sexes die after spawning.

The eggs float to the surface and soon hatch into slim, transparent larvae (glass eels). The sex an eel becomes is thought to be partly determined by environmental conditions such as crowding and food abundance, but it is not determined until they are about 8 to 10 inches long and living in their freshwater habitat.

The larvae drift and swim for one year (American) or three years (European) with ocean currents toward river mouths. Males stay near the mouths of rivers, whereas females travel upstream, mostly at night. Eels can absorb oxygen through their skin as well as their gills and are known to travel overland, particularly in damp, rainy weather. Balls of intertwined eels have been seen rolling up beaches in search of freshwater for overwintering.

Distinctive terms are used to identify the size, coloring, and behavior of these eels at different life stages. They are as follows:

Glass eels are those in the young larval stage called leptocephalus; they are shaped like willow leaves and have ribbonlike transparent bodies with a distinct black eye. These range from approximately 1 to $2^{1}/_{2}$ inches in length and are attracted to coastal estuaries and freshwater, where they are the target of intense commercial fishing interest.

Elvers are small eels in the stage of adapting to freshwater. They range from $2^{1}/_{2}$ to $3^{1}/_{2}$ inches in length and are darker in color than glass eels, being fully pigmented and ranging from gray to greenish brown. Mass upstream migrations of elvers have been observed. Although inconspicuous as they swim along river bottoms, they are especially visible when they encounter obstructions like dams and waterfalls.

Yellow eels are growing eels that exist in freshwater. Some biologists refer to them as adults, whereas others call them subadults. In any event, they are sexually immature, and yellowish to olive brown on the back and lighter on the belly. They swim freely along river bottoms, through shoreline rock crevices, and into silty lake bottoms in search of prey.

Silver eels are sexually mature adults that are dark with a bronze black hue on the back and silver on the underside. Many have enlarged eyes, which is believed to give them better vision in the ocean. These fish are ready to migrate, or they are in the process of migrating, out of freshwater to their ocean spawning grounds, a process that is believed to last three to five months during the fall and winter.

Food. The diet of the nocturnal feeding American and European eels includes insect larvae, small fish, crabs, worms, clams, and frogs. They also feed on dead animals or on the eggs of fish, and are able to tear smaller pieces of food that are too large to be swallowed whole.

Their feeding habits are rather unusual with respect to large quarry. These eels have relatively weak jaws that are mainly suited to grasping, yet they possess many small, round, and rather blunt teeth. Because they are palindromic—that is, they can move equally well forward or backward forcefully—they are able to pull, twist, and spin when tearing apart prey that is too large to be consumed whole. The habit of spinning, which also occurs when they are caught by anglers (with some consternation about line twist and grasping), deserves explanation.

Spinning habits. When food cannot be consumed whole, or when it cannot be broken into morsels for swallowing by jerking and pulling, an eel spins at a dizzying rate. Researchers have recorded a rate of 6 to 14 spins per second (Olympic ice skaters can spin five times per second). The purpose of this is to break apart food into edible pieces; what is edible is determined by the width of its mouth, which is said to seldom exceed 2 inches. It also serves the purpose of gaining access to interior portions of food items, such as entering the body cavity of a dead fish to consume its eggs.

The habit of spinning, however, is also one that brings attention to the eel itself. Eels may spin several times in succession for a protracted period, during which they are less alert to predators and more vulnerable. This tendency may in part account for the effectiveness of wavy and spinning lures and bait rigs in sportfishing applications.

Angling. Fishing for these eels is more popular in Europe than in North America, perhaps owing to less overall diversification in fisheries opportunities and also to a greater cultural inclination toward eel consumption. In North America, these fish are not considered game species and are seldom the deliberate target of anglers using lures, flies, and most conventional sportfishing techniques. They are captured, however, by design and accident, by anglers bottom fishing with natural baits. Worms, small dead fish, pieces of fish, and some aromatic processed and natural baits are used on bottom rigs. They are also taken in freshwater by spearing or gigging, where legal, as well as on trotlines and in eel weirs, eel pots, fyke nets, and the like for commercial purposes.

Using eels as bait. Live eels are a popular bait for striped bass fishing in estuaries, rivers, and along the coast, and are often responsible for larger catches. These are universally fished on the bottom and may be employed by anglers drifting or stillfishing from an anchored boat or a fixed shore position. Enthusiasts use fixed and sliding sinkers, heavy enough to stay on the bottom, usually with a 2- to 3-foot length of leader from hook to sinker.

Eels are hooked through the lips from bottom to top, using 4/0 to 6/0 hooks. They may be kept in a cold cooler, which renders them less active for handling and hooking; they regain energy in the water. When there's a pickup, it's best to have the reel in freespool mode and to let the fish take the eel. Once the fish starts to move off steadily, it's time to set the hook.

Skinning an eel. The skin of an eel can be removed by tying a strong line or string around the head and also to a secure object like a well-fastened nail. Cut the skin around the fish just below the head. Peel the skin back enough to get a grasp on it with a pair of good-gripping pliers, then quickly jerk the skin back and down the entire length of the eel. The skin may be used over certain lures or metal bodies; this was more common in the past before eel-like soft bodies were available.

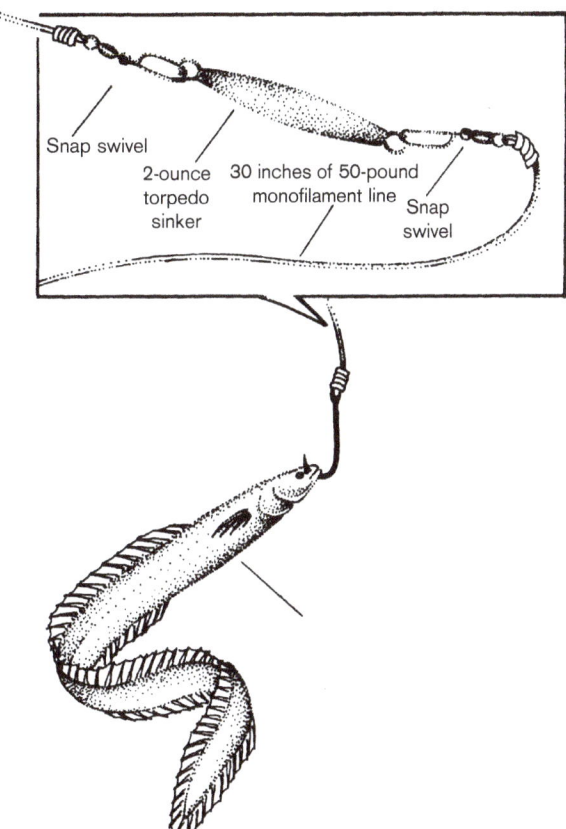
This is one of various rigs used for fishing live eels.

To further clean the eel, cut the head off, cut the eel open and clean it out, then use scissors to remove the fins. Use it as is for cooking, smoking, and so on, or fillet it by cutting through the flesh on both sides of the backbone.

See: Eels.

EEL, AMERICAN CONGER *Conger oceanicus.*
EEL, EUROPEAN CONGER *Conger conger.*
Other names for the American conger eel—conger, dog eel, sea eel, silver eel; French: *congre d'Amerique;* Spanish: *congrin americana.*
Other names for the European conger eel—conger, sea eel; Dutch: *congeraal, kommeraal;* Finnish: *meriankerias;* French: *congre d'Europe;* Italian: *grongo;* Norwegian: *havål;* Portuguese: *congro, safrio;* Russian: *morskoi ugor;* Spanish: *congrin americana;* Swedish: *havsål.*
Conger eels are widely distributed members of the small Congridae family of marine eels that inhabit temperate and tropical waters.

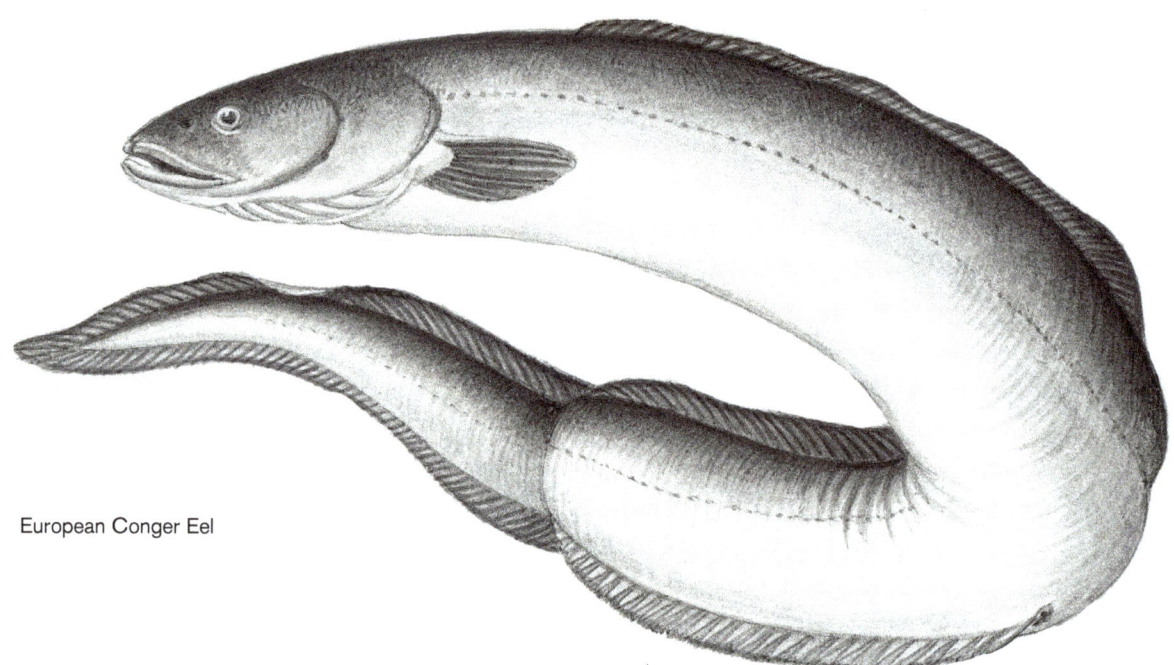

European Conger Eel

Identification. Conger are distinguished from moray eels by having pectoral fins (morays have none) and by the dark or black margin on their dorsal and anal fins. Conger eels are scaleless, and the dorsal fin originates over the tips of the pectorals. They grow much larger than American and European eels *(see: eel, American; eel, European)*, with which they are sometimes confused in inshore environs.

Size/Age. The American conger is reportedly capable of growing to $7^1/_2$ feet and 87 pounds, although it is most frequently encountered at 10 to 20 pounds and 5 feet in length. The European conger is capable of growing to nearly 10 feet and 142 pounds, although most are under 50 pounds. Females grow larger than males.

Distribution. The American conger occurs in the western Atlantic from Cape Cod, Massachusetts, to Florida and in the northern Gulf of Mexico. The European conger occurs in the eastern Atlantic from Norway and Iceland to Senegal, including the Mediterranean and western Baltic Sea.

Habitat. Both species range widely from shallow inshore waters, occasionally in brackish environs, to waters hundreds of feet deep. They usually suspend over rocky or broken bottoms. Shallow-dwelling fish may linger around wrecks, piers, pilings, and jetties.

Life history. The life history of these fish is similar to that of the American eel, although these fish enter freshwater or spawn in one place. Sexual maturity occurs between 5 and 15 years of age, and spawning fish migrate seaward, spawning in summer in water that may be more than 1,000 feet deep.

Food. The diet of the nocturnal feeding conger eels includes fish, shrimp, small shellfish, and crustaceans.

Angling. Anglers use stout tackle to take conger, which are strong fish that have to be muscled away from rocks and obstructions so they don't wrap their powerful tails around them and hold on. Heavy weights and bottom fishing rigs for natural baits (squid, crabs, cut or whole fish) are employed. This fish is difficult to remove from the hook, so anglers must take care to avoid being caught in its powerful snapping jaws. Fish brought to boatside often resort to furious spinning, a maneuver that often gains them freedom by pulling the hook or causing some item of terminal tackle to fail.
See: Eels.

EELPOUT
See: Burbot.

EGG FLY
A small, bright, artificial fly imitating a fish egg or eggs, usually made from yarn and used in fishing for Pacific salmon, steelhead, and some trout species.
See: Fly.

E-GLASS
A term for alkalai borosilicate glass, a type of high-tensile modulus fiberglass used in fishing rod construction.
See: Rod, Fishing.

EGYPT
Although some opportunity likely exists for pelagic

species in the Red Sea and its arms—the Gulf of Suez and the Gulf of Aqaba—as well as possibly in the Mediterranean, virtually nothing has been reported in the Western world about the present status of saltwater sportfisheries off the 1,520-mile-long Egyptian coast and the availability of sportfishing boats. Historically, visiting anglers, mostly European, have paid more attention to freshwater fishing in Egypt, although news is scant in this regard as well.

Nile perch are known to populate the Nile River and its lakes throughout Egypt and neighboring Sudan. Lake Nasser, formed by the Aswan Dam, is 300 miles long and up to 10 miles wide, with its upper third in Sudan; it contains huge Nile perch, huge vundu catfish, and tigerfish, as well as tilapia and numerous other species.

Anglers have caught Lake Nasser tigerfish to 12 pounds, and vundu to 74 pounds, although vundu over 100 pounds reportedly exist. In late 1997 a 213-pound all-tackle world record Nile perch was caught by angling in Nasser; reports also indicate that a larger fish, unweighed but estimated at 250 pounds, was landed by a visiting Indian angler some years before. The latter fish boasted a length of 6 feet, 2 inches and girth of 4 feet, 11 inches. Shore anglers have hooked Nile perch over 100 pounds, although the larger ones had to be landed from a boat. The lake record is purportedly a 392-pound Nile perch, although it is unknown if this was caught by a commercial or a recreational angler. These larger perch greatly exceed all existing International Game Fish Association (IGFA) world records for the species.

Trolling is the most common method of catching the biggest specimens, and safari operators select overnight shore campsites for shore fishing opportunity. There are few organized freshwater sportfishing operations in Egypt, however, and little is presently known about opportunities elsewhere, particularly along the rest of the Nile (which covers more than 960 miles in Egypt alone), in other inland lakes such as Birkat, and in brackish lakes near the wide and rich Nile Delta.

EL NIÑO

El Niño is a disruption of the ocean-atmosphere system in the Equatorial Pacific due to unusually warm ocean temperatures. It has important consequences for weather around the globe, among them being drought, sometimes associated with devastating brush fires; and increased rainfall in certain areas, some of which has caused destructive flooding.

For anglers, El Niño is one of the most prominent natural global phenomena that can have beneficial or adverse implications for sportfishing in saltwater or freshwater. Floods, droughts, and changed ocean temperatures impact the presence and availability of many species, not to mention the conditions under which they are sought. Its harmful effect can be seen when heavy flooding raises the levels of rivers or impoundments to such extremes that gamefish are widely scattered and nearly impossible to locate, assuming that it is even safe to be on such waters. A beneficial effect occurs when warmer-than-usual currents bring pelagic fish closer to shore than normal or extend their northerly range; this happened in 1997 off California.

In normal, non–El Niño conditions, the trade winds blow toward the west across the tropical Pacific. These winds pile up warm surface water in the western Pacific, resulting in the sea surface being about one-half meter higher at Indonesia than at Ecuador. The sea surface temperature is also about 8°C higher in the west, with cool temperatures off South America, because of an upwelling (see) of cold water from deeper levels. This cold water is nutrient-rich, supporting high levels of primary productivity, diverse marine ecosystems, and major fisheries. Rainfall is found in rising air over the warmest water, and the eastern Pacific region is relatively dry.

During El Niño, the trade winds relax in the central and western Pacific, leading to a depression of the thermocline in the eastern Pacific and an elevation of the thermocline in the west. This reduces the efficiency of upwelling to cool the surface and cuts off the supply of nutrient-rich thermocline water to the euphotic zone (the upper layer where photosynthesis occurs). The result is a rise in sea surface temperature and a drastic decline in primary productivity, the latter of which adversely affects higher trophic levels of the food chain and hurts commercial fisheries in this region.

The weakening of easterly trade winds during El Niño means that rainfall follows the warm water eastward, with associated flooding in Peru and with drought in Indonesia and Australia. The eastward displacement of the atmospheric heat source overlaying the warmest water results in large changes in global atmospheric circulation, which in turn force changes in weather in regions far removed from the tropical Pacific.

El Niños have been experienced in the periods 1986–87, 1991–92, 1993, 1994, and 1997–98. It is unusual for El Niños to occur in such rapid succession as they did between 1991 and 1994. They are sometimes followed by La Niña, which is unusually cold ocean temperatures in the Equatorial Pacific. Global climate impacts from La Niña tend to be opposite those of impacts from El Niño. In the tropics, ocean temperature variations in La Niña tend to be opposite those of El Niño. Different La Niña and El Niño events vary in strength; the 1997–98 El Niño, for example, was unusually strong.

El Niño means the little boy or Christ child in Spanish. This name was used because of El Niño tended to arrive around Christmas and because the phenomenon was originally recognized by fishermen off the Pacific coast of South America. La Niña means the little girl; it is sometimes called El Viejo, or simply "a cold event" or "a cold episode."

At higher latitudes, El Niño and La Niña are two of the factors that influence climate, and their impacts there are most clearly seen in wintertime. In the continental United States during El Niño years, temperatures in the winter are warmer than normal in the North Central States, and cooler than normal in the Southeast and Southwest. During La Niña years, winter temperatures are warmer than normal in the Southeast and cooler than normal in the Northwest.

See: Current.

EL SALVADOR

Sportfishing in El Salvador has been virtually non-existent in recent times due to the country's politics and economics and to the availability of other opportunities along the Pacific coast of Central America. The effect of commercial fishing and netting is uncertain, but it seems reasonable that El Salvador should have many of the same species found in bordering Guatemala and Honduras.

The smallest country in Central America, El Salvador is well situated along the coast to support pelagic species, and the excellent sailfish population found not far up the coast in Guatemalan waters is likely to be reflected to some degree offshore from El Salvador. Densely populated and mountainous, El Salvador has several small rivers and one larger one, the Lempa, that flow into the ocean. A few lakes and reservoirs (on the Lempa) exist, with unknown species and potential. The coastal area around the mouth of the Lempa, especially eastward to El Cuco, is distinguished by an extensive network of bays and estuaries, and snook may be present.

ELECTRIC MOTOR
See: Motor, Electric.

ELECTROFISHING

A method of biological survey in which waters are electrified with special equipment to temporarily incapacitate fish, which can then be gathered for quantitative and qualitative data. This method can be used to build a baseline of biological data trends and has been used to monitor fish, especially to determine the effect of length limits and habitat change. Electrofishing, which is also called electroshocking or shocking, is carried out only by trained biologists and technicians. Anglers are prohibited from using an electrical device to stun fish.

Electrofishing has been a preferred method of taking a census, or survey, of fish since the 1940s. For fisheries managers, electrofishing has long been preferable to such other survey methods as gillnet sampling, which is ineffective in many places and for some species, or rotenone (chemical) poisoning, which kills all fish captured. Electrofishing is quicker and more economical than angler surveys, which also don't produce sublegal-size fish or prey species. Biologists generally believe that electrofishing produces more reliable information than other sampling methods, especially angler surveys. It is not without some controversy, however, and can have adverse effects on fish. Some states have limited or prohibited their use of electrofishing, especially in trout waters and where there are fragile or threatened species.

Electrofishing is done from boats and from the bank, and portable backpack devices may be used. Alternating current (AC) was used originally, but that has given way to safer direct current (DC), which provides variable levels of electricity to probes in the water. Fish in the vicinity experience a muscle contraction and are temporarily stunned, whereupon they are immediately captured in a long-handled net. They are usually measured and weighed, and a scale sample may be taken; then the fish are released, or held briefly in a holding tank before release.

Studies have shown that certain fish may be susceptible to injury, stress, and fatigue, and that some delayed mortality may occur, particularly when the equipment is adjusted too high. Trout are more susceptible to problems than other species. Concern has been voiced that electrofishing can harm fish eggs or impact spawning, or drive fish out of the sampled area, particularly since a lot of electrofishing takes place in spring and/or when fish are shallow. In some situations, especially lakes and along deeper water shorelines, only a portion of existing fish are sampled, and nests are not affected. The effect on spawning or fish eggs has been hard to measure definitively, but some agencies have adopted a policy to avoid electrofishing in spawning areas containing eggs or larvae.

Some biologists feel that only a small portion of an overall population is available or vulnerable to electrofishing at any given time, and that the potential loss of a small number and small percentage of the overall population is not cause for concern, especially in light of the natural and angler-related mortality that is annually experienced, and because of the need to obtain reliable information to monitor management programs. In many places, electrofishing work has been successfully used to create or refine management regulations that have resulted in reduced angler mortality, increased numbers and sizes of fish, and development of trophy fishing and catch-and-release waters.

See: Fisheries Management.

ELECTRONICS

In a boating sense, the primary electronic accessories of interest beyond those associated with the operation of the engine include navigational devices such as GPS *(see)* and Loran *(see)*, various types of sonar *(see)*, remote or automatic steering devices, marine radios and other communications instruments, radio direction finders, and radar. For many people with mid- to large-size boats, or who navigate on large inland waterways or in marine environs, having sonar, a VHF radio, and some type of electronic navigational instrument (mainly GPS) is essential.

In a fishing sense, the primary electronic accessories of interest also include sonar and GPS, as well as electric motors, electric downriggers, temperature sensors, and speed gauges. There are other devices that might be used, primarily by freshwater anglers; these include oxygen meters, pH meters, and light meters. All of these devices are discussed in more detail in their respective entries. To most anglers who fish from a boat, and to all avid anglers, some type of sonar instrument is indispensable. To freshwater anglers who cast and seek fish that are oriented to structure, an electric motor *(see)* is close to being indispensable. To anglers who seek roaming fish, a temperature gauge *(see)* is extremely important; the same is true of speed gauges to trollers and electric downriggers to big water boaters and freshwater charter boat captains.

Electronic accessories have been a major part of the angling and boating scenes for decades. The primary emergence of electronic accessories started in the 1960s with the blossoming of both the electric motor and the fishfinder, which are arguably the two most important fishing accessories and certainly the most prevalent electronic devices. Fish-finding sonar was first developed by Carl Lowrance in 1957 and was a major milestone in the development of sportfishing equipment; it had a profound influence on angling technique, and it unarguably made anglers more effective. Today, the use of sportfishing sonar is taken for granted, and many boats contain two or more such devices.

The creation of that first lantern battery-operated fishfinder was nevertheless one in a long line of important advancements that helped open new eras in fishing. Similarly significant innovations included the modern hook, the outboard motor, the fiberglass rod, and the spinning reel.

Electronics, however, as a group of products, have moved forward faster and quicker than others, in keeping with general technological advancements. The advent of microprocessors, liquid crystal displays, and digitizing have helped rush electronic accessories to levels that were previously unimaginable, and that will continue. Whereas many electronic accessories were viewed with suspicion in the 1970s and 1980s—because of the introduction of products that did not live up to manufacturers' claims or that were sold to the public before being perfected—the contemporary era has seen a more uniform level of quality in

This protected center console contains the key electronics instruments used by anglers: VHF radio, navigational devices, and sonar.

this arena, befitting the high cost of research and development as well as relatively high retail prices. Electronic accessories for sportfishing have a better contemporary reputation and are being used by ever more people for increasingly diversified applications.

Questions have been raised about the effects of using electronic equipment for sportfishing, especially about the impact on fisheries resources. Obviously most of the same technology used in electronics sold to anglers is also in the electronics employed so effectively by commercial fishermen. Sonar, in particular, was once the target of some governmental entities, which unsuccessfully sought to ban them for recreational fishing.

These efforts failed for the logical reason that sonar is just one of myriad factors that contributes to increased pressure and effectiveness on the part of the recreational angler. Some other factors include the four-wheel-drive or all-terrain vehicle that allows a person to access a remote spot; the state-of-the-art graphite rod that makes hooksetting more effective; the swift boat that permits rapid coverage of expansive waterways; the high-tech fishing line that makes strike detection easier; the publication that details the characteristics of every pool on a given river and enumerates all of the fly hatches and all of the access spots; and so on. So who is to say what is and what is not fair, and where the line is to be drawn?

As always, anglers need to concentrate on quality fishing experiences, sportsmanship, and catch- and-release *(see)* efforts. There is no doubt that some electronic accessories, when skillfully used, can lead to greater and quicker success. Some of the devices help educate anglers so quickly that it almost seems unfair when compared with the education that pre-electronic-era anglers earned only after years and years of trial-and-error experience. Nevertheless, these devices cannot lead to success unless anglers have a good idea of what they are doing. Although these devices can provide you with increased confidence and can show you where the fish are or help you locate the places where they should be, they still cannot make the fish strike. Electronic wizardry does not equate with automatic sportfishing success, as any guide or charter boat captain whose clients have not been able to catch the fish that are plainly shown on a sonar screen can affirm.

Furthermore, having a boatload of electronic accessories has the potential for overdosing on technology and either losing some of the simple charm of angling or neglecting to use your own wits and knowledge to figure out where the fish are, what they are doing, and how to attract them. There is a likelihood that some anglers, especially novices, could become mere technicians manipulating a lot of sophisticated paraphernalia, who wouldn't know what to do if they didn't have sonar to tell them the depth, GPS to direct them to the hotspot, a gauge to tell them the temperature or the speed, and so on.

Yet, for many people, electronic devices have not only increased their effectiveness but added to their understanding and appreciation of aquatic environments, particularly by providing them with a lot of information. And if nothing else, as charter captains, guides, and big-water boat operators have found out, some of this electronic stuff is very entertaining to the passengers onboard, especially when the fish aren't biting.

See: Downrigger; Light Meter; Navigation; Oxygen Meter; pH Meter; Radio; Radio Direction Finder; Speed Gauge.

EMERGER

An aquatic insect evolving from the larval (nymph) to adult form on the water's surface; also an artificial fly (nymph) that represents this surface-emerging insect.

See: Aquatic Insects; Fly.

EMPEROR, RED *Lutjanus sebae.*

Other names—sea perch, government bream, king snapper, red kelp, redfish, emperor red snapper, emperor snapper; Arabic: *hamra;* French: *bourgeois, empereur rouge, pouatte;* Japanese: *sen-nendai;* Malagasy: *zazamanango;* Malay: *merah, jenehak;* Thai: *pla kapong dang.*

This fine sportfish, a member of the Lutjanidae family of snappers, is also a highly rated table fish that is much prized. In Australia, it is especially favored by anglers who fish the Great Barrier Reef, where they are a common target using handlines or traps baited with pilchards or other oily fish. Red emperor are not known to carry the toxin ciguatera, though caution should be exercised where large specimens (over 10 kilograms) are taken, and this poison is known to occur in other related snappers.

Identification. Red emperor are deep pink with three, bright red, crosswise bands across the stout, compressed body. These bands are the reason for the fish being called the government bream in Australia, as they bring to mind the shape of the Government "broad arrow" that was once worn by convicts in early Australian history. All the fins are pink, the caudal fin is emarginate, and there is a distinctive preopercular notch.

Size. This fish is known to reach a weight in excess of 32 kilograms, and specimens commonly weigh from 1 to 6 kilograms.

Distribution. The red emperor occurs in Indo-Pacific waters from the southern Red Sea and East Africa to New Caledonia, north to southern Japan, and south to Australia. It is found along the East Coast of Australia from Sydney to the Great Barrier Reef, and across the top of Australia to the coastal waters of western Australia as far south as Shark Bay. The principal recreational fishery in Australia is along the Great Barrier Reef and, in particular, the Cairns region.

Habitat. The habitat of red emperor ranges from reefs, coral reef lagoons, shale bottoms, and sand flats, in waters from a few meters to 180 meters deep. As they grow, they move to deeper water where they tend to form into schools that prefer fast-flowing currents in channels around reefs. They will often move into shallow water during winter months.

Life history/Behavior. Red emperor are highly fecund, with large females producing at least five to seven million eggs during a season; both the eggs and the larvae are pelagic. On the Great Barrier Reef, spawning usually takes place at night during the summer, between October and April. In Northern Territory waters, spawning takes place throughout most of the year. By the time red emperor are a year old, they have reached a fork length of 20 to 21 centimeters. They reach a maximum length of about 115 centimeters and are said to live for at least 10 years.

Food and Feeding Habits. The red emperor is a carnivore, feeding mainly at night as it forages for fish, crustaceans, octopus tentacles, and squid. It can also be fed cut fish baits of tuna, trevally, and shark.

Angling. Although red emperor can be caught during daylight, fishing usually takes place at night from a boat anchored in up to 50 meters of water. Knowledge of reef conditions and locations is imperative, lest weather blow up to make the outing dangerous; a quick getaway at those times can be lifesaving. Tackle is heavy, with short, stout boat rods fitted with revolving spool, spinning, or sidecast reels holding 15- to 30-kilogram line rigged with 6/0 to 9/0 extra-strong hooks. Handlines in excess of 40 kilograms are common and are used with gloves to prevent line burns. Sinkers must also be heavy to cope with currents. Baits of fresh-cut fish flesh, squid, and pilchards, are fished close to the bottom. When hooked, the red emperor quickly demonstrates its strength, and a major league tug of war ensues.

See: Snapper.

ENDANGERED SPECIES

In the United States, a species is classified as endangered if it is in danger of extinction throughout all or a significant portion of its range. Elsewhere, a species is classified as endangered if the factors causing its vulnerability or decline continue to operate, as defined by the International Union for the Conservation of Nature and Natural Resources (IUCN).

See: Threatened Species.

ENGLAND

Angling is a popular activity in Britain. Of the officially estimated 3.5 million anglers here, most pursue specific disciplines. About half of these are bank fishing coarse anglers; the remainder equally comprise sea anglers and people who pursue game fish (trout and salmon). The majority of the coarse anglers are English, and certainly England can lay claim to the most renowned angling writer of all time in Izaak Walton. His book, *The Compleat Angler,* written in 1653, illuminated his fishing exploits in the seventeenth century on such rivers as the Thames, Dove, Lea, and Test, and served not only as a guide to the techniques of the time but also as a chronicle of rural life and contemplative sport. He famously likened angling to poetry, and his words inspired millions to cast a line. But Walton would not recognize much of the angling sport in England today, which is like big business in many respects.

The majority of freshwater fishing is controlled by profit-making individuals or by nonprofit clubs. Season or day tickets (permits) must be purchased either in advance or on the bank and, in addition, anglers must buy a national fishing license, the proceeds from which go into a national fund. That fund is used to maintain the quality of freshwater fishing throughout England and Wales, fight pollution, and provide law enforcement. Daily and weekly licenses are available for the short-stay or holiday visitor, and discounts are granted to certain age groups.

Angling is strongly divided in the United Kingdom into coarse, sea, and game fishing, with many divisions within each branch. Coarse anglers use floats or leger fish with baits for nonpredatory species, and fish lures or baits for predators (coarse fish that are piscivirous such as pike, perch, and zander). Coarse fish are targeted for the sport only and are almost always returned alive. The rules governing when you can fish vary from region to region. As a general guide, you can fish most still waters (in a broad sense anything that is not a river, stream, or tributary) year-round, whereas on rivers

An angler fishes for trout on the Itchen, one of England's classic chalk streams.

there is a closed season from March 15 through June 15 inclusive.

The many man-made canals and drains that crisscross the industrial areas and farmlands of England create a complex fishery. Coarse anglers can fish for species such as carp, bream, roach, chub, and barbel with baits such as maggots, worms, and luncheon meat, all of which can be bought in the hundreds of tackle shops that dot the country. Interestingly, many thousands of anglers are happy just to fish for bites from small or large fish rather than targeting only big fish, and as a result a thriving match fishing circuit has built up. During match competitions, anglers fish for five hours and then weigh in their catch, which is kept alive during the match in a keepnet with a mesh fine enough to prevent even a minnow from escaping. The winner takes the spoils (including money), and fishing can be so hard that some matches in winter are won with just a few ounces of total catch.

So accomplished are the English in this field that England is broadly recognized as one of the world's top three match fishing nations (with France and Italy). The English have secured more team and individual world championship medals than any other nation, with one Cambridgeshire angler taking the individual title a record-equaling three times.

There are no freshwater bass in Britain, the main predators being pike, perch, and zander, which are caught by using lures, live bait, or dead bait. The country's largest native predator is the pike, which grows to more than 40 pounds. With the opening of large artificially stocked trout fisheries for seasonal pike angling, many pike over that mark have been landed, including several British record fish. Zander, which are very similar to walleye, grow to around 18 pounds, and perch up to 5 pounds.

The biggest native coarse fish of all, growing to more than 50 pounds, is the carp. Regarded as a pest in some countries, in England carp are all but revered as intelligent and hard-fighting fish that quickly become wise to anglers' techniques and baits. So respected are carp—they are never taken for food—that a thriving Carp Society has evolved, as well as a weekly newspaper and several monthly magazines dedicated purely to techniques for catching this species.

Small carp have been the driving force behind a wholesale change in coarse fishing in Britain. Artificially stocked coarse fishing waters have sprung up all over as the perceived general standard of river fishing has declined. Anglers can fish small, manageable venues (sites) knowing big fish lie before them waiting to be caught. These venues are often heavily stocked with carp from 1 to 10 pounds, and virtually all are run as a business. For the price of their day ticket, anglers benefit from high stocking levels and comfortable fishing (platforms are created for ease of fishing), they can often hire tackle on site, and they can buy lunch at some locations. Purists, however, wouldn't be seen dead at such venues, preferring to fish for what they regard as "wild" river coarse fish.

English coarse anglers, more than those from any other European nation, arguably have a strong tendency to specialize in one branch of the sport. The Carp Society is far from the only single-species group; societies for anglers who like to concentrate on catching zander, perch, chub, barbel, catfish, eels, and tench also exist. Members pay an annual fee, hold regular meetings, and publish newsletters to ensure familiarity with the latest techniques and catches. The level of devotion and sophistication is high.

The one element that joins all coarse anglers is a respect for their quarry. Coarse anglers almost never kill and eat the fish they catch and, outside the match fishing scene, fish are usually returned quickly and carefully to the water. The challenge is in the catching, and size is not everything. Catching a 3-pound roach would be a much more meritorious accomplishment than, say, catching a 20-pound pike.

As coarse fishing methodology has evolved, especially over the past few decades, it has brought this sport to an extremely sophisticated level. English anglers in Sheffield pioneered long-distance float fishing with rod and reel in the 1800s, and this became known as the Sheffield, or fine and far off, style. Float fishing on fast-flowing rivers was developed in Nottingham on the River Trent and became known as the Nottingham style. A third prominent style—called tight-lining, or London style, in England and known throughout Europe as *Peche Anglaise* (the same as *roubasiane* in France)—developed more recently. These styles have been adopted throughout Europe and have become known in North America only since the late 1980s.

More expensive licenses are required for game fishing in England and Wales, although there is no license requirement for either coarse fishing or game fishing in Scotland, which is the best bet for quality salmon experiences. In general, salmon fishing is only allowed from March through October, and in Scotland, tradition prohibits salmon and sea trout fishing on Sundays, although coarse fishing and brown and rainbow trout fishing are allowed.

The majority of English fly anglers concentrate on artificially stocked put-and-take trout stillwaters, where rainbow and brown trout up to and over 20 pounds are stocked. There is no season for rainbow trout, as they are not believed to breed in England, but there is a closed season on taking brown trout in the winter.

Sea fishing around Britain, including the offshore islands of the Hebrides, Orkneys, and Shetlands, plus the Isle of Man in the Irish Sea and the Isle of Wight off the south coast, is among the most varied in the world, considering the size of the fishery. The Gulf Stream, which flows north from the Atlantic Ocean, brushes the southwestern corner of England and continues north through the Irish Sea, past the

Welsh coast, up past Lancashire and the world-famous seaside resort of Blackpool, and along the western coast of Scotland. This has a warming effect on the sea temperature, and often brings with it strange, exotic species from the tropics.

In contrast, the eastern coast of England and Scotland is bordered by the colder North Sea, and tends to offer both shore and boat anglers different species than those encountered on the western coasts, although some species are common to both areas, and global warming appears to be making the differences smaller each year. The seasons vary considerably because of the changeable weather, and some summer species are never caught in winter. Since the 1980s, however, global warming appears to have considerably changed the pattern of fish movements, whereas other changes have doubtless been brought about by overfishing—especially following the huge influx of commercial fishing boats from the rest of Europe and Russia, which have been allowed to fish all around the coast.

The most striking example, however, concerns the overfishing of herring after World War II. Tunny used to follow the herring shoals north from the Bay of Biscay along the eastern coast of England, and were regularly caught off Scarborough, where there was a big trade for them. Tunny numbers peaked in the 1930s, but after the war they declined rapidly as the herring shoals declined. Despite a total ban on herring fishing for decades, the species has never properly recovered, and tunny fishing is now extinct around England, although the odd tunny has been reported off southern Ireland in the Gulf Stream, mainly taken in nets.

The result of general overfishing of species like mackerel and cod, as well as sand eels—which formed a major part of the diet of many other fish—has been a definite decline in fish populations, and a resultant decline in the numbers of fish caught on rod and line. Sea fishing is still a big industry all around the coast, however, with hundreds of charter boats dedicated to taking out parties of anglers, usually up to 12 at a time, and considerable numbers of shore-based clubs, as well as some clubs dedicated to private boatowners who own seaworthy fishing dinghies powered by outboard motors.

The rocky nature of the continental shelf around the mainland offers a certain amount of shelter from commercial netters in many localized areas, and the charter boats know where these marks (sites) are. The seas around the mainland are among the most dangerous in the world, and extreme caution is urged at all times; drownings of both boat anglers and those fishing from the shore are not uncommon. Due to increased safety regulations, the standard of charter boats is quite high compared with many other countries. There are several charter boat associations, and they will not accept members who do not meet certain minimum requirements. Virtually all charter boats have sonar equipment for locating fish.

In summer, many charter boats offer fishing trips that last about three hours; frequently these cater only to holiday makers who are content to fish with handlines. The more serious trips last longer. Some modern charter boats are fast, with planing hulls, but most boats have displacement hulls, which ride deeper in the water and give a better ride in choppy seas but are much slower. Charter boats advertise in the many angling journals, although the very best skippers rarely advertise, because they are fully booked in advance. The best advertisement is word-of-mouth.

There is no true American-style sportfishing in England, but blues, porbeagles, and the very occasional mako sharks do frequent these waters. Methods of sea fishing here differ considerably from those in America. Sea conditions and the lack of big-game fish rule out downriggers and outriggers, and fish are generally pursued on or near the bottom. The main boat methods are downtiding (putting a bait overboard to the bottom and fishing it downtide), uptiding (casting uptide and out from the boat and allowing a bow to develop in the line), and drifting with heavy pirks (from 50 grams to 1 kilogram) that are either baited or unbaited. With 12 anglers on a boat, it's almost impossible for everyone to use different styles, so anyone who wants to fish a particular style—drifting, downtide baitfishing, or uptiding—should always check with the skipper first.

To get the best day's fishing by boat, it's often better to book with a small party who have agreed to fish the same method; this is more expensive but likely to be more productive. Bait, at extra cost, is usually provided by the skipper, who will ask whether you need any when you make a reservation. Shore fishing is free and no license is needed. There may be an entrance fee for piers and jetties. Britain tends to observe size limit rules to a greater extent than any other European country, and these rules are strictly enforced in matches. In addition, it is an unwritten rule that all tope, common skate, and sharks are returned alive; most skippers now insist on this. Some skippers expect, though, to keep part of the catch of other sizable species such as cod, which they sell to defray their costs. The size limit for bass (European sea bass) is also strictly enforced, and many anglers return all bass. Other catch limits are introduced from time to time.

On boats, tackle up to 80-pound rating is used on the deep-water wrecks, with 20-pound to 30-pound rating sufficient for most inshore marks. Few Britons bother to chase International Game Fish Association (IGFA) line-class records, so there is scope for the visitor who fancies beating some of these.

Coarse Fishing

Probably the top English coarse river is its longest: the mighty, powerful River Severn, which rises in Wales before flowing east into England, then

Norman and Breton fishermen are believed to have fished for cod off Newfoundland as early as 1504.

turns south and empties into the Bristol Channel. Virtually every species of coarse fish thrives here, with superb summer barbel fishing around the Bewdley area in particular.

Barbel are regarded as the hardest fighting of all the river coarse fish. They are not native to the Severn, but have bred and grown so successfully since being stocked in 1956 that the river boasts a British record barbel of more than 16 pounds. Another nonnative fish that has thrived in this river is the zander. These were first stocked into the drains of eastern England but have quickly spread across the country. The Severn also lays claim to a record zander of more than 18 pounds from Upton.

Much of the River Severn is controlled by Britain's biggest angling club, the Birmingham Anglers Association, which has more than 20,000 members. Other top areas to try include Arley and around Worcester and Tewkesbury. The majority of specimen (large or trophy) fish are caught from Bewdley downward.

Another great river is the Avon, which joins the Severn near Tewkesbury. Scenic and fruitful angling with floats can be enjoyed in and around Stratford and Evesham. Pegs behind the theater at Stratford are noted for excellent roach sport. Luddington, Twyford Farm, and Offenham Weir are other noted roach spots, and anywhere below Pershore is good for plentiful big bream, with 80-pound catches possible.

Farther north, the most famous coarse angling river is the Trent, which starts life north of Birmingham and flows north, meeting the sea at the Humber estuary. For years this venue was fed by warm water from several power stations situated along its length, which led to sensational fishing all year for bream, roach, and chub. Such quality fishing is harder to come by now that these stations have closed, and the river is known more as a summer venue, with good fishing to be found in and around Nottingham.

The rivers of northeastern England are mostly spate (rain-induced) rivers that are not controlled by reservoirs and therefore rise and fall quickly in flood conditions. Flows are swift and the water clear, conditions the barbel in particular enjoy. The rivers Ure, Swale, and Wharfe all hold excellent barbel and chub stocks. Famous fishing spots include Boroughbridge (Ure), Topcliffe (Swale), and Ulleskelf (Wharfe).

Quality river coarse fishing is not easy to come by in the northwest, with better sport on the canals. Big barbel and chub can be caught from the River Ribble, however. In the south, the Hampshire Avon and the Dorset Stour still offer the kind of fishing Izaak Walton would have written of, with specimen barbel, chub, pike, roach, and dace thriving in crystal clear water. Much of the fishing is privately controlled, but anglers can enjoy excellent day-ticket fishing around Ringwood in Hampshire, where there is a first-class tackle shop. The more famous River Thames is at its best outside London, and excellent localized fishing can be enjoyed around Oxford.

Closer to the capital, Teddington Lock holds plenty of fish, including big river carp. Quality fishing is localized toward the east of England. Huge barbel are caught on the Great Ouse around Newport Pagnell. Specimen chub are worth targeting on the River Wensum in Norfolk. Good fishing for pleasure is available on the River Nene around Peterborough, on the River Welland around the scenic town of Stamford, and on the River Yare around Norwich.

Many of the big cities are also home to a network of canals used during the Industrial Revolution to transport coal and goods. These once-polluted waterways have been transformed, and where once there was no sign of life there are now thriving fish populations. South Yorkshire's Sheffield Canal, for instance, was once one of Europe's most polluted waterways, yet it is now full of fish. And the nearby River Don, which was also once devoid of life, now remarkably holds trout.

Generally speaking, canals are places to catch a lot of small fish, usually with fishing poles, and top venues include Regents Canal (London), Bridgewater Canal (Manchester County), Erewash Canal (Nottingham), Exeter Canal (Devon County), Grand Union Canal (Buckinghamshire County), and Oxford Canal (Oxfordshire County). Most canals can be fished on a day ticket.

In East Anglia more than 1,000 miles of man-made drains were built from the 1600s onward to drain water off farmlands to The Wash, and these have become excellent fishing venues, particularly for predator species. It was here that zander first thrived in England, and during the 1970s venues such as the Forty Foot Drain, the Middle Level Drain, and the Relief Channel became known as England's pike angling Mecca, where a 20-pounder was quite easily attainable and a 30-pounder possible.

It can take plenty of legwork to find the preda-

Portions of the Thames are known for coarse fishing.

tors on these long, straight, featureless bodies of water. Fish are localized, but once found they are generally easy to catch, and you can land one after another. Artificially stocked lakes are plentiful throughout the country, and a chat with the local tackle dealer will put you onto the in-form venue.

Gravel pits are another form of stillwater angling that warrants mention. Once mining has been completed, gravel pits are flooded, creating deep, clear venues. Fish thrive in these conditions and, because stocking densities are usually low, they grow to outsize proportions. This has resulted in a growing army of anglers (known as specimen hunters) who target gravel pit complexes. Many of Britain's record coarse fish, including carp, bream, and tench, were taken from gravel pits. Pike also thrive in such complexes and have been known to achieve 20 pounds in just six years.

Gravel pit complexes exist all over England, but sites famous for consistently producing specimen fish include those around Oxford, those close to the west side of the M25 motorway near Heathrow Airport, and the South Cerney complex near Cirencester, Gloucestershire.

Game Fishing

Trout. The majority of game fishing in England is for trout, mainly rainbow trout and the indigenous brown trout. This sport is largely pursued in the hundreds of commercially operated stocked stillwater fisheries that sprang up in the 1970s. These vary in size from perhaps half an acre up to 40 acres or more, with a few dozen much bigger reservoirs and lakes, such as the famous Rutland Water (3,000 acres), or Blagdon, which is the oldest stillwater brown trout fishery in the UK. These fisheries vary greatly in configuration, from recently dug barren holes in the ground to beautifully landscaped waters or natural lakes surrounded by forests and hills or mountains. The number of trout that may be taken is always limited, and a report form (return) showing the number of fish landed must be filled in, to enable restocking of fish and thereby maintenance of the population.

Some waters specialize in stocking considerable numbers of very big fish, and these tend to be more expensive. If you are content to catch smaller fish—those up to 2 pounds—the cost is less. Most waters give you the option of purchasing a less-expensive ticket, allowing you to take fewer fish. Some allow catch-and-release, which is usually cheaper. After having been caught a few times, these fish can become very wary, but then the pursuit becomes a rewarding challenge for the angler.

It is possible to find rainbows over 20 pounds at a considerable number of these fisheries, and brown trout over 15 pounds at a few. These have all been bred artificially, although in any case rainbows rarely breed naturally in the UK.

On many of these waters it is possible to obtain instruction, and rent tackle; some outfits have their own tackle shops on site, with food available either on site or in a nearby public house. Offerings include weighted flies (banned on some waters) like Dog Nobblers and Tinheads, and smaller, more natural patterns such as Damsel flies, Hare's Ears, various buzzers, various Pheasant Tail Nymphs, and floaters like Adams, Shipman's Buzzers, and sedge and olive patterns.

Rental boats are available on larger reservoirs and lakes, and advance booking is advisable. Match fishing for trout is big in the UK, and these events take place largely on the bigger reservoirs, mainly by boat; hence, most of the boats might be booked in advance on a particular day. Boobies fished on a sinking line are a favorite early-season pattern, followed by various lures, with smaller flies like Shipman's Buzzers working well when fish start rising in summer, and fly patterns from August onward. Otherwise, fly patterns are very similar to those used elsewhere.

Wild brown trout inhabit some rivers in England and are quite small; a 2-pounder is considered a good fish. But the thrill of catching a wild brown of any size makes trout fishing a popular activity. Rivers with wild brown trout include the upper reaches of the Severn, Tamar, and Fowey in the west; the Hampshire Avon and its tributaries; the Dove (where Izaak Walton started fishing) in the Midlands; the Wharfe, Yorkshire Derwent, Ribble, Swale, Nidd, Coquet, Wear, Derwent, and Tees in the northeast; the Lune and Eden in the northwest; and the Dart in the southwest.

The fishing is controlled either by private owners (often estates), who may or may not allow fishing, by syndicates who do not normally allow outsiders to fish except as guests of members, or by local clubs who will frequently allow outsiders to fish after paying a fee. The local tackle shop or post office is a good starting point for information.

The two most famous chalk stream trout fisheries in the world, the Test and the Itchen, have been stocked with rainbows and bigger brown trout, and some stretches can be fished. Costs vary enormously, corresponding roughly to the density of fish in the water. Other rivers have been artificially stocked also, and some of these are run in conjunction with a stillwater fishery; with easy access, you just show up and pay (advance booking is advisable on the smaller waters).

Grayling thrive in most of the rivers that hold wild brown trout, and there is a growing interest in restocking these fish into the waters from which they have gradually disappeared. Baitfishing for trout is allowed on very few fisheries; otherwise, the rule is flies only, and many sites limit the size of the fly.

On trout rivers there may be some restrictions as to methods allowed. The English place great store on tradition, and some purists still would not dream of casting downstream or using a wet fly. For up-to-date information, the best bet is to telephone

one of the many angling magazines that have access to the latest publications, and indeed may even publish some. The staff are invariably anglers themselves and will be only too pleased to help.

There is no closed season for rainbow trout, which can be fished year-round. There is a closed season for brown trout, and where a stillwater is attached to a river there may be a general closed season. All the big reservoirs have a closed season for brown trout. The big reservoirs close in winter, for commercial reasons, but some small stocked stillwaters are open year-round, some including Christmas and Boxing Day, when special festivities take place. Hard winters, which cause small stillwaters to freeze over, will bring trout fishing to a halt.

There is a closed season on all rivers; the approximate dates of the trout season are April 1 through September 30, but these vary from area to area. The grayling season is generally June 16 through March 13 inclusive, but local rules may apply.

Salmon and sea trout. Salmon and sea trout fishing are far less popular in England than in Wales and Scotland. Main English rivers include the Lune, Ribble, Eden, and Cumbrian Derwent in the northwest; the Tyne, Tees, Wear, Coquet, and Yorkshire Esk in the northeast; the Hampshire Avon and Test in the south; and the Camel, Tamar, Torridge, Exe, and Severn in the southeast. Atlantic salmon were reintroduced to the Thames in the 1980s, but there is no significant run up the river yet. Other rivers have odd salmon and sea trout runs, but these are insignificant compared with the ones mentioned.

Although the odd spring fish is caught, stocks of Atlantic salmon have dwindled since the 1960s. From August to the end of the season (which is roughly September, although seasons vary), however, the autumn runs of salmon can offer superb sport, with fish in excess of 20 pounds.

Although the traditional method of catching salmon and sea trout is by fly, certain waters allow fishing with spinners, worms, and, in some cases, prawns. Prawns are such a deadly bait, however, that they are banned on the majority of such waters.

Salmon flies include Willie Gunn, Stoat's Tail, Thunder & Lightning, Munro Killer, Garry Dog, Hairy Mary, and Ally's Shrimp (one of the most effective). Variations of these patterns tied as weighted tube flies will allow you to cope with any river conditions. A 15-foot double-handed salmon rod rated for a 10- or 11-weight line will be necessary to fish the majority of these waters. Chest waders are also advisable.

Sea trout fishing is best at night. Flies for sea trout include Teal Blue and Silver, Lethal Weapon, Silver Butcher, Peter Ross, Black Pennell, and tube flies based on these patterns.

The majority of salmon and sea trout fishing is privately owned. Fishing is available by booking a private beat, or it is controlled by an association that allows daily or weekly tickets. For details contact local tackle shops or purchase one of the national trout and salmon magazines for latest details and some contacts.

Sea Fishing

In northeastern England, fronting the North Sea, the area from Berwick on Tweed southward to Newcastle offers codling (small cod) to 5 pounds to shore anglers in winter, flounder and silver eels (not conger) most of the year, and red codling in among the kelp on rocky shores in summer. Expect to lose a lot of terminal tackle in the rocks here, but the fishing is great fun.

Small sea bass started to appear here in numbers in the late 1980s, and they always turn up on the same beaches, mainly in summer, when small turbot—one of the most prized British flatfish—may also appear. Charter boats take mainly codling and haddock over inshore rough ground, with ling and cod to 30 pounds–plus from deep-water wrecks, using heavy pirks to beat the strong North Sea currents. The main charter ports are Berwick on Tweed, which is on the border with Scotland, and Tynemouth.

From Newcastle down to The Wash, the main summer shore species are mackerel and small coalfish, taken from piers and jetties (there's exceptional fishing around South Shields), codling from rocks and cliffs, and flounder from open sandy beaches. The flounder linger near estuaries during winter. A winter run of codling is also available. Crabs are a popular bait for codling and flounder, as they can be gathered locally. The main charter ports are Hartlepool, Whitby, Scarborough, and Bridlington, and boats here produce huge catches of codling and cod if conditions are right. Deepwater wreck fishing produces cod over 30 pounds and ling over 20 pounds, both of which are invariably taken on baited pirks.

The bulge of East Anglia, south of The Wash, used to produce huge catches of codling for shore anglers, but these have dwindled dramatically, although codling are still taken in numbers as soon as the sea is fishable after a good easterly blow. With few rocks in this area, soft-backed crabs are rare, so the popular baits are lugworms (available fairly easily from tackle shops or local bait diggers) and ragworms, which are a little scarcer. Whiting appear in September, codling in November and again in March, and bass are found year-round, although many are undersize. The sole and dab fishing can be quite exceptional from May through Christmas, and long casts are not needed.

These beaches are almost invariably shallow. For codling, casts of 100 yards are usually needed, so this area has produced many casting champions. Some can cast distances approaching 300 yards over grass without bait, which equates to 180 yards with bait. Yarmouth and Lowestoft are the charter ports; no ports exist to the north because there are so few estuaries.

Essex County, just north of the Thames estuary, sees fantastic sport with thornback ray, tope, smoothhound, and bass, and excellent charter boats offer opportunities around the small port of Bradwell on Sea in the Blackwater estuary, and at Southend. The best skippers are always booked on weekends, often for years ahead, so a midweek trip is the visitor's best bet. Shore fishing can be good from the various sea walls, and in the many creeks and inlets, but access can be long and tortuous as much of this area is marshland.

South of the Thames estuary, the Kent County coast is one of the codling hotspots, and anglers land these fish all winter, although not in the fantastic numbers of the 1970s, when 20 codling per angler per night was not uncommon. The famous Dungeness Beach is still a favorite mark, as it offers deep water close to shore. Numerous easily accessible marks are available on the various seaside parades in Kent coastal towns. A top mark is Dover breakwater, which can be reached only by the daily boat service (details are available at Dover Harbour). Fishing by boat in the Thames estuary is brilliant for bass upward of 10 pounds, tope, and thornback ray, and these are found around the entire Kent coast. The area's main charter ports are Ramsgate, Deal, Dover, Folkestone, and Hastings.

The whole south coast, from Eastbourne west to Lyme Regis on the Dorset/Devon County border, offers highly varied fishing, with whiting, flounder, and codling available in winter from the shore, plus the chance of ray and hard-fighting triggerfish, which now appear in numbers. Mullet are extremely popular here; go at first light or at dusk to the marinas, where the fish can be seen cruising between boats until disturbed. Anglers land them on bread bait, or small scraps of worm, often by using floats. Most common is the thick-lipped mullet, found in saltwater; the scarcer thin-lipped mullet inhabits a few rivers.

Notable shore marks include rocks below the famous Beachy Head cliffs, where bass are taken; Poole Harbour, which is a flounder hotspot; the Hurst Castle shingle bank at Milford on Sea; and the 18-mile-long bank of shingle known as Chesil Beach, which offers a host of species, including mackerel in August, triggerfish in summer, and codling in winter.

Boat fishing appeals most to anglers here, however, with some of the best sport around the Isle of Wight. All of the south coast of the island regularly produces cod to 30 pounds as well as a host of other species, including thornback ray, conger eels over 50 pounds, tope and smoothhound in summer and autumn, blonde ray over 20 pounds, plaice to 7 pounds–plus, big bass, and many other species. Black bream inhabit these coasts, favoring certain localized reefs in summer and autumn. Shore fishing on the Isle of Wight is excellent; ask for details at tackle shops on the island.

Anglers can easily reach the Isle of Wight via regular crossings from Lymington, Southampton, and Southsea. Mainland charter ports are Eastbourne, Newhaven, Brighton, Littlehampton, Hayling Island, Poole, Weymouth, and the little town of West Bay. The bigger ports offer some of the most modern, fast charter boats in the country, and some travel on three-day or five-day trips to the Channel Islands, where huge cod, ling, and conger are taken. There are several charter ports on the Isle of Wight also.

Devon and Cornwall Counties, in the southwest corner of the mainland, offer particularly easy shore fishing. Anglers land mackerel, as well as wrasses and mullet, from the dozens of piers and rocks. Casting and float fishing are productive. Long-distance casters pursue several species of ray, big bass, and plaice. The best flounder fishing in the country exists in the mouths of the Teign and Exe Rivers, and there's excellent flounder action in most of the other estuaries, plus some cod mainly on the northern coasts. Summer shark fishing is again becoming popular here after the peak in the 1950s and 1960s, when every blue shark caught was slaughtered. The policy of releasing them is paying dividends now. Plymouth, Mevagissey, and Looe are the main ports, with Padstow and Boscastle the prime sites for porbeagles, which are caught off the west coast.

Cornwall and Devon offer probably the most varied boat fishing in the UK, and anything can turn up, although the area is perhaps best known for the huge conger eels taken by Plymouth charter boats; fish over 100 pounds are not uncommon, but it's tiring work winching them in. There's also excellent pollack and coalfish to be had, and big bass shoals, which don't get much publicity to limit leaks of their whereabouts to commercial fishermen. Also expect thornback ray, blonde ray, and the biggest turbot in the country. The main charter ports are Dartmouth, Plymouth, Falmouth, Rock, Padstow, Ilfracombe, Lynmouth, Porlock, and Minehead.

The English coast north of Wales is known as the North West, and the main boat species here are cod, mackerel in season, thornback ray, tope, plaice, and bass, plus conger, ling, and pollack over the wrecks. Gurnard are more prolific here than in most other areas of the country, and anglers land spurdog and haddock in season in some areas. The main charter ports are Fleetwood, Barrow, and Maryport. Several large small-boat clubs are in the area, particularly around Blackpool. Shore anglers tend to focus on flounder, dabs, and eels; the Dee and Ribble estuaries, Arnside in the Kent estuary, and Silloth on the south bank of the Solway Firth are quite outstanding at times. As winter approaches, the quarry changes to whiting and codling, although along the rocky edges of Cumbria, pollack, coalfish, and conger are taken from shore. Crabs are a popular bait along this coast, as they are easily found in certain estuaries.

This area also includes the Isle of Man in the Irish Sea, which offers fine and little-explored fish-

 Sixty percent of the world's 3.4 billion people lived within 60 miles of a coastline in 1997; 75 percent of a projected world population of 6.3 billion is expected to do so in 2025.

ing. Tope to 40 pounds are taken from its northwest coast; wrasses, pollack, mackerel, coalfish, conger, bass, and plaice, among other species, are regularly taken from shore. Contact the helpful Isle of Man Tourist Board, which is keen to promote sea fishing on the island. Charter boats operate here, with Peel the main location, or you can make arrangements with one of many small-boat owners.
See: Scotland; Wales.

ENTOMOLOGIST
A person who studies the forms and behavior of insects. Some stream trout fly anglers become so engrossed in fly tying and fly fishing that they become amateur entomologists.

EPILIMNION
The upper and warmer layer of water in a lake or pond that is stratified; the layer of water above the thermocline (see).
See: Stratification.

EPIRB
Acronym for Emergency Position Indicating Radio Beacon. Used in emergency situations and carried primarily by large boats and by anglers who venture far offshore, this transmitter issues a constant signal on a distress frequency; the activated signal indicates a distress situation and allows rescuers to determine the boat's position.

There are several classes of EPIRBs. The class A version is at the top of the list in both cost and function. It sends a homing signal on 121.5 MHz and communicates directly with satellites on 406 MHz frequency. The class A version is encoded with an identifier that is unique to the owner, so authorities can not only pinpoint your location anywhere in the world, but also tell who is in trouble. The class A EPIRB turns itself on automatically as soon as it gets wet, but it is bulky, expensive, and best for those who spend a lot of time far offshore.

The class B version requires manual activation, is cheaper, less bulky, and is preferred by most small boaters. It comes with a six-year lithium battery and a continuous operating life of at least 48 hours. Both A and B operate on 121.5 MHz and 243 MHz, and their signals are picked up by aircraft and shore stations that monitor their frequencies.

You can test a class A or B EPIRB yourself by holding it close to an AM radio and turning it on for just a few seconds. There will be a warbling tone through the radio's loudspeaker.

Federal regulations require that all EPIRB tests be as brief as possible and that they be conducted only during the first five minutes of each hour.
See: Boat.

ESTIMATING WEIGHT
See: Measuring Fish.

ESTUARY
In simplest terms an estuary is a body of water where freshwater from rivers and streams meets the saltwater of the sea. It may be called a bay, a sound, or a lagoon. Most estuaries are partially enclosed by islands, beaches, and the mainland; they may get freshwater from one large river, from several large rivers, or from hundreds of small rivers, streams, creeks, canals, and even springs. In addition to inlets and incoming freshwater sources, estuaries may contain barrier islands that protect estuary mouths, open water areas, oyster bars, salt marshes, mangrove forests, submerged seagrass beds, and mud flats. Much sportfishing is done in or near estuaries.

In an estuary, freshwater draining from incoming sources dilutes the saltwater to varying degrees. In a positive estuary, more freshwater meets the sea than evaporates; in a negative estuary, more freshwater evaporates than enters; and in a neutral estuary, evaporation and inflow are about the same. Freshwater is also diluted by tides, which push saltwater upriver to varying extents depending on the strength of the tide, geologic formations, offshore currents, and the quantity of freshwater entering the estuary.

The mixture of saltwater and freshwater in estuaries provides a plentiful supply of food that supports abundant plant and animal life. Tons of nutrient-rich materials washed from the uplands accumulate to make estuaries among the most productive natural systems known. In many coastal states and countries, 80 to 90 percent of all marine species of fish and shellfish spend some portion of their lives in estuaries. For many, these are nursery areas. Estuaries also provide homes for huge numbers of birds, protect the mainland by absorbing the force of storms from the sea, and provide an outlet for flood waters from the land.

Estuaries have been adversely impacted in many places because of pollution, siltation, and habitat loss through development.
See: Inshore Fishing.

ETHICS AND ETIQUETTE
Before delving into the murky waters and sometimes hot button issues of angling ethics and etiquette, it is necessary to provide some definitions, which are quoted from *Webster's New World Dictionary* and re-stated (in parentheses) in synonymous general terms and concepts.

Ethics: "The system or code of morals of a person, group, religion, profession, etc." (Moral principles and/or rules of conduct.)

Etiquette: "The forms, manners, and ceremonies established by convention as acceptable or required in social relations, in a profession, or in official life." (Rules, conventions, protocol, ceremony, formalities, custom, decorum, manners, politeness, courtesy, civility, and seemliness.)

Sportsman/sportswoman: "A person who can take loss or defeat without complaint, or victory without gloating, and who treats opponents with fairness, generosity, courtesy, etc."

Sportsmanship: "Qualities and behavior befitting a sportsman." (Fair play, fairness, honesty, honor, probity, scrupulousness, integrity, uprightness, justice, justness.)

Although etiquette is technically different from ethics, both are often discussed interchangeably, especially regarding matters pertaining to manners and courtesy. The definition of ethics is especially important because it establishes that ethics are different from laws *(see: regulations)*. What is legal may not be viewed by a majority of people as ethical, or may not fit an objective view of the proper behavior of a sportsman or sportswoman. Sportsmanship is essential to any discussion of ethics because it is the notion of fair play, and angling by sporting means, that should separate the recreational angler from the commercial fisherman *(see: angler; angling; commercial fisherman; recreational fisherman)*.

As George Reiger, North America's foremost fishing and hunting conservation writer, notes: "We're at a crossroads in angling today—a fork in the evolution of sportsmanship made all the more perilous by the fact that few anglers can define angling ethics. Most assume it's the same as law. The law, however, involves public obligations; ethics involve personal ones. Breaking the law entails public expense; the only cost—but it's a significant one—of betraying an ethical standard is the damage it does to one's soul. This confusion between ethics and law provides fertile ground for the agenda of groups who oppose angling."

"Any culture that allows law to become the arbiter of all human behavior runs the risk of losing its soul. Back about the time Pericles was refining a legal system for ancient Athens, a Chinese philosopher by the name of Kung Futzu (alias Confucius) was developing a social system based on personal conscience and peer pressure for every imaginable activity, including angling. Confucius believed that legalistic societies eventually fall apart because people come to believe that whatever isn't specifically forbidden by law is condoned by it. That's why he resisted the idea that an institution or the state should arbitrate personal behavior. Rules of conduct agreed on by the majority should be enforced by peer pressure, not the police. But all activities should have peer-pressured rules."

In angling today, and especially in North America, there is a lack of spoken and written attention to ethics. Many people, particularly fly anglers, believe that they adhere to a generally understood but seldom expressed code of ethics; most often this revolves around the act of harmlessly releasing fish (the catch-and-release ethic) or around the methodology (casting and/or fishing exclusively with flies or artificial lures, for examples, as ethics unto themselves).

Ethical Issues

The purpose of this entry—which is unfortunately rare in books about sportfishing—is to raise awareness of some of the major ethical issues that exist. Some, though certainly not all, of those issues are briefly noted here.

Casting. As mentioned, casting with artificial lures (which includes flies) is a sportfishing methodology especially favored by many anglers, in some cases to the exclusion of various forms of bait presentation. In Europe, a clear distinction is made between coarse fishing *(see)*, in which some form of bait is used in a still manner, and gamefishing, which primarily means the act of casting with artificial lures, especially flies, for trout and salmon.

Many people who cast artificial lures believe that doing so is more challenging, or more interesting, or more sporting, than fishing with any form of natural or processed bait or fishing by means of trolling; this view is derived from centuries of tradition of fishing with flies in streams, mainly for trout.

There is little doubt that the vast majority of anglers prefer to catch fish by actively casting and retrieving an artificial lure and by always holding the rod in their hand. However, it is not feasible to fish exclusively by casting with artificial lures for all species and for all sizes of fish in all places where they're found (rivers, big lakes, ocean reefs, blue water, and so forth), although one can certainly argue that the means are more important than the results. Some environments and some species clearly lend themselves to casting, making a personal casting ethic for those species one that is also practical and not counterproductive.

Artificial lures. The ethical issue of using artificial lures in lieu of natural or processed bait likewise involves the subject of practicality and incorporates questions about releasing fish, which are discussed in detail in the entry on catch-and-release *(see)*. Many people who use only artificial lures (especially flies) assume moral superiority because of this, which is not necessarily justified. The artificial lure versus bait issue is one of many ethical concerns that has been addressed in specific instances by laws.

Fishing for spawners. One of the few ethical issues that is raised from time to time is that of angling for spawning largemouth and smallmouth bass, which are vulnerable to detection and catching when on their large and easily observed shallow nests in the spring. The effect of deliberately or incidentally catching (and in many cases releasing) spawning bass has triggered a few scientific studies,

Estimates have it that 50 million plastic worms are produced annually. Most popular size: 6 inches. Top colors: black and purple.

and perceived potential negative effects from fishing during the spawning season are the main reason why a minority of fisheries agencies close the angling season (especially for trout, bass, walleye, pike, and muskellunge) during the spawning period. Such closures, however, are inconsistent among fisheries agencies, some with neighboring jurisdictions, which logically raises questions about validity.

Although the personal ethic of some anglers is that it is unsportsmanlike to deliberately angle for spawning bass, many anglers do so (it is legal in most states). Curiously, questions regarding the propriety and sportsmanship of angling for other species when they are spawning or specifically on their spawning migration—such as salmon, steelhead, trout, charr, striped bass, shad, and tuna—is almost never raised, perhaps because of their generally fleeting availability.

Fishing/catching to excess. The propriety of keeping a limit or excessive number of fish each time an angler goes fishing, even if legal to do so and even if the fish will be consumed, raises ethical questions. Many anglers have done this, whether for bluefish in saltwater or crappie in freshwater, and this practice long ago gave rise to game hog and other derisive terms ("game hog," incidentally, was coined by publisher George O. Shields in editorials in his magazine *Recreation* in the 1890s). Likewise, continuing to catch and release high numbers of fish when the angling is very good is viewed by some people as excessive, somewhat like running up the score in a lopsided athletic contest or piling onto the ball carrier in a football game.

Assistance. Ethical concerns exist with the very act of setting the hook on a fish and playing it. The International Game Fish Association *(see)* long ago established ethical rules for catches that were acceptable as world records *(see)*. Anglers who do not set the hook themselves on a potential record catch, for example, and/or who allow someone else to handle their rod while playing or landing that fish, cannot receive a record, no matter how stupendous the fish is. Although the wisdom of this is widely supported, similar mandates do not exist in many state record programs and most anglers are generally unfamiliar with these principles. Many other aspects of the equipment used and means of fishing are covered by these record establishing rules.

Foul hooking. Although it is generally addressed in laws and agency regulations, foul hooking of fish is another area that raises ethical questions and has caused a lot of controversy. Unfortunately, it does not raise ethical concerns for enough anglers, as some are willing to keep a gamefish that has been accidentally foul hooked, which many people view as unsportsmanlike.

The legal foul hooking of fish, known as snagging *(see)*, is another matter entirely, and one that is still supported by some fisheries agencies (previously for salmon and, in many if not all cases, for paddlefish).

Its adoption by a significant number of people, and advocacy by some fisheries agencies (New York, for example, until the early 1990s) has fostered a great deal of such activity, legal and illegal, especially for salmonid species in Great Lakes tributaries. This has lead to atrocious behavior by people who are unconscious of fair play ethics, and disapproval by a small number of anglers, with the vast middle ground of the sportfishing fraternity being silent.

Mismatched tackle. Many anglers fish with tackle that is either too light or too heavy for the intended species or common size of the species they seek. This includes rods and reels but especially the breaking strength of line used. With modern fine-diameter lines, it is possible to use a product that has 25-pound strength but the diameter of a conventional 10- or 12-pound line; the fairness of using this for 1- and 2-pound largemouth bass, for example, is extremely dubious. Many situations exist where anglers use heavy tackle on the off chance that they'll hook a huge fish, thereby ensuring that there is little contest in landing the much more plentiful smaller specimens.

On the other hand, using extremely light tackle for some species, especially those that are hard, strong fighters, is also unfair if the fish will, or must, be released, because it is likely that the fish will have a harder time recovering and/or escaping its other predators when released. Fair play is again the main issue here (although there is a question of the well-being of the fish and its ability to escape predators as well), and in their zeal to use productive methods in the right places, anglers may overlook this.

Selling fish. Some saltwater sportfish (especially tuna and dolphin) are legally sold by people using recreational angling methods to capture the fish. The lack of ethics in this is pretty obvious, not to mention the fact that commercial fishermen are rightly accused of overexploiting most ocean fisheries resources (particularly tuna) by the angling community at the same time that some of their own brotherhood are selling fish that have been caught on rod and reel.

Killing fish. The subject of killing fish that are kept for personal consumption is poorly addressed by the outdoor sports media, although it has been covered elsewhere in this book *(see: fish preparation—care)*. Anti-angling groups object to catch-and-release fishing because fish "are only let go to be hooked and tortured all over again,"and the criticism is that even when fish are kept, most are not killed immediately; they're put in boxes where they slowly suffocate. Although British sporting magazines recommend that anglers carry a "priest," or club, to kill fish instantly and humanely, North American writers rarely broach the subject. Perhaps many people feel that the growing popularity of catch-and-release fishing is proof of its moral superiority, or that what isn't actually written into law is ethically acceptable.

Pollution. It is ironic that anglers—who have a lot to gain from clean environments and healthy fish populations—number amongst themselves people who discard trash on the shore or into the water. Used fishing line, for example, is especially harmful, as it can entangle birds or other animals, but there are many examples of ways in which some anglers (albeit a small minority) despoil the environment through their personal behavior, both while fishing and not fishing.

Competitions and equipment. Competitive fishing events are commonplace and raise ethical concerns that are rarely addressed because many of these events are important business and tourism tools. Concerns include the use of public resources for private gain, the philosophy of angling, methodologies used by competitors, the handling and disposition of fish, interfering with and/or usurping the rights of the general public, the well-being of fish that are caught/transported/handled/released, and more. Many competitions, especially catch-and-release events for bass and walleye in freshwater, cause anglers to temporarily break the law and certainly abrogate ethical standards when they cull *(see)* a limit of fish in a livewell.

The kinds of equipment employed in recent decades has mushroomed enormously, and much of it is profiled in some way within this book. Electronic developments have lead to some attempts to curb or eliminate by law their use; these have been unsuccessful but included proposed bans on using sonar equipment and underwater viewing cameras. The use of some of these items has raised regionally isolated ethical debates.

In a related sense, the amount of fish-finding equipment used, and how it is used, is questioned by some people, among them George Reiger, who notes: "Confucius believed that the 'true angler' must fish with only one hook and line at a time and never use a net, not even to help land a fish. The measure of an angler's worth is in how he captures a fish, not in what he does with it once it's in hand. An angler who fishes with more than one hook and line, or uses a net, tips the balance of the sport in his favor and, thereby, reduces the ethical value of its experience.

"Confucius believed that while we're all born with conscience, it must be cultivated to serve us and society. Neglected or corrupted by false standards of fair play, conscience grows rank and unwanted like a weed. Since Confucius believed he was only articulating what everyone intuitively knows to be true, he called himself 'a transmitter, not an originator' of the precepts he codified. What makes his teachings so remarkable is that 2,500 years later, his disciples are still practicing what Confucius preached—including fishing with only one hook and line at a time.

"Even as recently as a century ago in the United States, anglers held themselves to a number of standards higher than those we accept today. A commercial fisherman might fish more than one line, but never a sportsman. In addition, many 1890s anglers felt it was unethical to fight a fish sitting down (unless the angler were in a canoe), wear a harness, or accept assistance of any kind while the fight was going on, unless he were handicapped, a novice, or—forgive those Victorian gentlemen—an 'anglerette.'

"In 1894 off California's Catalina Island, General Charles Viete hooked and fought for two hours a giant sea bass that eventually took refuge in a kelp bed. Determined to win the battle, the general tightened up his line and tied it to the rod. He then lashed the rod to an empty oil drum and left it adrift while he went back to the island for lunch. When he returned some hours later, he brought a grapnel and succeeded in tearing away the kelp without breaking the line. After another half-hour of stand-up combat, the 227-pound sea bass was gaffed and hauled over the side. It was a remarkable victory, but was it a fair catch?

"'Of course not,' the general replied. 'I had lunch; the fish didn't.'

"When big-game fishing came into vogue in the 1910s, some anglers—including most charter operators—thought it too much to ask the average angler, especially newcomers to the sport, to hold a rod all day and then fight a tuna or billfish standing up. Yet in 1913, William C. Boschen did precisely that when he landed the first broadbill swordfish (a 358-pounder) ever taken on rod and reel. He subsequently caught dozens of billfish single-handedly, without a harness, and all standing up.

"Another member of the Catalina Tuna Club, J. A. Wiborn, was so fearful he might accept assistance if it were available, he fished by himself and earned the sobriquet, 'Lone Angler.' A number of anglers, such as 89-year-old Frank Mather, keep this tradition alive today. Mather does so less because he's too proud to accept assistance than because he can find few younger men willing and able to maintain his pace in pursuit of giant bluefin tuna and billfish. He has caught, tagged, and released dozens of such big fish single-handedly.

"Why do we no longer teach the ethical validity of fishing only one line per big game angler and then fighting fish unassisted and standing up?

"The answers involve money and competition in a legalistic society. Right from the outset in what was called 'deep-sea fishing,' guides—not sportsmen—set ethical standards based on minimal levels that would enable even the most inexperienced or inept anglers to catch records 'according to the rules.' Four, six, up to a dozen lines at a time were trolled for half as many anglers aboard a boat. While it may be too much to expect a greenhorn to tackle his first tuna standing up, it also belittles the skill of an expert to establish standards that put him on a par with the greenhorn. Even worse, big game trolling has become a team sport in which the skipper and mate play roles that are as or more important than the angler.

Bluefin tuna have been known to make journeys in the western Atlantic Ocean exceeding 4,000 miles in less than two months.

"What's allowed in charter fishing has gradually become the standard in most fishing. The goal is to capture the largest or the greatest accumulated poundage of fish under the most rudimentary rules of sportsmanship. There are notable exceptions, of course, but increasingly the moral 'hows' of angling have been overwhelmed by the amoral 'how-tos.' And whereas competition was once seen as a corrosive influence on good sportsmanship, even conservation groups now use angling contests as a means of raising money and publicizing their cause.

"Writing in the September, 1922, issue of the Izaak Walton League's *Outdoor America,* 'Lone Angler' Wiborn spoke for a now forgotten generation's view of the matter when he noted that 'competition creates a false standard of sportsmanship. The best interests of conservation are debauched by prize contests. The joy of a day a-stream, or a-field, often is deadened by false desire to be number one.'

"A century ago, our angling forefathers thought they could best perpetuate the sport by giving certain species 'gamefish' status, thereby putting them off-limits to commercial exploitation. Trout and bass were soon followed by other freshwater fishes, and, in recent years, coastal states have begun doing the same for certain marine species. At the same time, however, recreational fishing is increasingly haunted by a different kind of commercial enterprise (and an oxymoron) called 'tournament angling' in which the most successful (meaning 'richest') anglers depend on corporate sponsorship to provide their fortunes.

"They're more like golf pros than recreational anglers. Fishing for them has lost its innocence and much of its charm. It's a job. Yet it's precisely these jaded pros who their corporate sponsors encourage us to emulate, not the ethical champions of the past. But unless we find ways to offset the increasing commercialism of recreational fishing with a revival of ethical standards, angling will not only lose the moral high ground to groups who oppose this activity, but the sport as a sport will die, and we'll have lost one of our species' best ways to immerse ourselves in nature while reinforcing the one ingredient that separates us from nature: our conscience."

Etiquette

In the modern era in which few people hold doors open for others, where a decreasing number say "thank you," and where people fight over street and mall parking spaces, it is no surprise that recreational fishing (and boating) has its share of issues pertaining to manners and courtesy.

Because there's no Emily Post or Miss Manners for the sportfishing world, there is no established guide to proper conduct on the water for anglers, many of whom are also boaters. There are certain conventions that are followed in some places and by some groups of anglers, however. For example, many North American Atlantic salmon anglers gather at a river pool and take turns rotating through the pool, fishing from the head of the pool to the run-out, with following anglers entering the water only when their predecessor has moved sufficiently downstream, depending on the size of the pool. This is one of the more civilized forms of angling behavior on crowded water, made bearable in part by a general lack of fish.

On the other hand, the presence of large numbers of fish has a tendency to bring out some of the worst behavior in people. A large school of chinook salmon in a small river, a huge school of surface-busting stripers or white bass in an inland reservoir, and a mass of bluefish rampaging in the surf along a beach are just a few examples of incidents that can draw a flock of wide-eyed people in a desperate bid to catch fish, often with the result that they get in the way of other anglers, cut off fish that are hooked by others, do things that cause the fish to be spooked, or act in ways that are unsafe or may cause harm.

Although the number of people who might be called "slobs" are a minority, their actions are detrimental to the way in which all anglers may be perceived. Some are simply anglers who don't know what is good etiquette on the water because they don't understand enough about the sport or the particular circumstances.

Trespass is probably the number one problem in freshwater and needs little explanation. If it isn't yours and isn't clearly public, then it's private. You must obtain permission to fish on private waters, to cross private property to access public or private waters, and, in some cases, even to stop briefly on private property while wading or navigating through public waters.

Trespass, of course, is a legal matter, but courtesy and manners are not, and they apply to all aspects of angling. For example, if you're fishing a small stream and come upon an angler working a pool, you should pass that pool up or wait until the angler fishing it departs. Likewise, when fishing in

Anglers crowd a New York river during the fall chinook salmon run.

a lake or reservoir, it is bad form to come into an area that another boat occupies. Allow a reasonable amount of space, and assume that they are, and will continue, working the area and not just the immediate spot where they're located. Crowded waters, however, make breaches of such reasonable etiquette too frequent. So do competitive fishing events.

Although common sense prescribes that proper behavior is necessary when sharing waters with others, this becomes complicated when anglers don't realize the extent of the circumstances. For example, a person fishing along a saltwater flat by poling and stalking fish will generally be heading downtide to spot and cast to fish that will be moving or facing uptide. Another person who runs by downtide or who pulls up to start fishing downtide, even within a hundred yards, is more than inconsiderate; this action is likely to spoil a careful stalk by spooking fish. In such an instance the pre-positioned angler should be given a very wide berth by a passing boat, should be allowed its original course by the newly arrived angler moving uptide (like the Atlantic salmon river anglers), or should be asked by the newcomer where he can fish (only after approaching quietly from uptide or via radio communication) without interfering.

Most examples of proper etiquette involve common sense. For example, trollers shouldn't run their boats too close to other trollers or anchored boats to avoid cutting or hooking lines, and should stay well away from shore anglers; well away is out of casting range. Boaters who cast along a shoreline should swing away from shore anglers (or swimmers) and leave this area completely to their less mobile counterparts.

Boating anglers should always give the right of way to a boat that has a fish; pull in your own lines if necessary and swing far away from their area. Sometimes in crowded situations this requires quick action.

Most boating anglers don't think of themselves as being a problem for non-boaters, although they're very aware when they are on the receiving end of poor conduct by water-skiers, some pleasure boaters, and many operators of personal watercraft. However, the wake of fast-moving fishing boats (bass boats in particular), especially in narrow places like canals and near-shore areas, can cause people in a small boat to grip the gunwales while the boat rocks, and does little to engender goodwill. Idling away from shore, observing no-wake zones and speed limits, and giving a wide berth to shores (100 to 150 feet is the minimum and a legal requirement in some waters), especially where there are homes and docks, are examples of good etiquette.

Boating anglers should be aware of others in a variety of not so immediately obvious ways. For example, boaters greatly interfere with duck hunters in the fall by getting anywhere near an active

When waters are fringed with docks and boathouses, as this Ontario lake is, anglers should be mindful of private property and steer clear of those in use.

blind; sometimes it's difficult to know which blinds are currently in use, even if decoys are on the water, but boating or angling activity may too easily destroy the duck hunter's already limited chance of success.

Fishing around docks and boathouses, which are popular fishing targets for bass anglers, requires common sense courtesies as well. Those who don't have pinpoint casting control should avoid fishing around these objects, as owners do not appreciate having lures and hooks bounce off their property, get tangled in dock lines, or stuck on foam dock supports. Do not fish docks when they're being used, and leave the area politely if asked to do so, even though the surrounding water is public.

Boating anglers should also make sure that they spend minimal time launching and loading a boat from active or crowded access sites. Boat preparation for fishing, and unloading, should take place away from the launch ramp and the public dock. When fish are kept, they should never be cleaned on the beach or shore; do so in designated fish cleaning areas at a launch site, or at home.

Kick boaters who fish flowing waters, as well as drift boaters and anglers fishing while floating in canoes, kayaks, jonboats, or other craft, need to steer clear of wading anglers. Sometimes this is not possible, and they wind up floating right in front of anglers and over the pool they're fishing. Where possible, it's best to go behind a wading angler, or directly in front of that person (if it is too shallow behind them) so as to minimize your impact on the pool or run. You may have to explain your intentions as you approach.

These are just a few examples of ways in which common sense dictates courteous behavior. The golden etiquette rule should always be do unto others as you would have them do unto you.

Eulachon

EULACHON *Thaleichthys pacificus.*
Other names—candlefish, hooligan; French: *eulachon, eulakane.*

The eulachon is a member of the smelt family, Osmeridae. It is one of the largest members of this family of small, Pacific coast fish, and has been important to the Chinook Indians. High in oil content (15 percent of body weight), eulachon used to be dried and fitted with a wick for use as a candle.

Like other smelts, the eulachon is important as forage food for Pacific salmon, as well as marine mammals and birds. It is also harvested or caught commercially and is a highly esteemed seafood by Native Americans from California to Alaska. Although some are hard-salted, these surf smelts are too delicate to be preserved and are generally smoked.

Identification. The eulachon is a small slender fish with a stubby adipose fin just in front of the tail. The lower jaw projects slightly beyond the tip of the snout. Its coloring is bluish black on the back, fading to silvery white on the belly. Smelts are so similar in appearance that it is difficult to differentiate among species. Its larger size, however, helps distinguish the eulachon from its relatives.

Size/Age. The eulachon can reach up to 12 inches. It generally lives two to three years.

Distribution. This fish is common throughout cool northern Pacific waters, with a range from west of St. Matthews Island and Kuskokwim Bay in the Bering Sea, and Bowers Bank in the Aleutian Islands to Monterey Bay in California.

Habitat. This fish is found near shore and in coastal inlets and rivers. It spends its life at sea prior to spawning.

Spawning behavior. Eulachon spawn between March and May when they enter freshwater tributaries from Northern California to the Bering Sea. They mature when they reach two to three years of age, and die following spawning.

Food. The eulachon feeds on planktonic crustaceans.

EUTROPHIC

In a lake, high nutrient levels and a natural aging; an increase in the rate of nutrient supply to a water body, characterized by an abundance of nutrients.

A eutrophic lake is one that is old, with a soft mucky bottom. Rooted plant growth is abundant along the shores and out into the lake, and algae blooms are not unusual. The water is often colored, with suspended and organic matter reducing its clarity; oxygen is limited or absent in the hypolimnion, especially during the summer. Eutrophic lakes support only warmwater fish such as perch, catfish, panfish, and bass, plus coarse species.

Lake aging goes through a process from oligotrophic *(see)* to mesotrophic *(see)* to eutrophic. Lakes age at different rates depending on natural and human-influenced factors. When plant growth is accelerated, particularly the growth of algae, and when the water body receives little or no flushing, the lake undergoes eutrophication, a hastening of the aging process. If this continues unabated, dense mats of algae choke off the surface and block the water column's access to sunlight. The algae below the surface begin to die for lack of light. The resultant decaying mass deoxygenates the water as it decomposes and makes the water unfit for anything to live in. There is a rapid die-off of many species; eventually the water may become clean again, but unless it is restocked, it will not exhibit the same populations it once had. If it does not come clean, it may simply fill in and die.

Eutrophication is most often associated with freshwater lakes and ponds, but can occur in fairly constricted saltwater bays.

See: Algae Bloom.

EXOTIC SPECIES

Organisms introduced into habitats where they are not native are called exotic species. They are often the agents of severe worldwide, regional, and local habitat alteration. Also referred to as nonindigenous, nonnative, alien, transplant, foreign, and introduced species, they can be the cause of biological diversity loss and can greatly upset the balance of ecosystems.

Exotic species have been introduced around the world both intentionally and accidentally; occasionally exotic species occur in new places through natural means, but usually the agent is some action of humans. That includes transportation of fish or larvae via the ballast of ocean freighters and the bait buckets of small-boat anglers, passage of new species via newly constructed canals, the introduction of plants by using them in packing shellfish that are shipped transcontinent, the dumping of aquarium plants and fish into local waterways, the experimental stocking of predator and prey species by scientists and nonscientists, and many other means. Exotic species can be transported by animals, vehicles, commercial goods, produce, and even clothing.

While some exotic introductions are ecologically harmless, many are very harmful and have even caused the extinction of native species, especially those of confined habitats. Freed from the predators, pathogens, and competitors that have kept their numbers in check in their native environs, species introduced into new habitats often overrun their new home and crowd out native species. In the presence of enough food and a favorable environment, their numbers explode. Once established, exotics rarely can be eliminated.

Sometimes the introductions of exotic species have generally beneficial results. Anglers consider the importation of coho and chinook salmon from the Pacific Ocean into the Great Lakes, for example, to be a highly successful introduction of a nonnative species. Certainly in terms of providing recreation, this is true. The same can be said for brown trout, first imported from Germany to the United States in the 1880s, and also spread to many countries on others continents. But the same cannot be said for carp, imported in the late nineteenth century and spread throughout North America, resulting in the destruction of spawning habitat for other species and the alteration of many environments into which they were placed. Likewise, the introduction of Nile perch into Lake Victoria in Africa is generally viewed as one of the most destructive exotic introductions of all time, having resulted in the apparent extinction of hundreds of small native tropical species.

Exotic species include other aquatic animals and plants as well as fish. These include such organisms as zebra mussels, hydrilla, the spiny water flea, purple loosestrife, and watermilfoil. Many exotic

Clusters of zebra mussels cling to the stalks of vegetation.

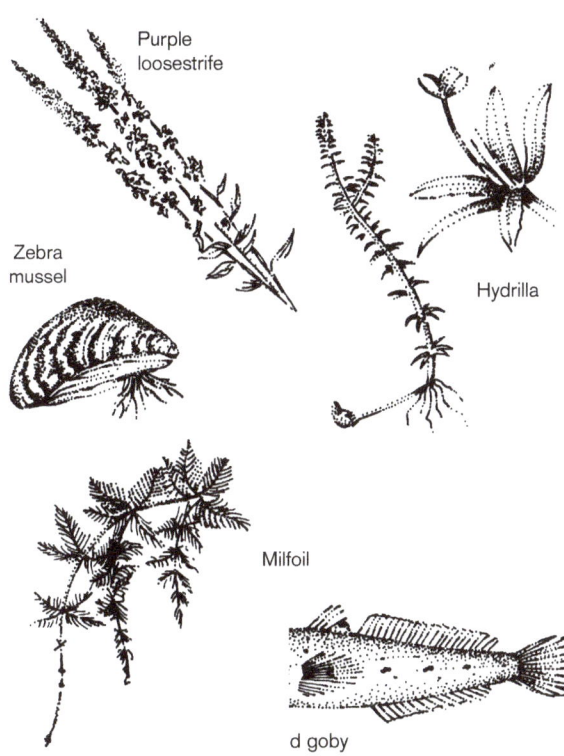

North American Exotic Species

Purple loosestrife
Zebra mussel
Hydrilla
Milfoil
d goby

plant introductions have been especially harmful. Several examples from the Great Lakes reflect this.

The zebra mussel *(see)* invaded the Great Lakes from its native habitats in Europe and has become a nuisance by clogging the intakes of water pipes and outboard boat engines. It has received much attention because it can be common in shallow water near shore and is large enough to be easily seen. During the 1980s, the 1-centimeter-long zooplankton called spiny water flea *(see)* entered the Great Lakes, and may have as profound an effect on the ecosystem as a larger invader. The sea lamprey *(see)*, aided by overfishing in the early to mid-1900s, decimated lake trout, which used to reproduce naturally in all the Great Lakes, and now reproduce naturally primarily in Lake Superior, with isolated occurrences in the other lakes.

Prevention. Anglers and boaters have an obligation to make sure they do not assist in transplanting any organisms to places where they don't belong. This pertains to the known problem exotics and also to not so obvious ones (like yellow perch being introduced into a small trout pond). This prevention starts with not deliberately planting or stocking species from one environment to another, which may also be illegal *(see: regulations)*. However, since many introductions are accidental, and many of the organisms moved are so small they cannot be readily seen (like larvae), anglers must be diligent at all times. These are some of the precautions to take:

- Empty a bait bucket on land before leaving the water; do not transport bait from one water body to another.
- Inspect the boat, the motor, all parts of the trailer, and any boating equipment that gets wet, and remove any plants and animals that are visible before leaving the water body.
- Drain livewells, bilge water, and transom wells at the access site before leaving the water body.
- Where zebra mussels and spiny water fleas are known or suspected, wash and dry your boat, tackle, trailers, and other equipment with hot water when you get home. Flush water through the motor's cooling system and other parts that get wet. If possible, let everything dry for at least three days before transporting the boat to another water body. Flushing with chlorinated tap water may be helpful.

Conversion Charts

THE SYSTEM OF WEIGHTS AND MEASURES USED IN MOST COUNTRIES AND IN ALL SCIENTIFIC work is the International System of Units (SI), which is commonly referred to as the metric system. A notable and influential exception to this is the United States, where the general public, and non-scientific publications, use the U.S., or U.S. customary, system of weights and measures. Throughout the *Ken Schultz's Fishing Encyclopedia & Worldwide Angling Guide*, there is a liberal use of both metric and U.S. customary weights and measures without parenthetical conversions to equivalent weights or measures. Some anglers, especially those who travel widely and those who pay close attention to world-record fish weights and fishing line classifications, are accustomed to both systems, which are often found mixed at boat docks, fish camps, and tackle shops throughout the world. The following information is provided to help the reader make the conversion from one system to another.

U.S. To Metric Conversion Formulas

When You Know...	Multiply By...	To Determine...
Inches (in)	25.4	Millimeters (mm)
Inches (in)	2.54	Centimeters (cm)
Inches (in)	0.0254	Meters (m)
Square Inches (sq in)	645.0	Square Millimeters (sq mm)
Square Inches (sq in)	6.45	Square Centimeters (sq cm)
Square Inches (sq in)	0.00064	Square Meters (sq m)
Feet (ft)	30.5	Centimeters (cm)
Feet (ft)	0.305	Meters (m)
Feet (ft)	0.0003	Kilometers (km)
Square Feet (sq ft)	0.093	Square Meters (sq m)
Fathoms (fath)	1.827	Meters (m)
Fathoms (fath)	0.0018	Kilometers (km)
Yards (yd)	0.914	Meters (m)
Square Yards (sq yd)	0.836	Square Meters (sq m)
Statute Miles (mi) (5,280 ft)	1.61	Kilometers (km)
Nautical Miles (n mi) (6,020 ft)	1.852	Kilometers (km)
Square Miles (sq mi)	2.56	Square Kilometers (sq km)
Miles per hour (mph)	1.61	Kilometers per hour (kph)
Knots per hour	1.84	Kilometers per hour (kph)
Acres	0.405	Hectares
Ounces of Weight (oz)	28.3	Grams (g)
Ounces of Weight (oz)	0.0283	Kilograms (kg)
Ounces of Fluid (fl oz)	29.6	Milliliters (mL)
Pounds (lb)	454.0	Grams (g)
Pounds (lb)	0.454	Kilograms (kg)
Pints (pt)—U.S.	0.473	Liters (L)
Pints (pt)—Imperial	0.568	Liters (L)
Quarts (qt)—U.S.	0.946	Liters (L)
Quarts (qt)—Imperial	1.14	Liters (L)
Gallons (gal)—U.S.	3.79	Liters (L)
Gallons (gal)—Imperial	4.55	Liters (L)
degrees Fahrenheit (°F)	0.555 (after subtracting 32)	degrees Celsius (°C)

Metric To U.S. Conversion Formulas

When You Know...	Multiply By...	To Determine...
Millimeters (mm)	0.039	Inches (in)
Centimeters (cm)	0.394	Inches (in)
Centimeters (cm)	0.0328	Feet (ft)
Square Centimeters (sq cm)	0.155	Square Inches (sq in)
Meters (m)	39.37	Inches (in)
Meters (m)	3.281	Feet (ft)
Meters (m)	1.09	Yards (yd)
Meters (m)	0.547	Fathoms (fath)
Square Meters (sq m)	1.2	Square Yards (sq yd)
Kilometers (km)	3,279.0	Feet (ft)
Kilometers (km)	1,093.0	Yards (yd)
Kilometers (km)	546.0	Fathoms (fath)
Kilometers (km)	0.621	Statute Miles (mi)
Kilometers (km)	0.545	Nautical Miles (n mi)
Square Kilometers (sq km)	0.386	Square Miles (sq mi)
Kilometers per hour (kph)	0.621	Miles per hour (mph)
Kilometers per hour (kph)	0.545	Knots per hour
Hectares	2.47	Acres
Grams (g)	0.035	Ounces of Weight (oz)
Grams (g)	0.002	Pounds (lb)
Kilograms (kg)	35.2736	Ounces (oz)
Kilograms (kg)	2.2	Pounds (lb)
Milliliter (mL)	0.034	Fluid Ounces (oz)
Liters (L)	2.11	Pints (pt)—U.S.
Liters (L)	1.76	Pints (pt)—Imperial
Liters (L)	1.06	Quarts (qt)—U.S.
Liters (L)	0.880	Quarts (qt)—Imperial
Liters (L)	0.264	Gallons (gal)—U.S.
Liters (L)	0.22	Gallons (gal)—Imperial
degrees Celsius (°C)	1.8 (and add 32)	degrees Fahrenheit (°F)

Table Of Metric and U.S. Equivalent Line Strengths

Metric	U.S. Customary	Metric	U.S. Customary
1 kg	2.2 lb	10 kg	22.0 lb
2 kg	4.4 lb	15 kg	33.0 lb
3 kg	6.6 lb	24 kg	52.8 lb
4 kg	8.8 lb	37 kg	81.4 lb
6 kg	13.2 lb	60 kg	132.0 lb
8 kg	17.6 lb		

Table of Fish Weights

Metric	U.S. Customary	Metric	U.S. Customary
1 kg	2.2 lb	60 kg	132.0 lb
2 kg	4.4 lb	70 kg	154.0 lb
3 kg	6.6 lb	80 kg	176.0 lb
4 kg	8.8 lb	90 kg	198.0 lb
5 kg	11.0 lb	100 kg	220.0 lb
6 kg	13.2 lb	200 kg	440.0 lb
7 kg	15.4 lb	300 kg	660.0 lb
8 kg	17.6 lb	400 kg	880.0 lb
9 kg	19.8 lb	500 kg	1,100.0 lb
10 kg	22.0 lb	600 kg	1,320.0 lb
20 kg	44.0 lb	700 kg	1,540.0 lb
30 kg	66.0 lb	800 kg	1,760.0 lb
40 kg	88.0 lb	900 kg	1,980.0 lb
50 kg	110.0 lb	1,000 kg	2,200.0 lb